Series in
Legal Information and
Communication Technologies

Volume 5

LAW VIA THE INTERNET

Free Access
Quality of Information
Effectiveness of Rights

Proceedings of the 9th International Conference
"Law via the Internet"

(30-31 October 2008 – Florence, Italy)

Edited by

Ginevra Peruginelli and Mario Ragona

EUROPEAN PRESS ACADEMIC PUBLISHING

Publication funded by the
Italian National Research Council

LATEX editing by
Giuseppina Sabato and Teresa Balsamo

Book cover photo: *Old Bridge, Florence*

ISBN 978-88-8398-058-9
Copyright © 2009 by European Press Academic Publishing
Florence, Italy
www.e-p-a-p.com
www.europeanpress.it
Printed in Italy

Contents

PREFACE   9

I Section
The Right to Access Legal Information

Fifteen Years of Free Access to Law
Daniel Poulin   15

Legal Information as an Essential Aspect of Citizenship
Vincenzo Zeno-Zencovich   33

The Right of Access to the Internet Network as a New Social Right:
Problems and Prospects
Marina Pietrangelo   41

Online Access to Legislation in the EU: from Fee-based to Free Information
Albrecht Berger   49

Italian Legislation on the Internet: Citizens' Access to Legislation in
Force and Regulatory Reorganisation
Italo Scotti, Enrico Seta   57

The Role of CNIPA in Accessing Legal Information
Floretta Rolleri   65

Problems of Privacy in Online Court Materials
Iain Currie   73

II Section
A Legal Framework for Open Access to Legal Information

Legal Information Services: The Policies of Publishing
Jon Bing   83

Open Access to Legal Scholarship and Copyright Rules: A Law and
Technology Perspective
Roberto Caso   97

Theory and Reality of the Official Publication of Legal Acts on Internet
Pasquale Costanzo, Marina Pietrangelo   111

Open Access and Legal Exceptions to Copyright: Towards a General
Fair Use Standard?
Davide Sarti   123

6

Problems Arising for BAILII from the History of Law Reporting
Philip Leith, Cynthia Fellows   129

Open Access to Outcomes of Publicly Funded Research
Sebastiano Faro   139

An Unexplored Legal Issue for the Provision of Free Legal Information
in Hong Kong
*Kevin Pun, Hak-wai Chan, Chun-fung Chong, Kam-pui Chow, Lucas
Hui, Wai-wan Tsang*   151

III SECTION
FREE ACCESS TO LAW: INFORMATION SYSTEMS AND
INSTITUTIONS IN EUROPE

Free Access to Legal and Legislative Information: The French Approach
Through the Enlightenment of the Strategic Reviews of Better Reg-
ulation in the European Union
Stéphane Cottin   163

Free Access to Legislation in Finland: Principles, Practices and Prospects
Aki Hietanen   177

Free Access to Legislation in Denmark: Advantages in Inter-institutional
Cooperation - Design and Production
Nina Koch   187

Free Access to Legislation in Italy: The Role of Standards for the Integration of Information Systems
Caterina Lupo   193

Free Access to Legal Information in Switzerland
Michel Moret   199

Free Access to Legal and Legislative Information: The Austrian Approach
Günther Schefbeck   207

Legal Documents as Core Public Sector Information: From Professional
Information to Internet Development Support
Fernando Venturini   219

An Easy Way to Find a Rule Among a Lot of Legislation in Disability
Area
Raffaello Belli   227

7

IV Section
The Global Scope of Free Access to Law

Free Access to the Law in Latin-America: Brasil, Argentina, México and Uruguay as Examples
Fernando Galindo 237

Access to Judicial Information via the Internet in Latin America: A Discussion of the Experiences, Trends and Difficulties
Carlos G. Gregorio 245

Free Access to Law in Africa: Issues for Network Society
Abdul Paliwala 253

Re-thinking "Open" in Free and Open Access to Law
Mariya Badeva-Bright 261

Towards Free Access to Law: Research Experience and Prospects
Roberta Nannucci, Mario Ragona 271

Free-access Case Law Enhancements for Australian Law
Andrew Mowbray, Philip Chung, Graham Greenleaf 285

V Section
ICTs and the Quality of Legal Information

Legal Information Systems: Some Aspects on Quality and Access
Roland Traunmüller, Maria A. Wimmer 301

Beyond the Internet Hype; How Law Can Be Made Effective
Tom M. Van Engers 311

An Approach towards Better Legislation to Improve Law Accessibility and Understanding
Tommaso Agnoloni, Lorenzo Bacci, Enrico Francesconi, PierLuigi Spinosa, Daniela Tiscornia, Simonetta Montemagni 327

Norms in the Interaction between Citizen Users and the Administrative Apparatus
Manola Cherubini 337

Justice via the Internet: Hopes and Challenges of Law and the Semantic Web
Pompeu Casanovas, Marta Poblet 347

SIAM: A Semantic Tool for Improving the Legal Information Access and Knowledge
Antonio Cammelli, Elio Fameli 359

Free Access to Law and Judicial Decisions: Solutions and Challenges
from a Belgian Viewpoint
Hans Van Bossuyt, Bertel De Groote   371

ARIA: Automated Regulatory Impact Analysis
Pietro Mercatali, Francesco Romano   385

IS-LeGI. A New On-line Dictionary for a Better Access to the Historical
ITTIG Archives Documenting Italian Legal Language
Antonio Cammelli, Paola Mariani   399

VI SECTION
STRATEGIC SOLUTIONS AND SUSTAINABILITY MODELS FOR THE DIFFUSION AND SHARING OF LEGAL KNOWLEDGE

Foundlings on the Cathedral Steps
Thomas R. Bruce   411

AustLII's Business Models: Constraints and Opportunities in Funding
Free Access to Law
Graham Greenleaf   423

The Evolving Ecology of the Legal Information Market
Pierre-Paul Lemyre   437

Introducing the Legal Taxonomy Syllabus (LTS) on EU Consumer Law
Gianmaria Ajani   455

After 15 Years, is Free Access to Law Here to Stay?
Ivan Mokanov   465

POSTFACE: Reflecting on Cross-Language Retrieval of Legal
Information as an Essential Component of Open Access
Ginevra Peruginelli   477

APPENDIX

Montreal Declaration on "Free Access to Law"   487

LIIs - Legal Information Institutes   489

Author Index   491

PREFACE

Provision of free access to legal information worldwide has progressed considerably in the last decades: this phenomenon has its origin in the rapid development of new information and communication technologies available at relatively low cost as well as in the increasing demand of open and reliable access services to law material.

The establishment of legal information institutes specifically dedicated to facilitate access to law material is the starting point of this whole process. The initiative of the Cornell University Law School in 1992 establishing a legal information institute providing free access to law on the Internet with a number of databases primarily of US federal law, was followed in 1995 by two Law Schools in Sydney, Australia, and then by the LEXUM team at the University of Montreal in Canada.

The establishment of new legal information institutes in other countries has been greatly facilitated by these pioneer efforts.

At the moment the Legal Information Institutes (LIIs) network gives access, through the World Legal Information Institute (WorldLII) portal, to over 900 databases from 130 countries and territories via the The Free Access to Law Movement (FALM). This is a loose affiliation, a decentralized and cooperative initiative of legal information institutes, formed in 2002 during the "Law via the Internet" Conference in Montreal, where the Declaration on Free Access to Law was adopted.[1] The participating institutes, including government-based organizations, are a sub-set of the worldwide legal data providers, which have decided to collaborate both politically and technically in the provision of free, independent and non-profit access to law and in publishing legal information via the Internet from multiple sources. The FALM commitment is to assist organizations operating in any country which wish to provide free access to law, participate in regional or global open access to law networks, and share software, technical expertise and experience on policy questions such as privacy, while promoting and adopting standards for quality legal material production and dissemination. At the forefront the freedom to republish official sources is at the heart of the Free Access to Law Movement and essential for the operation of LIIs.

The "Law via Internet" International Conferences have been the principal means by which cooperation between LIIs has been established and developed. The first was hosted in Sydney by AustLII in 1997, followed by annual conferences. The latested was held on October 30-31, 2008 in Florence, entitled

---

[1] See the Appendix of this volume.

"Law via the Internet: Free Access, Quality of Information, Effectiveness of Rights",[2] and organized by the Institute of Legal Information Theory and Techniques of the Italian National Research Council (Istituto di Teoria e Tecniche dell'Informazione Giuridica, ITTIG-CNR, formerly called IDG, Istituto per la Documentazione Giuridica), acting as a member of the LIIs network. It was an honor and a challenge to host around 300 participants coming from 39 countries of the 5 continents as ITTIG is one of the institutions where legal informatics started in Europe, supporting free access to law without interruption since its origin.

Increased use of information in the field of law has played an important role for the development of methodologies for legal data creation and access. Using this as a well-established basis, the Florence Conference focus was on digital legal information, analyzing its aspects in the light of the free digital legal culture paradigm and of the actual technological development that is shaping law. The Conference explicitly addressed the topics of quality of legal data as an essential requirement ensuring completeness and reliability of information and of access to law as a fundamental right. Full knowledge of quality legal information enables citizens to exercise their rights in a conscious and effective way: in this context the use of new technologies becomes an essential tool of democracy for the citizens of the e-society.

This volume, containing the contributions of legal experts from all over the world, reflects the crucial aspects of free access to law, which are visible in all sessions of the Conference, including the following:

- The Right to Access Legal Information;

- A Legal Framework for Open Access to Legal Information;

- Free Access to Law: Information Systems and Institutions in Europe;

- The Global Scope of Free Access to Law;

- ICTs and the Quality of Legal Information;

- Strategic Solutions and Sustainability Models for the Diffusion and Sharing of Legal Knowledge.

Besides the invited papers presented during the Conference, the volume includes 7 accepted papers prepared by ITTIG researchers who, for Conference schedule reasons, decided not to give oral presentations.

This impressive list of contributions clearly shows how the free access to law approach is fully accepted worldwide, deserving full analysis in all aspects and now enjoying a success in practice.

---

[2] Further information, including abstract and .ppt presentations are available on the Conference web site: <www.ittig.cnr.it/LawViaTheInternet/>.

The debate covered 4 main points. The first one is that official free access is not enough. Additional systems providing different quality services are needed as full free access requires a range of different providers and competitive republishing in the light of an anti-monopoly policy. This means that institutions providing legal data sources have a public duty to offer a copy of their output (judgments and legislation) in the most authoritative form that they can to anyone who wishes to publish their output, whether for free or for fee.

Another main point regards finding a balance of the potential for commercial exploitation and users' requirements. This is particularly relevant with reference to the question of open access to the outcome of publicly funded research.

Another important issue concerns effectiveness of access and reusability of legal information. Effective access requires that most governments promote the use of technologies to improve access to law, abandoning approaches borrowed from the past like technical restrictions on the reuse of legal information. What is important is to allow and facilitate others reproducing and re-using their legal materials, removing any impediments to re-publication.

Finally, international cooperation in providing free access to law is a fundamental requirement. The LIIs community, one week before the Conference, participated to an expert meeting concerning Global Co-operation on the Provision of Online Legal Information organised by the Hague Conference on Private International Law Permanent Bureau, discussing how online free resources can contribute to resolve disputes with trans-border elements. Following this meeting (further confirmed at the Florence Conference) a general consensus was reached on the need for States parties to preserve their legal materials, in order to make them available as necessary; to make historical legal material available; where possible, to provide translations in other languages, to develop multi-lingual access functionalities, and to use open standards and metadata for primary materials.

The key issue that emerged from the Conference discussions is that the marketplace has changed and the ultimate goal is to reach new models of legal information distribution through equal market opportunities for legal providers so as to achieve equality, quality of justice and quality of legal services. In this context legal information is to be considered an absolutely public good on top of which everyone should be free to build.

In conclusion we would like to thank the ITTIG Scientific Board as well as the Organizing Committee; in particular we want to express our appreciation and very grateful thanks to Sebastiano Faro, Enrico Francesconi and Daniela Tiscornia (our colleagues of the Program Committee), who has provided us with useful suggestions and support in preparing the Conference Program.

Furthermore we are in debt to Thomas Bruce, Graham Greenleaf and Daniel Poulin for their efforts and scientific support in making the Conference a success.

Finally a special thanks is extented to Simona Binazzi for her great secretarial activity and to Giuseppina Sabato and Teresa Balsamo for their precious editing work of this volume.

Ginevra Peruginelli and Mario Ragona

I SECTION

The Right to Access
Legal Information

Fifteen Years of Free Access to Law

Daniel Poulin
LexUM, University of Montreal, Canada

Abstract. Free access to law on the web began with the seminal initiative of two law professors at Cornell University in 1992. Rapidly, others researchers and professors adopted the idea, and created their own legal information institutes. Later, government also joined in by establishing free access for some law. In general terms, the movement to make law accessible for free on the Internet is now fifteen years old.

As the number of stakeholders involved in making the law free and open grows, it is useful to take stock of the progress, try to identify what has been demonstrated by pioneering actions, pinpoint what is still disputed and look at what needs to be done to further extend open and free access.

The LexUM laboratory at the University of Montreal had been involved in the open access to law initiative since its inception. Drawing on experience gained in Canada and in supporting access to law abroad, we offer our reading of the open and free access to law movement at fifteen.

1. Introduction

A mix of idealism and technology drove those who started publishing the law on the Internet in the 90s. Idealism was frequent at the outset of the Internet and web. Many actors were not working in line with the usual profit-driven dynamic; they were instead developing and employing technology in a way that made sense to them because it was a useful thing to do and could contribute to making the world better and fairer. Besides, an information revolution was underway, and some academics could not help themselves: they wanted a part of it.

It must be remembered that at the time, law publishers were explaining to all who wanted to listen, and to many who did not, that publishing law was so costly that they could not charge less than a couple of hundred dollars an hour for use of their systems. With the advent of microcomputers in courts and the development of the Internet many stakeholders were no longer convinced. The pioneers were not interested so much in the potential commercial benefits as in serving those needing access and in proving wrong those who claimed that putting decisions online was that costly.

The whole movement was also technology driven. Those who had used arcane technologies, such as legal database systems developed in the 70s and still in their glory in the early 90s, and who were discovering the nascent web could envision what could be achieved with it and a comprehensive public communication network. They knew the tools, they saw what the tools were starting to do for other disciplines, and so they were looking for what they could do in their own field, law. Of course, today, in some circles, technology-

driven projects sketched by IT lovers are doomed to be shot down on sight by
the sober and wiser boardroom crowd. Luckily, then, and still today, universities provide some safe havens for eccentrics who want to try things because
they are "interesting."

In this paper, we propose an assessment of the Free Access to Law (FAL)
movement's achievements, formulate questions, and suggest some future steps
to be taken to extend the spirit of the pioneer efforts but also to build necessary
bridges to other players, who began elsewhere, but have done very well in the
field.

2. Findings and achievements

Overall, the FAL movement has been successful. Modest and not-so-modest
initiatives – AustLII having been part of the mix since the beginning – have
significantly contributed to establishing a new understanding of what "access
to legal information" means. In what follows, we identify some of FAL's results,
with an admitted bias in favor of positive achievements. The results presented
here may appear as a mix bag, for some outcomes are measurable and some are
not, but all together they provide a good overview of what has been achieved.

Furthermore, the goal is not to establish which proportion of the positive
developments can be linked directly to the legal information institutes: LII,
AustLII, BaiLII, and CanLII and all the others. This is beside the point; this
paper aims at identifying what has been learned and demonstrated by all who
have chosen to make the law freely accessible on the Internet.

2.1. PRIMARY LEGAL DOCUMENTS MUST BE IN THE PUBLIC DOMAIN

For centuries, citizens have been presumed to know the law. Such a presumption certainly entails a duty for the state to make the legal rules as accessible as
possible. In older times, laws evolved slowly and the body of rules was limited.
When a rule has been around since time immemorial, informing people about
it is less a problem. Over the last century, the body of legal information has
grown tremendously and the pace of its evolution has significantly accelerated,
making it unrealistic to presume that one could be aware of all of the huge
body of regulations based on what filters through the media alone. Printed
legal documents are costly to distribute. Of course, official publications are
offered to local libraries at a cheap price, but nevertheless reliable documents
used to be difficult to access. For instance, a rapid query of the catalog of the
City of Montreal library system using "Lois révisées du Canada" or "Supreme
Court of Canada" will not return much and it is one the largest public library
systems in the country. However, let's assume for now that print did not lead
to a good distribution system.

The first wave of electronic systems, the commercial legal databases, such as SOQUIJ and Quicklaw in Canada, did not help much in terms of access, at least as far as individual citizens were concerned, for they required pricey subscriptions. Only with the advent of Internet did it become feasible to provide the general public with access to the law.

Today in most economically advanced countries, and for most of the people living in them, it has become possible to know the law, or at least to access the documents containing the law. In other words, in a significant part of the world, the law is now available to be accessed and consulted by the people it was designed to guide and rule. What the free access to law movement did is prove that this could be done in a very cost-effective manner.

It was not clear at the outset whether a site offering access to legal documents would find an audience outside the legal community. Legislative texts are at best boring, if not so convoluted as to be barely understandable. At first glance, a casual reader might think court decisions are easier to understand; however they are not court dramas or crime novels. The facts can be sketchy and learned judges can drag on for pages, discussing the recent addition of a full stop between two sentences of a statute. So, it was not certain that free access to law initiatives would find an audience beyond the usual crowd of lawyers and law students.

Well, it so happens that the documents have been used and consulted not only by lawyers and journalists but also by a significant segment of citizens trying to figure out how to prevent or get out of trouble. Evidence of such use lies in the nature and the quantity of questions we receive from users. Some try hard to help themselves. This said, figuring out how the law is organized and works and finding a way through the maze of texts, let alone understanding legal language, remain huge obstacles.

Of course, in most cases, when facing serious legal difficulties, people end up consulting a lawyer. However, with the advent of CanLII and the likes they could try to understand their situation and the rules by themselves, just as they look on the web for information about a new drug that they have been prescribed. They are not planning to fly solo or to order medicine from some dubious source on the Internet. They still trust physicians and pharmacists, but a little medical information cannot hurt and they can find it on the Internet. Now they can find legal information as well.

The pioneering efforts have shown that it is not so costly to provide free access to law and that this is within the reach of most states. The LIIs have also revealed that there is interest in legal texts, not only among lawyers, but also among members of the citizenry itself. To conclude, primary legal material, statutes, regulations and cases must be accessible for free to people.

2.2. THE ROLE OF THE STATE IN ENSURING PUBLIC ACCESS TO LAW

The countries where the first free access to law initiatives appeared enjoy a legal and policy framework globally favorable to the broadest circulation of law. Governments can make the difference.

In Canada, there is still Crown copyright over statutes and judgments. As long as Crown copyright was used to control reproduction of primary legal documents, the development of a free accessible resource was undermined by the required license. Legal information vendors did not suffer much from the policy: they could just set high prices for their products and buy the licenses from the government. FAL's activists did not have that option. When Canada's federal government decided later on to adopt a new policy such that permission was no longer required to reproduce legal documents prepared by the government if the intended use was non-commercial, free access to information started to develop at a fast pace.

A second, and far more fundamental, illustration of the importance of government policies is that only governments can establish some features of the basic framework of a law-governed country. For instance, if legal information is not gathered and preserved, there is no way to publish it, for free or for money. In some countries, gazettes and official reports have not been published for years and court records are not kept. It is obvious that in such situations only the government can establish the foundation for the legal system to operate properly.

Public institutions must collect, organize and preserve the essential texts stating the law of the land. For legislative texts, a public institution must also act as the official publisher. In other words, an authoritative version of legislative acts must be available from the state. This said, in countries subject to extremely difficult economic conditions, simply collecting and publishing legislation can be a challenge, even though it is the obvious starting point.

Collection of judicial decisions, especially those with precedential value, is also of great importance. Today, collecting the essential components of primary legal information must be done for digital as well as paper versions. Preservation of archival copies of the legal patrimony on both supports is a fundamental responsibility of government. With regard to ensuring access to law, particularly to legislative texts and judgments, which is the central issue here, there are many government obligations.

A common obstacle for those who want to publish law for free comes out of some governments' desire to make money out of legal texts. The thinking goes like this: if publishers are to develop products out of very valuable public assets, it is normal that the government get its fair share of the profits from the sales of those products. Sometimes it is even simpler. In some Canadian jurisdictions, the government imposes financial self-sufficiency objectives on the provincial Queen's printer, which is the office in charge of publishing legislation. This forces it to extract revenues from its control over statutes and gazettes. In such situations, Queen's printers have a very demanding balancing act to perform: they must provide access and also make money.

Other jurisdictions take another route: the Government of Ontario and the Canadian federal government have chosen to offer free access to the best systems of legislative information they can produce – their legislation sites are both remarkable – and to liberally authorize reproduction. They have preferred access over cost recovery. In our view, their approach exemplifies best practices in the matter.

In courts and tribunals, the outlook is simpler. To our knowledge, no Canadian courts or tribunals have ever asked for money for a license to publish their decisions. Legal publishers operating for commercial or for free access purposes can contact any of them to establish channels for providing their publications with raw materials produced by the courts. However, in some Canadian provinces, and in some countries, a single outlet has been set up to provide access to decisions from all courts and tribunals, and it often follows that cost recovery issues appear. Some jurisdictions have found quite elegant approaches. In Quebec, admittedly after a Court of Appeal ruling that case law must be accessible to publishers, SOQUIJ reluctantly set up a web site on which citizens can find all Quebec decisions for free. Then, as the court asked, SOQUIJ established a channel to give other publishers access to decisions as well. The Quebec government and SOQUIJ even ensure the distribution of anonymized decisions when identity protection is required. Eight years later, SOQUIJ continues to operate the most successful commercial operation in the Quebec's legal information market, yet at the same time it ensures free access and makes accessible all the source material needed by other publishers. In the end, SOQUIJ really won in all respects. This is an impressive and inspiring example.

Elsewhere in Canada, as in many other countries, a large number of courts and tribunals have set up their own web sites to make their decisions available. Some of them are very good resources, but all of them are important. Their relevance, even when, as in Canada, a LII such as CanLII publishes the decisions anyway, comes from the commitment to transparency and access shown by the institutions.

In many European countries, governments have taken into their own hands the burden of providing free access to legal information. Legifrance is a good illustration of this approach to making law accessible. On Legifrance, one can find nearly 2 million documents and 100,000 more are added each year. Since 2002, Legifrance has been making constant progress, and today it serves its mission with the usual French flair. We all know that legal language is not easy to understand, so while publishing the case law and legislation of a country is a very laudable objective, it does not suffice to reach the higher and much more difficult goal of making the law itself accessible. The French government has risen to the challenge by setting up a companion site to Legifrance that may be even more remarkable.[1] Service-Public offers a simplified outlook on procedures, explains administrative processes, and clarifies the law from the citizen's perspective, starting with ordinary personal problems with landlords, in the workplace, and in dealings with the government. Together, Legifrance and Service-Public provide a good illustration of what can be achieved by a government committed to public access.

To sum up, the role of government is paramount. There are fundamental missions that only the government can carry out; collecting, managing and preserving law are government duties. Official publication of legislation must also be under state control. Thus, proper policy must be chosen to favor other initiatives that complement those of the government. Finally, governments with resources can prepare tools that nobody else can match.

2.3. OPEN ACCESS TO LEGAL INFORMATION SERVES ACCESS TO JUSTICE

In the seventies, in many of our countries and in many forums, public rights advocates, academics, civil servants and politicians met and discussed how to make the justice system more accessible. In Canada, what can be called the access to justice program took four main tacks: (1) attempts to simplify procedure, and establishment of small claims courts; (2) exploration and creation of alternate dispute resolution mechanisms and resources; (3) establishment of a legal aid system, to make sure that less well-off people could have the assistance of a professional lawyer; and (4) efforts to simplify legal language. All these initiatives succeeded at some level, except maybe the last one: at least in Canada, legislation drafters made no breakthroughs.

Pierre-Paul Lemyre, a colleague at LexUM, recently suggested that free access to legal information must now become part of the program to support access to justice and this sounds right. With the means at their disposal, governments that favour access to justice must act today to make sure that the primary sources of law are accessible to their citizens for free on the Internet.

2.4. LEGAL PROFESSIONALS AND LAW SOCIETIES COULD BE CRITICAL ALLIES FOR OPEN ACCESS

Governments have money and responsibilities; lawyers have money too, and they have needs. Canadian law societies invest a significant amount of money in improving the competency of their members by maintaining libraries and preparing various types of training material and publications. This is an important way of protecting the public. In Canada, in the 90s, law societies and lawyers alike were facing huge cost pressures from legal publishers. Legal

---

[1] Available at: `<Service-Public.fr>`.

information costs were spiraling. The worst of it was that the transition from paper to the new digital media was fundamentally changing the deal. Lawyers and libraries, which used to build documentary assets, were becoming licensees having to pay forever to access online databases and even to continue using their CD-ROMs. On top of that, a law society was sued by publishers over sharing its information holdings with its client-lawyers. This was the context when LexUM and the Federation of Law Societies of Canada started to talk about building CanLII.

There was already some legal information accessible for free in Cana-da. LexUM was involved in many of the projects, but overall the resources were scattered. Some were not even searchable, and the others employed a range of different search tools. Overall, it was, if not useless, certainly not conducive to supporting competent practice of law. In 2000, Canadian lawyers decided that by partnering with those who were already involved in publishing law for free, they could improve the service. The Federation of Law Societies of Canada and LexUM ended up as an odd couple. Some may say that LexUM married up, but we like to think that we have spoilt the spouse. Now Canadian lawyers have a one-stop shop with over 600,000 decisions from all Canadian courts and a hundred tribunals, as well as the legislation from all of Canada's provinces and territories. CanLII, a marriage of convenience, has become a happy union. Recent surveys have shown that CanLII is now the main source of primary legal information for Canadian lawyers. In our view, what CanLII has shown is that free access to law can make business sense.

Something more needs to be said about CanLII: people with professional and business interests can do nice things. When they chose the CanLII approach as the solution to their problems, Canadian lawyers turned their backs on many less innovative, more familiar, business-like, and – let's say it – selfish approaches. They preferred the high road of ensuring free access to law for everybody, laypeople and paying members alike.

Involvement of the legal profession in making the law accessible is not specifically Canadian. The legal profession played an important role in the establishment of BaiLII. Cornell has been receiving contributions from its users for years, and lawyers are significantly present among donors. AustLII recently campaigned to reestablish its funding, and individual lawyers, law firms, law societies have responded to the call and shown huge support for their Australian LII. Even in emerging countries, lawyers get involved. In Burkina Faso, the Ordre des Avocats played a central role in the establishment of Juriburkina. A similar involvement paved the way to the establishment of JuriNiger. Clearly, lawyers are allies, and indeed sometimes the initiators of FAL.

2.5. OPEN ACCESS IS NOT POOR ACCESS

Today, CanLII offers a very sophisticated search environment: comprehensive databases, a powerful search tool, a citator, a point-in-time system for legislation and more. Database comprehensiveness is constantly monitored. Usability is a constant concern for the production team at LexUM. CanLII is not a rustic tool; it is the tool that professionals choose. AustLII is almost as good, and at times may be even better. The LII at Cornell continues to impress owing to its tidiness, and especially because of the care taken to make the law accessible to laypeople: no one tries harder. PacLII, SAFLII, BaiLII and all the other members of the LII family are doing quite well too. The quality of government sites varies. There are extremely basic sites, extraordinary ones, and everything in between. Beyond the variety of the systems, what can certainly be concluded here is that some of the accessible-for-free resources are setting the bar very high, even for their commercial brethren.

2.6. OPEN ACCESS AND COMMERCIAL PUBLISHING CAN COEXIST

Finally it is worth mentioning that free access has not killed commercial legal publishers. (Not yet, mischievous observers would say.)

Our own view is that there is room for both and that in fact both are needed. At least in Canada, commercial entities are doing a superb job publishing law. The business has certainly evolved: the bygone days of selling raw court decisions have passed. However, forward-looking publishers are finding new ways and new places to lead their businesses. They innovate in content packaging and they design products targeted to practice communities: securities, labour, corporate and so on. Beyond that, they still produce and support a lot of secondary sources of law: treaties, commentaries, annotated text and more.

3. Questions and perspectives

The first part of this paper is mostly upbeat; indeed, very significant progress has been made. The outcomes of the issues discussed in the second part are less certain. The stakes relate to sustainability, extension of the free access to law program around the world and proliferation of legal information.

3.1. OPEN ACCESS IS SUSTAINABLE

Cornell's LII went online in 1992; LexUM and AustLII followed suit in 1993 and 1995. In Internet time, that was long ago and they are quite old places. In a less favorable context, PacLII has been leading an ambitious publishing effort in the South Pacific since 1998. Juriburkina has been hanging on since

2004, and SAFLII in South Africa is the same age. All these initiatives are of course happening outside governments, and by definition they are the most vulnerable to sudden lack of funding, but they keep persevering. Government-based free-access-to-law sites have proliferated in recent years. There are now hundreds of them in ministries, agencies, courts, and tribunals across the world. These sites, once started, tend to stay around. So, in one form or another, free access to law is far from a fad of the doc.com times and seems to be here to stay.

Study and analysis of the first 15 years of development of legal information institutes remain to be done. However, some of the ingredients of the successful projects can be identified, and they are probably the same whatever the level of development of the economy: the involvement of the various local stakeholders is certainly the most important factor for success. Generally, however, sustainability factors differ depending on whether we are talking about LIIs and the likes, or government-created FAL sites.

The LII scenario is produced when members of civil society, academia, ONGs or a law society decide to take the initiative to publish the law for free. The depths of the roots in the community are the major factor for success because the deeper they are, the more likely the project will survive to maturity. Establishing a new source of law takes time, especially for those wanting to avoid huge investment. In our experience, the initial phase takes five to six years. This is easy enough to understand, for at first the would-be LII offers only few databases that do not extend very far into the past. It is plainly not sufficient for legal research. That will come, but it will take time. However, this is not to say that LIIs are useless in their first five years. Absolutely not. LexUM started with 300 Supreme Court of Canada's decisions and the service was highly appreciated from its very first months. However, in such conditions and at that tender age, the LII has not yet reach the point where legal research can be conducted, and this entails frailty. Such a LII needs to be nurtured until its usefulness is proven to the community.

The clearest form of local involvement – and a special one – is when a government or government agency decides to take charge of making the law accessible for free. In those cases, often a large or at least a significant body of law is published at once. Such sites can become reputable and reach a significant level of use rapidly, so generally they will avoid the long starting phase of their LII cousins.

In the long term, sustainability means the same thing everywhere; one has to be able to pay salaries, the rent and the like. In both rich and poor countries, two main sources of funding exist: those who have the mandate to make the law accessible – governments – and those who need the service – lawyers, businesses, law schools, and... governments. In most cases, a LII's capacity to self-finance will depend on the usefulness of its product. This said, everything is easier in a richer society.

Government-funded free-access-to-law sites are certainly less exposed financially. These resources still have to face risks. In less stable countries, a change of government may entail the death of the initiative and loss of the data. In poorer countries, where the state struggles to fulfill many of its basic responsibilities, the support of foreign development agencies could be required for a while. For instance, New Zealand's development agency is supporting free access to law in the South Pacific. In Canada, the IRDC is funding research on FAL and as well as on some experimental sites in Africa. External funding may actually be needed for some time. It is certainly hoped that the LIIs established in emerging countries will end up being financed by local sources, but this can take time, especially since the real usefulness of some sites can take time to develop.

In many emerging countries, international development funding agencies are involved in legal reform, rule of law strengthening, judicial transparency and good governance programs. Unfortunately, issues surrounding accessibility of legal documentation do not always receive the attention they merit. Quite probably, the value of the free access to law approach as one of many practical ways of strengthening rule of law-related institutions has not been sufficiently demonstrated. Besides the fact that the issue is too often neglected, there are also issues around the approaches chosen to make law accessible.

In some cases, outside funds have been mustered for programs designed to reinforce a country's capacity to collect and disseminate its law without sufficiently securing the public nature of the legal information and with no ambition to make the law accessible for free. To some, trading official legal documents appears as a better business than giving them away. Unfortunately accessibility is too often the victim of such commercial schemes. Let's start by noting that in order to create a market for raw official legal documents, one needs first to ensure some scarcity. To do that, digital versions of documents are made difficult to obtain, and licensing schemes is introduced for controlling the reproduction of legal texts. When a market has been sufficiently created businesspeople in or outside government can start doing marvels, selling the law. Anybody could then assess that all this is done without costing anything to the government. However, the truth is that this sort of privatization of official legal information can work somewhat and for some time in a rich country. Most often, it will not work at all, not even for a minute, in an emerging country. For, however scarce access to legal documents is, the buying power is just not there.

The obvious solution – funding permitting – is to adopt a principled approach where official legal documents or primary materials are deemed to be public patrimony. The documents are made freely available and their reproduction is permitted. Then, because commercial activity is good and businesses do many things better than governments, all the rest of the legal information business is left to entrepreneurs wanting to offer value-added legal information products and services. In such a framework, they can enrich state-produced material, which they have perhaps acquired for a license fee, to prepare products users will buy. Furthermore, the creation of various free access to law remains possible, it is up to interested stakeholders to make it a reality.

3.2. STRATEGIES FOR FOREIGN LAW ACCESS

Most of the time, law has a local character. Ordinary citizens and even practicing lawyers rarely engage in full-fledged worldwide research. This said, globalization is constant, and our legal systems undoubtedly influence one another. Higher courts in neighboring countries are cited in our Supreme Court, some fields of law – cyberspace, intellectual property, and privacy law come to mind – are evolving in a global way, and probably more importantly business is now frequently conducted globally. Commercial publishers recognized this fact and started responding to this need years ago. Some actors in the FAL movement are stressing the importance of being able to access foreign law: "Those who value free access to law need to respond to the increasing global nature of legal research" (Greenleaf, Chung, Mowbray, 2007).

An empirical way to assess the importance of the global nature of legal research is to look at what the users do. On CanLII, it is possible to see how often a user has chosen to go to other countries' resources, and how many times someone went to us directly from another country or through a portal as WorldLII or Droit Francophone (DF). Of course, this is not rock-solid knowledge. However, we believe that these observations could give us an idea of how global legal research is today.

Usage statistics show is that the need for foreign law is significant. For instance, CanLII answered close to two millions of queries from users abroad in 2007. However, only a tiny fraction of these users came to us through worldwide portals like Droit Francophone and WorldLII.

The needs to access foreign law are important enough for us to look at solutions. One is the creation of hubs, à la WorldLII, and another is the creation of interoperability standards and protocols paving the way to federating all FAL sites. The latter approach would let any FAL provider to act as a hub. Let's call these solutions the hub model and the federation model, and look at each one in turn.

In a hub model, the hub promoter/operator creates a catalog, various indices, such as a search index and maybe a citation index, and sets up the service. From that point on, those who want to access foreign law visit the hub and do their research work there. Greenleaf and his colleagues develop such a strategy in detail (Greenleaf, Chung, Mowbray, 2007) in relation to WorldLII, a hub of the sort they advocate. Anybody who has visited WorldLII can testify that the approach chosen by AustLII has a lot of merit. The system is working, and beyond its utility as a catalog it could be especially useful for those needing to do global comparative studies or global searches. Creating WorldLII was no small undertaking, and maintaining it over the years is also an achievement in itself. WorldLII has been serving free access to law for over seven years.

The hub approach is not without shortcomings, though. Such a centralized resource limits everything to a common denominator, its current implementation asks for too much technological consistency, and in the end it is too centralized.

There is certainly a need to compare law, and this need is probably increasing, but it remains relatively uncommon. Sometimes someone may wonder what is the law regarding protection of the personal data in school records world-wide. Such needs occur, and when they do, WorldLII is now the starting point for finding more specific sources and resources.

What we believe is more frequent is the need to know the law of not just other countries in general, but a very specific one. For instance, a Canadian business person or a company lawyer may need to know specific environmental requirements for mining activities in Tunisia or Cambodia. A student may want to know visa requirements for Australia. An information technology start-up or its lawyer may want to know how intellectual property is protected in Barbados. This understand of the needs in relation with foreign law is supported by CanLII usage statistics. It can be said that the most frequent needs with respect to foreign law are needs with respect to another country domestic law. When you have a project or problem, you want to know the law of the land.

This analysis of foreign law needs lead us to examine what could be the best strategy for meeting them. What advice would we like to give a Swiss lawyer looking for Canadian legal information? Of course, it is to invite him to pay a visit to CanLII. Indeed, despite the quality and the value of the work done in consolidating all the law of the world in global hubs, such resources may be not a substitute for the real thing. Hubs serve global searches especially well, but global search needs are limited. "Local searches" made by foreigners are more frequent. This is the need we wanted to serve.

Greenleaf et al. have described various facets of legal hubs (Greenleaf, Chung, Mowbray, 2007). We want to add one more. Some hubs may be characterized as shallow and others as integrated. Using this terminology, traditional search engines would be classified as shallow. The "Droit Francophone hub" (DF), designed to provide a starting point for exploring legal content produced in French and developed for the Organisation internationale de la Francophonie (OIF), would also be qualified as shallow. So, a shallow hub would be one that has no requirement with respect to indexed sites other than to be "browsable"and to let indexing robots pass. Integrated hubs have more requirements, and WorldLII is closer to an integrated one. Actually, an important ingredient of the WorldLII recipe is that most of the sites that are globally searchable on WorldLII share the same search engine, the excellent SINO developed by Mowbray. This is no sin, but it works only as long as other people use SINO. As of today, the real basis for the main WorldLII's service is the uniformity of technological choices. In all fairness, it must be noted that WorldLII operators are not opposed in principle to other approaches, for instance, for some time WorldLII has been federating CanLII's search engine's results with results from other search engines.

Finally, WorldLII offers a centralized model. Everything is done in Sydney. With Droit Francophone (DF), LexUM has also ventured in the field of global portals. However, DF was designed from the start to be operated by a world-wide network of partners. In the end, the planned collaboration never took off and we have ended up doing everything from the central office too. So, in that case everything is done in Montreal. When the collaborative approach did not work, it taught us something: collaboration and cooperation require incentives and we were not offering enough of these to those we were inviting to work with us.

Again, centralization is not bad in itself. For instance, CanLII is a very centralized model within Canada's borders. AustLII is also a centralized solution for Australia. Where it starts to get more complicated is with centralized solutions for outside jurisdictions. This said, it is probable that to many stakeholders, the centralized approach is the way to go. Their law can be searched and easily located, and it costs nothing. Many users as well find that WorldLII is great: it is a one-stop shop for finding legal information on the web, to do global searches. Others would prefer a less hierarchical, less centralized approach. This leads us to the second model which can be seen as an alternative or complement.

The federation approach can be compared with peer-to-peer networks. According to this approach, LexUM, for example, could develop for CanLII some sort of connectors that are usable by outside programs from other LIIs. Thus, any LII recognized as so by LexUM/CanLII would be able to search CanLII. Much richer connectors could also be designed. For instance, a citation resolver could be offered and a CanLII resource description could be prepared according to a standard and made accessible in the same way. We don't intend to be obscure here. The plan is simple. Participating LIIs would connect by way of standardized APIs, so when a Canadian user using CanLII is interested in South African law, she will find a link to SAFLII or will be able to use SAFLII's search engine directly from CanLII, and vice-versa.

This sort of approach is more scalable. These days, moving data between LexUM and AustLII is no small feat. With the suggested approach there would be no need to index huge external LIIs or to replicate enormous quantities of data. Such replication can be impossible, many LIIs has a duty to "control" the data entrusted to them. The approach also lends itself to offering complete freedom of choice with regard to technologies. Any site participating in the free access to law program would have only to support the standard API to join the access exchange. The approach would also be extensible; various levels of service interchange could be developed in the future.

The federation approach is not hub hostile. Actually, if LexUM offers an API to access the CanLII search tool ELIISA, a hub – more specifically WorldLII – will be able to use that API to send CanLII the query, get the results and federate them with other results obtained elsewhere. However, the API will be accessible not only to WorldLII but to other LIIs as well. Reciprocal agreements come to mind. To make sense, the approach requires standardization at the API level so the would-be hub operator does not have to talk to dozens of different programming interfaces. This makes sense though, and even if new in the FAL world, this seems to us the most obvious way to serve our desire to collaborate.

Finally, the federation model is closer to FAL's values. The resulting structure would be flatter. Relationships between free access to law sites could be between equals. In the end, we think that such an approach would even please those who are more attracted to the benefits of a hub approach. For them, this may mean that they would even get access to databases that were closed to them until now because some who provide free access to law may be reluctant to see their entire content copied abroad in order to be searchable on a hub.

Both approaches have advantages, and actually they may well complement each other. On our view, this would be the most promising way to serve the FAL movement.

3.3. ACCESS TO JUSTICE AND THE PROLIFERATION OF LEGAL INFORMATION

When we started publishing law at LexUM, we were eager to publish everything because so little material was accessible back then. We could not find enough of it, and the truth to be said we are still eager to publish more stuff today.

At CanLII, we are now publishing the decisions from all Canadian courts and over 100 administrative tribunals. We are also publishing the legislation from the fourteen Canadian jurisdictions. Overall we are publishing over 150,000 decisions a year not counting legislation. If one considers only Quebec, CanLII is publishing 20 times more decisions than used to be published there only 20 years ago. The publishing volume on CanLII is matched by commercial vendors. Legal information is now abundant, so abundant that some users are starting to feel challenged by the huge volume of information to be sifted and searched.

FAL's goals are to make the law accessible. Could it be that so many legal documents are published today that there could be a threat to access to justice, the end goal of FAL? Could the current proliferation of texts compromise actual access? Catherine Best, a member of the CanLII's board of directors, brought this issue to the attention of the FAL movement at the 8th International "The Law via the Internet" Conference (Best, 2007). Among the ideas expressed by Best is that lawyers can see their research work becoming more complicated if they have to face a tidal wave of published cases. The volume of available material seems to lead lawyers to take support from a larger number of authorities. At the same conference, Canadian judges also expressed concerns with the proliferation of case law. A flood of cited authorities can slow down the work of the judiciary. The FAL movement must meet this challenge, and for LexUM and CanLII, it means enhancing the tools provided to users.

The way this problem was dealt with in the more conventional world of legal publishing was by improving the organization of the data. Published pell-mell, even a thousand documents can be difficult to handle. Conversely, major legal publishers have demonstrated that users can utilize millions of documents when they are well organized. Legal publishers help users coping with large sets of documents by investing in editing to add head-notes with keywords; abstract, conceptual and thematic indexes; authorities cited, and so on. For FAL, the challenge is to provide the required but costly tools in a cheap way. In this respect, LIIs have fared well; however, as their holdings grow, some of them may want to do even more. Let's look at how FAL site operators have managed to add value in a thrifty way.

Firstly, one must respect the inherent structure of legal information. Cornell's LII site, the very first, offered good information architecture right at the origin of FAL. This inspiring model has generally been followed by other LIIs. Without going into minute detail, legislation is arranged and presented in a hierarchical way and cases are organized and browsed hierarchically and chronologically. The information is organized in directories and presented in pages in its "natural" structure. This way, URLs are meaningful, and navigating the material does not disorient users.

The second major element of the FAL approach is the search tool. It has also been a central part of the FAL offering since the beginning. The search tools are generally good and fast. Speed counts. CanLII's users send feedback to tell us how much they appreciate searching on CanLII: they can launch ten searches on it while they would be able to run just one or two on a commercial site. LexUM has always thought that search speed is paramount, for a fast search tool can compensate for weaknesses by letting users refine their query so efficiently that limitations are forgiven if not forgotten. This said, it is still best to have a search tool that is simple and powerful (and yet lightning fast).

Thirdly, hypertext linking helps users navigate information. In the olden days, checking a citation meant a visit to the library. With hypertext, checking is instantaneous. The massive legal hypertext built by AustLII in the 90s has become a FAL signature. The ingenious approach to building the hypertext systems is described by Mowbray (Mowbray, 1997). Let's summarize it in our own words: (1) citation recognition and markup is done around conversion time; (2) the well-designed information architecture makes it easy to set up links; (3) a note-up function makes it possible to find documents citing the current document by searching for the information added to citations at markup time. LexUM's Morissette found an astute supplementary trick by integrating the note-up with the full CanLII search function. The resulting search tool, entirely built by programmatic techniques, lets users mix concepts – or at least citations to documents strongly associated with concepts – and words in queries. For instance, CanLII's users can note up a Quebec Civil Code section with other search criteria.

LexUM hit a limit with the preceding approach when it was developing CanLII. The problem was that, quite often, cited documents were on CanLII but cited by reference to a printed report. The information needed to attach a citation referencing a reported decision to the very same decision published on CanLII was simply not available. A fourth enrichment strategy, the development of a citator or a database of citation information, was needed, and it has been developed by LexUM under the name of Reflex (Poulin, Paré, Mokanov, 2005). Over 200,000 citations were extracted from the leading Canadian reports by students in two consecutive summers. That operation added over 2 M of hypertext links to CanLII. The 36 report series have since been compiled on a monthly basis. Reflex adds chores to the editorial process for CanLII, but we feel that the hypertext linking makes the service much more complete and reliable, and so is worth the trouble.

Judicial history information is the fifth enrichment on CanLII. What is at stake here is to provide reliable information about later judicial treatment of the case at hand. For instance, a lawyer looking at an interesting Ontario Court of Appeal case needs to know whether the rule stated in the case is still good law, whether it has been overturned by the Supreme Court of Canada. Compiling judicial history adds another bit of work to the case law publishing process but can be mostly automated.

Furthermore, if we turn our attention to the future, LexUM is envisioning mobilizing CanLII users in some sort of collaboration scheme. Various collaborative strategies have been discussed and imagined to partner with our users so as to add even more value. At some point, experiments will have to be done. We are considering many avenues at this point; user interactions as they are reflected in the logs can tell us something about what users search for, how, what they look at and so forth. Personalization could also give us information on the content. Letting users create their "own CanLII" could pave the way to the enrichment we have in mind. Overall, making the most of users' interactions appears to be the strategy to further enrich CanLII. Hopefully, an efficient strategy will be identified to help us add some sort of classification of CanLII content. If the classification is dependable enough, it could be used to enhance the search tool and bring us closer to solving the difficulties related to proliferation of legal information.

4. Conclusion

In the first part of this paper, a list of findings was presented. We tried to analyze the FAL contribution to the establishment of the public nature of primary legal documents. We have looked at how legal information is now published, who are its users and what we can envision as the role of the state in these matters.

One of the findings that appear especially important is that free access to law is now more frequently provided by government bodies than by legal information institutes. This cannot be surprising to anybody, for most governments have the resources, and access to law is for a large part their responsibility. What follows is that a Free Access to Law movement must define itself as comprising the organizations working to achieve precisely that: free access to law. What started small in a quaint village in upstate New York has now become one of the various missions of a democratic state: providing access to the law for free.

Three issues have merited a longer treatment: the sustainability of FAL initiatives, strategies for providing access to foreign law and pressure on larger LIIs to improve and add value so that their users can exploit their huge holdings.

References

Best, C.P. (2007), *Everything old is new again: the proliferation of case law and whether there is a remedy*, oral presentation at 8th International Conference Law via the Internet, Marriott Château Champlain, Montréal, October 25-26.

Greenleaf, G., Chung, P., Mowbray, A. (2007), *Emerging global networks for free access to law: WorldLII's strategies*, SCRIPTed, Vol. 4, No 4, pp. 319-366, available at: <www.law.ed.ac.uk/ahrc/script-ed/vol4-4/greenleaf.asp>.

Mowbray, A. (1997), *Managing large scale hypertext databases*, Journal of Information, Law and Technology, Vol. 2.

Poulin, D., Paré, É., Mokanov, I. (2005), *Reflex – Bridging Open Access with a Legacy Legal Information System*, oral presentation at 17th International Conference Law via the Internet, Port Vila, November 17–19.

Legal Information As an Essential Aspect of Citizenship

Vincenzo Zeno-Zencovich
University of Roma Tre, Italy

Abstract. The relationship between law and citizens has significantly changed in the last quarter of century. Legal provisions, increasingly, are no longer simply an order, but offer to citizens access to social services, rights, freedoms, liberties. Enforcement of the legal order requires informed citizens who not only abide by the law but also take full advantage of its provisions. The sources of the law have multiplied and can no longer be confined to acts of Parliament. This requires a different basical approach to the issues of legal information. The argument is that public authorities are under a positive obligation to inform in a complete and substantial way the "consumer" of their legal products.

1. As new notion of citizenship

Information societies change many social and economic relations. They change also the nature of citizenship.

Citizenship is, traditionally, qualified as a political status which confers upon the holder a bundle of relations, both active and passive, which reflect his position towards public authorities and other member of the community. There are participation rights such as voting rights, right of association and assembly, having a saying in decision-making processes. There are also rights to public services such as education, health-care, and essential social services. There are rights in employment relations such as freedom to work, contractual conditions, welfare, right to form and join trade-unions. And there are rights which pertain to the family sphere such as marriage, parental relationship, and succession rights.

The status of citizen is well defined in modern constitutions which in setting out fundamental rights clearly distinguish between human rights and citizenship rights, following a centuries old tradition which dates back to the French *"Déclaration des droits de l'homme et du citoyen"* of 1789.

On the other hand, going even further back in time the notion of citizenships finds its theoretical and legal foundations in the Greek πολις and the powerful Latin expression *civis romanus sum*. In the modern age citizenship is strongly related to the theory of social contract which sees it as the status conferred upon a person in exchange of obligations towards the institutions such as taxation and military service.

After World War Two the notion of citizenship has gradually expanded both subjectively, including persons which up to then were only "half citizens" (*e.g.* women did not hold voting rights), and objectively with the increasing intervention of the State in the social sphere and in the economy. From the 19th

Century liberal theory approach – which considered citizenship a civilised privilege for the affluent, we have moved towards "second" and "third generation"
rights, generally ensured through wider and heavier taxation or by imposing obligations on private businesses such as non-discrimination in employment, contractual conditions for monopolists and public service enterprises,
protection of the weaker party in consumer transactions.

A further step towards modern citizenship can be found in EU law, and
in particular in 2007 Lisbon Treaty: there is no longer a direct relationship
between being the citizen of a State and citizenship. And increasingly social
rights – and even voting rights – are extended to persons who are not even
EU citizens.

2. Information and citizenship

Against this background one can evaluate the role that information plays in
constructing the notion of citizenship. The first, and most examined, aspect is
that of the so-called "right to information". Historically this is seen as symmet-
rical to freedom of expression and freedom to disseminate one's ideas through
any means. The relation between the two aspects is clearly indicated in article
11 of the European Charter on Human Rights, now incorporated in the Lisbon
Treaty. A caveat is, however, necessary: the traditional perspective which sees
information as an activity which is run by media enterprises (newspapers,
periodicals, radio, TV), is very reductive if one considers the immensely wider
dimension of information processes which in contemporary societies involve
institutions, enterprises and citizens in a two-way flow of communications.

If one considers information not exclusively from the point of view of news-
gathering and news dissemination, one can easily realize that in order to have
an "informed citizenship" a vast effort – direct or indirect – of the public
authorities is strongly needed.

3. Public information and awareness of social services

In the first place one must consider that in order to benefit from the numerous
social services that welfare states offer to their citizens it is necessary that they
be adequately informed on the nature of the services, who is eligible, how they
are delivered.

One can appreciate here a fundamental difference between the private
and the public sector. While the former lives on communication – mostly
advertising – in order to offer its goods and services to the public and tries
to simplify all the various procedures, the latter – owing to its monopolistic
position and the absence of for-profit goals – generally has rather opaque

communication policies which render it not easily understandable or simply creating a significant difference between the message which is sent to the public and the factual practices which are applied in order to render the various social services.

A further element of difficulty in public information over social services is the extreme complexity of some of them (*e.g.* health-care and welfare services) and the educational level of those to whom they are offered. It should not be forgotten that quite often social services are aimed at those citizens whose economic and cultural conditions are very low. It is sufficient to consider that even legal experts find it difficult to move through the maze of primary and secondary legislation, supplement by a thicket of by-laws, regulations and case-law. How can one ensure that a layman knows if and when he is entitled to social services, and to what extent.

Traditionally, education and information are two quite different processes. Without considering the issues related to the "digital divide" (which will be analyzed further on) one can not but stress the fact that the years spent by children at school cannot be aimed only at acquiring basic knowledge and abilities, but requires – in a modern State – that students should be made aware of their citizenship status and of the rights and opportunities that are offered to them.

Whilst children and teen-agers rapidly learn outside the school environment to enter in a private economic relationship (shopping, travelling, receiving or making presents, etc.), it is much more difficult to explain how to interact with public bodies which deliver social services and which appear – beginning with educational institutions – complicated, distant and foreign.

4. Electoral information

A different sector where, apparently, there has been for a long time a significant amount of public information is that concerning political rights. Traditionally participation in the various types of elections and public consultations is favoured directly through information by the State or local authorities on when, how and for what one is called to vote, and indirectly offering spaces – both physical and on the public media – through which parties and candidates may present their programmes.

These actions which are well experimented in modern democracies appear however inadequate in contemporary information societies. On the one hand the number of electoral engagements are increasing (in the European context one has municipal, provincial, regional, national elections; elections for the European Parliament; local and national referenda. Public awareness declines and abstentions surge. On the other hand it is increasingly difficult to explain convincingly why, for whom and for what one is called to vote, considering also the fact that within the same State there may many different electoral systems.

Surely voter participation depends largely on those competing and the ideas and programmes they represent and present. But at the same time it depends on public decisions which make voting a simple procedure, because citizens know how to vote e can do so easily. Electronic voting – with all the necessary cautions – is surely one of the technical way to enhance voter participation. But the solution to the apparent paradox of the multiplication of electoral moments and dwining participation lies, in information societies, in the amount of public communication aimed at reducing – on easily ascertainable targets – the percentage of those who decide not to make use of their citizenship rights. Voting participation appears to be the result of sharing information and knowledge on one's political rights.

Surely voting is an essential aspect of citizenship, but in contemporary democracies there are many more ways to express one's role as citizen, in particular in decision-making processes which concern the community one belongs to: from town planning to environmental protection, from public transport services to the development of health and educational services, the role of public communication is essential from a substantial point of view in order to promote awareness; and from a procedural point of view because it ensures transparency of public decisions. One can easily understand the profound difference between a market or opinion poll which is meant to orient industry or political parties, and the role of a public consultation for the legitimacy, in front of the courts, of a public procedure.

5. Legal information and common knowledge of the law

Legal information, throughout the last centuries, has become a growing concern of modern States. In the age of enlightenment the right to know the laws which governed the land became one of the main claims against absolutism. From the 19th Century the rule is introduced that laws come into effect only after they have received some form of publication. And at the same time the principle *ignorantia legis non excusat* become a general rule, especially in the field of criminal law.

One cannot avoid pointing out that, two centuries later, the axiom publication = presumption of knowledge still continues to stand and is the object of little controversy.

For a number of reasons that will be listed below, in information societies one can doubt of the wisdom of a formalistic approach to the effects of the publication of the law.

a) In the course of the last decades the amount of legislation has increased with amazing speed, reaching levels quite unprecedented. The sources of legislation have multiplied moving from Parliament to national and local government, to independent administrative authorities. To this one must add the overwhelming production of EU law. It is quite unrealistic - and contrary to the rule of reason - that an informed citizen should spend most of the day perusing the various types of "official gazettes" in order to know which are the laws or the rules he must abide by.

b) Traditionally it is up to the State to publish its legal provisions, while it is up to the citizen to inform himself if he wants to benefit from those provisions or does not want to incur into sanctions. In an information society the relationship should be seen in a different way. There surely is an obligation of each citizen to respect the laws of the State he belongs to. But there is a prior obligation of the State to inform its citizens on the existence, the extent, the purpose of the laws it introduces. The way through which the State performs its obligation is not irrelevant and reflects itself on the compliance by its citizens.

c) The principle of official publication of the laws has been developed mainly in relation to criminal laws as an aspect of the principle of legality (*nullum crimen sine lege*) and clearly reflects a punitive perspective. But in modern societies knowledge of the laws is only in a minimal aspect one of enforcement of the law against criminal behaviours. The huge amount of administrative legislation and regulation does not simply require compliance, but much more importantly cooperation by citizen. It is quite impossible that a modern State may achieve its goals if its citizens are not aware of them and therefore are not able to benefit from the public policies promoted via legislation and regulation.

d) The traditional form of publicity through printed communication is quite inadequate to ensure the level of knowledge and awareness which modern societies require and are accustomed to.

   i. In the 19th Century printed press was surely the most advanced form of public communication, much more than public announcements posted on some wall or the town crier. It is no longer so when there are much more efficient and pervasive ways to communicate.

   ii. Behind the publication of laws in official gazettes there clearly is a paradox: in order to perform his duty and comply with the law a citizen must buy a copy of the publication. The State has a duty to publish its laws but only those who are able to pay the price can have complete access to legal information. And a yearly subscription to the various gazettes bears a significant cost.

   iii. Official gazettes surely satisfy the primary exigency of certainty of the law - the text which is valid is the one that has been published - but that of substantial knowledge of the content of the law. One therefore must clearly distinguish between formal objectives and effectivity.

e) The modern techniques of communication have greatly evolved and the development of the science of public communication is extremely advanced. One is quite aware that the publication of a legal text is addressed not to all citizens but only those are able to understand it, possess the basic knowledge of legal language, know how a legislative text is structured, are familiar with the subject. Therefore only a minority of citizen are able to understand it, to posit it within the legal system, detect novelties and suppression of past rules. But the role of a modern State is to render its legislation to the great majority of its citizens, and not only those who have a legal education. This requires simplified forms of communication using the medium which is considered the most appropriate.

f) In early industrial societies messages could be disseminated only in a limited number of ways. In post-industrial societies any common person is submerged by messages. In any moment of the day he receives thousands of messages: through the radio and the television, the fixed and mobile phone, his computer, billboards, newspapers, road signs, stickers, leaflets, wall writing, shop windows and lights, banners. A public information policy requires a careful study of those to whom the rules are addressed, their age group, where they can be found. A one-size-fits-all approach, such as the official gazette solutions, is clearly formalistic and achieves no significant results in making citizens aware of the law and of the opportunities it offers, and not only of the sanctions it is announcing.

g) Traditional legal publication is once and forever. The day after one has to seek the gazette in a public library or wait until is reproduced in some publication, generally by a private publisher. Modern forms of communication are, and must be, permanently available and constantly updated.

6. Guidelines for the publication of norms

From what has been said one can model a new idea of publication of the law which, though maintaining some aspects of the past, is consistent with modern citizenship and the rights which are attached to it.[1]

i. The State and other public bodies with legislative and regulatory powers are under a legal obligation not only to publish the rules they enact

---

[1] One should consider the "Declaration on Free Access to Law" made by Legal Information Institutes meeting in Montreal in 2002, as amended at meetings in Sydney (2003), Paris (2004) and Montreal (2007). For the text see the Appendix of this volume.

but also to adopt appropriate measures in order to ensure their effective knowledge.

ii. Every legislative or regulatory act should contain specific provisions concerning the measures which must be adopted in order to render it effectively known by the public at large. These measures can be chosen from a wide range of solutions.

iii. In adopting legislative or regulatory provisions one should consider the economic aspects of the communicational measures, which are the first and unavoidable cost of legislation.

iv. With regards to certain provisions of wide social impact (*e.g.* health care and social security) information and communication policies must be envisaged on a continuous basis (*e.g.* call centres, on–line assistance) in order to ensure effective access to the relevant services.

v. One must gradually and conceptually establish a direct relationship between the text of the norm and its public communication, in a way not dissimilar to what is found in consumer legislation where, applying the *contra proferentem* rule, the advertising message prevails over the technicalities of the contractual text. Similarly one can adopt the well established rule in financial markets regulations which requires issuer to present the content of their offer to the public in a clear text of a limited number of words.

vi. If a citizen is mainly a "consumer of norms" obscure laws, because they have not been sufficiently publicized and made clear are a "defective (legislative) product" which entails not only disapplication but also a possible liability for damages.

vii. The State is under an obligation to make available to its citizens, freely, data banks constantly updated containing all the different types of legislation and all the case-law of its higher jurisdictions. This latter aspect is particularly important, especially in States which continue not to be aware of law-making role of jurisprudence. The rights of its citizens however - notwithstanding hard-to-die positivistic ideologies - depend largely on what is recognized by the courts.

viii. There are some indicia of awareness of the problem of access to publicly held information on behalf of the EU authorities. The most recent examples are Directive 2003/98 on the use of information belonging to the public sector or Directive 2003/04 on environmental information which implements the 1998 Aarhus Convention. This is, however, not enough considering the enormous role of information in the construction of an effective citizenship.

7. The right of access to network facilities

In order to analyze the issue of access to legal information it is not sufficient to set out the rules that should superintend to the communication of laws and regulations. It is not sufficient that public authorities inform citizens of all the relevant provisions and make them available through on-line data banks.

The problem of the accessibility of these essential sources of information is twofold. On the one hand there is in all developed countries what is currently defined as a digital divide, *i.e.* the exclusion of a significant part of the population from access to computer services owing to their digital illiteracy. This involves mostly citizens that for reasons connected to their age or their socio–cultural conditions are not able to operate a computer and are therefore cannot access the huge amount of information - of any kind, including legal information - made available on the Internet. On the other hand accessibility is made difficult for those who do have basic computer skills by the lack of adequate infrastructures or network capacity. This depends mostly on geographical and economic factors. The current debate on broad-band connections and "next generation networks" (NGN) is surely an economic issue, but puts also into the limelight the problem of "digital citizenship".

Nowadays that so many public services - from health-care to transport, from education to cultural events - are provided easily and at no extra cost on-line it is clear that those who are not able to have access to them have an impaired citizenship.

This brings up the issue of significant public investments in order to reduce digital illiteracy and promote the development of (at least) broad-band networks. The present definition of "universal service" contained in Directive 2002/22 is manifestly inadequate to cope with the technological developments of this last half decade and with the notion of digital citizenship.

The conclusion is that in the information society *tout se tient*: legal information is not an exclusive problem of lawyers, but of all citizens. Access to legal information cannot be separated from the general issue of access to the information and communication networks.

The Right of Access to the Internet Network as a New Social Right: Problems and Prospects

Marina Pietrangelo

Institute of Legal Information Theory and Techniques (ITTIG-CNR), Italy

Abstract. In this text I will address the legal issues related to the development of the Internet, the territorial diffusion of ICT facilities and the actual degree of free accessibility to this technology by individuals. I will, therefore, outline what can be defined as "right of access to the Internet network". I will also attempt to understand whether that right can and must be conceived, both within the frame of the Italian and that of the international law, as a new "social right".

Keywords: Right of access, social right.

***

The access to the new communication networks is certainly a pivotal issue in contemporary society. To this topic, the sociologist Jeremy Rifkin has devoted a valuable book, in which he stresses that participation and access rather than autonomy and possession are in fact "the most important indicators of individual freedom" within the workings of networks (seen not only as "infrastructure" but also as "relationships amongst individuals") (Rifkin, 2000).

Expanding on these premises, Rifkin argues that the State has the fundamental duty of granting each and every individual "the right of access to the boundless number of networks – both within the geographical space and the cyberspace – though which men and women interact with each other", and raises doubts whether as yet single States have really striven to achieve that.

Over the years, numerous works have been dedicated to the question of "access to technology". A common denominator, as it were, seems to emerge from each study: sizeable portions of the world population are completely left out of the new technological order. Furthermore, the differential sequence in the degree of accessibility to the new technologies observed in different countries depending on their geographic position certainly constitutes a major source of inequality in our society. Furthermore, the sociologist Castells maintains that the "cut-off areas" are "discontinuous in terms of culture and location", as they can be found in the French *banlieues*, in the African shanty towns as well as in the Chinese and Indian poverty-stricken peripheries.

All this appears in sharp contrast with the efficient connectibility to the new technological network available to organisations, social groups and predominant parts of the world (Castells, 1996). Today's multimedia system, or convergence system, Castells adds, is characterised by integration between different media and shows, above all, a high degree of interactive potential, which bring about an incipient social stratification amongst users, in striking opposition to the culturally unifying power exerted by mass television broadcasting.

Basing on these considerations, we may perhaps state that acknowledging the right of access to the network as a new, autonomous right in the era of technology will depend on the social and political decisions made at institutional level by each individual State and the international community as a whole.

A first proposal in this sense, that is. aimed at acknowledging this new modern right can be seen in a document issued by Eurocities, an association comprising the main cities of the European Union. This text contains in fact a "European Charter of Rights of Citizens in the Knowledge Society", or *Charter of eRights*, which appears to be the highest point reached by sociological elaborations on the topic of "right of access". This document seems to translate those elaborations into an out-and-out bill which encompasses, thereby, some authoritative indications regarding the urgent necessity for single States to adopt a common "Constitution for the Internet" (Cheli, 2003; Rodotà, 2004 *contra* Lyon, 2003).

Within the frame of reference of the rights now acknowledged by the Charter of Nice[1], the *Charter of eRights* advocates the acknowledgment of four categories of rights: "*The rights to access; The Rights to Education and Training; The Rights to Online Information; The Rights to Online Participation*". Despite the fact that the Charter is drafted in the form of a bill, it is, though, just a declaration of good intentions that in the EU countries, signed in Manchester by a number of willing local administrators on 7th July 2005.[2]

Along similar lines, also the *Declaration of the Committee of Ministers on human rights and the rule of law in the Information Society*, approved by the Council of Europe in May 2005, insists upon the relevance of access. Besides, the above-mentioned declaration invites the above committee's member states "[to] promote the opportunities afforded by ICTs for fuller enjoyment of human rights and counteract the threats they pose in this respect, while fully complying with the ECHR"[3], as "The primary objective of all measures taken should be to extend the benefits of ICTs to everyone, thus encouraging inclusion in the Information Society. This can be done by ensuring effective and equitable access to ICTs, and developing the skills and knowledge necessary to exploit this access, including media education".[4]

---

[1] The Charter of Fundamental Rights of the European Union.
[2] Available at: <www.eurocities.org>.
[3] CM(2005)56, cfr.§ II.1.
[4] *Ibidem.*

Somehow in line with this supernational tendency to promote citizens' sharing in the process of defining policies aimed at digital participation, regarding, though, the core issue of information accessibility (as an explicit reference to Art. 11 of the Charter of Nice clearly indicates)[5] the European Commission has, in the *White Paper on a European Communication Policy*, set in motion a public consultation aimed at drafting a document (a *European charter* or a *Code of conduct on communication*) which defines common principles concerning information and communication activities basing on the European guidelines. This document highlights the fact that every citizen should be granted access, in his/her own language, to all information on matters of public interest, and that, therefore, all information should be made available through an extensive network of channels comprising mass media and new technologies, such as the Internet. However, great emphasis is placed upon providing citizens throughout the European Union with the training and education necessary for them to accede to and make use of the information mentioned above.

We are therefore inclined to share the opinion of those who maintain that basically today's information society poses a "problem of right of citizenship, therefore of democracy" (Sias, 2002), as a high number of people are not able to use the new information technology. Those people's needs must be met by implementing a far-reaching process of alphabetisation and an effective IT access availability, at a price that does not discriminate socially or economically. The powers that be must grant access to the infrastructure, to the IT media itself, and adopt a cultural policy aimed at training and education, in order to enable people to benefit from the IT tools.

I would like to add that within the scope of both single States and the European community strict norms ruling organisation and activity of public administrative functions (online services, electronic signature, etc.) have been introduced, which in fact require that the citizens dispose of the know-how enabling them to use the new IT tools.

If now the lawmaker forces the public to use, as an option or as the only way, technological instruments in order to access a number of public services, the public administration must do its utmost to enable the public to make the best use of the new IT services, or else the information technologies used within public services (e-government) will not produce benefits but new types of inequality.

Stefano Rodotá writes that "digitalisation in the public administration and its appearance in the Internet does not necessarily grant democratic results. This happens only if this does not "bring out" the citizens, (*i.e. builds up people's self confidence, translator's note*) [...]. The *e-government* is not

---

[5] COM(2006)35.

democratic in itself. It becomes democratic if it helps create a context pursuing the aims of democracy, seen as "people's government" and "in-public government" " (Rodotà, 2004). The spread of new technologies is only meaningful if it brings about a decisive empowerment of the individual in accordance with the guidelines to be found in individual States' constitutions.

As clearly brought to light by the well-known sentence issued by the Federal Court of the USA, Federal District of Pennsylvania, on 11th June 1996, the Internet network constitutes a high-potential communication medium, contrasting, in its nature of both interpersonal communication tool and thought-diffusion means, with any other traditional media (for a comment see Zeno-Zencovich, 1996; Longhini, 2003).

What makes the new communication medium different from any other is indeed what makes it into an instrument which facilitates other human activities not necessarily connected to the exchange of messages, data and information. Those activities (online services provided by public administration bodies, online commercial transactions, work from home, e-learning)[6] are still carried out by a limited number of people, although their rapid diffusion is to be hoped for.

Consequently, the core contents of the right of access to informatics shows a wider scope than that of traditional forms of communication freedom. Better still, it appears to have an auxiliary function with respect to a wider range of traditional rights. And the new order of liberalised telecommunications has in fact given impulse to the need to think in terms of right to access the telecommunication network (whose maximum expression is the so-called "universal service"), to be conceived as a sort of "mother-right", as opposed to the mere right of connection to the internet (Costanzo, 2000).

"The discipline ruling accessibility – and, more broadly, interconnection – acquires now an ancillary function with respect to the fundamental rights"; to grant access we must then "set the minimum requisites of minimum transmission capacity for networks, introduce "IT literacy" training programmes,

---

[6] In the final declaration of the first part of the *World Summit on Information Society* (WSIS) organised by the UN (Geneva 2003 – Tunis 2005) we can read: «The usage and deployment of ICTs should seek to create benefits in all aspects of our daily life. ICT applications are potentially important in government operations and services, health care and health information, education and training, employment, job creation, business, agriculture, transport, protection of environment and management of natural resources, disaster prevention, and culture, and to promote eradication of poverty and other agreed development goals. ICTs should also contribute to sustainable production and consumption patterns and reduce traditional barriers, providing an opportunity for all to access local and global markets in a more equitable manner. Applications should be user-friendly, accessible to all, affordable, adapted to local needs in languages and cultures, and support sustainable development. To this effect, local authorities should play a major role in the provision of ICT services for the benefit of their populations» (§ 51). Cfr. Declaration of Principles. Building the Information Society: a global challenge in the new Millennium, 12 december 2003, Document WSIS-03/GENEVA/DOC/4-E.

foster policies aimed at reducing the generational and geographical divide in the level of technological competence, put certain subjects, both public and private, in charge of granting access to the network, discipline competition in the sector in order to curb service utilisation costs" (Zeno-Zencovich, 2004).

In conclusion, access to network becomes a "constituent part of citizenship" (Rodotà, 2004).

On the technology side, a greater diffusion of network accessibility depends on brad band availability, on the possibility to share language (therefore software), on the creation of shared standards, on the availability of the source code of programs. On the juridical side, it is now widely accepted that the Internet purports to be an instrument which caters for individual as well as social rights. These rights are upheld by a number of constitutional rulings. Therefore we must now ask ourselves whether we can envisage a general and pervasive right of access to this medium, which may serve the purpose of reinterpreting the constitutional norms, adapting them to the need for legal protection required by new situations arising from technological innovation.

Let us consider the thesis that the acknowledgment of new rights – beyond the boundary of both the existing and the ones stemming from social conscience – without modifying the constitution, and independently of their normative acknowledgment, is absolutely feasible (Modugno, 1995). Hence, we can assume that the right of access to the network and to IT instruments, if not as yet fully conceivable as a "freedom right", might be considered to be a "social right".

The thorough character of our constitution would allow us to extrapolate and surmise implicit rights as necessary and likely consequences of previously stated rights. These new rights could well be formulated as rights instrumental to those that have been enunciated, as transversal rights basing on the combination of a number of constitutional norms read in an evolutionary manner. These new rights have not been taken into account yet because they have not been recognised.

On the other hand, on the topic of those new rights, also known as "third-generation rights", it is worth remembering that the right to privacy itself entered our constitution in the form of a right instrumental to the rights of freedom present in the Constitution, which bears out the fact that rights are always a product of the time and society in which they originate and develop [...] and which first felt the need for them, then called for their protection and, finally, defined them (Busia, 2000).

Let us now try and figure out the right of access to information technologies as a right which cannot be immediately and unfailingly enforced. We will then realise to what extent the problem of its effectiveness is not so much, or not just a juridical one, as it rather depends on the cultural and economic development of society itself and on whether there exist within society organisations enabling the enforcement of such rights. Certainly, overcoming the so-called digital divide cannot just depend on the existence of adequate laws which, however can help see the process through. First and foremost, we must insist that access to the Internet be seen as "universal service" [7] by upgrading the EU legislation and consequently that of the individual member states.

However, the theoretical basis of the new right would remain anchored to the concept of liberation from a well-defined form of deprivation coinciding in our information society with the Internet, which has itself become the metaphor of this society. Besides, within this construction the question of its conflict with freedom rights would appear toned down, and yet perhaps reconciled, if we took into account that the right in question has a twofold valence. On the one hand it is an autonomous right, on the other hand it is a right functional to the exercise of other rights and, specifically, of the civil liberties.

In conclusion, we believe that underestimating the social role of access to information technology in today's information society is tantamount to failing to grant everybody those requisites, necessary (in our time) to establish relationships with other individuals and to ensure full expression of one's personality (see articles 2 and 3 of the Constitution; Principle of Dignity of the Individual and Principle of Substantial Equality).

In today's legal systems, in which telecommunication networks do not belong to the States any longer, as they have been privatised, public authorities are in charge of forcing network managements to grant the public service, in conformity with organisational and financial requirements and in concert with other constitutionally protected interests.

References

Busia, G. (2000), *Riservatezza (diritto alla)*, Digesto (diritto pubblico), Utet, Torino, pp. 476 and ff.

Castells, M. (1996), *The Rise of Network Society*, Blackwell, New York.

Cheli, E. (2003), *Introduzione al diritto commerciale nella "new economy". A proposito di un libro recente*, No. 2, pp. 667 and ff.

Costanzo, P. (2000), *Internet (diritto pubblico)*, Digesto (diritto pubblico), Appendice, Utet, Torino, pp. 347 and ff.

Longhini, P. (2003), *Internet nella giurisprudenza*, Giuffrè, Milano.

Modugno, F. (1995), *I "nuovi diritti" nella Giurisprudenza Costituzionale*, Giappichelli, Torino.

Rifkin, J. (2000), *The Age of Access*, Putnam Publ., New York.

---

[7] The directive 97/33Ce of 30 June 1997, issued by the Parliament and the Council of Ministers, defines Universal Service as follows: "a minimum, defined service system of a certain quality, available to each and every user regardless of their geographic location and, considering any condition or circumstance peculiar to a specific area within the nation, at an affordable price".

Rodotà, S. (2004), *Tecnopolitica. La democrazia e le nuove tecnologie della comunicazione*, Laterza, Roma-Bari.

Sias, G. (2002), *Società dell'informazione e conoscenza. Un futuro ineguale?*, Franco Angeli, Milano.

Zeno-Zencovich, V. (1996), *Manifestazione del pensiero, libertà di comunicazione e la sentenza sul caso «Internet»*, Diritto dell'informazione e dell'informatica, No. 4-5, pp. 640 and ff.

Zeno-Zencovich, V. (2004), *La libertà d'espressione. Media, mercato, potere nella società dell'informazione*, Il Mulino, Bologna.

Online Access to Legislation in the EU: from Fee-Based to Free Information

Albrecht Berger
Publications Office of the European Communities

Abstract. The paper describes the development from subscription-based legislation databases to free-of-charge services, which has been taking place at the EU level as well as in nearly all EU Member States since 1997. The most important issue was the conflict of the two main policies in the late 1990s: the dogma of fee-based value-added services vs. the principles of e-Government and free Public Sector Information. The paper also refers to the paradigm shift that has taken place in many countries since 2001, as far as the websites of legal gazettes are concerned. In many countries, these websites are no longer seen as a mere source of free information, but also as a way to rationalise the promulgation (official publication) of legislation. This means that the online publication of newly adopted legislation has become legally binding in these countries and has, in some cases, even replaced the official paper publication of legislation.

Keywords: Legal databases, free access to legislation, legal gazettes online, online promulgation of legislation, value-added information, e-Government, Public Sector Information (PSI), paperless legal gazette, Celex, EUR-Lex.

1. Introduction: legislation online in Europe - 3 milestones

1.1. LEGISLATION IN ONLINE DATABASES

In Europe, the development of legal databases goes back to the 1970s. These databases were first used in an in-house environment before they became accessible to external users during the second half of the 1970s. This external access was subscription-based, either with a pay-as-you-use fee or with a monthly or yearly flat rate.

This situation lasted about 20 years, and it must be said that the databases in question were, in most cases, rather user-unfriendly and their legislation section was not much used.

1.2. LEGISLATION IN WEBSITES

When from 1995 onwards the official publishers of legislation started to put a copy of their legal gazette on the web, this was done in parallel to the existing (official) legal databases. Therefore, it is not surprising that most of the new services on the web were initially offered as paying services as well, despite their vocation as public information systems in the framework of e-Government. But a turning point was reached already in 1997/98: many governments decided to offer access to these services free of charge, at least for the period immediately following the publication of the legal gazette (see fig. 1 and 2). This was the actual beginning of an unstoppable evolution, which led to a situation where the online legal gazettes have become accessible free of charge in all EU Member States but one (see fig. 3).

In parallel to the above-mentioned evolution towards free online access to the legal gazettes in Europe, a further development took place: having been modernised with the addition of a web interface, many of the traditional fee-based legal databases became free of charge. Very often, these databases and the websites of the legal gazettes were merged into one integrated service.

1.3. OFFICIAL PUBLISHING OF LEGISLATION ON THE INTERNET

Although it is only indirectly linked to the issue of free-of-charge access to legislation, another aspect of the above-mentioned development should be mentioned here, namely the new role of the legal gazette online. From 2001 onwards, many countries have attributed an official ("legally binding") character to the online edition of the legal gazette (see table I). In other words, in these countries publishing the legal gazette on the web has become part of the promulgation (official publication) of legislation.

Some countries have even gone a step further and no longer publish an official paper edition (see table II).

2. How online access to EU legislation became free of charge

The history of online access to EU legislation (before 1993: Community legislation) is a good illustration of the general development in Europe as outlined in part 1.

2.1. THE FEE-BASED CELEX DATABASE

In 1970/71, the European Commission set up the Celex (*Communitatis europeae lex*) database, first as an internal information system and thereafter for the use of all Institutions of the then European Communities. Although some external pilot users were already admitted during the 1970s, the official opening to the public took place in 1981, after the database had been converted to a multilingual system.

Initially, Celex was disseminated via a commercial host, but a few years later, a twofold dissemination scheme was introduced, which is still in force today: the database was licensed to more than 20 national hosts and other re-distributors (the Commission acting as a wholesaler) and was distributed directly to end-users as well (the Commission acting as a retailer).

The consequence of this double dissemination channel was that the end-user price of the authentic (Commission) version had to be set on a higher scale than merely a token fee. In the end, the fee was fixed at a level corresponding to the statistical average of the access fees for legal databases at the time in Europe. (It should be noted that the end-user and the license fees did not even cover the dissemination costs of the Commission, not to speak of the costs of the database management).

2.2. The free-of-charge EUR-Lex website ("Celex-light")

In the crucial years 1997/98 when the doctrine of free-of-charge access to legal information spread throughout Europe, the fee-based character of Celex was actually not put into question. Celex was indeed considered to be a value-added information service, intended for professional users, and the opinion that such services should remain fee-based was still predominant at the time: making those services free of charge would have been seen as being tantamount to subsidising professional information with tax payers' money.

Therefore, the Institutions of the EU decided the following in 1997:

— to give free access to the Official Journals during a period of 20 days following their publication (this period was later extended to 45 days, before access became entirely free);
— to grant free access to the texts (but not to the metadata) of the legislation in force and the preparatory acts, as well as to the case law of the Court of Justice "during the period granted by the Court", which was then one year.

For technical reasons, the free-of-charge access was not implemented within the Celex system but in a new website which was opened in 1998 under the name of EUR-Lex and which gave access to the texts stored in Celex. During the following years, EUR-Lex was enhanced with a common search interface which made it possible simultaneously to retrieve documents in distinct services. In addition, the coverage of EUR-Lex was extended beyond the limits determined in 1997 (e.g. all available Official Journals, the entire case-law of the Court of Justice, legislative texts in force in various formats, the EU legislation in its consolidated version as well as the legislation no longer in force). All these improvements turned the free-of-charge EUR-Lex into a fully-fledged "Celex-light" service which, despite the limitations of its search functions, quickly became a valuable complement to Celex for professional users.

2.3. The end of Celex and its merger into the new EUR-Lex

The Institutions of the EU thus provided two legal information services with approximately the same coverage but different search facilities, namely a fee-based database containing added-value information and intended for professional users (Celex), and a free-of-charge quasi-professional copy of the first service (EUR-Lex).

This was the situation in December 2002 when the European Parliament adopted a resolution requiring free end-user access to Celex (Resolution A5-0440/2002). The resolution was based on the political axiom of e-Government, namely the idea that online access to official legal information had to be free of charge, even if the database in question was a professional value-added service and despite the fact that a comprehensive layman-oriented free-of-charge version existed in parallel.

There were still other arguments in favour of maintaining the status quo of the two services (e.g. the risk of creating unfair competition with the commercial re-distributors of Celex), but the decision taken had the undeniable advantage of simplifying things: at the production level of the information service as well as at the dissemination level.

Therefore, further to the resolution, a project was undertaken in order to merge Celex and EUR-Lex into a new free-of-charge service under the name of EUR-Lex. This new service started in November 2004. Earlier on, in July 2004, Celex had also become free of charge, four months before the end of its existence as the then oldest legal database in Europe.

The following chronology of events shows that the whole process of making access to EU legislation free of charge lasted seven years.

July 1997: decision of the EU Institutions to create a limited free access service in parallel to Celex,
Jan. 1999: opening of EUR-Lex,
Jan. 2000: free access to the Official Journal in EUR-Lex is extended from 20 to 45 days,
Jan. 2000: free access to the Official Journal in EUR-Lex is extended from 20 to 45 days,
Jan. 2002: unlimited free access to the Official Journal,
Dec. 2002: Resolution of the European Parliament,
July 2004: (end-user) access to Celex becomes free of charge.

2.4. ACCESS BY RE-DISTRIBUTORS

Since the mid-1980s, when the Commission established the scheme of dual dissemination of Celex via national hosts and via direct access for end-users, the principles of the Directive on Public Sector Information (Directive 2003/98/EC of 17 November 2003, OJ L 345, 31.12.2003, p.90-96) have been applied (*avant la lettre*) to the wholesaling of Celex and EUR-Lex.

Today,

— the licence for the re-distribution of the database (texts and metadata) has remained fee-based,

— the texts of EU legislation can be reproduced and re-used for commercial purposes free of charge.

Some national hosts give access to their Celex/EUR-Lex version free of charge, others market it as a fee-based service. The re-distributors have, in general, not been very critical about the fact that the licences remained fee-based when end-user access became free of charge. In so far as they can continue to exploit their Celex/EUR-Lex database, they do not seem worried about their competition with a free-of-charge version of the same value-added database.

2.5. DIGRESSION: FREE ACCESS TO CASE LAW?

The situation concerning online access to case law is more complex than that of access to legislation. On the one hand, many courts publish their decisions (free of charge) on the Internet. On the other hand, the commonly used databases containing a comprehensive collection of the decisions of courts and tribunals are run by commercial companies and are thus subscription-based. There are also countries with public sector databases which are not free of charge.

In the case of Celex, pragmatic solutions were chosen:

— Since 1997, the Court of Justice provided its recent decisions free of charge on the *Curia* website, from which they were supposed to be removed after 1 year.

— From 1999 onwards, EUR-Lex provided unlimited free access to the case law stored in Celex, without any official decision being taken.

— From July 2004, when use of Celex was made gratis, access to EU case law became entirely free of charge, see subsection 2.3.

3. State of play in the EU

Since 2009, online access to legislation is free of charge in all EU Member States except one (see fig. 3). In about a third of the Member States, the legal gazette has official character (see tab. I). Official ("legally binding") online editions are often disseminated in parallel to the normal online gazette, in the framework of a special, technically protected service.

Six EU Member States no longer publish an official paper edition of new legislation (see tab. II); other Member States are preparing to take this step.

A. Berger

Table I. Legislation published officially on the Internet

(N.B.:) Norway	2001
United Kingdom	2002 (1 Jan.)
Estonia	2002 (1 June)
Belgium	2003
Austria	2004 (1 Jan.)
France	2004 (1 June)
(N.B.:) Iceland	2005
Slovenia	2006 (1 Jan.)
Portugal	2006 (1 July)
Denmark	2008 (1 Jan.)
Hungary	2008 (1 July)
Italy	2009 (1 Jan.)
Spain	2009 (1 Jan.)
Netherlands	2009 (1 March)

Table II. Paperless legal gazettes

Belgium	2003
Austria	2004
Portugal[1]	2007
Denmark	2008
Spain	2009
Netherlands	2009

Appendix

- Other official online versions: Greece, Finland, Switzerland.
- Projects under way: EU, Germany, Sweden and others.

Figure 1. Online access to the legal gazettes (and their equivalent in the United Kingdom and Ireland) in the European Union (May 1997).

Figure 2. Online access to the legal gazettes (and their equivalent in the United Kingdom and Ireland) in the European Union (October 2000).

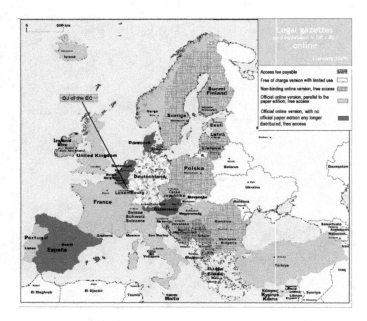

Figure 3. Legal gazettes (and their equivalent in the United Kingdom and Ireland) online (January 2009).

Italian Legislation on the Internet: Citizens' Access to Legislation in Force and Regulatory Reorganisation

Italo Scotti, Enrico Seta
Chamber of Deputies, Italy

Abstract. Together with the Senate and the Prime Minister's Office, Italy's Chamber of Deputies supports the so called "Normattiva" Project, i.e. the most significant attempt so far in Italy aimed to set up a free-of-charge public service enabling citizens to access online a highly stratified and extremely complex body of legislation.

The main challenge lies in determining the scope of the notion of "legislation in force" because of the coexistence of different sources of regulatory production, adopted at different times. Moreover it is only recently that the improvement of legislative drafting and of the quality of legislation have starter to attract increasing interest.

The following strategies were pursued in order to deal with those difficulties: a) the application of an XML mark-up for the automatic processing of measures explicitly amending previous legislation and the full tracking of linkages among legislative documents and among provisions; b) a notation system to flag implicit abrogating, amending or supplementing provisions; c) production of an editor enabling text consolidation; d) providing metadata in order to classify pieces of legislation and individual provisions contained therein according to subject-matter.

The "*Normattiva*" Project, which built upon the previous "*Normeinrete*" project, has already yielded good results in terms of data standardization, production of an editor for the consolidation of legislative texts in XML format, ex-post retrieval of all regulatory measures adopted as of May 2001 (the beginning of the 14th Parliament), the launching of the x-leges system for digitalising the entire rule-making process.

Major steps forward are expected in the coming 24 months.

Finally the paper analyses the strong interdependence between the availability of a digital system for filing, consolidating and classifying regulatory texts and the potential success of projects for regulatory simplification and reorganisation.

***

1. The title of this paper, "Italian Legislation on the Internet: Citizens' access to the Legislation in force and Regulatory Reorganisation", already highlights the two goals pursued by the "Normattiva" ("Regulactive") project launched in Italy by the Presidency of the Council of Ministers, the Chamber of Deputies and the Senate in the year 2000.

A more detailed description of the project and the extent to which it has been implemented will be given in the second part of this paper, whilst this first part will examine aspects of the context around the Italian.

2. From the 1990s onwards and partly in response to international and European demands, Italy has been paying increasing attention to issues concerning the quality of legislation. Such issues affect a series of aspects ranging from the formal ones of drafting legislative texts to both a preliminary and

a retrospective evaluation of regulatory impact. The quality of legislation is a cross-cutting theme that, in a multiple-level system, concerns all territorial levels and all the powers operating at each level. Therefore, in a system in which regulation is the result of complex procedures that increasingly have an impact on several territorial levels, even national policies pertaining to the regulatory quality are interwoven with regional ones and those stemming from the EU and affect the various legislative Assemblies and Government alike.

In recent years, the issue of the quality of legislation has also acquired importance in connection with policies related to economic development and competitiveness. This firstly by virtue of initiatives launched by the OECD from 1995[1] onwards and then as a result of the issue's inclusion in the Lisbon strategy.[2]

Within the international and European framework, both the Italian State and its Regions have recently adopted various measures directed not only at improving the quality of legislation but also, and primarily, at streamlining legislation and administration. The year 1997 marked a turning point at a national level, in this respect. Partly following in-depth studies carried out with the OECD, the Chamber of Deputies reformed its own Rules of Procedure around two guiding themes: the efficiency of parliamentary business (based both on tight timing rules and on the programming of the House's business) and pre-legislative scrutiny and consultation. That same year, Parliament passed Law no. 59 of 15 March 1997. This Act:

— launched a vast work of regulatory reorganization that was then further regulated by Law no. 229 of 29 July 2003. The latter singled out the "definition of the parameters of regulatory reorganization and codification of the primary legislation governing the subject, after obtaining the Council of State's opinion, (...) together with the determination of the basic principles for the subject-matters of concurrent legislation", from amongst the general guiding principles and criteria which the Government must comply with when rationalising the legislation in force; and

---

[1] On 9 March 1995, the OECD Council approved a *Recommendation on Improving the Quality of Government Regulation.* Appended to it was a *Checklist for Regulatory Decision-Making.* This comprised ten questions followed by a brief illustration and a note containing, *inter alia,* a wider-ranging commentary on the checklist's questions. The document recommended that Member States took effective measures to guarantee the quality and transparency of government regulations, whilst inviting the OECD's "Public Management" Committee to present a report within three years on the Member States' demonstrated ability to improve the quality of their regulations. The Committee's *Report on Regulatory Reform* was published in 1997 and was followed, in 1998, by the launching of a review of the Member States' regulatory systems. This project is still under way.

[2] So called because it was defined during the European Council meeting held in Portugal's capital on 23 and 24 March 2000, the Lisbon strategy assumes that the quality of regulation and a reduction of administrative burdens are fundamental factors for fostering competitiveness.

— entrusted to an Annual Streamlining Act the task of simplifying and rationalising administrative procedures by "delegislating" the rules governing
them.

3. The criteria for regulatory reorganization and simplification indicated
in Law no. 59 of 1997 are subject to constant updating and have been implemented at a national level through the enactment of about twenty Consolidation Acts and Codes, all told, as well as numerous delegislating Regulations.
At a regional level, their implementation has been achieved through an in-
tense work of regulatory simplification and reorganization carried out in ways
varying from Region to Region but always directed at streamlining and rationalising the regulatory "stock". Several of the new Statutes adopted by the
Regions following the reform of Title V of Part II of the Constitution have
dedicated important provisions to this aspect, too.

4. Both the central importance of this objective for everyone working with
the law and its growing political significance are demonstrated by another
important piece of legislation, namely, Law no. 246 of 28 November 2005.
Providing for regulatory simplification and reorganization for the year 2005,
this law contains four important novelties:

— section 1 amends section 20 of the above mentioned Law no. 59/1997
and provides that, as regards the subject-matters for which exclusive
competence lies with the State, the process of codifying each subject-
matter is to be accompanied by an comprehensive collection of all the
rules governing the same subject-matter;
— section 2 inserts section 20-*ter* into the above mentioned Law no. 59 of
1997 and provides for the possibility for the Government, the Regions
and the autonomous Provinces to reach agreements or understandings
(during the State-Regions Conference or the Unified Conference) for the
purpose of pursuing shared goals to improve the quality of legislation
within their respective legal systems. The first agreement was signed on
29 March 2007, during a Unified Conference;
— subsections 1-11 of section 14 reform the regulatory impact analysis to
be carried out ex ante and flank it with an impact analysis to be carried
out *ex post*. Thus they provide, one might say, a guide to the good
maintenance of a regularly running system once the work of "cleaning
up" has been carried out through a "Legislation-cutting" operation;
— subsections 12-24 of section 14 then introduce a special procedure directed precisely at reducing and simplifying the *corpus* of legislation (the
so-called "Legislation-cutting"). Such procedure provides for the repeal

(upon completion of the survey of the national laws in force now under
way) of all national legislative provisions published before 1 January 1970,
with the exception of those listed under subsection 17 and those that the
Government may deem indispensable by way of legislative decree. In December 2007, the Government presented both Houses of Parliament with
the report provided for under section 14(12) of Law no. 246/2005. The
report identifies the national provisions in force in the various Ministries'
areas of competence and highlights some regulatory inconsistencies and
antinomies relating to various sectors of law-making.

The report greatly aids an understanding of the progress already made
as well as the work's inherent difficulties. Such difficulties are tied, above all,
to a stratification of rules that often follow one another temporally without
"reckoning" with earlier ones and thus without an appropriate co-ordination
with already enacted provisions. This creates total confusion and gives *carte
blanche* to those who have to apply and interpret the law for the purposes of
establishing which pieces of legislation actually have legal force.

The Government has put the work done to implement the "Legisla-tion-
cutting" procedure to use in section 24 of Decree Law no. 112/2008 (and
related appendix), prior to the deadline envisaged in the enabling act and
inverting its mechanism (by identifying the rules to be repealed, instead
of those in force, and no longer applying the 1970 time limit). This brings
forward the fiscal measures for 2008 within a multi-year perspective. Section
24 provides for the repeal of 3,370 regulatory acts (other than those already
expressly repealed). This process was not without its problems that were
raised during parliamentary consideration, as regards provisions erroneously
included in the appendix. For example, the inclusion of the rules implementing
Sicily's Statute provoked a strong reaction from the island's "Governor" who
had them expunged from the appendix.

Section 25 of the decree deals with another fundamentally important issue,
namely, the quantification and reduction of administrative burdens. This, too,
is a commitment that is European in origin and one that requires Italy to make
a 25 per cent reduction in its administrative burdens by the year 2012.

This is an issue that clearly overlaps both with the "Legislation-cutting"
one and with the other challenge that Italy has to face, namely, the implementation of the well-known Services Directive (or Bolkestein Directive: Dir.
2006/123/EC) by 28 December 2009. Taking a horizontal approach towards
all services except those expressly excluded, this directive pursues the goal
of developing the internal services market, presupposing a major work of
simplifying the criteria and procedures laid down, in the individual Member
States, for the provision of the said services.

5. Thus, we are facing three challenges:

— "Legislation-cutting";
— a reduction in administrative costs; and
— implementation of the Services Directive.

All three require an in-depth survey of the regulation in force, within a general perspective of reorganization, regulatory and administrative simplification and liberalisation. They are three challenges that converge and are mutually supportive because they all presuppose activities moving in the common direction of finally creating a clear picture of the legislation in force, thereby necessitating and at the same time also fostering the "*Normattiva*" ("Regulation") project.

6. Such is the historical context into which the *Normattiva* project fits. Possibly one of the most technically complex Italian projects in the field of legal IT, this project is certainly the one that has, for years, been witnessing the greatest efforts made by the country's main institutions.

The proposal was first conceived at the end of the 1990s by the Legislation Committee of the Chamber of Deputies. The aim was to connect and create synergy between two highly important social and political needs:

— the need to create, in our country, too, a public service that could honour the citizens' primary right to know the laws in force. Today, a basic subscription to a private service providing access just to the legislation proper (Codes, Acts of Parliament and decrees) costs the citizen no less than 1,000 euros per annum. One should also consider that, in addition to their considerable subscription costs, these data banks also present the gaps and inaccuracies typical of a commercial product and do not achieve the degree of authority that is desirable in a field such as that of legal information and that ought necessarily to characterise a service provided by the State; and
— the need to offer the work of regulatory reorganization that basic technological infrastructure that is increasingly becoming one of the essential components for all the public administration's activities and that, given the dimensions and the chaotic nature of our legal system, constitutes a prerequisite for the success of every legislative simplification and rationalisation project.

On the basis of one of the Legislation Committee's debates held in 1998, a parliamentary amendment tabled the following year by the then Committee Chairman, the Hon. Giovanni Meloni, introduced what was to become section 107 of the Finance Act 2001 (Law no. 388/2000). This allocated 25 billion lire over 5 years to "realising free-of-charge computer access for citizens to the regulation in force and promoting its reorganization". The project's management was entrusted to the President of the Council of Ministers and was to be regulated by way of a special Decree of the President of the Council of Ministers, to be adopted in agreement with the Presidents of the two Houses.

7. In 2003, two years after the Finance Act was enacted, the implementing Decree of the President of the Council of Ministers was passed (the DPCM dated 24 January 2003). This established the project's steering bodies and further clarified the decree's provisions.

During this preparatory phase, some activities preliminary to IT processing were carried out. Of these, perhaps the most important – in terms of long-term effects – was the launch of the project "*Norme in rete*" ("*Laws online*") and the setting, as part of that project, of two national standards for the IT processing of regulatory texts. These standards were based on technologies for the mark-up and semantic processing of texts (see the AIPA circulars published in the Official Journal for November 2001 and May 2002, respectively).

Against this backdrop, two major achievements, that have had a highly positive impact on the Italian institutional and scientific "environment", have taken shape:

— the emergence of a scientific community that is highly specialised in the application of mark-up languages to regulatory texts (several of its representatives are present here today); and
— the standards' high level of penetration within institutions (most particularly, the administrations of national and regional legislative assemblies) and, therefore, a wealth of projects, applications and shared initiatives based on the exploitation of what the mark-up of regulatory texts has to offer.

8. Once the preparatory phase was completed, the project's Steering committee (comprising the three Secretary-Generals of, respectively, the Presidency of the Council of Ministers, the Chamber of Deputies and the Senate) and the working group operating under its mandate, began to tackle the more complex problems of:

1. designing the software for the IT processing of the texts; and
2. digitalizing the texts.

As far as the first point is concerned, results that may be considered definitive have been achieved. The "Editor" application, a database and a WEB interface are already operational. Under an agreement with the Court of Cassation (signed in August 2004), the Court's Data Processing Centre has been chosen to host the IT system, whilst the necessary IT equipment has been financed, for an amount of 3 million Euros, under a subsequent agreement drawn up in December of the same year.

As far as the second aspect is concerned, it became increasingly clear as the activities progressed that the main shortcoming of the "*Normattiva*" project was the lack of a complete collection of all the historical texts of the legislative acts in a digital format. Only such a collection and one enjoying the necessary quality requisites (i.e. conformity to the text published in the Official Journal) would be suitable to provide the "raw material" on which to apply the sophisticated automatic text-processing programmes (i.e. "Editor") that had, in the meantime, been realised.

Today, the project has therefore succeeded in:

1. producing a good part of the software required for the regular running of all the services provided by the "*Normattiva*" project; and
2. testing working methods for processing texts (input-checking-correc-tion-annotation-validation) on the basis of very wide-ranging experimentation relating to the laws passed since the beginning of the Fourteenth Parliament. Such testing has been carried out over the last three years, approximately.

As regards the now crucial aspect of acquiring the basic texts, the next phases will involve the Steering Committee's consideration of the results of a comparative study of the main electronic collections of Italian legislation existing today (this study was entrusted to CNIPA - the Italian National Centre for Information Technologies in Public Administration). Assessment of the results of this study should lead, by early 2009, to a strategy for the very demanding work of retrieving the entire regulatory inventory dating from 1861 to the present day in homogeneous formats with a high semantic content. Such task is estimated to involve approximately 90,000 regulatory acts.

9. Once the basic texts have been acquired, it will be necessary to "process" all of them with the software programmes required to produce the services to be supplied via the WEB.

Given the complexity of such operations and the high number both of documents and of exceptions and anomalies to be processed, it is envisaged that these activities will require the employment of several dozen operators, with varying levels of specialization, over a minimum period of two years.

From 2001 to date, moreover, the many preparatory activities carried out include execution of the tender competition for creating the site and the search engine. Thus the fruits of the gradual work of inputting the texts can progressively be published on the Internet.

Today, although it is being achieved only gradually (at least as regards the first phase of its implementation), the objective of equipping our country, too, with an authoritative system for accessing regulations in force totally free of charge appears to be within reach.

Thanks to the fact that the modern technologies of legal text mark-up have penetrated Italian institutions (which fact is largely due to the two linked "*Norme in rete*" and "*Normattiva*" projects), such system will be flanked by the launch of a "virtuous circle" for regulatory texts during their passage between Government, Parliament and the Offices responsible for their official publication.

We hope that new legislation governing the digital publication of texts enjoying the status of an official source may crown a long and unavoidably complex process such as the one just described.

The Role of CNIPA in Accessing Legal Information

Floretta Rolleri
National Centre for ICT in the Public Administrations, Italy

Abstract. CNIPA, the Italian National Agency for Digital Government, contributes to create added value for Citizens and Enterprises, through the achievement of digital government, supporting Public Administration, carrying out the e-Government policies, managing specific projects with significant innovation.

This paper describes the projects in the field of juridical documents in the framework of the Italian legislation, with regard to the Code of Digital Administration, the budget laws and recent bill. In addition, it is provided a brief description of European projects on this subject with the participation of CNIPA.

Keywords: CNIPA, juridical documents, legal information, Code of Digital Administration (CAD), System of Public Connectivity (SPC).

1. CNIPA - National Agency for Digital Government

In 2003 the privacy law (D.lgs. 196/2003 art. 176) established CNIPA, which operates under the *"Presidency of the Council to carry out the policies of the Minister for Public Administration, Reforms and Innovation"*. The founding of CNIPA brought together two pre existing entities: the Authority for Information and Communication Technologies in Public Administration and the Technical Centre for RUPA (Unified Network for Public Administration). CNIPA has a board of directors with *"technical, operational, administrative, accounting, financial autonomy and independence of judgment"*.

The reference law is huge and complex and, at the moment, it is subject to further implementation. (Many parliamentary and governmental initiatives affecting the scope and responsibility of CNIPA are in their final stage).[1]

The missions of the new entity are numerous and complex, but they can be summarized in different categories, so that Public Administration can contribute to create added value for Citizens and Enterprises, through the achievement of digital government:

---

[1] D.lgs. n. 39/1993 "Norms about ICT systems of public administration, according to art. 2 (1) (mm), of Law L. n. 421/1992"; D.P.R. n. 445/2000 "Consolidation Act of legislative and regulatory provisions and of administrative documentation" D.lgs. n. 196/2003 "Code of protection data"; L. n. 4/2004 "Provision to help along the access of persons differently able to ICT instruments"; L. n. 311/2004 "Provision for the annual and pluriennial financial programme (financial programme law 2005)"; DPR n. 75/2005 "Regulation for the implementation of law n. 4/2004 to help along the access of persons differently able to ICT instruments"; D.lgs. n. 82/2005 "Digital Administration Code"; L. n. 244/2007 Provision for the annual and pluriennial financial programme (financial programme law 2008).

- to give support to Public Administration, with an effective use of ICT to improve the quality of services and minimize costs of administrative actions;
- to collaborate to carry out the Government policies within the field of electronic Government (e-Gov);
- to carry out and manage specific projects with significant innovation, such as the SPC (System for Public Connectivity), RIPA (international Network for Public Administration).

In concrete, the objective is to promote the achievement of rights ratified by the Code of Digital Administration (CAD) *"with the innovative use of information and telecommunication technologies"*.

Indeed, CNIPA has a "constellation of roles". It functions as as a coordinator and controller of the development of information system of Public Administration.

CNIPA is responsible for:

- approving the triennial and annual plans of Central Public Administration (PAC)[2];
- formulating advice to PAC on the strategic, economic and technical adequacy of ICT projects and contracts;
- carrying out projects shared with other PAC and Local Administration (PAL);
- verifying the results of efficiency, effectiveness and quality of ICT.

There are also different ways of operating:

- consultancy and suggestions on strategies and exact actions to politicians, public administration and operators in the sector;
- legislation, namely to elaborate technical secondary level laws, such as guidelines, technical guides (which could also be produced with the support of PA), industry standards;
- evaluation of the following types: *ex ante* (in line with national strategy on digital Government), *in itinere* (during the carrying out of planned projects) and *ex post* (on results achieved) of ICT activities of PAC, either from strategic perspective for triennial plans, or single interventions, submitted to technical and economical advise.
- *definitions and management of demonstration projects* with high innovative impact, in the use of ICT for PAC, Regions and PAL.

New government strategy brings us to affirm the principle of unity of Public Administration for his users (citizens and enterprises) and to bridge

---

[2] "Public Administrations, including schools, public company and autonomous PAC, Universities, [. . .], and national agencies indicated by D.lgs. n. 300/1999".

the gap between innovation technologies and administrative technologies. Stop "computerizing" existing process, start reinventing them with ICT.

A more transparent control on spending flows of PA is needed to implement the Management Accounting System, as a measure of efficiency and effectiveness of administrative action.

It is also necessary to develop and expand the forms of "cooperative application", i.e., according to the CAD definition, "*interaction between information systems of PA*" to assure metadata integration and archive and information sharing.

To achieve the cited goals it is necessary to develop a "multilevel strategy":

- integrate and coordinate the PAC, Regions and PAL initiatives at sectorial and intersectorial level;
- use ICT to develop mature forms of e-democracy;
- support the innovation and development of the Country, utilizing the power of commissioning of Public Administration, in particular for ICT sector;
- incorporate the innovation of Italian administration into European directives.

There are several organizational instruments provided by CAD to sustain innovation, that join the "Responsible for Information System"[3] provided by D.lgs. 39/1993, which each Administration should distinguish "on the basis of specific competencies and professional experience" between their managers (general managers or equivalent) and constitutes the principle interface between the Public Administration and CNIPA:

- Permanent conference for Innovation Technologies, that represents the point of coordination of the PAC initiatives, that, for this purpose, constitute a "*competence centre*" for accomplishment of "strategic lines for reorganization and digitalization of the administration defined by the Government" (CAD, artt. 17, 18);
- Commission for the Coordination of SPC, in charge of strategic address for the development of SPC, with several tasks, such as:
  - to guarantee the connection between different PA,
  - to approve the guide lines and the operative manuals,
  - to further the evolution of organizational models and technological architecture, according to the new technologies,
  - to further the adoption of standards that guarantee connectivity, interoperability, cooperation at application level and security,

---

[3] The manager responsible for ICT "manages relationship between his administration and CNIPA and is responsible for the results achieved using technologies (...) contributes to the definition of the draft of the triennial plan and sends the the final report of the previous year specifying the technologies adopted, the costs sustained, human resources employed and benefits achieved" (art. 10 D.lgs. 39/93).

- to check the quality and trust of services provided by qualified providers of SPC.

In addition the Commission for coordination is responsible for subscription, suspension and deletion of SPC providers (CAD, art. 79).
- Permanent Commission for Innovation Technology, in charge of enforcement of art. 117 of the Italian Constitution that involves Regions and PAL that conduct preliminary investigation and give advice, under the auspices of the Unified Conference State-Regions.

CNIPA, on the basis of the "industrial programme" of the Ministry of Innovation and Public Administration, defines the content, terms and conditions and modus operandi for the facilitation of triennial plans and for the subsequent annual amendments (D.lgs. 39/93, art. 9) starting from the "drafts" which PAC should send to CNIPA.

The contents of the plan represent a fundamental guideline for PAL, local Public Administration, with the aim of increasing the level of integration and coordination between the initiatives of PA on all National territory.

To achieve his "mission", CNIPA organization has a matrix-like structure, with Departments and offices under the board of directors, operative departments and offices, operative departments and offices with a project responsibility.

With regard to the theme we are interested in, the Department for quality and organizational innovation, even if the strength of a matrix organization comes from the involvement of the support of the different Departments, is fundamental in the field of ICT.

Indeed, the cited department, includes, among his tasks, some important functions in the specific field of interest: the study, promotion and testing of "*methodologies, models and systems to represent destructured information and related search engine with semantic and knowledge functionality, with particular reference to judiciary information system*", as indicated in the resolution applied.

In particular, the Department study promotes and tests methods and instruments for the classification of textual documents, as well as those produced with voice recognition and for the analysis of aggregation obtained from the contents elaboration, also with the generation and the use of metadata.

The organizational instruments carry this out is the Office for the sharing and management of knowledge, which is responsible for promoting:

- the spread of web semantic standards and schema definition based on these standards to represent data and documents produced by PA;
- the initiatives to diffuse in the network metadata useful to support the integration of Public sector information that has different PA, in order to share them;

— the adoption and the development of metadata standards to create ontologies and automatic instruments to generate and manage them.

In conclusion, among all activities of the office, there is also the definition of standards and formats, search and test of methods and techniques
of information retrieval, automatic classification and automatic translation of
documents and mark-up languages, and, in addition, the sharing of catalogues,
set of metadata, thesaurus, ontologies.

Within this context CNIPA has important experience to offer. It is run
according to the CAD. The definition of Database of National interest[4] is the
starting point for several initiatives in order to create an unitary information system, with regards to territorial and institutional levels, which could
guarantee the alignment of information and the access by all interested PA
... (CAD, art. 60).

In line with all concepts expressed above, the set of public data that should
be considered "essential" has been defined by the programme e-Europe 2002
as data necessary for citizens and enterprises to exercise their rights.

There is no doubt that, considering the law definition, statutory data are
essential public data, because they consist of rules that citizens should respect
and know. "*Ignorantia legis non excusat*", or "a requirement of Law in any
modern legal order is the knowledge of the norms that is an assumption"
(from Wikipedia).

2. Projects in the field of juridical documents

CNIPA has a long-established experience in this field, in fact since the time of
AIPA the participation in sector initiatives has been highly significant, both
under the profile of the definitions of standards and metadata, and of the
support of initiatives in this sector.

The project Norme in rete (NIR) is an example, in collaboration with the
Ministry of Justice, the holder of this responsibility (the Minister of Justice
is called *Guardasigilli*, [that literally means "look-seal"] and the Office for the
publishing of laws and decrees), where over 40 public central and regional
administrations participate.

Currently the portal <www.normeinrete.it> represents the unique point
of access to the juridical documentation available on official web sites. It is
a model of "federation of web site" that overcomes the centralization of the
traditional systems of judiciary information technology, bringing added value

---

[4] "Series of information, homogeneous by typology and content, collected and digitally
managed by the public administrations, the knowledge of which can be used by public
administrations for the exercise of their functions in compliance with their respective
competences and the regulations in force" (art. 60 CAD).

to the complex of autonomous initiatives of legislation communications of each single PA through the sharing of standards and metainformation.

Another example comes from the program for the IT automation processes of current legislation (Normattiva), established by the art. 107 of law n. 388/2000 (budget law 2001), which aims to offer to citizens a free access through Internet to the norms in-force and to the legislator instruments to support the production and the simplification of norms.

The role of CNIPA can be summarized by the activities developed for the e-leges project, which has the aim of taking care care of the elaborations, experimentations and achievement of the programme "normattiva".

The adoption of NIR standards assures that the initiatives are complementary. Up to now the "federal model" has not been adopted. It which could be adopted in the future, but no long on a voluntary basis, but according to a precise allocation of fields of competences split between the different institutions.

The project e-Leges is composed of different sub-projects:

- x-Leges (x stands for transmission) to create a system to support the transmission and the management of document flow between the Presidency of Council, the Chambers and the Ministry of Justice;
- p-Leges (p stands for portal) to create the first version of the site to access the legislation in force, <www.normattiva.it>;
- c-Leges (c stands for classification): system able to support the activities of classifications of the measures of normative nature;
- r-Leges (r stands for reorder): to study, experiment and possibly realize a system able to support activities with the aim of legislative reorder.

The development of the project has found a new lifeblood in the budget law 2008 (L. 244/2007, art. 2, c. 584), which foresees the extension of the cited article n. 107 of the law n. 388/2000 to the coordination of programmes of ICT and of classification of regional legislation, in order to conform to standard adopted by European Union of the classification used in the public normative database and to the adoption of guidelines for the promulgation and electronic publishing of normative documents with the intention of overcoming the traditional printed edition of Official Journal publication.

It represents a typical example of "role constellation", because the coordination is put into the hands of a person responsible designated for three years by the Prime Minister and the Presidents of the Chambers. Superior Court of Justice, CNIPA and, for the special regional legislation people designated by the Conference of the presidents of legislative assemblies of Regions and autonomous districts carry it out.

Moreover, the project is connected with the ongoing activities for the implementation of legislative simplification (art. 14, L. n. 246/2005, named as reduce law).

Another aspect of the project implementation comes from the activities planned by Central Public Administrations on the publication of normative acts and on the standardization of criteria for the classification of legislative data.

In addition, at regional level, the CDPR (Centre for documents of regional parliaments) has been established. It is formed of all Legislative Assemblies of Regions and Autonomous Districts, which represent an instrument of cooperation to pattern the exchange of information and documentation. In this way, a virtual network is built to exchange information, documentation, experiences and good practise.

The project E-LEX represent the natural application of the experimental project "Norme in rete", to create a unique national interface to search the regional norms approved and "*in itinere*".

3. Projects in itinere

3.1. BILL OF XVI LEGISLATION SENATE OF ITALIAN REPUBLIC N. 1082

Implementation of economic development, simplification, competitiveness with regards to civil process.

A bill currently in discussion at the Senate, with the title "Disposal of waste related to the maintenance of paper documents" (art. 22) stipulates "the obligations of publication of acts and administrative measure with effects of legal notices are considered achieved by the public administration and by the persons obliged with the publication on their own web site. In order to guarantee and facilitate the access to the publications mentioned in c. 1, CNIPA create and manage a portal of access of web sites. Starting from the 1st of January 2009 paper publication will no longer be considered as legal notices".

4. European projects with the participation of CNIPA

There are several projects in this field, where CNIPA participate to create the prototypes.

N-Lex Unique portal to access to legislative database of Member States

Estrella ("European project for Standardized Transparent Representations in order to Extend LegaL Accessibility") which provides:

- creation of expert systems to search for information on financial subjects;

- definition of shared XML standards for the representation of information in the juridical field

DALOS ("DrAfting Legislation with Ontology-based Support") to create a multilingual ontology to support normative drafting

JUMAS ("Judicial management by digital libraries semantics") to experiment with technologies for the comprehension of spoken language

Metalex/CEN Working Group definition of an XML format for the Exchange of European legislative documents.

5. Conclusions

To all these tasks described above in this fundamental sector for the awareness of citizens of Public Administration activities, with special regard to the normative actions, we have also to add the project TAL (Language Automatic Processing), financed by the European Commission and related to the project "Language-based interaction" (Seventh Framework Programme) and "Multilingual Web" (ICT-PSP) and the collaboration with Universities and Search Institute with the Laboratory of CNIPA to develop initiatives in language comprehension.

The mission of CNIPA, according to the Digital Administration Code, declared in its mission statement: "create value for citizens and enterprises through the carrying out of digital administration" is again affirmed for the awareness of juridical information.

"*Citizens and enterprises shall be entitled to request and obtain the right to use telematic technologies when communicating with government bodies and with the operators of nationwide public services, in accordance with the provisions herein.*" (CAD D.lgs. 82/2005, art. 3).

Problems of Privacy in Online Court Materials

Iain Currie

University of the Witwatersrand, Johannesburg

Abstract. The Southern African Legal Information Institute publishes court information from Southern and East African countries on the internet. In many cases, the Institute will be the first publisher of the information in digital format. Providing internet accessibility to records that were previously entirely paper-based brings with it problems of privacy. As a further processor of personal information which was provided by data subjects to courts without any awareness that it might be subject to future electronic publication, SAFLII should take positive measures to minimise the impact of its activities on the privacy of data subjects.

Keywords: Privacy, data protection, internet, public legal information.

1. Background

This paper has its origins in a workshop organised by the South African Legal Information Institute (SAFLII) to consider a privacy policy for the legal materials published by the Institute. SAFLII, a member of the Free Access to Law Movement,[1] collects legislation, case law and some secondary legal material from Southern and East African countries and publishes it on the internet. In common with other members of the Movement, the principal purpose of the SAFLII collection is the provision of public legal information, free of charge and anonymously,[2] in the interests of promoting "justice and the rule of law".[3]

2. A brief history

SAFLII builds on the pioneering initiative of the Law School of the University of the Witwatersrand, Johannesburg, which, in 1995, published the first case law of the Constitutional Court of South Africa on the internet.[4] The idea of using the relatively new technology of the World Wide Web to distribute case law was borrowed (to be blunt, copied) from the Legal Information Institute of Cornell University which had, since 1992 provided internet access to the

---

[1] See the Appendix of this volume.

[2] 'Anonymously' meaning without requiring user registration and with safeguards against disclosure of the IP addresses of users. See the Institute's privacy policy at <www.saflii.org/saflii/terms_of_use.html>

[3] Free Access to Law Declaration, note 1 above.

[4] The Court was established by the Constitution of the Republic of South Africa, Act 200 of 1993 (known as the Interim Constitution). It gave its first judgment in 1995.

case law of the US Supreme Court. As I recall the initial negotiations, it took a little work to persuade the judges of the Constitutional Court to allow internet publication of their judgments for the first time in South Africa. The previous practice in the South African courts was for judgments to be provided only in paper form to the parties. Members of the public and press could obtain copies on application to the court Registrar's office and on payment of a photocopying fee. Publication in the Law Reports was at the discretion of the publisher's 'reporters', advocates who practised at a particular court who would collect judgments considered worthy of publication and forward them to the Law Report editors for consideration.

Though there were some initial misgivings, principally concerned with the technology of publishing a fixed 'official' version of the judgments, the Court agreed to this bold experiment and a website, operated from a second-hand Linux computer housed in the Law School library went live in 1995. Almost immediately, usage of the website was extensive and, particularly after publication of the Court's decision outlawing the death penalty,[5] the site recorded visitors from all over the world.

The success and popularity of the website encouraged other South African courts to follow suit, and the Wits Law School site was approached in 1996 by the Land Claims Court, the Labour Court and the Labour Appeal Courts, with requests to publish their judgments online. Significantly, these courts, like the Constitutional Court are 'new', post-apartheid, institutions.[6] The older courts were far more reluctant to take up the new technology, unsurprising perhaps given that some High Courts lacked even basic networking infrastructure well into the 1990s and remained very much creatures of the paper era. By contrast, the 'new' courts, equipped with modern technology and uninhibited by the weight of systems and practises from a pre-electronic age rapidly adjusted to the ease and immediacy of internet publication.[7]

The Wits Law School handed over responsibility for its collection to SAFLII in 2006. In addition, some of the South African courts now maintain their own official websites.[8] This last development, likely to spread to the other South

---

[5] *S v Makwanyane* 1995 (3) SA 391 (CC), available at: <www.saflii.org/za/cases/ZACC/1995/3>.

[6] The Land Claims Court was established by the Interim Constitution, principally to adjudicate disputes arising from the constitutionally-mandated programme of restitution of pre-apartheid land rights. The Labour Courts are created by the Labour Relations Act of 1995.

[7] And, in some cases, the convenience of electronic submission of filings by parties. Despite this, no court in South Africa has moved to a purely electronic case management system and all records are maintained in paper form. See rule 1(3) of the Rules of the Constitutional Court (25 copies must be made of every document submitted to court in addition to an electronic version).

[8] The two courts at the apex of South Africa's rather complicated appellate system, the Constitutional Court and the Supreme Court of Appeal, maintain official websites at <www.constitutionalcourt.org.za/> and <www.supremecourtofappeal.gov.za/>.

African courts, means that SAFLII will no longer be the only provider of electronic access to the materials of those courts, which will themselves take responsibility for the maintenance of an official record of their output and of authoritative versions of their documents.

But though the South African courts have grown less dependent on third-party provision of electronic access to their materials, most of the Southern and East African jurisdictions to be served by SAFLII lack any prior history of internet publication of court materials. Indeed, in some cases, material is unavailable in electronic format and has had to be scanned by SAFLII; the era of paper is far from over. The SAFLII initiative is therefore an extremely important step in increasing the accessibility of legal information from African countries.

3. Privacy

The shift from paper to electronic records of court materials and from paper archives to internet accessibility brings with it problems of privacy that are not equivalent to those encountered in the older system. 'Privacy' here is shorthand for an individual's interest in controlling information about them; it is the interest protected by what it is variously referred to in international jurisdictions as 'data protection' and 'information privacy protection', a body of regulation protecting against the processing of information that tells us something about someone.[9]

Court materials, since they deal with the rights, duties and actions of individuals, necessarily contain a great deal of personal information. All too often it is information dealing with what most people would intuitively regard as private, in the sense that it concerns human vulnerabilities, failings, intimacies: X is divorced, Y is an adulterer, Z is insolvent, A was raped, B can no longer deal with her own affairs, C is a thief. All of human frailty can be found in the most routine records of the courts, there are stories of unhappy families to rival *Anna Karenina*.

The conception of privacy that underlies data protection both encompasses this intuitive sense of what is private about personal information (call it "privacy as intimacy"[10]) but also reaches well beyond it. Though the openness and accessibility of court records is governed in general by the open justice principle,[11] most legal systems do have rules and practices concerning the

---

[9] For an international overview of this body of regulation see (Bygrave, 2002, pp. 30-36).

[10] Or, more accurately, privacy as control over access to information about the intimate sphere of an individual's life. See Julie Inness Privacy, Intimacy and Isolation (1992).

[11] The principle that judicial proceedings should take place openly and be accessible by any member of the public. The principle extends, the South African Constitutional Court has held, to public access to the full record of proceedings. *Independent Newspapers (Pty) Ltd v Minister for Intelligence Services* (CC, 22 May 2008) [35].

sealing, restriction of access to, or abridgement of court records dealing with issues of particular sensitivity. In South African law, for example, the names of criminal accused and witnesses under the age of eighteen cannot be disclosed. Similarly, a court may order that a rape victim's identity may not be disclosed and that all reference to the victim in the record make use of a pseudonym or an initial. These rules and practices certainly go a small way to protect against disclosure of certain intimate private information, but they do not make any attempt to regulate disclosure of personal information as such – information that simply tells us something, whether intimate or not, about someone.

The risks posed by unregulated access to personal information are a function of the rise of networked computing and the internet. 'Digital dossiers' are Daniel Solove's useful term for routine compilations of data about individuals drawn from publicly accessible electronic sources.[12] The dossiers are aggregations of sometimes widely dispersed pieces of data, capable of being assembled into remarkably detailed profiles which can be put to use in anything from marketing to criminal investigation to the prevention of terrorism. The harm that they cause to individuals is, Solove tells us, can be characterised as at once 'Orwellian' and 'Kafkaesque'. The Orwellian state operates under the gaze of Big Brother, with constant panoptic surveillance of the individual by electronic dossiers resulting in an inevitable diminishment of human freedom. The Kafkaesque state recalls Josef K's fruitless travails against an opaque bureaucracy, allegorising the extent to which our lives are increasingly controlled by the contents of mysterious, unknowable and opaque dossiers.[13]

Besides the, more or less, lawful use of publicly-accessible personal data by governments and the private sector, digital information is increasingly at risk from identity thieves and fraudsters. The aggregation of isolated pieces of personal information can yield sufficient detail to allow identity thieves to wreak considerable havoc on their victims. Beside direct harm, identity theft often pollutes an individual's dossier with discrediting information.[14]

These risks are associated with the networked accessibility of personal information in digital form. By contrast, the risks associated with the same information maintained only in paper records are minimal. This is because paper-based records are, though officially public, 'practically obscure'.[15] The expense and difficulty of obtaining physical access to records maintained only

---

[12] "We currently live in a world where extensive dossiers exist about each one of us. These dossiers are in digital format, stored in massive computer databases by a host of government agencies and private-sector companies. The problems caused by these developments are profound." (Solove, 2004, p. 13).

[13] Ibid chap 3.

[14] The problems that result are a function of the Kafkaesque nature of the dossier: "While their dossier remains defiled, victims have difficulty getting jobs, loans, or mortgages" (Solove, 2006, p. 515).

[15] *US Department of Justice v Reporters Committee for Freedom of the Press* 489 US 749, 762-64 (1989).

in paper form at the courthouse considerably raises the transaction costs of maintaining dossiers derived from them.[16] This fact has led, in some jurisdictions, to the creation of specific rules and guidelines governing electronic accessibility of official court materials that attempt to balance the principle of open justice with the protection of privacy.[17]

4. Developing privacy guidelines for SAFLII materials

SAFLII, a South African-based website is governed by South African law. South Africa currently lacks general data protection legislation, but there is some sector-specific legislation.[18] Currently, the only legislation with a bearing on privacy that is applicable to SAFLII is the Electronic Communications and Transactions Act 25 of 2002. Chapter VIII of the Act creates voluntary principles applicable to the processing of personal information by data controllers.[19] General data protection legislation is currently being drafted which is likely to result in a law which, following the familiar lines of the European model for data-protection regimes, will center on a set of 'information protection principles' which in turn flesh out a general and higher-level requirement that personal information must be processed 'in a reasonable manner in order not to infringe the privacy of the data subject'.[20]

---

[16] "Only those with a relatively strong interest in the information would take time out of their day, wait in line at the clerk's office, fill out the necessary forms, and pay the necessary copy charges. Once judicial records go online, however, computerized compilers can search, aggregate, and combine the information with information from many other public filings to create a profile of a specific individual in a matter of minutes, at minimal cost. Information in many different locations can be combined and aggregated in ways that previously were impossible, permitting entirely new uses of the information that could never have been intended before" (Winn, 2004, p. 316). A contrasting view is taken by Bepko A.B. (2004-2005), *Public Availability or Practical Obscurity: The Debate over Public Access to Court Records on the Internet*, New York Law School Law Review, Vol. 967 (court records should be as available on the internet as they are at the courthouse).

[17] See the useful state-by-state survey of the courts of the United States published by the Centre for Democracy and Technology 'A Quiet Revolution in the Courts: Electronic Access to State Court Records' (2007), available at: <www.cdt.org/publications/020821courtrecords.shtml>.

[18] Applicable to credit transactions (National Credit Act 34 of 2005) and information held by health-care services (National Health Act 61 of 2003).

[19] Briefly, personal information must be processed only with 'express written permission' unless specifically permitted by law. Unsurprisingly, few data controllers have opted in to these rather onerous standards.

[20] The legislative proposals emanate from South Africa's standing law reform Commission and are likely to be considered by Parliament in 2009. See Allan and Currie, 2007, p. 563.

The South African common law also provides limited protection of information privacy by way of an action in delict (tort) which allows recovery of damages or injunctive relief for breach of privacy.[21]

In sum, outside specific sectors, the processing of personal information is largely unregulated in South African law. Nevertheless, a general regulatory regime will be in place within a few years and SAFLII would be well advised in the meantime to strive for compliance with its general parameters. These parameters follow, with a few tweaks, the European Union's data protection regime as set out in the 1995 Data Protection Directive.[22]

What then might compliance with data protection principles entail for SAFLII? The principles aim to regulate the 'processing' of personal information, a term of art that easily covers SAFLII's activities of collecting court information, converting some of it to digital format and publishing it on the internet for unrestricted public access. Data protection does not seek to prohibit such processing but rather to ensure that it is conducted in such a way as to minimize its impact on privacy.[23] This is particularly important when the information has not been collected from data subjects themselves, who are consequently frequently unaware that material about them that they had thought to be languishing in a court registrar's office is freely circulating on the internet. Moreover, since it acts as a 'further processor' rather than a first collector of data, SAFLII frequently processes personal information that was provided by data subjects without any awareness that it might one day be given such visibility and accessibility.

It is also clear that the countervailing principle of open justice which considerably complicates the position for courts' own provision of electronic access to their material[24] does not apply to a third-party public-interest publisher like SAFLII. Moreover, SAFLII does not publish court information for the

---

[21] See, for example, *NM v Smith* 2007 (7) BCLR 751 (CC) (damages for reckless disclosure that someone is HIV-positive). The remedy is limited by the requirement of fault, in the form of intention (animus iniuriandi).

[22] Directive 95/46/EC of the European Parliament and of the Council of 24 October 1995 on the protection of individuals with regard to the processing of personal data and on the free movement of such data (EU Directive). On the Directive's remarkable degree of influence on the development of data protection laws around the world see Bygrave (note 9 above), pp. 30-36.

[23] See art. 6 of the EU Directive: personal data must not be 'excessive in relation to the purposes for which they are collected and/or further processed'. As Bygrave explains '[a] ...core principle of data protection laws is that there should be restrictions on the amount of personal data collected; the amount of data collection should be limited to what is necessary to achieve the purpose(s) for which the data are gathered and processed. This principle is summed up here as "minimality", though it could just as well be summed up in terms of "necessity" or "non-excessiveness". (Bygrave, 2001), available at: <www.austlii.edu.au/au/journals/PLPR/2001/9.html>.

[24] See Winn (note 16 above). Winn criticizes the approach, taken in some jurisdictions, that once material has been treated as public by virtue of the open justice principle it should always be public. This approach overlooks the difference between paper and electronic access; public access to paper records is limited by their practical obscurity.

purpose of maintaining a public archive of the activities of a particular court and is therefore not obligated to maintain comprehensive or complete records.

Put at its most abstract and general, compliance with the principle of minimality requires SAFLII to redact its materials to remove sensitive personal information such as medical and health information, financial information, identifying numbers and information such as dates of birth and addresses, intimate family information and intimate victim information. It cannot rely on courts to perform this process since many of the courts serviced by SAFLII have no experience of electronic accessibility to their materials and many of the materials are historical and therefore generated without any consideration of the particular problems posed by electronic access. Moreover, if this redaction process is automated this may well result in underinclusiveness, something that should be addressed by a 'takedown' procedure that can be initiated by a data subject.

Appendix 1

Extract from WorldLII privacy policy[25]

B. Personal information contained in WorldLII databases

B1. Some WorldLII databases contain personal information, including the decisions of Courts and Tribunals. WorldLII publishes these databases with the consent of the public bodies concerned. It is the responsibility of the public bodies which provide these databases to WorldLII to determine, subject to the requirements of the laws under which they operate, the appropriate balance between the privacy interests of individuals and the public interests in dissemination of the information. In particular, if personal data is to be anonymised before publication, this is done by the public body concerned. WorldLII does not and can not censor part or all of the information provided by these public bodies for publication.

Appendix 2

Extract from SAFLII privacy policy[26]

B. Personal information contained in SAFLII databases

B1. SAFLII publishes comprehensive collections of court decisions with the consent of the public bodies concerned. The electronic dissemination of

---

[25] Available at: <www.worldlii.org/worldlii/privacy.html>.

[26] Available at: <www.saflii.org/saflii/terms_of_use.html>.

judgments is in concordance with the open court principle, instituted to ensure the impartiality and transparency of the judicial process by allowing access to the record of judicial proceedings, including judgments. Therefore, SAFLII operates on the core principle that all citizens and organizations should be provided with free, unconditional and unrestricted access to basic legal materials.

B2. Some SAFLII databases contain personal information included in the decisions of Courts and Tribunals. SAFLII publishes these data-bases with the consent of the public bodies concerned.

SAFLII undertakes to monitor and delete from published judgments personal information as directed by law or a specific court order. SAFLII retains the right to remove personal information from judgments at its discretion where this is possible without distorting the meaning and context of the document.

B3. It is hereby expressly stated that SAFLII performs automated monitoring and, where necessary, de-identification of judgments prior to publication and does not guarantee that all sensitive material has been correctly de-identified.

Should you have concerns over personal information published on the SAFLII website, please contact us.

B4. SAFLII users should note that there are legal limitations on the use, publication and dissemination of some personal information contained in SAFLII databases. It is the responsibility of SAFLII users to comply with the laws of the land.

References

Allan, K. and Currie, I. (2007), *Enforcing Access to Information and Privacy Rights: Evaluating Proposals for an Information Protection Regulator for South Africa*, South African Journal of Human Rights, Vol. 23, pp. 572-596.

Bepko Bradford, A. (2004-05), *Public Availability or Practical Obscurity: The Debate over Public Access to Court Records on the Internet*, New York Law School Law Review, Vol. 49, p. 967.

Bygrave, L.A. (2001), *Core Principles of Data Protection*, Privacy Law and Policy Reporter, Vol. 7, No. 9.

Bygrave, L.A. (2002), *Data Protection Law: Approaching its Rationale, Logic and Limits*, Kluwer Law International, The Hague/London/New York.

Iness, J. (1992), *Privacy, Intimacy and Isolation*, Oxford University Press, Oxford.

Solove, D.J. (2004), *The Digital Person: Technology and Privacy in the Information Age*, New York University Press, New York.

Solove, D.J. (2006), *A Taxonomy of Privacy* University of Pennsylvania Law Review, Vol. 154, No. 3, pp. 477-564.

Winn, P.A. (2004), *Online Court Records: Balancing Judicial Accountability and Privacy in an Age of Electronic Information*, Washington Law Review, Vol. 79, p. 307.

II SECTION

A Legal Framework for
Open Access to Legal Information

Legal Information Services: The Policies of Publishing**

Jon Bing
Norwegian Research Center for Computers and Law (NRCCL), Norway

1. Challenging the legal publishers

The history of legal information retrieval has many aspects, and there may be different views of what many be the more important. But there cannot be any doubt that Ohio is one of the important places to start. At the end of the 1960s, there were numerous attempts of creating information or documentation systems. In 1964, the Ohio Bar Association created a working group for considering the adoption of a computerised system. However, the group concluded that no satisfactory solution was available, and recommended that a new system should be developed. They established a corporation, Ohio Bar Automated Research Corporation (OBAR), which contracted Data Corporation of Dayton to look into the problem.

Data Corporation had in 1964 developed a system for the retrieval of Air Force reconnaissance documents. In late 1968, it is told that two neighbours got talking across their fence, one being a partner with Data Corporation and one being the chief executive officer of Mead Corporation, a forest products, paper processing, pulp making company. But the two neighbours saw some possibilities of future synergy, and Mead acquired Data Corporation, including the OBAR project. They brought in Arthur D Little to give advice on restructuring; one of the consultants was Jerry Rubin. The advice was to carve out of the corporation the Information Systems Division, and concentrate on the legal business. In February 1970 this was spun off as Mead Data Central with Jerry Rubin as a vice president (cf. Bjørner and Ardito, 2004).

LEXIS was launched with flair. Jerry Rubin became the front figure; LEXIS established its own high-speed network connection to New York and Washington DC, over time developing into MEADNET. It brings to mind the network established around the ITALGIURE system in Europe more or less at the same time, and though the two front figures – Vittorio Novelli and Jerry Rubin – were very different as persons, they both had a vision, were able to communicate this vision to others and nurse enthusiasm.

From the beginning, LEXIS had an extravagant feel to it, like the use of colour terminals in 1970. One of the challenges for text retrieval is determining

---

** Much of the historical background until 1984 can be found, though organised in a different form, in (Bing et al., 1984). However, I have also relied on personal notes which are not documented elsewhere.

which of the retrieved documents are relevant. Even when a search request is adequate, there will be a certain share of the retrieved documents which are not relevant. These have to be discarded, and it will take too much time to read through the documents in full to make this judgement (though this is finally the test). Therefore, one traditionally adds to the document an abstract, this will provide an efficient strategy for making relevance assessment. But LEXIS did not in its original version have any editorial material, only the authentic text of the cases etc. Writing abstracts would represent a huge investment and long delay. Rather, the user was offered a keyword-in-context (KWIC) format, where the search term was highlighted and displayed with leading and following lines (much like the snippets giving the results of a current Internet search engine). In its 1970 implementation, LEXIS used the colour blue for this highlighting. It was seen as rather extravagant to use an expensive colour monitor only to highlight terms. People literary laughed at the Association of Computing Machinery (ACM) demonstration in New York 1970, Richard Giering remembers.

The establishment of the legal information service LEXIS was a huge operation. There was a historic back-log of cases which had to be entered by key-punching, LEXIS outsourced this to contractors overseas, where the cases were double-punched (to ensure high accuracy) by operators not knowing English. At the same time, new decisions had to be collected at home, which in principle implied a contract with each individual judge. LEXIS brought the approach of a modern computer system to this endeavour; it was also not constricted by a web of traditions. The vision was for the end user to operate the system, not any middleperson or paralegal. Based on this philosophy, LEXIS brought out the UBIQ terminal, a special purpose terminal for lawyers which had the help-text engraved on its keys: Press the key [next case], and the next case would be displayed. The red UBIQ was designed to sit on the desk of a partner in a big law firm.

LEXIS as a commercial system was launched 1973. And at the end of the 1970s, LEXIS announced that all the big law firms of the United States were their clients. By "big law firm" was meant all with more than 100 partners. This very clearly illustrates the difference between the United States and Europe. In Europe, there were in 1980 hardly any law firm with 100 partners, and in many countries there were regulatory restrictions to how large a law firm was permitted to grow.

It is my belief that at this time LEXIS was mainly used as a research tool. The user would have to walk up to the terminal, which typically would be in a library. He or she would type in the search request, and determine which cases might be relevant in a dialog with the system. But he or she would not print out the cases on the cumbersome and noisy line-printer connected to the terminal, which would result in folds of pyjamas-striped printout. Rather, the user would turn to the extensive library that any of the large law firms would have. LEXIS had provided the identification of the cases; the bound reporters would be collected for the cases to be read and studies in the conventional way. I believe this integration between computer research and extensive libraries is the clue to the success for LEXIS in the 1970s.

LEXIS challenged the largest legal publisher in the United States, West. In 1980, West employed 2,500 persons, among them 150 legal editors, and had a weekly export out of their warehouses in St Paul, Minnesota of approximately 250,000 books. It maintained the national reporter system, and its key index scheme was integrated in the legal system, part of the training of a legal mind. Though starting computerising typesetting in the middle of the 1960s, West had been slow to respond to the possibilities offered by computerised retrieval, and only when LEXIS had demonstrated that there was a market, West turned towards it.

There were interesting differences between the companies. LEXIS was rather glamorous, sparking of the ideas and the enthusiasm of new technology, while West was encrusted with experience, legal know-how and tradition. LEXIS was based on the programs originally developed by Data Corporation, West found its software across the border.

Since the early 1960s, a treaty project has been going on at Queen's University, Kingston, Ontario. The moving force behind this project was Professor Hugh Lawford, and in 1968 he initiated another project to support his collection and annotation of the treaties of the British Commonwealth, the Queen's University Institute for Computers and Law, which was given the acronym QUIC/LAW. Late in 1968, he had an exchange of letters with IBM or a joint project to explore the possibilities of computerised legal information retrieval. The basis was an in-house IBM program known as INFORM/360 for internal use at the corporate headquarter in Armonk, New York. It is believed that the program was developed to meet the need for litigation support in the major anti-trust proceeding to which IBM was party (and which contributed to the unbundling of software). One of the interesting features of the program was the use of ranking algorithms as alternatives to a plain Boolean query language. Richard von Briesen of QUIC/LAW further developed these into rather sophisticated strategies.

The QUIC/LAW system was from the start conceived as something larger than the Treaty Project of Professor Lawford, it was to be developed into a national legal information service. But the development period was rather stormy, several of the original supporters withdrawing, the Federal Department of Justice conducting a test in 1973. The result was the establishment of a new company, the QL-Systems Ltd with Professor Lawford, von Briesen and Canada Law Books Ltd as the original shareholders.

One of the first ventures of the new QL-systems was to sell their program to West. I believe IBM also used INFORM/360 to develop STAIRS, a general text retrieval systems which became the work-horse for many legal information systems, the first installation probably being the PRODASEN system of Brazil in 1972.

We return therefore to the United States, where West in 1975 launches its own computerised legal information service, the Westlaw, based on the QL-system program. West had many advantages, including it long established relation to the judiciary and the legal community. But West made at least one dubious choice in entering the market, the database only included the editorial headnotes. The headnotes were written by the editors, and it was believed that in restricting retrieval to these, retrieval performance would be enhanced. This was a presupposition contrary to known facts; such a document design would impair recall, though it might have a positive effect on precision.

I believe that West looked towards the use of the LEXIS system, where the computerised system was mainly used as a retrieval tool, while the cases were read from the books of the conventional library – books which actually were to a great extent published by West. West believed that by offering a superior tool for researching the headnotes lawyers were used to, they would in the computerised system open their conventional reporter system through a more efficient channel. West did not appreciate that though LEXIS was used as a research tool, the relevance function depended upon the ability to dip into the case at several points. Restricting the access to the headnotes, did in some way "blind" the user.

Therefore, it came as no surprise that West changed its policy in 1978 and included also the authentic text of the cases. Since then, Westlaw and LEXIS have competed in the market with comparable services. The services are different in detail with respect to coverage and features. But the monopoly of West in the paper based world has been broken, there is not a duopoly – and there are many specialised services.

The remarkable success of LEXIS also impressed operators in other markets. LEXIS decided to move into the French market in 1982, and with considerable success, but also with a lesson learned: The whole database had to be converted to a character representation permitting the French accents. LEXIS had then already moved into United Kingdom,[1] and this was to some extent a controversial move. The major English publisher, Butterworth, contracted to co-operate with LEXIS. One of the directors of Butterworth was Professor Colin Tapper, and as he had pioneered computerised systems, one had been waiting for Butterworth to make its move. One might have expected that a joint project with West would be an obvious solution, both companies being legal publishers and perhaps with a somewhat similar culture. The co-operation with LEXIS therefore came rather unexpected. I have learned that Butterworth in fact approached West and suggested a joint venture, but was

---

[1] This decision was announced at the 1978 conference of the British Society of Computers and Law.

turned down – West would not take any interest in activities outside its home jurisdictions.

In the UK market, the European Law Centre Ltd had taken an initiative in 1979 for a computerised service. The EUROLEX effort had a European perspective, and in 1981 a new and more aggressive phase was initiated with David Worlock as head of the organisation. The major legal publisher Sweet and Maxwell made an exclusive agreement with EUROLEX in 1982, which also made an agreement with Westlaw for making US material available to European users. EUROLEX was acquired by the Canadian based international publisher Thompson, and the competition between LEXIS and EUROLEX in the UK market became fierce, but brief. Legal policy arguments favoured EUROLEX, which was a "national" company compared to the LEXIS service, which actually was serviced also for its UK customers out of its facilities in Dayton, Ohio. But overnight the EUROLEX service was closed down by Thompson, as the CEO, David Worlock was told about this one hour before the rest of the company. It really brought home that legal information services no longer was something academics or enthusiasts fiddled around with in their spare time, it had become part of the more ruthless world of business.

The international publishing industry has now taken over both the US major services. Reed Elsevier owns LEXIS, and Butterworth is also part of that company. West – which for a long time remained a family company – has been taken over by Thompson, which has interests in a large number of legal information services throughout the world.

2. Early European developments

In understanding the early developments in Europe, it is also necessary to appreciate the role played by a small number of institutions. These forged the persons working with legal information services into a rather close-knit community, helped to communicate test results and experiences in an informal way, and they played a large part in reciprocal political support for the policies adopted.

First, the Council of Europe was an essential forum in the early developments. On the initiative of the "Committee of Experts on the Publication of state practices in the field of public international law", a "Committee of experts on the harmonisation of the means of programming legal data into computers" started its work in 1969. I believe no one will be offended by me saying that the longish name of the committee reveals that it was formed without a clear understanding of its objective or the means to achieve such an objective. And the committee changed its name to the more acceptable "Committee on

Legal Data Processing" in 1974.[2] For the rest of the century, this Committee was a central forum for an exchange of ideas and experiences with respect to computers and law. The substantive law was not part of the area for this committee – but it explored legal information services and justice administrative systems as well as teaching in the area of computers and law. Members of the Committee were a mixture of bureaucrats, policy makers and academics – and there would be annual international meetings with rather ambitious programs. Often the success of international committees is measured in the number of legal instruments adopted – the Committee certainly adopted such instruments,[3] but its main achievement was the facilitation of communications between European institutions, not only at the meetings of the Committee itself, but at the annual international events, which was organised in different member countries.

It is not possible to understand the co-ordinated development of legal information services in the different European jurisdictions without awareness of the exchanges taking place through the network built by this Committee. The Committee also strongly supported academic activity, not least through the adoption of recommendations of making introduction to computerised systems a compulsory part of legal education, and suggesting a curriculum in the teaching of computers and law.

One may see the Committee on Legal Data Processing as the pivot of a wheel with many spokes. Mention should be made of the congresses of the Corte Suprema di Cassazione, which attracted large audiences. There were also considerable activity and conferences centred around the Istituto per la Documentazione Giuridica[4] in Florence, and the enthusiasm of the Italian legal community embraced the whole of Europe, inviting them to join the march towards the future of law. In the United Kingdom, the British Society for Computers and Law[5] was founded; its meetings were also of an international nature and included barristers and solicitors as well as lawyers within government – all excited about legal information retrieval and how to bring its advantages to the UK (which by no means should prove easy).

In Germany there were formed societies, which still are very much active, of the same nature, and which addressed policy issues with considerable heat. These meetings perhaps did not contribute as much to the general international discussion – as German was the conference language, this tended to exclude a wider international audience, but it has an integrating effect on the German language areas of Europe.

---

[2] Formally, this was a new committee succeeding the former. I served as a chair for this committee 1981-82.

[3] An example is R(83)3 on the "protection of users" of legal information services.

[4] Which today has been re-named Istituto di Teoria e Tecniche dell'Informazione Giuridica (ITTIG), and still being very active within the field.

[5] The Society was founded 11 December 1973 based on an initiative of the Scottish Legal Computer Research Trust, which itself was founded in January 1970.

The main point of this small paragraph is to convey the feeling of enthusiasm and comradeship which was developed at this time – from the early 1970s and onwards to 1990. The European development cannot really by understood without considering this swell of common purpose – carrying us, it was believed, towards national, integrated – and probably monolithic – information services.

This was not realised. The obvious reason was the introduction of the PC and office automation. For the vision of the one, integrated national information service was to a large extent the shadow of the available architecture for computer systems: Mainframes with terminal networks. When office automation was introduced, this did not in the first years stimulate communication. Even the establishment of a local area network was not without its problems. The philosophy lead to the development of rather isolated islands, the PC on your desktop might be linked to some local resources like a printer – but not to central files like a national information system. When the CD-ROM was introduced in 1984, systems based on this became popular. Though the storage capacity of a CD-ROM seemed large compared to other media at this time, it was obviously insufficient for a truly national information systems. It was more suitable for sector-oriented systems, for instance tax law. But CD-ROMs were well suited for publishing and management of rights according to the same model as for books, which – it may be argued – made publishers more interested in the field, an interest which carried over into the next phase.

For the next phase came – communication was sorted out, LANs were linked into wider area networks. And then – at the beginning of the 1990s – the control of Internet was relaxed, permitting other institutions than those related to research having access to this international infrastructure.[6]

Nearly at the same time, World Wide Web was realised within Internet, web browsers became available and content could be reached from your desktop computer. This was the time when Content was crowned as King – computer technology had matured sufficiently to make vast libraries of text, images and sound available.

But again this did not bring back the vision of the integrated, national legal information services. There may be several reasons for this, but one certainly was that as the threshold of publishing material on the web was lowered, many institutions wanted their own home page and to make their own material available through this page rather than supply the material to some central facility.

---

[6] See for a more detailed story and analysis (Bing, 2009).

3. A changed technical context resulting in new legal policies

As the threshold for publishing went down, new parties took an interest in
the legal material. The new environment hungered for contents. A possibility
was to convert existing material for re-utilisation on the web. This strategy
had the attractive advantage that a lot of material could be made available
in a short time. But there usually would be formalities to be met before such
material could be uploaded, an obvious formality – which usually also cost
money – was clearing the copyrights associated with the material.

However, in the United States copyright was not claimed in the primary,
legal sources like statutes, regulations and case law.[7] Therefore, such material
was available to furnish a basis for new services supplementing the established
services or challenging them in the market place.

One of the United States systems was JURIS (an acronym for "Justice
retrieval and inquiry system"), developed in the early 1970s to serve the attorneys of the Department of Justice. In launching the service, it was emphasised
that "minimal standards of due process and equal protection of law" were to
be extended to all citizen, and that "fulfilment of these requirements depends
on timely access to reliable and up-to-date information" (Kondos, 1973).

The major objective of JURIS was to make available the legal material
generated within the department itself. In addition, JURIS was given from
another federal system[8] the total text of the United States Code. And since
1982, under a contractual arrangement with West, JURIS received weekly
updates of case law for its federal and digest files which otherwise was only
available through the commercial Westlaw service.

Unlike the "raw" legal sources, the West material was subject to copyright,
at least the material created by their editorial staff, like the headnotes. West
had also successfully claimed copyright in the pagination system[9] and other

---

[7] It is not quite clear how the doctrine of Crown Copyright applies to the different
jurisdictions of the United States. It is reported that in 1984, Crown Copyright was used as
a basis for state legislation in New York restricting the sale of data from the Legal Retrieval
Service of the Bill Drafting Commission of the state legislature to competing services. But
this is an exception; in general copyright in primary legal sources is not claimed. Cf. (Bing,
2003).

[8] Federal Legal Information Thru Electronics, operated by the Air Force Staff Judge
Advocate in Denver, Colorado.

[9] LEXIS was paying US$ 50,000 annual in license fees to West for incorporating the
pagination system, based on West Pub Co v Mead Data Cent., Inc, 616 F Supp. 1571
(D. Minn. 1985), aff'd, 799 F 2d 1219 (8th Cir), cert denied, 479 US 1070 (1986). In a
subsequent case, Matthew Bender and HyperLaw v West (SDNY 94-Civ 0589, 19 May
1997, United States District Court) Judge John Martin determined that West could not
claim copyright in its enhanced versions of decisions as included in its reporters. However,
Matthew Bender was acquired by Reed Elsevier in 1998; therefore the decisions were not
pursued. It is doubtful whether the copyright in the pagination system would be upheld
according to the Supreme Court's interpretation of the copyright originality test in Feist
Publications, Inc, v Rural Telephone Service Co, 499 US 340 (1991).

elements. The contractual arrangement with the Department of Justice was designed to avoid third parties through JURIS gaining access to Westlaw material and in this way avoiding paying fees or in other ways circumventing the policies of West.

The Department of Justice as a federal agency falls within the scope of the freedom of information legislation. Carole D. Hafner, herself a major figure in the history of legal information retrieval (Hafner, 1981), requested in 1991 samples of legislative texts from JURIS for research in computational linguistics. The request was denied. Public interest groups such as the Tax-payers Asset Project (TAP), National Technical Information Services (NTIS) and the American Association of Law Libraries (AALL) queried West on its willingness to make its database available to public access. In a press release of 30 September 1993 West announced that it would not seek renewal of the contract with the Department of Justice. The Clinton administration announced that the National Science Foundation would fund a project to enhance future access to government information. This announcement was made on a Friday, the following Monday the administration announced the permanent shut-down of JURIS from 1 January 1994.

The story is highlighted by the decision of the US District Court of Columbia.[10] After it had become known that the JURIS service would be discontinued, the information service Tax Analysts requested access to parts of the database containing West material. The court concurred with the Department of Justice, and held that "the West-provided data in JURIS is not an 'agency record' under [Freedom of Information Act] and this Court lacks jurisdiction to compel Defendant [Department of Justice] to disclose the information sought by Plaintiff".

The example of JURIS demonstrates some of the explosive policy power of the web technology, blowing away part of the older infrastructure designed and determined by technological circumstances. The exclusive arrangement between the department and West was discontinued – at least in this respect – and the money which used to go into the maintenance of JURIS would partly be used to purchase legal information services from West or LEXIS in the market place. At the same time, the court decided that a legal source was not an "agency record", and therefore not subject to access under the freedom of information legislation.

4. The Legal Information Institutes

Another major example of the possibilities stimulating new initiatives is provided by the Legal Information Institutes.

---

[10] *Tax Analysts*, Plaintiff, v. *United States Department of Justice*, Defendant, and *West Publishing Company*, Defendant-Intervenor, 913 F Supp. 599.

In 1992, the LII of Cornell Law School[11] was launched by Peter Martin and Tom Bruce, co-directors. "The legal information industry in the U.S. in the mid-'90s had focused totally on judges and lawyers and hadn't paid attention to the information needs of others," Peter Martin has stated. "One of our powerful early discoveries was how much demand outside those professional sectors there was – ordinary citizens trying to make sense of laws that impinge on their lives ... [12] The Cornell LII offers the United States Code, an organised compilation of current federal laws; and the collections of all recent opinions of the US Supreme Court and New York State Court of Appeals ... Making information accessible on the web in a manageable format has been a challenge – there are 13 US Circuit Courts, each putting its decisions on the web. The problem is that data structures and formats differ from site to site: researchers need some solution, for instance a search engine that reaches across those structures."

The Cornell Law School LII may have been the first service of its kind on the web,[13] and a Legal Information Institute has become a generic term indicating a certain type of operation on the web.[14] There are namesakes as far-flung as New Zealand, Zambia and Kazakhstan.

It may not be unfair to maintain that the LII represent a reaction to a protective attitude towards legal material. Though in most jurisdictions excluded from copyright as permitted under the Berne Convention art. 2(4), there remain exclusive arrangements designed to harvest profit from making the material available. But rather than restrict exploitation, the material should be made available for as low cost as possible to whoever want to build a value-added service on this basis. For instance, this is the policy underlying the EU re-utilisation directive.[15] It may further be argued that the LIIs have been most successful – and most needed – in jurisdictions where the legal material has been formally controlled, like in the countries applying the Crown Copyright doctrine, or something similar.[16]

One of the more remarkable LIIs, is the Australasian Legal Information Institute (AustLII), jointly established by the University of New South Wales and the University of Technology, Sydney with Professor Graham Greenleaf and Professor Andrew Mowbray taking the initiative in 1995. This is an effort with an impressive ambition, and a background in the policies of legal information services in Australia, where the doctrine of "Crown Copyright" prevails.

---

[11] Cf. <www.law.cornell.edu/>.

[12] Cf. (Myers, 2002).

[13] One will appreciate that 1992 is very early indeed for such a service.

[14] The term "Legal information Institute" (LII) refers to a provider of legal information that is independent of government, and provides free access on a non-profit basis to multiple sources of essential legal information, cf. (Greenleaf, Mowbray, King, van Dijk, 2002)

[15] Directive 2003/98/EC of the European Parliament and of the Council of 17 November 2003 on the re-use of public sector information.

[16] In general, see (Saxby, 1996).

AustLII is based on the belief that it is in the public interest that authorities should aim to maximise access to the "public legal information" that they control. AustLII argues that unless governments and agencies positively co-operate with non-commercial bodies by providing them with raw data in computerised form, non-commercial bodies are unlikely ever to be able to publish the data in any form (Greenleaf, Mowbray, King, van Dijk, 2002).

There are several characteristics of the AustLII that make the service remarkable – the scope of the database is one thing, the programs developed to enhance the service, and support search strategies is another. But perhaps most important are the standards AustLII sets itself for making legal sources available in a complete and authentic form, a service to integrate material and to be trusted.[17]

AustLII has also many offspring, one of them being the WorldLII, a co-operation several LIIs.[18] AustLII has taken upon itself to attempt creating a truly international information resource; not only are the materials made available by the LIIs listed under WorldLII, but a search engine has been developed to index legal sites around the world. There is a toolbar available for most browsers, and lawyers should download this – it will provide an on-screen visual evidence of future possibilities.

The enthusiasm for the LIIs should not obscure some important policy tensions. The needs of the professional users of legal sources require an efficient research tool. Certainly, the public should be given as easy access as possible to statutes and other important legal material. But use of the authentic legal sources is not trivial. There may be – and in my mind I am convinced there are different requirements for a service catering for the public and a service meeting the requirements of the professionals. And I am not at all certain that the specialised tools needed by a rather small number of professionals should be paid for by the public at large.

The services offered by the LIIs are often buffered by the policy of *publication legis* and a reference to the basic right of all citizens to know the law. This justification is not challenged. But it is challenged that it is wise, or even possible, to satisfy *both* the needs of the lay user *and* the needs of the professional user by the same information service. Even though much of the authentic material would be identical, the user requirements for a friendly service differ. The tension between these two objectives can be discerned in several aspects of services from LIIs. For instance, Cornell LII integrates it services with legal education, and AustLII has several features to help lay users.[19] And for the professional user we would like to see further develop-

---

[17] Also other LIIs have similar standards, for Cornell LII see (Bruce, 2002).
[18] Cf. <www.worldlii.org/worldlii/>.
[19] One of the innovative features of AustLII is an expert system integrated in the information service, when the user has identified a provision in a statute, the user may (where available) switch to an expert system mode that will guide the user through a series of

ments, for instance more sophisticated ways in presenting search results, better integration with in-house services (for instance for litigation support) etc.

5. The vision upgraded

Above, with a certain *tristesse*, it was observed that the vision of a consolidated national information service had been disrupted by the advances in information technology, first introducing office automation, and then web services. Of course, the vision never was realistic. A jurisdiction is too complex, there are too many possible perspectives that they could or should be contained within one system. The only way to ensure objectivity and a sufficient diversity is to support several systems.

The limiting factor may be the economical constraints within a jurisdiction. A large market like the United States may support several large scale and general legal information services like LEXIS and Westlaw. In other jurisdictions, there may be a need for the public sector to provide the necessary economic basis for a national service.

Because legal information services are not only a question about the market, it is also a question of what services have to be available for ensuring due process and the other ideal objectives of a society ruled by law.

But there is also a need to look towards an international solution. We need to find possibilities of exploiting the advantage of other jurisdictions having legal material which may be of interest. Current principles of using material across frontiers have been forged in a situation where it has been difficult to exploit case law or legislative reviews from other countries. Today, there are regional legal systems where it would make good sense to access decisions and other material from other countries. The European Union may serve as an example, regulations and directives are issued for a large number of jurisdictions, and it would be useful if the material generated by courts and other institutions in applying these provisions was available for the other countries within the union. There are examples of services offering such solutions, like CaseLex[20] reporting on national Supreme Court decisions from all countries within the region relating to European legal instruments.

But these attempts are still in the making. We should be guided by the vision of WorldLII, and look for knowledge based solutions which seek out and consolidate material on request of the professional user. And computational linguistics seem to have progressed sufficiently to offer the user the possibility to have the material rendered in a language he or she may understand, at least sufficiently to determine whether that material may be relevant.

---

questions in order to advice the user whether the provision will apply to the problem of the user

[20] Cf. <www.caselex.com/>.

If this is realised, we will see that the dynamics of the legal system itself, where a legal argument take into consideration prior decisions, may over time work itself into a more harmonised view as courts and other institutions puzzle together not only the pieces of their national systems, but also try to make them fit with a bigger, international picture.

References

Bing, J. et al. (1984), *Handbook of Legal Information Retrieval*, North-Holland, Amsterdam, also available at: `<www.lovdata.no/litt/index.html>`.

Bing, J. (2009), *Building Cyberspace: A brief History of Internet*, in Bygrave, L.A. and Bing, J., "Internet Governance – infrastructure and institutions", Oxford University Press, Oxford.

Bing, J. (2003), *The policies of legal information services: a perspective of three decades*, in Mirfield, P. and Smith, R. (Eds.), "Essays for Colin Tapper", LexisNexis UK, London 2003, p. 153.

Bjørner, S. and Ardito, S.C. (2004), *An Interview with Richard Giering*, January 2004, available at: `<connection.ebscohost.com/content/article/1036116093.html; jsessionid=D0437073C6647A193B3E827575CC0AE2.ehctc1>`.

Bruce, T.R. (2002), *Some Thoughts on the Constitution of Public Legal Information Providers*, available at: `<www4.law.cornell.edu/working-papers/open/bruce/ warwick.html>`.

Greenleaf, G., Chung, P., Mowbray, A. (2002), *Free access to law via Internet as a condition of the rule of law in Asian societies: HKLII and WorldLII*, available at: `<www2.austlii.edu.au/-~graham/publications/2002/HKLII_WorldLII_ Jan02/HKLII_WorldLII.html#Heading3>`.

Greenleaf, G., Mowbray, A., King, G., van Dijk, P. (2002), *Public access to law via internet: the Australasian Legal Information Institute*, available at: `<www.austlii.edu.au/ austlii/articles/libs_paper.html#RTFToC11>`.

Hafner, C.D. (1981), *An information retrieval system based on a computer model of legal knowledge*, UMI Research Press, Ann Arbor.

Kondos, G.R. (1973), *Introduction to JURIS – Justice retrieval and inquiry system*, Abidjan World Conference on World Peace through Law.

Myers, L. (2002), *CU Law institute web site has latest legal information, from Miranda to Elian*, available at: `<www.news.cornell.edu/Chronicle/00/4.27.00/Legal_Info_Inst. html>`.

Saxby, S.J. (1996), *Public Policy and Legal Regulation of the Information Market in the Digital Network Environment*, CompLex 2/1996, Norwegian Research Center for Computers and Law, Oslo.

Open Access to Legal Scholarship and Copyright Rules: A Law and Technology Perspective

Roberto Caso
Faculty of Law, University of Trento, Italy

Abstract. By applying copyright law, contracts, customs and technological standards it is possible to achieve two different kinds of control over digital information.

In the first form, control is based on the closeness of information and it is rigid and centralized: see, e.g., the Digital Rights Management systems (DRMs).

In the second form, control is based on the openness of information and it is flexible and decentralized: see, e.g., the GNU General Public License (GPL) and the Creative Commons Licenses (CCLs).

Those two models of control correspond to two opposite trends in scientific community. On one side, the risk is that a rigid and centralized control (such as the one based on DRMs), shaped by market considerations, invades the sector proper of the scientific community (which, on the contrary, is traditionally inspired by the logic of a flexible and decentralized control, based on customs and informal norms). This would strongly undermine the possibilities of access to scientific knowledge expressed in a digital format. This risk is prominent in the field of legal scholarship, where a vast amount of legal information (also covering the information that is, in theory, in public domain) is governed by rigid and centralized control.

On the other side, to counteract such a risk, part of the scientific community is promoting the logic of Open Access (mostly based on free licenses such as the GNU GPL or the CCLs) to scientific knowledge.

The Open Access (OA) movement is quickly growing in importance for legal scholarship. Nonetheless, the institutional arrangements and the technological features of OA to legal scholarship are variegated and pose a vast array of problems.

Keywords: Open access, legal information, legal scholarship, copyright law, digital rights management, creative commons licenses.

1. Introduction

We are confronting with a risk. A rigid and centralized control over digital information (such as that based on the Digital Rights Management systems), shaped by market considerations, may soon dominate the field of the scientific community at large (which, on the contrary, has been traditionally inspired by the logic of a flexible and decentralized control, based on customs and informal norms). This would strongly undermine the possibilities of access to scientific knowledge expressed in digital format. This risk is particularly acute in the field of legal scholarship, where a vast amount of legal information (also covering information that is, in theory, in public domain) is governed through rigid and centralized control. To counteract such a risk, part of the scientific community is promoting the logic of Open Access (mostly based on free licenses such as the GNU General Public License or the Creative Commons Licenses) to scientific knowledge.

Despite the initial delay, the Open Access (OA) movement is quickly growing in importance for legal scholarship. Nonetheless, the institutional arrangements and the technological features of OA to legal scholarship are variegated and pose a vast array of problems.

To understand the interaction between the law and technology in OA to legal scholarship Part 2 of this paper outlines the relationship between intellectual property and norms of science, Part 3 illustrates the two different kinds of control over digital information achieved by applying copyright law, contracts, customs and technological standards, Part 4 describes closed and OA models to scientific knowledge, Part 5 discusses the promises and perils of OA to legal scholarship. Eventually, Part 6 sketches some conclusions.

2. Intellectual property vs. [and] norms of science

Intellectual property has been shaped mainly by economic interests. In particular the ancestors of patents and copyrights emerged as privileges granted by the king to the representatives of merchant class, such as weavers and printers, to exercise their activity exclusively. The mechanism of privilege has then evolved to the exclusive right recognized by the law (David, 1993).

From an economic perspective, the exclusive right is a mechanism which is needed to balance the incentive to produce creative information with the possibility of accessing the same information. As distinct from material goods, information is a non-rival and non-excludable good (Arrow, 1962). Because of non excludability an information market cannot emerge. Intellectual property grants to the holder an artificial exclusive right, formally warranted by state law, mimicking the mechanism of ownership of material goods, thus laying the foundations of a market. The right holder can exclusively use the invention or the work, enjoying an advantage over competitors. In other words, the exclusive right is a sort of legal monopoly. Those enjoying the exclusive right can, indeed, charge a monopolistic price, i.e. a price higher than the marginal cost. This constitutes a benefit with regard to the incentive to produce information, but also a cost for society. The most important bundle of costs depends on the fact that anyone who is not willing to pay the monopolistic price will be cut out from the use of information protected by the exclusivity. Among these are also those who wish to re-elaborate the information in order to produce new inventions and works. It is, therefore, necessary that the social costs do not outweigh the social benefits. The limits of intellectual property rights are aimed at such goal and can consist in time limits (for example the patent for invention generally lasts twenty years; the copyright lasts usually for the lifetime of the author plus seventy years) and content limits (for example the patent for inventions concerns only new ideas; the copyright regards only the expressive form of an original work) (Menell and Scotchmer, 2005).

Instead, the institutional features of the production of scientific knowledge have been mostly shaped by the practices and customs of the community of scientists, the so-called Republic of Science (Polanyi, 1962). An authoritative trend of the sociology of science has singled out the main informal norms governing the production of scientific knowledge: "universalism", "communality", "disinterestedness" and "organized skepticism" (Merton, 1973; Eisenberg, 1987; Rai, 1999; Burk, 2006).

Universalism means that the truthfulness of the results of the research is not bound to the scientist's (national or institutional) identity.

Communality implies that the knowledge is the product of collaboration among colleagues and, therefore, it must be shared within scientific community. All the actual knowledge is built upon past knowledge and it is the basis for that of the future (as Isaac Newton said "if I have seen further it is by standing on the shoulders of Giants").

Disinterestedness requires that scientists aspire to research the truth, not their personal interests.

Organized skepticism expects that scientists' theories will be submitted to the critical evaluation of the community before being accepted.

These four norms are strengthened from the acknowledgement in terms of prestige (and of career progress) by the community. The scientific community, indeed, prizes those who make original contributions to knowledge. The emphasis on originality generates the incentive to publish the works as soon as possible, trying to avoid being anticipated by others. But, after having published the work, the scientist does not have any more exclusivity over the knowledge she has produced.

Even though intellectual property and the norms of science have different paths, they also intersect. In the complex historic process that has led from the "secret science" to the "open science" (Rossi, 2007; David, 2004), the invention of scientific journals by the Royal Society of London in early 1665 – when Henry Oldenburg created the Philosophical Transactions (or Phil Trans) - was probably the first of these intersections. At its beginning, the scientific journal was, overall, the "public record of original contributions to knowledge [. . .]". "[T]he Republic of Science claimed the right to grant intellectual property to scientific 'authors' and Phil Trans was its instrument of choice" (Guedon, 2001). Hence, it is paternity (i.e. the author's right) at the center of this scenario, not the commercial aspect (the editor's right) of copyright. In fact, for centuries scientific journals and scientific articles were not an editor's business.

The landscape changed after the World War II, when supply and demand of scientific publications quickly rose. Scientific journals become a flourishing business. The rise of the concept of "core journals" has shaped the peculiar features of the market for journal publications and has led to so-called "serial pricing crisis" (Guedon, 2001). As a recent European study pointed out: the market of scientific journals is "an intermediated market, where libraries are the key buyers, which leads to lower reader price sensitivity. Moreover, it is a market where the best authors want to publish in highly-read journals and readers want to read journals which publish the best authors. This leads to 'virtuous circles' for journals, and to associated 'natural barriers to entry'" (VV.AA., 2006). Moreover, "much of scientific activity is publicly funded: the output of research is typically not bought by journals but 'donated' by publicly-funded researchers" (VV.AA., 2006).

3. Digital technologies and access to information: closed models vs. open models

What role do digital technologies have in the access to scientific knowledge?

At a superficial glance, digital technologies multiply and speed up the possibility of access to scientific knowledge. Therefore, it is possible to think that their use within the scientific community has reinforced the trend of sharing the results of the research with the public.

Nonetheless, the picture is much more complex.

The information and telecommunication technologies present revolutionary features (Pascuzzi, 2006). In the context of this discourse, we can single out two of them.

1. On one hand, it is possible to foreclose information totally (for example, by making the open source code of software secret or by encrypting a text file), making it understandable only to the machines or, better, making it accessible and usable (by a human user) through pre-determined modalities, machines or software. For example it is possible to program software for reading an e-book in a way which is compatible only with specific hardware.

2. On the other hand, it is possible to transmit information in one language understood by the computer (binary code) and in an open format (the so-called open source code), a format modifiable by those who know the programming language.

Following the scenario depicted so far, two models of production of digital information can be sketched (Caso, 2008).

a) The first model is based on the closeness of information and, therefore, on rigid and centralized control. Such a model creates hierarchical forms of production and distribution in which the information holders can choose where, how, when and who will be able to use information: this is the case for Digital Rights Management systems (DRMs), based on technological protection measures (TPMs).

b) The second model is based on the openness of information and, therefore, on a flexible and decentralized control. This model generates non-hierarchical forms of production and distribution (called "Peer to Peer") where the actors, inspired sometimes by different incentives than payment in exchange for services, perform the functions typical of producers and consumers in a hybrid way: this is the case, for example, of the development of an open source software such as Linux or of the drawing of texts such as an on-line encyclopedia, where all the users can publish or amend the entries (Wikipedia).

Applying intellectual property law (patent, copyright, industrial secrets), contracts, customs and technological standards it is possible to obtain different forms of control over digital information.

Today, two forms of control are emerging, corresponding to the two models of production which have been previously indicated.

A) In the first form, the control is based on the closeness of information and it is rigid and centralized. This kind of control emerges from the market of the so-called "proprietary software" and finds its foundations on an (initially rudimentary) TPM: keeping the source code secret. The acknowledgment of the copyright protection and the diffusion of End User License Agreements (EULAs), have reinforced this control on a contractual basis.

This kind of control gives rise to DRM based on (cryptographic) TPMs (Bechtold, 2004; Caso, 2004). The control is extended from the source code of the software to any information which can be expressed in binary code (not only software, but also text, audio, video, etc.).

The goal of DRM is, indeed, that the conditions – written in the license - for access and use of information must be implemented by software and machines designed (on the basis of the standards proper of the DRM system) in order to enjoy the same information.

With regard to the control over information, the main components of the DRM systems are:

- the TPMs based mainly on the digital cryptography, but also on other technologies such as digital watermarking and fingerprinting;
- the metadata that describe restrictions in a language which is understandable by the computer;
- the content;
- the holder of the content;
- the user;

— the rules for enjoying the content (for example if it can be copied, printed, distributed, etc., where it can be enjoyed, through which machines it can be enjoyed), expressed in languages which are called Rights Expression Languages (RELs), such as the eXtensible rights Markup Language (XrML), which is one of the standard languages.

B) The second form of control is based on the openness of information and is flexible and decentralized. The first model of such control is represented by the GNU General Public License (GPL). These are general contractual conditions which, using copyright, are aimed at guaranteeing the right to copy (so-called "Copyleft"), modify and distribute software with open source code to anyone willing to accept such contractual conditions.

The mechanism of protection relies on the clause which declares that the software subject to the license is protected by copyright and that, at the same time, imposes on the users of the GPL to apply the same GPL, if the same software, or other derived software is distributed, to subsequent licensees. The GNU GPL model has inspired several different types of licenses. Among these, the Creative Commons Licenses (CCLs) are one of the most successful. Such licenses translate the GNU GPL model, successfully implemented in the field of software, to the broader field of all digital content and to all inventive works embodied in traditional media, such as books (Lessig, 2004).

4. Scientific knowledge: closed access models vs. open access models

The scenario described so far gives rise to the risk that rigid and centralized control (such as that based on DRM systems), shaped on market considerations, invades the proper domain of the scientific community (which is, on the contrary, motivated by the logic of flexible and decentralized control, based on customs and informal norms), decreasing the possibility of access to scientific knowledge expressed in a digital format. Such a risk depends on many factors.

— Digitalization, along with other causes – such as the shortening of the distance between base and applied research – means that the scientific community can perceive knowledge as economic goods tradable on the market through intellectual property rights and TPMs (Nelson, 2003; David, 2003; Eisenberg, 1987). The phenomenon also concerns institutions financed by public funds, such as universities (Monotti and Ricketson, 2003).
— The contemporary scientific press is controlled by few private big editors, who apply market rules and intellectual property rights to the circulation of information concerning scientific knowledge. Despite the fact that digital technologies allow huge cuts in the costs of production and distribution

of information, the price fixed by private editors to get access to digitized scientific information seems doomed to increase (Guedon, 2001).

– Western legal systems tend to strengthen and multiply intellectual property rights on digital (information) goods (David, 2003). New goods are subject to intellectual property (for example, software and databases); single goods can be subjected to many intellectual property rights (for example, in some cases software can be subject both to copyright and patent; databases in the European Union can be subjected both to copyright and to a *sui generis* right); a plurality of subjects can claim intellectual property rights (for example, not only private individuals or enterprises, but also research institutes, universities, etc.). Rigid and centralized control, such as that implemented on DRMs, is part, therefore, of a picture in which intellectual property rights appear to be strengthened. Despite the enormous power of control and the many effects that this rigid and centralized control has on different legal aspects, western parliaments have created a discipline of legitimization and protection (only) for some of the components of the DRM systems, often by making room for DRM provisions in general copyright legislation (see the U.S. Digital Millennium Copyright Act (DMCA) of 1998 and European Union Copyright Directive (EUCD) of 2001). Lobbying by traditional (the entertainment industry) and emerging (the DRM industry) interests has prevailed on the public interest to regulate the control over digital information.

– Intellectual property legislation on digital goods vary according to the legal system considered. For example, the US legal framework is different from that of the EU, but also within EU one can detect important differences between countries. This is a further hurdle to access to and circulation of scientific knowledge expressed in digital form.

To counteract this risk, part of the scientific community is promoting the logic of OA to scientific knowledge (Willinsky, 2006; Suber, 2004-2006; Guedon, 2001).

Many scientific communities publish their results on websites freely accessible to anyone through the Internet. This can be the case for the publication of drafts, articles already published in "for payment" journals or, again, it may be the sole manner of publishing the research (Guedon, 2004).

The logic of OA is also promoted in solemn declarations, such as the Berlin Declaration on Open Access to Knowledge in the Sciences and Humanities in 2003.

Nonetheless, the institutional arrangements and the technological features of OA are variegated and pose an array of problems (Burk, 2006).

For example, sharing the source code of software contemplated by the GNU GPL is based on contract and informal norms of the community of software programmers. On one hand, respect for the GPL is warranted by the threat to apply the law of contracts. This seems to be a different aspect than that of the traditional informal norms of the scientific community. On the other hand, respect is warranted by the reputation created by the norms of the software programmers. But this does not mean that such norms can be adapted to other communities (such as the communities of the biologists or lawyers).

To make a further example, the CCLs project is developing a program specifically dedicated to scientific knowledge called "Science Commons". However, the transplant of the CCLs logic in the scientific context gives rise to many questions.

CCLs are very recent tools, while the institutional arrangements of the scientific community are quite old. The CCLs are contracts which can be used for all the typologies of authors. The scientific community is formed by many scientific communities. Each of them has, along with the general informal norms already mentioned in Part 2 of this paper, specific informal norms. Moreover, the CCLs raises, like all standard contracts, the problem of the licensee's protection. In particular, an extremely interesting field of investigation is that aimed at improving the cognitive and informational position of the licensee, making it possible for him to choose preferred contractual arrangements with increased awareness (Hillman and Rachlinski, 2001). Such a perspective requires a major investigation also on the programming side, particularly with regard at the aim of improving the technologies for the digital management of the contracts (Mulligan and Burstein, 2003).

5. Open access to legal scholarship: promises and perils

The risk of rigid and centralized control based on market considerations invading the proper domain of the scientific community is acute if one considers the field of legal scholarship. A vast amount of legal information - also covering information that is, in theory, in the public domain - is presently accessible only through closed and proprietary databases such as Lexis and Westlaw. The increasing concentration of the market of legal databases has led to escalating prices for legal information (Arewa, 2006). The contractual and market power of databases holders is strengthened by new copyright laws (such as the EU directive 96/9 on the database protection and the DMCA as well as the EUCD on TPMs).

But, despite the initial delay, the OA movement is quickly growing in legal scholarship (Carroll, 2006; Hunter, 2006; Solum, 2007).

The OA model to legal scholarship has the potential to subvert the present dominant publishing model. Perhaps this is true as well as in other scientific fields. This impression depends on the peculiar features of the legal field.

- The peer review system (traditionally managed by commercial editors) is much less important in law than in the hard sciences.

- Some types of legal publications are for non academic lawyers (judges, attorneys, etc.). Besides, legal scholarship is more and more interdisciplinary and globalized (Carroll, 2006). Hence, the public interested in legal publications is very large and heterogeneous.

- The raw legal data (i.e., the primary sources like acts and judicial opinions) are – thanks to clear copyright rules - in many western legal systems in the public domain.

The emerging OA model the legal scholarship has the following institutional structure.

- The major functions of publications (selecting the best works, making the works accessible, publicizing the works, and archiving the works) is based on the old participants (commercial editors, university press, law reviews student-edited, etc.) and new intermediaries (legal scholarship repositories like Social Science Research Network's Legal Scholarship Network and Berkeley Electronic Press Legal Repository, Wikipedia, Internet search engines like Google Books and Google Scholar, social software, etc.) (Solum, 2007).

- Production costs are – as in the past – borne by the authors and their institutions (universities and law faculties). Dissemination costs – lower than in the past - are shared among the authors, their institutions and the old and new intermediaries. The incentive system is based on the "reader's attention". E.g., in the publishing of a post-print on the OA repository such as SSRN, the authors and law reviews increase the probability of reading and citation, while the repository multiplies the circulation of its own brand, and the Internet search engines increases the number of users and visits. Moreover, OA dramatically reduces the delay in publication (making the information more useful to potential readers, if it is true that time is an important variable in the contemporary legal arena, especially for attorneys and for judges) and the costs of reading/accessing that material.

- The author retains copyright (in particular, the right of attribution) over the publication and grants - through open licenses such as CCLs (see the Open Access Law Program of the Science Commons Project) (Carroll, 2006) – to public and intermediaries a limited set of rights.

This is a revolutionary approach. OA to legal scholarship changes the form of the legal publication - as a scholar has pointed out, we are facing new kind of publications such as the "idea-paper", the blog post, the Wikipedia article (Solum, 2007) - and shifts the "quality selection" function from the traditional intermediaries to the new intermediaries (e.g. search engines and social software) and the readers.

Nonetheless, the revolution has just started, and we are in the middle of it. The future of OA to legal scholarship is not clear. Some scholars have argued that the OA movement complements the old publishing model and is not a substitute. In particular, an author has pointed out that the success of the OA depends on the power to supply the so called "economy of prestige" that has been managed for centuries by legal scholarship through the old publishing model (Madison, 2006).

If it is true that the managing the economy of prestige is still (and will be) a cornerstone of (legal) scholarship, nevertheless the revolutionary power of digital technologies is modifying the features not only of the publishing model but also of the academic lawyer itself. As argued above, thanks to information and communication technologies, legal scholarship is more and more interdisciplinary and globalized.

Rather, the actual problems of the OA to legal scholarship seem the same as those of the larger OA movement. These problems can be synthesized in the following list.

— Until now OA has been a bottom up and decentralized movement, based on different policies, solemn declarations and contractual arrangements such as CCLs. In fact, there is no unified definition of OA. Yet, the formal law shows a growing attention to OA (see, in the USA, the National Institute of Health Public Access Policy implements the Division G, Title II, Section 218 of PL 110-161, Consolidated Appropriations Act, 2008). Hence, the future of OA depends on the intersection between formal law, OA policies and social norms of science. E.g., the CCLs are formal contracts (even if contracts with special features) and customs of (legal) science are informal norms. The future will tell us if the application of CCLs in the courts will be compatible with social norms of (legal) science.

— OA is a powerful instrument making work accessible. The success of the OA in the other three functions of publishing (selecting the best works, publicizing the work, and archiving the work) will depend not only on institutional arrangements but also on the development of a trustworthy technological system based on standardization of metadata (Carroll, 2006; Madison, 2006), search engines with sophisticated Boolean operators, and digital formats which guarantee long term preservation of the works. From this perspective the openness of software and formats will play a fundamental role.

— OA is not Nirvana. The dislocation of publishing functions to new intermediaries raises a number of new risks. E.g., Google's algorithm is not neutral. "Google ranks the relevance of any given Web site by determining the number of other sites that are linked to it" (Hunter, 2006). This is a value choice. Moreover, "the precise method for producing the rank order is a trade secret" (Solum, 2007). Last but not least, many have raised concerns about the Google's power to process an infinitive quantity of personal data (Guarda, 2008). In other words, dislocating publishing functions means also dislocating power, with new problems related to that power.

6. Conclusions

OA is an extremely powerful tool for the dissemination of knowledge made possible by digital technologies. It has some real advantages as regards the traditional publishing model. Moreover, through OA it is possible to counteract the risk that the rigid and centralized control (such as that based on the DRM systems), shaped on market considerations, will invade the proper domain of the scientific community. But the definitive success of OA (in legal scholarship as well as in other scientific fields) depends on our capacity to understand and manage the complex intersection among intellectual property law, contracts, norms of science and technological standards.

One may say that the OA is the revenge of "author's right" on the "editor's right". Nevertheless we must be conscious that - in the digital age - copyright law is only one (and not the most important) among many other instruments which may govern the production and distribution of information.

The dislocation of the publishing functions to new intermediaries raises a number of new risks. To counteract these new risks we have to take Internet governance seriously and to see beyond copyright law.

7. Acknowledgements

I wish to thank Pippo Bellantuono, Matteo Ferrari, Paolo Guarda, Umberto Izzo, Federica Lorenzato and Tina Piper for helpful comments on earlier drafts of this paper.

References

Arewa, O. (2006), *Open Access in a Closed Universe: Lexis, Westlaw, Law Schools, and the Legal Information Market*, Case Legal Studies Research Paper No. 06-03, available at: <ssrn.com/abstract=888321>.

Arrow, K. J. (1962), *Economic Welfare and the Allocation of Resources to Invention*, in Nelson, R. R. (Ed.), *The Rate and Direction of Inventive Activities*, Princeton, N.J.

Bechtold, S. (2004), *Digital Rights Management in the United States and Europe*, American Journal of Comparative Law, Vol. 52, p. 323.

Burk, D.L. (2006), *Intellectual Property in the Context of E-Science*, Minnesota Legal Studies Research Paper No. 06-47, August 18, available at:<ssrn.com/abstract=929479>.

Carroll, M.W. (2006), *The Movement for Open Access Law – Symposium*, Villanova Law/Public Policy Research Paper No. 2006-11, available at: <ssrn.com/abstract=918298>.

Caso, R. (2008), *Forme di controllo delle informazioni digitali: il Digital Rights Management*, in Caso, R. (Ed.), "Digital Rights Management: problemi teorici e prospettive applicative", Proceeding of the conference at the Law Faculty of the University of Trento, March 21-22, available at: <eprints.biblio.unitn.it/archive/00001336/>.

Caso, R. (2004), *Digital Rights Management: il commercio delle informazioni digitali tra contratto e diritto d'autore*, Padova, available at: <www.jus.unitn.it/users/caso/pubblicazioni/drm/download.asp>.

David, P.A. (2004), *From Keeping 'Nature's Secrets' to the Institutionalization of 'Open Science'*, available at: <www-econ.stanford.edu/faculty/workp/swp04006.html>.

David, P.A. (2003), *Can 'Open Science' be Protected from the Evolving Regime of IPR Protections?*, available at: www-econ.stanford.edu/faculty/workp/>.

David, P.A. (1993), *Intellectual property institutions and the panda's thumb: patents, copyrights, and trade secrets in economic theory and history*, in Wallerstein, M., Mogee, M. and Schoen, R. (Eds.), "Global Dimensions of Intellectual Property Protection in Science and Technology", National Academy Press, Washington, D.C.

Eisenberg, R.S. (1987), *Proprietary Rights and the Norms of Science in Biotechnology Research*, Yale Law Journal, Vol. 97, p. 177.

Guarda, P. (2008), *The Myth of Odin's Eye: Privacy vs Knowledge*, in "Proceedings The Future of... Conference on Law and Technology", Florence, 28-29 October 2008", upcoming, pre-print available at: <www.one-lex.eu/futureof/papers/guarda.doc>.

Guedon, J. C. (2004), *The 'Green' and 'Gold' Roads to Open Access: The Case for Mixing and Matching*, Serials Review, Vol. 30, p. 315, available at: <eprints.rclis.org/archive/00003039/01/science.pdf>.

Guedon, J. C. (2001), *In Oldenburg's Long Shadow: Librarians, Research Scientists, Publishers, and the Control of Scientific Publishing*, in "Proceedings Creating the Digital Future: Association of Research Libraries 138th Annual Meeting", Toronto, Ontario (Canada).

Hillman, R.A. and Rachlinski, J.J. (2001), *Standard-Form Contracting in the Electronic Age*, available at: <ssrn.com/abstract=287819> or DOI: <10.2139/ssrn.287819>.

Hunter, D. (2006), *Open Access to Infinite Content (Or 'In Praise of Law Reviews')*, Lewis & Clark Law Review, Vol. 10, No. 4, available at: <ssrn.com/abstract=952410>.

Lessig, L. (2004), *Free Culture. How Big Media Uses Technology and the Law to Lock Down Culture and Control Creativity*, New York, available at: <www.free-culture.cc/freeculture.pdf>.

Litman, J. (2006), *The Economics of Open-Access Law Publishing*, University of Michigan Law & Economics, Olin Working Paper No. 06-005, available at: <ssrn.com/abstract=912304>.

Madison, M. J. (2006), *The Idea of the Law Review: Scholarship, Prestige, and Open Access*, Lewis & Clark Law Review, available at: <ssrn.com/abstract=899122>.

Menell, P.S. and Scotchmer, S. (2005), *Intellectual Property*, UC Berkeley Public Law Research Paper No. 741724, available at: <ssrn.com/abstract=741424>.

Merton, R.K. (1973), *The Sociology of Science: Theoretical and Empirical Investigations*, Chicago, IL.

Monotti, A. and Ricketson, S. (2003), *Universities and Intellectual Property. Ownership and Exploitation*, New York.

Mulligan, D.K. and Burstein, A. (2003), *Implementing Copyright Limitations in Rights Expression Languages*, in Feigenbaum, J.(Ed.), "Security and Privacy in Digital Rights Management", New York, p. 137, available at: <crypto.stanford.edu/DRM2002/mulligan_burstein_acm_drm_2002.doc>.

Nelson, R. (2003), *The Market Economy and the Scientific Commons*, LEM Working Paper Series 2003-24, available at: <www.lem.sssup.it/WPLem/files/2003-24.pdf>.

Pascuzzi, G. (2006), *Il diritto dell'era digitale. Tecnologie informatiche e regole privatistiche*, II ed., Bologna.

Polanyi, M. (1962), *The Republic of Science: Its Political and Economic Theory*, Minerva, Vol. 1, p. 54, available at: <www.compilerpress.atfreeweb.com/Anno\%20Polanyi\%20Republic\%20of\%20Science\%201962.htm>.

Rai, A.K. (1999), *Regulating Scientific Research: Intellectual Property Rights and the Norms of Science*, Northwestern University Law Review, Vol. 94, pp. 77-152.

Rossi, P. (2007), *La nascita della scienza moderna in Europa*, Roma-Bari.

Solum, L. B. (2007), *Download It While Its Hot: Open Access and Legal Scholarship*, Illinois Public Law Research Paper No. 07-03, available at: <ssrn.com/abstract=957237>.

Suber, P. (2004-2006), *Open Access Overview*, available at: <www.earlham.edu/~peters/fos/overview.htm>.

VV.AA. (2006), *Study on the Economic and Technical Evolution of the Scientific Publication Markets in Europe – Final Report*, Commissioned by DG-Research, European Commission, Bruxelles, Belgique, available at: <ec.europa.eu/research/science-society/pdf/scientific-publication-study_en.pdf>.

Willinsky, J. (2006), *The Access Principle – The Case for Open Access to Research and Scholarship*, MIT Press, Cambridge, MA.

Theory and Reality of the Official Publication of Legal Acts on Internet**

Pasquale Costanzo*, Marina Pietrangelo°
* *University of Genova*
° *Institute of Legal Information Theory and Techniques (ITTIG-CNR), Italy*

Abstract. This paper offers an analysis of the main experiences faced by western democracies, experiences related to the official publication of legal acts on Internet against the demands traditionally linked to those kind of publications, pointing out new opportunities for democracy and protection of rights offered by Internet, as well as problems of cultural, technical and institutional character.

1. Foreword

The maxim "not all that comes after is progress" is attributed to the statesman Giovanni Giolitti. We could not be absolutely certain of the circumstances, even though the sense of the phrase could well match the object of this report. Without dwelling too long on the epoch in which "norms" were delivered to the recipients' homes to the sound of drums and trumpets (sonic attention effect), announced by bill-posting or even mural inscriptions (visual attention effect), we will mention the system still in force in revolutionary France and successively re-adopted on the other side of the Alps from the III Republic till recent times, whereby legal acts were not enforced following an abstract, chronological rule disjointed from factual reality, but exactly as soon as the official bulletin containing the act text had reached its destination located in the various territories.

At present, unless we are mistaken, we are under the impression that such sensitivity towards the demand for an effective (albeit mostly symbolic) knowableness of the law appears largely rather enfeebled. In the course of time, however, the assumption, stemming from the traditional brocard *ignorantia legis neminem excusat* and justified by social complexity, has increasingly revealed its theoretical character, to the extent that the unconditional enforcement of published acts as an answer to "the absolute need, of social and political relevance, for laws to be observed" (Ranelletti, 1937, p. 309) has come to appear even more genuine, as the core sense of this publication is unequivocally associated with maintenance of law authority and guarantees of right and social entrusting (Quadri, 1974, p. 14). The decision, in fact, to highlight the *bon côté* of the phenomenon, that is, what connects it to the legislation recipient's need to be granted juridical safety, once they are made aware of

---

** This text is the result of a common reflection of the authors. However, Pasquale Costanzo wrote paragraphs 1 e 4, Marina Pietrangelo wrote paragraphs 2 e 3.

their rights and duties, was made in a desultory way. As a result, insufficient attention, with sporadic exceptions, has been given firstly to the significance, essentially unilateral and not subject to the rule of acknowledgment of act text's receipt, secondly to the quasi symbolic, (if not at all deprived of sense in case of impellent enforcement) value of the *vacatio legis*, and lastly to the factual unsuitability and/or obsolescence of the communicative medium being used (for valuable ideas in this sense, see Grottanelli De' Santi, 1985, p. 229). Publication itself seems to be still dependent on the lexical formalism looked upon as text "neutrality" or "indifference" in respect of both its concrete effects on the systems (especially as regards abrogation), and the norms that can be extrapolated from its *provisions* (for this last meaning see D'Atena, 1974, p. 149). However, a more "substantial" conception of the norm accessibility had already emerged even in the preliminary drafting (session of 23 October 1947) of the Italian constitution (Codacci Pisanelli, 1970, p. 3479), according to which "To ensure knowledge of laws, issuing and promulgating them is not enough. Laws must also be set out and co-ordinated".

On the other hand, if we consider amongst the fundamental principles of contemporary democracy that of transparency on the part of the powers that be and that of preventive, exhaustive information to citizens regarding what is demanded of them in terms of conduct and performance (Constitutional Court, ruling of 24th March 1988, n° 364), to expect that the enforcement of law in a far-reaching and diverse reality such as a state organisation should be conditional upon the factual and widespread knowledge of it would end up being utopian and non-verifiable. Besides, it would also defeat its purpose (let alone what has been defined as the *"natural* inability" of a publication to achieve results without active law recipients' participation) (D'Atena, 1974, p. 149).

Nevertheless, such obvious, inescapable circumstance cannot alone deny the aforementioned publicity principle, which itself keeps acting as a generator (at least) of a force shaping up the most appropriate conditions, in order for at least the potential, general accessibility, if not the knowledge, of new legislative acts being generated to be considered more or less realised.

But this is the crux of the matter. If we believe that up until a recent past a better realisation of the principles in question had chiefly been hindered by the obsolescence of the available technologies, we must accept the fact that, at a time in which such technologies have undergone an extraordinary, unprecedented development, both in message delivery range and in speed, the die-hard devotion to antiquated transmission modules ends up gradually invalidating an essential aspect of the system.

Nowadays, this premise inevitably evokes the Internet phenomenon. If the Network has managed to strengthen those communication rights which up to then had remained at an "embryonic" stage owing to the well-known *dychotomy* between abstract entitlement to rights and the availability of means to exercise them (Costanzo, 2003, p. 73), it appears now legitimate to ask ourselves about its possible developments in the field of normative publication. And this not only concerning its more evident aspect, that is, the one coinciding with the communication of the norm by the law-maker to the law (norm) "user", but also in respect to less visible, albeit not less relevant aspects. In fact, on top of the more traditional function of accessibility as prerequisite for a law to be enforced, we can observe, by inverting the terms of the question, how publication fulfils two basics duties: to grant permanent accessibility to legal precepts and, equally important, to confer the necessary character of authenticity to them.

Finally, as we all know, normative publication has acquired, alongside the democratic evolution of the system, further significance. Let us try and consider it, for instance, to be a tool for, amongst other things, checking and evaluating the law-maker's work, whereas, in that sense, other activities linked to the drafting of the "normative product", in particular preparatory work, tend to be subject to publication. At the same time, we witness the re-publishing of "consolidated" texts bearing the successive normative amendments.

However, even if we keep within the boundary of mere technical publication of the law, what we try (we should try) to bring out is the core meaning of the law, by enhancing the quality of the message, namely its perspicuity, in the context of the relationship between governing and governed subjects.

These are some of the knots we will try to undo, despite the limited space of this report. Firstly, we will examine carefully the "state of the art" of this complex matter comparatively (paragraphs 2 and 3), and then we will focus on the most problematic aspects of electronic publication of legal acts, both from a techno-juridical and a more general, theoretical angle (paragraph 4).

2. The reality of legislative publication on the Internet in Italy e in some experiences abroad

To examine more closely the perspectives of the phenomenon being observed within the frame of present-time legal systems, a quick outline (merely by way of example) of the experiences made in some European countries, Italy included, within the scope of online availability of national normative production, may constitute a useful premise (thoroughly dealt with by Costanzo, 2006).

Since, as we will see, the different practices and their respective jurisdictions introduced in various states show numerous analogies, they lend themselves to be subdivided into some macro-categories, depending whether they are publications regarded either as reports – institutional communication (2.1) – despite being classified as official because of their source, or as electronic publication drafts with legal value, – in the eventuality that official bulletins have switched by law from traditional paper form to electronic format (2.3) – or else, besides that, whenever a mixed format (paper and electronic) is still the case (2.2).

2.1. Electronic publication whose value is merely informative

In a number of EU member states, and elsewhere, the advanced applications of information technologies to public administration started in the early nineties have as yet made available to the public sophisticated information systems granting citizens easy access to legislative texts published on line by public sources, for merely informative purposes.

In many cases, this is done by means of unified access to data banks containing norms and regulations (various sources, not only primary ones), which public administrations choose to publish on their own official web sites. The services in question are configured as "meta-engines" (the texts of the acts are made available by the individual public authorities on their own websites), normally within the framework of *civil law* systems, by reason of the high number of acts being issued. By way of example, we can mention the Italian portal "Norme in Rete"[1] and the French portal "Legifrance".[2]

Within other systems, in particular the *common law* ones, primary and secondary legislation are available online free of charge through access to an apposite, centralised database. We can mention the British example (*UK Statute Law Database*)[3] or the Irish one (*Electronic Irish Statute Book database*).[4]

These services aim at the highest degree of public accessibility and diffusion of legislative information and are complementary to digitalisation of official journals, which are also published on the official websites of most governments. Consultation and download of texts located on these online journals is in most cases unconditioned and free of charge (it is the case in the following countries: Bulgaria, Cyprus, Denmark, Germany, Greece, Latvia, Lithuania, Luxemburg, Malta, Low Countries, Poland, Portugal, Principality of Monaco, Czech Republic, Spain, Sweden, Hungary. As for Italy, gratuity is regretfully only temporary.[5] For the time being, though, the purpose of digital reproduction of such documentation is meant to be merely informative.

Additionally, official EU legislation is at present accessible through printed publication, whereas digital publication of EU acts within the EUR-Lex system is only a popularization tool. However, the objective appears to be that of a final changeover to digital publication: "*It is certain that the future of European Union law is eLaw – eLaw meaning law which id electronic, efficient, ergonomic and European law. The Official Journal of the Union in 2016 is*

---

[1] Available at: <www.nir.it>.
[2] Available at: <www.legifrance.gouv.fr>.
[3] Available at: <www.statutelaw.gov.uk>.
[4] Available at: <www.irish-statutebook.ie>.
[5] See: <www.gazzettaufficiale.it>.

probably an authentic electronic journal, with some paper copies distributed to the Member States" (Rissanen, 2006, p. 4).

2.2. CO-EXISTENCE OF PAPER AND ELECTRONIC FORM IN OFFICIAL PUBLICATION

Nowadays, some examples of "interregnum", that is, co-existence of traditional, paper-based and electronic official documentation, still survive.

Amongst the first examples of such experimentation we can certainly quote France, where since 2004 the digital version of the *Journal Officiel*,[6] in conformity with the ordinance 2003-591 implementing a more general process of legislation streamlining, enjoys the same legal validity as the printed one. The ordinance ruling modalities and effects of official publications states that the double standard must be the general rule for all acts. Besides, the possibility is envisaged that specific categories of administrative acts, to be defined by means of an apposite decree issued by the State Council ("Art. 5. *[omissis] la publication au Journal Officiel sous forme électronique suffit à assurer l'entrée en viguer"* of the ordinance 2004-164).

A similar solution to the French one has been introduced in the United Kingdom. The three editions of the British official gazette (*London Gazette, Edinburgh Gazette and Belfast Gazette*) are in fact also accessible in the digital form. Moreover, this relevant novelty has not been followed by any legislative intervention, as it was introduced only in the form of common practice (Costanzo, 2006, p. 11).

Also the Swiss and the Estonian legal systems have modified the norms and regulations concerning the publication of official statute laws. Legal validity has been conferred to electronic publication, even though traditional paper still prevails over electronic format in these two countries, at least in the event of discrepancy between the two versions. The Swiss federal act ruling the Bodies of Federal Laws and the Federal Charter (known as "act on official publications") of 18th July 2004 states that, in fact, the "bodies of federal laws and the federal charter are published in both printed and electronic forms" art. 16, co. 1. Furthermore, it rules that, as regards legislative acts and treaties between the Confederation and individual Cantons, the "determining version "is the one featuring in the printed form in the official Body of the Laws (art. 9). On enforcing this provision, the "Ordinance on the Bodies of Federal Laws and the Federal Charter" (known as "Ordinance on the Official Publications") of 17th November 2004 has made it clear that a hypothetical online version of the Official Body must be accessible and free of charge (art. 10.1.a). In addition, the ordinance states that "the systemised Body of Federal Laws can be published in the form of an adequate electronic databank support" (art. 29). A similar system to the Swiss one is in force in Estonia, where the *Rigij*

---

[6] Available at: <www.journal-officiel.gouv.fr/>.

Testaja (eRT: the Estonian state gazette) has apparently been published also in the electronic form since 2002, with the same legal validity as the printed form. Besides, on January 1st 2007 the electronic edition of the *Rigij Testaja* became the only official version. Only five printed copies of it remain today which, as in the Swiss case, are the ones to be deferred to in the event of discrepancy between the two versions.

2.3. ELECTRONIC PUBLICATION WITH LEGAL VALIDITY

The first government to have adopted the exclusive official electronic publication of legislative acts ids Austria. Since 1st January 2004, legislative texts have only been retrievable by access to the *Rechtsinformationssystem des Bundes* (*RIS*), the Austrian institutional information system. The legislative records printed on paper have literally ended up in the waste-paper bin of history!

In the same way, the Australian "*Legislative Instruments Act 2003*" ruled the enforcement of the new *Federal Register of Legislative Instruments*, on which, since 1st January 2005, legally applicable legislative acts have been published. However, publication on the printed journal resumes in the event of temporary interruption of electronic issue, as art. 41 of the *Legislative Act Instruments 2003* expressly states. In particular, provision is made that: "*If: (a) a legislative instrument is required to be registered under Division 2; and (b) because of technical difficulties the instrument is temporarily unable to be so registered; the Secretary may cause the instrument to be published in full in the Gazette*" (cf. point n. 2).

As for Italy, the act n° 23, issued by the Tuscan Region on 23rd April 2007 and in force since 1st January 2008 (Costanzo, 2007, p. 479), ruling that the *Official Bulletin* of the Tuscan Region (BURT), is worth mentioning. It is to be published exclusively in the digital form, in a way that grants both the authenticity and the integrity of the published acts", in compliance with the technical rules established by apposite act passed by the regional authority, in concert with the competent Regional Council. Publication of acts on the electronic BURT has obviously legal validity. Consultation of e-BURT on the Tuscan Region's website is in fact "free, gratuitous and permanent" (cf. art. 14).

In order to obviate limitations to Internet access, "Assisted Access Points" (PAAS) are provided by law at regional offices for the relationships with the public, local public libraries, local councils and Tuscan mountain communities.

3. The Network at the service of legislative publication: problematic aspects and technical solutions.

The aforementioned experiences are all characterised by a common intent. Nonetheless, they show, to some extent, some technical differences, which can be put down to three kinds of problems.

Stress is in fact being placed upon the use of "non-proprietary technology" (*open-source software*), more or less gratuitous, always re-usable at will.

The second question concerns whether standards for the publication, hence for the editing of legislative acts, are to be adopted or not.

The last points concerns the so-called multiple applicability, that is, the possibility to retrieve online not only the original, historical text of the provision, but more importantly the current text in force, and, last but not least, – as for texts subject to amendments or additions – the so-called coordinated text.

The choices made in relation to these three aspects obviously encroach upon other non-secondary problems, technical and juridical at once, such as those related to accessibility, authenticity and safety of the electronically published act.

More concisely, we can still observe how the attribution of legal validity to electronic publication chiefly stems from an amendment or an addition made to the discipline ruling official publications. On the other hand, the actual guaranty of accessibility, availability and safety of online legislative publication systems, aside from legal or informative value of such publication, stems exactly from which particular technology is adopted, in practice and quite often under the supervision of competent bodies.

Obviously, each of these questions are intrinsically interwoven with one another, even though it is easily observable that absolutely satisfactory solutions are hardly to be found in the systems considered so far.

3.1. OPEN SOURCE SOFTWARE (OSS)

It is a known fact that devising and implementing more or less advanced information systems for retrieving legislative acts on line requires specialist software.

In most countries, public administrative bodies place orders for such software with private firms, which produce *proprietary software*; in other cases, the user chooses to adopt public instruments to access legislative acts by means of *open source software* (OSS) both to retrieve mere information and to publish legislative literature with legal validity.

From this standpoint the Italian choice is clear: all items of software of the XMLeges family, devised within the Norme in Rete project (Ciampi, 2003), have been released with open source code (Agnoloni, Francesconi, Spinosa,

2007). These are instruments, devised by ITTIG-CNR within the Norme in Rete project aimed at backing up edition, revision and conversion into XML of legislative texts in conformity with legislative drafting rules and formatting standards and requirements. However, it is worth observing how, at present, such items of software are only being used to publish legislation online for informative purposes.[7]

3.2. STANDARDS

Some countries have adopted standards defined by the World Web Wide Consortium in order to remodel and restructure their legislation, making it suitable for online publication. In particular, XML (*eXtensible Markup Language*), a meta markup language stemming from a set of syntactic rules for structuring documents and data, has been adopted. Such rules are, in fact, standard ones, as they guarantee independence from a specific software and hardware platform or from a specific producer.

A whole range of technologies and languages is connected to XML, supporting its use and making it reliable and adaptable to any possible use. The XML standard is often applied together with DTD (*Document Type Definition*), a document describing the tags to be used in an XML document and their interrelation with the document structure, and giving further information on the characteristics of each tag.

All in all, such standards allow interaction between the various document bases and a better, more efficient research and elaboration work, thus enabling access to legislative bodies which, in reality, constitute one of the most important public data collections.

In Italy, such standards are already been adopted within the aforementioned project "Norme in Rete", aimed at the publication of legislation for informative purposes. Also worth mentioning are the project "Norma-System", developed at the university of Bologna (Palmirani and Benigni, 2007), and the aforementioned "xmLegesEditor" software developed by the ITTIG-CNR. Austria has even adopted them for the official publication of legislation online. In many other countries projects aimed at their adoption at institutional level are under way.

In the majority of cases, though, legislation is published online in the pdf format, even though a further step is envisaged, aiming at publication in the XML format. It is now worth reminding that an XML text can be modified in a semi-automatic way, that is, with an editor's minimum assistance. On the other hand, pdf texts require a significant degree of editing. Additionally, in this second case the publication of a text for each amendment is strictly required, which does entail a much heavier workload than any XML administrative requirement would do.

---

[7] See: <www.xmleges.org>.

3.3. MULTIPLE VALIDITY (APPLICABILITY)

Despite the high number of research projects on the subject of electronic publication of legislation in a multiple validity format, such applications still lack a firm institutional support.

However, some experimental, electronic publications of legislative multiple-applicability norms have appeared. In Italy, the project P.A.eS.I. (Public Administration and Foreign Immigrants), makes legislation on the matter on an apposite website accessible, as regards both the historical and in the current text, in XML format.

It is obviously a publication whose purpose is merely informative. Yet it deserves to be mentioned as it applied XML standards for publishing online multiple-applicability legislative texts.[8]

In other cases, it is possible to consult texts in both versions, the historical as well as the current, although the texts in question are published for information purposes in pdf, thus requiring much editorial work, as in the case of numerous regional legislative database.

It is still worth quoting the aforementioned Estonian experience concerning the publication in electronic format of the *Rigij Testaja*, which also features the legislative acts appearing in the consolidated text. From a technical point of view, it still lacks the application of the XML format, set to be introduced within few years, so texts are still in HTML, while charts, pictures and maps are in pdf.

However, this brief account purports to highlight the repercussions which some technical decisions might have, also in a strictly juridical sense.

Synthesising this theme in the extreme, it appears undeniable that accessibility to IT systems devised to retrieve legislative acts is more marked if proprietary software is not utilised. On the other hand, this very technical choice can guarantee system safety by virtue of transparency deriving from the utilisation of free source code software. Adopting the standards mentioned and described above can facilitate the "availability" of legislative acts contained in the current (and multiply applicable) text.

4. Questions of legitimacy and theoretical problems concerning the electronic publication of legislative acts: a "growth crisis"?

The aforementioned indications and comparisons between various experiences may have already provided some insight into some of the worries the introduction of electronic publication is likely to bring about.

This theme certainly deserves more attention than this report can offer. Yet we can at least observe that we are confronted with two kinds of questions.

---

[8] See: <www.immigrazione.regione.toscana.it/>.

The first is basically about whether online publication of legislative acts may grant reliability to the same degree as that as yet granted (*rectius*: supposedly granted) by printed publication.

The second rotates around the problems that, for good or bad reasons, have been associated with this recent sort of publication.

However, as we will see, dealing with these two levels of problems separately would prove difficult and counterproductive. Instead, we shall make distinctions between questions about, on the one hand, the "objective" accessibility of electronic publication (4.1) and, on the other, about the "subjective" accessibility to electronic publication (4.2).

4.1. OBJECTIVE ACCESSIBILITY OF ELECTRONIC PUBLICATION

By objective accessibility we mean the conditions that make publication in itself and *per se* apt to the purpose for which it was conceived in the first place. From this angle, we must preliminarily place stress upon the question of authenticity of the text published. There is no evidence, though, that this constitutes a specific profile concerning electronic diffusion of legislative acts, as this has, generally speaking, already been called in question in respect of electronic document, of which, to be exact, the various online journals constitute only one type, though it shows peculiar qualities and effects.

Hence there is no good reason, also in our case, to consider digital signature authentication technologies to be inefficacious, as long as we, of course, rely on its "stronger" version, on whose description we will not, in such a context as this one, dwell any further (earlier on in this text, we have already have the opportunity to examine the question of text format). Likewise, we must take into account the safety standards of the server from which the publication "departs", headed to the Network, in respect of both the ever possible "external attacks" and the possible malfunctioning of the IT system involved in the process. If we are in front of an unfortunate characteristic of the Internet, it is only a matter of scale anyway, as it no doubt affects especially the psycho-sociological sphere, the relentlessness shown by the Network as regards safety measures, as it appears now highly improbable that someone might question the authenticity of the printed publication he is holding in his hand!

Be it as it may, it is a proven fact that the system as a whole, in its complexity, does not lack protections and strategies granting it (at least statistically) a satisfactorily smooth running of the whole "clockwork", whereas, if anything, the most disquieting aspects concern the theoretical and general repercussions of an interruption, however temporary, of the service. If we tackle, though, the question right now, we can, for lack of time, refer to what has already been observed elsewhere, whereby the solution to the problem of "absence" of law caused by "interruption" of publication can only be that of keeping at least one, however low, instrumental threshold granting a "minimum hypothesis" that the legislative act, seen as lasting availability and potential accessibility, may exist (Costanzo, 2007, p. 493). After all, as already mentioned, some legal systems have opted either for double publication or, more problematically, for the printed edition of a limited number of copies of the legislative text. If from a technical angle the aspects hitherto mentioned advocate the adoption of solutions which, owing also to the rapidity shown by progress in the sector, ought to be regulated by productive sources of legislation such as the statutes of the various administrative authorities, from the angle of the juridical principles that are supposed to inspire and regulate the aforementioned solutions, the choice of the regulating source does not appear to be irrelevant. As this entails intervention in the *iter legis* whose final stage is the publication of the act, the constitution, that is, the core principle of the system, is no doubt to be fully referred to, both by the ordinary legislator and by the sources in charge of drafting the relative discipline.

For this purpose, we cannot fail to mention the enlightening example of the Austrian constitution, whose art. 49, in reference to electronic publication, insists that accessibility to legislative texts be granted permanently (*auf Dauer*) (Costanzo, 2007, p. 493).

4.2. SUBJECTIVE ACCESSIBILITY TO ELECTRONIC PUBLICATION

Proceeding along this line we come across the second of the levels indicated above, that is, that of subjective accessibility, in respect of which it may be more adequate to reason about a subjective, constitutionally protected claim to accessibility.

Such a premise, at least concerning continental legal systems traditionally based on the written form, stems not only from the above-mentioned rule stated by the Austrian constitution. It also appears to be corroborated by the "historical" stands taken by some constitutional jurisdictions, such as the French (*Conseil constitutionnel* dec. n. 99-421 DC), Belgian (*Cour d'Arbitrage*, arrêt n. 106/2004 of 16th June 2004) and Italian (Constitutional Court, sent. n° 364, 1988, cit.).

There is no possibility here to deal thoroughly with such a ponderous topic. However, there is little doubt that this must result in gratuity of publications and, more importantly, in equitable and general accessibility to them.

In this sense, the system still favours double publication, as it thereby purports to tackle the well-known problems of *digital divide* within a given community, which have even persuaded the Belgian constitutional judge to declare access to *Moniteur belge* unconstitutional because of its being exclusively configured for the Internet, despite the significant acknowledgment that such phenomenon is to be seen *dans l'évolution de la société, les techniques informatiques devenant un procédé de communication de plus en plus courant*." (*Cour d'Arbitrage*, arrêt n. 106/2004 cit.).

With reference to the specific purpose of this report, the scope of the aforementioned decision straddles beyond the starting legislative context. In fact, if on the one hand it might have cooled down hollow, facile enthusiasms, also due to the authority of the issuing source, on the other hand it has certainly called for a moment's reflection, not only on the practicability of a complete interchange between electronic and printed publication, but also, with a sort of feedback effect, on the real congruity of paper publication itself.

In this sense, going back to the initial critical considerations on the short-comings shown by the traditional way of publishing, distancing from an all-mechanical approach to this instrument appears not only justified (especially in the presence of an absolutely obscure legislative text). It also appears legitimate to doubt that the State might, only by virtue of that, regard its obligation to preliminary legislative information to citizens as adequately met as soon as the whole media system and particularly the Internet seem to be able, as elsewhere in the field of government-citizen relationships, to improve decisively the quality of communication with legislation recipients.

References

Agnoloni, T., Francesconi, E., Spinosa, P. (2007), *xmLegesEitor: an OpenSource Visual XML editor for supporting Legal National Standards*, in "Proceedings of the V Legislative XML Workshop", 2007, pp. 239 and ff.

Codacci Pisanelli (1970), Speech, in Chamber of Deputies – General Secretariat (Ed.), "La Costituzione della Repubblica nei lavori preparatori della Assemblea Costituente", Vol. IV, Roma.

Ciampi, C. (2003), *Legal Information on the Web. The NIR Portal for the Citizen*, in "Proceedings of the LEFIS Workshop on Legal Aspects of E-Government".

Costanzo, P. (2003), *Profili costituzionali di Internet*, in Tosi E. (Ed.), "Diritto di Internet e dell'e-business", 3rd ed., Vol. 1, Giuffrè, Milano.

Costanzo, P. (2006), *La pubblicazione normativa al tempo di Internet*, in: VV.AA. (Eds.), "Le fonti del diritto, oggi. Giornate di studio in onore di Alessandro Pizzorusso", Plus, Pisa, pp. 203-219.

Costanzo, P. (2007), *La pubblicazione delle leggi approda ufficialmente su Internet (osservazioni a margine della legge regionale toscana n 23 del 2007)*, Rivista dell'informazione e dell'informatica, No. 3, pp. 479-495.

D'Atena, A. (1974), *La pubblicazione delle fonti normative, I. Introduzione storica e premesse generali*, Cedam, Padova.

Grottanelli De' Santi, G. (1985), *La formazione delle leggi*, in Branca A. (Ed.), "La formazione delle leggi, sub artt. 73-74", Zanichelli, Bologna.

Palmirani, M. and Benigni, F. (2007), *Norma-System: A Legal Information System for Managing Time*, in "Proceedings of the V Legislative XML Workshop V Legislative XML Workshop", 14-16 June, European Press Academic Publishing, Florence, pp. 205-224.

Pizzorusso, A. (1963), *La pubblicazione degli atti normativi*, Giuffrè, Milano.

Quadri, R. (1974), *Disposizioni sulla legge in generale*, in Scialoja A. e Branca G. (Eds.), "Commentario del Codice civile, sub art. 10", Il Foro Italiano, Bologna-Roma.

Ranelletti, O. (1937), *Istituzioni di diritto pubblico*, Cedam, Padova.

Rissanen, K. (2006), *Access to EU law and eLaw – vision and challenger*, in VV.AA. (Eds.), "25 years of European law online", EU Publication Office.

Open Access and Legal Exceptions to Copyright: Towards a General Fair Use Standard?

Davide Sarti
University of Florence, Italy

Abstract. Copyright rights are probably the most important obstacles to open access of legal information. Actually, almost every source of legal information is protected by copyright, with the only exception of law texts and judgements texts. Last but not least, legal materials are often organized in databases, which are protected by copyright or sui generis rights, and which are made accessible to the public only under contractual agreements and payment of fees.

The European system provides for some exceptions to protection of copyright. A list of these exceptions can be found in art. 5 of the 2001/28/EC on the protection of copyright in the information society. The enumeration of these exceptions is considered exhaustive. On the other hand, Member States are not obliged to provide for these exceptions in their national systems. The European system doesn't provide for a general fair use exception, under which a free use of legal material for research purposes could be provided.

In the European system, an important exception is provided by art. 5.3.*a* of the directive. According to this article, Member States may provide for exception to reproduction, communication and distribution right "for the sole purpose of illustration for teaching or scientific research [...] to the extent justified by the non-commercial purpose to be achieved". This rule seems to be rather wide, and can be interpreted as providing for a general fair use exception in the field of research. Unfortunately, this rule is not mandatory for the Member States, and in some systems it has been implemented in a rather restrictive perspective. According to the Italian system, for example, only reproduction of excerpts or parts of copyrighted material is allowed.

The Italian system (and other similar European systems) is not incompatible with the European directive: as European rules about free use are not mandatory. Nevertheless, it should be considered that such rules probably hinder scientific research in the field of law. It seems especially strange that according to patent law a general free use for research purposes is provided, whereas no such use is provided in the field of copyright. On the other hand, use of legal texts is essential for legal research, and the cost to get access to these texts is the main cost that legal research must afford. For these reasons, hindering public access to legal texts could hinder research in the legal field, and a general rule should be introduced, according to which access to legal texts for research purpose should be made free: at least to the extent that these texts have been legally acquired by public libraries or institutions, or to the extent they rise from public funded research. This free access should probably be not extended to distribution of physical copies of copyrighted works, and could be limited to electronic copies of copyrighted works, which should be made available only in the circles of researchers and students of universities and other educational institutions.

Keywords: Copyright, exceptions, fair use standard, information directive.

1. Copyright as an obstacle to legal information

Access to legal information in the age of digital technology probably finds in copyright its main obstacle. Almost every source of legal information is subject to copyright, and almost every use of such information over the Internet constitutes an exploitation of copyright, which in principle should need an authorization of the author or of legal acquirers of copyright rights. Naturally, every rule has its exceptions, and even copyright has its own exceptions: law texts (including not only laws approved by parliaments, but also regulations of public authorities) are not considered as copyrightable, and similarly texts of decisions of legal courts are not protected by copyright. All of the others sources of legal information are on the other hand copyrightable: doctrine contributions, databases of legal information, and even abstracts of decisions, provided they are creative excerpts, drawn by researchers, are protected through copyright or are considered as works protected by neighbouring rights. As far as it concerns databases, it's interesting to remark that even data, which are not copyrightable as such, like court decisions, may be collected into databases, which are subject to copyright or protected through "sui generis" rights. Assuming that it's normally difficult for a researcher to know and to look for individual data, and that researchers need the access to databases to find what they're looking for, we must conclude that even access to not copyrighted materials is de facto made dependant upon the use of protected works.

On the other hand, copyright is an exclusive right, and access to copyrighted materials is normally made possible under payment of fees, which are determined by the copyright owner. That's why the general principle is: no payment, no access. In the field of law research, that means that access to legal texts is made dependant upon contractual agreements about payment of compensation to copyright owners, provided the copyright owner is interested in such agreements and doesn't want to reserve to himself the exploitation of his exclusive right. Somebody could object that such a system is perfectly coherent to a market economy and to competition, where resources are in principle accessible under property rules and free contracts. Under this point of view, it's improper to say that access to legal information is made dependant upon payment of fees that are fixed by the copyright owner; and it should be more correctly stated that fees are fixed according to market and competition rule. Although generally speaking I would agree with this view, I think the crucial point is not the question about the general function of copyright law, but the question about the opportunity of this function in the field of research. In other terms, the point is: should the market perform its function to allocate the resources in the field of research? Should a researcher who doesn't want or who can't pay for access to legal information be considered as an uncompetitive researcher, who should be expelled from market like any other manufacturing enterprise? The answer is not so simple, and is first of all a political answer. Not surprisingly, the European legislator didn't solve this problem. Anyway, it's interesting to remark that the European legislator considered the possibility to exempt industrial research from the general rules governing a market economy.

2. Exceptions and limitations to copyright in the EU directive

The European system provides for some exceptions to protection of copyright. A list of these exceptions can be found in art. 5 of the 2001/28/EC on the protection of copyright in the information society. The enumeration of these exceptions is considered exhaustive, but not mandatory (Abriani, 2002): Member States are not obliged to provide for these exceptions in their national systems. It's worth to remark that the European system doesn't provide for a for a general fair use exception. Under this point of view, the European system deeply differs from the US system. Under European law, any exploitation of copyright without the author's consent is in principle illegal, as far as this exploitation is not considered as free according to specific legal rules. Courts are not allowed to apply a general fair use standard, according to which some exploitation, although not considered in legal rules, may be deemed as lawful. It's somewhat disputed, if legal rules providing for free uses of copyright should be interpreted restrictively (Ubertazzi, 1994), or if they might be read in a broad sense (Spolidoro, 2007). In any case, even a wide or analogical interpretation of legal rules may consider only interests that have been considered by legislators. Courts may not apply a general fair use standard to protect interests, which have not been considered by the provisions concerning exceptions to copyright.

As far as it concerns scientific research, an important exception is provided by art. 5.3.*a* of the directive. According to this article, Member States may provide for exception to reproduction, communication and distribution right "for the sole purpose of illustration for teaching or scientific research [. . .] to the extent justified by the non-commercial purpose to be achieved". This rule seems to be rather wide. Under this rule, in the absence of a general free use exception, it could be inferred that such an exception exists in the field of research. In other words, the interests of research have been considered by EC law through a general rule that could be interpreted as providing for a fair use exception, although the fair use doctrine should be limited to the field of research, and couldn't be generalized to different fields.

Unfortunately, this rule is not mandatory for the Member States, and in some systems it has been implemented in a rather restrictive perspective. According to the Italian system, for example, only reproduction of excerpts or parts of copyrighted material is allowed. On the other hand, in Italy we don't have distinct rules for use of copyrighted materials for purposes of research and respectively for purposes of criticism (Galli, 2002), whereas the directive provides for two distinct free uses (5.3.*a* and 5.3.*d* respectively). Under such a system, we are far from a general fair use exception in the field of scientific (and legal) research.

The Italian system (and other similar European systems) is not incompatible with the European directive: as European rules about free use are not mandatory. Nevertheless, the non-mandatory character of art. 5.3.*a* of the information directive and the possibly different implementation by the Member States arise many questions. The first question concerns the opportunity that different Member States deserve a different treatment to the use of copyrighted works for scientific purposes. Scientific research seems a fundamental field of activity in the European Union, and the lack of a uniform regulation in this field seems rather odd and questionable.

The second question concerns the different rules governing patent and copyright law. It seems especially strange that according to patent law a general free use for research purposes is provided, whereas no such use is provided in the field of copyright (Galli, 2002): although technical research is in principle much more costly than (in our case) legal research, so that patented products should benefit of a more extensive protection in respect of copyright. On the other hand, use of legal texts is essential for legal research, and the cost to get access to these texts is the main cost that legal research must afford. Someone could argue that experimental use of patented material is rather costly and difficult, and a general free use in this field wouldn't harm the interests in fostering the research and costs that made the patented invention possible; while the use of copyrighted material is easy and inexpensive, and a general free use harms the interest in remuneration of creative work. Nevertheless, I would think such an explanation appears as very disputable: because it makes the application of a rule (i.e., the free use of patents) dependent upon the difficulty to apply the rule effectively.

The third question arises from the foregoing statements. Shouldn't scientific and legal research be ruled by uniform principles in the whole EC? And if yes, shouldn't these principles be based on a mandatory application of the wide general fair use standard actually provided (although not mandatory) by art. 5.3.*a* information directive?

3. A general fair use standard proposal

It must be conceded, that a general fair use exception in the field of scientific research could be under some aspects disputable. Someone could argue that some copyrighted works (such as doctrinal contributions, scientific reviews, legal databases) are essentially used in the world of research, and that a general free use of these works could deprive the authors of important sources of revenues, and after all could lessen the scientists' effort.

Personally, I think that the importance of intellectual property rights in fostering inventions and creations is probably overestimated, and that the main reason to grant patents and copyrights lies in the interest in giving inventions and creations a market price, which they wouldn't have if they were always accessible for free (Sarti, 2002). On the other hand, the importance of copyright in fostering creation is especially questionable in the field of scientific legal research, where most researchers are publicly funded, and are interested in earning a good reputation in a wide community, rather than in making money from their research. So, we're back to the previous question: are we sure a price system should work in the field of scientific and legal research? I admit the interest of book editors is important, and copyright might be essential for them to recover investments in publishing. Nevertheless it's also true that printed books should be les and less important in production and dissemination of scientific knowledge, which can now be more easily accessible in electronic form.

We should also consider that a general fair use standard is, precisely, a standard, not a strict rule. According to art. 5.5 of information directive "the exceptions and limitations provided for in paragraphs 1, 2, 3 and 4 shall only be applied in certain special cases which do not conflict with a normal exploitation of the work or other subject-matter and do not unreasonably prejudice the legitimate interests of the rightholder". It would be questionable the application of a general rule, which made free the reproduction and access to copyrighted works for scientific purposes. Probably it's a legitimate interest of the rightholder, that his work may not be freely reproduced in a physical form, especially when the physical copy is made possible by photocopy enterprises that earn money from this activity. The situation is nonetheless different when legal texts are made accessible in electronic form, inside the circles of researchers and students of universities and other educational institutions, through electronic communication networks, which have been realized and financed by the same institutions. This seems especially true, to the extent that legal texts rise from public funded research. It seems unacceptable, that public institutions pay three times the costs of research: the first time as they pay the researchers for their work, the second time when they acquire books and databases, the third time when they subsidize researchers to pay the cost of access to texts and databases. It should be obviously considered also the interest in recovering the costs of investment needed to organize legal texts and decisions, when these costs have been undertaken by private enterprises. Private enterprises could in any case recover their investment through contractual means: and typically making their databases disposable under payment agreements. Under this system, the use and the extraction of data from databases legally acquired by public research institutions for scientific purposes should in principle be free. And even the need of public institutions to pay for databases should be probably reconsidered, when these databases have been created with contributions of publicly funded researchers.

4. Conclusion

For all of these reasons, I think that research in the legal field is actually more hindered than fostered by copyright law. Therefore, I would suggest the introduction of a general fair use standard, which should be modelled according to article 5.3.*a* information directive, which should be made mandatory for all of the Member States, and interpreted according to the general principles of art. 5.5. The application of such a rule would imply a general principle: according to which copyright performs its function in a market context, where investment and resource allocation are determined by prices and disposability of money; while disposability of money is not necessarily a good measure of efficiency and resource allocation in the field of research.

References

Abriani, N. (2002), *Le utilizzazioni libere nella società dell'informazione: considerazioni generali*, AIDA, Vol. XI, pp. 98-124.

Celotto, A. (2004), *Diritto d'autore e circolazione delle informazioni: quale bilanciamento fra valori costituzionali (e comunitari?)*, AIDA, Vol. XIV, pp. 504-516.

Galli, C. (2002), *Le utilizzazioni libere: ricerca*, AIDA, Vol. XI, pp. 135-145.

Meli, V. (1997), *Le "utilizzazioni libere" nella direttiva 96/9/CEE sulla protezione giuridica delle banche dati*, AIDA, Vol. VI, pp. 86-109.

Reichman, J.H. (1997), *La guerra delle banche dati - Riflessioni sulla situazione americana*, AIDA, Vol. VI, pp. 226-236.

Sarti, D. (2002), *Proprietà intellettuale, interessi protetti e diritto antitrust*, Rivista di diritto industriale, Vol. 6, part. I, pp. 543-576.

Spolidoro, M.S. (2007), *Le eccezioni e le limitazioni*, AIDA, Vol. XVII, pp. 179-206.

Ubertazzi, L.C. (1994), *Le utilizzazioni libere della pubblicità*, Vol. III, pp. 63-87.

Problems Arising for BAILII from the History of Law Reporting**

Philip Leith*, Cynthia Fellows°
*School of Law, Queen's University of Belfast, Northern Ireland (UK)
°Institute of Advanced Legal Studies, University of London, England (UK)

Abstract. The history of publishing legal decisions (law reporting) in the UK has been that of a privatised system since its inception, and that history has encompassed several hundred years. The privatised nature of this has meant that the product (the law report) has been, except in limited cases, viewed as the property of the publisher, rather than the property of the court or public. In part the rise of the British and Irish Legal Information Institute (BAILII) came about because of the copyrighted, privatised nature of this legal information. BAILII is both affected by and making its own impact on the proprietary nature of that product.

In this paper, we will outline the problem of access to pre-2000 judgments in the UK and consider whether there are legal or other remedies which might enable BAILII to both develop a richer historic database and also work in harmony, rather than in competition, with legal publishers.

Keywords: BAILII, copyright in judgments, database right, legal education, National Law Library, benefits of deep linking.

1. What is a law report?

In simple terms, a law report is a document which provides an analysis of a court case and, frequently, is accompanied by the text of a judge's decision. This law report will have been produced by a lawyer, but one who did not participate in the case itself. It is, in effect, a third party view but a view which arises from the legal perspective. Thus a report of a case in a newspaper, although it is reportage, lacks the critical legal skills and qualities which comprise a law report.

Law reports have been published in the UK since the 13th century.[1] Legal historians have suggested various reasons for their existence – because of precedential, educational, record keeping and entertainment value. These reasons continue to be relevant, but the formal reason is that of precedent – i.e. legal principles developed through judicial decision-making. Common law systems are based on judicial precedent rather than by statutory. The courts interpret and clarify statutory law. The law reports are the repository of judicial reasoning and as such are vital to the common law.

** The authors are actively involved with BAILII, but this article reflects their own personal views.

[1] This has been a topic for legal historians for some time. See (Abbott, 1973) and (Stebbings, 1995), for example.

In 1865, the Incorporated Council of Law Reporting for England and Wales (ICLR) came into being in an effort to improve the quality of law reporting. The corpus of available reports was kept small – which judges prefer – and a formalised system arose to provide a quality product to a relatively small community of barristers and legal educators. Unlike in the U.S., the court did not see its role as legal publisher.[2]

By the 1980s, the system was beginning to be less attractive to lawyers. The expansion of the profession and the development of many sub-specialisations created a demand for more comprehensive access to legal information. Legal publishers, who were using a segmentation business model to cut the reports up into more profitable product types, were able to expand their products and charge more for their services. And electronic publication did not reduce the price of their products, but was viewed simply as a means of increasing their profits upon the back of the financially struggling legal profession (West-Knights, 1997).

In 1979, a report published by the Society for Computers and Law called for a 'National Law Library' – as a resource for both case law and legislation in electronic format which would be funded partly by the legal profession and partly by government – but since the government declined to provide one, BAILII came into existence to undertake that task. West-Knights' – an early proponent of BAILII – argument was essentially that the National Law Library approach should be reconsidered.

2. The publication of a law report: headnotes

The current law report is a formalised entity. It comprises a part produced by the judge or from a transcript of a recording of the judge's verbal decision, plus explanatory abstracts, annotations and subject keyword analysis – material generally referred to as "headnotes". The headnote material is produced by the law reporter. As a random example, consider the case of *Siggery v Bell* [3] which appears in electronic format in at least two published locations – Lexis and Westlaw. Both versions comprise "headnotes" that offer a case summary, subject keywords and list significant cases cited in the judgment.

There exists copyright in the text of the headnote, with the term of protection being life of the author plus 70 years. It is not always obvious who the author of the headnote was – he or she will be a barrister but will be somewhere between 25 to 75 years old, a fact which is clearly important to determining term of protection. It is a valuable intellectual property, requiring skill and substantial effort to produce and is thus rightly protected from copying.

---

[2] Only the Judicial Committee of the House of Lords published their own decisions. In 1996 they also produced internet available versions. The annual output of the Law Lords is approximately 100 cases a year.

[3] *Siggery v Bell* [2007] EWHC 2167 (Ch).

3. The publication of a law report: judgments

BAILII has no interest in impinging upon the intellectual property rights of the law reporter and has never seen itself as a provider of headnotes. The automated processing/publishing which is at the heart of BAILII's philosophy cannot provide competition to the intellectual property of the law reporters or publishers. What BAILII does have is an interest in making available the text of a judgment, which has legal status and precedential value. Unfortunately, law reporters and publishers take the view that the judge's text which they hold is also their intellectual property.

The difficulty for systems such as BAILII then becomes one of how to access the judge's decision in order to upload and make it available. Law Lords decisions are available, as are Court of Appeal decisions,[4] but for the High Court, County Court and the various Tribunals, informal means of harvesting of judgments is necessary. Even in the High Court, not all decisions will be made available to BAILII and not all will be in transcribed form. In the Royal Court of Justice, for example, when a judge reads a decision in the court (rather than 'handing it down' in printed form) it will have been recorded automatically and require transcription into readable format. BAILII does not have the funds to carry this out, so requires access to a transcribed version.[5]

There are two main copyright problems for BAILII in this process:

1. Who owns the underlying text and/or the transcription of a judgment?
2. What can BAILII do with judgments which have been processed by a commercial agent, whether of recent origin or from decades before?

These are not abstract questions. In a recent project to develop a more useful BAILII corpus for teaching of law, substantial problems were found in accessing sufficient well known and relevant judgments which form the basis of UK common law.[6]

4. Who owns the text and/or transcription of a judgment?

Under UK copyright law, the author is the first owner of copyright unless he or she is an employee. For most European observers, the assumption would be that the author is the judge and as an employee, copyright passes to the employer (in the UK, this is the Crown). Judgments being crown copyright is

---

[4] Through an agreement between the Court Service and the transcribers.

[5] Transcribed versions are usually given to the judge to correct (and thus become "approved versions").

[6] The JISC-funded Open Law Project, available at: <www.bailii.org/openlaw/introduction.html>.

advantageous to BAILII because, in the late 1990s, the decision was taken to allow free access and republishing of legislation and various legal materials.[7]

However, the matter of who owns judgments is not entirely clear. For example, a view from some of the UK intellectual property judges is that they are not employees, and thus the judgments are not Crown Copyright.[8] BAILII receives, every now and again, a letter from the author of a judgment requesting that we remove the copyright notice from his decision. Picciotto outlined the situation in 1996 as one which remains unclear, as there is still "a fog of ambiguity and disagreement as to copyright in court judgments" (Picciotto, 1996).

Another confusion is that the judgment – particularly those which are not produced in word processed format for the judge – will have undergone some form of transcribing, editing and/or revision by a commercial agent. The editors of these judgments assert that they have put sufficient effort and skill into this to gain copyright in the transformed judgment. Since recordings of judgments were destroyed after around 5 years (the tapes were reused) it is not possible to use these as evidence to argue in any particular case that the amount of effort and skill applied was less than required to gain copyright protection, and BAILII must accept the view of the publisher that they own the copyright in the available text of the judgment and since no other versions of these older judgments exist, the judgment is effectively privatised.

It is actually very difficult to resolve questions of ownership in the available text of judgments. Publishers may well intimate that they are the owners of the judgments which appear in their past publications, but in order for this to have been so there must have been some assignment of copyright from the author to the publisher, either through employment or agreement. If the "author" (in terms of the person who corrected the judicial transcript) was a barrister who was not employed by the publisher but contributed on a consultancy basis, then ownership resides with the barrister.

Most judgments prior to the mid 1990s would not have been produced in hard copy or digital format by the judge. Rather, they would have been recorded and transcribed by a commercial transcription service. In UK law, making a recording will give copyright in that recording which means that the transcription (usually the only available version) is the copyright of the transcriber. Judgments which are available in hard copy also have a copyright in their formatting – copyright in the typographical arrangement under S1 of the Copyright Designs and Patents Act 1988 – which lasts for 25 years. Finally, in UK law, when speech is recorded, there exists a further copyright

---

[7] Through what was known as the "Dear Publisher" communication. See <www.opsi.gov.uk/advice/crown-copyright/copyright-guidance/index.htm> for current information on what waivers exist and other forms of availability.

[8] (Laddie, Prescott, Vitoria, 1995, but also in later editions), first put the contrary view (para 22.39).

– the property of the speaker – in the original words.[9] The result is that there may be a number of versions of a judgment, each of which has copyright protection – the taped recording by the court, the transcribed version by the transcriber, the edited version by the publisher, and the approved version after the judge has commented upon the publisher's version.

BAILII's ideal source of a judgment is an approved version, either produced by the judge or read and corrected by the judge where the copyright clearly allows reproduction – ideally a judgment with a 'Crown Copyright' statement affixed. None of the available versions – apart from those which are now being made available via the Court Service from prior to approximately 2000 – are thus suitable for uploading. Expanding the corpus of judgments on BAILII requires a significant amount of effort in order to gain permissions from transcribers, hunt down available copies (perhaps from the lawyers involved in the original case who may have a copy of a decision produced by a judge), etc. BAILII simply does not have the resources to undertake this in any meaningful way.

5. Why does BAILII want to add pre-2000 judgments to its database?

In many ways, it would be simpler if BAILII ignored pre-2000 judgments. As time progresses, a large percentage of judgments lose value as precedent unless they are particularly striking. Non-precedent setting judgments that have lesser value may be discussed in newer cases; if not, they are quietly or explicitly dropped. Although it can be argued that BAILII can manage without many of these pre-2000 cases, the fact remains that older cases which are considered "leading cases" – those which establish and distinguish the judicial precedents which are the foundational pillars of the common law – are of vital importance.

The strongest reason for wishing to add older judgments to databases is, we suggest, the educational one – and the rational behind the JISC-funded Open Law project which BAILII recently undertook.[10] The aim of the Open Law project was to increase student usage of legal information systems generally because using them – we suggest – makes a better lawyer, and the more information literate a student is, the more likely they are to become a user of primary sources of legal information, as opposed to one who goes no further than a textbook during their studies.

The huge advantage of BAILII to law lecturers is that it is an open access system – there is no cost and no password requirement. Teaching materials

---

[9] The words are considered a literary work. It is only the recording of the spoken works (through fixation) which brings protection. If the words are not recorded, there is no copyright in them.

[10] Available at: <www.bailii.org/openlaw/introduction.html>.

can link directly to the full judgments from reading lists, or even link directly to a paragraph within a judgment, and we can integrate our teaching without requiring more effort from students. The Open Law project was thus interested in targeting a specific group of decisions – those which would be important for teaching of the core areas of law (contract, for example) and those areas in which a number of courses taught in the law school community would benefit from easy access to pre-2000 judgments.

6. What can BAILII do to add pre-2000 judgments?

We presume that the vast majority of available judgments from the period prior to 2000 are subject to commercial copyrights. This will not always be the case – but for the most part – it will be true. There are two main options open to BAILII.

First, 'the nuclear option': in this option BAILII takes the strident view that the text of judgments which have been published are Crown Copyright and now in the public domain (under current HMSO republishing agreements) and thus free to be republished at will. This has been a tactic used in the US,[11] and the Canadian Supreme Court has taken a similarly different approach to that of the US asserting that making trivial changes does not give a new copyright to judgments.[12]

But, as attractive as this option might appear, it is unlikely ever to be undertaken by BAILII due to the lack of resources to resist litigation from commercial publishers. Publishers may well view this as an attack upon a continuing source of revenue which they feel should be protected. The argument is certainly that they have put significant effort into collecting and publishing judgments and they should not bear the brunt of the lack of public expenditure in making judgments available in a non-commercial way. The counter view is that they have effectively privatised the common law.

The second option, and the one which was undertaken by the Open Law project, was to assume that judgments prior to around 1890 were most probably in the public domain and view these as suitable for processing. BAILII. Consequently BAILII, in collaboration with academics, librarians, and special interest groups such as the Society of Legal Scholars, and through review of subject syllabi, compiled lists of leading cases in core areas of law. Judgments prior to 1890 from this list were digitised first. BAILII then sought various sources of copyright-free materials for the remainder. BAILII successfully scanned and converted to html original transcripts in the Supreme Court

---

[11] *Matthew Bender v. West*, 158 F. 3d 674 (2nd Cir. 1998); *Matthew Bender v. West Publishing Co.*, 158 F.3d 693 (2d Cir. 1998), <u>*cert. denied*</u>, 526 U.S. 1154 (1999).

[12] *Para 35, CCH Canadian Ltd. v. Law Society of Upper Canada*, [2004] 1 S.C.R. 339, 2004 SCC 13 (CanLII).

Library of judgments where permission from the transcribers could be obtained. BAILII obtained word processor versions of judgments (52) directly from one cooperative transcriber. BAILII scanned and converted to html original copies or archived film copies of judgments from the House of Lords and Privy Council. BAILII negotiated permission from the ICLR (50) and SCLR (600) and from the Estates Gazette law reports (50) for permission to publish these limited numbers of pre-2000 "leading cases". The bar library in Belfast provided copies of Northern Ireland cases. As one can see, the Open Law project involved considerable effort in tracking down and getting permissions for the publishing of what is effectively part of our "common law heritage".

As of September 2008, the Open Law Project on BAILII offers 16 subject lists of Leading Cases and 2119 of these judgments are available on BAILII. These judgments can be accessed directly from links on the subject lists, or by citation, case name and subject searches. There are also hyperlinks to these judgments in all cases on BAILII that cite them. An analysis of usage patterns and online feedback indicates that both BAILII's use and usefulness have increased due in large part to the addition of leading cases. As one user put it, "As the older decisions are located and loaded into BAILII, an already very useful resource is going to become even more indispensable for legal researchers in all common law countries". And another: "I'm particularly happy with the new coverage of classic House of Lords cases. Everybody thinks they know what cases such as *Armory v Delamirie, Blyth v Birmingham Waterworks* and *Bolton v Stone* say, but one always wonders. I didn't think I'd ever see them online, except possibly as some grim PDF".

7. But BAILII wants protection, too

While extending BAILII is certainly useful to the wider community as an open system, it too wants protection for its contents. As a relatively easy to access system, BAILII can be targeted by web crawlers or others who simply wish to extract cases for republishing or re-use on their own systems. Although BAILII allows Google and other search engines to access case titles, it denies them direct search access to the full text of decisions and disables IP addresses which download too much material. The reasons for this protection of BAILII materials lie partly in economics and partly in obligations towards the data. First, as a charity, BAILII must prove that it is well used and functions as its goals suggest. If materials are removed to other sites and not accessed through BAILII, usage statistics will fall, funding will fall, and BAILII will fold. Second, BAILII has an obligation to the court to ensure that if a judgment has been wrongly made public, it is removed immediately and not be cached on someone else's server. BAILII is also obliged to take reasonable care that its data is held responsibly, given that cases contain information about individuals.

8. Conclusion: a new National Law Library?

The increasing dominance of electronic information services has significant implications for public access to legal materials. Open access systems such as BAILII play an important role in enabling free public access in a formalised and structured way but also taking reasonable care over the nature of that data, evidencing the approach which was suggested as the heart of the 'National Law Library' proposal – the report suggested that a successful system would indeed become the primary method of law publication in the UK. The view of BAILII as a national resource appears to be growing: judges will email in and complain that a paragraph indentation or numbering is wrong (this is usually corrected immediately and the Court Service informed), or that BAILII doesn't have such and such a judgment of theirs on the system. Several High Court judges will also send BAILII embargoed judgments and then they can inform those at court that copies of the transcript are available on BAILII.

BAILII positively encourages deep linking (hyperlinks to specific BAILII pages). Although allowing deep linking can enable attempts to gain commercial advantage from another's copyrighted works,[13] for BAILII, deep linking is totally advantageous – it ensures correct pointing to the relevant decision, does not require search processing, and generally encourages the use of the materials to the benefit of users. The deep-linked judgments all clearly demonstrate their origin, so BAILII's role is not hidden. Deep linking to a National Law Library would allow re-use of any individual judgment by publishers, students, teachers, legal practitioners and other professionals who need or desire access to primary sources of legal information.

Commercial publishers have historically served an important and useful function as intermediaries in the development of the legal information industry, but at a price many cannot afford to pay. In a digital era, open access systems providing legal information free from the constraints of commercial publication can actually facilitate the efforts of publishers, commercial firms, researchers or others who wish to develop search software and methodologies which utilise the underlying legal information corpus. It would be possible under a National Law Library approach to provide the data in a form which allowed creative usage, without the need to expend costs on the actual collection of the primary source data. The role of intermediaries – those who provide

---

[13] There have been no cases decided on deep-linking in the UK. The earliest litigation from 1996 (*Shetland Times, Ltd. v. Jonathan Wills and Another*, 1997 F.S.R. (Ct. Sess. O.H.), 24 October 1996) ended without a full judgment on the matter.

"added value" through tools such as headnotes, subject keyword analysis, sophisticated search engines, citation systems, and textbook analysis – would be encouraged through enabling more access rather than less access.

Furthermore, traditionally law publishers have been concerned with providing legal information only to the lawyer. But the nature of legal information suggests that open access models will need to consider and potentially meet the needs of a broad range of potential consumers, including practicing lawyers, legal academics, professionals in other disciplines (e.g. environmentalists and accountants), and the public.[14] The BAILII project is explicitly intended to provide an open access resource to potential users of legal information who might otherwise be excluded from such access to information. In so doing, BAILII serves as a 'National Law Library' and such a resource can only help increase the understanding of law in UK society.

References

Abbott, L.W. (1973), *Law Reporting in England 1485-1585*, The Athlone Press, London.

Laddie, H., Prescott, P., Vitoria, M. (1995), *The Modern Law of Copyright and Designs*, 2nd ed., Butterworths.

Leith, P. and McCullagh, K. (2004), *Developing European Legal Information Markets based on Government Information*, International Journal of Law and Information Technology, Vol. 12, No. 3, pp. 247-281.

Picciotto, S. (1996), *Towards Open Access to British Official Documents*, Journal of Information, Law & Technology, Vol. 2.

Society for Computers and Law (1979), *A national law library, the way ahead: a proposal for a computer assisted legal information retrieval system for the United Kingdom* (Milton: The Society).

Stebbings, C. (1995), *Law Reporting in Britain*, The Hambledon Press, London.

West-Knights, L.J. (1997), *The AustLII Paradigm*, Commentary, Journal of Information, Law and Technology, Vol. 3.

---

[14] See, for example, (Leith, 2004).

Open Access to Outcomes of Publicly Funded Research

Sebastiano Faro
Institute of Legal Information Theory and Techniques (ITTIG-CNR), Italy

Abstract. According to the Montreal Declaration on Free Access to Law, "Publicly funded secondary (interpretative) legal materials should be accessible for free but permission to republish is not always appropriate or possible. In particular free access to legal scholarship may be provided by legal scholarship repositories, legal information institutes or other means." This paper aims to outline the essential issues of the debate on open access to outcomes of publicly funded research. The debate is the setting for the topic covered by the Montreal Declaration. After clarifying the relevant key expressions ("outcomes", "publicly funded" and "open access"), the paper presents some national, international and supranational initiatives in this field, also giving attention to the main arguments in favour of open access. Finally, the paper discusses the emerging approach to the topic and its relevance for research in the legal field.

Keywords: Secondary legal materials, publicly funded research.

1. Introduction

The *Montreal Declaration on Free Access to Law*[1] gives specific attention to accessibility of publicly funded secondary legal materials (i.e. materials interpreting but also describing, analysing and evaluating primary legal sources such as statutes, regulations and case law). According to the Declaration:

> "*Publicly funded secondary (interpretative) legal materials* should be accessible for free but permission to republish is not always appropriate or possible. In particular free access to *legal scholarship* may be provided by legal scholarship repositories, legal information institutes or other means."[2]

This part of the Declaration focuses on an issue which is connected to the wider debate on open access to the outcomes of publicly funded research.

In recent years it has been a hotly debated issue, specifically with regards to scholarly publications.

The debate is based primarily on two phoenomena.

On the one hand, changes accompanying the evolution of scientific publication markets: over the last years the average annual increase in the prices of scientific reviews has approached a figure well in excess of the average inflation rate. The high prices of some journals raise significant worries concerning the ability of the system to deliver wide access and therefore efficient dissemination of research results, with the consequent risk of stifling further scientific progress.

---

[1] See the Appendix of this volume.
[2] Emphasis added.

On the other hand, the developments of new technologies and the internet have produced an explosion of dissemination and access possibilities. The potential for alternatives to existing scientific journals in performing research dissemination is strongly strengthened by, for instance, individual web pages or repositories or by open-access journals.

This issue is discussed in different contexts. Two examples among many can be cited. An online "Petition for guaranteed public access to publicly-funded research results"[3] was launched in January 2007 to promote and support the archiving of scientific publications in open repositories, after a (possibly domain-specific) time period to be discussed with commercial publishers. Currently more than 27,000 signatories from all over the world have signed this petition. The Alliance for Taxpayer Access,[4] in the U.S. supports the principle that American taxpayers are entitled to barrier-free access on the internet to the peer-reviewed scientific articles on research funded by the Government because they have paid for it.

This paper aims to outline the essential issues of the debate on open access to outcomes of publicly funded research. The debate is the setting for the topic covered by the above mentioned statement of the Montreal Declaration. After clarifying the relevant key expressions ("outcomes", "publicly funded" and "open access"), the paper presents some national, international and supranational initiatives in this field, also giving attention to the main arguments in favour of open access. Finally, the emerging approach to the topic and its relevance for research in the legal field are discussed.

2. Relevant key expressions

To better understand the topic it is useful to clarify the meaning of the three key expressions involved in the debate, namely "outcomes", "publicly funded" and "open access".

The word "outcomes" can refer to at least three different objects: research data, patentable inventions and copyrightable results.

Research data can be defined as factual records (numerical scores, textual records, images and sounds) used as primary sources for scientific research.

Patentable inventions are results of research activities which have three essential features: are new or "novel"; involve an inventive or "unobvious" step and are capable of industrial/useful application.[5]

---

[3] Available at: <www.ec-petition.eu/>.

[4] See: <www.taxpayeraccess.org/>.

[5] In this case, the ownership of the results from public funded research is governed by three different types of regimes, namely 1) employment and IP related legislation, 2) Government Research regulations, which vary from country to country and 3) contractual arrangements with industrial sponsors. See: European Commission (2006) *Management of intellectual property in publicly-funded research organisations: Towards European Guide-*

Copyrightable results are materials on which the author can claim copyright. Scientific literature belongs to this category. It can be royalty producing or royalty free literature. Books are an example of the former while scholarly publications in refereed journals and international conference proceedings are an example of the latter, because they do not involve payment (royalties) to the authors.[6] Scientists are rewarded by making advances to knowledge, and to their careers; through scholar publications, they aim to reach a large audience and increase impact of their research.

With respect to scholarly publications a distinction is made among pre-print, post print and publisher's version. *Pre-print* is any version of an article prior to peer review and publication. *Post print* is any version of an article which has been approved by peer review but not copy-edited. *Publisher's version* is the version that includes additional changes made by the journal's editorial staff after acceptance of the author's final manuscript.

As to "Publicly funded research", it is to pointed out that public funding of research activities usually takes one of two forms: general support to national research institutions and laboratories that perform research according to their mandate and designation (ordinary funding), or direct funding of specific projects according to specific priorities (selective funding). The latter could be carried out in public institutions, universities, both public or private, or in private companies. In some countries, in addition to the federal government, state or local governments provide substantial funding to research. The justification for publicly funded research (apart from mission oriented research in purpose created laboratories) remains based not only on cultural arguments and a sense that the primary justification of funding research is the pursuit of knowledge for its own sake, but also on the essential contribution that research gives to future wealth and other tangible benefits for society.

The third and last relevant key expression is "open access". Loosely speaking, open access (OA) is concerned with making digital content available free of charge without restriction. A more formal definition is provided by the Berlin declaration, according to which open access contributions must satisfy two conditions: (i) the author(s) and right holder(s) of such contributions grant(s) to all users a free, irrevocable, worldwide, right of access to the work publicly and (ii) a complete version of the work and all supplemental materials, in an appropriate standard electronic format, is deposited (and thus published) in at least one online repository that is supported and maintained by a public or private organization that seeks to enable open access, unrestricted distribution, inter operability, and long-term archiving.

---

lines, available at: <`ec.europa.eu/research/era/pdf/iprmanagementguidelines-report.pdf`>.

[6] Royalty free literature includes also "grey literature": material that usually is available through specialized channels and may not enter normal channels or systems of publication and distribution.

It is important to stress that OA is compatible with copyright, peer review, revenue, print, preservation, prestige, career-advancement, indexing, and other features and supportive services associated with conventional scholarly literature.

There are two primary vehicles for delivering open access to research articles. The first is Open access publishing ("gold" open access) which is based on a funding model that does not charge readers or their institutions for access; the costs of publishing are covered by authors or other sources (often university libraries) instead of readers paying via subscriptions. This type of publishing is offered by open access journals and by "hybrid" journals (subscription-based journals offering authors the option to pay for their article to be available open access). It ensures that research articles are immediately available in open access mode as soon as they are published. The second is Self-archiving ("green" open access): authors deposit the peer-reviewed manuscripts of their articles in repositories (also called open archives), to be available in open access mode.

It is generally accepted that OA can play a relevant role with respect to (i) archiving research publication, both now and in the future, by preserving research results and information for years to come; (ii) accessing research publications for all stakeholders and (iii) advancing science by creating information resources that make it easier for scientists to retrieve research publications and for public bodies to better manage their research investments.

3. Essential questions

The debate on open access to outcomes of publicly funded research focuses on some key questions. The first one concerns whether all outcomes of publicly funded research should be openly available to anyone and, if not, which outcomes should be made accessible. Moreover how they should be made accessible is discussed together with when they should be made accessible. The latter question involves the so called "embargo period", that is the length of time between the publication of an article in a journal and its public availability; it is meant to protect the journal's revenue.

Another fundamental question is related to identifying the legal basis for disseminating and accessing this material for free.

4. Some national, international and supranational initiatives

Some relevant national, international and supranational initiatives address the mentioned essential questions.

Since the beginning of this decade a movement in favour of open access to scientific information has gained scale in the research community and research-related organizations. Three major public statements of international scope in favour of open access to scholarly journal literature have been signed by thousands of individuals and by major research institutions and research funding bodies around the world. They are the *Budapest Open Access Initiative* (February 2002), the *Bethesda Statement on open access publishing* (June 2003) and the *Berlin Declaration on Open Access to Knowledge in the Sciences and Humanities* (October 2003).

In particular, signatories of the Berlin Declaration (more than 60 organizations) affirm:

"Our mission of disseminating knowledge is only half complete if the information is not made widely and readily available to society. New possibilities of knowledge dissemination not only through the classical form but also and increasingly through the open access paradigm via the Internet have to be supported. We define open access as a comprehensive source of human knowledge and cultural heritage that has been approved by the scientific community."

Following these initiatives in favour of open access (and the contemporaneous development of open access archives and emergence of new business models) several research funding bodies have established or announced policies supporting open access to the research output they have funded. The most relevant example of such policies is represented by the U.S. National Institutes of Health (NIH) public access policy.

The NIH is the largest funder of medical research in the world, and the largest funder of non-classified research in the U.S. federal government. Beginning 2 May 2005, NIH-funded investigators have been requested to submit PubMed Central (PMC) – which is the NHI free digital archive of biomedical and life sciences journal literature – an electronic version of the author's final manuscript upon acceptance for publication. The policy applied to all research grant as well as NIH intramural research studies, requesting that authors specify posting of their final manuscripts for public accessibility as soon as possible (and within 12 months of the publisher's official date of final publication).

As a matter of fact, since this policy was voluntary, it was not able to meet its goals. That is evident in the very low participation rate by researchers. Recently a legislative provision directs the NIH to change its policy so that participation is mandatory for agency-funded investigators. The Consolidated Appropriations Act of 2008 (sec. 218) states:

"The Director of the National Institutes of Health shall require that all investigators funded by the NIH submit or have submitted for them to the National Library of Medicine's PubMed Central an electronic version of their final, peer-reviewed manuscripts upon acceptance for publication, to be made publicly available no later than 12 months after the official date of publication: provided that the NIH shall implement the public access policy in a manner consistent with copyright law."

This provision was subject to annual renewal. The 2009 Consolidated Appropriations Act makes the NIH Public Access Policy permanent.

Similar policies have been proposed or put in place by other funding bodies like UK Research Council or the Wellcome Trust.[7]

However, the U.S. experience is relevant from a different point of view with respect to possible legislative regulation of the issue. In 2006 the Federal Research Public Access Act[8] was introduced in the U.S. Senate. The bill would require federal agencies with relevant extramural research budgets to develop public access policies. These policies developed by each agency would cover researchers that are employed, as well as those funded in whole or in part, by the agency. Specifically, they would require those researchers to submit electronic copies of their manuscripts, which have been accepted for publication in peer-reviewed journals, to the agencies that sponsored their research. The policies would also require that those manuscripts be deposited in a "stable digital repository". The public would gain free online access to manuscripts as soon as practical following publication, but not more than six months afterwards. As to the legal basis of open access, it is to point out that the bill does not alter copyright law or require that research be placed in the public domain. The bill has not been passed, but it represents a good example of a piece of legislation that, if enacted, would markedly increase public access to publicly funded research.

At the international level, the Organisation for Economic Cooperation and Development (OECD) adopted in 2004 a Declaration on *access to research data from public funding* and in 2007 a Recommendation on *Principles and Guidelines on Access to research data from public funding*. The Declaration recognizes that "open access to, and unrestricted use of, data promotes scientific progress and facilitates the training of researchers," as well as maximizing "the value derived from public investments in data collection efforts." It also recognizes that domestic laws in different countries, e.g., on national security, privacy, intellectual property rights, etc., may dictate constraints on open access, with "disparities in national regulations" affecting the uniformity of access. Nonetheless, the government that signed the declaration are committed to work towards the establishment of access regimes for digital research data from public funding in accordance with the objectives and principles of openness, transparency, legal conformity, formal responsibility, professionalism, protection of intellectual property, interoperability, quality and security, efficiency, and accountability. The *Principles and Guidelines* are meant to apply to research data that are gathered using public funds for the purposes

---

[7] See: Wellcome Trust (2006). *Position statement in support of open and unrestricted access to published research*, available at <www.wellcome.ac.uk/doc_WTD002766.html>.

[8] Available at: <cornyn.senate.gov/doc_archive/05-02-2006_COE06461_xml.pdf>.

of producing publicly accessible knowledge. They are intended to promote data access and sharing among researchers, research institutions, and national research agencies. OECD member countries are committed to taking these principles and guidelines into account in developing their own national laws and research policies, taking account of differences in their respective national context.

As to the supranational level, the European Union institutions and bodies have been considering the issue as both research funding bodies and policy-making bodies.

Both the Scientific Council of the European Research Council (ERC) and the European Research Advisory Board (EURAB) delivered statements on open access to results of publicly funded research. The ERC is the first European funding body set up to support investigator-driven frontier research. The EURAB is a high-level, independent, advisory committee created by the European Commission to provide advice on the design and implementation of EU research policy.

In its *Statement on open access* (2006)[9] the ERC Scientific Council stressed the attractiveness of policies mandating the public availability of research results – in open access repositories – reasonably soon after publication (ideally, 6 months, and in any case no later than 12 months). The *ERC Scientific Council Guidelines for Open Access* (2007)[10] requires that all peer-reviewed publications from ERC-funded research projects be deposited on publication into an appropriate research repository where available and subsequently made open access within 6 months of publication. In its report on *Scientific Publication: Policy on Open Access* (2006)[11] EURAB recommended that the Commission should consider mandating all researchers funded under Framework Program 7 (FP7) to lodge their publications resulting from EC-funded research in an open access repository as soon as possible after publication, to be made openly accessible within 6 months at the latest.

As to EU institutions, the Council's *Conclusions on scientific information in the digital age: access, dissemination and preservation* (2007)[12] include an invitation to the Member States to reinforce national strategies and structures for access to and dissemination of scientific information by defining clear policies and promoting access through the internet to the results of publicly funded research, at no cost to the reader, taking into consideration economically sustainable ways of doing this, including delayed open access.

Finally, the European Commission has been playing a relevant role in supporting open access to outcomes of publicly funded research.

---

[9] Available at: <erc.europa.eu/pdf/open-access.pdf>.
[10] Available   at: <erc.europa.eu/pdf/ScC_Guidelines_Open_Access_revised_Dec07_FINAL.pdf>.
[11] Available   at: <ec.europa.eu/research/eurab/pdf/eurab_scipub_report_recomm_dec06_en.pdf>.
[12] Available at: <ec.europa.eu/research/infrastructures/pdf/97236_en.pdf>.

Firstly, in 2006 the Commission published a study which examines the scientific publication system in Europe (*Study on the economic and technical evolution of the scientific publication markets in Europe*). The study drawn up for the Commission by a panel of experts, makes a number of recommendations for future action, including improving access to publicly-funded research. In particular recommendation A1 (*Guarantee public access to publicly-funded research results shortly after publication*) states:

> "Research funding agencies have a central role in determining researchers' publishing practices. Following the lead of the NIH and other institutions, they should promote and support the archiving of publications in open repositories, after a (possibly domain-specific) time period to be discussed with publishers. This archiving could become a condition for funding. The following actions could be taken at the European level: (i) Establish a European policy mandating published articles arising from EC funded research to be available after a given time period in open access archives, and (ii) Explore with Member States and with European research and academic associations whether and how such policies and open repositories could be implemented."

Open access is not presented as a substitute model but as a supplement to paid journals and the legal basis for open access is identified in a contract provision.

The Commission's support to open access is also expressed in its *Communication on scientific information in the digital age: access, dissemination and preservation* (2007) where it is affirmed that:

> "Initiatives leading to wider access to and dissemination of scientific information are necessary, especially with regard to journal articles and research data produced on the basis of public funding. With respect to journal articles, the Commission is observing and considering experiments with open access publishing. Fully publicly funded research data should in principle be accessible to all, in line with the 2004 OECD Declaration."

Finally, in August 2008, the Commission launched an open access pilot in the FP7. Under this pilot, grant recipients in seven areas (energy, environment, health, parts of information and communication technologies, research infrastructures, science in society, and social sciences and humanities) are required, on the basis of a special clause of grant agreement, to deposit peer reviewed research articles or final manuscripts resulting from their projects into an online repository; and to make their best efforts to ensure open access to these articles within either six (health, energy, environment, parts of information and communication technologies, research infrastructures) or twelve months (social sciences and humanities, science in society) after publication. The pilot covers approximately 20% of the Commission's FP7 research programme budget, and will run until the end of FP7.

5. Arguments for open access

If one considers all these initiatives, it appears that two major arguments justify open access to outcomes of publicly funded research.

The first argument is the taxpayer argument (Suber, 2003). The primary version of the argument is that it would be wrong to make taxpayers pay a second fee for access. Taxpayers pay for the research and very often the salary of the researcher, as well. Then they pay a second fee either directly, when they buy journals where research articles are published, or indirectly when journals are bought by publicly-funded researchers or by publicly-funded libraries. A secondary version of the argument is that tax money should be spent in the public interest, not to create intellectual property for the benefit of private publishers, who acquire it and profit from it without paying the authors or compensating the public treasury.

Even if this argument is a good argument it cannot be the defining one, as Velterop (2003) affirms: "The Americans haven't paid for the scientific results that come out of France; the British haven't paid for research done in the USA, and so forth. Tax is national, but science is global."

A second stronger argument concerns the economic and societal benefits that derives from a wide access to research results. As all research and innovation builds on earlier achievements, an efficient system for broad dissemination of and access to research publications and raw data can accelerate scientific progress and therefore economic and/or societal benefit (for example, increased productivity, greater wealth, improved quality of life); moreover it can help avoid duplication of research efforts and optimize investment of public funds.[13]

6. The emerging model

The above mentioned initiatives refer to different contexts and have different scopes, nevertheless they share a common approach with respect to some essential features. Therefore it is possible to outline an emerging common model for regulating the issue of open access to outcomes of publicly funded research. This model focuses on a specific outcome of research, namely royalty-free literature and then identifies online repositories as the most appropriate means of open distribution and access and finally foresees an embargo period

---

[13] From a different point of view, J. Willinsky in his 2006 book *The Access Principle: The Case for Open Access to Research and Scholarship* (available at: <https://mitpress. mit.edu/catalog/item/ebook.asp?ttype=2&tid=10611>) developed the idea that scholars have a *responsibility* to make their work widely available through open access mechanisms: "a commitment to the value and quality of research carries with it a responsibility to extend the circulation of such work as far as possible and ideally to all who are in interested in it and all who might profit by it."

of 6-12 months. Moreover, the legal basis for open access is identified in specific contract terms or existing copyright legislation. In particular, open access to research articles does not require articles to be in the public domain. It only requires that there are not copyright or licensing restrictions preventing open access (statutory or contractual barriers). The copyright holder's consent is sufficient to remove these barriers. In the context of publicly funded projects, the obligation to allow open access can be the subject of a contractual clause. The funding agencies can require open access as a condition for funding research activities. Concerning researchers, it is sufficient to create contracts with publishers that retain their authority to license research results for open access publication, even after an embargo period.

Analysing the different initiatives and this emerging model, it can be observed that all these initiatives aim primarily to affirm the principle that outcomes of publicly funded research must be accessible. Therefore these initiatives follow a "pragmatic approach", meaning that (i) they do not analyze in detail some issues (e.g. the concept of "publicly funded"); (ii) they consider those outcomes which seem the less problematic (royalty-free literature) and (iii) they do not aim to alter the existing economic and legal framework.

7. Conclusions

The current debate on open access to the results of publicly funded research focuses primarily on research in the field of natural sciences, technology and medicine, but arguments for open access can be applied also to research in the legal field.

In this field, another argument to be considered is the specific relevance of accessibility of primary and secondary legal sources (including legal scholarship), in the light of the impact of law on the daily lives of the public.

The Montreal declaration stresses the importance of free access to law, focusing primarily on cases, statutes, and other materials issued by bodies with law-making authority. Public legal information is defined as "part of the common heritage of humanity". According to the Declaration: "maximising access to this information promotes justice and the rule of law"; moreover "public legal information is digital common property and should be accessible to all on a non-profit basis and free of charge".

It is appropriate for a movement to make legal information freely and openly available to all to focus first on improving access to primary sources – legislation, case law, and treaties. But the same relevance must be recognized to secondary materials, including legal scholarship, that are strictly linked to primary legal sources. Legal articles are written by law professors, judges, lawyers, law students, and others to discuss, explain, or analyze the law (as it stands or as it should be). This literature serves to support and to influence the professional work of judges, lawyers, and legal scholars and to explain the law to the public. Legal scholarship gives an essential contribution to certainty of law and effectiveness of rights.

As a consequence, legal scholarship should follow the same approaches and solutions as primary sources regarding its accessibility.[14]

References

Berlin Declaration on Open Access to Knowledge in the Sciences and Humanities (2003), available at: <oa.mpg.de/openaccess-berlin/berlin_declaration.pdf>.

Danner, C.A. (2008), *Applying the Access Principle in Law: The Responsibilities of the Legal Scholar*, available at: <eprints.law.duke.edu/1698/1/Danner,_35_Int\%271_J._Legal_Info._355_(2007).pdf>.

de Blaaij, C. (2006), *Public funded research and open access: Perspectives and policies*, The Grey journal, Vol. 2, No. 1, pp. 7-16.

English, R. and Suber, P. (2006), *Public access to federally funded research: The Cornyn-Lieberman and CURES bills*, available at: <www.acrl.org/ala/mgrps/divs/acrl/publications/crlnews/2006/jun/fedfundedresearch.cfm>.

European Commission (2006), *Study on the economic and technical evolution of the scientific publication markets in Europe*, available at: <ec.europa.eu/research/science-society/pdf/scientific-publication-study_en.pdf>.

European Commission (2006), *Summary of the responses to the public consultation on the "Study on the economic and technical evolution of the scientific publication markets in Europe" commissioned by the Research Directorate-general*, available at: <ec.europa.eu/research/science-society/document_library/pdf_06/synthesis-consultation_en.pdf>.

European Commission (2007), *Communication on scientific information in the digital age: access, dissemination and preservation*, doc COM (2007) 56, 14.2.2007.

European Commission (2008), *Open Acces. Opportunities and Challenges. A Handbook*, available at: <ec.europa.eu/research/science-society/document_library/pdf_06/open-access-handbook_en.pdf>.

Martin, B.R. and Tang, P. (2007), *The benefits from publicly funded research*, SPRU Electronic Working Paper Series, available at: <www.sussex.ac.uk/spru/documents/sewp161.pdf>.

OECD (2004), *Declaration on access to research data from public funding*, available at: <www.oecd.org/document/0,2340,en_2649_34487_25998799_1_1_1_1,00.html>.

OECD (2007), *Principles and Guidelines for Access to Research Data from Public Funding*, available at: <www.oecd.org/dataoecd/9/61/38500813.pdf>.

Pielke jr., R.A. (2007), *The Honest Broker. Making Sense of Science in Policy and Politics*, Cambridge University Press.

Suber, P. (2003), *The taxpayer argument for open access*, SPARC Open Access Newsletter, issue No. 65, available at: <www.earlham.edu/~peters/fos/newsletter/09-04-03.htm>.

Suber, P. (2007), *Open Access Overview*, available at: <www.earlham.edu/~peters/fos/overview.htm>.

Velterop, J. (2003), *Public funding, public knowledge, publication*, available at: <eprints.rclis.org/3875/1/Serials_Vol_16-2_Velterop.pdf>.

---

[14] Some initiatives are underway to promote free and open access to scholarly articles in the legal field; see, for instance, the open access policy of Harvard Law School faculty (<cyber.law.harvard.edu/node/4289>).

An Unexplored Legal Issue for the Provision of Free Legal Information in Hong Kong

Kevin Pun*, Hak-wai Chan°, Chun-fung Chong°, Kam-pui Chow°, Lucas Hui°, Wai-wan Tsang°

*Department of Computer Science and Department of Law, University of Hong Kong, China

°Department of Computer Science, University of Hong Kong, China

Abstract. In Hong Kong, can a provider of free legal information website bring a legal action against someone who, without its permission, hosts a website containing the same materials obtained from the provider's website? Where the provider (such as HKLII) is not the copyright owner of materials on its website, it is not entitled to sue for infringement of copyright in the materials. And if the user interface of the offending website differs from the provider's, the provider may not be able to bring a copyright action in respect of the user interface. In these circumstances the provider may only rely on the copyright in its entire collection of online materials as a "compilation". However, in the absence of judicial authorities in Hong Kong, the requirements for such "compilation copyright" are unclear. Furthermore, in view of the conflicting decisions in other leading jurisdictions, there are serious doubts as to whether a free legal information website may in practice enjoy compilation copyright in Hong Kong.

Keywords: Copyright, compilation, database, free legal information, website.

1. Introduction

Provision of free legal information in Hong Kong is a relatively recent phenomenon. Following the establishment of the Judiciary website and the Bilingual Laws Information System (BLIS) by the Government in December 1997, HKLII became the 3rd provider of free legal information website in Hong Kong. Since October 2003, HKLII has been accessed more than 1.5 million times, which is a rather remarkable achievement for a website of its kind in Hong Kong.

However, unlike the Judiciary and the Government of Hong Kong, HKLII does not own the copyright in the materials on its website and has to rely on licences granted by the copyright owners. As such, doubts arise as to whether HKLII can instigate legal actions on its own against someone who, without its permission, hosts a website containing the same materials obtained from HKLII. Indeed, these doubts apply not only to HKLII but to all providers of free legal information websites in Hong Kong.

At first glance, since the provider is not the copyright owner of the materials on its website, it does not have the *locus standi* to sue for infringement of copyright in those materials. Furthermore, if the user interface of the offending website is different from that of the provider's, there would be insufficient basis for a copyright action in respect of the user interface. *Thus the provider is left with this practical question: what legal protection does it have for its website, apart from asking the copyright owners to take legal actions against the offender?*

2. Compilation copyright

The answer to the above question lies in the protection of the website as a whole, i.e., the copyright that subsists in the entire collection of materials in the website. In Hong Kong, a collection of materials, known as a "compilation", enjoys copyright as a literary work. This is expressly provided in s.4(1)(a) of the Copyright Ordinance[1]

" 'literary work' means any work, other than a dramatic or musical work, which is written, spoken or sung, and accordingly includes–

(a) a compilation of data or other material, in any form, which *by reason of the selection or arrangement of its contents constitutes an intellectual creation*, including but not limiting to a table;

(b) ... " (emphasis added)

The copyright in a compilation conferred by s.4(1)(a) is often referred to as "compilation copyright". It is important to note that the compilation copyright arises from the *selection or arrangement* of contents, which is distinct from the copyright in the contents themselves. Clearly, if the entire collection of materials in a website enjoys compilation copyright, the provider is entitled to sue any person who infringes the compilation copyright by copying the selection or arrangement of materials in the website. In this regard, it is important to note that infringement may arise from the copying of either the selection *or* arrangement of contents. Thus even if a person rearranges the materials extracted from the provider's website, so long as the extraction is substantial his act would infringe the compilation copyright in the website by copying its *selection* of materials.

The important issue for a provider of free legal information website in Hong Kong is therefore this: does the selection or arrangement of the contents of its website indeed constitutes an "intellectual creation" to qualify for compilation copyright under s.4(1)(a) of the Copyright Ordinance?

To date, there is no direct authority in Hong Kong on the interpretation of s.4(1)(a). If one applies the conventional UK doctrine of originality, then so long as the selection or arrangement of the contents of a compilation is the compiler's original effort and has involved the compiler's skill and labour, the compilation will enjoy compilation copyright. This is so even though there

---

[1] Laws of Hong Kong, Chapter 528.

is nothing creative about its selection or arrangement. The conventional UK doctrine of originality does not require a work to be creative in order to enjoy copyright, all that is required is that the work should originate from the author (i.e., not copied from another work).[2] and has involved the author's skill and labour.[3] It should further be noted that the UK threshold for skill and labour is a low one, which only requires the expenditure of more than trivial effort and skill in the creation of the work. Case law shows that trade catalogues,[4] street directories,[5] medical research questionnaires[6] and even TV programme listings[7] can have sufficient skill and labour to attract copyright.

Based on the conventional UK doctrine, there should be little doubt that providers of free legal information websites (such as HKLII), which put in skill and labour in collecting legal materials and arranging them on their websites, enjoy compilation copyright in their websites in Hong Kong. This is certainly good news for these providers. But unfortunately, as the law stands, it is by no means clear that this is the correct view. To see the fuller picture, one has to turn to the broader international scene where the conventional UK doctrine has been severely challenged and to which Hong Kong must pay heed.

3. International developments on compilation copyright

3.1. US FEIST DECISION

The first severe challenge to the conventional UK doctrine came from the US Supreme Court in 1991 in *Feist Publications v Rural Telephone Services*.[8] The case concerned copyright in a compilation, namely, white pages in a telephone book. Prior to this decision, it was generally assumed that compilations in the US were protected under the "sweat of the brow" doctrine, the equivalent of the UK "skill and labour" principle, which rewarded hard work that went into the selection or arrangement of the compilation without requiring such selection or arrangement to be creative. However, in a significant departure from the UK jurisprudence, the US Supreme Court in *Feist* firmly rejected the "sweat of the brow" doctrine as the test for originality of a compilation under the US law. According to the Supreme Court, sweat of the brow was simply not enough. For a compilation to be original, the selection, coordination or arrangement of the materials therein had to possess a minimal degree of creativity which went beyond mere sweat of the brow.

---

[2] *University of London v University Tutorial Press* [1916] 2 Ch 601.
[3] *Ladbroke (Football) v William Hill (Football)* [1964] 1 WLR 273 (HL).
[4] *Purefoy v Sykes Boxall* (1955) 72 RPC 89.
[5] *Kelly v Morris* (1866) LR 1 Eq 697.
[6] *Dr Lam Tai Hing v Dr Koo Chih Ling* [1993] 2 HKC 1.
[7] *Independent Television Publications v Time Out* [1984] FSR 64.
[8] 499 US 340.

Applying this principle to the case, the US Supreme Court found that the white pages in the telephone book did not meet the requirement for copyright protection of a compilation. The selection of materials – subscribers' names, towns, and telephone numbers – was too obvious and thus lacked the modicum of creativity necessary to transform mere selection into copyrightable expression. Moreover, there was nothing remotely creative about arranging names alphabetically in a white pages directory. It was an age-old practice, firmly rooted in tradition and so commonplace that it had come to be expected as a matter of course. Accordingly, the white pages, as a compilation, were not entitled to copyright. It followed that copying the contents of the white pages, which were all uncopyrightable factual information, did not infringe any copyright in the telephone book, whether in its contents or in its selection or arrangement of contents.

3.2. EC DATABASE DIRECTIVE

The *Feist* decision was the complete opposite of what one would expect based on the US "sweat of the brow" and the UK "skill and labour" doctrines, which would have held that copying uncopyrightable factual information from the telephone book would nonetheless infringe the copyright in its selection, coordination or arrangement of materials. The impact of *Feist* was quickly felt not only within the US but throughout the copyright world. Concern was raised about the criteria for copyright protection of compilations including, most importantly, electronic databases.

In 1996, the European Community issued what could be described as a response to *Feist* by way of a Directive on the legal protection of databases – Directive 96/9/EC of the European Parliament and of the Council ("EC Database Directive"). Article 3 of the Directive sets out the criterion for protection of databases in the following terms:

"1. In accordance with this Directive, databases which, *by reason of the selection or arrangement of their contents, constitute the author's own intellectual creation* shall be protected as such by copyright. No other criteria shall be applied to determine their eligibility for that protection.

2. The copyright protection of databases provided for by this Directive shall not extend to their contents and shall be without prejudice to any rights subsisting in those contents themselves." (emphasis added)

The term "database" is defined in Article 1 of the Directive to mean "a collection of independent works, data or other materials arranged in a systematic or methodical way and individually accessible by electronic or other means." The term thus covers not only electronic databases, but also conventional compilations which are accessible by non-electronic means. For all these databases, the level of originality required is that their selection or arrangement of contents must constitute "author's own intellectual creation", an expression similar to that in s.4(1)(a) of the Copyright Ordinance.

In the Explanatory Memorandum to the original proposal of the EC Database Directive,[9] it was stated that this standard for copyright protection – "author's own intellectual creation" – would be higher than the UK standard of "skill and labour". This was inevitable because of the different standards within the European Community for copyright protection. Unlike the UK, the continental civil law countries within the European Community all require a work to be "creative" in order to enjoy copyright. Thus to harmonise the law on database protection within the European Community, it was envisaged by the Database Directive that the UK had to raise its standard for copyright protection of compilations and databases, and that the continental civil law countries had to lower it. This intention was explained in an article published in 1995 by the Commission official directly involved with the drafting of the Directive:

> "Politically speaking the common law Member States will have to lift the bar for application of copyright protection, whereas the continental civil law countries will have to lower it. This bridging the gap between copyright and *droit d'auteur* is certainly not de minimis." (Gaster, 1995)

Hence under the EC Database Directive, copyright protection for compilations and databases in the European Community will not be granted merely because of the "skill and labour" that has gone into their selection or arrangement of contents, but because such selection or arrangement has a certain degree of creativity beyond "skill and labour". This is essentially the same standard for copyright protection as laid down by the US Supreme Court in *Feist*.

3.2.1. *Sui generis right*

The new copyright standard for compilations and databases adopted by the EC Database Directive has the most impact on the UK. To allay fears that compilations and databases hitherto protected under the UK "skill and labour" principle may become unprotected under the new standard, the Directive has introduced a new "sui generis right" to safeguard the database maker's investment in creating its database, namely, the obtaining, verifying or presenting of the materials contained therein. Article 7 defines the right as follows:

"1. Member States shall provide for a right for the maker of a database which shows that there has been qualitatively and/or quantitatively a substantial investment in either the obtaining, verification or presentation of the contents *to prevent extraction and/or re-utilization of the whole or*

---

[9] Proposal for a Council Directive on the legal protection of databases, COM (92)24 final, Brussels, 13 May 1992, OJ 1992 C156/4.

of a substantial part, evaluated qualitatively and/or quantitatively, of the contents of that database.

. . .

4. The right provided for in paragraph 1 shall apply irrespective of the eligibility of that database for protection by copyright or by other rights. Moreover, it shall apply irrespective of eligibility of the contents of that database for protection by copyright or by other rights. Protection of databases under the right provided for in paragraph 1 shall be without prejudice to rights existing in respect of their contents." (emphasis added)

By virtue of this sui generis right, it is clear that even when a compilation or database fails to attract copyright under the new standard of "author's own intellectual creation", the database maker's investment is still protected by being able to prevent anyone from extracting or re-utilizing the whole or a substantial part of the contents of the database. Pursuant to Article 10 of the Directive, the sui generis right "shall run from the date of completion of the making of the database" and "shall expire fifteen years from the first of January of the year following the date of completion."

3.2.2. *UK's implementation of the database directive*

The creation of the sui generis right represents a compromise between the UK and the continental European civil law countries in an effort to harmonise the law on database protection within the European Community. A year after the Database Directive was adopted, the UK implemented the Database Directive by its Copyright and Rights in Databases Regulations 1997.

Pursuant to the Regulations, a new s.3A was added to the UK Copyright, Designs and Patents Act 1988 providing that "a database is original if, and only if, *by reason of the selection or arrangement of the contents of the database the database constitutes the author's own intellectual creation*". The sui generis right was not created under the same Act but under s.13 of the Regulations which renamed it as "database right". The definition makes it clear that the database right subsists irrespective of whether the database is a copyright work. By s.16 of the same Regulations, the database right is infringed by a person who, without the consent of the owner of the right, extracts or re-utilises all or a substantial part of the contents of the database. All these have brought the UK law in line with the EC Database Directive, signifying a new chapter in the protection of compilations in the UK.

4. Status of compilation copyright in Hong Kong

4.1. DOES THE NEW UK STANDARD APPLY TO HONG KONG?

Although the UK Regulations have not been incorporated into Hong Kong law, the language therein for the new standard of originality for databases ("author's own intellectual creation") is virtually the same as that in s.4(1)(a) of the Copyright Ordinance ("an intellectual creation"). However, as of today, no Hong Kong court has been asked to interpret the meaning of "an intellectual creation" in the context of s.4(1)(a). Hence it is still open to debate as to whether the expression should be interpreted in the same way as the UK's new standard of originality for databases which requires creativity and not mere skill and labour, or the conventional UK standard of skill and labour which has always been part of Hong Kong law.

At first glance, it seems logical that Hong Kong should adopt the new UK standard for protecting compilations and databases. The reason is simple: since the Hong Kong copyright law has always been modeled on the UK and interpreted in the same way as the UK throughout Hong Kong's copyright history, there is no good reason to suggest that "an intellectual creation" as appeared in s.4(1)(a) of the Copyright Ordinance, which is virtually the same expression as "author's own intellectual creation" in s.3A of the UK 1988 Act, should be interpreted differently from the UK's interpretation of the latter. Based on this view, compilations and databases in Hong Kong must also possess certain degree of creativity in their selection or arrangement of contents to enjoy copyright protection.

This view would be fatal to providers of free legal information websites in Hong Kong such as HKLII. It is because in practice, these providers would invariably obtain contents for their websites from the few recognized sources – most notably, the Judiciary and the Government – and place them on their websites without much exercise of selection. Furthermore, these contents would typically be arranged alphabetically and/or chronologically, neither of which can be said to be creative in any way. Hence under the new UK standard, these websites would fail to qualify for compilation copyright. It follows that providers of these websites will not be able bring a copyright action against anyone who copies materials from the websites, even when it amounts to copying their entire selection and arrangement of materials.

In theory, providers of such websites may seek protection by arranging the contents of their websites in non-conventional ways so as to qualify for compilation copyright under the new UK standard. However, even then, a person who copies materials from these websites *without* copying their arrangement will not infringe their compilation copyright. In such a case, any copyright infringement will only be because of the copying of the materials, which is only actionable by the copyright owners of the materials and not the providers of the websites. This is so even though the provider has put in skill and labour and incurred expenses in obtaining and presenting the materials on its website. Similarly, if there is no copying of the user interface of the website, no action can be brought by the provider of the website for infringement of copyright in the user interface.

The argument that the new UK standard should apply to Hong Kong no doubt carries force. However, there is one important factor which distinguishes the situation in Hong Kong from that in the UK: namely, that there is no "sui generis right" (or "database right" as known in the UK) in the Hong Kong copyright law. Hence if Hong Kong simply raises the standard for compilation copyright to the new UK standard, it will be denying protection to compilations whose selection and arrangement of contents is by no means creative. But such compilations have all along been protected by copyright in Hong Kong. Given that Hong Kong does not have any law on unfair competition, this will mean that investments in creating such compilations – particularly the obtaining, verifying or presenting of their contents – are not protected in Hong Kong. This position is harsh and unfair to the makers of such compilations, and may not be something that Hong Kong, as its law currently stands, is prepared to adopt.

4.2. AN ALTERNATIVE FOR HONG KONG

As devised in the EC Database Directive, the new UK standard for compilation copyright is meant to go hand in hand with the sui generis right. This strikes a balance between the interests of compilers in having their investments protected and the interests of the public in having free access to information. Thus unless Hong Kong also amends its Copyright Ordinance to create a sui generis right for compilations, raising the standard for compilation right in Hong Kong will undoubtedly upset the balance between the compilers and the public.

An alternative for Hong Kong is to stay with the conventional UK standard of "skill and labour" for compilation copyright. While this will clearly be a departure from the UK path, Hong Kong will by no means be alone if it adopts this stance. In 2002, in a case concerned also with the copyrightability of white pages in a telephone book, *Desktop Marketing Systems v Telstra*,[10] the Australian Federal Court has firmly held that *Feist* was not supported by Anglo-Australian authorities. According to the Federal Court, there was no requirement in Anglo-Australian law for a work to demonstrate a threshold "spark of creativity" in order for it to be original. Originality could be found in the labour and expense of collecting, verifying, recording and assembling factual data. As ruled by the Federal Court, to deny copyright protection to telephone directories would be to allow anyone to appropriate the benefit

---

[10] 55 IPR 1.

of the substantial labour and expense put into compiling these databases and thereby to avoid the trouble and expense of doing that work for itself. This went against an important underlying principle for protection of factual compilations – preventing competitors from taking commercially unfair free rides on the labour and expense of others, or "reaping without sowing".

Thus despite the very influential developments in the US and the European Community as regards compilation copyright, the Australian Federal Court was clearly not persuaded and held fast to the conventional UK standard of skill and labour. After the Federal Court's decision, an application for special leave to appeal against it was declined by the Australian High Court in June 2003. To date, Australia remains the leading jurisdiction which upholds the skill and labour doctrine for protection of compilations. As the Australian copyright law and Hong Kong law are both modeled on the UK, the Australian position on compilation copyright may serve as a persuasive example for Hong Kong to follow.

5. Conclusion

In the absence of direct authorities in Hong Kong, it remains unclear as to whether compilation copyright in Hong Kong requires creativity or mere skill and labour in the selection or arrangement of contents. Arguments in favour of either position are equally persuasive, and all are awaiting authoritative guidance from the Hong Kong court. If it is confirmed by the Hong Kong court that mere skill and labour in the selection or arrangement of contents is enough to attract compilation copyright, then providers of free legal information websites in Hong Kong will no doubt be protected against anyone who copies materials from their websites. On the other hand, if it is held that compilation copyright in Hong Kong requires creativity in the selection or arrangement of contents, then providers of free legal information websites are unlikely to be able to sue a person who copies materials from their websites, particularly when the person also rearranges the materials thus copied.

When and how the Hong Kong court will resolve the issue of compilation copyright is unknown. But no matter what the outcome may be, it is perhaps advisable that providers of free legal information websites should not be overly concerned with legal means of protection but focus on making their websites useful to the general public. The features that render a legal information website useful – a good search engine, constant updates, and a friendly interface etc – are the basis for the success of a website which no legal protection can offer. In the case of HKLII, there is one more feature that other providers of legal information websites do not have: namely, the potential to collaborate with other LIIs to provide cross linking between cases hosted on HKLII and other LIIs. All these features cannot be easily copied. The presence of such features, and the constant improvement of them, is perhaps the most reliable protection for providers of free legal information websites in Hong Kong.

References

Gaster, J.L., (1995), *The EU Council of Ministers' common position concerning the legal protection of databases: a first comment*, Entertainment Law Review, Vol. 6, No. 7, pp. 258-262.

III SECTION

Free Access to Law: Information Systems and Institutions in Europe

Free Access to Legal and Legislative Information: The French Approach Through the Enlightenment of the Strategic Reviews of Better Regulation in the European Union

Stéphane Cottin
General Secretariat of the Government, France

Abstract. France has done and continues to do great efforts towards free access to the Law. These works have been built not only in the material ways to access to the legal data, but also in the logical elaboration of these documents, before the publication. All these efforts are made under the enlightenment of the studies lead by the European Union. The "European level" became certainly the right one to build best practices in the way to better regulation.

Keywords: France, access to the law.

✱✱✱

1. France has already a rather large know-how in term of free on-line dissemination of the Law. The French public powers have given for a long time a special attention to the dissemination of their national law. Not only in order to ensure the rule of law and the legal certainty, but also to assess in a certain manner the influence of the French law at the international level. These practices and each (good or bad) experiment, built since many years, should be exposed in detail. We'll try to expose quickly the state in 2008 of the French official efforts towards free access to the Law (paragraph 1). Most of these efforts have been done under the models and in the directions given by the European Union. The European directives and the present debates about "better regulations" offer many new ways and means to improve legal writing and, so, the legal and legislative information. Their direct impacts on the French efforts towards better access to the Law could be here exposed (paragraph 2).

1. French official efforts towards (free) access to the law

2. The most visible effort is the official portal Legifrance and public service of dissemination of the Law on the Internet (1.1). It needed solid foundations: those strong principles have been patiently built by the judges (1.2). Besides, a new direction of the effort has been recently given: a free access to the Law

needs not only downstream efforts towards dissemination through the different aims, but also well-built upstream procedures in order to better regulate (1.3).

1.1. THE PUBLIC SERVICE OF DISSEMINATION OF THE FRENCH LAW ON THE INTERNET

3. Electronic databases for legal information (acts, regulations, and case-law) have been created in France more than half a century ago. A public service of access to the Law has been built in 1984, and then an official website has been created in 1998.[1] In 2002, it has been decided to change its dimension, and its general organisation, it became the 'Public Service of Dissemination of the French Law on the Internet' (hereinafter SPDDI, standing for – in French – *Service Public de Diffusion du Droit par l'Internet*).

Its extent is thus defined by the Decree n° 2002-1064 of 7 August 2002 which takes over the previous decrees of 1984 and 1996 with subtle modifications (See the full text of the decree in Appendix 1). The field of application of the SPDDI seems therefore drawn. But this enumeration of texts is not saved of slight imprecision and, in practice, not all fields are covered in the same way. (See, on the Legifrance website, the column "A propos du droit", paragraph 7 on "the field of the disseminated legal data".

4. Content. It is therefore useful to make a point on the reality of the SPPDI's offer, by studying it with respect to what is made available on or via the site Legifrance.[2]

It (the SPDDI) makes available to the public for free the following data:

1° The normative acts, presented as they result from the successive modifications:

a) the Constitution,	Present up-to-date directly on Legifrance. More links towards the websites of the Constitutional Council or National Assembly for specifications.
the codes, Size: 95 codes	Part of the base LEGI (base of the full text of the codes, laws and decrees in force since 1978). **These codes are reproduced in their up-to-date version and "consolidated"**, the articles totally abrogated are not cited. There are all the codes, up-to-date and generally one week after the modification. The official codes, that is those which make the object of a parliamentary vote or which were codified by decree following the works of the superior Commission of codification.

---

[1] See: `<legifrance.gouv.fr>`.

[2] See also the explanatory note on the reuse of the data available on Legifrance, which briefly describes these bases `<www.legifrance.gouv.fr/html/licences/licences_notice.htm>`.

the laws and the acts with regulatory character (à caractère réglementaire) coming from the State authorities LEGI Size: 55,000 texts and 95 codes Annual growth rate: NA JORF Size: 444,000 texts Annual growth rate: 32,000 texts	Combination of bases: - LEX (references and summaries of texts published in the official journal since 1936) - JORF (full text of a great part of the texts published in the official journal since 1990) - also LEGI (full text of laws, decrees and codes in force since 1978) (The Direction of official journals, which makes this database of consolidated texts has the goal the exhaustion of documentary fund of legislation / national regulation, not yet totally achieved to date) Therefore we have the full text systematically since 1978 (rarely before, for some great texts), and especially only for laws (a hundred a year) and decrees (a thousand a year). For the other texts published in the official Journal (orders, circulars etc.) we have the rough versions since 1990. **The column "Other legislative and regulatory texts" is made of two data bodies:** - LEX: the documentary fund produced by the documentary Service of the general Secretariat of the Government, constituted of all the legislative and regulatory acts in force (or abrogated if they were in force during the last 40 years). Beside the identification data characterising this body, every legislative or regulatory text comprises analysis data. These are sorted by place of application, modification or abrogation: the link made between the references of the texts allow to consult the legal links of a given text, be it subsequent (modifying, abrogating or explanatory) or previous (modified, abrogated or sources) - JORF: the documentary fund of documents published in the edition "Lois et décrets" of the official Journal since 1990.
b) The national collective conventions having made the object of an extension order. Size: 124,000 art. Annual growth rate: 8,000 art.	ex-base KALI The documentary fund of the collective conventions, in simplified search, comprises the ensemble of brochures edited and published by the Direction of official journals, in their version into force. The advanced search refers to the ensemble of the documentary fund of the collective conventions, including the modified and abrogated versions. These works are updated from the official Bulletin "Conventions collectives" elaborated by the social affairs, labour and solidarity ministry.

2° The acts resulting from international commitments of France:

a) The treaties and agreements to which France is a party	PACTE base, Ensemble of treaties and agreements related to France. Sends to the PACTE base (Ministry of foreign affairs)
	`<www.doc.diplomatie.fr/pacte/>`, but also to a selection of fundamental treaties:
	`<www.legifrance.gouv.fr/html/`
	`traitesinternationaux/liste_traites.htm>`

b) The directives and regulations coming from the authorities of the European Union, as they are disseminated by these authorities.	A number of links to Eur-Lex The indicated transposition measures are the ones which were notified by France to the European Commission. This does not prejudge of the subsequent advice of the latter regarding the exhaustivity of each notified transposition and a fortiori of a decision of the Court of Justice on an action in an infringement proceeding.

3° The case-law:

a) The decisions and judgments of the Constitutional Council Size: 3,500 dec. Annual growth rate: 150 dec.	Base CONSTIT, full text of the decisions, actions since the origin (1958) and notices of the Government since 1995. The base offered directly by the services of the Constitutional Council is, in the general opinion, easier and more complete.
of the Conseil d'Etat, Size: 230,000 dec. Annual growth rate: 12,000 dec.	Base JADE (des Juridictions AdministrativEs/ of administrative jurisdictions). Comprises the full text anonymised of the decisions of the Conseil d'Etat since 1968. Comprises also a selection of judgments of administrative Courts of appeal and some very rare judgments of administrative tribunals.
of the Court of Cassation Size: 120,000 + 246,000 (unpublished) = 366,000 dec Annual growth rate: 11,130 dec	Bases CASS and INCA The CASS base is the oldest full text database in France. It dates from 1960. As it did take the origins only the published judgments, (approx. 10%), in 1984 appeared INCA (for INédits de la cour de CAssation.)
and of the conflicts tribunal;	(included in the CASS and JADE bases)
b) The decisions and judgments given by the Court of Auditors (Cour des Comptes)	Redirects to the site of the Court of Auditors (<www.ccomptes.fr>)
by the other administrative, judicial and financial jurisdictions which were selected on criteria suitable for every jurisdiction order; Size: 19,000 dec. Annual growth rate: 20,000 dec.	Before 2002, the old fee-based system Jurifrance had a passage to the service of the commercial base Jurisdata, produced by the editors Lexis-Nexis and having more than 500,000 judgments of the courts of appeal. Since 2002, and now organized under the provision of the article R433-3 of the Judiciary Organisation Code (<www.legifrance.gouv.fr/affichCodeArticle.do?cidTexte=LEGITEXT000006071164&idArticle=LEGIARTI00001892180>), the documentation service of the Court of Cassation holds a database with a selection of case-law "which are presenting a special interest", under the rules of the SPDDI.

c) The judgments of the European Court of Human Rights and the decisions of the European Commission of Human Rights;	Redirects to the website of the Court and especially the database HUDOC (`<www.echr.coe.int>`)
d) The decisions of the European Court of Justice and of the court of first instance	Redirects to CURIA (`<curia.eu.int/fr>`)

4° An ensemble of official publications:

a) The edition "Lois et décrets" / "Laws and decrees" of the official Journal of the French Republic;	Redirects to the site of the official Journal (`<www.journal-officiel.gouv.fr>`)
b) The official bulletins of the ministries;	Redirects to a list of links of the ministries proposing, unfortunately in a non-normalised manner, their production of official bulletins.
c) The official Journal of the European Communities	Redirects to Eur-lex (`<eur-lex.europa.eu>`)

5. This public service is held by the State towards everyone's' benefit: citizen consumers, legal professionals, and law vendors. It is a part of several technological innovations. One of the most important of them is the digitalization of the Official Gazette (Ordinance n° 2004-164 of 20 February 2004 on the modalities and effects of the publication of laws and of certain administrative acts: see the full text of the Ordinance in Appendix 2).

6. According the mentioned Ordinance, the publication of the official texts is ensured, on the same day, in conditions capable to guarantee their authenticity, on paper **and in electronic form**. The official Journal of the French Republic is put at the disposition of the public in an electronic form on a permanent and free of charge basis.

1.2. LEGAL PRINCIPLES

7. French supreme courts built also several principles directly linked to the better ways to make and disseminate Law: Intelligibility of the Law (1999); Accessibility of the legal rules (1999); Anonymization of the judicial decisions (2001); Legal certainty (2001-2006)...

These texts and principles strengthened the position of the French authorities in charge of the dissemination of the Law.

8. The SPDDI must respect the principles described above. This list is though not exhaustive.

On the first two goals, it is formally a matter of aim with constitutional value inferred by the Constitutional Council in its decision n° 99-421 DC of

16 December 1999[3] and which found a positive application in the review of an article of the finances' law of 2006, reversed by the Council for "complexity".[4]

9. One of the practical answers to these two first goals is in the guide for the elaboration of legal texts, a big work of more than 450 pages, present in full text on the homepage of the site Legifrance (SGG, 2007). It presents in detail the procedures applied by the public powers to elaborate and publish coherent and error-free normative texts. The work is comprehensive and didactic. It is filled with specific examples and regularly updated. Concerning the aim of efficiency of the norms, as described in the precedent paragraph, a whole chapter of the guide is dedicated to these issues.[5] We shall also retain that the chapters 1.4.1 and 1.4.2[6] respectively dedicated to Legifrance and to the codification take the description of the stakes of SPDDI.

1.3. SOLON: DIGITIZING AND MONITORING OFFICIAL TEXTS

10. Because a better access to the Law for the citizens, the administrative bodies and for the legal professionals needs obviously better ways and means to write it, huge efforts have been done to drive the legal writing process. So, upstream, an efficient workflow has been developed between the different actors of the law-making process: the software SOLON, standing for *Système d'Organisation en Ligne des Opérations Normatives*, or Online Organization System of Law-making Operations. It consists in the dematerialization and in the monitoring of texts from their origin to their publication in the Official Gazette.

11. Patiently built in coordination with every administrative bodies involved in the law-making process, the software has been in use since april 2007. More than 20,000 texts have been digitally transmitted by SOLON in 2007, and the system has already transmitted 15,000 texts and published 12,481 for the first half of 2008.

---

[3] See esp. para. 13 of the decision, available at <www.conseil-constitutionnel.fr/conseil-constitutionnel/francais/les-decisions/depuis-1958/decisions-par-date/1999/99-421-dc/decision-n-99-421-dc-du-16-decembre-1999.11851.html> (accessed 10 October 2008).

[4] See esp. in the attached documentation of the decision, pages 84 to 87, available at: <www.conseil-constitutionnel.fr/conseil-constitutionnel/root/bank/download/99-421DC-doc.pdf> (accessed 10 October 2008).

[5] Chapter 1.2 Efficiency of the norms, (SGG, 2007), available at: <legifrance.gouv.fr/html/Guide_legistique_2/121.htm> (accessed 29 September 2008).

[6] (SGG, 2007), available at: <legifrance.gouv.fr/html/Guide_legistique_2/141.htm> and <legifrance.gouv.fr/html/Guide_legistique_2/142.htm> (accessed 29 September 2008).

2. European dimension

12. Moreover, the European dimension of the issues must not be forgotten, at least in two directions. Access of the Law, so as all the information of the public sector, does have economic impacts, and the European Union managed in 2003 to organize the re-use of public sector information (paragraph 2.1). But the debate isn't, like in France, only facing this downstream dimension, and the ways to better write law became a great issue for Europe (paragraph 2.2). At the European level, best practices must be shared, and one of them found its place in the newly written French Constitution, with the compulsory procedure of Impact Assessments for each new Act (paragraph 2.3).

2.1. THE DIRECTIVE 2003/98/EC ON THE RE-USE OF PUBLIC SECTOR INFORMATION

13. The Directive 2003/98/EC of the European Parliament and of the Council of 17 November 2003 on the re-use of public sector information[7] has been integrated into French legal system by the Ordinance n° 2005-650 of 6 June 2005 on the free access to administrative documents and to on the reuse of public information[8] and by the decree n° 2005-1755 of 30 December 2005 on the free access to administrative documents and the reuse of public information, in application of the Act n° 78-753 of 17 July 1978.[9]

14. For the information of the legal sector, the 2002 decree is sufficient by itself and anticipates largely the integration of the European Directive. In exchange, this 2005 decree regulates the problem of the dissemination of legal texts produced by public persons (or holders of public power prerogatives) and which are not integrated in the first decree of 2002 (in the public service of dissemination of law by Internet).

2.2. "BETTER REGULATION" PROGRAMMES

15. The European Union has, over the years, developed a complex body of legislation, notably through the completion of the internal market. It has also become clear that the way in which we regulate has considerable impact on whether we meet the objectives efficiently. The Commission has launched a comprehensive strategy on better regulation.[10] The EU's Better Regulation

---

[7] Official Journal L 345, 31/12/2003 P. 0090 - 0096 available at: <eur-lex.europa.eu/LexUriServ/LexUriServ.do?uri=CELEX:32003L0098:EN:HTML> (accessed 30 September 2008).

[8] JORF n° 131 du 7 juin 2005 page 10022, texte n° 13 available at: <www.legifrance.gouv.fr/affichTexte.do?cidTexte=JORFTEXT000000629684> (accessed 30 September 2008).

[9] JORF n° 304 du 31 décembre 2005 page 20827, texte n° 119 <www.legifrance.gouv.fr/affichTexte.do?cidTexte=JORFTEXT000000265304> (accessed 30 September 2008).

[10] Available at: <ec.europa.eu/governance/better_regulation/index_en.htm> (accessed 30 September 2008).

policy aims at simplifying and improving existing regulation, to better design
new regulation and to reinforce the respect and the effectiveness of the rules,
all this in line with the EU proportionality principle.

16. The European Commission recognizes that considerable efforts have been
made since 2005 to make legislation of the member States clearer and more
effective. Nevertheless, the Commission intends to pursue with determination
the "Better Regulation" programmes (2005 then 2008) and proposes a series
of actions to be taken in collaboration with the European institutions and the
Member States.

17. Better Regulation strategy is based on several key action lines, including
the promotion of the design and application of better regulation tools at the
EU level, notably simplification, reduction of administrative burdens and impact assessment.[11] The accessibility and presentation of EU law are reinforced
by the quality of legislative drafting and by the role of the legal revisers.

18. Two Europa websites offer free access to general public to EU law:

- **EUR-Lex website** offers free access for the general public to the full
  range of EU law and treaties, including consolidated legislation, international agreements, parliamentary questions, case law, new legislative
  proposals and much of the EU Official Journal in all EU languages.
  EUR-Lex also contains a register of documents of the EU institutions.
- **Pre-Lex database** offers a possibility to follow the major stages of
  the decision-making process between the Commission and the other EU
  institutions starting from the Commission proposals. Commission communications are also accessible as well as various search possibilities.

19. Improving the quality of drafting of the EU legislation and clear use of language is a constant concern of the Commission and the other EU institutions.
To this effect, the three EU institutions involved in the legislative process -
the European Parliament, the Council and the Commission – have concluded
an **Inter-Institutional Agreement**[12] on the Quality of Drafting of EU
Legislation. This is complemented by a Joint Practical Guide[13] for legislative
drafting, available in all EU languages to all those within and outside the
institutions who are involved in drafting legislation. The **Joint Practical
Guide** is used together with other more specific guides, such as the Council's
Manual of Precedents, the Commission's Manual on Legislative Drafting and
the Inter-institutional style guide by the Office for Official Publications.

---

[11] Available at: `<ec.europa.eu/governance/better_regulation/access_eu_law_en.htm>` (accessed 30 September 2008).

[12] Available at: `<eur-lex.europa.eu/LexUriServ/LexUriServ.do?uri=CELEX:31999Y0317(01):EN:NOT>` (accessed 29 September 2008).

[13] Available at: `<eur-lex.europa.eu/en/techleg/index.htm>` (accessed 29 September 2008).

20. The legal revisers are part of the *'Quality of legislation'* team of the Commission Legal Service. They bear primary responsability within the Commission for the drafting quality of Community legislation. They ensure that Commission legislative proposals and draft Commission acts are drafted clearly and precisely and comply with the rules as to form. They check that the correct legal terminology is used and that the legal implications are the same in each official language. In line with the Better Regulation principles the legal revisers are involved early in the decision-making process, working closely with the department producing the first drafts, well before the texts are translated. They also cooperate various ways with the Member States to promote the quality of legislation and organize seminars to raise awareness of the effects of multilinguism.

2.3. IMPACT ASSESSMENTS AND NEW CONSTITUTIONAL PROVISIONS

21. France will for instance follow the indications of the Commission in continuing to reduce unnecessary administrative burdens by promoting the use of information and communication technologies. But another effort is also made towards the generalization of the procedure of impact assessments.[14]

22. Impact assessment is designed to help in structuring and developing policies. It identifies and assesses the problem at stake and the objectives pursued. It helps to identify the main options for achieving the objectives and analyses their likely impacts in the economic, environmental and social fields. It outlines advantages and disadvantages of each option and examines possible synergies and trade-offs.

23. Impact assessment is an aid to political decision-making, not a substitute for it. The impact assessment informs the political decision-makers of the likely impacts of proposed measures to tackle an identified problem, but leaves it to them to decide if and how to proceed.

24. Thus, the recent revision of the Constitution of the Fifth Republic (Act of 27 July 2008) went even further than the European strategies. It officially integrated impact assessment system is helping the Parliament design better laws (new articles 24, 39 and 51-2 of the Constitution). An impact assessment facilitates better-informed decision making throughout the legislative process. A Consulting Commission on the Evaluation of the Legislation[15] has been created by decree on 22nd September 2008. The new version of the article 39 of the Constitution, as it had been changed in July, imposes to take an institutional Act before March 2009 in order to establish the new conditions of the law-making process in front of the Parliament.

---

[14] The explanations of the procedure are available at: `<ec.europa.eu/governance/better_regulation/impact_en.htm>` (accessed 30 September 2008).

[15] Official website available at: `<www.ccen.dgcl.interieur.gouv.fr/>` (accessed 30 September 2008).

3. Conclusion

France seems to be the first European country having a compulsory procedure of impact assessment before each enactment of Act, written down in its
Constitution. This essential step of the law-making process is necessary to
build a better access to the law for every stakeholder. At the other end of the
process, publication and open access to the French Law are now strengthened
by several texts and procedures. All these ways and means are the multiple,
but connected, parts of a complex system aimed to the decreasing of the
ignorance of the Law, which is always no excuse, but it's also no excuse for
the public powers not to build a better access to it.

Appendix 1

Decree n° 2002-1064 of 7 August 2002 on the Public Service of Dissemination of the
French Law on the Internet. J.O n° 185 of 9 August 2002 page 13655, text n° 5, available at <www.legifrance.gouv.fr/affichTexte.do?cidTexte=JORFTEXT000000413818> (accessed 29 September 2008)

The Prime Minister,

According to the Law n° 2000-321 of 12 April 2000 on the rights of citizens in
their relationship with the administration, especially its Article 2;
According to the Decree n° 89-647 of 12 September 1989 modified as regards the
composition and the functioning of the Superior Commission of codification

Decrees:
Article 1

A public service of dissemination of the French law on the internet is created.

This service has the goal to facilitate the public access to the legal texts in force
as well as to the case-law.
It makes available at no costs for the public the following data:

1. The following normative acts, presented as they result from the successive
   modifications:

   a) The Constitution, the codes, the laws and the acts with regulatory character (à caractère réglementaire) coming from the State authorities;

   b) The national collective conventions having made the object of an extension order.

2. The acts resulting from international commitments of France:

   a) The treaties and agreements to which France is a party;

   b) The directives and regulations coming from the authorities of the European Union, as they are disseminated by these authorities.

3. The case-law:

   a) The decisions and judgments of the Constitutional Council, of the State Council (*Conseil d'Etat*), of the Court of Cassation and of the conflicts tribunal;

   b) The judgments and decisions given by the Court of Auditors and by the other administrative, judicial and financial jurisdictions, which were selected on criteria suitable for every jurisdiction order;

   c) The judgments of the European Court of Human Rights and the decisions of the European Commission of Human Rights;

   d) The decisions of the European Court of Justice and of the court of first instance of the European Communities.

4. An ensemble of official publications:

   a) The edition "Lois et décrets" of the Official Journal (Journal official) of the French Republic;

   b) The official bulletins of the ministries;

   c) The Official journal of the European Communities.

Article 2

It is created a website named Légifrance,[16] placed under the responsibility of the Government's General Secretary and exploited by the Direction of official journals.

This site gives access, directly or by links, to the ensemble of data mentioned at Article 1. It makes available to the public instruments meant to facilitate the search of this data. It offers the possibility to browse the other national public sites, those of foreign States, those of the European Union institutions or of international organisation having a mission of legal information. It informs on the legislative, reglementary and jurisdictional update. The other sites managed by the State administrations which participate in the execution of the public service of dissemination of law by Internet are mentioned by order of the Prime Minister, given after the advisory opinion of the committee mentioned in Article 5 of the present Decree.

Article 3

The Direction of official journals produces the databases corresponding to the acts of which it ensures the publication. It achieves especially a base ensuring the integration, in short time, of the modification of the legislative and reglementary texts. It can also create other bases mentioned in Article 1, upon request of the authorities which enact the data.

Article 4

Licences of reuse the data mentioned in article 1 and detained by the State can be granted to persons who ask to use this data in the framework of their activity, having or not a commercial character. A convention specifies the conditions of use of data and especially the commitment of the beneficiary to guarantee the use in accordance with the requirements of reliability imposed for the dissemination of such data.

---

[16] Available at: <www.legifrance.gouv.fr>.

The decision to grant the licence is taken by the authority which is responsible with the exploitation of the site on which the object of the licence is disseminated. The Committee mentioned in Article 5 of the present decree is consulted in advance. The licences are granted at no costs. The beneficiary supports the costs of the publication of the data. The licences cannot be given back.

Article 5

It is created, under the authority of the Prime Minister, a committee of the Public Service of Dissemination of the French Law on the Internet. This committee has the following attributions:

1. It gives the advisory opinions provided for by Articles 2 and 4 of the present decree; it can also deal with any conflict which would arise from the use of licences mentioned in Article 4;

2. It makes all proposals which seem useful with a view to improve the quality of the public service of dissemination of the law;

3. It establishes, every year, an evaluation report which is published on the site mentioned in the first paragraph of Article 2 of the present decree;

4. It brings its expertise to the administrations willing to proceed to the dissemination of legal data on the Internet. An order of the Prime Minister establishes the composition of the committee, especially the representatives of the companies specialised in the legal editing field.

Article 6

The Decree of 12 September 1989 above mentioned is modified as follows:

I. – It is added to Article 1 of this decree the following paragraph: "Finally, the commission is informed by the Direction of official journals of the difficulties that arise from the updating of the texts mentioned in Article 1, 1° of the Decree n° 2002-1064 of 7 August 2002 on the Public Service of Dissemination of the Law on the Internet as well as of any other problem linked with this activity. It formulates any proposal useful in this field."

II. – It is added to Article 2 of the same decree the following paragraph:

"In order to exercise the mission defined in the first paragraph of Article 1 of the present decree, the commission use the work of an expert group constituted under its authority, the composition of which is established by order of the Prime Minister."

Article 7

The dispositions of the present decree enter into force on 15 September 2002. The Decree n° 96-481 of 31 May 1996 on the public service of legal databases ceases its application on the same date.

Appendix 2

Ordinance n° 2004-164 of 20 February 2004 on the modalities and effects of the publication of laws and of certain administrative acts. J.O n° 44 of 21 February 2004 page 3514, text n° 5, available at <www.legifrance.gouv.fr/affichTexte.do? cidTexte=JORFTEXT000000435289> (accessed on 29 September 2008)

The President of the Republic,

Based the report of the Prime Minister and of the minister of justice, (J.O n° 44 of 21 February 2004 page 3512, text n° 4, available at <www.legifrance.gouv.fr/affichTexte.do?cidTexte=JORFTEXT000000796904> (accessed on 29 September 2008)

Considering the Constitution, especially its Article 38;
Considering the Civil code;
Considering the law n° 2003-591 of 2 July 2003 empowering the Government to simplify the law, especially its Article 4;
With the advice of the Conseil d'Etat;
With the advice of the Council of ministers,

Orders:
Article 1

Article 1 of the Civil code is replaced with the following dispositions:
"Art. 1. – The Acts and, when they are published in the official Journal of the French republic, the administrative regulations, enter into force at the date they establish or, in the absence of such an indication, the next day after their publication. However, the entry into force of those dispositions the execution of which needs application measures is postponed to the date of the entry into force of these measures."
"In case of emergency, the acts whose decree of promulgation so prescribes and the administrative regulations, for which the Government orders so by a special disposition, enter into force on the day of their publication."
"The dispositions of the present article are not applicable to individual regulations."

Article 2

The Acts, ordinances, decrees and, when a decree so prescribes, the other administrative regulations are published in the official Journal.

Article 3

The publication of the texts mentioned in article 2 is ensures, on the same day, in conditions capable to guarantee their authenticity, on paper and in electronic form. The official Journal of the French Republic is put at the disposition of the public in an electronic form on a permanent and free of charge basis.

Article 4

A decree of the Conseil d'Etat issued with the advice of the National Commission on Information Technology and Liberties (**la Commission nationale de l'informatique et des libertés**) defines the individual regulations, especially those related to the status and nationality of persons, who, in the present available state of technology must not be the object of an electronic publication.

Article 5

A decree of the Conseil d'Etat defines the categories of administrative regulations for which, taking into account their nature, their importance and the persons to whom they apply, the publication in the official Journal in an electronic form suffices in order to ensure their entry into force.

References

On "Better Regulation"

European Parliament (2008), *IPEX Dossier: COM/2008/0032, Communication from the Commission to the European Parliament, the Council, the European Economic and Social Committee and the Committee of the Regions Second strategic review of Better Regulation in the European Union {COM(2008) 33 final} {COM(2008) 35 final} {SEC(2008) 120}*, available at: <www.ipex.eu/ipex/cms/home/Documents/dossier_COM20080032/lang/en> (accessed 20 September 2008).

European Commission (2008), *Prelex File (European Commission legislative file) Second strategic review of Better Regulation in the European Union*, available at: <ec.europa.eu/prelex/detail_dossier_real.cfm?CL=en&DosId=196683> (accessed 20 September 2008).

On Legifrance

Belin, P. (2004), *La dématérialisation des procedures d'élaboration des textes à publier au Journal Officiel de la République Française* "6th International Conference Law via the Internet", Paris, available at: <www.frlii.org/spip.php?article62> (accessed 29 September 2008).

Cottin, S. (2006), *The Public Service of Dissemination of the French Law on the Internet*, published in the supplement of the issue 12/2005 of the Review Acta Universitatis Sibiu (Romania), available at: <www.servicedoc.info/The-Public-Service-of,1833> (accessed 29 September 2008).

Du Marais, B. (2002), *Dematerialized Procedures Without a Cyberjudge: A French Perspective on the Application of Information and Communication Technologies to Justice*, "4th International Conference Law via the Internet", Montréal, Presentation PDF, available at: <www.lexum.umontreal.ca/conf/conf2002/actes/dumarais.pdf> (accessed 29 September 2008).

Legifrance (2008), *About Law* (presentation of the French Law on the official website Legifrance), available at: <www.legifrance.gouv.fr/html/aproposdroit/aproposdroit_uk.htm> (accessed 29 September 2008).

SGG (2007), *Guide pour l'élaboration des textes législatifs et réglementaires* (also said "Guide de Légistique"), General Secretariat of the Government, La Documentation Française, 2e ed. 2007, available at: <www.legifrance.gouv.fr/html/Guide_legistique_2/accueil_guide_leg.htm> (accessed 29 September 2008).

Free Access to Legislation in Finland: Principles, Practices and Prospects

Aki Hietanen
Ministry of Justice, Finland

Abstract. In Finland there is a long tradition of free access to government files, actually already from the Access to Public Records Act in 1766, applied to Finland during the Swedish rule. Free access to legal information became a new issue with the use of Internet in the mid-1990s. In 1996 a governmental committee on access to legislation recommended that legal information (i.a. legislation, treaties and court judgments) should be made available on the Internet, free of charge.

The different aspects of free access are discussed, including the implementation of the PSI Directive on the re-use of public sector information and the role of commercial services of legal information. In Finland the key institutions of the government have been active in providing free access to government files.

Keywords: Access to legislation, databases, Finlex, Finland.

1. Free access to legislation - the Finnish principles

1.1. HISTORICAL BACKGROUND

Finland has a long tradition in the free on-line dissemination of legislative information. The current thinking on free access to government files and specifically to legislative information is based on one hand on historical traditions and on the other hand on recent analysis of the right to information by citizens. In Finland, a unique concept has been developed concerning the free access to information and especially legal information.

The tradition of open access to government files in Finland is among the longest in the world. As Finland was a Swedish-governed territory until 1809, the Swedish Royal Act of 1766 on Access to Public Records was applied also in Finland. It was actually drafted and introduced by a Finnish clergyman and scientist and Member of Swedish Parliament named Anders Chydenius. This act remained in effect in Finland until 1809 when Finland came under Russian control. For over a century, between 1809 and 1917, Finland was an autonomous Grand Duchy in the Russian Empire. During that period Finland had her own legislature and her own central administration, as well as her own legal system, inherited from the times of Swedish rule. Even during the Russian rule, openness policy continued through a series of laws and decrees on openness and publicity that were periodically adopted and overruled. The Finnish Legal Gazette of the Grand Duchy of Finland was established in 1861 and it was published both in Finnish and Swedish languages. In the upper corner of the Legal Gazette, there was a text "To be read out loud from the pulpit". Between 1902-1905, during the first oppression period of Finland, the Legal Gazette was published in Russian, Finnish and Swedish.

When Finland became an independent country in 1917, the new Constitution of 1919 provided for freedom of expression. the Constitution did not, however, include specific right of access to documents and therefore in 1919 Freedom of the Press Law created a general presumption of openness. The specific aspect of "principle of public access" (Offentlighetsprincipen, as it was called in Swedish) was still unclear and therefore in K.J.Ståhlberg, the first President of Finland and Professor of Law, began work on a new specific law. After the war in 1945 he co-drafted a proposal, which was adopted in 1951 as the Act on Publicity of Official Documents. It remained in effect until 1999. The same principle was adopted in the new constitution of 2000. In the Section 12 of the Constitution is written clearly: "Documents and recordings in the possession of the authorities are public, (. . .) Everyone has the right of access to public documents and recordings."

1.2. THE CURRENT APPROACH TO FREE ACCESS

In the Act on Openness of Government Activities of 1999, the scope of the openness principle was extended to e.g. state and municipal enterprises and private-law organisations and to preparatory documents. Simultaneously it was extended to both paper and electronic documents. In the Act, openness is the general rule and secrecy must be provided by law.[1] As regards the copyright to public documents, according to the Finnish Copyright Act (404/1961, section 9), there is no copyright in laws and decrees, or in decisions and declarations of public authorities and other public organs, or in translations of these documents.

In Finland free access to legislation and, in more general terms, free access to government information, is based on the Constitution, Acts of Parliament and a number of Committee reports by the Ministry of Justice and the Parliament. These texts and principles have created a uniform position of the Finnish authorities in charge of the dissemination of the legislation and other Government information.

In the Finnish concept of free access to legal information, there are some elements which are not necessarily well known elsewhere in the European Union member states. Firstly, it is based on the historical tradition of transparency and openness (the historical Principle of Public Access). Secondly, it is not limited to the access to legal acts, but in a broader framework it takes into account the accessibility of legal information.

Access to legal information in the Finnish thinking is a multidimensional issue. Knowing the law is not enough and making only the law available is

---

[1] Act on Openness of Government Activities (621/1999), English version at: <www.finlex.fi/fi/laki/kaannokset/1999/en19990621.pdf>.

not enough. Furthermore, a mere access to information is not enough as such, but also some elements are required, especially usability and acceptability.

The overall acceptability of a website or an information system is a combination of social acceptability and practical acceptability. Social acceptability refers to pluralism and to the possibilities for the user to find the information using different approaches, methods and websites. Practical acceptability refers to the cost, compatibility, reliability and usefulness of the service. Usability refers to an electronic service which is easy to learn, efficient to use, easy to remember, which includes few errors and which is subjectively pleasing. (Nielsen, 1993, p. 25)

According to the Finnish principles, also the practical implementation of the law by the courts (in judgments) or by state authorities (in decisions and orders) has to be made available. Furthermore, to find out and to analyse the objectives and intentions of legislation, the preparatory acts and information on the legislative projects and legal literature need to be accessible. In the Finnish concept of free access to legislation, also the access to legislative projects is emphasized. There is a specific database called Hare (project register) for the legislative projects. Via Hare it is easy to find information on the actual phase of the project, project publications, members of the project and the outcome of the project (government bill, act of parliament). Hare includes links to the database of the parliament and to Finlex.

One important aspect in the Finnish discussion has been the accessibility of disabled persons to legal information. Several Finnish websites, including the Finlex website, have been implementing the W3C Checklist of Checkpoints for Web Content Accessibility Guidelines (WAI). These guidelines explain how to make Web content accessible to people with disabilities. The primary goal of the guidelines is to promote accessibility. However, following them will also make Web content more available to all users (e.g., desktop browser, mobile phone, etc.) or constraints they may be operating under.[2]

With the emergence of the Internet and the new discussion on the access to information, the principles of free access had to be reformulated in the mid-1990s. This was done by a working group set up by the Ministry of Justice, revising the principles of access to legislation. A new direction for the dissemination of legislative information was given: it is not sufficient to provide only the material of the Legal Gazette to the citizens, but to provide free access to other legal materials, as well. The latest steps in defining the principles of access to legislation were during the drafting of the parliamentary act on the Legal Gazette in 1999. During the parliamentary procedure, the Constitutional Committee made a statement, that Finlex service should be complemented with databases of government bills and consolidated legislation within three years time. The database on consolidated law was opened to the

---

[2] Available at: <www.w3.org/TR/1999/WAI-WEBCONTENT-19990505/full-checklist>.

public in February 2002. Nowadays the database of consolidated law is the most popular database of Finlex.

The Finnish approach to the free access to legislative materials consists thereby the following elements:

1. The historical principle of Public Access (since 1766).
2. The right to information as confirmed in the Constitution and in the Act on the Openness of Government Activities.
3. The definition of the non-copyright of laws, decrees, decisions and judgments in the Copyright Act.
4. The broad concept of access to legislation by the Constitutional Committee of the Parliament and the Ministry of Justice, including access to

   a) Legal Gazette in Finnish, Swedish and Smi languages
   b) Consolidated legislation in Finnish and Swedish languages
   c) Index of legislation since 1734
   d) Government bills and parliamentary documents
   e) international treaties and conventions
   f) court judgments
   g) secondary legislation (norms of ministries and other state authorities)
   h) collective agreements
   i) specific legislation via the Suomi.fi website and the websites of ministries
   j) decisions of the supervisors of legislation (Justice Councellor and Parliamentary Ombudsman)
   k) translations of Finnish legislation
   l) Finnish legislation via the N-Lex service

2. Free access - the practices in Finland

2.1. THE FIRST STEPS OF FINLEX

Electronic databases for legal information (laws and case-law) have been created in Finland already over thirty years ago. In October 1972, the first pilot project was started, searching the text of the electronic Criminal Code and some other laws. Some months later, the first database of case law was established (the database of the Supreme Administrative Court). The databases were operated in the computers of the State Computer Centre, with software called IMDOC-T, which had been procured from Sweden. The brand Finlex has been used since 1981 and the first generation of Finlex was an information system including in early 1990s over 40 different databases and it was available until 2002 on the Internet. The Finnish Ministry of Justice has been responsible for the Finlex legal data bank from the very beginning.

The Finlex database service was established in a mainframe computer environment, with remote terminals connected to the databases. It was not until April 1996 that Finlex became available on the Internet and the www browsers. The elements of the first generation FINLEX were legislation, case law, literature and material of the European Union. The legislative section included laws and decrees in Finnish and in Swedish, index of international treaties and index of parliamentary documents. The case law section included over ten databases. The section of literature included references to case law in Finnish legal literature and Bibliographia Iuridica Fennica - Finnish Legal Literature.

EU section included i.a. the complete CELEX database (English version and CELEX in Finlex was (world-wide) the first database on European law opened on the Internet in April 1996.

In Finland the Internet era of legislative information started with website of the Finnish parliament in December 1995. During the same year, the Finnish Legal Gazette was made available on the Internet. The traditional FINLEX with user-fee was available until 2002 on the Internet.

2.2. THE NEW FINLEX AND THE NEW APPROACH

The preparation of the new Finlex Legislation Data Bank was started in 1996. A working group carried out a study on the duty of the government to disseminate legislative materials electronically. The report was published in March 1996, and in the end of 1996 a European call for tenders was published. The service was opened to the public in October 1997. The prime contractor for the new data bank is Edita Ltd, a Finnish company specialized in electronic publishing. The new Finlex Legislation Data System of the Finnish Ministry of Justice is using XML as a standard for structured documents and Oracle Text software as the retrieval system in the Internet service. The data system has been free of charge for all users since 1997. The concept of free access to legal information has reflected the actual contents of Finlex.[3] The following list describes the spectre and the main contents of the databases which constitute the Finlex service.

The Ministry of Justice makes available to the public free of charge the following data:

1. The normative Acts of Parliament and Decrees:

   a) the Constitution of the year 2000.

   b) the consolidated legislation (size: 1700 laws and decrees, annual growth: 100 doc.). The database of consolidated acts and decrees

---

[3] Available at: <www.finlex.fi>.

includes the consolidated full text of the laws and decrees in force since 1734. The texts are updated once a week.

c) the legislation in original form (size: 35,000 doc., annual growth: 1500 doc.). The database of acts and decrees in original form includes the full text of the laws and decrees in the form they appear in the Legal Gazette (Statutes of Finland). New texts are uploaded once a week.

d) the index database of legislation (size: 49,000 doc., annual growth: 400 doc.). The SMUR index database of all legislation includes reference information on all legislative acts (laws, decrees, decisions, orders, etc.) from 1734. The database includes a comprehensive list of all amendments made to the act and historical information on preceding acts.

e) The database of legislation in Smi language (size: 150 doc.).The database of legislation in Smi languages consists of translations into three official smi languages of Finland (Inari Smi, Skolt Smi and North Smi languages).

f) Translations of Finnish laws and decrees (size: 750 doc., annual growth: 50 doc.). The database of translations of Finnish laws and decrees included the updated texts of translations as pdf files. New translations are uploaded once a week.

g) A collection of the electronic Legal Gazette (Statutes of Finland):
   - The Statutes of Finland: laws and decrees appears daily in electronic form (as pdf files) in Finnish and Swedish.
   - The Treaty Series of the Statutes of Finland appears daily in electronic form (as pdf files) in Finnish and Swedish.

h) The international treaties and conventions (size: 1450, annual growth: 80). The treaty database has two part: reference data (information on the entry-into-force and ratification of treaties and information on additional protocols and a complete index of reservations made to multilateral treaties) and a full-text database. Both are updated by the Finnish Ministry for Foreign Affairs).

2. The case-law and decisions of State authorities:

a) The decisions and judgments of the Supreme Court and Courts of Appeal (size: 12,000 dec., annual growth: 150 dec.) The Supreme Court has three separate databases: Precedents, Judgments other than Precedents and the Pending Cases.

b) The decisions and judgments of the Supreme Administrative Court and Administrative Courts (size: 14,000 dec., annual growth: 240 dec.) Two databases with precedents and other judgments.

c) Special Courts (size: 2000 (MC) + 4600 (LC) and 1500 (IC), annual growth: 600 dec.). The Special courts in Finland are the Market Court (judgments in Finnish and Swedish), the Labour Court and the Insurance Court. All the judgments of Market Court and Labour Court are published electronically and appr. 1% of the judgments of Insurance Court.

d) Case Law in Legal Literature (FOKI) (size: 700,000 ref., in 120,000 judgements, annual growth: 8000 ref.). CLLL is a unique database with references to national and European case law. CLLL includes references to 2200 ECHR judgments and to 6000 judgments of the European Court of Justice. From the references there is a link to the text of the judgment.

e) The decisions of the Chancellor of Justice (size: 2500 dec., annual growth: 130 dec.). The Chancellor of Justice supervises the legality of the official acts and he also oversees the observance of basic rights and liberties and human rights.

f) Decisions and orders of Ministries and central agencies of government; (size: 4000 dec., annual growth: 300 dec.). The database is updated in a decentralised way by all ministries and agencies. The decisions are published both in Finnish and Swedish.

3. Future prospects of free access to legislation

3.1. THE COMMERCIAL DATABASES AND THE EU DIRECTIVE ON THE RE-USE OF PUBLIC SECTOR INFORMATION

In addition to the legal information provided by the state authorities, there is also commercial legal information available for citizens, judges and the private sector in electronic form. Compared to several other European countries, the information market in the legal sector is fairly small. It is clear that the broad concept of free access to legal information has had direct impact on the legal information market.

The commercial databases of legal materials are operated by two legal publishers, Edita Publishing Ltd and Talentum Media Ltd. In the Finnish legal information market there are no international operators, probably due to the small language area and the population of five million inhabitants.

The commercial service on Finnish Legislation ("Suomen Laki") of Talentum Media Ltd has been available on the Internet since 1997. Nowadays the electronic service[4] consists of consolidated texts of Finnish legislation, (with

---

[4] Available at: <www.suomenlaki.com>.

a small collection of EU legislation), case law of the Supreme Courts and the Government bills.

The legal information service Edilex by Edita Ltd. has been available on the Internet since 1995. Edilex [5] consists of consolidated legislation, court judgments, government bills, some special collections of legislation and case law of a certain field of law (e.g. environment law and taxation law) and expert writings.

The commercial companies in the legal publishing have been able to utilise the materials of legislation and case law available in Finlex. The impact of the EU directive on the re-use of public sector information (2003/98/EC) in Finland has not been notable. There has been fairly little discussion on the contents of the directive and on the practical implementation of the directive. In 2005 the directive was transposed into national legislation with amendments in the Act on the Openness of Government Activities and in the Act on Criteria for Charges Payable to the State (150/1992). In contrast to several other countries, no specific act was drafted on the re-use of public sector information and e.g. for the articles 7 or 8 of the Directive there are no detailed plans to promote the exchange of information between the public sector and the private sector.

3.2. THE NEW DEVELOPMENTS - TOWARDS FREE ACCESS TO AUTHENTIC LEGISLATION

The new developments in the free access to legislation have been emphasizing two important aspects of access. The first aspect is quality in the development of the legislative drafting process and the higher standards of legislation. Finland has been following and implementing the European projects of Better Regulation and Impact Assessment. The basic premise of the Finnish Better Regulation Programme is that good legislation, well drafted, will be a positive influence on both the welfare of citizens and the competitiveness of businesses. The promotion of welfare reinforces a just and safe society, in accordance with the rule of law, a society where people can expect their rights to be enforced in an equitable manner. In the impact assessment, when the legislative project is started the relevant impact areas and possible effects are identified. As the drafting process continues a more detailed assessment of the impacts of the regulatory options is made.

The Guidelines for Impact Assessment in Legislative Drafting are applied in drafting of legislation and decrees and other binding legal rules. The guidelines concern assessment of economic impact, impact on public administration, environmental impact and social impact.

The second new aspect of access is authenticity. The traditional approach in the definition of the legal status has been that the paper version is the only

---

[5] Available at: <www.edilex.fi>.

authentic and legally valid version of the Legal Gazette. The free access to electronic legislation has meant access to unauthentic electronic versions or databases of the Legal Gazette.

The new approach, which could be called the information society approach, defines the electronic version as the primary authentic version. In comparison to the traditional approach, the situation is upside down: it is possible to publish unofficial, unauthentic paper versions of the Legal Gazette, mostly for information purposes and for the archiving of the materials of the Legal Gazette.

Finland will be following in 2009-2010 the examples set by Belgium, Austria, France and Denmark in the publishing of authentic Legal Gazettes. Just like in Belgium and Austria, some paper copies of each legal gazette will be produced for archiving and accessibility.

3.3. CONCLUDING REMARKS

Finland has been among the first European countries to make legislation available free of charge on the Internet already in the 1990s. Furthermore, this approach has been complemented with a broader perspective, providing free access not only to legislation, but also to case law, collective agreements, parliamentary documents, secondary legislation and information on legislative projects. The Finnish way has emphasized the qualitative aspects of free access.

In the future development of free access, the needs of the users have to be analysed in detail. It is not clear that the user want to prioritize the access to authentic versions. Instead, they may want access to regularly updated and consolidated legislation in a plethora of ways (push and pull services, RSS, with lex alerts, etc.).

Appendix

Excerpts from the main legislative acts in Finland:

1. Finnish Constitution (731/1999)
Section 12 - Freedom of expression and right of access to information
Everyone has the freedom of expression. Freedom of expression entails the right to express, disseminate and receive information, opinions and other communications without prior prevention by anyone. More detailed provisions on the exercise of the freedom of expression are laid down by an Act. (...)

Documents and recordings in the possession of the authorities are public, unless their publication has for compelling reasons been specifically restricted by an Act. Everyone has the right of access to public documents and recordings.

2. Act on the Openness of Government Activities (621/1999)

Section 1 - Principle of openness

(1) Official documents shall be in the public domain, unless specifically otherwise provided in this Act or another Act. (. . .)

Section 2 - Scope of application

This Act contains provisions on the right of access to official documents in the public domain, officials' duty of non-disclosure, document secrecy and any other restrictions of access that are necessary for the protection of public or private interests, as well as on the duties of the authorities for the achievement of the objectives of this Act.

Section 3 - Objectives

The objectives of the right of access and the duties of the authorities provided in this Act are to promote openness and good practice on information management in government, and to provide private individuals and corporations with an opportunity to monitor the exercise of public authority and the use of public resources, (. . .).

3. Act on the Statutes of Finland (188/2000)

Section 11 - Languages of publication

(1) The Statutes of Finland and the Treaty Series shall be published in the Finnish and Swedish languages, unless otherwise provided in this Act.

(2) If a treaty is not authentic in either its Finnish or Swedish version, it shall also be published in at least one authentic language.

(3) Smi language translations of the statutes, treaties and the other instruments and communications referred to in this Act shall be published in The Statutes of Finland or the Treaty Series in accordance with the provisions of the Act on the Use of the Smi Language before Public Authorities (516/1991).

Section 12 - Format of publication

(1) The Statutes of Finland and the Treaty Series shall be published as printed bulletins.

(2) In addition, The Statutes of Finland and the Treaty Series shall be kept available to the public on an information network free of charge; they may also be published in record formats other than that referred to in paragraph (1) .

References

Hietanen, A. (2007), *Towards authenticity - publishing of electronic legal gazettes.*, in "25 years of European Law Online", Office for Official Publications of the EU, Luxembourg, pp. 97-128.

Nielsen, J. (1993), *Usability engineerings*, Academic Press, Boston MA.

Sarvilinna, S. (2006), *Finnish Law on the Internet.*, available at GlobaLex: <www.nyulawglobal.org/globalex/Finland.htm> (accessed 12 September 2008).

Free Access to Legislation in Denmark: Advantages in Inter-institutional Cooperation - Design and Production

Nina Koch

Departement of Civil Affairs, Ministry of Justice, Denmark

Abstract. The presentation will from a practical point of view give an overview of the advantages in the comprehensive cooperation between the Danish parliament (Folketinget) and the Ministry of Justice developing and operating the new production system for lovtidende.dk, the Official Journal online, and the legal information systems of the Folketing and the Danish state.

The Danish constitution states the separation of powers, but nevertheless the Folketing and the government since 1998 have cooperated in creating a common production system for legislation, where the work flow and user profiles reflects the separation of powers. Thus creating a very unique situation, where drafting, proof-reading, introduction, passing, promulgation, publication, end-user access is supported by one single system. No additional processing from other public bodies or private contractors is required to bring the passed bill or the promulgated act into the legal information systems.

One week before the opening of the new parliamentary session, on 2007, September 24, was our go-live with Lex Dania production. In the years before and during the development of the new system complex the inter-institutional cooperation secured a common document standard that meets all formal requirements in the legislative process (Lex Dania xml) , as well as a work flow that sustains the process from drafting a bill to promulgating the act.

Benefits of the cooperation in operating the legal information systems are numerous, but some of the most important are:

- A single system for production for all parties in the legislative process thus securing uniform and consistent data.
- Data capturing by legal experts
- A common document standard in XML facilitating presentation of data in different channels including the future electronic Hansard.

Vis-à-vis end users the cooperation secures a seamless integration of data from different sources.

1. Introduction

A few parameters combine to make it a lot easier to build legal information systems in Denmark[1] than in many other countries. We only have one language, and practically all primary and secondary legislation are national. Furthermore, we have a legislative tradition that supports proper administration of legislation, as every new act or statutory order will decide on its consequences by provisions on amending of and/or repealing current legislation.

---

[1] Greenland and the Faroe Islands have Home Rule. Though quite many subjects are regulated by national law, variations are often made, and national legislation that only are in force for Greenland and/or the Faroe Island are not included in Retsinformation. The origin for this decision was technical difficulties concerning different versions of the same acts in one system. Though one could argue that the basis for the decision has changed, the decision stands.

Retsinformation (translates directly into Legal Information) was established in 1985-1986 by the government. All primary and secondary legislation
end every treaty that was in force on 1985, January 1, were incorporated and
nothing has been removed ever since, but documents are marked as historical
as legislation are repealed.

The first – and probably the most important – strategic decision made by
the government was that datacapturing was established as part of the proces
of issuing legislation. When a bill is passed by the Folketing, the relevant
minister/ministry is responsible for presenting it for the Royal Assent – thus
becoming an act – for promulgating the act and since 1985 for publishing the
act plus the metadata concerning the act in Retsinformation. Exactly the same
goes for secondary legislation, so every civil servant in central administration[2]
know that if one issues delegated legislation or administrative orders, ones job
is not done, until document and metadata are available in Retsinformation.

The second very important strategic decision concerning Retsinformation
was made by the Folketing as an institution. It goes without saying that
Folketinget was not bound by the governmental decision concerning legislation. However, the Folketing decided to take on a similar obligation concerning
the legislative history behind the acts and have since 1985 uploaded the
legislative material, the Hansard and its annexes.

For a number of years Retsinformation was not successful, and the possibility that the legal information system in time would be a paying proposition
as originally expected was after nearly 10 years not even close. The reasons
were mainly the 3270 user interface, a rather difficult query language and the
pricing system based on use of time.

2. Close to All-in-One

Early in 1994 the government decided to call for tenders for a modernization
of Retsinformation. The decision also defined the framework for organisation
and economy and maintained important principles on content (totality in
legislation) and the obligation on all institutions in central administration to
publish every bit of legislation issued in Retsinformation.

During our work with the requirements specification the concept of a single
system to produce, organize and publish all legislation was born.

We realised that all the conditions for establishing a production system for
legislation that would support the legislative process from the first draft of
a bill made in a ministry through the parliamentary procedure to the Royal
Assent and transformation to an act were already present.

The organisation was there. The Ministry of Justice published both Lovtidende, our Official Journal, and Retsinformation. The government and the

---

[2] Alas, no similar decision was made concerning case law.

Folketing had a general contract with a private company concerning the production of legislation, which allowed us to decide on close to every "how to do" in production and publishing both on print and digital media.

The governmental responsibility for legislative technique lies with the Ministry of Justice and a close working relationship with the Office of Legal Services within the Folketing is a sine qua non. This and a teamwork of a more practical nature about Lovtidende and Retsinformation made the basis for a quite informal agreement that we should design a production system for legislation. From then and on the going got tough!

The short version is that the modernization project gave us our original database, BRS Search, on a mainframe, a client-server application with GUI and improved searching for end-users, fixed-price subscription and 3 years of very hard work on the production system.

In 1997 we skipped the client-server application and went onto the internet, and on August 28 the government decided to give access to Retsinformation free of charge from 2008.

And we were working on the production system. We build the backend with a textproduction application based on MS Word 6.0, 52 templates matching our 52 different doctypes and macros to match the Plagues of Egypt. Metadata, references, user administration, workflow etc was managed in a Oracle database using a tailor-made client, and in December 1998 we started production.

Since then all legislation are produced in our own production system either by the private contractor on behalf of the institutions or by the institutions themselves. The workflow allows government and the Folketing to pass data from one to another and back, and we only have one source whether we publish on print or digital media.

3. Lex Dania xml

The more they have the more they want. Working with the new system prompted a lot of ideas, what if's and wishes. Again, it was very easy to agree, as we were quite sure that we wanted to use xml in the production of legislation as soon as possible. The Ministry of Justice represented the legislative domain in the Danish xml committee under the Ministry of Science, Technology and Innovation, and the committee took part in the organisation of a new joint venture between the Ministry of Justice and the Folketing to create Lex Dania xml. Besides the obvious advantages in using the xml format in the production, the ambition was to be able to sustain the legislative technique in greater detail thus enhancing the quality of legislation and of data. We used lots of time and effort on this project, as we wanted to ensure that Lex Dania xml as far as possible could facilitate future developments of the production system, e.g. automatic consolidation of amended legislation.

The project was set up in 2002, and Lex Dania xml is the standard format in the production of Danish legislation since 2007, September 24.

4. lovtidende.dk

The governments duty to promulgate primary and secondary legislation is stated in the Constitution and the means has since 1871 been publishing in Lovtidende.

2004, on October 25 the Ministry of Justice decided to set up a committee on Lovtidende Online. The committee reported[3] one year later and recommended in unison that the Act on Lovtidende[4] should be amended to allow publication of Lovtidende electronically on the internet. The Bill[5] was presented 2005, December 12 and passed by the Folketing at the third reading 2006, March 30, and the Act[6] came into force on 2008, January 1, and from that day Danish legislation is promulgated on lovtidende.dk.

Access to lovtidende.dk is free of charge.

5. All in One

When the bill was passed by the Folketing, it was obvious that a new production system was compulsory, if we were to meet the standards set out in the act. An elderly close to all-in-on system is not enough to secure ePromulgation.

Our point of departure was the existing system that had established the chain of confidence,[7] given us a lot of experience and a great number of wishes to the new system – and an absolutely outdated platform. And if wishes were horses, beggars would ride. The keywords was reengineering, building the system on a sound platform, security, implementing Lex Dania xml, designing the process of promulgation and lovtidende.dk

We called for tenders, and the task was won by NNIT, a company with no knowledge or experience concerning the domain, and once again we went to work.

---

[3] Betænkning nr. 1464/2005.

[4] Lov om udgivelse af en Lovtidende og en Ministerialtidende, jf. lovbekendtgørelse nr. 608 af 24. juni 2008.

[5] LF 106 Forslag til lov om ændring af lov om udgivelsen af en Lovtidende og en Ministerialtidende. (Lovtidende i elektronisk form).

[6] Lov nr. 305 af 19. april 2006 om ændring af lov om udgivelsen af en Lovtidende og en Ministerialtidende (Lovtidende i elektronisk form).

[7] The number of subscriptions was diminishing from 1998 an on because end users had confidence in the information in the legal information system.

We faced every known challenge in this project, but our new contractor supplied organisation and people who were able to raise to the challenges – as were we - and the system complex was build within the stipulated limits of time and cost.

And now we have got Lex Dania production consisting of a drafting environment, Lex Dania converter and Lex Dania client.

Lex Dania client is the central component in the production system. It controls users, workflow – including the process of promulgation – metadata and every piece of rules and logic, we built into the backend.

It is an important improvement that Lex Dania client is the best ever to create and maintain the complex relations between legal documents due to advanced algorithms controlling and processing both active and passive relations to other documents according to legal definitions.

Our users are very satisfied with the new client and especially that it is possible to see previews of the document in html- and pdf-versions before one release it for publishing.

Lex Dania client is the user interface of the backend, and the technical platform is a client/server application with a SQL database and a client in .Net 2.0 and Click once for seamless deployment. Communication is secured with VPN to allow confidentiality on the Internet. It is basically a reengineering of the existing application, but we got a lot of nice stuff and in places some gold-plating.

The drafting environment is for the time being[8] also partly reengineering. We updated our existing editor to MS Word 2003 now with only 44 templates matching 44 Lex Dania schemas.

Lex Dania converter is a separate module servicing Lex Dania client, our online web validator and desktop converter. The conversion is rule based with post processing using an intermediate format ODF via OpenOffice.

After the final touch in Lex Dania client the documents are in the hands of a tailor-made service layer that controls consistent publishing to the different media.

We publish directly to lovtidende.dk/ministerialtidende.dk and retsinformation.dk, and pushes data to Web of the Folketing, RSS-feeds and a web service (free of charge) used by private publishers for reuse purposes.

retsinformation.dk is the legal information system that contains the documents in html-format and with all the additional information, we supply. The new website is designed according to current web usability conventions thus better facilitating access to law for lay users.

lovtidende.dk is the means of promulgation, and the process of promulgation has become more effective, that is more controlled, faster and cheaper. For example was a huge piece of primary legislation on the recent financial

---

[8] A prototype of a dedicated xml editor, Lex Dania editor, will be tested by the Ministry of Justice, the Folketing and 1-2 institutions in central administration during 2009.

crisis introduced to the Folketing and got the first reading Wednesday, second and third reading was Friday, the Royal Assent later the same day and Friday evening the Act was promulgated and coming into force Saturday at 00:00 according to its own provisions.

ministerialtidende.dk is a clone of lovtidende.dk and used for ministerial orders etc.

With Lex Dania production the Folketing and the Danish government have obtained a unique instrument, where civil servants can draft legislation guided by a set of drafting rules i.e. Lex Dania xml and immediately preview the document and send it further on in the work flow.

But not only do we have a solution, but both the Folketing and the government have acquired a platform with many possibilities. Most recently the Folketing has decided stop printing the Hansard, and a substantial part of the work has all ready been done in Lex Dania production. A foreseen project is a tool both supporting consolidation of amendments to bills and acts, where the comprehensive inter-institutional cooperation once again hopefully will prove it's worth.

Free Access to Legislation in Italy: The Role of Standards for the Integration of Information Systems

Caterina Lupo
National Centre for ICT in the Public Administrations (CNIPA), Italy

Abstract. Nowadays Internet is the most effective means to deliver information on demand. Its spread relies on the adoption of shared conventions to represent information, i.e. open standards to identify and expose content accessible through non proprietary software tools. Resources belonging to a specific domain usually present relations and structural and semantic peculiarities. Representing these peculiarities through open standards allows to automatically connect such resources detecting a thematic sub-net within the web. Based on these considerations, in order to achieve integration among different and independent legislative data bases and to automate legislation life-cycle workflow, standards for the identification and representation in XML of legislative resources have been defined within the project "Normeinrete" and then adopted among others also by Normattiva program.

Keywords: XML, URI, URN, standard, legislation in force, interoperability.

1. ICT for legislation: objectives and lines of action

1.1. GENERAL OBJECTIVES

In the last years several initiatives have been undertaken in Italy by public administrations in order to improve the efficacy in processing electronic legislative documents. These initiatives rely on a strategic view aimed at achieving three main objectives, that are

1. making completely effective citizens' rights to access public sector information concerning legislation through tportals delivering on line services;
2. support public administration in order to conduct more efficiently internal processes related to law production and publication;
3. creating a technological framework in order to move towards a completely paperless process, embracing all the stages from the early ones concerning drafting to the legally official gazzette publication on line.

1.2. LINES OF ACTION

In order to achieve the general objectives listed in the previous paragraph, CNIPA activities address several aspects through specific lines of action concerning:

   content, since, obviously, the quality of any service that relies on information depends upon the quality of information itself. Therefore it is clear that quality of electronic legislative documents has to be defined and measured with respect to a set of specific parameters significant for achieving desired results (i.e. completeness, precise transposition of paper official publication, corrige handling, etc.);

organization, considering that moving towards paperless processes within public administration has considerable impacts on the organization, thus requiring processes reengineering, sensibilization, training;

on-line services, being the means to deliver services to fulfil citizens rights, offering when possible advanced search and retrieval functionalities exploiting opportunities to deal with semantics;

cooperation, among information systems, considering the molteplicity of institutional entities involved in law production at different levels, with respect to primary or secondary legislation or to the geographical level.

The last line of action will be described more in depth in the following sections.

2. Standardization

Internet spread relies on the adoption of shared conventions to represent information, i.e. open standards to identify and expose content accessible through non proprietary software tools. Internet nodes (web sites) are easily reached by users through self-explanatory names (www.domainname) hiding the cryptic IP addresses that actually identify the resources. Content are published using an open standard language (HTML) that can be easily interpreted by browsers and delivered to users according to the presentation characteristics set by the author. Unambiguously identification and meaningful content representation can be seen as key factors to make information really usable.

Resources belonging to a specific domain usually present relations and structural and semantic peculiarities. Representing these peculiarities through open standards allows to automatically connect such resources and detect a thematic sub-net within the web. Based on these considerations, in order to achieve integration among different and independent legislative data bases and to automate legislation life-cycle workflow, two standards for the identification and representation in XML of legislative resources have been defined.

The first one concerns a unique identification mechanism for the norms, regardless of the physical address, the second one concerns XML mark-up. The standard have been defined within ad hoc working groups in which major PA and research institutions have taken part. The standards have been issued as national technical norms by CNIPA and published as regulatory acts in the Italian Official Journal. The definitions make use of IETF Uniform Resource Names (URNs) (RFC 2141) and eXtensible Mark-up Language (XML W3C) standards.

2.1. Uniform Resource Name (URN)

Each law contains several references to other laws. The whole legislative corpus can be seen as a net, in which each law is a node linking, and linked by, several other nodes through natural language expressions. Manual activity is required in order to build the hypertext of a distributed legislative corpus by means of the usual web link mechanism, based on the physical address of the linked document. Such activity is carried out through the following steps:

1. recognize in the source document the text containing a significant reference to another norm;
2. find the physical address (i.e., URL Uniform Resource Locator) of the resource corresponding to the referred document;
3. insert the URL address of the document to be linked, in the appropriate location within the source document, according to HTML syntax.

The hyperlink mechanism based on URL is inefficient with respect to the following problems:

1. the availability, at a certain time, of more than one resources corresponding to the norm referred to;
2. the need to discover the physical address(es) of the resource(s) to be linked;
3. the variability of such address(es);
4. impossibility to identify resources not yet published on the web or whose physical address is not known.

The disadvantages arising from the URL based approach include the significant editorial work that must be carried out before publishing a document and the subsequent continuous activities needed to prevent or to limit broken links. The uniform resource name (URN) is intended to enable persistent, location-independent, resource identification mechanism. The adoption of a scheme based on URNs allows to build an automated distributed hypertext, according to a model similar to the DNS (Domain Name System) used to resolve the self-explaining web sites names into numerical IP addresses. The opportunity to build such hypertext automatically relies on the following considerations:

1. the natural language expressions that refer to a norm usually contain repetitive patterns, making references automatically detectable;
2. the URN is built by combining data (almost) always included in the reference;

indexing process can collect the information needed to build the cross reference between each URN and the list of corresponding URLs, to be used for the resolution service. The URNs are defined as a combination of elements according to a specific grammar. The basic elements are the name of the promulgating authority, type of norm, date, number and a set of more detailed specifications when needed.

The grammar satisfies the following requirements:

1. each URN univocally identifies a norm and can distinguish different versions due to subsequent modifications;
2. the rules are easy, unambiguous and self-explanatory;
3. the URNs can be built automatically.

The grammar for building URNs adopts the Backus-Naur form.

2.2. DOCUMENT TYPE DEFINITION (DTD) OF ITALIAN LEGISLATIVE ACTS

XML representation of legislative documents has been adopted with the aim to improve effectiveness in managing , publishing and retrieving norms. NiR has defined specific Document Type Definition (DTD) and correspondent XML Schema for Italian legislation, considering the peculiarity of legislative documents structure, metadata representation and other significant information useful to provide additional functions. The availability of documents with XML mark-up according to shared XML language definitions allows the creation of advanced search and retrieval functions operating on heterogeneous data bases effectively. Other opportunities provided by standardized XML mark-up are, for example, the standard URN exploitation and the semi-automatic creation of legislation in force at any given date. Italian legislative and regulatory acts can be divided into three categories:

1. documents with a well-defined structure (i.e. laws, constitutional laws, regional laws, etc.);
2. documents partially structured (i.e. regulation act, decrees, etc);
3. generic documents (i.e. any kind of non-structured acts, enclosures, annexes, etc).

In order to avoid a proliferation of DTDs/schemata for each type of legislative document, it has been considered more convenient the definition of a single language containing many elements capable to represent all the types of documents. Throughout the years, the structural and stylistic principles, which the documents should conform to, have changed. Therefore, the whole Italian legislative corpus includes documents with significant variations in the structure.

The mark-up elements have been defined keeping into account several kind of information, concerning structure and semantic. They have been conceived in order to support not only searching and publishing, but also to support consolidation activities. The elements can be classifed into structural elements, special elements and metadata elements. Structural elements are used to identify the parts in which the document is structured (heading, preamble, articles, paragraphs, etc.). Special elements identify meaningful parts of the text in the legal context, (for instance references to other laws) or associating a formatted representation to text-embedded relevant entities (institutions, dates, places). Finally, metadata elements contain metadata information on the norm (for instance subject-matter classification, publication data, other documentation connected to enacting process, etc.).

3. National programs: Normeinrete e Normattiva

The Normeinrete project (NiR) aims to improve accessibility to legislation by providing a unique point of access to existing Italian and European Union legal documents published on different web sites through a specialized portal.[1]

The portal runs a search engine that operates homogeneously on distributed data sources. Its full-text search index is selectively built detecting only legislative documents. The federative approach relies on a distributed architecture that, due to the standards, allows to preserve independence of the participating systems while assuring complete interoperability and an unique search user interface.

The Normattiva project aims at providing free access to *in-force* version of national law and to support processes from the early stages till the official publication.

The main issues that have been identified in order to fulfill these objectives are the following: *(i)* making available over the Internet the in-force version of the primary Italian legislative corpus, by means of specialized document management systems; *(ii)* studying legislative drafting and classification problems and testing software products to simplify these tasks; *(iii)* designing and implementing a cooperative system to support exchanges of electronic documents among the institutions involved in the law production process.

This program has adopted the standards previously described, thus assuring interoperability with other legislative data base (i.e. at regional level) and with the Normeinrete portal, as shown in figure 1.

4. Conclusion

The projects illustrated in this paper involve all the main Italian institutions. They have an high level commitment, and thus gives high national visibility and raises the level of expectations. We underline that all the projects have

---

[1] See: <www.nir.it>.

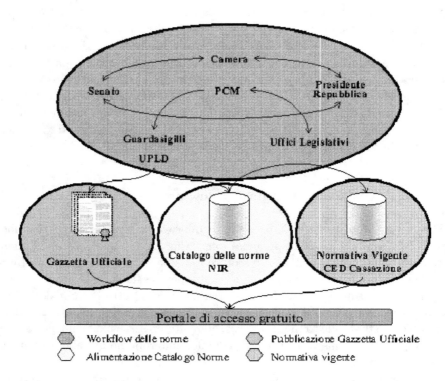

Figure 1. Final Architecture

a fundamental element in common: the NormeinRete standards. The standards adoption guarantees interoperability between this program and other independent initiatives, both public and private open to the implementation of the european directive on Public Sector Information reuse.

Free Access to Legal Information in Switzerland

Michel Moret
Centre for Official Publications, Swiss Federal Chancellery, Switzerland

Abstract. The contribution give a general overview of the institutions concerned by this issue at the federal and cantonal levels and of the systems used to offer such kinds of access. It will also provide information about the E-Government initiatives in this area and about the trends in new projects.

Keywords: Switzerland, official publications, e-government.

1. Switzerland – a State of diversity and federalism

Switzerland's 26 cantons are the federal states of the Swiss Confederation. For historical and geographical reasons, they differ widely: the largest canton (Graubünden/Grisons) has 192 times the area of the smallest (Basel-Stadt) but fewer inhabitants, while Canton Zurich has around 80 times more inhabitants than Canton Appenzell Innerrhoden.

Bern is the seat of the federal authorities, while the country's economic centres are its three global cities, Geneva, Basel and, above all, Zürich.

German (63.7%),[1] French (20.4%), Italian (6.5%) and Romansh (0.5%) are the 4 official languages.

Each canton normally has only one official language, either French, German or Italian. 4 cantons have 2 or 3 official languages:

- Fribourg and Valais: French (majority) and German

- Bern: German (majority) and French

- Graubünden: German (majority), Romansh and Italian

As far as the law is concerned, Switzerland has 27 different legal systems in various languages, i.e. one federal system and 26 cantonal systems.

---

[1] Federal Statistical Office, Swiss Population Census 2000.

2. Current situation in Switzerland

2.1. AT FEDERAL LEVEL

The Publications Act[2] approved by Parliament and the Publications Ordinance[3] approved by the Federal Council define what (content) and how
(quality and access) federal legislation has to be published. The Centre for
Official Publications within the Swiss Federal Chancellery is responsible for
the publication of federal legislation in 3 official languages (German, French
and Italian).

The three main products, the Official Federal Gazette,[4] the Official Compilation of Federal Legislation[5] and the Classified Compilation of Federal
Legislation[6] (consolidated versions) are available in print, offline and, for the
past 10 years, online versions. Online versions are free of charge,[7] but the
print and offline versions are available in return for a subscription fee, which
covers only a small part of the publication costs.

Only the printed versions of the Official Federal Gazette and the Official Compilation of Federal Legislation are legally binding. The number of
subscriptions is decreasing each year and is currently around 2000.

Consolidated versions are no longer legally binding (having been legally
binding until 1986). Despite this, they are the most used and consulted: the
consolidated online version has some 450,000 visitors every day, while the
online version of the Official Federal Gazette and of the Official Compilation
of Federal Legislation has around 10 times fewer.

2.1.1. *The Official Federal Gazette*
The Official Federal Gazette publishes:

- reports and documents submitted by the Federal Council to Parliament,
  in particular bills relating to new laws or decrees and related explanatory
  reports known as "dispatches";
- decrees and laws adopted by the parliament which may or must be subject
  to a referendum;
- decisions of the Swiss Federal Chancellery on the preliminary examination
  of popular initiatives and on the success or failure of requests for popular
  initiatives or referendums;
- federal decrees on the results of popular votes, with the full results for
  each canton;

---

[2] Act of 18 June 2004: <www.admin.ch/ch/f/rs/c170_512.html>.

[3] Ordinance of 17 November 2004, available at: <www.admin.ch/ch/f/rs/c170_512_1.
html>.

[4] Available at: <www.admin.ch/ch/i/ff>.

[5] Available at: <www.admin.ch/ch/i/as>.

[6] Available at: <www.admin.ch/ch/i/rs>.

[7] Article 19, paragraph 2 of the law.

- reports on elections to Parliament, with the full results for each canton;
- decisions of federal authorities (administration or courts) if the recipients are not precisely defined or if they cannot be reached by mail;
- directives of the Federal Council.

The Official Federal Gazette has been published since 1849 in German and French. Since 1918, it has also been published in Italian. For almost 10 years now, each weekly edition has been made available on the Internet. Thanks to a retro-digitalisation project in collaboration with the Swiss Federal Archives, all editions dating back to 1849 are also available on the Internet in German and French, and all the Italian editions since 1971 as well.

Publication in the Official Federal Gazette triggers the following legal effects:

- the period allowed to appeal against decisions begins;
- the period begins for collecting the signatures needed to force a referendum against new federal legislation (100 days, 50,000 signatures) or to force a popular initiative for a change in the Federal Constitution (18 months, 100,000 signatures).

The Official Federal Gazette has also a major influence on the application of the law, because Federal Council dispatches represent a principal source for the interpretation of the laws.

2.1.2. *The Official Compilation of Federal Legislation*

The Official Compilation of Federal Legislation contains all the legislation that is currently in force, as well as amendments to the following legislative instruments:

- the Federal Constitution and cantonal constitutions;
- federal acts and ordinances;
- federal decrees if they are subject to an optional referendum, if they ratify international treaties or if Parliament decides that they have to be published;
- international treaties, agreements and decisions. EU directives, regulations, etc., that may be implemented in their existing form under national or international law are not published verbatim: only the title and a reference to the publication concerned in the Official Journal of the European Union are published. More help is offered under the form of an online compilation[8] of the EU Law relevant to the bilateral agreements of 1999 and 2004;
- agreements between Confederation and cantons.

---

[8] Article 25, Publications Ordinance.

The Official Compilation of Federal Legislation has been published every week since 1849 in German, French and Italian. Since 1998, it has also been published weekly online.

Legislative instruments are published at least 5 days before they come into force.[9] If this is not possible, the law provides for an emergency procedure.[10]

2.1.3. *The Classified Compilation of Federal Legislation*

The Classified Compilation of Federal Legislation is published in French, German and Italian. The online version is updated constantly, while the printed and offline versions are updated 4 times a year.

The Classified Compilation is a consolidated version, classified by subject, of the legislation, international treaties and agreements between Confederation and cantons currently in force that have been published in the Official Compilation, together with the Federal Constitution and cantonal constitutions.

The Classified Compilation represents the current state of the legislation, which is continually evolving.

It was created in its current form in 1966, based on a loose-leaf folder system, which replaced the old Classified Compilation of Act and Ordinances that had been in force from 1848 to 1947.

Relevant international legislation was published until 2001. Since 1998, the texts have been available online.

Today the Classified Compilation contains around 4,400 legislative instruments, totalling 60,000 pages, in each official language.

The Classified Compilation was legally binding from 1974 to 1986. When the law was revised in 1986, Parliament decided that it could no longer be binding due to the loose-leaf folder system. 12 years later, the Classified Compilation is also published on the internet and this form is the most used!

2.2. AT CANTONAL LEVEL

The Federal Constitution[11] requires the cantons to implement federal law in accordance with its provisions and the provisions of federal legislation,[12] but also states that the Confederation should allow the Cantons all possible discretion to organise their own affairs and take account of cantonal particularities.[13]

This means that the cantons can organise the publication of their legislation as they want and that each canton has its own law on what must be published and its own specific ICT solution.

---

[9] Article 7, paragraph 1 Publications Act.
[10] Article 7, paragraph 3 Publications Act.
[11] Available at: <www.admin.ch/ch/e/rs/101/>.
[12] Article 46, paraprah 1 of the Federal Constitution.
[13] Article 46, paragraph 3 of the Federal Constitution.

Nevertheless, in keeping with the system at federal level, each Canton has in its official languages its own classified compilations of its legislation (consolidated versions) and either its official gazette and/or its official compilation, in which the changes in the cantonal legislation are published regularly (normally weekly).

Consulting the online versions of the compilations of cantonal legislations is also free of charge and print versions are normally subject to subscription fee defined by the Canton.

2.3. SUMMARY

Switzerland has to manage some 25,000 legislative instruments in various languages at federal and cantonal levels.

Despite its complexity and diversity, the law in Switzerland is freely accessible to any member of the public who has internet access.

In addition, there is online access, most free, to the decisions of the federal and many cantonal courts in order to keep up-to-date on how the law is being applied.

3. The portal to Swiss legislation – <www.LexFind.ch>

3.1. AN INTERESTING INITIATIVE TO GIVE FREE ACCESS TO THE LAW

This portal was created and is hosted by the Institute of Federalism[14] at the University of Fribourg, based on an initiative and sponsorship from the Conference of Directors of the Cantonal Departments of Justice and Police.[15]

The current version of the database has been online since April 2007. The database is updated every day and gives access to federal and cantonal legislation.

The user interface is available in German, French, Italian and English.

The index search is only possible in German, French and Italian:

— is based on around 150 Keywords on important legal topics;
— results are independent of the language of the search;
— if the text exists in the language being search, it will be displayed in this language;
— if not, it will be displayed in one of the official languages.

A full text search is possible in German, French and Italian: only results which have the word in the language being search are displayed – no cross-language results.

---

[14] Available at: <www.federalism.ch>.
[15] Available at: <www.kkjpd.ch>.

A professional search engine and a special page for each canton with direct links to the cantonal databases and web sites are also available.

Results are displayed either in PDF or in HTML, depending on the local systems at federal or cantonal levels.

3.2. AN ALTERNATIVE VIEW THROUGH THE SWISS PORTAL <WWW.CH.CH>

The website <www.ch.ch> is one of the successful initiatives under the E-Government Strategy at federal level approved by the Federal Council in 2002.

This Strategy was revised in January 2007 for the period 2007-2010 and expanded to an E-Government Strategy for Switzerland.[16]

The portal provides the public easy access to information from the federal, cantonal and municipal administrations and also allows people to do more and more business with these administrations online.

The portal also gives access to Swiss legislation based on the Lexfind Database.

This alternative access give two search options:

- full text search;
- selective search on the basis of about 80 topics spread over 9 different areas. These topics are consistent with the logic of the Swiss Portal and are different from those on LexFind's own portal. They are available not only in French, German and Italian, but also in English.

4. Trends for the future

4.1. THE NEW ICT SYSTEM FOR THE CENTRE FOR OFFICIAL PUBLICATIONS

The new ICT System project for the Official Publications Centre is now underway. It should be completed by the middle of 2010.

Beside the internal goals, such as optimisation of processes, facilities for editing new or existing laws, reductions in publication time, etc., this project will offer some benefits as far as free access to the law is concerned:

- it should be possible to compare laws at article level not only in the various languages, but also to navigate between the current version of each law and its previous versions or a future version that has been approved by Parliament but has yet to come into in force in order to see the changes;

---

[16] Available at: <www.isb.admin.ch/themen/strategien/00071/index.html?lang=en>.

— the new system should also offer solutions in relation to integrity and authenticity (e.g. electronic signatures) to compensate for the fact that consolidated versions are currently not legally binding and will not be legally binding for the new few years because there is currently no political will to change the Publication Act, which has only recently come into force;

— the new system should offer rapid accessibility to changes in consolidated versions, such as RSS-Feeds.

4.2. The "access to legislation" project in the e-government strategy 2007-2010 for Switzerland[17]

The goal of this project is that the law (legislation, decisions, etc.) at all levels of federalism is made available in uniform structures and is free to all.

This will reduce the time that the target groups spend searching and the time the authorities spend providing information to the public.

It is a very ambitious and difficult project due to the complexity and diversity of the current federal and cantonal systems, but a very important project for the community.

This project is at its very beginning and should offer its first results at the end of 2010.

Interested participants in and sponsors of this project are the Conference of Directors of the Cantonal Departments of Justice and Police,[18] the Swiss Federal Chancellery,[19] in particular the Centre for Official Publications, the Federal Office of Justice,[20] the Institute for Federalism[21] and the Swiss Association for Legal Information Technology.[22]

5. Conclusion

Free access to the law in Switzerland is already a reality, while at the same time a major challenge for the future.

---

[17] Available at: <www.isb.admin.ch/themen/egovernment>.
[18] Available at: <www.kkjpd.ch>.
[19] Available at: <www.bk.admin.ch>.
[20] Available at: <www.bj.admin.ch>.
[21] Available at: <www.federalism.ch>.
[22] Available at: <www.svri.ch>.

Free Access to Legal and Legislative Information: The Austrian Approach

Günther Schefbeck
Austrian Parliamentary Administration, Austria

Abstract.
The postulate of the Codex Justinianus in accordance to which "leges ab omnibus intellegi debent" has been implemented within the Austrian legal system, too. It has, however, been recognized that the amount of norms as well as the normative language makes it difficult for the citizens to know and "understand" the laws in force. The Constitutional Court, in its standing judicature, has established minimum qualitative demands on structure and language of laws. The quantity of laws is, however, continuously growing; legal informatics, in the past decades, has started to be a retention pond for the "flood of norms". Since legal and legislative information was first made available through the Internet by the responsible organs of the Republic of Austria, in particular by the Federal Chancellery and by the Parliamentary Administration, free access has been granted. The focus of legal informatics, meanwhile, is slowly shifting from information management to knowledge management.

Keywords: Law, legislation, legal information, legislative information, legal informatics, Internet.

1. The rule of law, and the transparency of law

With regard to the publication of laws, the Austrian Constitutional Court states in its classical decision, collection no. 3130/1956:

"The provisions of art. 49 and 97 of the Federal Constitution on the publication of the laws are based on the rule-of-law principle of the publicity of legal content. From this ensues the obligation of the legislature to clearly and exhaustively make known to the public the content of its legal enactments".

From this decision, which has become standing judicature (cf., e.g., collection no. 13.740), several different conclusions may be derived:

— First of all, the publication of laws is to be interpreted as an emanation and necessary implication of the rule of law, which, as a basic principle of the modern European state model, which in the past century has spread out all over the world, is being observed in a wide variety of different legal systems, and may be seen as their common denominator.

— Above that, the publication requirement would not be restricted to the laws being put in force but also include the legal enactments made by the legislatures. Thus, whereas publication of laws in most normative systems falls within the competence and responsibility of executive bodies, there is already a liability of the legislative bodies to make accessible to the public their enactments, in advance of the formal promulgation of the laws.

— Finally, and this is to be mentioned with exclusive regard to the Austrian constitutional system, by referring the publication of laws to the rule-of-law principle of the Austrian Federal Constitution, the Constitutional Court declares it part of the most sublime layer of Austrian positive law, namely of the constitutional principles that may be amended by referendum only.

The Austrian Federal Constitution refers to the publication of federal laws in art. 49 para. 1: "Federal laws ... shall be published by the Federal Chancellor in the Federal Law Gazette. Unless explicitly provided otherwise, they enter into force with expiry of the day of their publication, and apply to the entire federal territory ...". Thus, the entry into force of federal laws is construed as being a direct consequence of their publication. The other way round, in accordance with the judicature of the Constitutional Court, incomplete publication of a federal law would make it contradictory to the Constitution and would have the consequence of the respective law being rescinded by the Constitutional Court.

Para. 3 of the above-mentioned article carries on: "Publications in the Federal Law Gazette ... must be accessible to the public and obtainable in the form of publication completely and permanently". This provision, which in its present wording goes back to the Federal Law on the Reform of Promulgation (FLG I no. 100/2003), refers to the principle of accessibility as the very concept of publication, and it implicitly refers to the new means of electronic publication by defining the quality criteria to be met by publication using these media.

In a historical perspective, official publication of laws as a necessary condition for them entering into force rests on a tradition going back to antiquity, but in its present form of the "law gazette" is a relatively young achievement, as a theoretical concept and demand going back to the age of enlightenment, in practice mostly going back to the 19th century. Enlightened legal philosophers, but even legal practitioners, throughout the 18th century argued that the unsystematic ways of making laws known to the public, e.g. by having them read from the pulpit, were at least inefficient, if not principally preventing laws from being effective. But it was only the French Revolution that introduced the "Bulletin des lois" as the official and uniform publication media for laws, and it yet took several decades until other Europeans countries took over the concept (Ruppert, 1999).

In Austria, it was also a revolution that had to take place before an official publication organ for the laws was created. Though already since 1780 there had been the Judicial Law Collection, and since 1790 the Political Law Collection, both being official collections of the laws in force but not media for promulgating laws with binding effect, only in 1849, after and as a consequence of the revolution of 1848, the Imperial Law Gazette and the Provincial Law Gazettes were introduced as the official and exclusive publication media for laws. From that day, in Austria, too, the publication of laws was constitutive for them entering into force (Lukas, 1903).

The enlightened principle of publication of laws in print instead of reading them out unsystematically, in combination with alphabetisation of the people, had an important consequence, so to say the contrarius actus of publication, namely the possibility to legally establish the fiction of the laws being known by the public. Thus, section 2 of the Austrian Civil Code of 1811 (which is still in force) states: "Once a law has been appropriately promulgated, nobody may plead it has not become known to him". Likewise, section 9 para. 2 of the Penal Code of 1974 lays down that "someone who has missed to make oneself acquaint with the respective provisions ... is to be blamed for a legal error". This, of course, is a legal fiction. Thus, e.g., the Administrative Court has ruled that the validity of a regulation is not dependent on whether the subject of the regulation has in reality taken note of it (collection no. 8181 A). It is only this fiction that would allow efficient law enforcement.

On the other hand, it will always remain an issue to be seriously reflected upon what the classical rule according to which "leges ... intellegi ab omnibus debent" (Cod. Just. 1, 14, 9), would really mean. Three possible meanings have been identified:

- The laws are to be understood by the people subject to them, which would imply they are known.
- The laws are to be understandable to the people subject to them.
- The laws are to be appropriate to be substantially accepted by the people subject to them.

The first of these possible meanings would directly refer to the principle of the publication of laws. The second one would establish an elementary demand on legislative drafting, in particular on the quality of legal language. The third meaning, at last, would establish a connection to the basic issue of the legitimacy of the legal system, and thereby to the legitimatization of legislation.

2. The legitimacy of law, and the transparency of legislation

Proceeding from a view that identifies the political system as a sub-system of the societal system, we have to ask the question about the function of the former within the latter. Proceeding from the assumption that every system's primary function is its own stabilization, we can assume that its sub-systems are serving the same purpose. In this perspective, we can (with Luhmann) see the contribution of the political system to stabilization of the societal system in providing legitimation for the binding decisions that have to be made in order to ensure the framework of communication and interaction of the society's members. In modern societies, these rules usually would be established in the form of laws. In modern democratic societies, these laws usually would be enacted by Parliaments.

We can further assume that democratic legitimization of law-making is based on two concepts, namely that of representation (Kelsen, 1929) and that of "deliberative politics", which may be defined as the "interplay of the public sphere based on civil society with the institutionalised structures of opinion-making and decision-making in the parliamentary complex" (Habermas, 1992, p. 448). If by use of these concepts it can be ensured that the regulations established within a society would enjoy acceptance with its members, then the political system has completed its mission to stabilize society by producing legitimation.

It has been observed that there is a high correlation between the acceptance decisions are finding and the way, or rather the procedure in which they were produced; this is what Luhmann calls "legitimization by procedure". If a decision is made by the competent body in accordance with the appropriate procedural rules, it has the chance to be accepted even by those who would not be in line with the notion of the decision. If therefore a law is enacted by a Parliament elected in accordance with the electoral rules, and if Parliament has issued this enactment in accordance with the procedural rules to be applied, the law has a high chance to be considered legitimate. If in the process of legislation civil society has been involved, if at least the organised interests have been heard, and if there is at least a procedure for processing the opinions uttered, legitimacy enjoyed by the outcome of the legislative process is considered to be even much stronger.

In order to make procedure provide legitimation, however, procedure must not be a "black box" but has to be what might be called "transparent". In the words of Oberreuter, "transparency of the parliamentary procedure is func-tionally serving the inter-dependency of the (relatively) autonomous spheres of political communication, which is a basic requirement of democracy" (Ober-reuter, 1986, p. 73). Only if the spheres of political communication are ensured their inter-dependency, only if the processes of decision-making and opinion-making are overlapping, and, at least, only if it is evident that the formal requirements of the decision-making process are observed, legitimation can be obtained for the outcome of the decision-making process.

Parliamentary transparency, since the 19th century, has been based on three columns:

— public access to parliamentary proceedings;
— written documentation of parliamentary proceedings;

– mass media coverage of parliamentary proceedings.

The Internet revolution has affected all these instruments substantially:

– Public access to parliamentary proceedings no longer requires presence in person, trough live audio and/or video streaming.
– Written documentation of parliamentary proceedings no longer requires to be consulted in libraries, through parliamentary business made available via the Internet.
– Mass media coverage of parliamentary proceedings is conveyed electronically, too.

Generally, the new information and communication technologies today are allowing a much easier access to legislative information than ever before. Parliamentary websites have got an information broker function for legislative information, providing not only easy but in many cases even customized or customizable access. Nevertheless, there still remains a gap between the vast amounts of information on parliamentary business and proceedings available on parliamentary websites, and the more and more reductionist coverage of parliamentary proceedings in the mass media.

3. Free access to legislative information

After having started to electronically support parliamentary information management in the early 1990s, the Austrian Parliament entered the Internet era on 22 November 1996, when its website was launched. Today, only the Internet site[1] is hosting more than 200,000 pages (there is, of course, also an intranet site providing the internal users with even much more information).

To be able to provide the public with those amounts of information without any delay, it needs an architecture based on automatic generation of web pages out of the databases being located in the background, in which the information is processed. This background infrastructure consists of six core applications, among which the application "Parliamentary Business" is to process all kinds of information on parliamentary business and proceedings (except EU documents, which are processed in an application of their own). When the legislative process was analyzed in order to be able to model it in the application, more than 1000 different process steps were identified and defined. Based on this analysis done for sake of information management, it was easy to add workflow components to the application when in 2001 the Federal Chancellery together with the Parliamentary Administration started the "E-Law" project that was to develop a system to electronically support the whole process of law-making.

---

[1] Available at: <www.parlament.gv.at>.

Already since 1996, all parliamentary business have been made electronically available to the public, thus enhancing transparency of the parliamentary process as well as the opportunities for the public to get involved. Above that, since 1999 the documents of the pre-parliamentary consultation procedure that draft government bills are undergoing have been electronically available on the parliamentary website as well; this was even more a contribution to legislative transparency, since until then these documents (draft bills as well as comments) had not been accessible to the public even on paper.

4. Free access to legal information

Since 1849, as mentioned above, authentic publication of laws in Austria has been in a print Law Gazette, though, of course, on the ground of legal provisions undergoing some changes. The last major change was issued in the Federal Law on the Federal Law Gazette of 1996 (FLG no. 660/1996), by which the Federal Law Gazette was given a new structure consisting of three series for (roughly spoken) laws, ordinances, and state treaties, resp.

The Federal Law Gazette was obtainable from the State Printing Office, on a subscription basis as well as by purchase of single pieces. Altogether, about 6000 copies of the Federal Law Gazette were printed, a number that had been decreasing over the years. There were, of course, some individuals, mostly lawyers, subscribing for the Federal Law Gazette, but most people were restricted in their access to the Federal Law Gazette by being bound to public libraries and municipal offices.

This situation has fundamentally changed. It is true, the primary motivation for introducing authentic electronic promulgation of federal laws was finding a way to save money, namely the considerable printing costs for the Federal Law Gazette. That was why in 2001 the "E-Law" project was initiated, in the course of which, by joint effort of the Federal Chancellery and the Parliamentary Administration, the electronic workflow system was established that was the prerequisite for having the Federal Law Gazette authentically published in electronic form.

The Federal Law on the Reform of Promulgation (FLG I n. 100/2003) provided for authentic electronic promulgation of the federal laws from 1 January 2004 on (Eberhard, 2003; Laurer, 2004). In accordance with section 6 of the new Federal Law on the Federal Law Gazette 2004 (art. 4 of the above-mentioned act), this is to be done within the framework of the Legal Information System of the Federal Chancellery. Section 7 defines the URL at which the Federal Law Gazette is to be published,[2] and section 8 defines the criteria to be met in order to safeguard the authenticity and integrity of the documents published in the electronic Federal Law Gazette: In accordance

---

[2] Available at: <www.ris.bka.gv.at>.

with these criteria, and the state of the art, the file format chosen is XML, and the files are electronically signed. It may be mentioned that in the five years past no violation of the integrity of a federal law electronically published has been noticed.

Section 9, at last, entitles anyone to freely and without prove of identity access the Federal Law Gazette, and make printouts free of charge. Besides, non-authentic printouts may still be purchased, which, of course, is a service meanwhile rarely demanded. Besides the authentic XHTML representation bearing the electronic signature, three additional non-authentic electronic versions of the Federal Law Gazette are offered on the same site, to make possible different ways of re-use and further processing, namely a PDF, an HTML and an RTF version.

Having in mind that, according to recent polls, about 71% of the Austrian population older than 14 years are using the Internet (Integral, Austrian Internet Monitor-Consumer, Q2/08), and that about 69% of the Austrian households have Internet access (Eurostat, STAT/08/169), the shift not only in quantity but even in quality of free access to legal information achieved through authentic electronic promulgation becomes evident: In the former paper environment, there was, on an average, one copy of the Federal Law Gazette for more than 1300 people. Free access was possible but coupled with some trouble and investment of time, as well as restrictions in availability. Today, an Internet connection will do.

However, we have to be aware that even before this wide-scale free access to the authentic federal laws was created, people were enjoying free access to non-authentic kinds of electronic legal information, and that they used these kinds of information much more intensively than the authentic Federal Law Gazette, simply based on trust instead of a warranty of authenticity. Above that, it is due to the very nature of the legal system and its dynamics – indeed, in case of nearly all legal systems – that the authentic publication of laws in the respective law gazette would attract less attention than non-authentic (or, in a very few legal systems, authentic) consolidated versions of the law in force, at a given time.

For the practical use of law enforcement through courts and administrative agencies, for lawyers and laypersons involved in legal proceedings or just interested in a particular normative issue, such consolidated versions would be essential: They spare the users the requirement to reconstruct the will of the legislature, as composed of different layers in time, following the derogation principle, in each single case of a law to be applied. Theoretically, each act of application of law requires such an act of reconstruction – practically, it can be done once and for all (until the next amendment of a given law).

Whereas in some legal systems it has for a long time been the responsibility of the public authorities to regularly provide consolidated versions of the legal regulations, such as the Systematic Law Collection in Switzerland, in others this was traditionally seen as a market for private businesses, which produced, e.g., loose-leaf editions of the laws in force within a certain, e.g. national, jurisdiction. This was the case in Austria, too, until the 1970s.

It was only in the 1980s when legal information in Austria finally was put on an IT basis (Holzinger, 1982). Notably, private enterprises and public authorities simultaneously, and partly co-operating with each other, developed legal information databases: The first commercial databases of that kind went on-line in the mid-1980s (Svoboda, 1986; Jahnel, 1988), and at the same time the Legal Information System of the Federal Chancellery became operational, then addressing a restricted audience only, namely public administration and the courts (Wilfert, 1989).

The Legal Information System aimed at representing the legal regulations of federal law, including laws, ordinances, state treaties, etc., as well as court decisions; whereas the legal regulations were processed by the Federal Chancellery's own staff, the court decisions' databases were only to be built up by the staff of the respective courts. Thus, though in the end providing access to all kinds of legal sources, the documentalistic criteria followed within the Legal Information System were not fully coherent. This was also true for the legal regulations of the nine federal provinces that subsequently were integrated into the Legal Information System, too, fed from the provinces' own legal information systems.

Although, starting with 1983, the (non-authentic) full texts of the Federal Law Gazette were also made available within the Legal Information System, the main user interest was in the consolidated versions of federal laws, the full texts of which were collected after a systematic index to the federal regulations in force was compiled first (Holzinger, 1984). Establishing the Legal Information System meant a revolution in the field of legal information. For the first time, a complete collection of "law in time", though going back not equally far (but in all instances to 1983), had been created, which made it possible to precisely identify the federal law in force at a given point in time, by a simple online search, and retrieve the respective normative texts. For the first time it was feasible to get access to consolidated versions of the laws in force with a short delay in time only, i.e. a few weeks. Though these texts, of course, were non-authentic only, the simple circumstance that they were provided by the Federal Chancellery was to inspire confidence.

Thus, it may not be surprising that after some time there was an increasing public demand for the content of the Legal Information System being made directly and freely accessible to the public (instead of being indirectly available through a commercial legal database, the provider of which was co-operating with the Federal Chancellery, against payment). Finally, it was the Internet revolution that made the step towards providing free access to the Legal Information System inevitable. When in the mid-1990s the Internet, in the appearance of the World Wide Web, had its take-off, the public authorities in

Austria, too, felt urged to make their information resources available to the public; at the same time, the breakdown of the mainframe world made a system change in case of the Legal Information System, and a change in the way of providing access, necessary anyway. Only a few months after the Austrian Parliament made most of its legislative information services available on its website, the Federal Chancellery, in June 1997, opened up a web interface to accede its Legal Information System.

From that time on, the public was given free access to the diverse databases combined in the Legal Information System. As far as federal law was concerned, the Legal Information System the year before had been put on new legal grounds, when section 7 para. 2 of the new Federal Law on the Federal Law Gazette 1996 ordered: "The data produced for the Federal Law Gazette are ... to be made available to the Legal Information System of the Federal Chancellery, which does not contain authentic data". This was nothing else but legalizing the practice; a legal provision for public access to the data contained in the Legal Information System was not yet made in 1996 – once again, practice led the way, and law was to follow.

The decision to provide the public with access to the Legal Information System free of charge arose some critics from the side of the commercial information service providers busy in the field of legal information. At that time, in the late 1990s, the discussion about what kind of legal information services were to be rated "added value services" was in full swing, and some commercial information service providers argued already providing consolidated texts was an "added value service" to be left to them. Indeed, when early in 2001 a draft amendment of the Federal Law on the Federal Law Gazette 1996 was sent out for public consultation by the Federal Chancellery, it proposed to entitle the Federal Chancellery to charge a fee on public use of the services of the Legal Information System. Thereby, on the one hand revenue would have been raised, and on the other hand, the commercial information service providers would not have got rid of their public "competitor" but would have been given a better chance to regain market shares, against a service no longer being available for free.

However, the public consultation process made it clear. The public had got used to the free service, and was not willing to do without it anymore – the comments given on the draft bill within this specific consultation process may be read as a collection of all possible arguments in favour of free access to legal information. As a result, the proposal was dropped, and the remaining part of the amendment, as it was adopted by the National Council in March 2001, ordered: "The data of the Legal Information System produced by the Federation and the content of the Federal Law Gazette are to be made available via the Internet" (section 7 para. 2, 2nd sentence). Thus, practice, once again, was turned into law, and the assault on free access to legal information was repulsed (Bargmann, 2002).

Nevertheless, the fight was not yet over: when in April 2002 the draft Federal Law on the Reform of Promulgation was sent out for public consultation, it omitted the provisions of section 7 of the Federal Law on the Federal Law Gazette 1996 as amended in 2001. Once again, the Legal Information System received wide public support in the course of the consultation procedure, and the result was that the new Federal Law on the Federal Law Gazette 2004, as adopted by the National Council in October 2003, referred to the Legal Information System in its section 13.

As a matter of fact, section 13 of said law replaced the legal assignment by an entitlement saying non-authentic legal information may also be made available by the Federal Chancellery via the Internet, at the same URL where the authentic Federal Law Gazette is located. However, this need not be seen as weakening the free access policy, because the scope of this entitlement was extended to provincial and municipal regulations (following the practice, once again), and this extension, of course, would allow only an entitlement instead of an obligation, due to the federalist structure of the Republic of Austria.

Since the beginning of the era of authentic electronic publication of federal law in Austria, free access to the non-authentic consolidated versions of federal laws, as well as the other kinds of legal information contained in the Legal Information System, has never been seriously questioned again. Maybe this was due to an argumentum a maiore ad minus: if now even the authentic Federal Law Gazette was available free of charge, why charge the non-authentic legal texts, regardless in what kind of systematic arrangement they were presented? Anyway, the above-mentioned public consultation processes in the years 2001 and 2002 clearly proved that the Austrian public deemed it to be the responsibility of the public authorities to provide the public with legal information, in particular with the consolidated versions of legal regulations, and to do so free of charge.

The Legal Information System of the Federal Chancellery, therefore, will remain the central hub of legal information in Austria. Currently, it is undergoing not only a redesign of its website but also a major system change. All the documents contained in the system, the number of which amounts to more than 1 million, are being converted from ASCII text to XML, which is a difficult process but will, if successful, in the future offer additional structural functionalities (Stöger and Weichsel, 2008).

5. Perspectives

There is no way back. Free access to legal and legislative information, as a public service, has become an enforced standard throughout Europe.

Legal and legislative information systems, like those of the Austrian Federal Chancellery and the Austrian Parliament, however, are still expert systems, requiring the user to have at least some knowledge of the legal system as well as legal terminology.

That is why other and additional approaches to enable the citizens to deal with legal issues are to be developed. A fine example is given by the Austrian system[3] (Moser, 2000), which chooses a "life situation" approach, providing legal information not in accordance with the formal structure of the legal system but with a selection of "life situations" regularly occurring, like birth and decease, marriage and divorce, tax declaration, passport application, military service, habitation issues, etc. Instead of providing the texts of the relevant legal regulations, the system, which is, of course, freely available, as well, would give meta-information on the content of the provisions and on the procedures to be applied in the respective "life situations", and it does so in plain language; needless to mention that writing these texts, which, of course, are reviewed by legal specialists before being published, requires considerable editorial effort.

However, the system, as useful as it is, currently remains an island in the stream of legal information. It is neither connected to the legal texts as provided in the Legal Information System nor to the explanatory material as provided in the parliamentary information system. The same goes for court decisions, administrative decisions, legal doctrine, and all other kinds of sources that may be of use when it comes to dealing with legal issues, from different points of view, and from different levels of legal knowledge. This scope is what might be called the "legiverse" – the whole universe of legal and legislative information of all different kinds, substantially inter-related but kept within different information environments and therefore, in the best possible case, synoptically accessible to the legal expert only, even the expert's capacity being more and more restricted by specialization.

That is why what might be called legal knowledge management, instead of legal information management, will be the requirement of the future. Legal knowledge management will not aim at building larger and more compre-hensive databases but at making all the information already available in the existing databases, in practice regularly via the Internet, better synoptically accessible in a context-sensitive as well as user-sensitive way. Only then it will be possible for users with different personal knowledge backgrounds to find their own specific paths through the "legiverse", and to arrive at where they want to go, at a level of case-specific legal knowledge making the relevant legal regulations not only known but even intelligible to them.

Intelligibility of law, however, remains a challenge to law-making, and to legislative drafting, beyond the scope of legal information. In its famous "brain teaser decision", the Austrian Constitutional Court has clearly stated that the rule-of-law principle of the Austrian Federal Constitution requires normative

---

[3] Available at: <www.help.gv.at>.

regulations to be basically intelligible; this minimum intelligibility required cannot be attributed to a regulation "which is only to be understood on the ground of subtle expertise, extraordinary methodological capacity and some interest in solving brain teasers" (collection no. 12.420/1990).

References

Bargmann, M. (2002), *Das österreichische Rechtsinformationssystem zwischen öffentlichem und privatem Interesse* (Master thesis), Eisenstadt, Austria.

Eberhard, H. (2003), *Die Kundmachungsreform 2004*, Juristische Ausbildung und Praxisvorbereitung 2003/04, pp. 187-192.

Habermas, J. (1992), *Faktizität und Geltung*, Suhrkampf Verlag, Frankfurt am Main.

Holzinger, G. (1982), *Ein Rechtsinformationssystem für Österreich*, in Kindermann, H. (Ed.), "Studien zu einer Theorie der Gesetzgebung 1982", Berlin, pp. 102-116.

Holzinger, G. (1984), *Aufbau eines EDV-unterstützten Index des Bundesrechts*, in Öhlinger, T. (Ed.), "Gesetzgebung und Computer", München, pp. 250-269.

Holzinger, G. (1988), *Die Kundmachung von Rechtsvorschriften in Österreich*, in Schäffer, H. (Ed.), "Theorie der Rechtssetzung", Wien, pp. 303-341.

Jahnel, D. (1988), *Rechtsdatenbanken für Wissenschaft und Praxis*, Österreichische Juristen-Zeitung, pp. 301-305.

Kelsen, H. (1929), *Vom Wesen und Wert der Demokratie*, 2nd ed., Tübingen.

Lachmayer, F. (2001), *Die Rechtsdokumentation als moderne Form der Rechtsbereinigung*, in Bußjäger, P. and Lachmayer, F. (Eds.), "Rechtsbereinigung und Landesrechtsdokumentation", Wien, pp. 67-80.

Lachmayer, F. and Stöger, H. (1996), *Austrian Legal Information System*, in Ciampi, C. et al. (Eds.), "Verso un sistema esperto giuridico integrale", Milano, pp. 577-581.

Laurer, R. (2004), *Neues vom Bundesgesetzblatt*, Österreichische Juristen-Zeitung, pp. 521-533.

Lukas, J. (1903), *Über die Gesetzes-Publikation in Österreich und dem Deutschen Reiche*, Graz

Moser, L. (2000), *Amtshelfer online – www.help.gv.at*, in Schweighofer, E. and Menzel, T. (Eds.), "E-Commerce und E-Government", Wien, pp. 107-112.

Oberreuter, H. (1986), *Parlament und Öffentlichkeit*, in Langenbucher, W.R. (Ed.), "Politische Kommunikation", Wien, pp. 70-79.

Ruppert, S. (1999), *Die Entstehung der Gesetz- und Verordnungsblätter*, in Stolleis, M. (Ed.), "Juristische Zeitschriften", Frankfurt am Main, pp. 67-105.

Stöger, H. and Weichsel, H. (2008), *Das Redesign des Rechtsinformationssystems – RIS*, in Schweighofer, E. et al. (Eds.), "Komplexitätsgrenzen der Rechtsinformatik", Stuttgart, pp. 235-243.

Svoboda, W.R. (1986), *Rechtsdatenbanken in Österreich*, EDV & Recht No. 3, pp. 18-23.

Svoboda, W.R. et al. (Eds.) (1994), *Elektronische Rechtsinformation in Österreich*, Wien.

Wilfert, N. (1989), *Der Aufbau des Rechtsinformationssystems des Bundes (RIS)*, EDV & Recht, pp. 104-106.

Legal Documents as Core Public Sector Information: From Professional Information to Internet Development Support

Fernando Venturini
Chamber of Deputies Library, Italy

Abstract. Internet, creating a technological infrastructure common to all citizens, has deeply changed the nature of legal information now part of more general "public sector information".

Through the Internet, institutions which create and maintain legal documents become "visible". The legal profession becomes stakeholder in spreading legal information, legal data enter into the public debate and feed all processes of evaluating public decisions that take place on the network.

The "user generated information" related to the use of Internet as platform for e-democracy and public debate, seems to require high quality legal information characterized by free access, reliability, continuity and stability. These values were reaffirmed in a recent document of the Italian Library Association referred to "Italian Government information on the net: status and needs" (November 2007). The document shows the library professionals concern for quality and free access of public data and their importance for cross referencing, linking and dissemination of information.

1. Electronic legal data before Internet

Legal data, produced by public institutions, are subject to legal forms of advertising that should ensure effective knowledge. These two aspects have strongly influenced the development of legal documentation, particularly in the countries of continental Europe. Creators of legal data, almost always co-inciding with the bodies responsible for official publication and with top level public bodies (i.e. Ministries, Parliaments, Supreme Courts), have developed large archives over time. Since the '60s, these archives have been computerised. Consequentially, large centralized databases are now in the hands of public bodies. In some cases, management and dissemination of these databases have been subcontracted to private companies. In the case of Italy, electronic legal documentation was created using the archives of cases and legislation of the Corte di Cassazione, and the archives of both Chambers and the Poligrafico e Zecca dello Stato, the official printer for treasury notes, legislative documents and the Official Gazette.

2. Electronic legal data after Internet

The development of the Internet has completely changed this scenario. We can identify 5 important characteristics:

1. We have a common technological infrastructure that allows any producer of digital information to enter into our homes

2. The institutions that create and maintain legal information at any level suddenly become visible on the network and have the irresistible impulse to publish and communicate the documents produced. Because of the technical simplicity, any court, any central or local office can publish on the web documents that are issued by them or refer to their competencies.

3. The users' increasing demand for legal information very often leads to the origin of the information source or who is considered such. For example, the network user searches the text of new laws on Parliament's websites, not on the website of the Official Gazette. In both cases, the circuit which provides a formal place of publication is hidden in a process that is typical of many in the Internet, i.e. elimination of "middle man". Users tend to search for what they consider the original source and legal information often tends to loose the sacred feature linked to the official source and specialisation of intermediaries.

4. The legal professions that had been leaders in dissemination of data through legal magazines and directories and that had been partially put aside by the centralization of electronic legal data, again today play an important role, particularly in sector information and in updating (they do this through discussion lists, magazines on-line, legal blogs, etc.).

5. Reliability of legal information is in question. The proliferation of archives, the proliferation of versions of same legal documents, not always updated, causes the diffusion of unreliable legal information. This allows the private creators of legal information sources to maintain the commercial value of their databases which usually guarantee complete and updated content.

3. Legal information for all? Or one for professionals and one "for all"?

In this new situation, what happens to official legal information and large databases owned by public bodies? Web oriented applications have been developed and the problem of free access to these databases created for professional purposes has been posed.

The possibility for everyone to access information on the web can be considered a new way to obtain the knowledge of law as a condition for its effective application. Everyone agrees with this statement which dates back to the American and French revolutions. But there's also some tradition of believing that legal information is something to be provided to lawyers and other legal system professionals. As a result, we have different solutions for legal information access through the Internet in which professional and citizen oriented approach are balanced.

Generally speaking, maintaining the current distinction between professional users and citizens, involves the risk of having a parallel system that, in the worst case, we could describe in the following terms: reliable, comprehensive and stable legal information in databases for a fee. Legal information that is uncertain, incomplete and unreliable, free for all. In other words, Google for all; professional databases for professional users. A more frequent option is the creation of subsets of legal data dedicated to common citizens, with restrictions in content and research. For example in Italy only the last 60 issues of the Official Gazette are accessible free-of-charge and no consolidated legislation database is freely available on the Internet.

The risks of limiting the legal data availability and free access are exacerbated by the following:

1. Legal information may be considered like other kinds of information: an economic commodity subject to the laws of the market.

2. Private legal publishers, or other companies which disseminate legal information, have strong commercial interests in this matter. They tend to create obstacles to the complete free access to legal information provided by public bodies.

3. On the users' side, there's the so-called "illusion of availability." The easier accessibility of regulations and laws in comparison to the world of paper nearly seems to satisfy the average user who rarely has to deal with official journals and bulletins. Retrieving an official text by traditional research methods is so difficult that most people are satisfied with the results of their internet research and don't realize the difficulties and dangers that can arise from the use of disordered and unreliable legal information.

4. Overcoming the legal approach to legal information: legal information is made up of public decisions

It seems to us that in order to overcome any obstacle and have a really new approach to the problem of free access and knowledge of legal electronic information, it is necessary to overcome the legal and professional point of view from which we have seen these questions so far.

If we limit ourselves to look at the problem from a legal point of view, the prevailing aspect is that of *ignorantia legis non excusat*. The Internet is conceived as the instrument for resolving the ancient question of ignorantia legis. But this approach limits the problem only to regulations and, in particular, to rules deriving from laws and other acts that have the same impact of laws.

Adopting a completely new approach, let's try to place legal information in the context of government information or public sector information. In this way, legal information is closely linked to other categories of public information. When dealing with legal information, we talk about acts such as laws, judgements, circulars, general administrative acts (eg financial acts, territorial plans, environmental impact assessments and health directives) which are subject to public decisions and scrutiny.

Through these acts the public bodies express their willingness and have an effect on: single persons, companies, the entire national community (in the case of a law), local communities (for example in the Master Plan of any city), particular categories (in the case of a circular addressed to the employees of a ministry).

If we look at legal documents as to public decisions in the context of a democratic society, we realize that every general legal document is linked to many other legal and non-legal documents and data which stood before and stand after the decision: acts and parliamentary documents, acts of city councils, documents and certificates of advisory and control bodies, statistics, data from scientific surveys of public authorities (for example in the environmental and health sectors), reports prepared by public bodies and study commissions, consultation papers, etc.

Every decision has an impact on the interests that are represented in any area of social life. It has effect not only on judges, lawyers, administrators at the time of application of the law but also on the average citizen. Citizens not only want to know their rights or to avoid sanctions, they want to assess the local and national leaders also, to have the information necessary to try to change the rules and to compare decisions in different contexts (e.g. employment contracts). Naturally it involves not only the individual citizen but also the forms of social organization, special interests groups and lobbies, spontaneous or temporary aggregations and many other expressions of social vitality.

5. Legal information is the foundation for an electronic democracy

It has been said that "the Internet has resurrected the notion of freedom of expression as an individual liberty" (Zeno-Zencovich, 2008, p. 100). Everyone can disseminate his/her thoughts and opinions directly today. The media (press, television, etc.) are no longer necessary to exchange our own thoughts and involve other people.

Internet is not just a (potential) library of documents and data but also a place of interaction between citizens and between the citizenry and it's institutions.

Firstly, citizens tend to use Internet in order to control public decision makers, monitoring the behaviour of politicians, the use of resources, the consistency between statements and voting.

Secondly, single citizens, social organizations, political parties, companies and unions, lobbyists of all kinds, discuss the public decisions in the network openly, set new agendas and proposals, prepare alternative texts, develop campaigns to promote alternative decisions to those prevailing in the representative institutions.

Controlling and discussing are the two faces of every use of IT in enhancing democratic processes: what we call e-democracy.

To do this people need to cite public documents (legal texts of all kinds, judgments, legislative proposals, white papers and consultation papers, reports of research bodies, especially in sensitive areas such as health and the environment, statistical data, etc.). They need, in essence, the raw material which feeds public debate. If this raw material is not on the network immediately, if it is networked in formats that are not easily accessible, if it is networked only for a fee, if there are not simple tools for retrieving it, these debates will be seriously hampered or may be in vain. Indeed, the absence of reliable and updated public information hinders transparency of decisions and fuels the spread of unreliable and incomplete surrogates.

Information is the bridge between the structures of government and society through which consultation and participation pass.

6. Legal information is essential to facilitate the development of "user generated information" and the activities of so-called "data mashers"

In a recent report for the British Government (*The Power of Information*, June 2007) the strategic importance of public information for the development of Web 2.0 was emphasised, in particular for all activities in which network users create and rearrange information.

While the issue of re-use of public information is based on the idea of making the most of it for business purposes, the online communities approach tends to highlight the social value of public sector information:

> When enough people can collect, re-use and distribute public sector information, people organise around it in new ways, creating new enterprises and new

communities. In each case, these are designed to offer new ways of solving old problems. In the past, only large companies, government or universities were able to re-use and recombine information. Now, the ability to mix and "mash" data is far more widely available (Mayo and Stenberg, 2007).

From this point of view legal information has a crucial role because it permeates every social activity. This report recommends "that government should publish regulatory information on the internet in a format that consumers find easy to understand and that citizens and organisations can easily re-use and re-combine with other information". Citizen generated websites need to have a solid ground of all regulations and legal decisions related to their aims. As has been said, "Law not only applies to communities, but it has considerable power to create them; and law can be the vehicle by which the members of those communities share something in common" (Wise and Schauer, 2007, p. 268).

7. Legal information is made up of essential public data

Now we can understand that legal documentation is actually *essential* for an informed citizenry in the today's modern IT information society, as well as for the growing innovative use of Internet. Generally speaking, the use and importance of documents depends on technology and on social and cultural context. More people use Internet in their daily life, more people express themselves through the web, more legal documents are *essential*.

Ten years ago, in a famous report which declared the French strategy regarding the dissemination of public data on the Internet, the category of *essential public data* was identified. This report did not list a series of data to be considered *essential* but proposed a definition:

> Les données essentielles seraient définies alors comme les données publiques dont la mise à disposition est une condition indispensable à l'exercice des droits du citoyen, ainsi que de ceux des étrangers résidant sur notre sol.[1]

This definition is open and is closely related to the evolution of technology by which citizens exercise their rights. What was not essential in the realm of paper, can be essential in the world of Internet. Unfortunately, since the *Mandelkern Report* the debate on essential public data has come to a halt and the European e-government policy has been oriented towards *economic* exploitation of public data and the use of the network to improve the efficiency of public administrations and to facilitate 'interaction with citizens. Only in the eEurope 2002 Action Plan, can we identify some key objectives making Europe "the most competitive and dynamic economy in the world,

---

[1] Commissariat general du plan (1999), *Diffusion des données publiques et révolution numérique*, Paris, La Documentation française, available at: <www.ladocumentationfrancaise.fr/rapports-publics/994001620/index.shtml> (it is known as *The Mandelkern report*).

also exploiting the opportunities offered by the Internet". It provides for the spread of "electronic access to public services" in favour of the citizen:

> Making accessible online essential public data, including information of a legal, administrative, cultural, environmental and traffic information.[2]

8. Conclusions

If we disseminate legal information directly on the web, adopting the same approach we have been using in the past, we run the risk to have two parallel systems of legal data, one for professionals, one for the average citizen.

If we start from user's needs and from the Internet-based approach, we reach the full availability and free access of all legal data, since they are "food" for the effective functioning of the network.

Availability is the key word. In fact the Internet has already become, in part, the place of the availability of public information. Availability of public sector information and, above all, legal data, in a third place (the network) – a sort of condominium between society and state – could be the most simple and effective tool for information sharing between governments and citizens. In this "third place" – regulated and managed – governments and citizens can share information through which the participatory processes are being favoured.

This approach is another way to arrive to the statements of the Montreal *Declaration on Free Access to Law*.[3]

Appendix
An attempt of Italian librarians to promote these principles

Recently, the DFP group of the Italian Library Association has tried to formulate a series of statements about publication of Italian public sector information on the web.

DFP (Documentazione di fonte pubbica in rete = Italian Government Information on the Net) is a section of the Italian Library Association website and consists of a database[4] of Internet resources produced by the Italian public institutions and pages devoted to the description and comments about Italian public sector information. DFP includes updating services via e-mail and RSS.

---

[2] E-Europe 2002: Communication from the commission to the council and the European parliament: communication to the Spring European Council in Stockholm, 23-24 March 2001, COM(2001) 140 final, available at: <eur-lex.europa.eu/LexUriServ/LexUriServ. do?uri=COM:2001:0140:FIN:EN:PDF>.

[3] See the Appendix of this volume.

[4] Available at: <dfp.aib.it>.

The document adopted at the tenth anniversary of the DFP, November 2007 is entitled: *State and needs of the Italian Government Information on the Net.*[5]

The main contents of this document are as follows:

1. Internet must become the place for government information availability and free access. As with traditional means of official publication, Internet can be a common space where official public documents are published and where people can freely avail and eventually link to them.
2. Documents of general public interest are defined and listed, including all kind of public decisions and legal data.
3. Information and documents related to public decisions (before and after them) must have the same accessibility on the net.
4. Persistence of institutional and legal information on the net, is recommended.

Specific recommendations are made for Italian legal information. In particular:

1. It is recommended free availability of case law databases at least with regard to constitutional court, legitimacy and higher administrative courts.
2. It is recommended free availability of the Official Journal of the Italian Republic in all its series without time limits.
3. It is recommended that the site Norme in rete evolves towards the model of a national legal portal in which all regulatory databases and case archives are available at national and regional levels.

References

Mayo, E. and Stenberg, T. (2007), *The Power of Information: an independent review*, available at: <www.opsi.gov.uk/advice/poi/power-of-information-review.pdf>.

Wise, V.J. and Schauer, F. (2007), *Legal information as social capital*, Law library journal, Vol. 99, No. 2, pp. 267-283.

Zeno-Zencovich, V. (2008), *Freedom of expression: a critical and comparative analysis*, Routledge–Cavendish, Abingdon, Oxford.

---

[5] Available at: <www.aib.it/dfp/c0711d.htm3>.

An Easy Way to Find a Rule Among a Lot of Legislation in Disability Area

Raffaello Belli

Institute of Legal Information Theory and Techniques (ITTIG-CNR), Italy

Abstract. This paper gives and overview of the internet portal "Diritto e disabilità" (Law and Disability), <www.ittig.cnr.it/disabilita>. In this portal there are four parts. In the first part, "Legal databases", there are six databases (VIPDd, VIPDe, VIPDg, VIPDi, VIPDn, VIPDr); moreover there is an "Unified search based on a classification scheme". In the second part there is an "Investigation area": it is for researchers to investigate some legal items on disability. The third part, "Guide to Web Sites", has a database with web sites on disability. The fourth part, "Papers", has documents of the editor of the portal about some items on disability.

Keywords: Basic freedoms, disabled persons, independent living, self-determination

1. Forewords

At the url <www.ittig.cnr.it/disabilita> there is the internet portal "Diritto e disabilità" (Law and disability): unfortunately most of the documents are in Italian language only. It is because these legal documents were written in such a language and a lot of work would be necessary to translate them into English language. Moreover big problems could come as regards the authenticity of translations.

Nevertheless at the url <www.ittig.cnr.it/disability> there is an "homepage" with some documents in English language (or in other languages as regards some web sites).

As regards this internet portal another big problem is given by the lack of a scientific definition of disability or handicap. I mean that there is no scientific borderline between disabled and able-bodied people. As a consequence the editor of the portal had to decide where the borderline between disabled and able-bodied people could be. And it could happen that other researchers would like to include or to leave out some people from disability area.

According to editor choices any person with difficulties (physical, psychic, mental and sensorial) in daily living has to be included into disability area.

Of course editor choices can be improved and discussed. It is to be remarked that, according to these choices, drug addicted people are not included into disability area. But people with HIV virus are included into disability area. It would be to discuss if some other people should be included into disability area. Nevertheless this discussion could require a lot of time.

Nowadays in this internet portal there are more than 6,000 documents and more than 1,600 records. These documents are in html language and most of them are unstructured, while records are structured. When the portal will be finished more than 15,000 documents will be available in the legal database (as regards Italy only) and some thousands of records will be available as regards the database on web sites.

2. VIPDd – Legal literature

In this database there are abstracts of legal literature. They are structured documents. Abstracts are of works from legal reviews, but also of monographs. They are of works both on papers and on line. Most of documents are in Italian language.

Nevertheless there are some documents in English language. This is a reason because sometime there is no abstract but details of the work only. Sometime there are some of the most important sentences of the work.

When works are freely available on line, there is the url of the document, and it is possible to click it.

Nowadays there are 2,350 documents on line. The final database will have more than 7,000 documents.

3. VIPDe – Documents of European Union

As regards legislation and other documents of the European Union in this database there are those regarding disabled people only. Nowadays there are 65 documents. They do not include internal documents of European Union. Documents are in Italian language as it is an official language of European Union.

It is to be remarked that "inclusive legislation" is very used in the European Union. When this is the type of the documents, in the database there are sentences on disabled people only. Full text is replaced with some "omissis" and a link to the full version of the document.

A problem is due to the fact that European Union produces a very big amount of documents: this is a reason because it is very difficult to have a comprehensive view of all the papers on disability. Well, thanks to this database, just a few clicks are enough to have such a view.

There are some decisions of the European Court of Justice too, but these are on the database on case law.

4. VIPDg – Case law

In this database there are all the case law on disability, if they are of any interest for Italian situation. There are decisions of summon judges and of all Courts. (Court of Cassation, Constitutional Court, European Court of Justice and European Court of Human Rights included).

Whenever it is available, there is the full text of the decision. There are maxims of the decisions both when they are of a special interest and when the full text is not available. Most of the maxims are from the Italgiure database of the Court of Cassation.

Nowadays there are 2,400 documents on line. It is to be remarked that there are all the decision as regards the upper Courts (Constitutional Court, European Court of justice and European Court of Human Rights). The database has to be updated as regards Court of Cassation and lower Courts decisions.

In Italy there is a lot deal of case law on disability. This is due to many reasons. A mean reason is due to the fact that many able bodied people are used to ask facilities as if they were disabled people. It is shocking to see how many people try to be recognized as disabled because they have been impaired while working as civil servants. It is also shocking to see how many people sue for an allowance for home help in Campania Region.

5. VIPDi – Documents of international organizations

In this part of the portal there are documents on disability passed by international organizations. Nowadays there are 11 documents: this is because there are ONU documents only. OMS and ILO documents are to be added.

It has to be remarked that there are most important documents only. Otherwise a very big amount of documents would be to be processed. It is to be observed that the generic world "documents" is used because they have a different legal role in Italy.

As regards international organizations "inclusive legislation" is not very used. This is a reason because in this database there are few documents. Nevertheless, when the document is a matter of inclusive legislation, it is processed in the same way as the other documents of the database. I mean just sentences on disability are in the database. There are some "omissis" for the sentences on different issues and there is a link to the full text of the document.

When it is available, the Italian translation of the document is in the database. Usually it is a not official translation. This is a reason because there is a link to the full text in English language, if available on line.

6. VIPDn – National rules

In Italy there is a very big amounts of rules on disability: therefore it is very difficult to have a comprehensive view of this matter.

It is more difficult to have a comprehensive view of the consolidated text of all of these rules. In this database there is a such comprehensive view. Nowadays there are 1,200 documents on line in this database. Some of these documents are no more in force and it is pointed out with a sentence at the top of these documents. Two different sentences are used: one of them works for documents no more in force. The other sentence is used for documents with some sentences no more in force.

It is a very big problem to have consolidated text at any time. It is difficult because both the amount of the legislation is very big and some changes in the sentences of documents are often passed. This is the reason because it is very difficult to have consolidated text quickly.

Until some years ago in Italy there was not inclusive legislation. This made easer to find all the documents on disability, but it made more difficult social integration of disabled people. For example, in the plans for a new cinema, architect had to look for accessibility into disability legislation. That is the architect had to move from rules on cinemas to legislation on disability.

Nowadays, thanks to "inclusive legislation", there are some laws on disability only. But it often happens that rules on disability are on legislation for all the community. For example, in the law for cinemas there are some rules on accessibility for disabled people. This means that architects have not to look for rules into disability legislation.

Nevertheless it makes more difficult to have a comprehensive view of the rules on disability.

In this database there is "inclusive legislation" too. For this pieces of legislation just sentences on disability are in the database. Sentences not involving disability are replaced with "omissis". It is to remarked that, as regards some documents, it happens that hundreds of pages are replaced, with just an "omissis" and one or two sentences in disability are on the database.

Because of the cut of a so big amount of pages it happens it is not possible to understand fully the meaning of the few sentences on disability. This is the reason because at the top of the each document there is a link to a "parser". The user clicks at the top left of the document on the button "Mostra riferimenti normativi". Links to all the documents involved with text will be available. Moreover a link to the full text of the document will be available. Such a parser is very powerful.

Sometimes links are to .pdf documents. This format is very difficult for blind people. "Istituto Poligrafico dello Stato" is the official publishing house of Italian legislation. It should solve the "pdf problem" making every document fully accessible to blind people.

When the parser is switched on, links will appear within the name of laws, decrees etc.: it is to be remarked that these links have an "urn", instead of an "url". It only works properly with documents which are in internet with some standards. The big advantage of the "urn" is that it works any time the document is available in internet, regardless the physical location where it is. That is, if the document is moved to another location, the "urn" works in the same way.

7. VIPDr – Regional rules

In the year 2001 Italian Parliament passed a big change in the Title V of the Constitution. Afterwards Regions have many competences as regards disability. Therefore, in the portal we are discussing about, it is essential to collect all the regional rules on disability. And it is very important to make easy access to them.

Moreover it is essential to be aware that there will be many more regional documents on disability in the future. Another difficulty is due to the fact that a lot of work is necessary to have consolidated text of so many documents.

Finally, most of regional documents on disability are of administrative law, and a lot of work is necessary to keep updated consolidated text as regards this sort of documents. Because of these difficulties, nowadays just documents on "independent living" are collected in this portal.

Nowadays there are 85 documents in this database. Some updates are necessary. Most of the documents deal with many items: this is the reason because there are many "omissis" to replace sentences unrelated to independent living.

8. The classification

All the documents in the legal databases are classified according to the same classification scheme.

Indeed it could be misunderstanding to say it is a classification scheme. It is correct to say that items are in two levels. But items of the upper level do not include documents involved with items of the lower level. Nevertheless it is possible to say that it is a classification into two levels because those of the upper level are general items while those of the lower level are detailed items.

Nowadays, if we sum items of the upper level and items of the lower level, there are 687 items altogether. Moreover there is a filter of the classification items. It makes possible to type a word and to search for all the classification items with such a word.

It is possible to say that disability requires many more affirmative actions than other areas. This is a main reason because there are many items involving disability. Searches are much easier thanks to classification scheme: just a click can be enough to go to the case in point. It would be necessary to refine items. It is likewise that it would be necessary to add some items and to take away some others of them. It is an open classification because it could be necessary to add some more items in any time.

Each document can be classified according to several items. As regards legal literature and case law each item involves all the document. On the contrary, as regards rules, each item of the classification scheme can involve all the document or just a paragraph.

9. Unified search for each item of the classification scheme

Nowadays this search facility involves 5 of 6 databases, that is it does not involve the database on regional rules. This is because nowadays in this database there are rules on the item of independent living only.

Such a possibility of "unified search" can be very powerful: this is because just a click on an item is enough to have a comprehensive view of all documents on such an item as regards all the 5 databases. That is just a click is enough to have all the documents as regards international law, European Union documents, Italian law, legal literature and case law.

As regards international, European and national law, this search is much more powerful because an item of the classification scheme could be assigned just to a paragraph.

Nowadays, for example, just a click on the item "Accessibilità architettonica: edifici pubblici" (access to public buildings) is enough to have this result:

VIPDd (Legal literature)	1	documents
VIPDe (Documents of European Union)	2	documents
VIPDg (Case Law)	5	documents
VIPDi (Documents of the International Organizations)	1	documents
VIPDn (National Rules)	11	documents

After getting these results, it is enough to click on each database result to have a look at all documents of the item we chose. A longer time would have been necessary to get the same documents by searching them in each database. Moreover it would have been more difficult to have a comprehensive view of all documents of the item. These difficulties make a big difference for people with some disabilities.

10. Investigation area

This area is for some papers of the editor of the portal. Whenever it is necessary and it is possible, the editor of the portal writers an investigation on an item involved with disability. Any expert in legal science and in disability can send comments or further investigations on the same item and they will be on line.

This area is of a special importance because Italian rules on disability are very many, and they often are good too. Nevertheless there are some difficulties to enforce them. One of these difficulties is due to the fact that these rules are often read and enforced with a superficial approach.

Another difficulty is still more important. It is due the fact that rules are often enforced without taking into account inviolable freedoms protected in the article No. 2 of the Italian Constitution. This point is particularly important because basic freedoms of each human being are protected in this article. These freedoms are protected regardless the human being is Italian citizen. As a consequence it has to be remarked that these basic freedoms are inviolable as regard disabled people too, at least because of equality principle.

There is another reason because inviolable freedoms are of special interest. It is due the fact that independent living is included in the item of inviolable freedoms. It has to be remarked that independent living is spreading all over the world as the most advanced approach to disability. And it is in the UN Convention on the Rights of Persons with Disabilities. It is interesting to note that Italian Constitution was passed 60 years ago but in the article No. 2 there is a very advanced approach to disability.

Unfortunately it is necessary to be aware that most of people have old-ashioned notions of disability. As a consequence it is essential a change in the mind of people involved into disability at least. This is the mean reason because it is necessary to investigate some questions more in deep and this "investigation area" can be important.

11. Guide to web sites on people with disabilities

In this area of the portal there is a database with web sites on disability all over the world. Unfortunately in this database there are just some web sites. This is because all over the world there is a very big amount of web sites on disability. Some more difficulties come from the fact that urls often move to different locations and a lot of time has to be dedicated to this database in order to have all these urls working.

As regards this database there is a web page in English language at the url <www.ittig.cnr.it/BancheDatiGuide/Disabilita/RicercaEng.php>. Of course each website is in the language they chose regardless the English or Italian web page of the database in this portal. There is a main advantage coming from the English web page for access to the database: from this web page there is access to the classification scheme in English language.

The main advantage of this database is that each web site is searchable through a classification scheme: this is not the same of the legal databases as web sites deal with many more items.

This database has a special advantage if compared with searches through internet search engines. These search engines give as a result all the web pages where the word of the research there is just once at least. On the contrary this database gives as a result just web sites where some lines are given for each item for the the classification scheme.

12. Papers

This area of the portal mainly is for records. It means it contains some papers of the editor of the portal. They are documents on disability which can be helpful for a better reference of the portal.

IV SECTION

The Global Scope of
Free Access to Law

Free Access to the Law in Latin-America: Brasil, Argentina, Mexico and Uruguay as Examples

Fernando Galindo
University of Zaragoza, Spain

Abstract. The paper presents, shortly, the state of the art on free access to the Law in four Latin-american representative countries. They are Brasil, Argentina, Mexico and Uruguay. The reason of the selection resides in the fact that Brasil, Argentina and Mexico, three big Latin-american countries in relation with the number of population, have experiences on the topic several years ago: the seventies. The experiences have different origin: initiatives of the legislative power in Brasil and initiatives of the executive power in Argentina and Mexico. The citizens of the three countries, also, speak different languages: Portuguese and Spanish. Uruguay is an example of small country that has began initiatives in recent times: the adopted solution is different and accommodated to the recent context. The paper makes a short presentation of their respective experiences and will conclude with an initial approach to go from the examples to a complementary ideal state of the art on free access to the Law in the Latin-american situation and in another countries, according to the today state of the technique and the democratic principles of the State of Law.

Keywords: Legal documentation retrieval systems, semantic web, democracy, access to the juridical documentation.

1. Introduction

The paper likes to expose, in exemplary and symbolic form, initially (section 2), the state of the question on the access to juridical documentation retrieval in Brazil, Argentina, Mexico and Uruguay. The objective is to show that in those countries, like it happens in another, there are several real initiatives that facilitate the free access to the juridical texts via Internet to all interested that, having the appropriate knowledge, want to retrieval this information.

The next section (3) will present the fact that the problem resides in that, the democratic ideal referred to that the citizens as co-authors of the law through their political representatives can consent to these texts, doesn't take place with the technical solutions developed until this moment. It is important to consider that this ideal is present, in an or another way, in the fundamental principles of the State of Law and the initiatives that promote the free access to the juridical texts via Internet.

The last section (4) will present an intent of solution of the problem by means of the proposal of mechanisms that would allow to increase, in relation to concrete questions, the number of people that access to juridical documentation and their knowledge and understanding on the same.

2. Free access

There are several initiatives in the history directed to facilitate the access to juridical texts to the citizens. It is a precedent, for example, the fact that in the European Middle Age (starting from the XI century in Bologna) was reimplanted the Roman Law as government's instrument of the new Emperor by means of the study in the Universities of the Corpus Juris Civilis of Justinianus. The lawyers ought help to the exercise of the Imperium by means of the exegesis and study of this juridical text (Lalinde, 1970, p. 104). The measure also had for object to propitiate that the Emperor's citizens could hire the services of the experts in case they had conflicts with others in matters whose resolution was prescribed by this Law to the Emperor's judges.

It is easy to conclude that this is a limited precedent: the objective of the initiative was not to provide directly access to the juridical texts to the citizens, that they were servants of the Emperor or the King, but to intermediary people as the lawyers.

We won't continue this "archaeology" that would force us to extend profusely. It comes very good here, to help to expose the question, to remember with words of Rousseau why at the present time it is a basic and unquestionable principle of the State of Law the principle of facilitating the free access to juridical texts to all the citizens. Let us remember that Rousseau said that the social contract, government's origin form collected in the Constitutions, laws and institutions of the State of Law, is the solution to the following problem: "The problem is to find a form of association which will defend and protect with the whole common force the person and goods of each associate, and in which each, while uniting himself with all, may still obey himself alone, and remain as free as before." (Rousseau, 1975, p. 42). These words have implicitely, without doubt, the idea that the citizen must can access freely to the juridical texts. It is neccessary because to be obeyed itself it is indispensable to know the text of the laws and another juridical documentation that the social contract and his consequence: the State of Law through its three powers, settles down (Zippelius, 1994, p. 21).

Starting from these principles, considered implicit in any basic juridical text of the democratic States, it is a logical consequence that from the moment in that instruments like Internet exist, that it allows, at least in theory, that the juridical texts of all type can be accesed by all the citizens, resources have been developed that facilitate freely this access. Free means that the juridical texts (laws, regulations, sentences, customs ...) can be accesed by all the citizens without necessity of paying for the access.[1]

Indeed there are numerous manifestations of this free access. Limiting the consideration to what happens in countries like Argentina, Brazil, Mexico or Uruguay, the free access to juridical texts happens in all countries, and it is

---

[1] See Montreal Declaration in the Appendix of this volume.

referred to documents or juridical texts emitted by the three state powers: the legislative, the executive and the judicial.

It can be proven the reality of this statement considering the contents referred to legislative and reglamentary documentation (coming from the executive) starting from that settled down in the following web pages:

1. Argentina
   `<infoleg.mecon.gov.ar/>`
2. Brazil
   `<www.presidencia.gov.br/legislacao/>`
3. Mexico
   `<www.dof.gob.mx/>`
4. Uruguay
   `<www.presidencia.gub.uy/>`

With respect to judicial documentation, this is to the access to resolutions or sentences emitted by the instances that have the power conferred by the State to solve conflicts of judicial character, the following pages exist also:

1. Argentina
   `<www.csjn.gov.ar/>`
2. Brazil
   `<www.jf.jus.br/juris/>`
3. Mexico
   `<www.cjf.gob.mx/>`
4. Uruguay
   `<www.poderjudicial.gub.uy/>`
   (remote consult of judicial files only)

The consultation to these pages in all the cases (with the exception in Uruguay of the judicial files: the user needs to know previously the information on the basic characteristics of the judicial case stored in the file) allows to check that any citizen of one or another country that wants to access to juridical texts and that has a computer and access to Internet, can make it freely simply using the access mechanisms that are established in the pages of the mentioned web.

We must consider here these questions: Is it fulfilled the principle of free access to the juridical texts with the realization of these activities? Or, like we said above, are the citizens able to know and to understand all the retrieved juridical texts to effects to assume an obligation in relation to concrete problems as active part of the social contract? The following sections give answers to these questions.

3. Problems

If we study the interfase of communication of the mentioned web pages that allow to access freely to juridical texts, we can conclude inmediately that the answers to give to the questions of the previous section must be negative.

The fundamental reasons of the negative answers reside in that or the formulation of the consultation to the stored juridical texts requires the use of juridical knowledge of those that the citizen lacks normally, or when the use of the free text is allowed (it is necessary to carry out the question in natural language) the documentation retrieval becomes impossible, once the answer gives such a quantity of information that no user can have the minimum security on which it is the juridical text that can be precise to solve the problem for which the consultation is made.

Let us observe shortly in the requirements of use of the considered systems and their answer. We take as reference several consults made to, for example: <www.jf.jus.br/juris/> and <www.cjf.gob.mx/>.

All the systems offer a mechanism that uses a of similar interface. This is: it is possible to carry out questions in free text, that is the use of words (isolated or in combination with other), or to execute categories of indexation of the juridical documents as: norm type, dates of the norm (promulgation or publication), authority that emits it, title (total or partial) of the norm, juris-diction type, presenter, number of identification of the norm in the consulted collection, place of emission of the norm ...

In the case of the consultations in free text the answers related with a single term or word are so numerous that it is impossible the handling of the documentation that result as answer. The same thing comes to happen when the consultation is made using several words unless the consultant person has articulated it foreseeing the result: or what is the same thing knowing the characteristics of the problem to ask.

The consultation that requires to keep in mind the indexation categories, advanced consult is the denomination in many occasions, requires inevitably to know the meaning of the categories, that is to say to have knowledge and instruction of juridical character.

This takes us to consider that the access systems to juridical texts that exist provide help to the experts in Law more than to the citizens, once the jurists have enough technical knowledge to formulate the question using several words in the modality free text, or responidng to the interrogation categories in the advanced modality. They also know the reasons for those that is necessary to gather documentation: the juridical problem for which they ask the question.

All this has the signification that each juridical database becomes to be in the practice a new "Corpus" with which the jurists aid to the establishment of the empire of the States, the exercise of the three powers and to approach, as middlemen, their operation to the citizens. The conclusion is that the responsible participation and aware of the citizens in the government of the State of Law is not possible, when they can not be able to access to the juridical texts.

Is this the only possibility to access to juridical texts? We will answer to the question in the following section.

4. Solution

There is some intents to solve the problem. Let us notice that the solution has to do with initiatives of the XVIII century as those of Diderot and D'Alambert in the Encyclopedia.

These authors summarized their object in the following words: "L'Ouvrage ... a deux objets: comme Encyclopédie, il doit exposer autant qu'il est possible, l'ordre & l'enchaînement des connoissances humaines: comme Dictionnaire raisonné des Sciences, des Arts & des Métiers, il doit contenir sur chaque Science & sur chaque Art, soit libéral, soit méchanique, les principes généraux qui en sont la base, & les détails les plus essentiels, qui en font le corps & la substance. Ces deux points de vùe, d'Encyclopédie & de Dictionnaire raisonné, formeront donc le plan & la division de notre Discours préliminaire. Nous allons les envisager, les suivre l'un après l'autre, & rendre compte des moyens par lesquels on a tâché de satisfaire à ce double objet" (Encyclopédie, 1751, p. 1).

The solution would be centered in our case to offer to the users of access systems to juridical texts, basic juridical knowledge existent on a matter or problem in comprehensible terms, as it is made by the Encyclopedia, for citizens interested in consulting juridical documentation. This solution would be the articulation of access mechanisms to documentation that were not reduced or to use formal categories, characteristic of experts, or to use words or texts without context. The proposed solution would be to make consults on concrete problems exposed by people that didn't have juridical formation and whose interest is limited to know and to understand juridical texts. This proposal is connected with the possible technical solutions that are bound to the development of the "semantic web" (Casanovas, Noriega, Bourcier, Galindo, 2007).

The proposed solution is developing, by way of example, from some years, in the context of knowledge referred to Law and Technologies of the Communication and the Information.[2] The example, finally, has to provide juridical documentation to university students that learn several disciplines in the following environments: juridical, technological, management, economy, business admnistration and documentation. An example of the initial development

---

[2] Available at: <www.lefis.org> and <courses.lefis.unizar.es>.

is in: <www.lefis.org/index.php?option=com_wrapper&Itemid=464>. The interface can be seen in Figure 1.

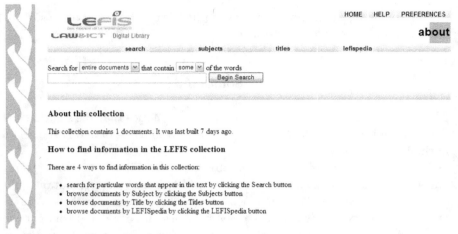

Figure 1. The interface in development

The example consists on the design of a digital library integrated by documentation on the matter Law&ICT and whose content is accessible by means of the use of these systems:

1. Brief definitions of basic concepts on the matter
2. A classification of the stored knowledge using systems of documental classification accepted universally

The brief definitions of basic concepts on the matter are constituted by definitions carried out by students of the different imparted disciplines.

The list of basic concepts has been established by experts in the matter . The list is located in: <www.lefis.org/app/vcampus/outcomes/concepts_facets/concepts.xls.>

The knowledge classification has been elaborated using universal systems of documentation classification: facets, and the inclusion in the same of the concepts settled down by experts on the matter. The list of facets is located in: <www.lefis.org/app/vcampus/outcomes/concepts_facets/facets.pdf>.

The virtue of the example resides, therefore, in that the consultation categories are being elaborated in plural or collaborative form: by experts on the matter and by non experts, using thesaurus and facets or ontologies (Boccato, Ramalho, Fujita, 2008).

The results of the tests, when the system is fully elaborated, will prove if it is possible to aid to the citizens in the moment to access to juridical documentation, and the modifications that must be developed. It must consider that the system is open to the participation in its construction of interested citizens: have or not juridical knowledge.

5. Conclusion

The work has shown that in Latein-america countries, like it happens in another countries, it is not closed the possibility to design access systems to juridical documentation open to the citizens that with it, like Rousseau said, allow them to be free and to participate in the established government by means of the setting in practice of the principles of the social contract, increasing practically in the pointed out form the grade of the citizens' digital inclusion.

Acknowledgements

This research is supported by the European Union, Lifelong Learning Programme 2007–2013, ref.: 133837-LLP-1-2007-1-ES-ERASMUS-EVC.

References

Boccato, V.R.C, Ramalho, R.A.S., Fujita, M.S.L. (2008), *A contribuçao dos tesauros na construçao de ontologias como instrumento de organizaçao e recuperaçao da informaçao em ambientes digitais*, IBERSID, pp. 199-209.

Casanovas, P., Noriega, P., Bourcier, D., Galindo, F. (Eds.) (2007), *Trends in Legal Knowledge the Semantic Web and the Regulation of Electronic Social Systems*, European Press Academic Publishing, Florence.

Encyclopédie, ou Dictionnaire raisonné des Sciences, des Arts et des Métiers, par une société de gens de lettres (1751), *Discours préliminaire des editeurs*, Mis en ordre & publié par M. Diderot, de l'Académie Royale des Sciences & des Belles-Lettres de Prusse; & quant à la Partie Mathématique, par M. D'Alembert, de l'Académie Royale des Sciences de Paris, de celle de Prusse, & de la Société Royale de Londres, Paris, 1751.

Lalinde, R. (1970), *Iniciación histórica al derecho español*, Ariel, Barcelona.

Rousseau, J.J. (1975), *Contrato Social*, Espasa Calpe, Madrid.

Zippelius, R. (1994), *Rechtsphilosophie*, Beck, München.

Access to Judicial Information via the Internet in Latin America: A Discussion of the Experiences, Trends and Difficulties**

Carlos G. Gregorio
Instituto de Información para la Justicia, Argentina

Abstract. Judicial branches in the Latin American region are conducting an extensive reform. The principal causes which lead to this reform are: overload and congestion, excessive delays and lack of transparency. The judicial information management represents one of the pillars of the reform and once the judicial information has been disseminated via Internet the next issue to be considered is how to manage the access policy.

With this change the judiciaries launched services via Internet: access to case tracking and management, access to massive databases of case law (where practically all the decisions are included), and recently other creative services such as viz. criminal records (particularly related to sexual *offences*), cases already filed, names of individuals who failed to pay child support, names of imprisoned convicts, names of fugitives of the law, lawyers and notaries suspended, crime victims, personal bankruptcy and successions, law notices.

All these processes are taking place in a complex scenario: legal gaps within the rights of access and personal data protection, social claims for a more transparent, efficient and speedy justice system, and an growing number of loaded cases (as an example, approximately 6 millions cases are filed annually by the trial courts in Brazil). In addition, experiences and experiments occur isolated and intermittently.

This presentation intends to analyze the trends, the adverted risks and to discuss best practices and further recommendations.

1. Introduction

Depending on what the information pertains to, there are different ways to access it, which vary from one country to another. This variety goes from free access to the judicial information (e.g. Brazil, where the only limit is having to use the name of the employer in the search engine of labor cases or child support cases in Peru); to registered users (e.g. child support debtors in Argentina); or to all interested persons in criminal records – by paying – in Peru. Meanwhile in Venezuela access to case management is restricted to the parties and their lawyers, in Argentina (province of Chubut) every lawyer can access to every case. However, in most of the countries the access is open free and unrestricted when having the case identification number.

The balance among the right to access and other fundamental rights (mainly privacy, right to defense, and presumption of innocence) has a wide set of solutions, which could be on one extreme full annonimization of case management like in Mexico (Nayarit state) and on the other extreme displaying

** The research reported in this paper was supported by a grant from the International Development Research Centre, Canada.

all the information – including the victims' names even if they are minors – like in Mexico (Tabasco state). A controversial subject is if the right to access has to be applied to all judicial databases of cases: e.g. access is limited in the courts of Rio Grande do Sul state (Brazil) and civil courts in Buenos Aires (Argentina), in other countries the access (download) is fully allowed: e.g. Guatemala and Mexico where there are private companies that reorganize this information and sell it to paid users (by subscription).[1] In Argentina and Costa Rica the name of voters are accessible through complete databases.

The limited access to law notices ("edictos" or "editais" that involve the right of defense) in the region is contradictory compared with the trend of free access. Only in Ecuador there is a search engine which allows free access (sometimes requires registration) to law notices. Recently in Brazil, due to Act 11.419, they created a website which enables access to all law notices in all states (*Diario da Justiça Eletrônico*). In some states of Mexico, law notices can be accessed at the judicial websites by date of edition. In addition, a great number of countries publish law notices in private newspapers.

The most advanced and complex issues are arising in Brazil where the level of access to judicial information reaches its maximum in the region. Based on the high level of congestion and delays the 11.419 Act establishes the electronic dossier and a full computerization of all judicial process that must be implemented in only one year.

2. Access to judgments

There are legal publishers that collect and select judgments to create databases that are accessible only by subscription – only a few of these services have really some value added. On the other hand, there are two main means of free access to judgments in Latin America. These two means are: by the official website of each judiciary (normally Constitutional Court, Supreme Court or Appellate Court); and via non-profit private publishers, that could be NGOs or regional institutions that publish case law linked to a specific thematic, Bar Associations, law offices or also judges' personal websites that publish their own opinions (e.g. <www.gracielamedina.com>).

El Salvador and Honduras recently enacted legislation that entitles the judiciaries to publish all the judgments. Currently, the access to first instance judgments is possible in Brazil at the judiciaries' websites using search engines. In other countries the access to first instance decisions is only possible when using the case tracking system (i.e. the user needs to know the case number, enter it to the case tracking system to retrieve the history of events, and then access to the full text of the judgment) or in the Bar Association or law offices websites.

---

[1] See: <www.bil.com.mx>.

Interlocutory decisions are also published in some countries but the access is only allowed by case (i.e. via the case number using the case tracking system, and then access to full text of interlocutory decisions).

Access to a list of judgments is only possible by tribunals, they are ordered by date or they provide a search engine. This means that it is possible to search full text of judgments using particular names. Undoubtedly, this is opposite to the purpose for which opinions are disseminated. While some statutory laws specify the purpose of judgments dissemination, in the vast majority of regulations the purpose is not defined or it could be interpreted by the context of the law *i.e.* transparency.[2] The transparency of the judiciaries in Latin America is a reiterative citizen demand because of a past of suspected corruption or influences on the decisions sense. In practice the judiciaries accelerated the publication of judgments and discarded or omitted the discussion and prevention of the invasion of the privacy of the parts, witness and other people mentioned in the decisions. A very illustrative example is that initially the judgments published included the full names of children (as parts, victims of abuse, or offenders) and just recently a few jurisdictions started anonymizating their names.

3. Access to case tracking systems

The citizens and lawyers claims for faster judicial processes encouraged the judiciaries to allow the access to the processes via Internet. This represents a problem depending on the means of access. There are many ways of accessing in Latin America.

The most extended one is a search engine in which it is possible to search the existence of a case by the names of the parties (plaintiff, defendant or respondent), it is also possible to search by the name of the lawyers or their numbers of registry in the Bar Association. (e.g. Brazil). Once the case history is retrieved all documents can be displayed in full text.

In Monterrey courts (Nuevo León state, Mexico) – for instance – every user of the website should be a registered user. As registered users they can search the existence of cases searching by the names of the parties (this application also includes family and domestic matters). The case history is visible for every user, but the access to full text documents is only allowed to the lawyers that represent the parts of each case.

Other forms of access also include the possibility of searching by the names of the parties or entering using the case number, but only registered lawyers are allowed to see the documents. This is possible at the courts of the province of Chubut in Argentina.

---

[2] See Equator Constitutional Court publication policy <www.tribunalconstitucional. gov.ec/politicas.asp>.

In Paraguay and Venezuela courts, the access is allowed only to the parts and their lawyers, and the general public is not allowed to find cases by the names of the parties.

In some countries or courts there is no access to case tracking systems, but it is possible to access to a list of new cases. Equator courts and commercial courts in Buenos Aires, (Argentina) publish a list of the new cases filed with the names of the parties and a short description of the conflict (type of case) on a daily basis.

State courts in Mexico issues a daily *Boletin*, which is a short list of all cases that had an event the previous day (that could be an interlocutory decision or a petition of the parties). This list includes the names of the parties, the type of case in civil matters and the offence in criminal cases, and a short description of the event. There are two states with particular differences: Nayarit state does not include the names of the parties and Tabasco state includes that information and the names of the victims (when the victim is a child with the addition of the word "minor"). This list was used to discriminate and investigate persons. A company in Mexico named Buró de Informaciones Legales (Legal Information Bureau)[3] downloads every day all these lists and joint them in a CD that sells to their subscriptions. Once the information is all together in a unique file, it is easier to search by name and determine if a person has promoted a divorce, has a claim to pay a debt or has been processed by an offence.

4. Hearings, schedules and videos

The dissemination of scheduled hearings is also a problem. On one hand its publication is part of the open and public justice administration (a constitutional guarantee in all the countries), on the other hand the names of the persons processed in criminal cases appear with the offence, that represents – in an indirect way – a conflict with the presumption of innocence right. A few courts issue these lists on the Internet; one is the Costa Rica judiciary but they take the precaution of removing the list once the hearing has taken place. A conflict was originated between the Supreme Court of Costa Rica and the WayBackMachine[4] an Internet cemetery that store old occurrences in the Costa Rica judiciary website, including the hearings schedule. This storing broke the delicate balance between publicity of hearings and presumption of innocence that constructed the Supreme Court allowing the access for a minimum time. Finally, WayBackMachine removed the lists.

It is unquestionable that the hearings are public (only with the exceptions established by the law, as juvenile justice or family matters). But recently in

---

[3] Available at: <www.bil.com.mx>.
[4] Available at: <web.archive.org/web>.

Latin America the hearings have been recorded in videos that have become accessible at the judiciaries websites. This is the case — for instance — of hearings of criminal cases listed and available in the website of Nuevo León state in Mexico; it is not a live transmission, it gives the possibility of watching the hearing in video.[5] The technology used does not allow downloading it but still it does not seem difficult to achieve it in the future.

5. Access to legal notices

Legal notices (named *edictos* in Spanish and *editais* in Portuguese) are orders or subpoenas with unknown address that a judge publishes in a newspaper or posted in designated area in court house. The text of legal notices includes the names of the parties, the type of case and the purpose. Normally, legal notices are used to inform a party that failed to be in the process of the judicial decision that compromises his/her right to defence. For this reason legal notices are the judicial information that needs the most extensive and accessible system of dissemination (that probably could include indexation in universal search engines like Google or Yahoo). Paradoxically, only a few judiciaries include legal notices in their website and what is even worst without search engine capabilities. A newspaper *La Hora* in Equador – <www.lahora.com.ec> – receives judicial orders to publish legal notices (this newspaper offer a free access to law website <www.derechoecuador.com>) that were published in paper in daily editions and there is also a search engine in the website.

Recently in Brazil, the *11.419 Act* created a website which enables access to all law notices in all states (*Diario da Justiça Eletrônico*).[6]

6. Other forms of access that enforce specific laws

Other uses of judicial information have also emerged in Latin America. There are several examples mainly related to enforce particular laws.

One use is to enforce child support payments. If a parent fails to pay the child support his/her name is entered into a data base that could be accessible by different means. This is widespread in Argentina provinces. The province of Mendoza gives access to this database in its website but only for registered users. In Peru the access to the database of parents that failed to pay child support is fully accessible without need of registration.[7]

---

[5] In Colombia hearings videos are accessible in Internet at: <almacenamiento.ramajudicial.gov.co> but only for registered users.

[6] See: <portal.in.gov.br/in/pesquisa/avancada> and <inbuscatotal.in.gov.br>.

[7] In Peru according to the Law 28970 the Supreme Court must administrate the Registro de Deudores Alimentarios Morosos del Poder Judicial, <www.pj.gob.pe/CorteSuprema/redam> that is accessible in lists <servicios.pj.gob.pe/redamWeb/_rlvid.jsp.faces?

Databases of sexual offenders were created in order to protect children's rights which can be consulted anonymously. An example are a recent legislations of the provinces of Mendoza and Neuquén in Argentina, but it is still being implemented (the same thing happends with databases of parents that obstruct the rights of visit in the province of Santa Cruz, Argentina). In Chile the law allows each person to obtain information from the Criminal Register on sexual offences of a person that will be contracted to work in particular homes. Access to Criminal Records in Latin America is restricted to the concerned person. Recently the Supreme Court of Peru established a change, in practice it allows any person to pay a fee and obtain criminal records of another person. In Latin America (with the exception of Costa Rica, where it is of restricted use) a person normally needs to present a negative certificate about his/her criminal records to postulate for an employment or entering in a University. Another problem is related to the emigrants: Latin Americans who settle down in other regions need a criminal records certificate to regularize his/her immigration status. Understanding this situation – and that there is not such service in the consulates – some countries e.g. Paraguay, allow an authorized person to obtain a certificate, but presumed abuses could occur.

The access to personal bankruptcy and successions supposes a high level of access. Not allowing access to bankruptcy cases could derive in a wrong discrimination among creditors. The province of Mendoza in Argentina offers free access to these databases.[8]

In Uruguay the Supreme Court allows any user to search in the database of lawyers and notaries suspended in their habilitation. Obviously this access reinforces the sanctions that the Court orders to punish professional misconducts.[9]

In the past, there were databases in Brazil about people incarcerated and fugitives of the law (access to these databases was allowed by name in the website of Paraiba state) but currently they are not accessible without explanation.

7. Analysis and conclusions

The dissemination of judicial information in Latin America seems clearly related to transparency and efficiency. The value and use of precedents as

---

_rap=pc_Index.buscarTodo&_rvip=/index.jsp> and also searching by names <servicios. pj.gob.pe/redamWeb/>.

[8] See: *Registro de Juicios Universales*, available at: <www.jus.mendoza.gov.ar/ registros/rju/index.php>.

[9] See: <www.poderjudicial.gub.uy/pls/portal30/portal30.rentrar> and there Profesionales Suspendidos at the main menu.

a source of law in Latin America are different that of the *Common Law*.[10] Notwithstanding the dissemination of judgments makes judicial decisions more predictable and leads the custom to cite precedents specially in appellations. It was observed quantitatively that the dissemination of precedents produces a significant reduction into the volatility introduced by judicial decisions into the quantification of personal injuries of damages cases in Argentina (Álvarez, Gregorio, Highton, 2004).

Assuming that in Latin America the dissemination of judgments were used for transparency purposes and web services like case tracking systems to increase efficiency, the promotion of rules or recommendations about the balance with privacy rights is essential. In Latin America, only Mexico has a public protocol to regulate the anonymization of judgments that includes cases specified by law (normally minors and family matters) but also creates a presumption of privacy interest. Other countries use unwritten rules and informal practices (Bahia, Minas Gerais, Paraná, Santa Catarina states in Brazil: Córdoba and Mendoza provinces in Argentina and partially in Costa Rica).[11] In Uruguay the Supreme Court approved a detailed rule ordering the anonymization of practically all persons mentioned in judgments, but now this rule is indefinitely suspended. The judiciaries not only need recommendations about how to proceed in different types of cases but also need to be provided with software for anonymization and adequate training.

Among the mentioned standards about the access to case tracking systems the recommendations must consider an adequate balance between the privacy rights. For example, the Nayarit (Mexico) system which allows any user to access to the processes information without showing the names of the parties becomes to be useful and efficient to the purposes defined. There is no reason to reveal in Internet the names of the parties if a secure case number system is designed.

Naturally the solution ruled in Brazil, i.e. a unique national website to publish all legal notices, is the preferred standard. Search engine capabilities are very important to enhance the right of defense; this could include the indexation in Google, Yahoo or other universal search engine. Nevertheless, it is important to understand that in some case the names of children are shown in these legal notices and that there are not standards to solve this contradiction.

---

[10] See   in   Equator   <www.estade.org/temasdeinvestigacion/ FallosdeTripleReiteracionCSJ.htm>. The *Ley de Casación* establishes "La triple reiteración de un fallo de casación constituye precedente jurisprudencial obligatorio y vinculante para la interpretación y aplicación de las leyes, excepto para la propia Corte Suprema" <www.derechoecuador.com/index.php?option=com_content&task=view&id= 4008&Itemid=410>.

[11] In Brazil the Law 11.111 allows explicitly to the judiciaries the anonymization, but judiciaries in other countries understand that without a rule like this they cannot anonymizate ex officio.

The dissemination of hearings videos is extremely new (this year) and it is too early to evaluate its consequences (it depends on the technology to identify and search faces in video files) but it also must be evaluated to uphold the privacy rights. The publication of hearing schedules must be available for a minimum time needed. Searching by name of parties or offenders into the hearings schedules is a very controversial matter. Independently, hearing schedules could be published as images to counterbalance the risks.

These experiences show that the access rights are more complex now than before the use of information technology. Privacy rights, presumption of innocence, right to defense in trial, risk of discrimination appear to be necessary regarded, but the list is not closed; it probably depends on future technological developments. If the right of access is more complex (depending of the type of case, the parties involved in a case, e.g. if they are public figures, if the user is identified or anonym, the date of the information) regulatory instruments must need permanently updated.

Another lesson learned from Latin America experience, (perhaps characterized with extensive legal gaps) is the need to avoid the reuse of information, particularly if the new use involves practices that could be considered discriminatory, as the systematic download using robots.

Latin America appears – comparatively – to be a laboratory of experimentation where technological innovation comes first and regulatory instruments go after, with considerable delay.

References

Álvarez, G.S., Gregorio. C.G., Highton, E.I. (2004), *Capacidad regulatoria de la difusión de información judicial*, in "Internet y Sistema Judicial en América Latina", Ad-Hoc, Buenos Aires, pp. 75-89, available at: <www.iijusticia.edu.ar/docs/alvarez.htm>.

Free Access to Law in Africa: Issues for Network Society

Abdul Paliwala

University of Warwick, UK; Law Courseware Consortium, Electronic Law Journals

Abstract. This paper explores the link between the development of a network information society/economy and its capability for delivering social justice in the context of the development of African legal information systems. In particular, it asks the question how collaborative free and open content ventures such as SAFLII, CommonLII and WorldLII and Droit Francophone can interconnect with social justice organizations.

1. Network society

In the paper on Free Culture and Global Commons (Paliwala, 2007), I suggested that networked information technology has produced fundamental social and cultural changes. These have been variously described by Castells and Benkler as resulting in paradigmatic Network Information Society or Network Information Economy. Baxi takes a broader position on this and describes changes towards a "techno-scientific mode of production".

Castells further suggests a negative consequence for those who are not part of networks:

> Be in the network, and you can share and, over time, increase your chances. Be out of the network, or become switched off, and your chances vanish since everything that counts is organised around a world wide web of interacting networks (Castells, 1998).

Thus, the network as a social medium of information 'flows' seems to transcend the geography of 'spaces'. However, this does not go unchallenged. Even Castells would suggest that power in network society is not uni-dimensional; that there is potential for 'counter-power' or 'counter-public' networks. However, while he would locate this in an alternative network culture, others such as (Shackleford, 2006) suggest that these counter-publics may be located in a much more complex interaction between physically located social interaction and contemporary network logic. Thus the Inuit use new media in ways that enhance their communal solidarity within their physical location. Therefore, it is the combination of the social information flows and spatial which results in a counter-culture ethos which emphasizes collaborative and cooperative action (Travers, 2003).

It may be that it is this distinction between grounded networks which emerge out of local geographies and ones which emerge from wider social activism or international organizations which constitute the distinguishing logic between the activities of organizations such as Oxfam, Amnesty and Transparency International and more locally based networks emerging from local protest and social action such as the South African Treatment Action Campaign or Human and Legal Rights Centres. On the other hand, village based telecentres are more of a hybrid in the sense that while they are locally based, the initiative for their development and funding has often come from international organizations. That is, the underlying issue is not so much whether an organization is local or global, an organization may benefit from cosmopolitan linkages, but the relations of power become a significant issue. Thus, Santos (2002, ed. 2005) relies on the concept of counter-hegemonic cosmopolitanism to distinguish between subaltern counter-publics and those forms of social action which are dominated by Northern organisations. His model is that of activisms involved in the World Social Forum.

Juris (2004) identifies four elements of these counter-public social justice movements utilising cyberspace:

a) Building horizontal ties and connections among diverse autonomous elements
b) Free and open circulation of information
c) Collaboration through decentralized coordination and democratic decision making
d) Self-directed or self-managed networking

Therefore, organizations which provide legal information and support exist within the same complex matrices as wider social organizations. They might be identified clearly as being part of the global capitalist system or of an alternative subaltern counter-hegemonic public. However, frequently, it may not be possible to provide these simple binary labels.

The next section of the paper therefore offers some thoughts on how the developing African legal information systems fit into a network culture of complex mainstream and counter-networks.

2. African legal information networks

Compared with the very problematic state of African legal information even a decade ago, there have been significant changes in the provision of legal information in African countries. African legal information systems are constituted within the dominant network ideology and the counter-network ideologies.

3. Commercial legal information systems

Commercial legal information systems have not proved adequate for sub-Saharan Africa other than South Africa. In the case of the commonwealth

common law jurisdictions, for example, most countries have found it difficult
to maintain effective systems for the production and delivery of basic legislation and case law. This has been partly ameliorated in the era of 'good
governance' with its emphasis on judicial and legal reforms (World Bank Law
and Justice Institutions website). Clearly the provision of good public legal
information has been an essential aspect of this. Unfortunately for a long
time aid was provided for printed legal publications on the basis that the
publication was an expensive one based on a contract with an international
commercial publisher. There was a requirement of the aid agreement that
the publication was sustainable. To achieve this, the host government had
to charge an 'economic' price to users, often to government users. However,
this could put additional strain on already strained legal department budgets.
This led to a bizarre consequence in one country that unsold volumes of laws
were piled up in the Justice Department while magistrates had no access to
them because of budgetary constraints. Thus the main market for the laws
therefore consisted of a few government lawyers, elite law firms in the country
and an international market consisting of international agencies, developed
country foreign ministries, law firms and university law libraries: That is, the
dominant network.

Commercial eLegal Information essentially satisfied the same network.
LEXIS/NEXIS and WESTLAW have a presence in Africa but their coverage of African legal material is very limited.[1] Its significant objective is to
provide for those who are part of the same global legal network. African
based commercial systems may have different objectives. JUTAStat has developed a significant commercial presence because of the strength of the South
African legal market and JUTA continues to extend its coverage to other
African jurisdictions because these jurisdictions are relevant to expanding
South African interests. Perhaps most interestingly, the innovative Kenya Law
Reports, which commenced as a subscription service has moved to become a
free service provided by an essentially government agency which has been
supported by aid funds.

4. Free and open content material

If commercial provision has been as aspect of the dominant networks, the free
and open content movement might be seen to have been filling some of the
void. The Droit Francophone and the SAFLII, CommonLII and WorldLII
datasets provide an impressive range of material for the users. I will not

---

[1] Inevitably there is coverage of South African material and very limited Nigerian material. LEXIS/NEXIS also provides free access to the ABA Rule of Law project which includes
African information, but this is primarily for academics and development practitioners.

describe these here as others have done it or will do it at this session. What I would like to consider is how they fit into the counter-network framework.

Firstly, it is clear that these providers fit the four criteria of outlined above of horizontal autonomy, free and open information, decentralized and democratic collaboration and self-directed and managed networking in accordance with the *Montreal Declaration on Free Access to Law.*[2]

The most significant aspect of the provision is that information provided is free and open. Secondly, this Conference is an iconic tribute to the interconnected, decentralized, collaborative and democratic histories of the Legal Information Institutes which have resulted in the provision of African legal information. Of course, these achievements would not have been possible without impressive leadership of colleagues at this conference, but the ethos is non-hierarchical. The network is essentially self-directed and managed.

The networks are clearly much more efficient in providing basic legal information than the commercial ones in the sense that they have already enabled vaster libraries of African material than the commercial sector. Their essence as networking enables collaboration within the ever growing WorldLII umbrella. Because of this umbrella African lawyers have access not only to the legal material in their own jurisdictions but also to material in other African jurisdictions and in effect in the world. Reciprocally, of course, the world also has access to African legal material. In essence these datasets are an exciting force for legal cosmopolitanism.

5. Social justice and African counter-publics

However, my next question is somewhat more perplexing. In essence the LII movement is a counter-public for legal professionals based on the underlying principles as enunciated. In the developed countries, by promoting the idea of free law, it has enabled not only lawyers to have good free access to law but also those members of the general public who would otherwise find such access difficult or impossible. However, how different are African issues in relation to this? What information about the law would be relevant to an African counter-public?

Firstly, I take SAFLII as an example to see the types of legal information it provides. In principle, SAFLII is a provider of primary legal information. Even in relation to its most advanced jurisdiction, that of the Republic of South Africa, it concentrates on providing mainly case law and legislation. This of course, may be an issue of priorities. In this context, it is interesting to note that AustLII with which SAFLII has strong links, does provide a significant alternative model of material of interest to specific user groups such as Indigenous Law, Access to Justice etc. although AustLII's main role seems

---

[2] See the Appendix of this volume.

to be the provision of primary legal materials. The WorldLII, CommonLII and Droit Francophone datasets pick up a wider range of material than is available directly from SAFLII.

The question then arises, how does this range of information serve activist networks which are grounded in African society? The obvious answer is that when these networks need primary information, they can refer to the SAFLII website, and one should not undermine the significance of this service. However, it is still relevant and important to consider how the activist groups themselves conceive of their legal role. Here we may use the South African based Treatment Action Campaign as an example. The TAC has been an enormous influence in South Africa and the world in resisting both global pharmaceutical companies and their own government in relation to medical and legal rights of hiv/aids sufferers. Its website contains significant information about legal campaigns and practical information of how to obtain justice. For example:

I have been discriminated against because I have HIV. Where can I get help?

ProBono.org offers free legal services to people with discrimination cases who cannot afford legal assistance. Email address is `info@probono-org`. Tel: 011 336 9510 Fax: 011 336 9511. Although they are based in Johannesburg they work with partners across the country and will attempt to assist you wherever you are based.
`<www.tac.org.za/community/hivhelp>`

The website ProBono.org then can be explored to provide legal assistance in the following way:

ProBono.Org is a non profit organisation. It provides the following services:

- Consultations with individuals or groups who cannot afford commercial legal fees and who have matters which are in the public interest
- Referrals of public interest matters with good merits to law firms in line with their expertise and/or interest
- Referrals to relevant institutions should the matters not be suitable for legal resolution
- Maintains working relationship with the Johannesburg Bar Council
- Maintains working relationships with a range of NGO's active in different areas of public interest work
- Arranges training / workshops / seminars on relevant public interest topics for either NGO's or law firms
- Publicises positive impact of pro bono legal assistance
- Tracks developments in public interest jurisprudence
- Alerts NGO's and law firms of developments in public interest jurisprudence
- Facilitates collaborations with public interest law research facilities

  - Facilitates collaborations between law firms and public law organisa-
    tions and / or NGO's
  - Accesses support from foreign and international pro bono entities

Alternatively, the user may refer to the AIDS Law Projectoriginated by Wits University from which they can cross-refer to other
organisations.

For further information about a range of issues including hiv/aids the user
may refer to the South African Street Law site <www.streetlaw.org.za/
main.html> which provides a range of information including easy to read
leaflets etc.

> Street Law (South Africa), and all its projects, work towards making people
> aware of their legal rights and how the legal system can be used to protect
> them. This practical course encourages the use of alternative dispute reso-
> lution methods and critical thinking through debates, mock trials and the
> teaching of human rights.
>
> The lives of thousands of people have been changed through their partici-
> pation in the Street Law programme. See some of the quotes from previous
> employees, learners, students and workshop participants.
>
> Street Law is currently co-ordinating *Sexual Harrassment in Schools* and
> *HIV, the law and human rights projects* and whilst continuing its school
> programme.

It may be significant that none of these sites cross-refer to SAFLII although
WorldLII and CommonLII cross-refer to some of these sites. However, the
significance probably lies in the general absence of interconnectedness between
networks rather than something specific about SAFLII.

I have suggested earlier that geographical groundedness may be a basis for
a different politics. However, this groundedness needs to be related to issues
of power. Thus, Telecentres, which have an enormously useful role in relation
to rural communities tend to have less of a success when they are not clearly
allied to the specific politics of the local. The Nakaseke Telecentre in Uganda
is a well publicized institution (Etta and Parvyn-Wamahiu, 2003). However, it
does not seem to be promoting any role in relation to people's rights and has
had mixed success as far as use of the Centre resources is concerned. Could it
be that part of its problem lies in it being part of a pilot African Information
Society Initiative?

India also provides a variety of examples of activist related legal information and action cultures in which the emphasis is on specific user needs to
promote justice. Indian activism was given a significant boost through the
struggle by subaltern activist groups for a Right to Information. For example,
the IS Watch website makes it a point to emphasise its specifically South perspective "the dominant information society discourse has been North-centric,
and does not take the development needs of the South into due consideration."

<www.is-watch.net> The Alternative Law Forum promotes legal information advice and assistance in the context of radical society change towards social justice. On the other hand, the more mainstream UNDP funded e-Justice pilot project intends to provide information and legal services for the citizen from kiosks, but does not have a radical dimension.[3]

Both the South African and Indian information suggests that movements located in subaltern activism may be better able to provide information which works for their audience but also to network effectively. However, it would be difficult to generalise this principle too greatly.

6. Possibilities for African based Legal Information Institutes

I have suggested that in Castell's terms, unlike Commercial organizations, Legal Information Institutes have their ethos in counter-publics. What I have tried to explore in this paper is the relationship between their form of counter-public and organizations which provide legal information from a more social justice perspective. As a minimum, it can be stated that an organizations such as SAFLII, CommonLII, Droit Francophone and WorldLII provide valuable primary material to those involved in social justice action. Apart from SAFLII, they go further in cataloguing and connecting to many of the relevant datasets. However, the question arises as to whether they could or should do more. There are three possibilities here. The first is to appreciate that these are distinct roles and should not be confused. That is, it is upto activist organizations as with any civil society or commercial groups to make what use it can of the access to primary materials. This may go against the ethos of organizations such as WorldLII in the sense that the objective is to provide *effective* access to legal information. This leads us to a second possibility, that LIIs take on the role of providing information in a form which is appropriate to the ordinary literate African audience. On current evidence this would require enormous co-operation between LIIs and activist groups and it may be that the task may be better carried out by activist groups or others who already have experience in these areas. The third possibility is to acknowledge that it is entirely appropriate for there to be a division of labour between providers of primary legal information and the activist groups who can best provide appropriate secondary legal information. Nevertheless, LIIs have to develop approaches which make interconnection and access more meaningful for the user in the activist community. This can be achieved for example by ensuring cross-links between the different networks especially including 'deep-linking' as

---

[3] From the e-Justice website (<www.ejustice.org.in/home.do>), a pilot initiative funded by United Nations Development Programme (UNDP) is a citizen centric approach for providing access to justice through Information and Communication Technology (ICT). It will help to provide a crucial link between rule of law, poverty eradication, human rights and sustainable human development and to provide better access to justice.

appropriate. It could also be achieved by ensuring that collections of material which may be of specific interest in the advancement of rights are organized with explanatory information and material. In this respect, AustLII's practice of providing community based information must be a valuable precedent although the strength of LIIs may not necessarily lie in ensuring regular editing. What may be needed is a co-operative dialogue between activist groups and the LIIs to determine ways in which they can be of mutual benefit within a specifically African context of activism around law.

References

Alternative Law Forum Website (2008), available at: <www.altlawforum.org/>.

AustlII Website (2008), available at: <www.austlii.edu.au/>.

Castells, M. (1998), *Information Technology, Globalisation and Social Development*, Conference on Information Technology and Development (Geneva, UNISRD), available at: <www.unrisd.org/infotech/conferen/castelp1.htm>.

Castells, M. (2000), *The Rise of the Network Society: The Information Age: Economy Society, Culture*, Vol. 1, Blackwell, Oxford.

CommonLII Website (2008), available at: <www.commonlii.org/>.

Droit Francophone Website (2008), available at: <droit.francophonie.org/df-web/>.

E-Justice Project India Website (2008), available at: <www.ejustice.org.in/home.do>).

Etta, F. and Parvyn-Wamahiu, S. (2003), *Information And Communication Technologies For Development In Africa*, in Etta F. and Parvyn-Wamahiu S. (Eds.), "The Experience with Community Telecentres", Vol. 2, CODESRIA/IDRC, Ottawa / Dakar.

Juris, J. (2004), *Networked Social Movements: Global Movements for Global Justice*, in Castells, M. (Ed.) "The Network Society: a Cross-Cultural Perspective", Edward Elgar Publishing Ltd, Cheltenham, UK, pp. 341-362.

Juris, J. (2005), *The New Digital Media and Activist Networking within Anti–Corporate Globalization Movements*, Annals of the American Academy of Political and Social Science, Vol. 597, No. 1, pp. 189-208.

Kenya Law Reports Website (2008), available at: <www.kenyalaw.org/>.

Paliwala, A. (2007), *Free Culture, Global Commons and Social Justice in Information Technology Diffusion*, Law, Social Justice & Global Development Journal (LGD), Vol. 1, available at: <www.go.warwick.ac.uk/elj/lgd/2007_1/paliwala>.

SAFLII Website (2008), available at: <www.saflii.org/>.

Santos, B. and Rodriguez-Garavito, A. (2005), *Law and Globalization from Below*, Cambridge University Press, Cambridge.

Santos, B. (2002), *Towards a New Legal Common Sense: Law, Globalization and Emancipation*, London, Butterworths.

Shackleford, L. (2006), *Counter-Networks in a Network Society: Leslie Marmon Silko's Almanac of the Dead Postmodern Culture*, available at: <muse.jhu.edu/journals/pmc/v016/16.3bios.html#shackelford.bio>.

Travers, A. (2003), *Feminist subaltern counterpublics in cyberspace*, Sociological Perspectives, Vol. 46, No. 2, pp. 223-237.

Treatment Action Campaign Website (2008), available at: <www.tac.org.za/>.

World Bank Law and Justice Institutions Website (2008), *Introduction to World Bank Law and Justice Reform Projects*, available at: <web.worldbank.org/WBSITE/EXTERNAL/TOPICS/EXTLAWJUSTINST/0,,contentMDK:20746118~menuPK:1980807~pagePK:210058~piPK:210062~theSitePK:1974062,00.html>.

WorldLII Website (2008), available at: <www.worldlii.org/>.

Re-thinking "Open" in Free and Open Access to Law

Mariya Badeva-Bright
Southern African Legal Information Institute (SAFLII), South Africa

Abstract. The paper discusses the provision and consumption of free access to legal information in a developing country context. A variety of factors in such a context necessitate taking a, not only free, but also open access to legal information stance. The paper further explores parallels with other open access initiatives and philosophies, notably open access to knowledge and open source and free software. Finally, policy and technical challenges and solutions are discussed. The anticipated impact on a LII of such changes in policy are canvassed.

1. Access to legal information in a developing country context

The rationale of this paper is based on observations on the state of access to legal information in a developing African country, particularly countries in the scope of the operation of the Southern African Legal Information Institute. In this context, the proposals for a model of access to legal information based on the principle of openness, is informed to a great extent by pragmatic considerations, but also on moral grounds.

Free public access to law strengthens the rule of law through the creation of the potential for increased knowledge of the law; through the establishment of an environment of openness and transparency in the judicial system; by creating the possibility for legal exchange on a regional and international level, thus bringing consideration of jurisprudential standards into the national legal systems (Poulin, 2004). It has been SAFLII's experience that the provision of free access to legal information in Southern and East Africa has provided a viable alternative for smaller legal practices to the heavily over-priced commercial legal information products. In some countries, SAFLII has been the sole provider of access to the law – in a situation of lack of, or sporadic publication of national primary law.

The Southern African Legal Information Institute (SAFLII) became operational in 2003, as a website featuring primarily South African information. In the years leading to SAFLII's re-birth in 2006, the project had failed to produce a noticeable impact on the South African legal information scene. There are a number of reasons for the difficulties facing free access to law in the region, the least of which is the reliance on old arrangements with commercial publishers.[1]

---

[1] For example, a quasi-judicial tribunal in South Africa is unable to participate in the SAFLII project because of an agreement with commercial publishers whereby access to the decisions of the tribunal is given in exchange for legal publications.

There were only a few producers of primary legal materials at the time who were making their work easily available for publication. Initially SAFLII saw the task of publishing case-law and legislation to be as easy as mobilizing courts in sending judgments to the service for publication on the website or collecting the legal information from the institutional repositories available on the Internet (e.g. the Constitutional Court of South Africa). In late 2006, and in fact, until today, very few producers of legal information in SAFLII's countries of operation place the product of their work online in a format readily accessible for re-publication in a meaningful way. The progress in bringing institutions to establish their own online digital repositories has been unsatisfactory. SAFLII has had to adjust its strategy to one of collection, and increasingly, digitization of information, sometimes even current information, for placement on the Internet. This situation, perhaps unique to a developing country context, has adjusted the position of the legal information institute to one of a primary publisher of legal information. In some countries, SAFLII remains the only provider of legal information, as even commercial legal publishers have pulled out of the legal information market.[2] In a sense, SAFLII holds the only repository of digital case-law in some of the jurisdictions of its operations – this places the Institute in a position necessitating a different policy approach to the dissemination of the information in its possession.

Producers of primary legal material in the region experience difficulties in setting up and maintaining an up-to-date ICT infrastructure and related human resources capital to support the operation of dissemination of their work. The SAFLII team observed the difficulties facing courts and court libraries in the region in terms of computerization and access to the Internet. This affects not only the production and dissemination of the digital version of a judicial decision. The strained state of ICT resources, coupled with the, generally, low level of ICT literacy remains a contributing factor to the slow progress of the free access to law projects in some of SAFLII's member countries. Difficulties range from the lack of standards, including low-level ones, in the production of the case law material to the communication of the case-law to a central repository – either within the courts or on SAFLII.

There was and continues to be little appreciation of the benefits of free access to primary legal materials over the Internet. While this is partially due to limited access to the Internet and less developed information research skills and reliance on older legal research methods, it is exacerbated by concerns over the quality, authenticity and re-use of the legal information thus provided.

SAFLII's long-term approach here focuses on training and local capacity building by seeking out and enabling local actors to participate in the publication of free law as well as engaging stakeholders and producers of information

---

[2] Such is the case with Uganda and Zimbabwe. Both countries currently do not produce printed, neither hard-copy, nor electronic, law reports, save for the cases published on the SAFLII website.

on policy and functional level. The local capacity building envisioned includes the propagation of legal information skills and legal information standards across the creation, archiving, publication and use of legal information. The aim is to create a legal knowledge economy[3] where knowledge of the local law will grow through application. The creation of abundance of freely and openly available legal information will incentivise the creation of local legal information industries[4] building additional knowledge value onto the basic legal material delivered electronically or in print. The creation of a working legal knowledge economy – with its free and commercial sides – will have the effect of creating a demand for access to primary legal materials further pressuring governments and courts to make the product of their work openly available for citizens to use and organizations to build products and services around.

In the short term, however, SAFLII aims to utilize all means in its disposal to bring public legal materials to users particularly in Africa. Thus far, this has required changes in copyright and access policies and technical and functional modifications of the SAFLII website and distribution model, so as to enable a wider acceptance and usage of the primary legal materials. SAFLII, as a member of the Free Access to Law Movement, has pledged to provide free, full and anonymous access to public legal information. A year after its rebirth, SAFLII's operational environment necessitated the re-examination and expansion of the service's access and usage policies and the meaning of free and full access to the collection held.

2. The meaning of open access

2.1. WHAT IS FREE AND WHAT IS OPEN?

When one thinks of free access to information, it is usually the dichotomy of free versus subscription models for access to information that come to mind. However, a cursory review – sufficient for the purposes of this presentation – of the available literature on free and open access shows that there are distinguishable nuances in the meaning of free and open access. In view of the outlined challenges to the provision of access to basic legal material, SAFLII has taken lessons from the philosophies of some of the available free and open access initiatives in other areas of knowledge and attempted to incorporate into its own free and open access to law policy.

---

[3] The term knowledge economy was coined by Peter Drucker to mean the production and management of knowledge in the frame of economic constraints, to the end of production of economic benefits. (Wikipedia, *Knowledge Economy*, available at: <en.wikipedia.org/wiki/Knowledge_economy>, accessed 18 October 2008).

[4] Daniel Poulin from LexUM was among the first to recognize the potential of developing national legal information industries and its benefits for the building of a well-functioning legal system (Poulin, 2004).

2.2. FREE AND OPEN SOURCE SOFTWARE

The GNU/Free Software project was one of the first free movements to emerge in the 1980's as a reaction to the commercialization of software. It later became the starting point for open source software. Today the GNU General Public License[5] protects most open source as well as free software today.[6] Richard Stallman, the ideologue of the free software movement, is careful to make the distinction that "free software" is about *freedom*:

"Free software" is a matter of liberty, not price. To understand the concept, you should think of "free" as in "free speech" not as in "free beer" (Stallman, 2002).

Free software allows users the freedom to run, copy, distribute, study, change and improve the software. Free software also means access to the source code of the software – the accessibility giving meaning to the freedom to run the programme on any computer, to modify, use and build on in subsequent works. The free software movement explicitly recognises the freedom to distribute copies of the software in binary, executable and source code formats; and to build on the previous work.

Stallman's rationale for *freeing* software is based on a moral obligation to share programmes, to keep software transparent, control-free and open to change. The harm in non-free software can be seen on three levels: fewer people use the programme, none of the users can adapt or fix the programme; and other developers cannot learn from the programme, or base new work on it (Stallman, 1992). If software were free there would be increased software productivity at all levels through better education of programmers and the elimination of duplication of effort.

The inroads that the free software movement made into the realm of proprietary information (be it in the form of source code/computer programme or any domain-specific information) remain philosophically and pragmatically sound and became the foundation for further developments in the concept.

2.3. OPEN ACCESS

The concept of "open access" today is exclusively associated with the initiative to provide free access to scholarly literature via the Internet. While it is not within the objective of this paper to analyze the open access initiatives in the scholarly realm, a few recourses to the rationale and meaning of the concept shall be pointed out.

---

[5] The GNU General Public License is available at: <www.gnu.org/copyleft/gpl.html> (accessed 18 October 2008).

[6] Though "open source", in Stallman's words, focuses more to the technical potential to make high quality, powerful software, but does not necessarily embrace the ideas of freedom, community and principle.

The initiative's roots can be traced back to the Budapest Open Access Initiative,[7] which defined the meaning of open access. Two more statements followed: the Bethesda Statement on Open Access Publishing[8] and the Berlin Declaration on Open Access to Knowledge in the Sciences and Humanities.[9]

All initiatives recognize the unprecedented potential of technology, specifically the Internet, to distributing knowledge. The knowledge is to be disseminated not only via free, but also through open access to all "curious minds".[10] All three declarations permit *"any users to read, download, copy, distribute, print, search, or link to the full texts of these articles, crawl them for indexing, pass them as data to software, or use them for any other lawful purpose, without financial, legal, or technical barriers other than those inseparable from gaining access to the internet itself".*[11] The Bethesda and Berlin statements go further to also permit derivative works without mention of copyright restrictions.

Peter Sauber (2008), in his recent Open Access Newsletter distinguished between *gratis* and *libre* open access – where *gratis* open access will mean the removal of the price barrier and *libre* would mean the removal of both the price and permission barriers to research. Apparently satisfying either of these two conditions would qualify a repository as open access.

The ultimate goal of open access, as defined in the Berlin Declaration, is to create a global and accessible representation of knowledge where open access is a comprehensive source of human knowledge and cultural heritage that has been approved by the scientific community. The road to achieving this goal, is through a Web that is sustainable, interactive, and transparent, where content and software tools are openly accessible and compatible.[12]

Open access initiatives recognise that open access information is costly to produce. While new cost recovery and financing mechanisms are needed, the benefits of the reduced cost of electronic dissemination is seen as making the goal attainable.[13]

2.4. FREE ACCESS TO LAW MOVEMENT

The Free Access to Law Movement (FALM)[14] is the collective of organizations from across the world providing free online access to legal information. The philosophy and objectives of the movement are embedded in the Montreal Dec-

---

[7] Available at: <www.soros.org/openaccess> (accessed 18 October 2008).

[8] Available at: <www.earlham.edu/~peters/fos/bethesda.htm> (accessed 18 October 2008).

[9] Available at: <oa.mpg.de/openaccess-berlin/berlindeclaration.html> (accessed 18 October 2008).

[10] Budapest, *supra note 7.*

[11] Budapest, *supra note 7.*

[12] Berlin, *supra nota 9.*

[13] Budapest, *supra nota 7.*

[14] Generally on the FALM see (Greenleaf, 2008).

laration on Free Access to Law, 2002 to which all legal information institutes (LIIs) subscribe. LIIs define public legal information as "legal information produced by public bodies that have a duty to produce law and make it public. It includes primary sources of law, such as legislation, case law and treaties, as well as various secondary (interpretative) public sources, such as reports on preparatory work and law reform, and resulting from boards of inquiry. It also includes legal documents created as a result of public funding".[15] Public legal information is declared by the LIIs "digital common property" that should be accessible on a not-for-profit and free basis as it forms part of the "common heritage of humanity".

A Legal Information Institute that is part of the Free Access to Law Movement, such as SAFLII, participates in the LII community via the regional and global free access to law networks on the development of open technical standards, research and training and:

— Publishes via the internet public legal information originating from more than one public body;
— Provides free, full and anonymous public access to that information;
— Does not impede others from publishing public legal information.

Similarly to the open access and free movements outlined above, the Free Access to Law Movement and its operations are seen as a vehicle for, *maximizing* access to public legal information to the end of promoting justice and the rule of law. Professor Greenleaf, one of the founding members of the FALM and drafter of the Montreal Declaration, however, explains that the policy stated in the Declaration does not intend that a "LII must declare its content to be 'open content' (available for re-use by anyone), but only that it must not hinder others from obtaining the data from its official sources and republishing it" (Greenleaf, 2008). It is clear though that different LIIs have interpreted the meaning of "free, full and anonymous" access differently under their operational environment and implemented their distinct policies with respect to it. For example, Cornell LII claims no copyright in its collection, but do make use of a Creative Commons Attribution-Noncommercial-Share Alike license to permit use of the markup, navigation apparatus, and other value-added features of electronic editions of government publications for non-commercial use.[16] AustLII, on the other hand, does not make an explicit statement with regards to the use of its collection of public documents but states that depending "on the type of material, and the method of reproduction" license to use information published on AustLII may be granted. AustLII prohibits the commercial reproduction of its detailed mark-up.[17]

---

[15] See the Appendix of this volume.

[16] The Legal Information Institute's Policy is available at: <www.law.cornell.edu/comments/credits.html> (accessed 18 October 2008).

[17] AustLII - About AustLII: Frequently Asked Questions (FAQs), available at: <www.austlii.edu.au/austlii/faq/#q5> (accessed 18 October 2008).

CanLII has taken still another approach – in its Reproduction and Copyright policy licenses the copying, printing and distribution of legal material in their collection, including CanLII inserted editorial enhancements free of charge, provided CanLII is cited as the source.[18]

SAFLII has adopted an approach similar to that of CanLII for reasons outlined below.

3. Policy and technology choices for open access to law

3.1. OPEN AND FREE ACCESS TO LAW IMPACT ON AN AFRICAN DEVELOPING COUNTRY

Analyzing the lessons of the open and free philosophies as outlined above, perhaps it is only suitable to describe Lawrence Lessig's equation of code as law. Code defines the architecture of and regulates cyberspace, law regulates the behaviour of individuals. Both code and law need to be transparent to preserve liberty (Lessig, 1999). Transparency in the control of law is best achieved via free and open access to the source code of law – the basic public domain primary and secondary legal materials. SAFLII sees this access as allowing individuals – legal researchers (in the broadest sense) to study and build on the existing law to create better laws and commentaries on the existing ones. Some will go on to build free and open legal knowledge using the existing resources for the benefit of the common citizens.

SAFLII is sometimes the primary holder of the basic public legal material in digital format. Furthermore, the digitization of this public information has been achieved with the use of public and private funds granted to fulfil the objectives of strengthening democracy and the rule of law, through availing access to primary legal materials. The natural choice, in application to the achievement of this goal, is placing the available public information in the public domain free of conditions on reproduction and distribution, including commercial one – making maximum use of funds granted and avoiding duplication of costly digitization efforts, thus truly maximizing access to law. The type of open access that can impact a developing country in building a proper legal knowledge economy and associated know-how and skills, is the type of *libre* open access – removing both price and permission barriers – where open legal information and technical standards are used to represent content and ensure compatibility of information systems. Open technical standards for representation of legal information and open architectures shall contribute to the building of regional and international legal information systems and integration with scholarly services (such as open access scholarly literature

---

[18] CanLII Terms of Use Reproduction and Copyright, available at: <www.canlii.org/en/info/terms.html> (accessed 18 October 2008).

repositories) allowing for cross-border legal research and cross-pollination of
the legal systems. In the African, context, this brings the promise of sharing
solutions to regional problems at a much reduced cost and increasing the
possibility of developing intensive local and regional legal research networks.

3.2. PRACTICAL STEPS TO EFFECT CHANGE: CHANGE IN COPYRIGHT POLICY

Throughout its existence until October 2007, SAFLII operated under a copyright policy allowing limited reproduction of the case-law and legislation collections freely available on the website. The old copyright policy permitted
any user to reproduce up to 30 pages from the SAFLII service for non-
commercial and reasonable purpose. In October 2007, the copyright policy
changed allowing users to reproduce all public domain legal material, including
all editorial enhancements inserted by SAFLII free of charge and without prior
authorisation, for any use, including commercial, subject only to attribution to
the source of the material. SAFLII has followed in this regard and approach
very similar to CanLII's approach to licensing reproduction of material on
the service. The decision stems for the earlier outlined position of SAFLII as
a primary provider of, otherwise difficult and costly to obtain, public legal
material. SAFLII observes the creation of the first services around material
found on its website.[19] The attribution component of the policy remains for
the strategic purpose of increasing the visibility of the free law available on
the SAFLII website.

The change in copyright policy facilitates the proper addressing of the
issue of lack of Internet connectivity to access the legal material available
on the website. For example, in a recent trip to Malawi, judges expressed
concern over the value of the SAFLII project for the judiciary which had sparse
access to the Internet and outdated computer facilities.[20] SAFLII changed its
publication strategy to packaging case-law collections for off-line distribution
via CDs and DVDs. However, the task of maintaining updates on all such
distributions of the collection has become cumbersome for the organization.
SAFLII has looked to partner with Freedom Toaster – a project, born out of
the necessity of the constrained African broadband environment, specialising
in the offline distribution of free digital content. Since SAFLII content is free
of copyright restrictions, Freedom Toasters placed in strategic public places
– such as universities across the region, would be able to dispense updated
versions of SAFLII's collections.

[19] South African dedicated labour law websites: <www.labourguide.co.za> and <www.
erisa.co.za> – intending to build case books and subject indexes on South African labour
law based on SAFLII collections.
[20] Similar concerns were raised in other member countries, e.g. Zimbabwe, Uganda.

3.3. PRACTICAL STEPS TO EFFECT CHANGE: CHANGE IN ACCESS AND PRIVACY POLICY

It was mentioned earlier that SAFLII sees the success of the objectives of the project to be best served by increased visibility of the law. Visibility includes discoverability. In SAFLII's operational environment of poor information research and computer literacy skills maximizing access to the law means opening all channels for users to be able to find the law. This includes opening up, similarly to open access to scholarly literature, of the SAFLII legal collections for crawling by search engines. The move, effected in late 2007 for select databases and later, in February 2008, for all SAFLII databases, saw, as per SAFLII statistics, a rise in unique visitors on the website from a mere 7352 in August 2007, to a peak 93342 in June 2008 and over 880,000 hits in September 2008. Opening up SAFLII for crawling has proven to be a successful move to increase the visibility of African law.

The opening of the collection required that special attention be paid to the issues of privacy in personal information published. Most of the courts in the region pay little attention to the fact that judgments disseminated out of the court's registry may contain sensitive personal information and little is done to redact such information. While SAFLII continues to engage with courts with the view of sensitizing the judiciary to the problem, the Institute has taken a number of measures to prevent certain personal information, as required by statute or common law, from being disseminated via the website, irrespective whether the judgment is exclusively discoverable via SAFLII's search facility or via a general Internet search engine. SAFLII is of the view that it is the *court's* discretion to include or exclude facts and information from, otherwise available for public scrutiny, judicial decisions.

3.4. PRACTICAL STEPS TO EFFECT CHANGE: TECHNOLOGY CHOICES FOR MAXIMUM ACCESS

SAFLII is actively involved in the development and implementation of open technical standards for the representation and publication of legal information. Most notable here is SAFLII's contribution to the AKOMA NTOSO XML standards for the representation of judgments. AKOMA NTOSO is a UNDESA-led African initiative.[21]

AKOMA NTOSO forms part of a wider initiative to harness the power of ICT through technical assistance, capacity building and standards and associated tools building for more efficient parliaments. The partnership with UN/DESA on this level brings the promise of integrating legislative texts, produced in open standards into SAFLII's service. It is also envisaged that

---

[21] AKOMA NTOSO for Judgments available at: <www.akomantoso.org/schema/ akoma-ntoso-standard-for-judgments/rationale> (accessed 18 October 2008).

courts, and ultimately citizens and organizations, will benefit from workflow solutions based on open XML standards for the production and publication of their judicial decisions. SAFLII, which already makes extensive use of free and open source software to aid publication,[22] has included in its strategy the promotion of such free and open source tool for integration into the court workflows for production and dissemination of judgments as means of ensuring that open standards are used from the creation stage of the law.

To counter the lack of electronic legal research skills, SAFLII is exploring technical means of using added value content built into judgments to enhance legal research. The end of October 2008 will see the pilot of a subject index database on select SAFLII collections.

In 2009, SAFLII will continue its efforts to removing technical barriers to access to African law and facilitating a distributed model of access to law in the region.[23] SAFLII and Kenya Law Reports are working towards the establishment of a federated search facility between the two collections, and further building the African network as new African LIIs join. It is clear that the federated search model based on open access and open standards is the appropriate choice to increase the potential for building a comprehensive African legal research platform.

References

Greenleaf, G. (2008), *Legal Information Institutes and the Free Access to Law Movement*, available at: <www.nyulawglobal.org/globalex/Legal_Information_Institutes.htm> (accessed 18 October 2008).

Lessig, L. (1999), *Code and Other Laws of Cyberspace*, Basic Books, New York.

Poulin, D. (2004), *Open Access to Law in Developing Countries*, First Monday, Vol. 9, No. 12, available at: <www.firstmonday.org/issues/issue9_12/poulin/index.html> (accessed 18 October 2008).

Sauber, P. (2008), *Gratis and Libre Open Access*, Open Access Newsletter, No. 124, available at: <www.earlham.edu/~peters/fos/newsletter/08-02-08.htm> (accessed 18 October 2008).

Stallman, R. (1992), *Why Software Should Be Free*, in Gay, J. (Ed.), 'Free Software, Free Society: Selected Essays of Richard M. Stallman', 2002, GNU Press, p. 41.

Stallman, R. (2002), *Free Software Definition*, in Gay, J. (Ed.), "Free Software, Free Society: Selected Essays of Richard M. Stallman", GNU Press, p. 122.

---

[22] For example, our document conversions are exclusively handled with OpenOffice and a free and open source conversion tool, called UnoConvert.

[23] As announced at the 8th Law via the Internet Conference, SAFLII's strategy is to build local capacity in its member countries by supporting the set-up of country-specific legal information institutes. The approach sees the establishment of a technical network, based on standards and open access, for research into the collection of the country collections hosted in the respective national institutes.

Towards Free Access to Law: Research Experience and Prospects

Roberta Nannucci, Mario Ragona
Institute of Legal Information Theory and Techniques (ITTIG-CNR), Italy

Abstract. By means of new ICT technologies implemented for making documents related to different law sources available to the public a set of support tools were built moving towards free access but trying at the same time to make the use of these data banks easier and more friendly. Free access demonstrated to be an excellent means of open and democratic approach, but practically insufficient for a fruitful exploitation by expert and non expert stakeholders of materials which are by their nature scarcely comprehensible.

A more than twenty years old experience of a research institute is described here, enriched also by its participation to a variety of national and international projects.

Some strategic guidelines derive from this experience aiming at developing effective services capable of meeting the needs of a widespread audience such as Internet stakeholders. It is worthwhile to keep on free access, but also to devote energies to develop tools able to support effectively the comprehensiveness of legal materials. In this way free access will not be a mere empty expression, but will correspond to a real and effective right to legal information access.

Keywords: Legal information, free access, retrieval support tools.

1. Introduction

The research world involved in the development and dissemination of legal data banks from the very beginning focused its attention on how these systems could be used by the widespread and variegated public of the Internet: since its origin the net immediately appeared as a powerful tool for enhancing a democratic approach in any section of social life but also capable of making the technological community closer to expert professionals and non expert citizens.

Many efforts were devoted to the building of large legal databases for rendering data pertaining to different law sources (legislation, case law and legal literature) available to the great public by exploiting the means deriving from the implementation of new ICT technologies. It became also immediately apparent that these types of databases had to be available free of charge as anybody would in this way be allowed to have the chance to access data which were so far not easily available and anyhow only to certain categories of users.

Contemporarily a set of support tools were conceived and built in order to make the use of these data banks easier and more friendly. Free access demonstrated in fact to be an excellent means of openness and democratic approach, but practically insufficient for a fruitful exploitation by expert and especially non expert stakeholders as materials such as legal documents (laws, court decisions) are by their nature scarcely comprehensible by not sufficiently competent persons.

This was also the experience of a research institute such as ITTIG, which with its activity going on for more than twenty years has become one of the best known institutions "par excellence" in the European scenario, enriched also by its participation to a great variety of national and international projects, within the scope of free access (bibliographies, databases) or aiming at experimenting and developing semantic-oriented supporting tools such as classifications, thesauri and ontologies or content-oriented tools.

Some strategic guidelines derive also from this experience aiming at developing effective services capable of meeting all the needs of large and widespread audiences that is any user can retrieve the database information in an easy way but comprehending the deep substance of the information content.

2. ITTIG's experience: free access to law

ITTIG's research activities were concentrated in two major directions: a large variety of different databases (bibliographical, legislative, historical and lexical) were built, as can be seen consulting its website, following the free access approach to legal information, but a variety of supporting tools facilitating such access was also implemented.

Among the built and distributed databases two services in particular are to be mentioned here.

2.1. DoGi – Dottrina Giuridica

DoGi is the name of a bibliographical database (`<www.ittig.cnr.it/dogi-e>`) started in 1970 which in the Italian legal world is one of the most precious sources for searching legal literature. Its main goal is to provide law professionals, scholars and university students with exhaustive and updated information as can be found in Italian law reviews. It offers abstracts of articles (scientific contributions, summaries of cases, commentaries to statutes, conference papers and book reviews) published in the most important legal periodicals (more than 250). At present it consists of more than 330,000 records containing value-added items (abstract, classification, references to major national, European and international case law and legislation cited by the author, links to some citation full-texts, and other metadata) (Peruginelli, 2006).

DoGi has been freely accessible from its origin and for more than thirty years, as the Institute management was convinced that the data-base – and not only this - should be available without any charge as it could be of relevance for the users, irrespective of their affiliation and utilization and a good means for enhancing democracy in the country. However, since 2004, this was no

Figure 1. ITTIG Databases

longer possible due to a drastic reduction of the financial support by public bodies such as the CNR head administration, the Chamber of Deputies and the Ministry of Justice.

On the basis of its long outstanding role as witness to Italian legal literature's evolution and reputation in the scientific community, and wishing to maintain a service with high quality features, ITTIG sought the support of new institutional partners and accepted the idea to disseminate the database through commercial publishers. To this purpose an agreement was signed with Infoleges and in the last five years the DoGi database has been distributed on pay through subscriptions to <www.infoleges.it>. A demo version of the database is still accessible on the ITTIG's website free of charge for marketing purposes.

Although ITTIG's policy would preferably address towards a free access dissemination, certain that the service is highly appreciated by the scientific, academic and professional community, DoGi sustainability cannot be any longer publicly afforded in the present general and national financial situation.

The question is then how can a public institution afford the costs of such an important service for the community free of charge? For the moment there are no positive answers. Anyhow, the Institute is trying to persuade public institutions that DoGi is a patrimony for the expert and non expert stakeholder and therefore should be a service assured to all of them free of charge. It is also to be considered that in Italy, contrarily to the approach followed in other countries, such as Canada and Australia, private organizations (bar associations, legal publishers, large law firms) do not want to support the service financially although very interested to it in their practising activity.

2.2. CASELEX – EUROPE'S PREMIER CASE LAW SERVICE

A second database produced by ITTIG of relevance here is Caselex. It is an Internet based "one-stop-shop" service for national case law developed with the support of the EU Commission under the eContent and eTEN programmes (<www.caselex.com>). It collects decisions of Supreme and High Courts of Member States, within selected areas of law connected with the implementation and application of EU law. The knowledge of the decisions taken by national courts is important in the European Union, as the experience of the courts of other Member States can help a national court to better comprehend and interpret the same EU measure. The distribution of decisions made by national courts and the building of a sort of dialogue may enhance their role as *juges communautaires de droit commun* and contribute to guaranteeing the uniform application of EU law (Biasiotti and Faro, 2007; Faro and Nannucci, 2008).

Cases are collected in Caselex only when: (i) a national court interprets a term mentioned in an EU rule; (ii) a national court says something about the 'value' of a certain EU rule; (iii) a national court *de facto* applies an EU rule in a new way.

Caselex focuses predominantly on commercial law, presently consisting of 12 areas, being: Company law; Competition law; Consumer protection law; Environmental law; Freedom of movement; ICT law including e-commerce, telecom and privacy; Intellectual property law; Private international law; Employment law; Public procurement law; Social security law. It covers all EU Member States together with the four EFTA Member States and the EU and EFTA courts.

Cases are offered in their native language full text, integrated with a headnote, a summary and additional metadata in English and enriched by a multilingual thesaurus translated into the major European languages. A typical Caselex summary is between 250-400 words, and does not represent a legal analysis of the case but rather reflects key facts, holding, decision and results. This is meant to help the user to obtain a qualified opinion about the merit of the case when reading its headnote and summary.

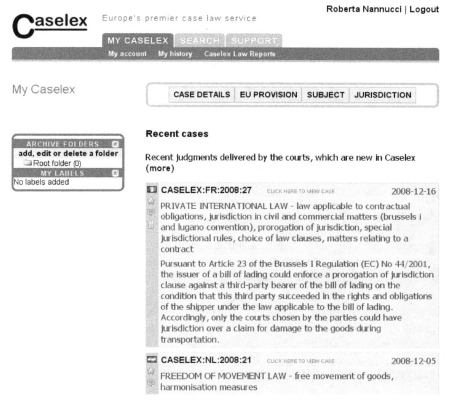

Figure 2. Example of a Caselex record

Caselex knowledge infrastructure is designed for facilitating its access through a semantic layer supporting the user in his searching needs to understand what the content is like and to link it with the knowledge already existing in his experience and skills. The semantic layer is particularly useful when the stakeholder may lack of those capabilities to manage multicultural and multilingual data, although he might be interested in entertaining good relationships with enterprises and institutions of other European countries. The knowledge of national case law is essential for better understanding the legal order of the different countries.

The implementation of the Caselex service is the result of a strong alliance between public institutions (content holders and public sector organisations) and private actors such as publishers. At present Caselex is funded by the European Commission (e-TEN program) for experimenting if this type of service is sustainable without the support of public funds. The Consortium publishers involved in the Caselex dissemination through subscriptions find quite difficulties to organize a business venture with good revenues. Therefore it becomes apparent that free access to this kind of systems can be rarely sustainable if distributed only by private enterprises, although appreciated by stakeholders.

3. ITTIG's experience: support tools enhancing access

ITTIG has been always aware that many efforts should also be devoted to develop tools able to support the comprehensiveness of legal materials. Only in this way free access could become not an empty expression, but would correspond to a real and effective right to legal information access.

The developed support tools can be subdivided, as to their nature, into semantic, structural and knowledge-oriented tools.

3.1. SEMANTIC SUPPORT TOOLS

The semantic tools have the function to identify the linguistic and content meaning consistency of the information. Their typologies can be distinguished into Classification Schemes, Thesauri and Ontologies.

3.1.1. *Classifications*

Almost all ITTIG's databases are equipped with systematic domain-oriented classifications, but the DoGi classification scheme is worth of being mentioned. It is hierarchically structured (up to three levels) and composed by alphanumeric codes expressing specific concepts. Codes are associated with descriptors (6,600 at the moment). An authority list of descriptors is maintained and updated on the basis of indexing suggestions as well as of statistic analysis of user searches. The classification scheme is a dynamic instrument periodically reviewed: new codes are established reflecting additional topics dealt with by the literature. The language used to index DoGi documents is a controlled language, based on the areas of law as structured in the Italian law faculties, so the classification scheme is a good means not only for retrieving legal literature items in the database, but also to understand the organizational structure of Italian law. The system is utilized also in academic and professional contexts as well as in specialized legal libraries (Peruginelli, 2006).

3.1.2. *Thesauri*

Among thesauri already implemented two experiences cannot be neglected.

Thes/BID (a multilingual thesaurus on computers and law). It is a structured thesaurus of descriptors (keywords and phrases) implemented in 1992 and used in the "International Bibliography on Computers and Law" (BID) and its computerized database for indexing and retrieving bibliographical material relating to computer science, its application to the law and to computer law problems. It is the first attempt at giving a general structural systemization to recurrent concepts within a new discipline such as legal informatics and computer law. Thes/BID was compiled electronically by means of a specially prepared automated checking and printing procedure designed to facilitate its development. About 2000 descriptors were chosen from the technical literature present in the analyzed journals on the basis of the frequency in their use. Once normalized, they were numbered progressively and then classified with a code number taken from a special scheme, the Classification Table also used for classifying the BID bibliographical units.

The most important relations of a vertical kind (conceptual hierarchy) and of a horizontal kind (synonymy, quasi-synonymy and other associative-type relations) existing between the various descriptors selected were identified, as well as a distinction was made between non-preferred and preferred terms. The developed thesaurus consists of a Structured Alphabetic List containing all keywords and phrases examined (including non-preferred terms) and with the indication of the different relation types between them. It is integrated and enriched by a Class list, a Geographic list and an Acronym list. Still nowadays it is a fully utilizable tool for identifying the most relevant concepts related to legal informatics with all relations among concepts.

Eurovoc studies. Most recently (2008) a feasibility study was carried out in favour of OPOCE within a tender on interoperability between European thesauri. The study concentrated on thesaurus mapping, considering five thesauri of interest for EU activities with the aim of promoting cross-collection retrieval facilities (that is providing a query from a single user interface, using for example Eurovoc as support, and retrieving pertinent documents from different collections, indexed by Eurovoc or by other thesauri). In this context a methodology to describe thesauri terms semantics and to provide a semi-automatic mapping procedure between thesauri concepts was also proposed.

3.1.3. *Ontologies*

Within the Semantic Web Community, the term 'ontology' has acquired several meanings and specifications, such as lightweight, core, domain, and foundational (or upper) ontology. In the Wonderweb project (Masolo et al., 2004) differences are explained as follows:

> "In most practical applications, ontologies appear as simple taxonomic structures of primitive or composite terms together with associated definitions. These are the so-called lightweight ontologies, used to represent semantic relationships among terms in order to facilitate content-based access to the (Web) data produced by a given community. In this case, the intended meaning of primitive terms is more or less known in advance by the members of

such community. On the other hand, however, the need to establishing precise agreements as to the meaning of terms becomes crucial as soon as a community of users evolves, or multicultural and multilingual communities need to exchange data and services. To capture (or at least approximate) such subtle distinctions we need an explicit representation of the so-called ontological commitments about the meaning of terms, in order to remove terminological and conceptual ambiguities. A rigorous logical axiomatisation seems to be unavoidable in this case, as it accounts not only for the relationships between terms, but – most importantly – for the formal structure of the domain to be represented".

Lexicons are therefore considered lightweight ontologies, linguistic expansions of the description of a way of perceiving reality, with limited formal modelling. Their role is mostly to support the conceptual retrieval of information. They intend to improve the functionalities of traditional search engines for legal information retrieval which do not include legal knowledge into their search strategies. In other words, there is no semantic relationship between information needs of the user and the information content of documents apart from text pattern matching.

These aspects are more emphasized in multilingual environments. Given the structural domain specificity of legal language and the concepts involved, the expression "translating the law" cannot be used to ascertain correspondences between legal terminology in various languages, since the translational correspondence of two terms satisfies neither the semantic correspondence of the concepts they denote, nor the requirements of the different legal systems. There is a lack of a clear language level where the equivalence has been set up. In "translating the law" the distance between the statute and the law or, more generally, between the law and its verbalisation is to be negotiated.

The attention here is focused on two European projects, which were co-ordinated by our Institute: LOIS - Lexical Ontologies for Legal Information Sharing (2002-2004), and DALOS - DrAfting Legislation with Ontology-based Support (2006-2008).

LOIS. The project aims to remedy this semantic lacuna by means of the development of a multi-language legal lexicon, whose structure is based on the WordNet methodology, an existing *de facto* standard for lexical ontologies construction. The architecture ensures the coverage of the semantic peculiarities of the legal domain, and facilitates the capture of essential semantic differences between the legal systems involved (Peters, Sagri, Tiscornia, 2007).

As its methodological starting point, LOIS adopts the structure of two widely known and used thesauri. WordNet (Fellbaum, 1998) is a lexical database which has been under constant development at Princeton University. EuroWordNet (EWN) (Vossen et al., 1997) is a multilingual lexical database with WordNets for eight European languages, which are structured along the same lines as the Princeton WordNet. Both thesauri are organized around the notion of a synset. A synset is a set of one or more uninflected word forms (lemmas) with the same part-of-speech that can be interchanged in a certain context. For example, case, cause, causal, law suit form a noun synset because they can be used to refer to the same concept.

A synset is often further described by a gloss. Synsets can be related to each other by semantic relations, of which the most important are hyper-onymy/hyponymy (between specific and more general concepts), meronymy (between parts and wholes), and antonymy (between semantically opposite concepts). Cross-lingual equivalence relations are made explicit in the so-called Inter-Lingual-Index (ILI). Each synset in the monolingual WordNets has at least one equivalence relation with a record in this ILI. Language-specific synsets from different languages that are linked to the same ILI-record by means of a synonym relation are considered conceptually equivalent. The database holds 33,000 synsets in Italian, English, Dutch, Ceckz, German and Portuguese (around 5,000 per legal system), which originate from European Community definitions, national legislation and lexical databases.

DALOS. Not only from a general user perspective, but also from the European legislator perspective, it is necessary to allow citizens to access "understandable" legal and legislative information in order to enhance the law comprehension process and to improve the quality and readability of legislative texts, thus contributing also to the "certainty of law".

In this context, the aim of the DALOS project (Francesconi, Tiscornia, 2007) is to foster the quality of the legislative production, to enhance accessibility and alignment of legislation at European level, as well as to promote awareness and democratic participation of citizens to the legislative process. In particular DALOS aims at ensuring that legal drafters and decision-makers have control over the legal language at national and European level, by providing law-makers with linguistic and knowledge management tools to be used in the legislative processes, in particular in legislative drafting.

Based on the assumption that in a legal domain one cannot transfer the conceptual structure from one legal system to another, it is obvious that the best approach consists in developing parallel alignments with the same methodology and referring to a shared conceptual model.

The methodological approach chosen in the DALOS project is based on the definition of mapping procedures between semantic lexicons, driven by the reference to an ontological level where the basic entities which populate the legal domain are described. Such an approach has been followed to obtain a correspondence between terms of different languages as well to align corresponding terms towards a common conceptualization at a higher knowledge level.[1]

---

[1] See also Agnoloni, T. et al., *An Approach towards Better Legislation to Improve Law Accessibility and Understanding*, in the present volume.

3.2. STRUCTURAL SUPPORT TOOLS

Some important tools were also implemented for organizing information from a formal and substancial point of view. Three experiences are to be mentioned.

NormeInRete (NIR - Italian legislation on the net) project was launched in 2001 (`<www.nir.it>`). It was proposed by CNIPA in conjunction with the Italian Ministry of Justice. It aimed at defining standards for Italian legislation, allowing the creation of a unique access point for legal documents in a distributed environment with search and retrieval facilities, as well as a mechanism of stable cross-references capable of guiding users towards relevant sites of public authorities participating at the project.

The NormeInRete project proposed the adoption of standards for identifying and representing legal documents, basically legal provisions and regulative acts. These standards (xml-based NIR-DTDs), an unambiguous identifier based on URN technique allowing references to be expressed in a stable way, independently of document physical location (URL) are now implemented by Italian public administrations (Francesconi, 2007).

xmLeges - An Open Source Application Suite for Legal Drafting (`<www.xmleges.org>`). The production of new documents, as well as the transformation of legacy contents according to the NormeInRete standards, can be a hard problem to face without an editing system guiding and supporting the user. To allow the production of legal texts according to the NormeInRete standards, a specific editor (*xmLegesEditor*) has been developed. It includes modules able to manage legacy contents and to work on native XML-NIR and URN-NIR formats (Francesconi, 2007).

Law Making Environment (`<nir.ittig.cnr.it/lme>`). The project aim is the effective knowability of the legal order through IT systems capable of reducing its complexity, giving legislators the opportunity to draft self-explaining legislative texts and giving citizen friendly access to them. It is a system of integrated knowledge models and module tools, to support the production and management of legislative sources and direct search of relevant provisions.

LMEmetaEdit is an XML open source editor for drafting support. It allows the semantic mark-up of legal texts, when the drafting is going on, or already drawn up, by inserting metadata according to a provision and concept model developed. *MetaSearch* is a system for researching cases-in-point in legislative sources. It can be used as a conceptual guide for consulting organic and complex legislation. The system is also able to run inferences: deductions in the rules context and deductions in the concepts context.

Finally the module *metaPlan*, in progress, should be able to guide the legislator in drafting a new bill from a conceptual point of view (Biagioli and Grossi, 2008).

3.3. KNOWLEDGE-ORIENTED SUPPORT TOOLS

Some tools were also implemented to catch the substantial meaning of accessed information, that is capable to convert available information into achievable knowledge.

ELIOS - Environmental Legal Information Observatory System (`<www.ittig.cnr.it/BancheDatiGuide/elios/Home.html>`). It provides the analytic description of relevant websites dealing with environmental law all over the world. They are integrated and regularity updated in a database which can be visited free of charge. Data are retrievable in two ways: by browsing or by searching. In the former data are organized into geographical areas and then per country, in the latter the retrieval is based on the keywords that the user can select or through the search channels connected with the various fields into which the documentary unit is subdivided (title, web address, author, description, resource type, language, country, geographical coverage and keywords). The user is therefore supported in his search navigation towards useful concepts of environmental law (Fameli, 2008).

ABC for the Law (`<www.nir.it/abc/html/indice.htm>`). It supports citizens when accessing the NiR Portal, from where Italian legislation can be retrieved. It aims at explaining some basic legal concepts the knowledge of which is essential for aiding users, especially non experts, to comprehend what they are searching. The user can perceive the substance of the legal concepts related to his search and therefore understand the deep meaning of what he is looking for. In his search the citizen right to effective access is therefore substantiated (Biasiotti and Nannucci, 2007).

4. Conclusions

Although these experiences were carried out during many years of research activities not only by our institution but also by other organizations belonging to the scientific community, it is apparent that results are still not sufficiently adequate. So an imperative and an obligation should be shared by all world-wide research institutions, which should endeavour for making easy and free access to legal knowledge an effective and widespread right for all citizens of the world.

This means that when implementing and distributing legal databases for rendering them freely accessible a particular attention should be addressed to the creation of tools facilitating the comprehension and searchability of legal contents.

The widespread increasing development of globalization affecting all aspects of social and economic activities all over the world assigns a fundamental role to the use of ICT technologies and to the Web. The Internet facilitates the comprehension of the different legal systems but has also an impact on different social systems contributing to harmonizing citizens rights and to establishing a positive dialogue among different cultural backgrounds. The Web is not only a huge repository of legal information, but is also ever more becoming an open forum where legal issues can be easily debated: it is the place where the user can find information about legal events when they occur in the reality, but is also becoming an essential part of the legal world, a place where many legal events take place officially. In all these cases the citizens of the world can increase their awareness and become more participative.

With the hope that it may happen in our near future, we would like to conclude our contribution leaving the answers to some key questions open to the scientific community:

— Is access to raw data to be conceived as real access to information?
— Is it possible to guarantee free access to legal information without taking care of its quality?
— Is sustainability possible without any external fund?

References

Biagioli, C. and Grossi, D. (2008), *Formal Aspects of Legislative Meta-Drafting*, in: Francesconi, E., Sartor, G., Tiscornia, D. (Eds.), "Legal Knowledge and Information System", Amsterdam, IOS Press.

Biasiotti, M.A. and Faro, S. (2007), *Caselex - Case Law Exchange: An Unprecedent Service for the Dissemination of National Case Law Applying EU Law*, in: Cunningham, P. and Cunningham, M. (Eds.), "Expanding the Knowledge Economy: Issues, Applications, Case Studies", Amsterdam, IOS Press.

Biasiotti, M.A. and Nannucci, R. (2007), *ABC del Diritto. Conoscere il diritto per navigare il Web giuridico*, Florence, European Press Academic Publishing, 195 pp.

Fameli, E. (2008), *ELIOS Presentation*, available at: <www.ittig.cnr.it/BancheDatiGuide/elios/Present.html> (accessed March 2009).

Faro, S. and Nannucci, R. (2008), *Trans-European Access to National Case Law: The Caselex Project*, in: Janowski, T., Pardo, T.A. (Eds.), "ICEGOV 2008 - Proceedings of the 2nd International Conference on theory and practice of electronic governance" (Cairo, December 1-4, 2008), pp. 76-81.

Fellbaum, C. (Ed.) (1998), *WordNet: An Electronic Lexical Database*, Cambridge, MIT Press.

Francesconi, E. and Tiscornia, D. (2007), *Building Semantic Resources for Legislative Drafting: The DALOS Project*, in: Casanovas, P., Sartor, G., Rubino, R., Casellas, N. (Eds.), "Computable Models of the Law", Lecture Notes in Computer Science, 4884, Berlin, Springer.

Francesconi, E. (2007), *Technologies for European Integration. Standards-based Interoperability of Legal Information Systems*, Florence, European Press Academic Publishing, 174 pp.

Masolo, C., Gangemi, A., Guarino, N., Oltramari, A., Schneider, L. (2004), *The Wonderweb Library of Foundational Ontologies*, technical report.

Peruginelli, G. (2006), *Legal Information on the Web: the Case of Italy*, International Journal of Legal Information, Vol. 34, No. 2, pp. 327-357.

Peters, W., Sagri, M.T., Tiscornia, D. (2007), *The Structuring of Legal Knowledge in LOIS*, in Biasiotti, Lehmann, Francesconi and Sagri (Eds.), Journal of Artificial Intelligence and Law, Special Issue on Legal Ontologies, Vol. 15, pp. 117-135.

Vossen, P., Peters, W., Díez-Orzas, P. (1997), *The Multilingual Design of the EuroWordNet Database*, in Mahesh, K. (Ed.), "Ontologies and multilingual NLP", Proceedings of IJCAI-97 workshop, Nagoya, Japan, August 23-29.

Free-access Case Law Enhancements for Australian Law

Andrew Mowbray*, Philip Chung°, Graham Greenleaf§
* *University of Technology, Sydney, and Co-Director, AustLII, Australia*
° *Law Faculty at UTS and Executive Director, AustLII, Australia*
§ *University of New South Wales and Co-Director, AustLII, Australia*

Abstract. Sophisticated use of case law is essential to the work of Courts, Tribunals and the legal profession. This paper describes a research project which aims to automate the extraction of many types of data from case law available through collaborating free access services, so as to create various types of enhanced case law facilities. A prototype case citator developed by automated means is described, one of the first outputs from the project. This paper focuses on enhancements to free access Australian case law, and refers to international extensions.

1. Background: AustLII and the courts

This paper describes a research project[1] that aims is to develop new ways to take advantage of the salient features of legal texts (in particular, case law) so as to create far more useful legal documents. The project involves the Australasian Legal Information Institute (AustLII)[2] as well a number of major Australian courts and legal publishers.[3] The current work utilises automated interconnections between documents achieved primarily by the use of heuristics. One of the early outcomes of the project has been the development of an international case citator (LawCite). This citator has been built without editorial intervention and currently contains around two million cases and law journal articles.

AustLII, a free access non-profit facility operated by two Law Faculties, is Australia's largest online provider of legal information, measured in terms of accesses. It is consistently rated by the Hitwise Internet ranking service as Australia's most used online legal service, receiving 20-25% of all internet traffic in Australia related to legal research. On business days AustLII receives up to 800,000 hits (not counting cached traffic), measured from its own logs. AustLII is a non-profit free-access joint facility of the Faculties of Law at the University of New South Wales and the University of Technology, Sydney.

Almost all of the 120 Courts and Tribunals in Australia provide access to their decisions online. AustLII publishes the decisions of over 90% of them and

---

[1] The project is an Australian Research Council Linkage Project, "Improving online case law". Details are available at: <www.austlii.edu.au/austlii/research/2008/linkage/>.

[2] Available at: <www.austlii.edu.au>.

[3] The Industry Partners are four Australian Courts and Tribunals (the High Court, Federal Court, Family Court and Victorian Civil and Administrative Tribunal (VCAT), the Australian Institute of Judicial Administration (AIJA), and the publishers Thomson Legal & Regulatory Australia, and Justis (a UK case law publisher).

is working toward completion. About one third of the Courts and Tribunals on AustLII do not otherwise publish their own decisions, so AustLII is the *only* free-access provider of their decisions.[4] The commercial legal publishers do not comprehensively publish the decisions of most of these Courts and Tribunals. They concentrate primarily on the decisions of the superior Courts, and publish relatively few other decisions. Improvements to the quality and functionality of case law on AustLII will therefore have a substantial effect on Australia's legal profession, Courts and the general public.

2. Project aims: citations as a key factor in best practice public access case law

The overall aim of this cooperative research is to develop practical outcomes to advance world's best practice in the online provision of free access to case law. The 'free access' constraint requires AustLII to develop solutions at a low cost for sustainability. Value-adding through extensive editorial input, as is typical of commercial legal publishers aiming to satisfy a smaller but better resourced market, is not an option. Goals must be achieved by largely automated means. The key to creating more sophisticated case law is recognising and automating both interconnections between cases (the basis of the precedent system in common law jurisdictions) and interconnection between cases and other documents (eg Acts, Treaties, Law reform reports, and commentary such as Law Journal articles). Interconnections between cases include both later cases citing earlier cases and the hierarchical relationships between cases caused by appeals. Cases also cite sections of legislation, treaties and law reform reports commentaries (eg journal articles) which analyses and explain cases. The more efficiently these other sources can be accessed and understood, the better the system of case law operates. Solutions must be applicable not only to current Australian case law, but also to the decisions of considerable antiquity that are still cited, and to decisions of foreign and international courts and tribunals.

Once such interconnections can be identified, many elements of dealing with case law can be automated in ways not previously possible. This project aims to achieve hypertext linking to and from cases, 'noteups' of cases, grouping of cases related by appeals, better relevance ranking of search results, and links from cases to the correct versions of point-in-time legislative provisions. Creating these interconnections in a cost-effective way is a significant research task. Once this is done, a wide range of software-based innovations become possible which will provide methods of better access to and usage of case law and other types of legal documents. These improvements will be provided for free public access on AustLII. They will also be shared with other free-access Legal Information Institutes (LIIs) around the world that wish to collaborate

---

[4] See: <www.austlii.edu.au/cgi-bin/cases_status.cgi>.

on this project. Most of them participate in the Free Access to Law Movement (Declaration FAL)[5] and collaborate on its data networks, particularly the World Legal Information Institute (WorldLII – <www.worldlii.org>) which is operated by AustLII on behalf of all LIIs. A high level of interconnection will arise between data on all participating LIIs, to the benefit of system users both in Australia and overseas.

The project must address a number of core research problems in order to deliver the desired innovations. The proposed solutions build upon each other and are heavily inter-related. This paper focuses on these issues from the perspective of AustLII and Australian users.

2.1. RECOGNISING PARALLEL CITATIONS OF CASES

The largest problem is to identify all subsequent cases which have considered an earlier case, which is essential in order to assess how authoritative that earlier case is now. This is difficult because subsequent Courts do not refer to earlier cases consistently. The names given to the same case have considerable variation depending on the publisher. Furthermore there may be multiple law reports by commercial publishers each with its own citation system ("parallel citations"), so the same case may have numerous unrelated citations. Finally the same case may have been published online by the Court, AustLII or a government, using yet other citations. Even well-established citation methods are not followed with complete uniformity (preliminary research shows there is not even a 1:1 correspondence between cases and citations). For AustLII, creating a parallel citation table is a huge task. AustLII holds approximately 250,000 Australian cases, and each of those cases may have somewhere between one and eight parallel citations and may be referred to by different names. There are between 30 and 40 current Australian series of printed law reports, 30 of which are online. Each provides a different form of citation. The result can be thought of as a table with about 200,000 rows and about 40 columns (8M cells), sparsely populated with (say) 1M entries. Creating such a table by editorial means would be prohibitively expensive for a free-access service such as AustLII or other free-access LIIs. Commercial legal publishers have painstakingly created such tables over many years largely by editorial means but they are all very limited in scope, both in terms of Courts covered, and also which publishers' report series are covered.

2.2. RECOGNISING OTHER PARALLEL CITATIONS

Other legal documents share variations of the parallel citation problem. A treaty may be cited by name, common name, Australian Treaties Series number (ATS), UN Treaty Series number (UNTS) etc. Law reform reports have

---

[5] See the Appendix of this volume.

barely anything that can be recognised as a consistent citation method. Effective research, and linking, requires heuristics and techniques to recognise parallel citations that share much with case law, but present unique issues.

AustLII's hypertext links from cases to sections of legislation presently go only to the current version of a section. This is not necessarily the same as the section as it was at the time of the facts considered by the case (which is not the same as the date of the case). Links to the current version are potentially confusing, leaving the user to do more work to find the correct version. Links to the correct version, by contrast, would greatly facilitate research.

3. Previous research on citation recognition

Free access law providers have made some progress on these issues. Lexum 2005 has made good progress on case citations, with heavy editorial input supported by some automated processes. Caselaw NSW has editorially tracked cases which cite law reform reports. Some Legal Information Institutes (eg AustLII) use mark-up software to provide hypertext linking to current legislative sections and to cases which cite other cases by a court-designated citation, but not by the parallel 'publishers citations' still most commonly used. Other free access sources also have some hypertext linking through relatively simple pattern matching. Commercial legal publishers often have some of the functionality that we seek to develop in their online case law, but they have achieved this largely by editorial means exerted over many years at great expense, and possible by proprietary automated means that are not public. This editorial value-adding is to a large extent what commercial legal publishing is about. Examples are 'Shepardizing' or 'Keyciting' cases (equivalent of what we call 'noting up') and 'case citators' which identify parallel citations, appeal status of decisions, and editorial judgments of how cases are interpreted by later cases. This project seeks to achieve as much of that functionality as possible by low cost largely automated means, and to share the results.

There is no literature of significance on heuristic-based linking of legal materials (Rugh and Lennen, 2003) uses fuzzy logic instead). Outside law, there is a knowledge base on the use of heuristics and other techniques for citation recognition. While it is useful it does not solve the problems posed by legal information or even address many of them. For scientific and technical literature, an approach known as autonomous citation indexing (ACI) has been effectively implemented in the CiteSeer system `<citeseer.ist.psu.edu/directory.html>`, (Lawrence et al., 1999; Giles et al., 1998). While the CiteSeer conceptual framework might prove useful in the legal domain, its algorithms are grounded in scientific and technical documents. As detailed herein, many more variations of case citations are possible, and the information needed for CiteSeer to work effectively may not be available or be as consistent and obvious in legal documents. For example, cases are often cited with page numbers missing, without a date, by different names, with different formatting and punctuation, with typographical errors, or with nothing but the case name. Thus "Mabo and Others v The State of Queensland (1992) 175 CLR 1" May be cited as "Mabo & Ors -v- Queensland 175 CLR, 1", "Mabo v Queensland (1992) 175 C.L.R.", or simply "Mabo".

The problem of resolving legal citations cannot be solved by simple application of existing algorithms. For example, the Naïve Bayes Classification fails in the legal domain because of the complex web of interdependencies between the various elements of legal citations. Whereas more correlations between components of non-legal citations generally indicate a greater likelihood of a match, this does not apply for legal citations. For example, "175 CLR 1" refers to the same case as "[1992] HCA 23", but not the same case as "174 CLR 1". Further, two cases may have the same name and occur in the same year and jurisdiction and yet be distinct from one another. This makes a Naïve Bayes approach unsuitable. (Borkowski, 1969) developed an algorithm for extracting legal citations. However, it was only tested on formal citations with no variations in structure or format. The algorithm produced extremely poor results when tested with cases in AustLII's database, due to the many variations in format, structure and style of today's legal citations. Consequently, his algorithm is only of limited use. Fuzzy logic approaches have been used to resolve legal citations in the past, but these have used complete, high quality, manually entered data sets. Because AustLII does not have the resources to enter all parallel citations manually, it must obtain data by isolating and extracting legal citations from cases through automated means. Consequently, the data is of much lower quality and so the fuzzy logic does not work well. Other approaches for citation resolution combine extraction and co-reference so as to obtain a higher quality of data (Rugh and Lennen, 2003), and use overlapping canopies to efficiently cluster citations (Nigam et al., 2000). These approaches do not transpose all that well into the legal domain. Nonetheless, elements of these approaches have been used in AustLII's initial algorithms.

4. Elements of the proposed research

The core of the research is to develop automated methods, primarily heuristic-based programs (described below) at AustLII. This project is innovative primarily because, in the legal domain, the problems posed by case citations are very different from other domains because the same case is likely to be published in multiple differently cited locations. Many other legal documents share this feature. Scientific journal articles, in contrast, are usually published in one location only.

4.1. BUILDING CITATION AND STATUS TABLES

The building blocks for many of the improvements proposed here will be the development of parallel citation tables, including recording of appeal status of cases. The initial approach taken is to obtain wherever possible reliable seed/training sets of parallel citations, perhaps from a Court or Tribunal, and to develop heuristics which will then use them to find other parallel citations. If no other citations are available the 'Court designated' citations on AustLII can be used for this purpose. To the extent that this data mining does not find parallel citations, or additional seed/training citations are needed to make it work, minimal editorial input should suffice to augment the automated processes. The process is then iterative: the new seeds are used to mine further citations, the result assessed, and the process completed after several iterations. To a large extent the same iterative process will be used with treaties and law reform reports. A further set of heuristics is being developed to build citation recognition based on case names. Some cases are not referred to in other cases by a recognisable citation, but only by name - in widely varying forms. This is often so with cases frequently referred to by other cases in the same tribunal but which are not reported in publishers' law reports. Since 1998 (when adopted by the High Court), Australian courts have started to assign a simple and uniform citation of their own (Court-designated) citations to judgments at the time they are made, see (Mowbray et al., 2000; Greenleaf et al., 2005). This is slowly reducing this problem of citation by case name, but is not applicable to past cases. Such heuristics must avoid significant numbers of false hits or user confidence will be undermined. Factors which may prove valuable to heuristic development are the relative in-frequency of the names of the parties (determinable from AustLII's concordances), the extent of match with a known case name, time information and so forth.

4.2. HYPERTEXT LINKS AND NOTEUPS

Creation of a Court's citation table will result immediately in hypertext links between cases, through changes to AustLII's hypertext mark-up software to read the table. Once a table is populated sufficiently to be valuable (even if not yet 'complete'), every case from the Court can be given a 'Noteup' link which finds all other documents referring to it (cases, articles, law reform reports etc). Because the citation tables include commercial publishers citations, the concept of 'Noteups' can be extended to include automated searches of all online materials from cooperating publishers (as occurs with CCH, and may with Thomson). This helps create a seamless research environment for users who have access to that publisher's materials.

4.3. CONTEXTUAL RANKING

These hypertext links created through citation tables will also be used to build a new form of relevance ranking of search results suitable for legal materials. Traditional methods of relevance ranking (as AustLII currently uses) based on word-occurrence density and position are effective but require improvement to take account of legally specific features of text. Approaches utilising the number of links to a document such as implemented by Google (Brin and Page, 1998) may be an indicator of significance, but taken alone are too coarse a measure, because 'popular' cases which are often cited for general principles will be unduly highly ranked whenever found. A more precise approach requires consideration of the relative frequency of links from documents in the retrieved set: we call this 'contextual ranking'. The aim of this approach will be to rank within a set of results that have known relevance. Preliminary work shows that, whilst computationally expensive, this might yield far better ranking results than any existing legal search retrieval system. This would also give much better ranking of the 'noteup' results discussed above. This difficult research will draw on work done in comparing the effectiveness of using 'local' versus 'global' link information in improving document retrieval (Calado et al., 2003; Kleinberg, 1998).

4.4. INTELLIGENT USE OF EXPLICIT DATA IN CASES

There is often other explicit data which can be mined from cases in addition to parallel citation data, and this project will aim to extract such data comprehensively from decisions provided by Australian Courts and Tribunals. It will aim to do so irrespective of the variations in formats (while also encouraging greater standardisation). Two likely examples are: *(a) 'Catchword' clusters as search vectors* - Some of the data which AustLII receives already contains 'catchwords', indexing terms added by the Courts. Greater use could be made of this data, particularly to create search vectors which could complement the 'Noteups' of cases, particularly in cases decided recently. We will examine the usefulness of such search vectors in relation to vector-based search approaches (Salton, 1989; Wong et al., 1987). *(b) mining for case status information* Similarly, it may be possible to develop automated mechanisms to extract data regarding the appeal status of cases as well as finding references to other cases and legislation.

4.5. INTERNATIONAL AND HISTORICAL EXTENSIONS

Various members of the global network of Legal Information Institutes (LIIs) have for some years agreed to share parallel citation data. The LIIs agreed in 2004 on a protocol of the exchange of parallel citation information, and a standard location on each LII where such tables may be found and extracted.[6] (For the LIIs collaborating in this research, which are mainly from common law jurisdictions, a richer set of citation data than these known parallel citations becomes available because other parallel citations are extracted from the texts of the cases by heuristic means. One purpose of this collaboration is so that they can use this data to create hypertext links to cases found on other LIIs: 'cross-LII hypertext links'. Cases in common law jurisdictions frequently cite precedent cases from other jurisdictions, so cross-LII links can create a very high degree of improved utility of cases. By an extension of the 'noteup' facilities described above to 'global noteups' which also search the cases from all LIIs on WorldLII, Australian users will also find valuable foreign cases citing Australian cases (and vice-versa for other participating LIIs).

A different international element will be added, by testing how far the heuristic citation extraction techniques developed for Australian case law can be effective for cases of international courts and courts from civil law jurisidictions.

Industry partner Justis has made a vital in-kind contributions to extend the research in historical depth by providing the complete texts of the English Reports from the 13th to the 19th centuries in digital form (both images and OCR text of the original cases, and metadata). AustLII has re-formatted the reports into an English Reports 1220-1783 database of nearly 125,000 cases on the Commonwealth Legal Information Institute (CommonLII).[7] Hypertext links can be developed from citations in any Australian cases to those historical sources, 'noteups' developed from the old cases to cases that have subsequently cited them, and citation records developed for these old cases in the LawCite citatory now described.

5. First project outcome – LawCite citator

One of the early outcomes of the project has been the development of a fully automated case citator. The current test system includes records for about 1.5 million cases and law journal articles (as at 1 December 2008). These include cases actually held as part of the AustLII collections or those of other collaborating LIIs, as well as entries for cases that are referred to in those cases but for which copies are not held. The system currently recognises around 2.1 million individual unique citations (of which 600,000 can be considered 'parallel citations' to other known citations), which have been identified from about 14 million citation references in the texts used to construct the citator. The eventual scope of the system is estimated to be around 3 million cases representing most of the case law that has been cited in a common law courts

---

[6] See: <www.austlii.edu.au/citations.txt> for example.
[7] Located at: <www.commonlii.org/int/cases/EngR/>.

within the last decade or so, plus an additional undetermined number of cases from civil law jurisdictions.

The system is built via a process of extracting citation data from data on AustLII and other collaborating LIIs as well as from other freely available external sources. At the moment, the main source of information is judgments, but provided that documents contain references to cases and journal articles and include their citations, any reliable source of data can be used, such as law reform reports and law journal articles.

5.1. HEURISTICS TO RESOLVE CITATION AMBIGUITIES

A major problem that the system has to deal with is the presence of incorrect citations and citation sets in the source data (being mainly judgments, but also including secondary materials such as journals and law reform reports). Fairly sophisticated conflict identification and correction mechanisms have been developed to deal with this.

Consider the following example. Here are a set of references that might be identified for the case Dietrich v The Queen:

Dietrich v The Queen [1992] HCA 57; (1992) 177 CLR 292

Dietrich v The Queen [1992] HCA 57; **(1992) 177 CLR 291**

Dietrich v The Crown [1992] HCA 57; (1992) 177 CLR 292

Dietrich v R [1992] HCA 57; (1992) 177 CLR 292

Dietrich v The Queen **[1991] HCA 57**; (1992) 177 CLR 292

(1992) 177 CLR 292; **[1992] HCA 77**

Dietrich v R [1992] HCA 57; (1992) 177 CLR 292; **[2000] 2 All ER 12**

This set of references contains a number of typographical and other errors (indicated in bold) including incorrect court designated citations, an error in the publishers' citation and a stray reference to an unrelated English decision. Note also that the name of the case varies.

The LawCite conflict resolver resolves all of these entries by counting the most frequent associations for each individual citation, rejecting conflicts based upon reports from different jurisdictions or courts and tracking the most commonly used case name. The above example set is reduced to:

Dietrich v The Queen [1992] HCA 57; (1992) 177 CLR 292

Whilst the approach is highly heuristic, we believe it achieves high levels of accuracy that are rapidly becoming comparable or better than manual editorial approaches. Further testing will be needed to demonstrate this.

5.2. DEVELOPING A CITATOR

An early application of the extracted citations was to facilitate richer markup of the AustLII databases. Where possible, this is used to insert court designated citations into materials and link these to cases that are referred to. This has been live on the AustLII system since February 2008.

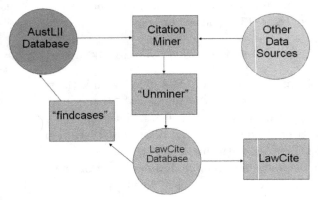

Figure 1. LawCite Anatomy

The next logical step was to use the data to produce a traditional case citator. A version of this that contained only Australian cases was demonstrated in October 2007 at the *8ᵗʰ Annual Conference on Law via the Internet* in Montreal. Since that time, it has been extended to include international data from collaborating LIIs and also data from other databases maintained by AustLII on AsianLII, CommonLII and WorldLII. While the current citation data is predominantly from common law jurisdictions its coverage of decisions from civil law jurisdictions is growing. An alpha version of LawCite was released for public use on 1 December 2008.[8]

The interface is fairly straight forward and allows for searching cases by party name, citation, court, jurisdiction, year and so forth (fig. 2).

Case records include all of the information that can be generated from the case itself (if available) and that can be deduced from the citation itself (e.g. jurisdiction, court, etc.). These are stored as a separate searchable XML database. Records are currently displayed as shown in fig. 3 and fig. 4.

As part of the entry a number of other elements are also generated. These include a list of all cases referring to the present decision, transcripts of decisions and law journal articles referring to the case. This will be expanded to include law reform reports and other secondary materials.

Cases that are heavily cited are annotated with a series of stars. This is based upon the number of times that a case is referred to. The interface allows sorting by citation, date or court. Where available, the parallel citation list

---

[8] See: <www.austlii.edu.au/lawcite/>.

Law**Cite**_ALPHA_

LawCite is an international case citator and is the first product of a 3 year Australian Research Council funded project to research into automated systems for citation recognition. The LawCite database is generated on an entirely automatic basis with no editorial input and includes a fairly complete collection of all common law cases cited in the past decade plus most of the important uncited decisions before this. Please note that this is an Alpha version. It is still being built and refined and is not intended for public release.

Law**Cite**_ALPHA_

Citation:		eg [1963] 2 All ER 575
Parties:	v	
Court:		eg Supreme Court
Jurisdiction:		eg Australia
Article Title:		eg "Human Rights"
Author:		eg Michael Kirby
Year:	to	
Cases Cited:		
Legislation Cited:		Section:
Full Text:		Search Reset

Figure 2. LawCite interface

will include a link to the text of the actual decisions or journal articles (via AustLII and collaborating LIIs).

LawCite does not include editorial judgments of whether a case was distinguished, reversed, etc by subsequent cases. It concentrates on demonstrating the patterns of case citation, and also provides parallel citations for cases.

A. Mowbray, P. Chung, G. Greenleaf

[Home] [LawCite Search] [WorldLII] [Feedback]

LawCite ALPHA

[Legislation Cited] [Cases Cited] [Cases Referring to this Case] [Law Journal Articles Referring to this Case]

Dinsdale v R
(2000) 202 CLR 321; (2000) 175 ALR 315; (2000) 74 ALJR 1538; (2000) 115 A Crim R 558
High Court of Australia
Australia
12th October, 2000

Legislation Cited

Legislation Name	Provision
Crimes Act 1900 (ACT)	
Crimes Act 1914 (Cth)	s20
Constitution	s73
Crimes Act 1900 (NSW)	
Crimes (Sentencing Procedure) Act 1999 (NSW)	s12, s39
Penalties and Sentences Act 1992 (Qld)	s144
Criminal Law (Sentencing) Act 1988 (SA)	s38
Sentencing Act 1997 (Tas)	s7, s24
Sentencing Act 1991 (Vic)	s27
Sentencing Act 1995 (WA)	s6, s24, s39, s76

Cases Cited

Case Name	Citations	Court	Jurisdiction	Date ↑	Full Text	Citation Index
Worp v R	[2000] WASCA 154	Supreme Court of Western Australia - Court of Appeal	Australia - Western Australia	01/06/2000	AustLII	
Dinsdale v R	[2000] HCA 54; 202 CLR 321; 175 ALR 315, 74 ALJR 1538	High Court of Australia	Australia	2000	AustLII	
Lowndes v R	[1999] HCA 29; (1999) 73 ALJR 1007; (1999) 163 ALR 483; (1999) 195 CLR 665; (1999) 8 CA 29	High Court of Australia	Australia	17/06/1999	AustLII	
Pelechowski v Registrar, Court of Appeal	[1999] HCA 19; (1999) 198 CLR 435; (1999) 73 ALJR 687; (1999) 162 ALR 336	High Court of Australia	Australia	05/05/1999	AustLII	
State Rail Authority of New South Wales v Earthline Constructions Pty Ltd (in Liq)	[1999] HCA 3; (1999) 73 ALJR 306; (1999) 160 ALR 588	High Court of Australia	Australia	09/02/1999	AustLII	

Figure 3.

[Home] [LawCite Search] [WorldLII] [Feedback]

LawCite ALPHA

[Legislation Cited] [Cases Cited] [Cases Referring to this Case] [Law Journal Articles Referring to this Case]

R v Dudley and Stephens
(1884) 14 QBD 273
United Kingdom - England and Wales

Cases Referring to this Case

Case Name	Citations	Court	Jurisdiction	Date ↑	Full Text	Citation Index
Luavex v R	[2007] SBCA 13	Court of Appeal of Solomon Islands	Solomon Islands	11/10/2007	PacLII	
R v Maygar	[2007] QCA 310	Supreme Court of Queensland - Court of Appeal	Australia - Queensland	21/09/2007	AustLII	
Abigail Alliance for Better Access To Developmental Drugs and Washington Legal Foundation v Von Eschenbachs	[2006] USCADC 84; 445 F3d 470	United States Court of Appeals, District of Columbia Circuit	United States	02/05/2006	WorldLII	
De La Espriella-Velasco v R	[2006] WASCA 31	Supreme Court of Western Australia - Court of Appeal	Australia - Western Australia	10/03/2006	AustLII	
Espriella-Velasco v R	(2006) 31 WAR 291		Australia - Western Australia	2006	AustLII	
Oswald v Bertrand	[2004] USDA7 377; 374 F3d 475	United States Court of Appeals, Seventh Circuit	United States	12/06/2004	WorldLII	
State v Seniais	[2004] FJHC 44	High Court of Fiji	Fiji	27/07/2004	PacLII	
R (Anderson) v Secretary of State for the Home Department	[2003] 1 AC 837		United Kingdom - England and Wales	2003	BAILII	
R v Japaljarri (formerly known as Hocking)	[2002] VSCA 154	Supreme Court of Victoria - Court of Appeal	Australia - Victoria	01/10/2002	AustLII	
R (Anderson) v Secretary of State for the Home Department	[2002] 3 WLR 1800		United Kingdom - England and Wales	2002	BAILII	
Cheung v R	[2001] HCA 67; (2001) 209 CLR 1; (2002) 76 ALJR 133; (2001) 185 ALR 111	High Court of Australia	Australia	22/11/2001	AustLII	
Shayler, R v	[2001] EWCA Crim 1977	England and Wales Court of Appeal - Criminal Division	United Kingdom - England and Wales	28/09/2001	BAILII	
Riley v Fuchs	[2001] QDC 85	District Court of Queensland	Australia - Queensland	18/05/2001	AustLII	

Figure 4.

6. Conclusions

This paper has outlined a relatively ambitious but achievable research project. The LawCite citatory, its first significant outcome, has been described but a full explanation of the heuristics on which it is based (which are still developing) is not covered in this paper. The implications of achieving a more complete set of interrelations between case law and other legal documents are, however, much wider than then the development of a citator. The identification of clusters of documents sharing similar citation information has many applications and it is hoped that many of these will be built over the three year life of the project.

7. Acknowledgments

Thanks to Nicholas Tobias for his considerable assistance on prior theoretical work on citation identification.

References

Borkowski, C. (1969), *Structure, Effectiveness and Uses of the Citation Identifier*, "International Conference on Computational Linguistics", Stockholm, Coling. Association for Computing Machinery, 1969.

Borodin, A., Roberts, G.O., Rosenthal, J.S., Tsaparas, P. (2005), *Link analysis ranking: algorithms, theory, and experiments*, ACM Transactions on Internet Technology (TOIT), Vol. 5, No. 1, pp. 231-297.

Brin, S. and Page, L. (1998), *The anatomy of a large-scale hypertextual Web search engine*, in "Proceedings of the 7th International World Wide Web Conference", Brisbane, Australia, pp. 107-117.

Calado, P., Ribeiro-Neto, B., Ziviani, N., Moura, E., Silva, I. (2003), *Local versus global link information in the Web*, ACM Transactions on Internet Technology (TOIT), Vol. 21, No. 1, pp. 42-63.

Giles, C.L., Bollacker, K., Lawrence, S. (1998), *CiteSeer: An Automatic Citation Indexing System*, Digital Libraries 98: Third ACM Conf. Digital Libraries, ACM Press, New York, pp. 89-98.

Greenleaf, G., Chung, P., Mowbray, A. (2007), *Emerging global networks for free access to law: WorldLII's strategies*, SCRIPTed, Vol. 4, No. 4, pp. 319-366, available at: <www.law.ed.ac.uk/ahrc/script-ed/vol4-4/greenleaf.asp>.

Kleinberg, J.M. (1998), *Authoritative sources in a hyperlinked environment*, in "Proceedings of the ninth annual ACM-SIAM symposium on Discrete algorithms", San Francisco, California, United States, pp. 668-677.

Lawrence, S., Giles, C.L., Bollacker, K. (1999), *Digital Libraries and Autonomous Citation Indexing*, IEEE Computer, 32, No. 6, pp. 67-71, available at: <clgiles.ist.psu.edu/papers/IEEE.Computer.DL-ACI.pdf>.

Lexum (2005), *RefLex: CanLII's Citation Resolver*, available at: <www.canlii.org/reflex_en.html>.

Mowbray, A., Austin, D, Chung, P. (2000), *Scalability of Web Resources for Law: AustLII's Technical Roadmap: Past, Present and Future*, The Journal of Information, Law and Technology (JILT), Vol. 1, available at: <www.law.warwick.ac.uk/jilt/00-1/austin.html>.

Mowbray, A., Greenleaf, G., Chung, P. (2000), *A Uniform Approach for Vendor and Media Neutral Citation – the Australian Experience*, Citations Workshop, University of Edinburgh, Scotland.

Nigam, K., McCallum, A., Ungar, L.H. (2000), *Efficient clustering of high-dimensional data sets with application to reference matching*, in "Conference on Knowledge Discovery in Data", Proceedings of the sixth ACM SIGKDD international conference on Knowledge discovery and data mining, ACM, pp. 169–178.

Olsson, (1999), *The Honourable Justice L T Guide to Uniform Production of Judgments*, (2nd Ed.) AIJA Rogers I 'The Google Pagerank Algorithm and How It Works' IPR Computing Ltd, available at: <www.iprcom.com/papers/pagerank/>.

Rugh, J. and Lennen, J. (2003), *Using Fuzzy Logic to Create Links: Resolving References to Court Decisions*, XML Conference and Exposition, available at: <www.idealliance.org/papers/dx_xml03/papers/05-05-03/05-05-03.html>.

Salton, G. (1989), *Automatic Text Processing: The Transformation, Analysis, and Retrieval of Information by Computer*, Addison-Wesley Series in Computer Science. Addison-Wesley Longman Publishing.

Wittfoth, A., Chung, P., Mowbray, A., Greenleaf, G. (2003), *Can One Size Fit All?: - AustLII's Point-in-Time Legislation Project*, in "Proceedings of the 5th Law via Internet Conference", Sydney.

Wittfoth, A., Chung, P., Greenleaf, G., Mowbray, A. (2005), *AustLII's Point-in-Time legislation system: A generic PiT system for presenting legislation*, Launch of the Point-in-Time legislation system, 7 April 2005.

Wong, S.K.M., Ziarko, W., Raghavan, V.V., Wong, P.C.N. (1987), *On Modeling of Information Retrieval Concepts in Vector Spaces*, ACM Transactions on Database Systems, Vol. 12, No. 2, pp. 299-321.

V SECTION

ICTs and the Quality
of Legal Information

Legal Information Systems: Some Aspects on Quality and Access

Roland Traunmüller*, Maria A. Wimmer°

* *Institute for Informatics in Business and Administration, Johannes Kepler University of Linz, Austria*
° *Institute for Information Systems, Research Group eGovernment, University of Koblenz, Germany*

Abstract. In recent years, the increasing focus on e-Governance has prompted issues such as citizen participation, policy modelling, legal drafting, etc. For these fields, information quality and information access have become basic needs. These features are essential for both, public agencies performing their tasks, and citizens who participate in democratic deliberation. Governmental and Legal Information Systems have become crucial support means for information provision and quality assurance. The development and maintenance of such systems has also been challenged with new requests of participation and policy modelling. This contribution investigates such challenges along key aspects of information: quality, access, presentation, communication, etc.

Keywords: Public governance, participation, legal information, information quality, information access.

1. E-Governance has emerged as a prime issue

In recent years e-Governance has emerged as prime issue. Surely, e-Governance comprises many points already covered before in Legal Informatics as well as in e-Government. Yet, e-Governance brings these points to vivid attention, develops special aspects, combines them in a new way and connects them with the practical life of citizens.

The permanent transformation towards electronic service provision of the public sector (transforming Government, tGovernment) spurs the discussion on entirely new ways for Public Governance. Good governance is an important target and in that way Public Governance is top on the political agenda. Whatever the domain of carrying out activities may be, it is this electronic transformation that has changed nearly everything: redefining the mental models of performing work, changing methods and tools and restructuring relationships.

Transformation takes place for any kind of relationship, citing a common example: seller-to-buyer relationships in the commercial sector. In the same way, the relation between governmental institutions and citizens is transformed. The scope of Public Governance has become rather broad:

- democratic and cooperative policy formulation;
- citizen and civil society involvement;

- transparent and efficient implementation of policies;
- continuous evaluation of their results;
- accountability of public decision makers;
- ways to improve policy making in the future.

The following sections touch three key themes of current research and implementation activities in transforming Governments, which result from above topics of public governance: citizen participation, policy formulation and legal drafting. For all these topics legal and administrative knowledge are decisive.

2. Improving e-Participation

Among the points of Public Governance that recently received broader attention is increased democratic participation. This means empowering citizens and including them in policy making and implementation. Government has to support the formation of a democratic culture. So the initiative of the European Parliament identified three main challenges:

- the perceived democratic deficit requiring new relationships between State and citizens;
- reconnecting Europeans with politics and policy making;
- competing with the complexity of decision making and legislation.

Thus e-Participation develops and implements new forms of participation in decision and policy making processes for citizens, thereby involving citizens, public authorities, elected representatives and other key stakeholders. Aims of e-Participation are to improve public responsiveness and to enhance public satisfaction. This reinforces democracy and helps fighting against corruption and fraud. Many projects are aimed at citizen voting and participation. They show the efficiency of linking people, bringing together persons, giving support services for participation. In particular these are advantages for areas where communities are scattered and resources are scarce. So e-Participation is a major point in the EC e-Government Action Plan (European Commission, 2006).

The early foci of e-Participation were laid in e-Voting and transparency. There were several projects using the web for voting. Yet, most projects ran without digital signature and were often directed to rather particular circumstances. This included voting on special issues or covering areas of less sensitivity such as professional bodies. One successful example is e-Petition, which gives communication to the Prime Ministers Office. Active participation is a further item – so supporting community development and the building up of democratic knowledge.

3. ICT for Policy modelling

Recently, working on policy formulation has become a strong issue in Public Governance. The European Commission launched within the 7th Research Framework Programme the Work Programme 2009-2010. It contains the objective of ICT for governance and Policy modelling. The fan of issues is broad: policy modelling tools, opinion visualisation, mass collaborative platforms, and large-scale societal simulations. For details we refer to (European Commission, 2008). For example online collaborations have the potential to trigger and shape significant changes. Governance and participation toolboxes may comprise advanced tools from gaming and virtual reality technologies. This would include opinion visualisation and simulation solutions based on modelling, simulation, visualisation, mixed reality technologies, data mining etc. Further, employing systems dynamics methodology helps analyse and model complex systems. For all these tools it is necessary to exploit the vast reserves of data and knowledge resources which are collected in public agencies. Thus, having legal data are a must, legal modelling becomes essential and quality of information is crucial.

4. Legal modelling and drafting

There exists a long history of legal modelling. Here listing some spotlights may suffice (more on history in Traunmüller, 1997). After some precursors legal modelling started in the Eighties with legal expert systems. It covered various subjects, ranging from practical applications such as decision support systems and configuration of legal documents to methodical issues such as non monotonic reasoning and neuronal nets. In the Nineties legal modelling has been improved by knowledge engineering offering a sound methodological basis including essential work on ontologies and tools.

Our decade has brought continuous development as well as a new application – legal modelling for data exchange.

Legal modelling has become essential for running online one stop services. The data involved in a specific administrative decision are dispersed over many locations, under the competencies of diverse agencies and residing on several systems. That data have to be brought together from diverse data sources and disseminated vice versa. Such exchange of data needs interoperability; for that goal modelling legal notions in the form of XML descriptions has become essential. Going cross border, interoperability needs automatic translation from one system to another one as well.

There has been substantial development in legal drafting. First prog-ress is going totally electronically in handling the information flow between diverse stakeholders from the beginning to the authentic publication. Such stakeholders are ministries, parliaments, parties, consulting bodies etc. In such a project in Austria 60 tons of paper is saved by electronic handling. Another example is the DALOS project which ensures that legal drafters and decision-makers have control over the legal language at national and European level by providing law-makers with linguistic and knowledge management tools to be used in the legislative processes, in particular within the phase of legislative drafting. The project is built over a well structured multilingual domain-specific ontology (DALOS, 2007).

5. Legal and administrative domain knowledge

In e-Governance and in e-Government the task of managing legal and administrative domain knowledge is central. Knowledge management in the public sector has become an important issue and managing legal knowledge is a major part. A series of conferences has taken place treating KM in the public sector (Wimmer, 2001 and 2002, 2003, 2004 as forerunners).

Specific questions for the public sector are among others: Governments are not mentally prepared to KM. Administrators do not conceive themselves as knowledge workers. They are not conscious that in their agencies respectable and extensive riches of knowledge exist. Most hindrances are in the pronounced distinctiveness of the legal domain. Legal information is collected in special forms and is organised following types of legal sources (norms, decisions, legal facts etc.). It is this conventional form of legal documentation that makes retrieval onerous and causes problems for administrators and for citizens. Finding the right information is even troublesome for professionals; even more problems arise in the case when lay persons seek information. Some help is promised by tools for case based retrieval, attribute based search and ontology-based information retrieval. Progress is slow as nearly all systems using deontic logic, probabilistic measures, neuronal nets etc. belong to the scientific realm.

6. The cosmos of administrative knowledge types

Information sources grow in number and diversity; also the amount of unreliability and fuzziness increases. As an example we regard activities in public agencies. Here a citation on the number of information/knowledge types involved from an earlier publication (Traunmüller and Wimmer, 2002):

1. Knowledge on legal regulations
2. Knowledge about the policy field to be influenced
3. Knowledge about the respective environment

4. Knowledge on the own means and modalities of action
5. Knowledge on the effectiveness of various measures and about the evaluated effects of previous actions
6. Knowledge how to protect basic citizen rights
7. Knowledge about standards
8. Knowledge about attitudes of stakeholders
9. Knowledge concerning the cases to which the actions of the administration are directed.
10. Knowledge about the potential effects that the communication of an administrative act entails on the environment of the administrative body.
11. Knowledge about the own resources and abilities to influence this environment and to enforce the law.
12. Knowledge about the internals of the administrative system in general.
13. Expertise knowledge when applying the general knowledge to particular cases.

It is a broad cosmos of knowledge involved in administrative decisions – and legal is just a part of it. Nevertheless legal information is quite crucial for decision – so the quality of legal information is crucial.

7. Quality of legal and administrative information

Governments, enterprises, and individuals increasingly need well-defined, timely, accurate, reliable and appropriate information. The fact is an enormous dependency on the quality of data; thus guaranteeing information quality has become a major objective in the information society. Especially systematic evaluation of commercial databases has taken place in order to improve the quality of Customer Relationship Management. So a better quality of customers' address data makes marketing more successful. For commercial databases also metrics measuring quality have been used.

The picture changes considerably when turning from the private to the public sector. The case for legal and administrative information is quite different. On one hand the starting situation is easier: administrative registers are much more accurate than private collections, and for legal data, exactness of official repositories is quite high. On the other hand in the public sector, the situation becomes much more complex compared with using marketing data. Thus the situation is quite different:

1. Legal information is by far more complex as marketing data are.
2. Tasks occur that are considerably more complex as found in marketing – just thinking on using data for town planning decisions.
3. In the public sector also non-professionals, such as plain citizens, should be able to use the data (citizen information, citizen participation).

To resume from these considerations: in the public sector, the quality of information is not self-evident. Thus the Roadmap e-Government 2020 (Codagnone and Wimmer, 2007) treats several questions on quality of legal and administrative information: What mechanisms are need-ed to find and qualify information for a given use? How to ensure trust and proper use of information? Which kind of framework is needed to ensure information quality? How to certify information resources?

Information quality per se is abstract and only one side of the coin; one has to consider the access-side as well. It is necessary to regard both, the objective and the subjective aspect. The first one concerns the question: How good are the data stored in the system? The second one relates to the subjective side: What is the quality of that information which a certain user gets out from the system.

Concerning legal information one asset is clear: the objective quality is noticeably high – as most data are official. Also for administrative information the quality level is high, yet in some cases fuzzy data may come in. Examples for data that may have some fuzziness are census data or social data. Turning to the subjective quality – the access by the user and the obtained information –, quality is uncertain. The quality for the user heavily depends on special factors: complexity of data and questions; form of presentation, way of dissemination, exactness of translation, opportunity of web-access.

8. Complexity of information

Complexity is a key factor deciding the quality. In case of common civic advice, system quality is high and access is easy. An example is the Austrian <www.help.gv.at> which gives also detailed information in English to the following items:

1. Birth Certificate
2. Certification for Ability of Marriage
3. Copy from the Birth Register
4. Documentary Proof of Academic Degrees
5. Identity Witness
6. Marriage Certificate
7. Official Identification with Photo
8. Primary Residence
9. Proof of Citizenship
10. Residence Registration Form
11. Social Insurance Card
12. Tenancy Agreement

9. Presentation of information

Presentation of information is a key factor influencing the quality of the part of information which can be obtained by users. Especially in the legal field providing information that can be understood by citizens is a big challenge. Giving the textual information of the administrative-legal wording does not suffice; information has to be "palatable" for citizens. Exemplifying this aspect concerning citizen advice systems, smaller improvements are easily possible: working on better comments, drawing clearer scenarios, adding help functions. Giving the complexity of the field, there is need for bigger improvements as well. Software systems give help, e.g. describing illustrative scenarios or offering clarifying dialogues.

Software agents may embody detailed knowledge – on both, on the field in question and on the interaction.

Legal ontologies significantly help in searching. Other developments comprise intelligent multi-lingual and multi-cultural personal assistants being integrated in service portals. A software-only-solution for advice is not the only option; another is using multimedia for contacting human expert. In next section a vision of a dialogue system is sketched.

10. Actively disseminating information

Systems which actively communicate information offer a considerable service to the citizen. So more and more common agencies do not only present legal and administrative information on the web; they actively communicate relevant pieces of information. That might be pieces of more general information as well as quite special information for an individual case. For the first, information concerning more addressees can be sent via mailing lists. For the individual case an example from taxation follows. In several countries tax offices offer the service of communicating to taxpayers a suggestion for the tax declaration. They mail how according to their data the individual tax declaration would look like. Then taxpayer can simply agree or make additions like submitting deductible items.

All these solutions are less or more automatically. When an issue is rather complex multimedia dialogues become an option. Multimedia offers the possibility to invoke service by getting advice from a distant expert. Just imagine a citizen going to a kiosk or accessing the service shop from home via multi media. With remote experts themselves using knowledge repositories ultimately human and machine expertise become completely interwoven.

11. Exactness in translation

Transformation for data exchange may be source of error. Data exchange is based on eXtensible Markup Language (XML). Several approaches in description exist mostly based on XML languages amended with RDF (resource description facilities). Standardisation is a burdensome way due to the intricacy and complexity of law. Troubles start because legal terms themselves all too often are not adequately defined. This is due to several reasons: vagueness that may be on purpose, genuine inconsistencies and fuzziness, dynamics in law, etc.

Further problems appear in translating terms for cross border usage. Sometimes it is not easy to find adequate meaning of terms. Difficulties comprise adequate meaning of terms (taking licenses, certificates). Also different connotations of terms occur: boundaries of professions as in the case of lawyer and barrister. Non-existence of counterparts poses problems: public honours, awards, and titles.

12. Access to the Web

Last but not least: general web accessibility influences usage. Common web access is given for professionals. It may be lacking in the case of lay-persons. In last years data from EC basic services for citizens have an availability of 36%, and 24% of citizens use some of them. Thus initiatives for reducing exclusion are quested as web accessibility is a social responsibility for any organization having a web presence. Accessibility contributes to good society and environment as a whole. Accessible web not only increases effective and efficient information access, but also expands the level of opportunities. There have been several initiatives since years. One is to install free internet access in public buildings. Examples are post offices in France, parish churches in Portugal and tobacco shops in Austria. Further policies point to these directions, counterbalancing deficiencies and starting promotions for special groups. Later ones concentrate on individual groups of addressees: rural areas, traditionally under-served communities, youth in disadvantaged districts, etc.

References

European Commission (EC) (2006), *i2010 eGovernment Action Plan: Accelerating eGovernment in Europe for the Benefit of All*, COM (2006) 173 final, Brussels: EC, available at: ec.europa.eu/idabc/en/document/5763/254>.

European Commission (EC) (2008), *FP7 Consultation Workshop on ICT for Governance and Policy Modelling*, Brussels, 28th May 2008, available at: <ec.europa.eu/egovernance>.

Codagnone, C. and Wimmer, M.A. (Eds.) (2007), *Roadmapping eGovernment Research: Visions and Measures towards Innovative Governments in 2020*, MY Print snc di Guerinoni Marco & C, Clusone.

DALOS Project (2007), *DALOS - Drafting Legislation with Ontology-Based Support*, available at: <www.dalosproject.eu>.

DEMO-net Project (2007), *DEMO-net, Report on current ICT to enable Participation*, available at: <www.demo-net.org/>.

Traunmüller, R. (1997), *Rechtsinformatik auf dem Weg ins nächste Jahrzehnt*, in Lenk, K., Reinermann, H., Traunmüller, R. (Eds.), "Informatik in Recht und Verwaltung: Entwicklung, Stand und Perspektiven", R. v. Decker's Verlag, Heidelberg, pp. 3-24.

Traunmüller, R. and Wimmer, M.A. (2002), *KM for Public Administration: Focusing on KMS Feature Requirements*, in Karagiannis, D., Reimer, U. (Eds.), "Practical Aspects of Knowledge Management", Proceedings of PAKM'02, LNAI 2569, Springer Verlag, Berlin, pp. 314-325.

Wimmer, M.A. (Ed.) (2001), *Knowledge Management in e-Government*, in "Proceedings of the 2nd International Workshop of IFIP WG 8.5 (KMGov-2001)", Schriftenreihe Informatik 5, Trauner Verlag, Linz.

Wimmer, M.A. (Ed.) (2002), *Knowledge Management in e-Government*, in "Proceedings of the 3rd International Workshop of the IFIP WG 8.5 (KMGov-2002)", Copenhagen, May 2002, Schriftenreihe Informatik 7, Trauner Verlag, Linz.

Wimmer, M.A. (Ed.) (2003), *Knowledge Management in Electronic Government*, in "4th IFIP International Working Conference Proceedings", Springer LNAI 2645, Heidelberg.

Wimmer, M.A. (Ed.) (2004), *Knowledge Management in Electronic Government*, in "5th IFIP International Working Conference Proceedings", Springer LNAI 3035, Heidelberg.

Beyond the Internet Hype; How Law can be Made Effective

Tom M. Van Engers

Leibniz Center for Law, University of Amsterdam, The Netherlands

Abstract. During the last decade governments throughout Europe and the rest of the world discovered the Internet at an important vehicle for dissemination (legal) information, 'modern' legislative practice however in many aspects still reflects the practice in upcoming democracies at the beginning of the 19th century.

Public administrations use ICT-support for many legal task. Since the vast majority of the constituency bound by the legislation and by the regulations has neither means nor wish to directly understand and apply the large body of knowledge reflected in the law, public administrations have developed various eServices to assist citizens with meeting these legal demands or receive the benefits the are entitled to. These eServices are in fact legal services that are intended to improve legal access. Examples of such legal services are electronic tax returns, criminal reporting over the internet and automated traffic violation ticketing.

In this paper I will argue that innovation of the legislative chain is needed to really improve access to the law. I will explain how methods, techniques and ICT tools can be used to improve various aspects of legal quality, such as formal qualities, adherence to technical legislative requirements, absence of internal conflicts, but also its implicit understanding and achieved compliance by the constituency, the cost of legislation enforcement by government agencies and the realization of intended effects and the avoidance of unintended effects.

1. Introduction

The last decade governments throughout Europe and the rest of the world discovered the Internet at an important vehicle for dissemination (legal) information. Some authors such as Francesconi even see technology as a vehicle for high ambitious goals like European integration (Francesconi, 2007). This might eventually be true but at this moment many governments are mainly using technology for the purpose of proliferation of legal documents and use the Internet as an additional channel to other communication channels. Except for the introduction of this additional communication channel modern legislative practice in many aspects still reflects the practice in upcoming democracies at the beginning of the 19th century. Also then specialised legal experts wrote their drafts that after being amended in the parliament became the law that then was published in an official gazette.

In our modern society legislative drafting still is challenging and daunting task with many stakeholders varying from politicians to interest groups, civil servants, citizens and businesses. Even more, the need for effective regulations at low costs led to additional requirements and especially the (side) impact in society including administrative costs, operational cost such as the costs for law enforcement and administrative procedures etc. should be taken into account in early stages of the drafting processes. More and more the awareness grows that legislative drafting is just one (essential) process in a chain of processes and the effectiveness of the law as a steering instrument for society is high dependent of the overall quality of these connected processes.

Information and Communication Technology (ICT) can and already does play an important role in improving legal quality and legal effectiveness. Governments realise themselves that citizens can not be expected to act compliant to the law if they have problems accessing those laws, Internet publishing of legislation and court decisions became an obvious goal. Today legislation can easily been accessed using governmental portals such as the Dutch portal <www.wetten.nl> and the European <www.eurolex.eu>.

Also law enforcement agencies and public administrations use ICT for many legal tasks. Since the vast majority of the constituency bound by the legislation and by the regulations has neither means nor wish to directly understand and apply the large body of knowledge reflected in the law, public administrations have developed various eServices to assist citizens with meeting these legal demands or receive the benefits the are entitled to. These eServices are in fact legal services that are intended to improve legal access. Examples of such legal services are electronic tax returns, criminal reporting over the internet and automated traffic violation ticketing.

Public administrations have always had a need for data from citizens and business as input for their processes. With the growing maturity of Internet technology data exchange between citizens, businesses and the government has now shifted from paper based forms through eForms to electronic data exchange using EDI protocols or recent world wide web standards such as XML. The various legal demands that regulate business administrations these days include obligations, at least for businesses, to use specific protocols and provide the administration with specifically addressed data elements. This of course requires very detailed and technical specifications that are communicated over the Internet as well.

All the above mentioned developments have made Internet publication the most important legal source and the user requirements may not be covered sufficiently by the state gazettes, if ever.

While a lot of progress has been made in smart internet access to legal sources, either using simple search and retrieval of legal documents or intelligent support systems that can solve legal problems and support automated decision making, the legislative processes themselves have successfully preserved a relatively low ICT acceptance rate. Except for the introduction of the PC as a modern typewriter and the use of email legislative drafters have not yet made benefit of the advantages of ICT supporting their daily practice until recently.

This paper describes some recent technological developments that are aimed to improve legal effectiveness. These developments are not limited to one single process in the legal chain and in this paper we will show how ICT can support the legislative production chain including the work of legislation drafters.

ICT support is not only intended to making the life of those drafters a bit easier, it will also help to improve legal quality. ICT support includes software components that assist legislative drafters and other stakeholders involved in the legislative drafting processes, but also the introduction of methods and techniques that haven been developed over time by information scientist and especially knowledge engineers. Some of these methods and techniques have been proven to provide useful handles that help to acquire insights in the legal quality of legislation at hand, and can be used to systematically translate legal source texts into (electronic) services that support both law enforcers, citizens and business to comply with the law.

In this paper some practices, results of recent projects and some insights from academic research in the field of Legal Informatics will be described. Furthermore this paper will explain how methods, techniques and ICT tools can be used to improve various aspects of legal quality, such as formal qualities, adherence to technical legislative requirements, absence of internal conflicts, but also its implicit understanding and achieved compliance by the constituency, the cost of legislation enforcement by government agencies and the realization of intended effects and the avoidance of unintended effects. This will hopefully shift the attention of decisions makers from their current bias on Internet publication to a more fundamental approach that will lead us beyond the Internet hype.

2. Legislative processes and the role of ICT support

(Kollár, 2007) describes a comparative study on the legislative processes of three European countries which we conducted in order to analyse the main characteristics of their legislative processes. The purpose of the comparison was to create a common ground for a legislative drafting tool suite that was to be developed and tested in a large European project sponsored under the eParticipation regime.[1] For this study we examined the legislative processes in those countries in detail. Comparison between the legislative drafting practices of these three countries show that beside some distinctiveness which comes from the historical and cultural differences between the countries, these processes are largely similar. In this paper we will therefore leave out the specific details and describe the general practice of what we will call the unified model for legislative processes (UMLP, see also fig. 1).

In the model we can distinguish three prime process phases of which the processes are loosely coupled. Acts becomes a law in a series of these three processes:

1. Initiation of a bill (a new law or an amendment of an existing law)

---

[1] See: <www.eu-Participation.eu>.

2. Parliamentary phase (discussion and voting)

3. Promulgation and publication

In every country the national constitution defines the group of people who are allowed to propose bills. Initiation of a bill means that given people (most of the cases ministry officials) create a draft text for it. Before sending this to the Parliament various processes may be needed, like in the Netherlands for example the new bill needs to be passed to the State Council (in Dutch: Raad van State). That Council acts as the advisory body to the government and can propose amendments to the bill. In recent initiatives under the European Commission's eParticipation programme projects have been initiated that address deliberation processes with different stakeholders including citizens.[2]

The second phase start when the bill is introduced to the Parliament. The steps within this stage depend on the working procedures of the particular national parliament. In the Netherlands and Italy, like in many West European countries, the Parliament is divided into two chambers (the House of Representatives and the Senate); while in Hungary for example it is unicameral which means that this country has only one legislative or parliamentary chamber. However despite these differences for every chamber the process starts with a preliminary phase, when an appropriate committee discusses the bill to possibly find out mistakes made during the drafting stage. The chamber members also have the rights to suggest amendments for the bill before the members of the houses start to debate it. During the detailed debate the chamber may also propose amendments for the bill or for a previous amendment. The last step of this phase is to vote in favour of organist the law. Different voting procedures exist, varying from passing the whole law in once or voting article by article.

After the Parliament adopted the bill, the final stage before it becomes a law is that it needs to get the assent of the leader of the country. If the leader signs the bill, it turns into a law and will be published in the official way (in most European countries still publication in the official gazette). If the leader does not agrees with some point of the law, before the promulgation he (or she) may ask for further deliberation from the Parliament.

The main steps and stages are displayed in Fig. 1.

In the next sections of this paper we will refer to the different UMLP phases.

Since the beginning of 19th century when most modern states were formed, the legislative drafting processes have not changed fundamentally. In many European countries even the way that bills (or amendments) are communicated still reflect the original procedures despite the availability of Internet technology.

---

[2] See e.g.: <www.eu-participation.eu/>.

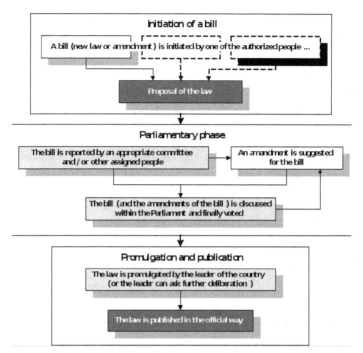

Figure 1. Unified model of legislative processes

Many legal experts involved in these processes however, do not realise themselves that the official documents that are produced in the legislative processes are shaped the way they are shaped because they should finally enable printing by the publisher of the official gazette. The current practice in many European country that changes to the bill are published and usually these published changes are the only documents that have an official status as the applicable law goes back to the time that documents containing those changes were not only treated as a service to the stakeholders involved but more important as a print instruction for the publisher enabling the construction of a new consolidated version of the bill at hand. As stated before this practice still exist in many European country despite the fact that almost any word processor contains the option track changes and publishing the new law as a consolidated whole using internet technology has become extremely easy and potentially making the role of the traditional publishers obsolete.

Some European countries such as Italy and Austria have already decided benefit from the advantages of ICT and especially the Internet and have changed the official publication process. After a new law or changes to existing law have been approved by the parliament they simply publish the consolidated version on their official web sites. This digital version has become the authentic legal source. Sometimes changes to the previous version of the law can be produced as a service. This change in legislative procedure has dramatically reduced publication time and effort but even more important prevents the constituencies to figure out what the consolidated law would be and what the implications thereof for their cases would be. The trend is obviously to that direction. Most countries have already recognized that trend, but it usually takes some time to actually change procedures that were in place for a long time, while it is often in the interests of the publishers to delay this process as much as possible.

Since the practice of publishing changes will vanish sooner or later we will not go into too much details of the practical aspects of writing legal documents that just contain such changes. These documents we can easily generate on demand. The recent SEAL project sponsored by the European Commission in the already mentioned eParticipation programme shows that the editorial processes for legislative drafting can be improved this way and several editors have been developed for this purpose.

In the next section we will describe how we can use ICT not merely as a communication vehicle, i.e. as a means for publishing legal documents over the Internet, but how we can use ICT to improve the legislative drafting processes and to improve the implementation of legislation in operational processes.

3. ICT support during the creation and structuring of legal texts

Many different stakeholders play a role in legislative processes, focussing at different aspects of the legislation. To make it even more complex, every level of government has to deal with forms of legal pluralism and many differences exist between the different legislative cultures and European countries.[3]

Several ICT support tools have been developed over the years to support legislation drafters in fulfilling their difficult task. In the past a common approach was to build some software components that could for example automatically check the numbering of the different structural elements in the legislative text, such as the numbering of chapters, sections, articles and members, according to the standards for the particular legal document type given the legislative drafting culture. Examples of such tools are the Dutch LEDA system (Voermans and Verharen, 1993) and the Italian Norma editor (Palmirani and Brighi, 2002).

The Leda tool was developed to automatically support legislative drafters the Dutch Directives for the Legislative Drafting (DLD) that was renewed in 1993. The DLD consists of 346 directives and guidelines addressing various

---

[3] Legislative processes at regional or municipal level have much in common with the processes at national level, but also have some distinguishing features. While we focus at national level in this paper, many of the issues addressed in this paper however are also applicable at those governmental levels.

aspects of legislation. These guidelines address legislative technical issues, like terminology and model clauses, the directives also cover policy aspects, methodological issues, legislative procedures, structural design amongst other issues. The directives can be categorized according to the stages of the legislative process into:

- directives concerning preparatory activities;
- directives addressing regarding the structural design of the draft;
- directives addressing phrasing and terminology;
- directives concerning procedures.

The DLD was rather ad-hoc organised and the authors thereof didn't make a proper distinction between these categories. This makes it quite difficult for legislators to use the DLD. The main goal for the LEDA-project was to create a system to offer systematic access to the DLD. LEDA was aimed at offering the legislative drafters support in their primary task, without requiring the legislation drafters to constantly worry about compliance to the DLD. LEDA offered the users both a procedural support guiding the user step wise through the steps a legislation drafter has to take when creating a bill, a directive etc.. LEDA furthermore allows template-based creation of the legal draft.

The LEDA system was one of the first attempts to assist the legislative drafter by semi-automated support of the complex task of drafting a bill. Nevertheless the uptake in practice was proven to be extremely difficult. Legislation drafters felt they were forced to adapt to a new way of working which they didn't like. Furthermore technical problems, the CDP was for instance very slow, and the dependency on the right version of MS-Word required updates every time Ms-Word was updated, resulted in stopping the further development and implementation after many years of trying to build support amongst the intended users.

A second example of a project that aimed at supporting the legislative drafters is the Italian Norma in Rete project (translated: Norms in Law). The project was co-ordinated by AIPA[4] in conjunction with Italian Ministry of Justice (Biagioli, Francesconi, Spinosa, Taddei, 2003) The primary goal of the project was to construct a specialized portal which guides the user through to the sites of public authorities participating in the project, and also equipped with a search engine, for retrieving legal documents. In order to improve the accessibility of the legal documents the project decided to use a then recently developed set of standards which was adapted to particular characteristics of the Italian legislative culture and the structure of the legal texts within that culture. This so-called Norme in Rete standards or NIR standards was based upon the URN and XML standards. Uniform names (URN)[5] technique was

---

[4] AIPA: Italian Authority for Information Technology in the Public Administration.
[5] URN: Uniform Resource Name.

used for identifying legal documents and for cross-referencing legal documents. The legal documents were described using XML[6] with a DTD[7]. This way it was much easier to guarantee that the legal documents were compliant to legislative drafting rules. For creating new legal documents an editor was developed. This xmLegesEditor was developed at ITTIG/CNR[8] and is a specific editor for legislative documents based on NIR standards. The whole editor was written in Java, based on open source standard libraries, which is particularly suited for a project involving different subjects (e.g. parliament, public authorities, regional assemblies and research institutes). The tool is a native XML editor, so it directly works on and produces XML documents compliant to the NIR-DTD. The program is currently under experimentation at the Italian Senate and Chamber of Deputies. According to the results an extension has been planned to extend it to support Parliamentary Acts. The lifecycle of the bills in both chambers is being studied as the requirements for textual and partial modification mark-up. Parsing formal structure of bills into XML and creating support for bills lifecycle management will be included in new extension on the xmLegesEditor.

Like we saw in the LEDA example the xmLegesEditor also supports an a priori validation preventing legislation drafters form producing documents that violate the directives for legislation drafting.

A third example is the Norma System, which has been developed and maintained by the University of Bologna (see e.g. Palmirani and Brighi, 2002). The prime goal of the system was to create an architecture that allows marking-up normative text into XML, and consolidating existing acts to create a legal database. The documents stored in the resulted database can be published and searched on the web.

The system supports the control of the chronological coherence, maintenance of the versioning chain and support editing during the consolidation operation.

Like LEDA the Norma Editor was implemented in VB.Net[9] as an extension for MS-Word, which also made it depending on the versions of MS-Word. Therefore the designers decided recently to rebuild the Norma Editor but this time as an XML-based editor more or less following the NIR editor's architecture.

The Norma system is not a real legislative drafting tool, but rather a consolidation tool for marking-up pre-existing texts and converting them to XML format. These documents were originally created in Word, which explains why this way of the implementation was chosen. The XML versions of the legal

---

[6] XML: Extensible Mark-up Language.

[7] DTD: Document Type Definition.

[8] ITTIG: Istituto di Teoria e Tecniche dell'Informazione Giuridica (Institute of Legal Information Theory and Techniques of the Italian National Research Council).

[9] VB: Visual Basic.

documents are produced automatically, so users don't need to know about the actual mark-up of the documents. The mark-up function of the editor works in steps and the editor guides the user. The editor tries to recognize the structured parts of the text in an automatic way (following the NIR-DTD), and allows the user to manually correct possible mistakes. The tool also offers an automatic technique to detect references. The text parsing is done using structural rules and a multilingual external vocabulary. After that, the software marks-up the metadata such as dates, keywords and (automatically calculated) URNs. During the consolidation procedure the editor connects to the database and stores the legal text while maintaining the coherence with the rest of the documents in the collection.

The team responsible for developing the Norma system has recently started to develop a legal-drafting module, which should support the legislator through the process of producing a legal document.

The last example is the MetaVex edit environment developed at the Leibniz Center for Law of the University of Amsterdam. MetaVex is a XML based editing environment that is specifically designed for supporting the creation and modification of legal documents marked up in the European CEN standard for legal sources MetaLex.[10]

MetaVex uses XML as a basis because other document formats such as MS-Word, PDF, ODF etc. lack the structural information that is required to adequately refer from and to parts of sources in a explicit and publishing channel free way. The MetaVex edit environment ensures that a legal document remains valid (i.e. compliant to the XML schema definition) during composing or editing. This is realised by providing a list of elements that are allowed at a particular position in the text. These elements and their order are recorded in an XML Schema file, which is processed by the editor. In contrast to normal word processors such as MS-Word, where a legislator can just start typing and need not bother about creating the structure of the document the MetaVex supports the user to create a well structured text using the permitted elements. After creating a permitted element, such as an article, the user can continue creating the actual text of the element. Of course deciding on the permitted elements would require knowledge about the structure defined by the schema, knowledge that can not be assumed present at most users. Therefore the MetaVex editor is designed such way that even inexperienced users will be supported by offering predefined templates (i.e. blocks of texts and element structures, which can be inserted to a given point of the document). These templates can already contain some standard phrases.

Legal drafters have begun standardising typical structures and words used for certain "legal statements" and the designers of the MetaVex edit environment made benefit of that. These typical structures, key words and standard

---

[10] See: <www.MetaLex.eu>.

phrase are of course legislative culture depending and also are language dependent. The MetaVex edit environment was designed for international use and users can easily create their own templates or edit existing ones using the same MetaVex editor.

Legal documents typically contain different kinds of references. These external links can point to other legal documents, varying form regular legal texts or for example spatial plans or "concepts" in some formal domain model. MetaVex supports automatic generation of links, for any reference inserted, allowing drafters to easily validate such references. If the legislator would like, he can follow the link, and navigate inside documents stored in the system. The position of a document in the complete legal framework is also made clear through references.

The MetaVex edit environment is intended to support different languages and corresponding XML Schemas, it allows the user to choose between the different languages of the text, or to specify a date and check the effective version of the legislation in a given time period.

The MetaVex environment also supports the legislative process, e.g. during the parliamentary phase, where the content of the draft bill is oftend changed through proposed amendments. The content management functionality containing support for storing, versioning and controlling of the composed and edited documents enables the user to create amendments to either other amendments or the original draft bill and help the user to keep track of changes.

All documents and amendments created with MetaVex are saved in a data repository, which allows fast access to relevant documents. It also offers functionalities to control access to certain (parts of) documents e.g. to restrict access to those (parts of) documents. This means that different rights can be assigned to different users. Depending on the user rights, specific functionalities can be restricted, such as editing, approval or administrative features. Controlling documents also includes groupware facilities. Especially in this stage the legal document needs to be locked for other users, preventing conflicting changes in the same part. At the same time, if one ore more person is involved in creating a document, their collaboration needs to be guaranteed by the architecture.

The MetaVex environment also supports the last phase of the legislative process where the accepted bill needs to be promulgated. It supports publishing in various formats through different export functions, allowing publishing in for example PDF format or web-based format (XHTML file).

4. ICT support for supporting the implementation of legislation

In the previous section we described how we can use ICT support for supporting the legislative drafting processes. We already mentioned some of the many stakeholders that are involved in the legislative process. Usually drafting is restricted to adapting an existing piece of legislation, but even then several legislation drafters may be involved. Although 90 percent of the legislative drafting considers adapting existing legislation, which usually is limited to inserting small changes, a job that can be easily done by one legislative drafter, the number of involved legislation drafters may increase when larger changes have to be inserted of when a completely new law has to be created. When the income tax law in the Netherlands was renewed in 2001 for example more than 80 legislation drafters were involved. One can imagine the increased complexity of organising the cooperation and alignment issues that are to be solved in such cases. But legislation drafters are not the only stakeholders in the process of creating a new law or adapting existing legislation. Also department heads, politicians and institutions such as the state council for the judiciary and the operational departments responsible for implementing the law when it passed the parliament play a role in the drafting process.

While the editorial environments such as MetaVex offer the required basic facilities needed to adequately supporting the many stakeholders involved in the legislative drafting process, including content management and workflow management support, other forms of ICT support are required for further improving the quality of the legislative process chain.

Legal quality is not a singular concept and it depends on the legal content but also on the quality of the forth-bringing processes (legitimacy), the quality of the court system etc. The subsidiarity of a law is one of the elements that we have to look at if we want to judge the legal quality thereof. Checking the subsidiarity, that is checking the balance between the negative effects such as the disturbance caused by the law, the administrative costs, the law enforcement efforts etc. are worthwhile given the supposed benefits the law will bring, is the one of the most important focus points of the State Council when giving advise to the government about a draft proposal. These days operational issues of legislation may enjoy quite some political attention. Discussion about the administrative burden for example take place all over Europe and possibly due to the ever raising cost of labour governments are also keen on reducing operational costs for administration, law enforcement and judicial processes.

ICT systems can help governments to realise these aims, since ICT can help to improve transparency, and provides support for civil servants responsible for administration and law enforcement, citizens and businesses. One early attempt to support the whole chain starting from legislation drafting to the operational processes was made by the Dutch Tax and Customs Administration (DTCA) with different partners in the so-called (E-)POWER project that was started end of the ninety nineties (see e.g. Van Engers and Kordelaar, 1999; Van Engers and Glassée, 2001; Van Engers and Vanlerberghe, 2002.) The approach developed then has become influential and while the actual Power methodology has not yet become the default it could have been, it does play an important role in different large governmental projects.

Central to the (E-)POWER project was the development of an integrated method that supports the process of 'translating' legal sources into operational processes and supporting information systems. The context of the POWER method was defined as a regulation-intensive integrated organization of automated systems and knowledge workers, established to service customers and enforce the defined regulations. A formal analysis of legislation and regulations enables the cooperation of such an organization on the operational level in the design of legislation. Also such formal analysis enables the organisation to implement new legislation more quickly and accurately. An abstract picture of the approach is depicted in figure 2.

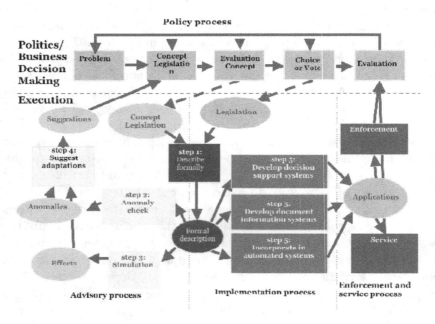

Figure 2. Position of the (E-)POWER method in the advisory and implementation process. With the POWER approach we aim to support the legislative chain from drafting to implementation in an integral way.

The POWER method resulting from the (E-)POWER project is aimed to support the implementation of new or adapted legislation, but also is intended to help legislation drafters to get better insights in quality issues of their drafts and the operational consequences thereof. In order to support the actors involved in such task the relevant legal sources including the draft legislation is *translated* into a formal model, i.e. an explicit and executable form. Relevant sources are broader than just the draft legislation, since other legal sources including case law is usually needed for being able to determine the semantics of a piece of law. Also operational policies have impact on the effectiveness of new legislation and therefore is included in the analysis. A law can only be effective if the law enforcement organizations involved manage to design and implement their law enforcement strategies and offer services to the stakeholders.

Central to the POWER-method is the formalisation of legal sources. This can be the law itself, possibly in draft form, additional regulations, case law, or policy statements. Normally concept legislation is the starting point since we have to adjust to the political process. The speed of this process may however vary significantly. The speed of the POWER-approach therefore ideally meets the fastest political decision-making process (sometimes this takes place within one or two days). Obviously this cannot be realised in case of substantial changes, since formalising a piece of law is a labour intensive process, which requires highly trained experts. For this purpose the so-called POWER-light approach was developed (Van Engers and Vanlerberghe, 2002). This method is based upon the original POWER method but instead of actually translating the law into a formal representation, this analysts read the legal sources as if they would actually translate that into such representation. This form of close reading with a certain mind set has proven to already be beneficial in case of limited time. Normally after a draft law has been created it has to be implemented which implies that the public administrations, law enforcement organisations etc. have to adapt their systems, and in many case this holds for citizens or business as well. The formal representation that will result from the regular POWER method can speed up those processes.

These formal descriptions of the law can be used for the development of decision support systems, for incorporation in document information systems or automated systems that are developed to support law enforcement and service provisioning to the citizen. When the draft legislation has been formalized, the approved legislation can be transformed into the implementation process very quickly.

But these formal representations can be used in a very powerful way during the drafting stage as well. Then these formal representations of the legal sources are used for anomaly checking and building simulations (see e.g. Spreeuwenberg et al., 2001). Anomaly checking provides us with a list of anomalies, e.g. potential reasoning defects, which would occur when implementing the legislation. Simulations provide us with insights in enforceability and in the desired or undesired effects that would result from implementing the law. The results of these activities can be used to formulate suggestions for change and fed back to the legislation drafters, in order to enhance the quality of legislation. Even when the legislation is already approved, or if these suggestions are not effectuated in a new draft it is important for government agencies to be aware of the potential problems in the legislation early on. Business processes may have to be adapted to cope with these problems. Executive decisions may be required to ensure consistent implementation.

Within the Dutch Tax and Customs Administration POWER is effectuated as an integrated approach. According to this approach, teams are established with representatives from different domains. Jurists, fiscal experts, information scientists, knowledge engineers and system engineers co-operate in advisory projects or projects responsible for the implementation of law enforcement processes. The POWER method has been applied in several projects varying from pure advisory projects to implementation projects and combination of these two. In all of these cases this form of co-operation proved to be very effective. As a result better regulations have been established, while at the same time its accessibility has been significantly improved. Implementation consequently can be speeded up, while execution becomes more consistent and more cost effective. Furthermore the quality of the law enforcement processes is increased as a result from better consistency and better support by knowledge based systems.

Despite the obvious advantages the POWER method had to offer the DTCA being involved in endless reorganisation programmes reduced its efforts to continue the development thereof. In the European Estrella project sponsored under the EU's 6th Framework Programme however many of the ideas of the original (E-)POWER project were brought another step forwards.[11]

In new projects we will continue to work on amongst others reducing the time needed to produce formal models from legal sources, using natural language processing (NLP) tools that are used for automated concept extraction. We had these tools in prototype form already in the (E-)POWER project but these tools would certainly need further improvement. Such tools would not only speed up the modelling process but would also improve model uniformity across analysts, and put the maturing tools at the disposal of not only analysts, but also involved experts of other disciplines. If we would also succeed in creating NLP tools that can cope with different natural languages, investigating and assisting harmonization within the European community will become achievable. We could then assist in translation of legal sources and compare the consequences of different legislation in member countries in specific situations. This would also increase the accessibility of legal sources because multi-lingual interfaces to the legal knowledge-based systems will be easier to realize at relatively low costs.

---

[11] See: <www.Estrellaproject.org>.

5. Conclusions

Many governments still struggle with using the Internet as a vehicle of disseminating legal documents. The impact of ICT as a support tool for legislative processes however is by far not exploited to the full extend. Examples such as the SEAL project, the (E-)Power project and the Estrella project show us a pathway to more effective legislative processes supporting all processes not just the communication process. Using methods, tools and techniques from different disciplines such as Artificial Intelligence we can further improve legal quality and the effectiveness of the legislative processes. Legal knowledge-based systems were seen a promising technique in the nineteen eighties but could play an even more important role these days. Legal pluralism and the complexity of our society is not going away. We need to go beyond current Internet hype and extend our perspective by learning from past experiences and combining them with new opportunities offered by Internet technologies. With respect to the latter especially the semantic WEB technologies are promising. The W3C community has already provided us with interesting knowledge representation formalisms (also the basis for the Estrella project) that are both decidable and tractable and provided that they are expressive enough this might allow us to create an open environment for assembling legal services out of building blocks that are maintained by the owners of the legal sources they are based upon and which computational behaviour can be guaranteed. In the AGILE project sponsored by the Dutch Science Foundation (NWO) we will look into these issues in more detail. It may turn out that Francesconi proves to be right in the end with his claim that technology is the vehicle for European integration. But even if this ambitious claim fails we can still use technology to make our lives a little bit easier.

References

Agnoloni, T., Francesconi, E., Spinosa, P.L. (2006), *xmLegesEditor, an opensource visual XML editor for supporting Legal National standards*, paper presented at the V legislative XML Workshop, 14-16 June 2006, ITTIG-CNR Institute of Legal Information Theory and Technique, San Domenico di Fiesole (Florence - Italy), available at: <www.ittig.cnr.it/legws/Presentations/AgnoloniFrancesconiSpinosa.pdf>.

Biagioli, C., Francesconi, E., Spinosa, P., Taddei, M. (2003), *The NIR Project, Standards and Tools for Legislative Drafting and Legal Document Web Publication*, paper presented at the ICAIL - Workshop, E-Government: Modelling Norms and Concepts as Key Issues, available at: <www.cirfid.unibo.it/~agsw/icail03/e-gov03/slides/08_francesconi.pdf>.

Boer, A., Hoekstra, R., Winkels, R., Van Engers, T., Willaert, F. (2002), *METAlex: Legislation in XML*, in Bench-Capon, T., Daskalopulu, A., Winkels, R.G.F. (Eds.), "Legal Knowledge and Information Systems. Jurix 2002: The Fifteenth Annual Conference, Frontiers in Artificial Intelligence and Applications", IOS Press, Amsterdam, pp. 1-10.

De Maat, E., Winkels, R., Van Engers, T.M. (2006), *Automated detection of reference structures in law*. in Van Engers, T.M. (Ed.), "Legal Knowledge and Information

Systems. Jurix 2006: The Nineteenth Annual Conference", Vol. 152 of Frontiers in Artificial Intelligence and Applications, IOS Press, Amsterdam, pp. 41-50.

Francesconi, E. (2007), *Technologies for European integration, standards-based interoperability of legal information systems*, European Press Academic Publishing, Florence.

Kollár, A. (2007), *IT architecture for legislative drafting tools in a multicultural Europe*, Master Thesis, Corvinus University of Budapest.

Palmirani, M. and Brighi, R. (2002), *Norma-System: A Legal Document System for Managing Consolidated Acts*, in "Database and Expert Systems Applications", 13th International Conference, DEXA 2002, Aix-en-Provence, France, September 2-6, Springer, Berlin / Heidelberg.

Spreeuwenberg, S., Van Engers, T.M., Gerrits, R. (2001), *The role of verification in improving the quality of legal decision-making*, in Verheij B., Lodder A.R., Loui R.P., and Muntjewerff A.J. (Eds.), "Legal Knowledge and Information Systems. Jurix 2001: The Fourteenth Annual Conference", IOS Press, Amsterdam, pp. 1-15.

Van Engers, T. and Glassée, E. (2001), *Facilitating the legislation process using a shared conceptual model*, IEEE Intelligent Systems, Vol. 16, No. 1, pp. 50-58.

Van Engers, T. and Kordelaar, P.J.M. (1999), *POWER: Programme for an ontology based working environment for modeling and use of regulations and legislation*, in: "Proceedings of ISMICK'99: Management of Industrial and Corporate Knowledge", Rotterdam, The Netherlands.

Van Engers, T. and Vanlerberghe, R.A.W. (2002), *The power-light version; improving legal quality under time pressure*, in: "Electronic Government, Proceedings of the first international conference E-Gov 2002", Aix-en-Provence, France.

Van Gog, R. and Van Engers, T.M. (2001), *Modeling legislation using natural language processing* in "2001 IEEE International Conference on Systems, Man & Cybernetics", Tucson, Arizona.

Voermans, W. and Verharen, E. (1993), *LEDA: A Semi-Intelligent Legislative Drafting-Support System*, in Svensson, J.S., Wassink, J.G.J. and van Buggenhout, B. (Eds.), "Legal Knowledge Based Systems: Proceedings 6th International Conference JURIX '93".

An Approach towards Better Legislation to Improve Law Accessibility and Understanding

Tommaso Agnoloni*, Lorenzo Bacci*, Enrico Francesconi*, Simonetta Montemagni°, PierLuigi Spinosa*, Daniela Tiscornia*
*Institute of Legal Information Theory and Techniques (ITTIG-CNR), Italy
°Institute for Computational Linguistics (ILC-CNR), Italy

Abstract. The quality of legislative drafting process at European and national levels is highly influenced by the legal drafters control over the multilingual complexity of European legislation and over the linguistic and conceptual issues involved in its transposition into national laws. The DALOS project aims at ensuring coherence and alignment in the legislative language, providing law-makers with a knowledge (ontological-linguistic) resource and knowledge management tools to support the multilingual legislative drafting process. This paper outlines the activities within DALOS, aiming at the definition of the characteristics of the knowledge resource, at its implementation, at its integration in a legislative drafting environment for the project prototype.

Keywords: Multilingual legal drafting, legal ontologies, NLP techniques.

1. Introduction

Quality in European and national legislation is one of the main purposes of the current initiatives of the European Commission. In the Mandelkern report on Better Regulation (Mandelkern, 2001) the need for a coordinated action by Member States was solicited to simplify the EU regulatory environment, to enhance the quality of EU legislation as well as to rationalise the transposition of Community legislation into national law. The Mandelkern Group on Better Regulation in particular stressed on "quality of regulation" as an essential precondition to enhance the "credibility of the governance process" and to contribute to "welfare of citizens, business and other stakeholders". Coherence, interoperability and harmonization in the legislative knowledge of, and control over, the legal lexicon is therefore considered as a precondition for improving the quality of legislative language and for facilitating access to legislation by legal experts and citizens. In a multilingual environment and, in particular, in EU regulations, only the awareness of the subtleties of legal lexicon in the different languages can enable drafters to maintain coherence among different linguistic versions of the same text, as well as over their transposition in national laws.

To face these problems the DALOS[1] project has been launched within the "eParticipation" framework, the EU Commission initiative aimed at promoting the development and use of Information and Communication Technologies

---

[1] DrAfting Legislation with Ontology-based Support.

in the legislative decision-making processes. The aim of such initiative is to foster the quality of the legislative production, to enhance accessibility and alignment of legislation at European level, as well as to promote awareness and democratic participation of citizens to the legislative process. In particular, DALOS aims at ensuring that legal drafters and decision-makers have control over the legal language at national and European level, by providing law-makers with linguistic and knowledge management tools to be used in the legislative processes, in particular within the phase of legislative drafting.

Nowadays the key approach for dealing with lexical complexity is the ontological one (Boer, Van Engers, Winkels, 2003), by which it is possible to characterize the conceptual meaning of lexical units, as well as to provide a detailed description of the semantic properties of the related concepts as well as of their relationships.

In this paper the development of a two level (ontological and linguistic) knowledge resource for DALOS is described. In particular, in Section 2 the design principle of the DALOS knowledge resource and the characteristics of its Knowledge Organization System (KOS) are presented; in Section 3 and 4 the implementation of the DALOS knowledge resource organized in two levels (lexical and ontological) is illustrated; in Section 5 a description of the prototypical integration of the DALOS resource in a legislative drafting environment is given; finally in Section 6 some conclusions are reported.

2. Design of the DALOS resource

As discussed, DALOS is targeted to provide a knowledge resource for legislative drafting. For the aim of developing a project pilot, the "consumer protection" domain has been chosen. The DALOS resource is organized in two layers of abstraction (see Fig. 1):

- the *ontological layer* containing the conceptual modeling at a language-independent level;

- the *lexical layer* containing lexical manifestations in different languages of concepts at the ontological layer.

Basically, the ontological layer acts as a layer that aligns concepts at the European level, independently from the language and the legal order, where possible. Concepts at the ontological layer act as a "pivot" meta-language in a N-language environment. They are linked by taxonomical as well as object property relationships (`has_object_role`, `has_agent_role`, `has_value`, etc.).

On the other hand, the Lexical layer aims at describing language-dependent lexical manifestations of the concepts of the ontological layer. At this level

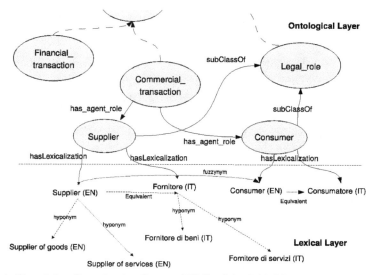

Figure 1. Knowledge Organization System (KOS) of the DALOS resource.

lexical units are linked by pure linguistic relationships (**hypernymy**, **hyponymy**, **meronymy**, etc.). It uses the semantics of WordNet and EuroWordNet, which is centered around the notion of "synset". A synset is a set of one or more uninflected word forms (lemmas) with a synonymous meaning.

The connection between these two layers is represented by the relationship between concepts and their lexical manifestations: within a single language (different lexical variations (lemmas) of the same meaning (concept)); in a cross-language context (multilingual variations of the same concept). In the DALOS KOS this link is represented by the **hasLexicalization** relationship. The use of a two-level knowledge architecture provides a higher degree of modularity to the knowledge resource:

1. the lexical layer is a lexical database which can be upgraded and reused in different domains with respect to the one considered in DALOS;

2. the ontological layer provides a more detailed semantic description of the lexical units at the lexical layer, as well as relationships between concepts.

Entries and relationships at both levels are described by exploiting the expressiveness of RDF/OWL semantic Web standards. The combination of these two levels of knowledge allows synsets at the lexical layer to obtain two different kind of properties:

— *linguistic properties*, namely EuroWordNet lexical relations that come directly from a linguistic and statistical analysis of texts;

— *semantic properties*, deriving from the classification of synsets into classes of the ontological layer, describing the consumer protection domain for

the pilot case; such semantic properties are valid only within this particular domain.

For example, a statistical analysis of texts on consumer protection law revealed
that `consumer` and `supplier` are related lexical units. Therefore, in our model,
at the lexical layer they have been linked by a `fuzzynym` WordNet property.
At the Ontological layer such relation can be more semantically characterized
as regards the consumer protection domain: such lexical units are considered
as lexicalizations of the classes `Consumer` and `Supplier` respectively, while the
relations between them pass through the concept `Commercial_transaction`
which links `Consumer` and `Supplier` by a `has_agent_role` property (see
Fig. 1). Next sections will focus on the DALOS ontological-linguistic resource
implementation activities.

3. Lexical layer implementation

The starting point for the construction of the lexicons is a selected corpus
of documents on the domain of "protection of consumers" economic and legal
interests, including Directives, Regulation and Case Law on the subject.

From a methodological point of view, of great importance is the fact that
the source documents for the construction of the resource are made available in
parallel translations in the EU languages because of the obligation to publish
directives in the national languages of the member states, making possible a
subsequent automatic terms and concepts alignment

Domain lexicons in the four European languages (Italian, English, Spanish, Dutch) supported in DALOS have been constructed in a semiautomatic
way applying Natural Language Processing techniques to the set of selected
documents.

For the extraction of Italian terms we used T2K (Text–to–Knowledge), a hybrid ontology learning system combining linguistic technologies and statistical
techniques (Dell'Orletta et al., 2006).

For the other languages two term extraction applications have been used.
TermExtractor[2] (Sclano and Velardi, 2007) offers a comprehensive package of
algorithms for the selection of relevant terms from any text corpus. GATE[3]
(Cunningham et al., 2002), developed by the University of Sheffield, is a framework for Language Engineering (LE) applications which supports efficient and
robust text processing.

A key requisite for both the automatic tools was the possibility to keep
track of the links to document fragments in the domain corpora from which
each relevant term has been extracted. To this end a preliminary fragmen-

---

[2] Available at: `<lcl2.di.uniroma1.it/termextractor/>`.
[3] Available at: `<www.gate.ac.uk>`.

tation of each document in its formal partitions (paragraphs of normative documents *e.g. Part, Article* etc.) have been performed.

More important, this made possible the exploitation of the peculiarity of the domain corpus to be parallel. Interlingual alignment could in fact be automatically established exploiting the origin of extracted terms in different languages from parallel contexts.

A particular treatment is reserved to terms identified by automatic tools to be definitions, *i.e.* terms preceding a definition in the directives. For this terms a translation in the different languages keeping the original meaning is guaranteed. Defined terms are highlighted in the lexicons and corresponding definitions are entirely reported in the knowledge base as special contexts.

After a manual clean-up phase due to the noise introduced by automatic tools, the average size of the four lexicons is about 1500 terms.

The automatic construction of lexicons should be seen as a starting point for the setup of a dynamically growing resource. A manual update of the lexicons will be possible and should be done at a second stage directly by the users through terms insertion, deletion and inter-linguistic alignments editing.

4. Ontological layer implementation

The Ontological layer of the DALOS resource is aimed at providing an alignment of concepts at language-independent level. It acts not only as a pivot structure for language-dependent lexical manifestations, but it provides a more semantically characterized description of the chosen domain in terms of concepts and their relations, exploiting the expressiveness and reusability of the RDF/OWL semantic Web standards for knowledge representation. This allows also to validate the developed knowledge resource with respect to existing foundational or core ontologies.

As discussed in Section 2 the ontological layer is the result of an intellectual activity aimed at describing the domain of the consumer protection. An intellectual approach has been chosen to strictly reach the project objectives with a predictable degree of reliability in describing semantically qualified relations between concepts.

Classes and properties have been implemented on the basis of the terminological knowledge extracted from the chosen Directives on the consumer protection law (see Section 3), in particular from the "definitions" contained, maintaining coherence to the design patterns of the Core Legal Ontology (CLO)[4] (Gangemi, Sagri, Tiscornia, 2005) developed on top of DOLCE foundational ontology (Masolo et al., 2004a) and on the "Descriptions and Situations" (DnS) ontology (Gangemi, 2007) within the DOLCE+ library.[5] The

---

[4] Available at: <www.loa-cnr.it/ontologies/CLO/CoreLegal.owl>.
[5] DOLCE+ library, available at: <dolce.semanticweb.org>.

DALOS ontology copes with the entities of the chosen domain and their legal specificities. In this knowledge architecture the role of a core legal ontology is to provide semantic characterization to entities/concepts which belong to the general theory of law, bridging the gap between domain-specific concepts and the abstract categories of formal upper level or foundational ontologies such as, in our case, DOLCE.

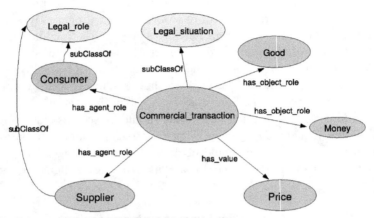

Figure 2. Excerpt of the DALOS Ontological Layer.

The ontological layer is therefore populated by the conceptual entities which characterize the consumer protection domain. The first assumption is that all concepts *defined* within consumer law are representative of the domain and, as a consequence, that several concepts *used* in the definitional contexts pertain to the ontology as well, representing the basic properties or, in other words, the 'intensional meaning' of the relevant concepts. Similarly, the Ontological layer contains generic situations having a legal relevance in the chosen domain.

Such domain-specific concepts are classified according to more general notions, imported from CLO, such as `Legal_role` and `Legal_situation`. Examples of some concepts obtained by the definitions from the consumer law domain are `Commercial_transaction`, `Consumer`, `Supplier`, `Good`, `Price`. The specific roles they play (Masolo et al., 2004b) are illustrated in Fig. 2.

The first version of the DALOS ontological layer contains 121 named classes with necessary and sufficient definitions, resulting in the OWL-DL language.

5. The application prototype

An application prototype has been developed within the project in order to show how the DALOS resource can be accessed and exploited to provide multilingual lexical and semantic support in legislative documents drafting concerning the "consumer protection" domain.

xmLegesEditor is an open source legislative drafting environment developed at ITTIG-CNR (Agnoloni, Francesconi, Spinosa, 2007) for supporting the adoption of legal national standards (XML and URN NIR[6] standards). Briefly, xmLegesEditor is a visual XML editor able to support legislative drafters in the production of standard compliant normative documents, providing advanced features for structural and semantic markup.

The DALOS extension of xmLegesEditor provides integrated access from the drafting environment to the knowledge resource produced in DALOS.

5.1. ACCESSING THE DALOS RESOURCE WITHIN THE APPLICATION PROTOTYPE

Following its multiple components architecture a set of views on the Knowledge Base have been been implemented in the editing environment to provide access to the different resources (Fig. 3). Once the KB in a specific language is loaded in the application, users can access the controlled vocabulary from different perspectives exploiting:

- terms classification accessed from a browsable hierarchical view of the ontology;
- direct search of terms in the lexicon from a plain list view from which the user can perform textual queries over the lexical forms of the extracted synsets
- access to detailed information over a synset as well as to hyperlinked external document fragments in the domain corpus where each term, as well as its variants, have been defined or used;
- view and browsing on sets of terms clustered according to their lexical relations (*i.e.* "hyponymy", "fuzzynymy") or semantic relations *i.e.* relations inherited from the relations between the ontological classes under which each synset is classified (see sect. 2)
- interlingual relations provided by terms alignment for "horizontal" browsing in the multilingual resource

---

[6] NormeInRete, available at: <`www.normeinrete.it`>.

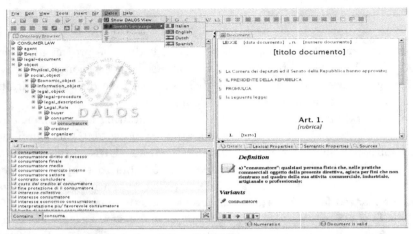

Figure 3. A screenshot of xmLegesEditor DALOS prototype

5.2. USING THE DALOS RESOURCE TO IMPROVE THE QUALITY OF LEGISLATIVE TEXTS

The integration of the DALOS resource into xmLegesEditor provides users with facilities which aim at enhancing the quality of legislative documents in different scenarios, which can be grouped into three main working situations:

1. new legislative documents drafting; in this case the user has the possibility to browse the ontological layer, identifying concepts which are relevant for a situation to be regulated, as well as clusters of related concepts and semantic relationships which give a view of the actors and their relationships in the situation to be regulated. Going down to the lexical layer the user may choose, in a specific language, the most appropriate lexical manifestations of such concepts, checking also the contexts in which they are used within the European legislation and insert the chosen lexical unit, with a proper XML annotation, within the text.

2. existing documents checking; the system may check all the lexical units of the text also contained in the DALOS lexical layer, as well as verify their pertinence to the context, and, in case, replace them with more appropriate terms.

3. transposition of European directives into national laws. Usually European directives use general concepts and terminology to better cope with different Member States legal cultures; the use of the same term in a transposition law and in the transposition language version of the related directive might not be appropriate for a national legal culture and legislation. By using the DALOS resource the legal drafter can be supported in choosing the more appropriate concept and terminology to be used within the transposition law.

6. Conclusions

The main purpose of the DALOS project is to provide law-makers with linguistic and knowledge management tools to be used in the legislative processes, in particular within the phase of legislative drafting. The aim is to keep control over the legal language, especially in the EU legislation multilingual environment, enhancing the quality of the legislative production, as well as the accessibility and alignment of legislation at European level.

In this paper we presented the DALOS resource, which is organized into two knowledge layers (the ontological and lexical layers). The motivations for this kind of architecture and the methodologies for its implementation have been presented. In particular, we have discussed the principle on the basis of which the ontological layer has been developed, as well as NLP techniques used to implement the Lexical layer. Finally we have illustrated the use of the DALOS resource in the xmLegesEditor legislative drafting environment, along with facilities aiming at enhancing the quality of legislative texts.

The availability of a document archive marked up with a vocabulary of normalized terms derived by DALOS modules can also be useful in documents indexing to provide Semantic Web-oriented retrieval services. Moreover, as terms in XML texts will be linked to the ontological layer through the lexical layer, it will be possible to provide more advanced query features exploiting semantics for extracting norms or document fragments using more complex retrieval inferences.

References

Agnoloni, T., Francesconi, E., Spinosa, P. (2007), *xmLegesEditor: an opensource visual xml editor for supporting legal national standards*, in "Proceedings of the V Legislative XML Workshop", European Press Academic Publishing, pp. 239–251.

Boer, A., Van Engers, T., Winkels, R. (2003), *Using ontologies for comparing and harmonizing legislation*, in "Proceedings of the International Conference on Artificial Intelligence and Law", Edinburgh (UK), ACM Press, pp. 161–172.

Cunningham, H., Maynard, D., Bontcheva, K., Tablan, V. (2002), *Gate: A framework and graphical development environment for robust nlp tools and applications*, in "Proceedings of the 40th Anniversary Meeting of the Association for Computational Linguistics (ACL'02)".

Dell'Orletta, F., Lenci, A., Marchi, S., Montemagni, S., Pirrelli, V. (2006), *Text-2-knowledge: una piattaforma linguistico-computazionale per l'estrazione di conoscenza da testi*, in "Proceedings of the SLI-2006 Conference", Vercelli, pp. 20–28.

Gangemi, A. (2007), *Design patterns for legal ontology construction*, in Bourcier, D., Galindo, F., Casanovas, P., Noriega, P. (Eds.), "Trends in Legal Knowledge. The Semantic Web and the Regulation of Electronic Social Systems", European Press Academic Publishing, pp. 171–191.

Gangemi, A., Sagri, M.T., Tiscornia, D. (2005), *A constructive framework for legal ontologies*, in Benjamins, R., Casanovas, P., Breuker, J., Gangemi, A. (Eds.), "Law and the Semantic Web", Springer Verlag.

Gangemi, A., Sagri, M.T., Tiscornia, D. (2003), *Jur-wordnet, a source of metadata for content description in legal information*, in "Proceedings of the ICAIL Workshop on Legal Ontologies & Web based legal information management".

Lame, G. (2005), *Using nlp techniques to identify legal ontology components: concepts and relations*, "Lecture Notes in Computer Science", Vol. 3369, pp. 169–184.

Mandelkern, D. (2001), *Mandelkern group on better regulation*, Final report. European Commission, 13 November 2001.

Masolo, C., Gangemi, A., Guarino, N., Oltramari, A., Schneider, L. (2004a), *Wonderweb deliverable d18: The wonderweb library of foundational ontologies*, Technical report.

Masolo, C., Vieu, L., Bottazzi, E., Catenacci, C., Ferrario, R., Gangemi, A., Guarino, N. (2004b), *Social roles and their descriptions*, in Welty, C. (Ed.), "Proceedings of the Ninth International Conference on the Principles of Knowledge Representation and Reasoning", Whistler.

Sais, J. and Quaresma, P. (2005), *A methodology to create legal ontologies in a logic programming based web information retrieval system*, "Lecture Notes in Computer Science", Vol. 3369, pp. 185–200.

Sclano, F. and Velardi, P. (2007), *Termextractor: a web application to learn the shared terminology of emergent web communities*, in "Proceedings of the 3rd International Conference on Interoperability for Enterprise Software and Applications (I-ESA 2007)".

Norms in the Interaction between Citizen Users and the Administrative Apparatus

Manola Cherubini

Institute of Legal Information Theory and Techniques (ITTIG-CNR), Italy

Abstract. Free access to a norm via Internet cannot ignore dealing with practical modes of application, on which all legal knowledge about specific topics is founded, where inevitably they involve and link provisions, jurisprudence, local practices and legal authority.

To precisely reconstruct all the information relating to the functioning of the State and its peripheral administrations is a very arduous task, also for those working in the sector. Information in this domain, for the use and consumption of both the citizen user and the service provider user involves the integration of the two different approaches that determine the possibility of taking in both directions a bidirectional knowledge route that ranges from "specific behaviour" ("how do you do it?") to its normative justification ("based on which norms?").

All the considerations mentioned above have been made on the basis of a precise working methodology and its related technical solutions that permit the implementation of increasingly easy, aggregate, complete, updated and innovative accesses to the services supplied by the public administrations.

Keywords: Norms, administrative processes, legal ontologies, open source, standards.

1. Introduction

By now after several decades, legal informatics has has taken on the role of a necessary tool for innovation within the legal domain.

The scientific world has, for some time, been confronted with issues ranging from the organisation and processing of legal information and documentation, the automated drafting of norms and documents, information technology applications for the different offices of the public administration, legal portals, the use of formal logic and new methodologies for knowledge representation in legal systems, to experimentation with decision support systems. Attention paid to the free access to norms, the open source philosophy and the quality of online information are strictly related to these topics.

The challenges faced by advanced technological applied to the law have, up to date, been mainly focused on data par excellence, knowledge that the individual cannot ignore – whatever the "life event" he/she is involved in, whether voluntarily or not – or, in other words, the norms (laws, decrees, regulations, circulars, etc.).

But when the focus is on the citizen and, therefore, on systems concerned with greater and better interaction with the end user of the norm, then it is necessary to reflect on the fact that it is not sufficient to know what the norms are but it is important to know how to identify and apply them properly. And it is here that the importance of dealing with information relating to administrative processes, for which the various institutional bodies are responsible, also comes into play.

2. The importance of the effective interaction between norms and administrative processes

Each administrative process,[1] regulating a specific legal situation, can be placed within a specific life event and, in most cases, it is more important for citizens to know how to behave properly in order to manage the event in which they find themselves in the best possible way, more than about the norm itself.

So it becomes important for citizens to have a description of the practical modes in which to begin processes with the public administration, to do their duty, to assert their rights, etc. And, therefore, it is important to know, when faced with a particular objective (to obtain certain documentation, access specific services, etc.), how to start the processes, what forms to fill out, what documents to present, etc.

Norms relating to individual administrative processes must be identified, reconstructed according to their life cycle (amendments, repeals, etc.), interpreted and placed within their proper relationships.

Full knowledge of the administrative processes, in all their facets, ranges from a careful study of all the regulations involved, including specific cases, not explicitly provided for in the regulations, that give rise to interpretation, as a result of the innumerable cases offered in actual fact.

A careful reconstruction of all the information relating to the functioning of the State and its peripheral administrations, that gives a useful overview, is a very arduous task, also for those working in the sector, even when it is only concentrated on single legal matters.

In many cases, users do not even know which administrative body to go to for complying with certain processes or what the main points of the regulation of a given procedure are (cases in which it is more or less possible to obtain a certain measure, income ceiling for activating a procedure, what rules are valid everywhere and what, instead, depend on the autonomy of the local administration and so on).

The study of the regulations presents different general critical factors, independently of the sector of interest.

---

[1] An administrative process is a set of acts aimed at producing the legal effects of a specific case that affect public and private interests. It begins as the result of a private initiative (for example, application, appeal, etc.) or ex officio, even on the part of the office that is not competent to make the final decision. The act of external importance is the administrative process, coming from a public administrative body in the exercise of an administrative activity.

Above all, the wide range of acts involved is striking, for their number and type, and their competences, in fact, they are divided up amongst numerous central and peripheral administrative bodies, without there necessarily being a direct passage of competence from the central to the local level (for example, Ministry – Municipality).

Still more complicated are the different and sometime diverging, interpretations in legal authority, in case law and in the different practices left to the discretion of the individual administrations.

All these critical factors often translate into inadequacies and legal disputes and lead to the necessity for co-ordination and close collaboration among the administrative bodies, at least on a territorial level, for defining clear and codified procedural passages for each process.

3. Towards a precise working methodology for improving online access to information about the services provided by public administrations

The considerations discussed earlier have all been based on a precise working methodology that currently guides the project development capabilities implemented by the Institute in collaboration with the public bodies and institutions with which, on each occasion, it works (public bodies of national importance, Regions, Municipalities, Prefectures). This is an oganised methodology with related technological solutions that lead to the choice of tools targeting interoperability that pay careful attention to standards.

All this in the light of increasing complexity and the greatest possible sharing of knowledge and technologies and legal knowledge representation (norms, procedures and practices), that make information retrieval systems very efficient (for organising and retrieving information and for the semantic representation of documents), used by both specialists as well as ordinary citizens and companies.

To build a model dedicated to the innovation of the bureaucratic apparatus means, above all, taking into account both the roles played by public administrations:

1. the front-office, or the client interface, the help desk for accessing public services, used by very diversified kinds of users;
2. and the back-office, or the analysis, planning and testing of the tools and in-house working processes and information flows, for the benefit of the front-office and the basis for interoperability among the various administrations and individual offices.

The implementation of information retrieval systems on norms and processes involves a uniform structuring of the knowledge found in the documents and the use of universal linguistic tools, being able to count on a semantic analysis of the documents, that strengthens processing and retrieval capabilities.

In this field, it is possible for the person who produces them to work on two fronts in inserting the elements of the semantic recognition in a predefined structural model and in the development of automated recognition techniques that identify the structural parts of the documents, the type and the class they belong to, etc.

The methodologies linked to knowledge representation are among the key elements in realising intelligent and advanced information systems, because a well structured set of concepts considerably increases interoperability and information sharing between systems and can be used for learning, supported by "intelligent" systems.

A tool for knowledge conceptualisation and modelling is represented by ontology or, in other words, by an organisation of concepts and their reciprocal relations, whose objective is to provide models for describing a knowledge domain and, therefore, legal sectors that can be used for more than one purpose.[2]

The choice of ontology involves the special tagging of the document in the appropriate languages (XML, RDF) with semantic meta-data, the use of the OWL language for formalising the domain[3] (defining classes, properties and individuals up to the level permitted by OWL's formal semantics) and of the Protégé open source editor for its definition.[4]

More specifically, regarding the processing of norms and administrative processes, it should be remembered that the norms already have their own precise formal structure, corresponding to the articles or a pre-established sequence of the logical partitions (heading, preamble, enacting terms, final formula, etc.),[5] whilst administrative processes do not have a consolidated standard that describes them fully and exhaustively.

In this regard, the Institute carried out a series of studies in order to identify the relevant information, giving a uniform reference structure that enables this information to be extracted from the so-called macro-partitions. Furthermore, attention was focused on the substantive aspect of the processes, so the entities involved could be represented with meta-information (concepts, relations, roles, actions, conditions, etc.).

---

[2] An ontology may represent concepts common to a specific domain and their relations, defining their semantic meaning according to different levels of fomalism and provide a common "semantic vocabulary" that can be used for reutilising, sharing and exchanging knowledge among applications.

[3] See W3C Recommendation of 10 February 2004 "OWL Web Ontology Language Overview".

[4] Software developed by Stanford University.

[5] The representative effort is concentrated on the identification of standards that are sufficiently general to be able to be specialised based on the types of normative acts and on the representation of the operative part of the normative text (permission, obligation, sanction, etc.).

Next, it was essential to concentrate on the need for the representation model to be able to clearly express the link between the process and the generating norm or, better still, the generating provision.

Norms and processes, therefore, consist of two comparable knowledge representation structures based on similar functional models that share part of the entities that populate them and that can interact between them thanks to numerous points of contact.

In this way, the possibility arises of sharing the same representation formalism and tagging for the two objects (norms and procedural forms) concerning formal structuring, functional analysis, unambiguous identification and concepts.

For modelling the regulations, the path was opened up by the "Norme in Rete" [Norms on the Net] (NIR) Project,[6] whose standards have been implemented in the AIPA Circulars of 6 November 2001, No. AIPA/CR/35 "Assigning Uniform Names to Legal Documents" and of 22 April 2002 No. AIPA/CR/40 "Format for the Electronic Representation of Normative Measures through the XML Markup Language".

Regarding the representation of administrative processes, instead, there are absolutely no online examples of national standards for identifying and structuring information.[7]

The activities carried out in this sense by the Institute have led to the definition of a detailed proposal within the ambit of specific domains and/or ge-

---

[6] The project, begun in January 1999, promoted by the Ministry of Justice and financed and co-ordinated by the Centro Nazionale per l'Informatica nella Pubblica Amministrazione (formerly, AIPA), aimed at aiding and simplifying the retrieval of legal documentation made available on Internet by institutional bodies through a unified access point and it was part of the development activities of RUPA (Rete Unitaria della Pubblica Amministrazione) [Unified Network of the Public Administration], for providing greater efficency within the administrative machinery, especially in its relations with citizens. ITTIG/CNR has collaborated in the project beginning with the preparation of the feasibilty study entrusted to it. The architecture resulting from this assigns a fundamental role to the adoption of shared standards (for the representation, description and identification of the materials), as a tool for data access and exchange, in accordance with the autonomy of the individual institutions participating in the project.

[7] Many institutional Web sites do not provide information about competence processes, or they only give a list, or, in any case, do not contain all the really basic information. Attempts to uniform the structure of the forms of the processes is found within the environments of some Public Relations Offices or some sites of the institutional bodies, especially local bodies.

ographically defined territories,[8] that takes on the job, among other things, of further distinguishing respectively administrative procedures and processes.[9]

Once the users of the system to be implemented have been identified, who always also involve those working in the public administration (especially help desk officials and workers) and those working in the law in general, and their operational and training needs, the study of the regulations in the sector enables the administrative processes belonging to the analysed legal domain to be set out, for the purpose of processing all the phases of the administrative path, enjoying advanced functionality for searching and retrieving the documents, permitted by the representation in accordance with NIR's national standards.

In this regard, a series of innovative choices were made relating to the implementation of multiuser distributed environments, with versatile editors, always based on open source technologies, that make the end user independent of technicians, paying special attention to the interoperability among the administrative bodies and to multilinguism.

The choices of the formalisation of the standards for the information forms on the processes and the appropriate guidelines for their compilation, the adoption of the NIR standards for the regulations to be put online and the alignment of these same standards also for the publication of the forms of the processes, as well as the development of special "Laboratory" areas with reserved access, as tools for participation and transparency for confrontation with those working in sectors belonging to different initiatives were in line with the objective to encourage interoperability among administrations.

The norms identified as specific for the legal domain under examination are always marked up in XML according to NIR standards, by using the support tools designed by ITTIG,[10] for the purpose of reaching the greatest formal detail of the tagging and for building legislative data banks in a multi-in force mode (that is, by displaying the text in force at any amendment date) and enabling the processing and retrieval functions to be used more efficiently.

---

[8] In particular, the P.A.eS.I. - Pubblica Amministrazione e Stranieri Immigrati [Public Administration and Immigrant Foreigners] project, that is part of the e.Toscana Regional Action Plan, approved in implementation of the "A More Efficient and Less Bureaucratic Tuscany" special programme, has involved all the members of the Territorial Council for Immigration of Florence. The main objective of the project is to implement a Portal for electronically accessing services involving public administrative bodies and non Italian citizens and stateless persons.

[9] Beginning with the study of the regulations, the administrative procedures, on which the individual administrative processes are based, were represented by means of flow charts. The chart represents in a simple and direct way the sequence of parties and activities involved.

[10] This is a family of modules of xmLeges-Editor, a legislative drafting environment for producing legislative documents adhering to the NIR standards that allow documents with automated and/or guided functions to be converted or produced ex-novo.

In a similar way, the processing of the administrative processes and, therefore, of the information forms, set out, as we have already mentioned, in precise standardised fields then begins.[11]

The articulation of the form is based, among other things, on the functional analysis of the process, currently in the phase of research that, in turn, derives from the functional analysis of the norm. Here, the user is also able to take advantage of the the the formalisation of the semantics of the process for having more intelligent access to the documents and he/she is able to make inferences.

The possibility of linking, similarly to the regulations, unambiguous identifiers of the processes, that are constant and independent from their collocation on the Net, is also currently in the phase of research.

All this in order to benefit by the possibility of establishing symbolic references between competence processes of the same body or different bodies, inferring the relations existing between norms and processes and representing the different versions of the same process over a period of time, as a result of legislative amendments.

In this way, the identification, then, of a methodology for analysing legal knowledge able to be carried out in an incremental way on single domains, lays the bases for a specialised legal ontology for individual sectors that, built in a precise legal domain, can act as the head of a uniform structure for all sectors.

4. A new overview of norms and administrative processes

The advantages of a scientific overview of the norms and administrative processes, as we can see from the methodology described here, can only be considerable for users, even the most specialised users, who will see that they are given increasingly easy, aggregate, complete and updated accesses to the services supplied by the public administrations.

Information in this domain, in fact, for the use and consumption of both the citizen user and the service provider user, cannot ignore the integration of the two different approaches that determine the possibility of taking in both directions a bidirectional knowledge route that ranges from "specific behaviour" ("how do you do it?") to its normative justification ("based on which norms").

That is, free access to the norm via Internet cannot disregard dealing with practical modes of application, on which all the legal knowledge on the specific topics is based, in which provisions, jurisprudence, local practices and legal authority are necessarily involved and linked.

---

[11] The title of the process, the type of users for whom the information in the form is valid, the time required for implementation, duration and revocation indicated in the regulation, the responsible body, access mode to the service, etc.

Among other things, the new overview of the legal domains examined has further significant repercussions in terms of scientific research and practical applications.

These repercussions are very closely connected to matters like administrative simplification, professional training, computerisation and the improvement of administrative offices in terms of efficiency, effectiveness, and running costs, carrying out checks and simulating the impact of normative innovations on processes.

With regard to the last of these objectives, the amendment of a norm, to which a process refers, will impact on the updating of information found in precise sections of the relative form, also exploiting the added value contributed by the ontology.[12]

Navigating by way of the ontology enables the user to access documents by concepts, independently of the terms used in them and allows the implicit amendments between the norms to be understood (or better, the cases in which the amendment of a norm linked to a conceptual node of the ontology affects other norms, conceptually linked to the same node).

As in processes that do not expressly refer to a norm, they can be interested in an amendment of the norm, if logically linked to the same node. Moreover, the inferences between processes and norms become evident and usable, being able to automatically identify the norms (or provisions) that generate processes and the processes that are generated by them.

And regarding the possibility of verifying or simulating the impact of normative innovations on processes, it easily becomes possible to learn which processes are affected by the amendment or repeal on one or more norms and in what measure.

Finally, another possible spin-off of the model relates to breaking down language barriers.

In fact, the integration between mechanisms of semantic annotation based on functional analysis and concept ontology will enable the user to manage, with the application of special mark up languages and software tools, searches formulated in natural language.

A natural language search is particularly useful both for the fundamental differences between technical legal language and everyday language,[13] and when faced with problems connected to multilinguism and the comparison of legal orders.

---

[12] A link between documents (or the individual sections) and a specific node of the ontological model is necessary whereby, at every node of the model, all the documents logically linked to it can be selected.

[13] In everyday language, we talk about a "sale", instead of a "conveyance".

References

Blaquier Ascano, M., et al. (1995), *Navigating in the Law through Hypermedia*, in Di Giorgi, R.M., Nannucci, R. (Eds.), "Informatica e diritto", Special Issue "Hypertext and Hypermedia in the Law", No. 1, pp. 69-83.

Borruso, R., Di Giorgi, R.M., Mattioli, L., Ragona, M. (2004), *L'informatica del diritto*, Milan, Giuffrè.

Cherubini, M. (2007), *Norme, procedimenti amministrativi e web semantico. Un approccio ontologico per il diritto*, ESI, Naples.

Cherubini, M. and Tiscornia, D. (2008), *An Ontology-based Model of Procedural Norms and Regulated Procedures*, International Conference, eGov 2008, Turin.

Di Giorgi, R.M. (2002), *Informatica e Pubblica Amministrazione: le politiche per l'innovazione e i progetti*, in Nannucci, R. (Ed.), "Lineamenti di Informatica giuridica. Teoria, metodi, applicazioni", ESI, Naples, pp. 365-400.

Di Giorgi, R.M. (2006), *Lo stato essenziale. Semplicità, cultura e democrazia al tempo della rete*, Naples, ESI.

Palazzolo, N. (2002), *Strumenti per l'accesso all'informazione giuridica*, in Nannucci, R. (Ed.), "Lineamenti di Informatica giuridica. Teoria, metodi, applicazioni", ESI, Naples, pp. 85-118.

Rescigno, G.U. (1998), *L'atto normativo*, Bologna, Zanichelli.

Rescigno, G.U. (1996), *Tipi di regole*, Rassegna parlamentare, No. 4, pp. 3-96.

Rossi, P. (1996), *Ontologie applicate e comparazione giuridica: alcune premesse*, in: <www.dsg.unito.it/ut/data/papers/ontologie\%20applicate\%20e\ %20comparazione\%20giuridica.pdf>.

Sartor, G. (1996), *Riferimenti normativi e dinamica dei testi normativi*, in VV.AA., "Il procedimento legislativo regionale", Cedam, Padova.

Smith, B. (1996), *Ontologia e sistemi informativi*, in: <lgxserve.ciseca.uniba.it/lei/ai/networks/06/Barrysmith.pdf>.

Spinosa, P.L. (2001a), *Assegnazione dei nomi uniformi ai documenti giuridici*, in "Informatica e diritto", No. 1, pp. 233-264.

Spinosa, P.L. (2001b), *Identificazione dei document giuridici tramite URNs (Uniform Resource Names)*, in "Informatica e diritto", No. 1, pp. 149-164.

Tiscornia, D. (2001), *Il diritto nei modelli dell'intelligenza artificiale*, in: <www.di.unito.it/~guido/ontologie/Diritto_modelli_IA.ppt>.

Tiscornia, D. (2002), *Intelligenza artificiale e diritto*, in Nannucci, R. (Ed.), "Lineamenti di informatica giuridica. Teoria, metodi, applicazioni", ESI, Naples, pp. 119-156.

Uschold, M. and Gruninger, M. (1996), *Ontologies: Principles, Methods and Applications*, in "Knowledge Engineering Review".

VV.AA. (2000), *Studio di fattibilità per la realizzazione del progetto 'Accesso alle norme in rete'*, in "Informatica e diritto", No. 1.

VV.AA. (2001), *Progetto NIR – Fase 2 'Accesso alle norme in rete'*, in "Informatica e diritto", No. 1.

Justice via the Internet: Hopes and Challenges of Law and the Semantic Web

Pompeu Casanovas*, Marta Poblet°
* *UAB Institute of Law and Technology (IDT), Spain*
° *ICREA, UAB Institute of Law and Technology (IDT), Spain*

Abstract. The legal market is an emerging domain for the Semantic Web (SW). However, legal professional knowledge is unequally distributed among legal professions, and some Semantic Web promises have not been fulfilled yet. SW strategies should be grounded on detailed cognitive and sociological studies showing the daily behavior and real needs of ICT users. Second generation of SW applications is coming up but, still, some well-known problems remain, especially regarding knowledge acquisition and ontology building. SW and new trends in legal knowledge, such Online Dispute Resolution (ODR), easier citizens' access to justice or the needs of the law firms for a more efficient organization and information retrieval are evolving along to the new functionalities and services orientation of the Web 2.0 and the Web 3.0. We will stand that only a multifunctional and hybrid strategy may cope with citizens' needs for a better and more efficient justice through the web. Some examples will be provided from our IDT studies on judges and lawyers in Spain.

Keywords: Internet, web 2.0, web 3.0, semantic eeb, lawyers, spanish lawyers, online dispute resolution (ODR), legal ontologies, justice, access to justice, AI and law.

1. ICT impact in law

The legal domain is becoming one of the most relevant targets for technology developments. Law firms spend a substantial part of their budget specifically for technology: in 2008, over 40% of the firms indicated an average $ 8,000-$ 17,000 spending per attorney (ILTA, 2008). Besides, 72% of respondents report that the firm files court documents electronically, up from 55% in the 2007 survey (ILTA, 2007, 2008).

Thus, we think that there is room for semantic technologies in different legal scenarios. To be sure, these areas would include legal information research (LIR), e-discovery, web-based communications, collaborative tools

---

** A first version of this paper was presented at ESTC-08, Vienna, September 22nd-24th 2008. Some parts of the text have been used in (Breuker et al., 2008).

(wikis, blogs, etc.), xml technologies, metadata,[1] multimedia contents, and e-courts.[2]

If we consider the broad landscape of AI and IT law, we will notice that, generally, researchers in Artificial Intelligence and Law divide IT and Law into two different domains: (i) IT law (data protection, copyright, security, domain names ...), (ii) IT for lawyers (e-government, e-court, Online Dispute Resolution, Multi-Agent Systems ...) (Apistola and Lodder, 2005; Lodder and Oskamp, 2006; Lauritsen, 2006). The first area covers regulations and protocols. The second one refers to all the languages, tools, software, that bring support to legal activities at the workplace. This seems quite reasonable, from the legal point of view. However, recent developments in semantic technologies, NLP, legal ontologies, information retrieval technologies (IR) and the Internet 2.0 and 3.0 contribute to the convergence of the two approaches into a single techno-legal one. A lawyer seriously interested in tags and semantic conflicts cannot ignore OWL. A computer scientist developing legal ontologies for procedural legal knowledge must have a clear picture of the court proceedings. The usual perspective on technology and law, therefore, is no longer possible.

2. Law and the Semantic Web

The development of legal markets and the Internet new regulation devices foster the rapid evolution of law practices. Traditional fields of legal drafting, private contracting, judicial sentencing and administrative management have been enlarged with all the Online Dispute Resolution (ODR) initiatives and new forms of self-regulation and access to justice. Citizens require a greater participation and faster and more effective ways of facing their legal activities. Less lawyering, less judging, more dialogue, more participation, more flexibility and autonomy seems to be the aim of new legal forms of relational Administration and relational justice (Casanovas and Poblet, 2008). It is worthwhile to quote here explicitly a forthcoming paper by Colin Rule,[3] from e-Bay:

---

[1] XML technologies are in fact involved in the production of metadata. Currently, the adoption and development of standards for legal information, electronic court filing, court documents, transcripts, or criminal justice intelligence systems has become the core activity of a number of initiatives and projects (i.e. the non-profit OASIS LegalXML, a subgroup within OASIS, and the LEXML community, which defines itself as a "European network searching for the automatic exchange of legal information". European standards are being developed, stemming from previous national projects [Norme in Rete (Italy), Metalex (the Netherlands), LexDania (Denmark), CHeXML (Switzerland), or eLaw (Austria)] (Benjamins et al., 2005; Biagioli et al., 2006; Francesconi, 2007).

[2] Technology has been one of the main concerns of national and European Courts, but the degree of application to court offices and sentencing shows a great variety of solutions (Fabri and Contini, 2001).

[3] We thank Colin for allowing us to quote his still unpublished paper.

"If you have any doubt that consumers are moving to online commerce, take a look at eBay, the online auction company. In the 13 years since it was founded, eBay has grown into the largest marketplace in the world. In the first half of 2008, there were more than one billion product listings added to eBay worldwide. At any given moment, there are more than 100 million listings around the world, and approximately 7.1 million listings are added each day. eBay users trade almost every kind of item imaginable, in more than 50,000 categories. On eBay, a pair of shoes sells every 7 seconds, a cell phone sells every 7 seconds, and a car sells every 56 seconds. The daily volume of trade on eBay is greater than the daily volume of the NASDAQ.

Unsurprisingly, all of these transactions generate a lot of consumer disputes. Even though less than 1 percent of purchases generate a problem, the incredible volume on the site means eBay handles more than 40 million disputes a year, in more than 16 different languages" (Rule, 2008).

It has been highlighted the democratic model that the Web 2.0 implies. People can cooperate and build up in common their ideas (Motta, 2006). Enriching this process seems a quite natural move from the Semantic Web perspective. However, this is not an easy task. First, oddly enough, the science of the Internet and the science of the Web have not been developed yet. Several economic, political and legal obstacles are hindering scientists from measuring the real size and volume of connections (Hendler et al., 2008; Claffy, 2008). The account by K. C. Claffy et al. makes it clear:

"Because no systemic measurements activities exist for collecting rigorous empirical Internet data, in many ways, we don't really know what the Internet actually is. Thus, we don't know the total amounts and patterns of data traffic, the Internet's growth rate, the extent and locations of congestion, patterns and distribution of ISP interconnectivity, and many other things that are critical if we're to understand what actually works in the Internet. These data are hidden because ISPs consider such information proprietary and worry that competitors could use it to steal customers or otherwise harm their business. The information might not even be collected because no economic incentive exists to do so, nor do any regulations require this collection" (Claffy et al., 2007).

Second, Semantic Web developers themselves have pointed out some technical obstacles or limitations to the SW original purposes (Benjamins et al., 2008). E.g., search in the World Wide Web is the great unfulfilled promise. Bridging SW and information retrieval technologies faces scientific problems on knowledge representation and natural language understanding that remain still unsolved. In Baeza-Yates's (2008) words "IR research is strongly driven by a problem, whereas Semantic Web is driven by a solution".

This may be true. However, hybrid approaches and perspectives seem to guide the ontological work, as long as folksonomies, data mining, NLP techniques, and upper, middle and domain ontologies develop. Moreover, to optimize the possibilities of success, SW strategies should be grounded on detailed economic, sociological and cognitive studies on the daily behavior and real needs of professional ICT users and consumers. At least, this is our approach towards the Spanish legal market and institutions.

3. Tailoring the Spanish legal profession

In recent years, the Spanish legal market (law and auditing firms) has emerged as one of the most expansive in Europe. Despite growing competition and ongoing influx of US and UK firms in the domestic market, annual turnover of law firms has risen up to 63.4 percent in six years (1999-2004). In 2002, the value of the market was 6.4 billion €, which represented more than the South Korean, Chinese and Japan market altogether. Legal services in Spain largely depend on the market structure. This is a segmented market. Thus, solo practitioners tend to offer general legal services to individual clients, while large law firms exclusively provide services to companies, offering highly specialized counseling. Between these two poles, mid-sized law firms have both individuals and small or mid-sized companies as clients in their portfolios. In some cases, they also offer specialized services such as labor law, criminal law or urbanism.

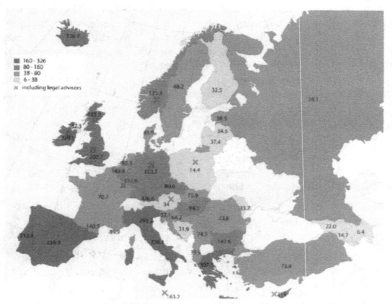

Figure 1. Lawyers in Europe (per 100,000 inhabitants). Source: Council of Bars and Law Societies of Europe, 2005.

As shown in Fig. 1 and Fig. 2, Spain clearly ranks first in number of lawyers in Europe (above 140,000 lawyers, 259.3 lawyers per 100,000 inhabitants, 2004

Figure 2. Lawyers in Europe. Source: Council of Bars and Law Societies of Europe, 2005.

data) (Council of Europe, 2006). In 2006, there were 833,763 lawyers registered in the national bars of 31 European countries.[4] We think that a legal

---

[4] Council of Bars And Law Societies Of Europe, CCBE Statistics 2006, available at:
<www.ccbe.org/index.php?id=29&L=0>.

culture based on such numbers may have problems in the future, because this legal market heavily relies on other services and financial markets. However, this would speed as well the need for citizens' more efficient access to legal information.

In the study we conducted in 2006 for the EU Project SEKT, based on 40 semi-structured interviews and field research in law firms (Poblet et al. 2007), we found that the average spend almost one third of their working day (26.27%) in front of the computer. This percentage does not include dealing with their e-mail accounts (12.83%) and managing the firm (5.73%). Meetings with clients (14.07%) and with other lawyers (9.27%) consume an important share of their working day, as well as talking with them on the phone (7.97% with clients, 8.37% with lawyers). Finally, the average lawyer spends 10.93 percent of its time in court, and a 4.93% performing other tasks.

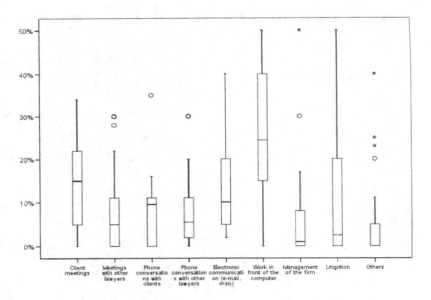

Figure 3. Working day, in percentages. Source: Poblet et al., 2007.

The box and whisker plot (fig. 3) offers a clearer view on how lawyers spend their working day, showing where the central data is clustered, the median, and the existence of outliers. We can distinguish between those activities of the working day shared in a similar proportion by all kind of organizations and lawyers, for instance working in front of the computer, from those which follow different tendencies depending on the type of organization and the specialization, such as the litigation level.

4. Adding semantics to the legal field: some trends and problems

Relying in our data, we think that lawyers are professionals with a specialized knowledge and the cognitive skills and tools to work it out through the web. Thus, the kernel of their experience and their legal knowledge is dynamically rebuilt and updated through their daily interactions and searches. Not only attorneys, but even judges and magistrates are currently browsing through the web when they gather information to build their legal strategy to construct and solve the cases they have before them.

This goes far beyond the practice to look and seek for information through the existing legal databases. We think the reason for what they do this is because they save time and effort. Therefore, expert knowledge, personal and professional experiences, and common knowledge combine in a new way that reduces the differences among experts and lay people or, at least, approaches the legal perspective to the social perspective of non-legal users. Thus, lawyers (and magistrates) practice law through and within the web.

According to the *The American Lawyer 100 Report* – the top-grossing law firms in the United States – total revenues reached $ 64.6 billion and increased 13.6% in 2007. At the top rank, two big firms, Skadden Arps Slate Meagher & Flom and Lathan & Watkins, reached more than 2 $ billion (gross revenue) and 1.17 and 1.05 $ million per lawyer. We may wonder whether such numbers are sustainable in the new economic landscape after the crisis of the Wall Street financial model. Some prudence is required before answering such a question.

We are not saying that expert knowledge operates in the same way common sense does when facing a legal case. This is not certainly so. However, lay people and experts tend to rely on the web to seek for the information they need, and the web increasingly offer more accessibility to documents containing legal rules and procedures, past cases and accumulated experiences.

Results of the 2008 ABA and ILTA Surveys focus again on e-mail management, collaborative tools and mobility (Smartphone / Blackberry).[5]

Legal chats and blogs can be found along with public or private legal databases. Moreover, e-mailing boxes are currently being used as personal databases. And, as stated before, more and more people rely first on the web accumulated information to find a solution for their administrative or legal problems. This situation makes the legal activity of citizens and the daily routine of experts suitable to be treated with the Semantic Web initiatives. In this sense, changes of the legal field are close to the change which is experiencing the Semantic Web itself.

Personalization, user-centered approaches, semantic wikis, hybrid ontological solutions, synergies between folksonomies and ontologies, scalability and

---

[5] 2008 ABA Legal Technology Survey Report: Online Research, available at: <www.iltanet.org>.

meta tagging of great amount of web-stored available data, and web-services orientation seem to be the next step (Benjamins et al., 2008; Davies et al., 2008; Warren et al., 2008; Fensel, 2008).

Comparing first and next generation of Semantic Web applications, (Motta and Sabou, 2006) identify several features of the new orientations: (i) reuse (vs. semantic data generation); (ii) multi-ontology systems (vs. single-ontology systems); (iii) openness with respect top semantic resources, (iv) scale as important as data quality, (v) openness with respect to Web (non-semantic resources), (vi) compliance with the Web 2.0 paradigm, (vi) openness to services.

It is worthwhile to point out that scalability affects reasoning (D'Aquin et al., 2008):

> "[...] because the Semantic Web combines heterogeneity, variable data quality, and scale, the applications we envision will exhibit intelligent behavior owing less to an ability to carry out complex inferencing than an ability to exploit the large amounts of available data. That is, as we move from classic KBSs to Semantic Web applications, intelligence becomes a side effect of scale, rather than of sophisticated logical reasoning. An important corollary here is that, as logical reasoning becomes less important and scale and data integration becomes key issues, other types of reasoning – based on machine learning, linguistic, or statistical techniques – become crucial, especially and because they frequently need to integrate and use other, nonsemantic data".

D. Fensel says a similar thing with different words, but insisting in that integration and scalable interoperability rely on meaning, that is on semantic processes: "the process that establishes the facts must be included as an aspect of the reasoning process itself" (Fensel, 2008).

We do agree with these statements, and we are aligning our SW prototypes for the legal field according to them (Casanovas et al., 2008a). Especially the idea of building up platforms for SW Online Dispute Resolution (ODR) services assumes this approach. We are doing this in our preparatory work for the general law of mediation in Catalonia.[6] Statistical and NLP techniques are exploited as well in our work with Wolters Kluwer-La Ley legal databases, going along with the relevance algorithms that the WK research team has been developing in its search engine (Sancho-Ferrer et al., 2008). However, our experience with legal services and the SW prevents us to be too optimistic with respect to the classical "knowledge acquisition bottleneck" (as E.A. Feigenbaum termed it in the early times of AI).

The problem we face is that legal knowledge is not only implicit and disseminated through the Internet or into the content of sentences, statutes and academic works stored in the available legal databases. Dynamic legal knowledge is implicit in the professional behavior of people working in the legal field, and it is not easy at all to elicit, organize and structure in a feasible way.

---

[6] Available at: <idt.uab.cat/llibreblanc>.

To produce the second prototype of IURISERVICE, e.g., an i-FAQ for judges in their first appointment that gives to them answers on practical judicial problems, we ought to work for five years with the team of magistrates of the Spanish Judicial School. They were very cooperative, indeed, and they really wanted to contribute with their answers to the nearly eight-hundred questions that have been raised by inexperienced judges.

However, they were constrained by time, effort and the daily duties they had to comply with. So, patience, joint work of magistrates and researchers, and adapting the lifecycle of the engine to the rhythm of the institution became key issues. We had to literally invent how to deal with their constraints, and we learned that we could not simply apply standard knowledge on SW applications and ontology building to be successful in the implementation of a new service for the Spanish Judicial Council. Knowledge acquisition and ontology building, for instance, have not been successive stages, as they have evolved at the same time (Casanovas et al., 2008a).

Let's put another example, the E-Sentencias prototype tackles the problem to classify automatically the legal video records of Spanish Civil Court proceedings (Casanovas et al., 2008b). The aim of E-Senten-cias is to develop a software-hardware system for the global management of the multimedia contents produced by Spanish civil courts. The Civil Procedure Act of January 7th, 2000 (1/2000) introduces the video recording of oral hearings. As a result, Spanish civil courts are currently producing a massive number of DVDs which have become part of the judicial file, together with suits, indictments, injunctions, judgments and pieces of evidence.

This multimedia material is used by lawyers, prosecutors and judges to prepare, if necessary, appeals to superior courts. Nevertheless, video recording of Spanish courts are neither officially transcribed nor digitally stored in large databases. Security is an important issue, and judges, lawyers and legal drafters prefer to rely on individually-based management of the records (CVDs).

Again, we had to proceed from scratch to understand the typology of civil cases to be modeled. Within the building process of the procedural ontology, we discovered that court proceedings followed behavioral patterns that did not match the prescribed legal stages under the Spanish procedural law. Professional lawyers, prosecutors, judges and magistrates usually do not "go by the book", but produce patterns of legal behavior that are most suitable to their work and to the hearings.

Capturing those patterns in workflows to obtain a first typology of dynamic proceedings before tagging them constituted, again, a knowledge acquisition problem in itself. And, within the annotation and ontology building processes, we learnt that a general solution for the "semantic gap" problem of the difference between semantic and visual content cannot be taken for granted either.

Therefore, even accepting the new trends of SW orientation, old problems remain.

Our particular strategy to overcome these problems is hybrid as well. We try to understand, first, what and where the problems are, and then we combine all types of available technologies to tackle them. This is not an original move. Most researchers adopt this approach as well. We try to bear in mind the users' needs to draw a clear picture of what they want. That is to say, to what extent they are willing to be responsible for what they need (their cooperative involvement with projects), and, at the end, to what extent they are willing to pay (in efforts, time or money) for what they want. We think that free access to justice, free access to legal information may be balanced with final users' responsibility as well.

Full cooperation of users is a necessary condition to build SW solutions. Sometimes, they like the idea of having a better access to their documents or having a better organization of their knowledge, but they discover that they have to spend too many efforts and they decide to give up. This should not be viewed as a problem (although sometimes it may become one). The point is that once people enter into a satisfactory technological cycle, they become used to it and they enter into daily routines. Then, there is no way back. This is what happened with mobile telephony and with Google, and what may happen with Semantic Web services for the legal field if they are efficient, user-friendly and free or, at least, cheap enough.

5. Acknowledgements

(i) *SEKT*-EU-IST Project IST-2003-506826; (ii) e-Sentencias FIT-350101-2006-26); (iii) Metabuscador FIT-350100-2007-161), (iv) *OCJ* SEJ2006-10695; (v) DALOS EU 2006/01/024; (vi) NEURONA TSI-020100-2008-134.

References

Apistola, M. and Lodder, A. (2005), *Law Firms and IT. Towards Optimal Knowledge Management*, Journal of Information, Law and Technology, No. 2/3, pp. 1-28.

Baeza-Yates, R., Mika, P., Zaragoza, H. (2008), *Search, Web 2.0, and the Semantic Web*, in Benjamins, V.R. (Ed.), "Near-term Prospects for Semantic Technologies", IEEE Intelligent Systems, pp. 80-82.

Benjamins, V.R., Davies, J., Baeza Yates, R., Mika, P., Zaragoza, H., Greaves, M., Gómez-Pérez, J.M., Contreras, J., Dominguez, J., Fensel, D. (2008), *Near-term Prospects for Semantic Technologies*, IEEE Intelligent Systems, pp. 76-88.

Biagioli, C., Francesconi, E., Sartor, G. (Eds.) (2006), *Proceedings of the V Legislative XML Workshop*, European Press Academic Publishing, Florence.

Breuker, J., Casanovas, P., Klein, M.C.A., Francesconi, E. (2008), *The Flood, the Channels and the Dykes: Managing Legal Information in a Globalized and Digital World*, in Breuker, J., Casanovas, P., Klein, M.C.A., Francesconi, E. (Eds.), "Law, Ontologies and the Semantic Web. Channeling the Legal Information Flood", Amsterdam, IOS Press.

Casanovas, P. and Poblet, M. (2008), *Concepts and Fields of Relational Justice*, in Casanovas, P., Sartor, G., Casellas, N., Rubino, R. (Eds.), "Computable Models of the Law: Languages, Dialogue, Games, Ontologies", LNAI 4884, Springer Verlag, Berlin, Heidelberg, pp. 323-339.

Casanovas, P., Casellas, N., Vallbé, J.J. (2008a), *An Ontology-based Decision Support System for Judges*, in Breuker, J., Casanovas, P., Klein, M. and Francesconi, E. (Eds.), "Legal Ontologies and the Semantic Web Channeling the legal informational flood", IOS Press, Amsterdam, *in press*.

Casanovas, P., Binefa, X., Gracia, C., Teodoro, E., Galera, N. et al. (2008b), *The e-Sentencias prototype. A procedural ontology for legal multimedia applications in the Spanish Civil Courts*, in Breuker, J.,Casanovas, P., Klein, M. and Francesconi, E. (Eds.), "Legal Ontologies and the Semantic Web. Channeling the legal informational flood", IOS Press, Amsterdam, *in press*.

Claffy, K.C., Meinrath, S.D., Bradner, S.O. (2007), *The (un)Economic Internet?*, IEEE Internet Computing, May, June, pp. 53-58.

Claffy, K.C. (2008), *Ten Things Lawyers should Know about the Internet*, available at: <www.caida.org/publications/papers/2008/lawyers_top_ten/> (accessed October 10th 2008).

Council of Europe (2006), *European Judicial Systems 2006 (2004 data)*, available at: <www.coe.int/t/dg1/legalcooperation/cepej/evaluation/2006/CEPEJ_2006_eng.pdf> (accessed September 15th 2008).

D'Aquin, M., Motta, E., Sabou, M., Angeletou, S., Gridinoc, L., Lopez, V., Guidi, D. (2008), *Toward a New Generation of Semantic Web Applications*, IEEE Intelligent Systems, May/June, pp. 20-28.

Davies, J., Grobelnik, M., Mladenić, D. (2008), *Challenges of Semantic Knowledge Management*, in Davies, J., Grobelnick, M., Mladenći, D. (Eds.), "Semantic Knowledge Management. Integrating Ontology Management, Knowledge Discovery, and Human Language Technology", Springer Verlag, Heidelberg, Berlin, pp. 248-251.

Fabri, M. and Contini, F. (Eds.) (2001), *Justice and Technology in Europe: How ICT is Changing the Judicial Business*, Kluwer Law International, The Hague.

Fensel, D. (2008), *STI Technical Report 2008-01-10*, STI Innsbruck, available at: <www.sti-innsbruck.at/fileadmin/documents/SemanticTechnology.pdf>.

Francesconi, E. (2007), *Technologies for European Integration. Standards-based Interoperability of Legal Information Systems*, Florence, European Press Academic Publishing.

Friedman, R. (2008), *Why and What Lawyers Should Consider Outsourcing, Law and Technology Resources for Legal Professionals*, available at: <www.llrx.com/features/legaloutsourcingoptions.htm> (accessed September 12th 2008).

Hendler, J., Shadbolt, N., Hall, W., Berners-Lee, T., Weitzner, D. (2008), *Web science: An Interdisciplinary Approach to Understanding the Web*, Communications of the ACM, July, Vol. 61, No. 7, pp. 60-69.

ILTA (2007), *ILTA 2007 Technology Purchasing Survey*, available at: <iltanet.org/pdf/2007PurchasingSurvey.pdf> (accessed September 10th 2007).

ILTA (2008), *ILTA 2008 Technology Purchasing Survey*, available at: <www.iltanet.org/communications/pub_detail.aspx?nvID=000000011205&h4ID=000001315505> (accessed September 15th 2008).

Lauritsen, M. (2006), *Artificial Intelligence in the Legal Real Workplace*, in Lodder, A., Oskamp, A., (Eds.), "Advanced Technology in the Legal Domain. From Challenges to Daily Routine", Springer, Dordrecht, pp. 165-176.

Lodder, A. and Oskamp, A. (2006), *Law, Information Technology and Artificial Intelligence*, in Lodder, A., Oskamp, A. (Eds.), "Advanced Technology in the Legal Domain. From Challenges to Daily Routine", Springer, Dordrecht, pp. 1-22.

Motta, E. (2006), *Knowledge Publishing and Access on the Semantic Web: A Sociotechnological Analysis*, IEEE Intelligent Systems, May/June, pp. 88-90.

Motta, E. and Sabou, M. (2006), *Next Generation Semantic Web Applications*, in Mizoguchi, R., Shi, Z., Giunchiglia, F. (Eds.), "The Semantic Web", LNCS 4185, Springer, Heidelberg, Berlin, pp. 24-29.

Oskamp, A., Lodder, A., Apistola, M. (Eds.) (2004), *IT Support of the Judiciary: Australia, Singapore, Venezuela, Norway, the Netherlands, and Italy*, TMC Acer Press, The Hague.

Poblet, M., Benjamins, V.R., Casanovas, P., Pérez, E. (2007), *Exploitation strategies for the Spanish legal market*, SEKT D12.5.5. EU-IST Project 506826, pp. 1-54.

Rule, C. (2008), *Making Peace on eBay: Resolving Disputes in the World's Largest Marketplace*, ACResolution Magazine, Fall (forthcoming).

Sancho-Ferrer, A., Rivero, J.M.M., García, A.M. (2008), *Improvements in recall and precision in Walters Kluwer Spain legal Search engine*, in Casanovas, P., Sartor, G., Casellas, N., Rubino, R. (Eds.), "Computable Models of the Law: Languages, Dialogue, Games, Ontologies", Lecture notes in Computer Science, Vol. 4884, Springer, Berlin, pp. 130-145.

Warren, P., Davies, J., Brown, D. (2008), *Conclusions*, in Warren, P., Davies, J., Brown, D. (Eds.), "ICT Futures. Delivering Pervasive, Real-time and Secure Services", John Wiley, Chichester, pp. 229-233.

SIAM: A Semantic Tool for Improving the Legal Information Access and Knowledge

Antonio Cammelli, Elio Fameli

Institute of Legal Information Theory and Techniques (ITTIG-CNR), Italy

Abstract. Free access to legal information is, by now, a widespread reality for the most European Union Countries, but we are fully aware that the mere access to the legal information is only the first step for its understanding and knowledge. In order to achieve this necessary result, we must promote research activities oriented to the development of informatic and telematic tools able to support the common citizen in understanding legal information retrieved on the Web. The present contribution aims at describing a model of a knowledge-based system which allows a natural language dialogue between the user and the system, providing an easy integration with (also external) databases that can be consulted with the support of lexical and semantic tools.

In the field of Law the first rule-based systems date back to Seventies; by that time many system prototypes have been implemented, but with disappointing practical results. Actually research activities oriented to knowledge-based systems development are propelled by an easier Internet accessibility and by the introduction of new technologies for the "Mobile Web".

Keywords: Legal information access, intelligent integrated system, effectiveness of rights.

1. Introduction

Simple access to legal information is only an essential, but not sufficient, requirement for its understanding and, therefore, for an effective knowledge of law. In order to achieve this fundamental goal, without which the mere acquisition of information doesn't produce effects socially significant and considerable, it is necessary to propel research activities aimed at developing informatic and telematic tools able to support common citizens in understanding legal information.

The present contribution profiles the SIAM Knowledge Based System (KBS) [1] as a Law specifically oriented project; its fundamental features are the user-system interaction performed through natural language dialogue and the acquisition, representation and management of a legal knowledge including not only statutory texts but also case law and legal literature. Moreover, in system developing the problem of the knowledge of Law has been regarded both

---

[1] These systems use knowledge-based techniques in order to support human decision-making, learning and action. On this matter see "Knowledge-Based Systems", an international, interdisciplinary and applications oriented journal published by Elsevier. Emphasis of this journal is on the "practical significance of such systems in modern computer development and usage". With particular reference to Law and legal knowledge, for a recent review see (Casanovas et al., 2007).

from the point of view of the legal operator and in terms of common citizens requirements.

2. Sources of online Italian legal information

Thanks to most recent developments in informatic and telematic technologies, the documentary material needed for the legal theorist and operator to conduct their activities – in any sector of law and as concerns any related professional function – can now be retrieved for the most part by consulting the many online legal archives. In Italy, these differ in structure and features and are available especially in the systems of the Court of Cassation, Chamber of Deputies, Senate and State Mint and Printery, in addition to the various specialized information systems created by public authorities and bodies, but also by institutions and private concerns, and distributed through the channels of traditional and electronic publishing, or on the international telematic networks, especially Internet.[2]

The ease of use, reliability and efficiency of retrieval systems (and thus also of search engines) for obtaining legal information online, have been targeted mainly through the realisation of "friendly interfaces," that can be general or personalised in relation to the user profiles. In this regard, it is well worth noting that progress in this nodal sector of documentary informatics has been assisted not only by techniques and methods consolidated in the science of documentation and informatics, but also by the most recently tools of Artificial Intelligence.

In considering the various phases of the complex procedure whereby the user moves from singling out the information of interest to him to directly using it in pursuing a concrete objective, let us draw attention to one fact. Once obtained, by means of traditional retrieval systems or by the most complex and sophisticated search engines available on telematic networks, the legal information capable of satisfying the demands of study and work of the theorist as well as of the operator of law can not – usually – be immediately used for the particular purpose it was intended. Indeed, in most cases, it must first be analysed, commented, annotated, connected, co-ordinated, organised and reprocessed along alternative logical routes, functional to precise objectives, which are often complementary but can also prove to be antithetical.[3]

---

[2] For an up-to-date picture of the extraordinary wealth and considerable complexity of online legal information, see the websites: *Globalex* (<www.nyulawglobal.org/globalex>); *Guide to Law Online: International* (<www.loc.gov/law/guide/multi.html>); *Juraportal* (<Juraportal.dk/?lang=en>); *Legal Research Engine* (<library.lawschool.cornell.edu/guides/researchengine.asp>); *RASK: Find your way on the net* (<rask.ub.uu.se/index.cfm?eng>); *LLRX.com* (<llrx.com>); *Intute* (<www.intute.ac.uk>).

[3] As an example of both cases, consider the documentary activity performed in the course of their specific functions by the judge and court-appointed expert, on one hand, and the

In this sense, at least in an initial approach to the problem, quite a difference can be noted between the information acquired by consultative information systems and the information effectively useable in the legal activity conducted: there is, between the two, a conceptual space where, while man's creativity remains primary and irreplaceable, the machine is already capable of providing an assistance which is efficient and can gradually be increased.

In any event, in moving from one type of information to the other – whether using a computer or not – the documentation on which the information is based undergoes a complex series of analyses and elaborations which, given the data dealt with, produces an actual "added value" usually of wide interest and, at times, even of general interest. In the abstract context of the considerations presented thus far, the specific hypothesis of creating – starting from general archives – printed bibliographies or specialist databases (sectorial, mono- or pluri-thematic) in a certain sense only clearly defines and formalises an activity which is always inevitable and typical for legal activity.

3. From legal information retrieval to legal knowledge representation and management

In developing the "integrated intelligent system" SIAM ("Sistema Intelligente integrato per l'Acquisizione e la Manutenzione dell'informazione giuridica in linea" – "Intelligent Integrated System for Retrieving and Managing Online Legal Information"), at the Istituto di Teoria e Tecniche dell'Informazione Giuridica (ITTIG) of CNR, our objective was to create a working tool specifically conceived to support both the legal theorist and operator in the complex intellectual activity which – from structuring and organising documentation retrieved from external electronic archives using the tools of formal, linguistic and conceptual analysis – gradually transforms "data" into "information" and "information" into "knowledge."

A fundamental requirement in conducting analysis to create software corresponding to the objective indicated is the awareness that "knowledge" is formed and progressively structured starting from the retrieval of data which, initially disaggregated, are increasingly more often extracted from online sources of a general or specialist character. The novelty of the proposed approach therefore firstly consists in pointing out and clarifying the nexus, both logical and physical (as concerns software architecture and the integration of its constitutive modules), which should exist between the operations of a unitary procedure on the basis of which, starting from the consultation of one or more information systems (heterogeneous databases), we obtain the data of interest ("Data Mining"). Then, following a definite series of intermediate phases, the

opposite (or in any event, not immediately convergent) activity performed by the parties to a suit, on the other hand.

data are organised into forms and contents that can be effectively used towards established objectives ("Knowledge Discovery", with the consequent creation of coordinated and integrated "Knowledge Bases").

Taking as reference the typical working procedure of the legal theorist or operator in the performance of his activity, we can assume that the following operations are presented not only as specific tasks of the system, but also as elements of a general value and, therefore, also as constant steps of the corresponding formalised procedure.

1. The first step of the sequence under consideration consists in retrieving documentation relative to the diverse typologies of principal legal sources (legislation, case law, legal literature, praxis) as pertains to the subject matter or the topic of interest. Functional to this objective is the consultation of pertinent specialist legal archives (accessible on line, or available on CD-Rom or paper support). In relation to this point, "Expert Systems" can be configured which not only incorporate knowledge relative to structure, contents and query features of the diverse and most often consulted legal databases, but also can be further personalized by means of automatic learning from the user (adapting to the "user profile").

2. Immediately following documentation retrieval, comes formal analysis and, therefore, the structuring and organisation of the data previously extracted from online archives or from various kinds of sources (databases that can be consulted on the Internet or recorded on CD-Rom or published in print). Regarding this procedural phase, the research project conducted the analysis necessary to develop the so-called "importation filters", functional to loading into a management general archive data extracted from external and heterogeneous sources. The special software developed is able to recognize the formal structure of the documentary units, comparing them with the model attributed to the corresponding typology.

   On account of the considerable practical interest and numerous application possibilities of this particular module of the overall system, collaboration is required across various sectors to verify and integrate analysis as concerns its extension to the most frequently consulted legal archives. It involves researchers belonging to other work groups engaged in documentary activities relative to realising specialist (sectorial or thematic) legal archives and analysing formal models of statutes and sentences.[4]

---

[4] A first software version – limited to practically experimenting the module formed by the "importation filters" – has been revised and verified at the Istituto di Teoria e Tecniche dell'Informazione Giuridica. Also under study is the integration of software relative to structurally analysing documents of a legislative type with programmes realised at the Institute, as part of the research project on applying information and communication technologies to

Let us bear in mind that the study necessary to develop software oriented toward formally analysing and structuring different legal data categories, draws a very clear picture of the lack of homogeneity presently existing among different information systems, as concerns structuring and managing data belonging to the same typology.

3. At this point, linguistic and semantic analysis is performed on the previously retrieved and structured lexical material. Software is developed for this phase, integrating the tools disposed for: a) language check and definition (spelling, grammar and stylistic checks with linguistic and statistic verification functions, but also clarification and elimination of semantic ambiguity, and the possibility for competent users to increase the system's learning by means of gradually integrating its dictionaries: etymological dictionaries; dictionaries of synonyms and opposites; "analogical dictionaries", where terms are grouped by relation and association into families of large semantic areas; online legal glossaries and dictionaries); b) documentary analysis of the information contained in the material collected (this kind of analysis is typically conducted by means of "indexing:" each document is "indexed" attempting to represent its essential content with a limited number of words or expressions – metadata, keywords – intended as descriptors consisting of one or more terms selected from a controlled dictionary of the reference sector's specific terminology). The hierarchical structuring of the terms used for indexing – based on identifying the relations of generality, specificity and correlations – would make it possible to pass from the "List of descriptors" ("Keyword List"), as a mere list of significant terms selected from the specialist dictionary considered, to the "Thesaurus", as a logically organised and structured dictionary of descriptors.

4. The ordering and systematic organisation of documents, already subjected to the structuring and analysis procedures previously illustrated, occurs when the individual document units are arranged on the basis of one or more ordering criteria (alphabetical, numeric, chronologic), referring to one or more fields (author, title, publication date, etc.) within their structure. Furthermore, the same document units can be inserted into groupings on the basis of their belonging to specific formal typologies (articles in periodicals, books, proceedings of conventions, etc.) and subject classes of a completely preconstituted schema. By means of "classification"

law drafting and sentences modeling. For an essential bibliography on the research themes dealt with in this paper and for references to the evolution of applications developed in relation to these at the Istituto di Teoria e Tecniche dell'Informazione Giuridica, please refer to the "Bibliographical Appendix" in (Fameli, 2004). For a general view of the system development over the time see (Fameli et al., 1992; Fameli and Turchi, 1994; Fameli and Cammelli, 1995; Fameli, 1996a; Fameli, 1996b).

each document unit is attributed a code (numeric or alphanumeric) corresponding to one of the "entries" and "subentries" hierarchically structured
within a general schema of the matter considered. It is evident, of course,
that several ordering criteria and several classification codes can combine
and integrate in varying manner.

The software tools conceived to support this phase, on one hand, come
under different sorting techniques typical of the most common word processors, while on the other, they may evolve to the point of configuring
forms of automatic (or semi-automatic) classification of documents, using
algorithms capable firstly of considering the occurrences of pre-classified
descriptors within each document unit, assuming that the classification
can be based on verifying the presence/absence of certain descriptors inside the document unit. The use of a technical Thesaurus, that is specific
of the domain considered and recallable by the procedures of the general
management archive, should enable the system to perform conceptual
type searches on the basis of data managed in a coordinated manner
inside the general work archive, but also to propose a rough classification
for the single documents gradually introduced.

From the viewpoint of programme instructions – inside the SIAM system considered as a whole and therefore formed by several modules
which, though integrated, have distinct and integrated functions of a
documentary, management and decisional type –, the automatic (or semi-
automatic) assignment of a given classification code to documents has, in
turn, been configured as the condition for the emergence of new "events"
such as, for example, the attribution (or proposal to the system manager)
of a certain link typology or particular print features (so-called "context
sensibility").

5. At this point, the logical analysis of information leads to identifying
   and building links of different typologies among the document units of
   databases, among the logical units of knowledge bases and, again, among
   the document units and the logical units inside the SIAM integrated
   system, considered as a whole.

The software tools designed to perform these functions, as far as relational
network implementation is concerned, belong to hypertext techniques, but
also to Artificial Intelligence, in particular as concerns the construction of
nexus of the «If-Then» type («if <condition> then <consequence>,» or
«if <condition> then <action>»). Links and production rules can be combined, giving rise to "epistemic networks" of the following type: «if A then
select B and C and D»; «if A then B or C or D»; «if A and B and C
then D»; «if A or B or C then D» (Greenwell, 1988).

In turn, on the level of logical connection, "hypertextual navigation" between the network nodes can be "guided" in at least two different ways: a) in
the sense that, within the general archive intended as a set of heterogeneous
databases, the search can expand or contract – moving from specific to general
or from general to specific – advancing along the hierarchical structures of the
conceptual trees inside the Thesaurus predisposed for the selected domain; b)
in the sense that the different link typologies logically connecting not only the
single document units within the databases and the single logical units within
the knowledge bases, but also them to one another, can in turn be activated
or deactivated by a network of conditions on a higher logical level.

4. System general architecture

Starting from what can be called – in a broad sense – "personal legal documentation", for the afore-mentioned functions of retrieving, organising, representing and managing legal knowledge, the project aims at realising a complex
information/advisory system formed by four fundamental modules: a) the
"Conversion Filters", for importing and structuring documents extracted from
heterogeneous databases; b) the "Local Managing Archive", configured as a
heterogeneous database capable of ordering and maintaining the data retrieved from external sources (online databases, specialist archives recorded
on CD-Rom, bibliographic publications on paper, etc.); c) the "Integrated
Advisory System", intended as an "Expert System" oriented toward organising,
representing and managing knowledge bases connected with local databases;
d) finally, the "Meta-System", incorporating the functions necessary to coordinate and verify the many operations assigned to the single modules of the overall system (transactions among heterogeneous, local and remote databases,
among knowledge bases, between databases and knowledge bases).

4.1. System fundamental components

The architecture of the system makes it possible to integrate the following
components: a) "Conversion Filters": software modules able to analyse and
rebuild (by means of configuring the corresponding masks) the structure
of different data typologies to import from online archives; b) "Databases":
formed by "document units" belonging to different structural typologies, but
whose consultation can be coordinated by means of using both the access keys
to the fixed fields in which the document units are structured and information retrieval and hypertextual navigation techniques; c) "Knowledge Bases":
constituted by "dialogue units" grouped into interconnected "logical (or procedural) blocks"; d) "Maps": consisting in graphic representations ("dynamic"
and "interactive") of the knowledge bases; e) "Linguistic Tools": configurable as

Grammar/Spell Checkers, Dictionaries, Glossaries, and Thesauri, functional to analysing, revising, explaining, interpreting, indexing and classifying texts contained in "document units" and "dialogue units."

It is possible to implement heterogeneous local archives (databases), but having a predefined structure; each local archive is formed by a set of "document units", with regards to which many functions can be performed. A knowledge base is constituted by logically interconnected "dialogue units" and the flow of the dialogue units consulted can be visualised in graphic form by means of maps. The individual dialogue units can be grouped into "logical" or "procedural blocks", corresponding to the elements of a reasoning or to the phases of a procedure. The definition of logical connections must furthermore be extended to all the components of the integrated environment, so as to enable the creation of logical links within all the modules of the system: not only documents in the local archives, but also individual constitutive elements of the knowledge bases.

"Map" is intended as a representation in graphic form of the "nodes" and "logical links" defined to interconnect the "dialogue units" of the knowledge base. Depending on the analysis performed, the Map should become "dynamic and interactive," in the sense that not only does it allow knowledge base representation, but also the direct management – by the qualified user – of its constitutive elements.

As for the usability of the tools the project provides for pertaining to revising (Checkers), explaining (Dictionaries, Glossaries), classifying and indexing (Classification Tables and Thesauri) "document units" and "dialogue units," it is first of all necessary to study integration with the various types of linguistic supports already available and with the corresponding management techniques. Moreover automatic experimental techniques can be configured for classifying and indexing the individual, logical or documentary, units dealt with by the system.

4.2. INDEXING AND DESCRIPTORS

Words or expressions significant for indexing the units analysed are configured as mono- or pluri-terms descriptors. It will be possible to browse the hierarchical list of descriptors and, in particular, the entire structure of the relations connected to the descriptor each time considered; correspondingly, with respect to the initially selected descriptor, the research can be broadened, narrowed or expanded by choosing – and therefore selecting – the connected descriptors having, respectively, a broader meaning (BT - Broader Term), a more specific meaning (NT - Narrower Term) or a conceptually associated meaning (RT - Related Term).

In the phase of marking the words or expressions in the text of "dialogue units" (in knowledge bases) or of "document units" (in databases) the task of indexing will prove considerably simplified by implementing several specific functionalities, even taking on the form of a (semi)auto-matic procedure. Indeed, the alphabetical and structured lists of descriptors will gradually increase with the retrieval of new document units in the databases and the introduction of new dialogue units in the knowledge bases. Every time a significant word or expression has been selected as descriptor and properly placed in the corresponding conceptual structure, the system's knowledge will increase and successively can be profitably used when inputting new documents or dialogue units.

On the basis of the previous considerations the system will be able to interact with the user according to distinct modalities: a) submitting – for each new text introduced – indexing and classification proposals based on an automatic comparison between the new terms and expressions and those memorised in the lists of descriptors and the classification headwords; b) pointing out that the proposed term does not exist in the system dictionaries and then suggesting words or expressions similar with reference to the semantic area of interest. Therefore while, on one hand, the performance of this function can be integrated by a series of automatic checks on the coherence and consistence of the conceptual hierarchical structures in relation to observing precise formal rules, on the other hand, it must always be based on the system-user interaction, in particular on the user specialized knowledge.[5]

4.3. THE MANAGEMENT LOCAL ARCHIVE

The management local archive is configured as an environment where the user collects, organizes and manages all documentation extracted from the various specialist databanks consulted in order to both theoretical and practical functions, from study and research to consultancy and decision. It must primarily correspond to the demands of document organization set by the user, providing him with adequate and flexible tools; in any event, however, as it contains data extracted from a plurality of external databases, the archive is necessarily qualified as a heterogeneous databank, in turn, formed by a plurality of databases representing well-defined subsets.

As they belong to different typologies, the databases composing the local archive also present a different structure: consequently, the information originating from archives such as those of legislation (State, Regional, international), case law (civil, penal, administrative, State Council, Constitutional Court, etc.), legal literature (books, articles, conference papers, etc.) and opinion press, must be visualised following opportune modalities and therefore configured according to the corresponding document structure.

---

[5] For the outlooks and problems of more or less complex forms of automatic indexing, see (Ferber, 1997).

The management archive can be consulted in the "browsing" modality – by scanning documents and selecting those of interest –, in the "hypertext" modality – navigating through links and conceptual paths either pre-constituted or to be created, – and in the "search" modality – using words or expressions interconnected with Boolean operators (AND, OR, NOT) or following the parameters of the "NEAR" function. The various functionalities indicated act transversally on all the databases composing the manager general archive, enabling the simultaneous use in effecting searches of data heterogeneous by typology, but complementary by topic.

5. General considerations

In relation to project finalities, the overall system has been conceived so as to provide the following functions. It is possible: a) to flexibly construct analysis and identification filters for documents from external databases (of diverse typologies) as concerns inputting them in structured form into a heterogeneous manager archive; b) to memorize the documents identified in local archives, manageable in a specific integrated environment.

In the manager archive environment it is possible to perform: a) full text search as concerns the texts in natural language contained in the various fields of memorized documents (title, abstract of articles or volumes, maxims or integral text of sentences, text of laws, etc.), with the use of Boolean operators and of the "near" function; b) search by "field" and "sub-field"; c) search by descriptors (mono- or pluri-term). Furthermore, in local archives documents it is possible to create and utilize hypertexts to facilitate the user's navigation in the system.

The procedures of data analysis make it possible to a) index and classify the documents by means of semi-automatically assigning descriptors and classification codes; b) develop semi-automatic generation functions of hierarchical dictionaries of descriptors as concerns the control of the specialist lexicon (sectorial technical language) and the performance of assisted conceptual searches in the manager local archive databases. As far as distribution and propagation functions are concerned, we can: a) configure the database documents so as to make them directly useable for their printed publication; b) structure the documents identified with the standard format corresponding to their typology, as concerns putting them on telematic networks (particularly Internet).

In order to make easier and improve the integration between knowledge bases and databases – and therefore between "organized" data and "structured" data – it has been found necessary to carefully analyse the various phases through which unfolds the activity of specialist-type legal archives, destined to be consulted (on line and/or on paper support) not only by experts, but also – generically speaking – by all concerned citizens. Finally, an "Integrated Intelligent System" adequately developed around the indicated functions should be capable of supporting both the theorist and the operator of law throughout the various work phases necessary to organize, manage and concretely utilise the legal information retrieved; moreover, it could induce a substantial enlargement and a considerable enhancement of the common citizen legal knowledge.

References

Casanovas, P., Noriega, P., Bourcier, D., Galindo, F. (Eds.) (2007), *Trends in Legal Knowledge. The Semantic Web and the Regulation of Electronic Social Systems*, European Press Academic Publishing, Florence.

Fameli, E., Nannucci, R., Di Giorgi, R.M. (1992), *A Legal Expert System Prototype Integrated with Databases*, in "Expert Systems with Applications", IV, 3.

Fameli, E. and Cammelli, A. (1995), *Ambiente e diritto: Modelli di sistemi integrati per l'informazione giuridico-ambientale*, paper presented at the annual AICA Congress, Chia-Cagliari, September 27-29, in "Proceedings '95", Vol. I, pp. 521-529.

Fameli, E. and Turchi, F. (1994), *ELP Advisor: A Prototype of an Integrated Expert System in Italian Environmental Law*, in "Proceedings of RIAO '94 Conference on Intelligent Multimedia Information Retrieval Systems and Management", New York, Rockefeller University, October 11-13, 1994, Paris, Vol. I, pp. 493-518.

Fameli, E. (1996a), *Osservatorio sui sistemi informativi giuridico-ambientali in Italia e all'estero: i sistemi esperti*, in Fameli, E. and Cammelli, A. (Eds.), "Diritto all'informazione ambientale e sistemi informativi orientati al cittadino", CEDAM, Padova, pp. 77-107.

Fameli, E. (1996b), *Modelli di "sistemi esperti integrati" nel Diritto: Problemi di configurazione e metodologia di sviluppo*, in Fameli, E. and Cammelli, A. (Eds.), "Diritto all'informazione ambientale e sistemi informativi orientati al cittadino", CEDAM, Padova, pp. 355-403.

Fameli, E. (2004), *SIAM/Lav: un "sistema intelligente integrato" come supporto alla consulenza e alla decisione nell'applicazione delle clausole generali di correttezza e di buona fede alle procedure concorsuali private*, Informatica e diritto, Vol. XIII, No. 1-2, pp. 177-258.

Ferber, R. (1997), *Automated Indexing with Thesaurus Descriptors: A Co-occurrence Based Approach to Multilingual Retrieval*, in Peters, C. and Thanos, C. (Eds.), "Research and Advanced Technology for Digital Libraries: Proceedings of the First European Conference, ECDL '97", Pisa, September, 1997, "Lecture Notes in Computer Science", 1324, pp. 233-252.

Greenwell, M. (1988), *Knowledge Engineering for Expert Systems*, Ellis Horwood Limited, John Wiley & Sons, New York.

Free Access to Law and Judicial Decisions: Solutions and Challenges from a Belgian Viewpoint

Hans Van Bossuyt*, Bertel De Groote°
* *Judge Court of Appeal, Ghent; President Management Board Informatisation of Judicial Organisation, Belgium*
° *University College Ghent; University of Ghent; University of Liege, Belgium*

Abstract. Public authorities have an important role in guaranteeing a broad and easy access to an objective and representative selection of judicial decisions. In this regard information and communication technology has a facilitating role. Belgian legislation therefore developed a regulatory framework to sustain the electronical availability of court decisions through the portal site of the Belgian Judiciary. In its analysis, the paper draws attention to the regulatory framework, to privacy concerns that are related to the online publication and to the structure of database itself. The latter mainly concerns the module that enables consultation as well as the module for the decentralized input of decisions. Accessibility of judicial decisions can also be enhanced by standardizing the drafting process and thereby enabling an optimal use of ICT. This paper develops arguments regarding the opportunities, for instance in view of facilitating electronic publication and enhancing accessibility, and challenges in this regard. They focus moreover on the question whether standardization could endanger a judge's independency, how it could facilitate the "drafting" as a business process and how labeled information facilitates its interconnection.

Keywords: Access to legal information, e-justice, standardization of court decision.

1. Introductory remarks

It is important that legal decisions are broadly notified to the public. Moreover they have to be easily accessible. It thereby has to be ensured that the distribution of the decisions gives an as objective and representative as possible view of the decisions that are given in the different law branches. An arbitrary selection must be avoided. It must absolutely be avoided that decisions are published to sustain certain theses, serving the interests of certain groups, by creating a misrepresenting picture of the jurisdiction in a certain branch of law. Since long, both in Belgium and abroad, it was warned for these dangers.[1]

Information and communication technology facilitates a problemness distribution/publication of court decisions. Such is unfortunately not (yet) a

---

[1] (Popovici, 1972), cited in Quebec Superior Court, September 21, 1998, Wilson & Lafleur Ltée c. La Société québécoise d'information juridique, R.J.Q 1998, 2499: "Si le choix définitif est celui de l'arrêtiste et les critères de sélection les siens, son choix est limité par les sources mises à sa disposition. Il n'y a aucun 'système' de cueillette des jugements. Certains juges, fiers de leur oeuvre judiciaire l'envoient à l'arrêtiste. D'autres sont trop modestes pour le faire. Certains avocats agissent de même. De sorte qu'en définitive c'est autant l'arbitraire du choix de l'arrêtiste (qui ne l'oublions pas, est limité par le nombre de pages à sa disposition dans la publication qu'il dirige) que la disparité hétéroclite et incohérente de ses sources qui laissent à désirer et devraient être remédiées". Cf. (de Terwangne, 2006, p. 151, note 6).

guarantee for the impartial distribution of court decisions. Moreover, the access to the available information can be refrained as users have to pay a subscription rate.

In view of the forementioned objectives and concerns, the public authorities have an important role to play.

This role can be twofold. In first instance, legislation can develop a framework wherein free and convenient access to a wide and representative range of judicial decisions can be guaranteed. From this perspective, this paper analyses the Belgian initiative, and its regulatory framework, to make court decisions electronically available through the portal site of the Belgian Judiciary ("Juridat").

Secondly, authorities can streamline the drafting process. This standardization can optimize the use of information and communication technology, which consequently contributes to court decisions' accessibility. In this regard, this paper intends to develop arguments that may encourage authorities, especially the Belgian government, to balance the opportunities and challenges of the standardization of the drafting of court decisions... especially in view of the implementation of the distribution that contributes to widespread information regarding the legal framework people and social entities live in.[2]

2. Online publication of court decisions

2.1. ONLINE PUBLICATION OF COURT DECISIONS – REGULATORY BACKGROUND

As soon as September 11, 1995, the Committee of Ministers of the Council of Europe recognized the phenomenon of dissemination of information by automated systems.[3] As a consequence it recommended that the governments of the member states should:

1. bring the general principles and guidelines set out below to the attention of the persons responsible for the creation, the management and the updating of legal information retrieval systems;
2. take appropriate steps to ensure that these principles and guidelines are applied to automated jurisprudence retrieval systems in the public

---

[2] Guidelines for the standardization of the drafting process (especially from a Belgian viewpoint), as well as the legal and technical difficulties that have to dealt with in this regard, are not enclosed in this paper. They can be found however in a paper, drafted for the workshop "Civil Procedure" of the Ius Commune Research School 2007 Conference held at Liège (29 & 30 november 2007) (work in progress available with the author: Bertel.DeGroote@hogent.be).

[3] Council of Europe, Recommendation No. R (95) 11 of the Committee of Ministers to Member States concerning the selection, processing, presentation and archiving of court decisions in legal information retrieval systems (11, 1995).

sector, and to facilitate their application, and see to it that automated jurisprudence retrieval systems are objective and representative;

3. take appropriate steps to ensure that all users have easy access to legal information retrieval systems that are open to the public.

The aforementioned recommendations have to serve the following objective:

"to facilitate the work of the legal profession by supplying rapid, complete and up-to-date information; to provide information for all persons directly or indirectly interested in a matter of jurisprudence; to make available more quickly new court decisions, especially in areas of law under development; to make available a large number of Court decisions concerning both questions of law and questions of fact; to contribute to the coherence of jurisprudence; to enable law-makers to analyze the application of laws; to facilitate research on jurisprudence; in certain cases, to furnish information for statistical purposes".

In line of this recommendation of the Council of Europe, the Belgian legislator drafted the law of August 10, 2005 regarding the establishment of the information system "Phenix" (the so called "Phenix-I law"). Art. 7 of this law stated that an external database will be created, that has to enable to disseminate among the public court decisions that are important for the knowledge and development of the law. Since court decisions are official acts of the public authority they're not protected by copyright.[4]

The external database, called "Juridat",[5] is freely accessible by means of the internet.[6]

The public authority has meanwhile opted for an active policy regarding the publication of judicial decisions. It hereby challenges the "Judiciary". Formerly, the publication of court decisions was more or less the concern of some publishers and editorial boards of journals that published court decisions. They hereby relied on their proper "scientific" criteria to select the court decisions that were brought to them, mostly by individual judges.

Since not all court decisions are publication-worthy (for instance, the usefulness of the publication of a standard-decision or a decision whereby the case is merely sent to another court, is highly questionable), selection in one way or another is inevitable.

The Council of Europe recognized already the relevance of selection and embedded that option in the recommendation that is referred to.

---

[4] Art. 8 §2 Belgian Copyright Act.

[5] Available at: < jure.juridat.just.fgov.be >.

[6] Apart from the external database, the legislator has introduced an internal database. The latter will be fed mechanically. A selection won't take place and the identifying particulars needn't to be removed from the decisions it will contain. The decisions can only be consulted professionally by the judges of the instance that rendered the decisions. The database has an internal documentary added value, since it may for instance be useful to guarantee unity in an instance's decisions, since it may facilitate the consultation of certain useful standard formula.

It stated as follows:

"Selection means the type of choice among the court decisions currently given in a member state to be inserted in the database. Selection of court decisions can be carried out according to one of the following criteria:

- hierarchical selection
- geographical selection
- selections by fields of law
- selection by substance (the choice of court decisions according to whether they are or not considered of sufficient legal interest)".

The recommendation comprises a number of guidelines for the selection of court decisions. Those guidelines are formulated both in a positive and in a negative way. Nonetheless, they're not inhibiting a potentially broad selection of decisions.

One has to notice, that the Belgian legislator gave every court the authority to select sovereignly the to be published decisions among the ones it rendered. In this regard, the Belgian solution is not in line with the recommendation of the Council of Europe. The latter suggest that the selection should be done on a central, out of court level, by properly legal trained staff.

It states as follows:

"The selection should be carried out by one or more persons that have proper legal training. This selection can be carried out in steps, for example by using the method of pre-selection. Selection by substance should be carried out in such a way that broad expertise is used and different opinions and points of view are represented. This/these person/s selecting the decision could be judges, university lawyers, advocates (barristers, solicitors), prosecutors or other civil servants. Representatives of associations, of law reviews and of other legal information services may also be included in this group of persons".

"Juridat" is conceived differently. The Belgian Judiciary chooses another approach against the background of the principle of independence of the court magistrates ("judges"). Since the latter give great weight to their independence, in Belgium judges (i.e. the "chamber" that rendered the court decision) traditionally decide autonomously whether they want their judgment to be published or not. This implies the risk of a non-objective selection, while almost all judges who wish so can enter decisions in the data system or refuse to do so.

To decide which court decisions are eligible to be recorded in the external database, the "management committee" (Beheerscomité/Comité de gestion) established selection rules, after having consulted the "Users' Committee". The positive and negative rules were published in the Belgian Official Journal of Laws ("Belgisch Staatsblad/Moniteur belge").[7]

These rules rely on the background that a broad selection is sound and even has to comprise decisions that concern the factual background of a case

---

[7] B.S. 05.10.2007, p. 52449.

when these are thought to be relevant. The criteria that were established are mostly conform to what is intuitively considered to be important.[8]

The question remains whether the rules for selection can avoid that there will come a too massive supply of court decisions. When such would be the case, it can not be excluded that mainly the case law of the higher courts (for instance the Consitutional Court, The Supreme Court [Hof van Cassatie/Cour de cassation], the Council of State [Raad van State/Conseil d'Etat], the European Court of Human Rights, Court of Justice of the European Communities) will be consulted to the detriment of the lower courts.

2.2. ONLINE PUBLICATION OF COURT DECISIONS – PRIVACY CONCERNS

Especially during the last twenty years, great attention is given to the protection of the privacy.

Art. 6 of the Council of Europe's Convention for the Protection of Human Rights and Fundamental Freedoms requires that the judgment has to be announced publicly. For the media, such is a signal that court decisions may be published.[9] The main goal of this pronouncement in public, is not to share the verdict concerning an individual citizen with the public/the community. Publicity rather has to enable the community to exercise control whether the administration of justice was sound and to protect the citizen before court against abuse of powers. The presence of public, and possibly press, as well as the way in which court decisions are evaluated in contributions regarding legal theory, will incite a judge to proceed more carefully since he is subject to control by the public opinion.[10]

The fast evolution of information technology as well as the growing performance of automated search engines (for instance Google, Yahoo), allow to collect systematically information that belongs to persons' individual privacy/private life.

Since ten year now the Commission for the Protection of Privacy in Belgium draw attention to and warned for these questions.[11] In Belgium, great attention is given to the protection of privacy of natural persons. The law concerning the protection of the privacy (regarding data processing), dating form December 8, 1992, severely constrains the processing of court decisions. It is indisputed that the publication of such a decision has to be qualified as the processing of personal data as described in the law of December 8, 1992. Consequently, some basic principles have to be taken into account. They

---

[8] In neighbouring countries selection criteria were established as well. See, for instance for the Netherlands: <www.rechtspraak.nl/Uitspraken/Selectiecriteria>.

[9] The Belgian legislation is very restrictive regarding prohibitions for publication or terms for the publication of court decisions. If such restrictions exist, they mainly concern family and juvenile matters as well as hearings for the examining magistrate [onderzoeksrechter/juge d'instruction].

[10] Cour d'appel Paris, 12.12.1956, J.C.P. 1957, II, p. 9701.

[11] Advice 07/96 from April 22, 1996 as well as Advices 42/97 from Decmeber 23, 1997.

concern the presence of a justified goal for which personal data are processed. Furthermore data may only be processed in a proportional and transparent way (de Terwangne, 2006, p. 155 ff.).

The question whether identifying particulars have to be removed from court decisions in order to guarantee that the personal data are processed in a proportional way, especially with regard to the names of natural persons, is much debated. Anyhow, according to the Commission for the Protection of the Privacy "privacy" prevails to the "right of access".

Against this background, the Phenix-I law states that selected decisions that contain personal data will generally have to be "anonymized" if they will be brought in the external database.[12] [13]

Following the proposal of the management committee and after having received the advice of the "monitoring committee" (Toezichtscomité / Comité de surveillance, the King ($\rightarrow$ the government [executive branch] by Royal Decree) establishes the rules regarding the "anonymisation" of court decisions. He enumerates the exceptions on the rule that are necessary for the intelligibility of the decisions. Furthermore he defines how persons who are mentioned in published decisions can oppose the fact that personal data related to them are included in the latter decisions. Up till now, the Royal Decree is not yet issued.[14]

Removing identifying particulars concerning parties and third parties who are implied in a case before court may be required. This is not the case for the names of judges, the registrar, the expert at the trial, or other persons that are due to their professional activity involved in a case. Their names have not to be barred, since the law on the protection of personal data does not apply to them. Anonymisation has to be limited to what is absolutely necessary to guarantee the balance between privacy and transparency. Therefore, other data that could lead to the identification of the parties may only be barred exceptionally. Furthermore it is not allowed to remove data that are in themselves related to the decision.

2.3. ONLINE PUBLICATION OF COURT DECISIONS – THE STRUCTURE OF JURIDAT

Juridat, the external database for judgments is operational since april 2007. It's realized by three cooperating partners: The federal ministry of Justice

---

[12] Art. 9 of the "Phenix-I law".

[13] There are however cases for which the legislation prescribes the integral publication of the court decisions. This means that personal data of the parties involved will remain included. One may think of prohibitory injunctions or criminal cases, whereby the integral publication is a complementary punishment, is a compulsory measure of information or a compensation for damage.

[14] For rules regarding "anonymisation" in neighbouring countries, see for instances the guidelines issued by the Hoge Raad voor de Rechtspraak in the Netherlands (May 19, 2006). Available at: <www.rechtspraak.nl/Uitspraken/Anonimiseringsrichtlijnen>.

(Federale overheidsdienst justitie/Service public fédéral Justice), the Juriciary and a private partner.

It's based upon three modules:

- Consultation
- Input
- Administration

2.4. MODULE 1 – CONSULTATION

Since Juridat contains selected data of all judicial instances, its users have access to online published case-law of these instances through one single application.

Professional as well as non-professional users have free access. The demands of professional users may differ from those of non-professional users. For this reason, the search engine is established in such a way that professional users can search the database in a targeted and specific way.

All inputted decisions are obligatory related to a unique keyword. This keyword is part of a universal thesaurus. For every sector of the law, a number of keywords are selected. They are ranked by as well in tree structure as alphabetically at different levels. For the users, this approach is advantageous, since they can search by keyword or sectorally through the tree structure.

For the moment, the Universal Thesaurus comprises more than 6,000 keywords. It is maintained by a Scientific Committee.

2.5. MODULE 2 – INPUT

The input of the selected decisions is organized in a decentralized manner. The Juridat-application contains a separate module for input. In every court instance one or more persons are (or will be) trained, since they will receive access rights that enable them to upload decisions locally. This approach has to enhance the processing speed. As a consequence "sensitive" decisions can be made accessible (for instance for the press) in a very short period of time. It may be just a matter of minutes.

There is no preparatory control on the judgments that are uploaded. Nevertheless a number of measures are taken to avoid abuse of the external database.

Three of them are enumerated hereinafter:

- a limited "Technical Committee" distributes the "access rights"; the committee can decide that a person – on the advice of a hierarchical supervisor – can no longer upload judgments (on his own);

- judgments which are contrary to the law can immediately be removed from the database by the technical committee (for instance in case of privacy infringement or if the publication violated the law), and set aside awaiting further investigation;
- it is recommended to establish local selection committees.

2.6. MODULE 3 – ADMINISTRATION

For the maintenance of the application as well, a separate module is developed. (Partial) access to the module and the right to modify it, is restricted to a very limited number of persons.

3. Law via the internet: standardization of the drafting process as a lever to access to court decisions

The second part of the paper deals with some of the opportunities that are related to the standardization of the preparation of court decisions. It develops, in a non-exhaustive way, some arguments in favour of this standardization, since it can amplify the effects of the Juridat-application in view of enabling access to court decisions.

While the latter dealt with the development of a system to publish the judgments, this part deals with the judgment in itself. Crucial for this part of the paper is the question whether a judgment's value – more precisely as a crucial element in the "communication" of the Judiciary – can be enhanced in dealing with the judgment's structure. One may suppose that a sound structure of a judgment can contribute to its readability, as well as to the easiness and usefulness of its dissemination.

While Belgian literature regarding this theme is almost non-existing, very inspiring was a note, dated 1996 and revised in 2002 by the Canadian Citation Committee, regarding this theme. It is entitled: Canadian Guide to the Uniform Preparation of Judgments.

3.1. STANDARDIZATION FAVOURS ELECTRONIC PUBLICATION

Giving access to judgments is giving access to basic legal information. Electronic publication favours the publication of legal texts. The growth of the internet stressed this evolution, enabling publication at limited cost and making it possible to hop from one text to another by intertwining information.

Indeed, the development of information and communication technology effects society as a whole, therefore including justice as well. In order to fully benefit from the opportunities new technologies bring along, the question of standardization emerges.

First of all, since judgments are practically all prepared electronically, there is a huge potential for electronic publication. The public at large, as well as the legal professional, can easily get access to a huge amount of juridical information. In as far as different interdependent sources of juridical information can be published, and if possible and useful, interlinked by efforts of public bodies, publishers and others, the development of information and communication technology broadens the platform for accessible juridical information. It may be clear that the growth of the Internet strongly attributes to the widening of the accessibility of intertwined information sources.

One may hereby refer to the Canadian Guide to the Uniform Preparation of Judgments (nr. 2), which enumerates the advantages that characterize electronic publication of juridical information, i.e. of judgments. It concerns internet-supported, wider and timely distribution as well as a reduction of costs regarding storage, reproduction and publication. Moreover citation can be facilitated and information can be improved. Therefore structuring is crucial however. It enables factual accessibility and interlinking by improving the efficacy of search engines and hypertext functions.

Although electronic publication sometimes leads to the impression that there is an overkill of information, it has clear advantages, as set out above. Therefore the fact that standardized texts are easier to publish is self-evident, since the adopted guidelines regarding structure can lead to documents that are ready for publication. Furthermore, it will be set out that the advantages of electronic publication are enhanced by standards that favour the functionalities linked to it.

As the efficacy of the use of information and communication technology driven tools is depending from its input, the necessity of shared standards for preparing judgments, leading to standardization of their structure, is inevitable. It is helpful for dealing with large and constantly growing amounts of juridical (information) sources.

3.2. INDEPENDENCY ENDANGERED OR IMPROVED

In order to get the best out of the use of information and communication technology, it is important to introduce standardized formats. It is important to stress that those formats regard the structure of information, not touching the core of its content. From this point of view, standardization is not contrary to the independence that constitutionally has to be guaranteed to judges exercising their judiciary power.

The contrary is true. Standardization is helpful to more clearly and accurately express a decision and its arguments. Enhancing efficiency gives judges more time to consider their judgment's content. Moreover they can concentrate on the "material" aspects of the question brought for them, since they have to bother less about formal aspects of the decision.

Since the judgments will be easier to access and understand, standardization may add value to the judge's efforts. Moreover, in the drafting phase will the judge himself have better and easier access to other judgments that can inspire him or to which he can refer.

3.3. STREAMLINING THE DRAFTING PROCESS

Alongside the reduced costs of publication, standardization streamlines the business process of drafting. From this point of view, one can gain efficiency. Standardizing the structure of judgments is indeed in line with the finding that, business processes tend to unity in order to gain efficiency. Standardization is necessary to fully gain from positive effects of scale. From this point of view it can be seen as complementary to a tendency of growing "specialisation" within the courts. It facilitates the integration of different business processes, for instance by enabling automation. From this point of view, this paper intends to express some thoughts regarding the advisability of adopting a standard structure.

Furthermore, drafting guidelines, leading to harmonisation, is a first step in the preparation of software tools that can sustain the drafting process. Such tools can contain optional/mandatory – depending from the procedural law requirements – fields to be filled out, mechanisms of auto-correction and functionalities that enable easy or even automated integration of information that yet exists at other places (one may think of information regarding a party's address and identity). It sustains the drafting process and contributes to the quality of the judgments (for instance an auto-correction tool can make sure that all mandatory elements are integrated in the judgment; if possible they can be taken automatically from the "primary source" in order to avoid mistakes in processing the concerned data). In the end may this integration may lead to an electronic file.

3.4. ENHANCING ACCESSIBILITY

Also, regarding accessibility, intelligibility and searchability of documents, is consistency in structure of great importance, especially in a computational context. In print-based information systems, the need for consistency is moderated by the need of visual consultation every single time a document is used and re-used. At this occasion the information is recognized and identified, which is very demanding. Furthermore in the process of reuse of documents, which often constrains to re-entering them, differences in structure and presentation could be bypassed. On the other hand, with every "manual" re-use the risk of mistakes is growing.

Anyhow, it is not advisable to neglect or under-exploit the advantages of electronic means regarding re-use and reproduction by not structuring the information embedded in the documents in a way that information can only be retrieved form a document by consultation of every single document. Standardization is necessary to permit re-use without the necessity of physical consultation.

This advantage may not be neutralised, since it is of major importance that electronic information can for instance be compared and searched through with the necessity of recognition and identification by the human eye. Effectiveness, in line with the potential of the technology, results in automatic searches covering a bunch of documents, electronic interlinking of documents, as well as comparison of documents and so on without having to consult "materially" each single document.

Referring to the fore mentioned Canadian Guide to the Uniform Preparation of Judgments however, it may be clear that "standardization is the only way to achieve more effective information systems that will reach the full potential of the technology".

Standardization gives way to automation in processing (f.i. presentation) of as well as information technology sustained recognition and identification of documents. Computer languages make it possible to mark identified data (XML/HTML). Meaningful tags are placed on pieces of data, whereby software can be instructed to interpret the marks. Furthermore the tagged data can be presented variably. Tagging facilitates contextual searching as well. However, tagging has to rely on a clear vision of what data have to be tagged. This selection (a) has to be completed with directives on how the data are composed and represented (b).

Such uniformity can facilitate the process of reading and interpreting texts and probably facilitates the development of software that optimizes the efficiency and efficacy of searching routines. It for instance raises the question whether certain data, that are especially helpful for the parties and the court's staff members involved in a process and that mainly contributes to the judgment's identification, shouldn't rather be detached from the core of judgment's arguments. This could definitely optimize the readability and the attractiveness of legal documents for parties that are not directly involved in the related case, but in the more general questions of law that are related to the conflict between the parties.

Moreover uniform labels that mark up these data could be of great help in order to announce the relevant data and make them recognizable. The use of preconditioned labels can furthermore lead to a(n automated) checklist for judges and clerks of the courts relating to data that legally have to be mentioned in order to avoid a void document.

3.5. INTERCONNECTIBILITY

Structured elements containing information that is clearly isolated, identified and labelled, can easily be compared. Furthermore they are easy to gather (for instance: one can gather all cases filed on a specified date) and to connect. Therefore they can be the gateway to other information that is related to the same element (for instance: the party's name is a link that gives access to all cases in which party X was claimant, which can in theory further give access to all cases in which the defending parties where party and so on). The label these elements bear is the key to link them (and therefore enables the integration and re-use of existing information). Analogous to the way in which the WWW functions, the labels form the basis on which a web of intertwined information can emerge.

4. Concluding remarks

In regard of the importance of a wide dissemination of court decisions. The internet has a growing role to play. Taking this into account, the Belgian Judiciary, in line with the Recommendations of the Council of Europe, developed "Juridat": an exernal database containing court decisions that are selected to make them publicly accessible.

Four characteristics of "Juridat" ought to be outlined.

Firstly, "Juridat" is a decentralized system. Courts and individual judges are autonomously responsible for the input of the court decisions in the external database as well of the selection of the judgments that are eligible for dissemination. Therefore, it remains unclear what the consequences will be of the fact that the application of the selection criteria is not centralized and monitored by a dedicated person or institution. The same goes for the attribution of keywords to the decisions that will be subject to publication. Moreover it is not yet clear whether court instances will be keen enough or rather too keen on disseminating judgments. Moreover it is to be seen whether the disseminated court decisions guarantee a representative image of the way in which case law evolves contributed to the evolution of the Belgian legal order.

Secondly, great effort was given to the development of a powerful retrieval system. Keywords that are linked to a sectoral tree structure and an alphabetical thesaurus have to facilitate access by legal professionals as well as interested non-professionals.

Thirdly, though privacy concerns do not prohibit the publication of court decisions they generally require a removal of identifying particulars of natural persons.

Fourthly an internal database of non-selected court decisions will exist, apart from the external database and for internal documentary reasons. It contains information of which the judge can dispose though it is not publicly accessible.

(Online) dissemination of judgments and its effects could be positively influenced by investing in the development of guidelines for uniformity in the creation of court decisions. It is a relatively cost-friendly measure that is necessary however for and could have great (cost-reducing) effect in case of further automation of the drafting process of court decisions and the integration of different applications, "Juridat" included, and data-sources with regard to the drafting and publication of judgments. Hereby, one has to notice that "Juridat", as the portal of the Belgian Judiciary, gives access to a database with Belgian legislation as well.

Agreements in this regard do not affect the judge's independence. On the contrary, the guidelines regarding structure of judgments must facilitate the drafting process as they create the best circumstances for doing so. Furthermore standardization creates added value, since it favours the distribution of, the access to and understanding of the judgment.

While developing a standard structure for the drafting process of judgments, it has to be taken into account that standardization basically has to lead to great accessibility. Furthermore it has to contribute to easier distribution, understanding and searchability – as all relevant and isolatable elements have a distinctive marker – and comparability of the judgments. These goals can moreover better be reached due to the growing potential and functionalities of at high pace evolving information and communication technology. Standardization is hereby necessary in order to optimally use and exploit information technology.

Furthermore, as standardization leads to interconnectibility, information technology makes it possible to integrate structured information, by means of electronic references [hyperlinks]. This can be helpful in drafting the judgment ("import" of data) or in exporting information of judgments in other systems. Structured information can more easily be combined. This combination, whereby a growing "web" of data emerges, leads to added value on the basis of "integration".[15]

This linking can therefore positively affect both the (pre-)drafting and the post-drafting process.[16]

Lastly, harmonized guidelines for the structure of judgments can be a perfect basis for systematic sustaining of the drafting process by information

---

[15] One may hereby remind the use of authentic sources in judgments and the export of judgments to information systems, where it can be combined with other information (for instance "doctrine") that is, by means of the structured elements, linked in one way or another. An example of the usefulness of interlinking structured information could for instance be related by the automated export of judgments to criminal records or the import of data concerning someone's criminal records in the drafting process in as far as it can influence the measure of punishment. This linking can therefore concern the pre- and post-drafting process.

[16] "Hyperlinking" information may eventually lead to an electronic integration of all elements of a case from the introduction of the litigation up to the execution of the final judgment. The result of it may be one (virtually) centralized electronic case file.

and communication technology, where a software driven tool guides the judges through the drafting process and can automatically supply or correct elements on which the judgment's validity is depending.

Efforts regarding structure are rather necessary than regarding form in view of accessibility as well in view of optimizing the drafting process. Standardization has to deal with the definition of the judgment's constituent elements rather than with its design.

References

de Terwangne, C. (2006), *Banques de données de jurisprudence et protection des données personnelles*, in Henrotte, J.F. (Ed.), "Phenix et la procédure électronique", Commission Université – Palais, Vol. 85, Larcier, Louvain-la-Neuve.

Popovici, A. (1972), *Notes sur l'état inadéquat des recueils de jurisprudence au Québec*, R. du B., No. 32, pp. 93-100.

ARIA: Automated Regulatory Impact Analysis

Pietro Mercatali, Francesco Romano
Institute of Legal Information Theory and Techniques (ITTIG-CNR), Italy

Abstract. In Italy, we need to amplify the tools for Technical Normative Analysis (ATN), for Regulatory Impact Analysis (AIR) and, more generally, for the assessment of public policies especially at regional level, given that many Regional Charters give regional councils a central role in controlling the effective implementation and results of legislative policies. The aim of this paper is to illustrate, also through applications given as examples, how tagging techniques and the electronic processing of the text validly support the assessment of: the quality of the legislative text; the impact of the law on the legal order; the impact of the law on society. Impact assessment supported by ICT tools can be conjugated with forms of participation in the legislative decision-making of local bodies together with individual citizens or associations.

Keywords: Legimatics, regulatory impact, information extraction.

1. Assessment of regulations

Since the 1980s, a fear that overabundant and cumbersome drafting of legislation could hinder social and economic development has prompted an increasing number of government institutions (amongst the earliest those in the USA, Canada, Japan, Australia and the countries of Northern Europe) to develop tools for controlling the quality and assessing the impact of legislative instruments. In order to carry out Regulatory Impact Analysis (RIA), each national government builds its own model or creates an assessment method, calling it by different names. Therefore, we talk about Regulatory Impact Analysis or Regulatory Impact Assessment (RIA), Regulatory Impact Statement (RIS), or Regulatory Impact Analysis Statement (RIAS), etc.

However, we can summarise the purposes of these analyses as follows:

– quality control of legislation;
– cost-benefit analysis of legislation;
– assessment of the social and economic effects of regulations.

In Italy, starting from the 1980s, assessment techniques were defined and organised within the domain of legislative drafting (Ielo, 2008; Lazzaro, 2005; Giachi, 1997; Romano, 2003).[1]

Later, several legislative provisions recommended or established their use in the law-making phase[2].

---

[1] See also the Seminar "*Le regole di tecnica legislativa tra strumenti consolidati e possibili sviluppi futuri. Esperienze a confronto*" Consiglio regionale della Toscana, Florence, 26 May 2006.

[2] The itinerary that has paved the way to the use of RIA and TNA in Italy starts from the Law on Simplification of 1998 (Law No. 50 of 8 March 1999). The Law on Simplification

A model was, therefore, designed which provides for and regulates three different types of analyses.

1. ATN (Analisi tecnico-normativa): Technical Normative Analysis assesses the quality of the normative text, verifies the impact of the proposed legislation on the legal order in force, from the point of view of its conformity with the Constitution and Community law as well as matters relating to its compliance with the powers of the regions and the local authorities and to prior acts of deregulation.

2. AIR (Analisi d'impatto della regolazione): Regulatory Impact Analysis assesses, in advance, the effects of cases of normative action affecting the activities of citizens and enterprises as well as on the organisation and operation of public administrations.

3. VIR (Valutazione d'impatto della regolazione): Regulatory Impact Assessment assesses ex post, also periodically, whether the objectives have been reached and estimates the costs and the effects produced by the normative acts that have been passed on both the activities of citizens and enterprises as well as on the organisation and operation of public administrations.

For the purposes of this paper, we propose a different classification for making assessments from the perspective of textual analysis. We, in fact, prefer to talk about a continuous assessment process in which it is possible to make an ex post de iure condito assessment introductory to the ex ante assessment to be made about the law condenda; likewise the ex ante simulation will then constitute the benchmarking for ex post assessment.

1.1. ASSESSMENT OF THE QUALITY OF THE TEXT (TEXTUAL)

We, therefore, more correctly call the ambit of the analysis textual. It can be said that this analysis is aimed at assessing the capacity of the text to carry the regulatory contents. It is centred on linguistic aspects and on the logical conceptual organisation of both the full text and the single provisions. The parameters of reference for this initial kind of assessment are the rules for drafting normative acts, adopted by both the Regions and the State and linguistic conceptual models based on legal authority (Bolioli, Mercatali, Romano, 2003).

---

of 2005 (Law No. 246 of 28 November 2005) consecrated legislatively the mechanism for verifying the final impact of regulations which was drafted in the D.P.C.M. of 21 September 2001: regulatory impact assessment.

1.2. Normative impact assessment (intra textual)

This relates to the relations that the text establishes within the legal order in which it is to be found. It focuses on so called "normative links" (Sartor, 1996) that is, on all those textual elements (but also only conceptual elements) useful for linking the text to the legal order. It assesses the consequences that the new text and the single provisions in it have not only on the legislation with which relations are established but also on the entire legal order.

1.3. Factual impact assessment (extra textual)

This relates to the fitness of the normative text for producing its desired effects, on the reality sought to be regulated or actually regulated. It centres on a comparison between the content of the text and the acts, facts, situations, that it will regulate or has regulated, that it will constitute or has constituted, that will be or have been the consequences of it.

We have already mention that it is indispensable for factual impact assessment to make a comparison between the normative text and other information external to it. Obviously, to have these data available presents considerable difficulties such as:

- the production of data on the effects produced in actual fact by the normative act. These data are not always kept or made available by the assessing body;
- the online availability of the datum that can be electronically compared to the normative datum.

To avert this problem, a solution is also being found in Italy. It is the addition within legislation of assessment clauses with (more or less detailed) directions about contents, methods and tools for the assessment.[3]

With regard to the second difficulty, we must keep in mind that there is a great deal of online data relating not only to the socio-economic situation but also to administrative activities (administrative measures, plans, reports, etc.) generated by the parties implementing the normative provisions.

All Italian municipalities, for example, have their own web sites, even if the formats and contents of these pages are extremely varied and do not respond to any systematic criteria. Furthermore, analyses and experiences on the organisation and processing of online date already exist for identifying the relations between administrative activities and normative provisions

---

[3] In US legislation, there are now examples of actual assessment clauses. In this regard, see (Martini and Sisti, 1999).

2. Automated tools for processing regulations

Apart from offering citizens a single point of access to legislative and other legal documentation published on the web by public institutions, the NormeIn-Rete project has attempted to encourage cooperation among Public Administrations, proposing methods and software tools to support the computerisation of processes linked to the drafting and publication of normative documents.

This latter aim of the project has, in fact, lead to the definition of two standards: the first for unambiguously identifying normative documents based on the technique of uniform resource names (URNs), the second, the XML standard, for describing the content of normative documents defined through three DTDs.

These models describe a normative texts according to two profiles:

- one relating to the physical structure of the document that takes into consideration the formal partitions of the legislative text;
- the other of a functional kind which, instead, describes, through meta-data, the logical structure of the document, considering the law as the result of elementary components called provisions (Biagioli, Francesconi, Spinosa, Taddei, 2003).

The use of this mark-up code (textual and meta-textual) for computerising the processes of legislative drafting allows us to propose the implementation of systems for monitoring the impact of a bill on both the legal order in force and on the administrative activities generated by it.

In Italy, we need to amplify the tools for Technical Normative Analysis (ATN), for Regulatory Impact Analysis (AIR) and, more generally, for the assessment of public policies especially at regional level, given that many Regional Charters give regional councils a central role in controlling the effective implementation and results of legislative policies.[4]

The aim of this paper is to illustrate, also through applications given as examples, how tagging techniques and the electronic processing of the text validly support the assessment of textual, intratextual and extratextual quality.

---

[4] In particular, powers of the Councils related to:

- assessing the effects and results of regional policies;
- controlling of the process for implementing the laws;
- promoting and safeguarding the quality of the normative texts.

In Italy, the Conferenza dei Presidenti delle Assemblee Legislative delle Regioni e delle Province Autonome has promoted the CAPIRe project to stimulate the use of policy assessment within the legislative assemblies.

3. Automated Regulatory Impact Assessment

We need to begin by mentioning that we are not proposing an "absolute" assessment of the text, based on general parameters that can be used for any kind of assessment. The types of analyses, in fact, depend on the methodologies employed and, above all, on the objectives to be achieved. In fact, a legislative text has many uses, interpretations and effects also depending on circumstances and situations which cannot always be determined in an unambiguous manner: therefore, we have to decide, on each occasion, which text elements to take into consideration and which analyses and processing to carry out (what meaning and what function to examine, which data to put into a relation with them).

It follows that even the marking-up that, especially with regard to the metadata, is a semantic annotation which, as such, contains an interpretation of the text by the person who has done it, can only be functional to the desired assessment objectives.

Although we can, therefore, talk about a non *a-priori* reductionistic system, it is, on each occasion, to be traced back to a predefined set of parameters for each specific assessment.

3.1. AUTOMATED ASSESSMENT OF THE QUALITY OF THE TEXT

3.1.1. *Textual analysis and assessment on the status of the legislation*
One kind of assessment which met with wide approval in the national Parliament and regional councils is the reports on the status of the legislation which the President's Office and legislative offices prepare every year for their relative assemblies.

These reports describe the legislative activity from both the point of view of the law-making process (with data regarding the number of acts passed, the time required for their enactment, the number of amendments, the numbers of acts awaiting approval, etc.) and the point of view of the types of acts passed (for example, listing the sectors of legislative intervention, the matters to be regulated, emergency measures, etc.).

Some quantitative information about the contents of the text are also presented such as: the length, the number of articles and other partitions, the referrals to other provisions, the number of abrogations, the types of acts, etc., which make up all the elements useful for assessing the textual quality of the acts. Measuring this quantitative type of information can easily be done electronically on texts that have been tagged according to the national standards, with tools that many legislative assemblies already possess.

3.1.2. *Index of the quality of laws*

In the area of qualitative assessment, we would like to mentions the experience of the Regional Council of Tuscany which has created a quality index of Tuscan laws, on the assumption that this is the measure of the relationship between the legislative text and the rules for legislative drafting (VV.AA., 2003).

The rules taken into consideration are those which, having a high technical profile, can be directly applied by the regional legislative offices and, in particular, 21 of the 30 rules for legislative drafting found in Annex D of the Manuale on Drafting of 2002. From the viewpoint of quality = proper application of the rules, it is obvious that the individual rules constitute the elementary units of quality, that is, they correspond to what we can call quality factors. Therefore, the quality index provides the representation of the degree of the proper application of the selected rules to the laws under examination. The steps for approaching the measurement of quality have been called the qualitative standard, qualitative deviation, quality profile and have been defined in the following way:

— Qualitative standard: identifies the sum of all the values corresponding to the individual frequencies of quality factors that have been applied positively. The more widespread the positive application of a rule is, the higher its contribution is to the quality of the norm. Theoretically, the standard to which each law should aspire is solely represented by the positive application of all the quality rules-factors found in that law.

— Qualitative deviation: identifies the sum of all the values corresponding to the non proper frequency of quality factors. Non proper application can be assessed as a kind of departure from proper application which has lead to the definition of the qualitative standard.

— Quality profile: is equivalent to the difference between the values highlighted by the qualitative standard and those expressed by the qualitative deviation and represents the first synthetic indication of quality.

From the set of these qualitative elements, the drafting quality index of the individual laws originates as a relationship between the quality of the law, as it is provided for by the qualitative standard, and the quality effectively possessed as indicated by the quality profile, and, therefore, a synthetic representation of the degree of application of the rules.

The completion of the quality index has been called the improvement index and it is expressed by the relationship between the qualitative deviation of a law and its qualitative standard. Being made up of the qualitative elements that have been found but not properly applied, this index provides useful information for improving legislative drafting.

With this method, we can highlight the weak points of an individual normative text and build up scores of how serious, detectable and frequent errors are.

Obviously, apart from making all the operations related to textual analysis more rapid, the availability of software for the automated detection of the application of the rule would enable the quality indices for single provisions or structures or the type of rules (sectoral) to be processed and would make the comparison between different normative texts easier.

An initial application (Mercatali and Romano, 2004a) to use as a support for this particular form of text assessment could be the Lexedit XXI.

The prototype, which was designed in order to correct the text in the drafting phase, is based on a parsing system for recognising the structure of the enacting terms, the normative provisions and other propositions or expressions resulting from the application of the legislative drafting rules.

Precisely the function for which it was designed enables it to identify whether the structures are well-formed or malformed, elements which, as we have seen, use the method created by the Tuscan region, for computing the textual quality indices.

3.2. AUTOMATED NORMATIVE IMPACT ASSESSMENT

As we have mentioned, normative impact assessment cannot ignore the analysis of so-called "normative links", that is, of all those conceptual and textual elements useful for linking the text to different normative texts; a particularly important function for the purpose of reconstructing the inter-textual dimension that, together with the conceptual dimension, is fundamental for assessing the consequences of a normative text.

Clearly, the automated assessment we propose relates, at present, to the explicit text elements usually found in duly defined structures, both legally and linguistically, of the legistic rules and other very binding normative rules.[5] Nothing, however, excludes the fact that, once the texts annotated with metadata regarding the conceptual links are available, we can also extend these automated normative impact assessment techniques, by making them more efficient. Some initial indications of the use of tagging texts and the relative classifications with metadata for normative impact assessment concern links that are important for making automated checks on:

- the constitutional legality and consistency of the trends in Regional Charters;
- conformity with Community law and international obligations;
- co-ordination with existing legislation;

---

[5] Information extraction systems can enable us to recognise and extract the structures which create so-called normative links. In particular, they can recognise and extract textual structures that define provisions such as explicit textual amendments, legislative derogation, suspension, extension, and referral to future norms. According to NIR standards, they can even support this phase just considering the URN and tools created for the automated creation of the links between normative texts.

— referrals to future implementing provisions.

3.2.1. *Relations with the Constitution, Regional Charters, Community and international law.*

This is the case of tagging which, for example, enables the references to a Regional Charter contained in the promulgated legislation to be identified, in order to assess whether the incorporation in the text is positioned in a proper way for the function it is to perform. This tagging also enables the modes and effects of the application of the article of the cited Charter to be assessed. In the following, we describe an experiment of a completely provisional mark-up for verifying the compatibility of a provision, in this case a delegation, with the Charter.[6]

Umbria REGIONAL LAW No. 7 of 2 May 2006:
Art. 1

1. The Regional Council authorises the Regional Assembly, <**consistency with the Charter - delegation**> in accordance with Article 70(2)(j) of the Regional Charter, </**consistency with the Charter - delegation**> to adopt regional regulations concerning the processing of sensitive and legal data [. . .].

Art. 2

1. Regional regulations referred to in Article 1 shall identify: <**consistency with the Charter - object delegation**> a) the types of data that parties under Article 3 may process; b) the types of processing that may be carried out on the data referred to in (a). </**consistency with the Charter - object delegation**>

3.2.2. *Co-ordination with existing legislation*

Information extraction systems also permit the recognition and extraction of those particular types of links represented by explicit amendments. In other words, all those provisions that link the text to other texts in the legal order, affecting the textual structure or the meaning of one and the others.

In particular, they can recognise and extract the textual structures that define provisions like:

— explicit textual amendment,
— derogation,
— suspension,
— renewal.

---

[6] We can also imagine a similar method for impact assessment with regard to the Constitution and Community and international law.

Regarding explicit amendments of a textual type, research on the formalisation of the text and the electronic processing of those provisions have already lead to a considerable number of results and some applications (Palmirani, 2005; Boer, Winkels, Van Engers, De Maat, 2004; Mercatali and Romano, 2004b).

Among the latter, the LexLooter prototype, exploiting the recognition and tagging of explicit textual amendments, through UML notation, automatically co-ordinates normative texts and the reconstruction of the text in force (Mercatali, Romano, Boschi, Spinicci, 2005). Already developed technology in the prototype can be re-used for simulating the impact of amended texts of the amendments found in a bill for the purpose of assessing the consequences on both the structure of the text and its content. One of the possible assessments could, for example, consist in verifying whether the amended text has already undergone many prior amendments. This could suggest to the legislator that it is necessary to completely rewrite the law or even to reorganise the entire legislative sector. Or it may be possible to verify whether the amending provision amends one of the texts that have already amended the root-text instead of the latter.

3.2.3. *Referrals to future norm*
When the normative act refers the integration and implementation of the rules of the act itself to another legislative measure, we are faced with a referral to a future norm. Monitoring this type of link is especially significant whenever we intend to verify whether the activity referred to has effectively been carried out by the appointed body, within the period and in the manner provided for in the referral law. The presence of this kind of referral is, for example, very important within the legislation of the Italian Regions. It is, therefore, possible that the legislative assemblies are interested in monitoring, electronically, the regulatory activities, limited by law, of other bodies (the regional executive, local authorities, etc.).

Examples to future norms found in some regional laws are of the following kind:

[...] After hearing the opinion of the competent commission, the Regional Executive shall adopt, within 60 days from the date on which this law enters into force, an outline of the regulations [...]

and yet again:

[...] the associations of municipalities shall adopt Regulations within sixty days from the date on which this law enters into force [...].

Once again, we have experimented with Information Extraction[7] tools for recognising, tagging and extracting this type of link from a legislative text

---

[7] For a detailed illustration of the linguistic parser used in more than one project for processing legislative texts, see the Celi website (`<www.celi.it/>`) and also (Mercatali and Romano, 2004c).

and attempted to implement some rules in the grammar of the parser. The initial brief analysis carried out on a sample corpus allowed us to identify the referrals to the future norms set out in the example above (Romano, 2007).

3.3. AUTOMATED FACTUAL IMPACT ASSESSMENT

We have already explained how comparison between the normative text and other information external to it is indispensable for factual impact assessment.

It is obvious that there are considerable difficulties involved in having this data available, such as:

- the presence of data relative to the effects generated in the real world by the normative act, data that are not always processed and accessible to the assessor;
- the online availability of the datum in a format that can be compared electronically with the normative datum.

To avoid the first problem, a solution which appears particularly efficient is to add assessment clauses with detailed information on content, methods and tools for assessment within the legislation.[8]

As far as the second difficulty is concerned, we need to keep in mind that there is a great deal of online data concerning not only the socio-economic reality but also administrative activities (administrative measures, plans, reports, etc.) generated by the actuators of the normative provisions.

It should be noted that, for example in Italy, the New Code of Digital Administration (Arts. 53 and 54) dictates that state bodies publish a wide range of data relating to administrative procedures and measures as well as many of their activities in a systematic and easily accessible manner on web sites. Furthermore, whilst not being able to impose these obligations on the Regions and local authorities, the Code (Arts. 2 and 3) lays down a framework of normative reference that stimulates the Regional bodies to legislate so that local authorities can also reach the same objectives.

The relations between the text being drafted and its "factual" impact can be grouped into three categories:[9]

---

[8] There are various examples of actual assessment clauses in legislation in the United States. In this regard, see (Martini and Sisti, 1999).

[9] A grid of "institutional" assessment can be found in the Directive of the President of the Council of Ministers of 27 March 2000 which is briefly outlined here:

- identification of the administrations, addressees and interested parties involved in the proposed normative intervention: a1) identification of the "addressees" which are those included in categories expressly mentioned in the Bill; a2) identification of any "interested parties" that is socio-economic categories on whom the intervention will, in any case, have an effect;
- conditions relating to the organisational, financial, economic and social spheres: b1) conditions necessary public administrations, intermediary organisations and the ad-

1. socio-economic impact. The objective of the economic analysis is to determine the contribution of the option with reference to the objectives of the development of the country and its social and economic impact on the whole of society, assessing not only direct economic effects but also indirect effects;

2. financial impact. The financial part of the cost-benefit analysis lies in the analysis of the cash flow, constituted by financial income and expenditure;

3. administrative-procedural impact. The aim of the administrative impact analysis is to assess the impact of the proposed regulations on the organisation of public administrations operating locally (so-called "internal impact").

The automated tools for implementing the assessments we have just listed are, in some cases, easy to carry out, instead, in others, they appear to require considerable research and planning in various different ways.

In any case, it is, in the first place, necessary to determine the elements to be extracted as useful for assessing the factual impact of the normative text so we can then compare them with the real (or simulated) data that make this assessment possible.

Concerning the third type of impact, administrative-procedural impact, an initial example relates to the monitoring of the impact that an authorisation provision may generate on administrative organisation and on the activities which are the object of the authorisation. In particular, we showed (Romano, 2007) how it is possible to define a model of authorisation provisions based on legal and linguistic rules and how this model can then be translated into the formalisms of information extraction systems so that information pertinent to this type of assessment can be extracted from normative texts.

---

dressees to properly implement the normative intervention; b2) financial conditions: availability of funds for implementing the intervention; b3) economic conditions: that there are impacts on one or more economic sectors that are not directly included within the objectives of the intervention; b4) social conditions: that there are impacts of a social nature;

— assessment of the areas of "criticality", that is, those options that cause a risk to the successful outcome of the proposed normative intervention;

— assessment of alternative options to regulations and regulatory measures: d1) assessment, in the first place, of the so-called "do nothing option", that is, the alternative of leaving the existing situation unchanged; d2) assessment of options that do not require legislative or regulatory interventions in the strict sense: adoption of codes of self regulation, economic policy actions, enactment of informative or explanatory guidelines.

4. Conclusions: from assessment to participation

It should be noted that the proposals we are making have been presented in very heterogeneous stages of processing among them.

In fact, in some cases we have only mentioned the possibility of electronic supports for assessment, in others we have indicated, even if briefly, operational solutions, and finally in others we have described procedures and tools that have already been implemented and are already in use, even if experimentally, using, in this way, these descriptions as examples of the methodologies and techniques that can then be also re-used in other tests.

Applying these test procedures and the exchange of data, also via the web, will, nevertheless, provide new opportunities to add additional content to at least two of the objectives the legislative assemblies wish to achieve: transparency and participation. The availability of this data on line, in fact, will not only allow the legislative assemblies, on the one hand, to carry out the monitoring and checks listed above but it will also give even citizens the possibility of assessing the quality, implementation and performance of normative measures and of acting in a conscious manner in the law-making process.

Therefore, impact assessment (in particular, factual assessment) can be conjugated with forms of participation in the legislative decision-making of local bodies together with individual citizens or associations in sectors such as:

- analyses of addressees (evaluation of direct and indirect beneficiaries, localisation, etc.);
- economic analysis (the economic effects prompted by a proposal, impact of actions on the labour market, environment, company competitiveness and, in general, the economic/productive system, also in reference to specific trends in planning, etc.);
- qualitative and quantitative identification of parties involved in the processes and any responsibilities attributed to the local bodies;
- institution of organisms to be regulated.

An additional element of participation may be furnished by the creation of a taxonomy enabling norms to be searched from the point of view of the parties who are the addressees of the provisions, especially social intermediaries (local authorities, associations, etc.). Introducing a taxonomy of addressees of the provisions will, for example, permits us to foresee the activating of tools for e-dialogue with citizens and civil society to be activated during the process of the adoption of legislative acts. Finally, information targeting the addressees could activate the same channel in an interactive sense: that is, it would enable addressees to intervene in the process of law making and the drafting of other measures. This could occur either informally or officially, if provided for by the legal order. Also in the direction of conjugating control over public policies and citizen participation, it seems that decisive impetus has been given by the European Union which, with programmes focused on E-participation in legislative and decision making processes, stimulates research aimed at developing automated tools for assessing the costs-benefits of adopted or proposed legislation and at developing tools that permit interaction between those who have been elected and citizens or economic groups and civil society in general.

References

Biagioli, C., Francesconi, E., Spinosa, P.L., Taddei, M. (2003), *The NIR Project. Standards and tools for legislative drafting and legal document Web publication.* in "ICAIL 2003 Proceedings", Edinburgh, 24-28 June 2003.

Boer, A., Winkels, R., van Engers, T., de Maat, E. (2004), *A content management system based on an event-based model of version management information in legislation*, in Gordon, T. (Ed.), "Legal Knowledge and Information Systems". Jurix 2004, IOS Press, Amsterdam, pp. 19-28.

Bolioli, A., Mercatali, P., Romano, F. (2003), *Legimatics Methodologies for the Implementation of a Legislative Grammar.* in "ICAIL 2003 Proceedings", Edinburgh, 24-28 June 2003.

Giachi, G. (1997), *Tecniche per l'analisi di fattibilità dei testi normativi*, Naples, ESI, 238 pp.

Ielo, D. (2008), *L'Analisi di Impatto della Regolazione tra limiti al Leviatano e teoria dei giochi*, available at: <www.mi.camcom.it/upload/file/1335/667540/FILENAME/Ielo.pdf> (accessed 28/8/2008).

Lazzaro, F. (2005), *L'apporto della scienza e dell'analisi giuridica per la radicazione dell'AIR*, Studi parlamentari e di politica costituzionale, Vol. 38, No. 147-148, pp. 89-97.

Martini, A. and Sisti, M. (1999), *Fatta la legge... con quali strumenti è possibile valutarne l'attuazione*, National Seminar "Formazione per le tecniche legislative" of the *Conferenza dei Presidenti dell'Assemblea, dei Consigli Regionali e delle Province Autonome*, Turin, 17-18 June 1999, available at: <www2.prova.org/Doc/relaz17giugno.doc> (accessed 28/8/2008).

Mercatali, P. and Romano, F. (2004a), *Analisi preliminare per la progettazione di uno strumento di analisi e correzione di testi normativi.* Technical report No. 11/2004, Florence, ITTIG/CNR, 10 pp.

Mercatali, P. and Romano, F. (2004b), *Modelli formali per una grammatica normativa. La modifica testuale esplicita*, Parlamenti regionali, No. 11, pp. 261-281.

Mercatali, P. and Romano, F. (2004c), *Grammatiche normative e applicazioni legimatiche*, Informatica e diritto, Vol. XXX, 1-2, pp. 259-280.

Mercatali, P., Romano, F., Boschi, L., Spinicci, E. (2005), *Automatic Translation from textual representation of laws to formal models through UML.* in "Proceeding of the 18th Annual Conference on Legal Knowledge and Information Systems (JURIX 2005)".

Palmirani, M. (2005), *Dynamics of Norms over Time: a Model for Legislative Consolidation*, in "Proceedings of the Workshop on legislative XML", Quaderni CNIPA No. 18 November.

Romano, F. (2003), *Drafting legislativo e controllo di qualità: esperienze e proposte*, Technical report No. 3/2003, Florence, ITTIG/CNR, 8 pp., available at: <www.ittig.cnr.it/Ricerca/Testi/Romano2003.rtf> (accessed 28/8/2008).

Romano, F. (2007), *Identification of normative provisions by NLP tools for impact assessment of legislation*, Technical report No. 2/2007, Florence, ITTIG/CNR,

10 pp., available at: <www.ittig.cnr.it/Ricerca/Testi/romano2007.pdf> (accessed 28/8/2008).

Sartor, G. (1996), *Riferimenti normativi e dinamica dei nessi normativi. Il procedimento normativo regionale*, Cedam, Padoa.

VV.AA. (2003), *Indice di qualità: la sperimentazione del Consiglio regionale della Toscana. Percorso e metodologia, a cura del Gruppo di lavoro per la applicazione del manuale unificato di drafting, l'applicazione e il monitoraggio delle regole applicabili d'ufficio*, in the Proceedings of the Workshop "Regole di uniformità redazionale e indice di qualità della legge: l'esperienza del Consiglio regionale della Toscana", Florence, 19 September 2003.

IS-LeGI. A New On-line Dictionary for a Better Access to the Historical ITTIG Archives Documenting Italian Legal Language

Antonio Cammelli, Paola Mariani

Institute of Legal Information Theory and Techniques (ITTIG-CNR), Italy

Abstract. The Institute, like its primary objective, had the creation of a *Vocabolario Giuridico della lingua italiana* (Italian Language Law Dictionary) that documented that language's historical development, considering that this objective would be better accomplished with the help of computer technology rather than via traditional methods. This led to the creation of electronic lexical archives that were able to provide the user with a considerable quantity of data on legal terms and meanings, as well as search modes that would have been inconceivable in traditional paper archives.

In this context what really matters is the study of techniques and methods of information access that guarantee the retrieval of documents whatever their content, and which have the possibility of diversification with respect to the legal culture of other countries.

The *Lingua Legislativa Italiana* LLI (Italian Legislative Language) is the first archive created by the ITTIG. Today it is accessible on-line and constitutes a valuable and unique consultation tool for understanding the historical development of legal language. *Lessico Giuridico Italiano* LGI (Italian Legal Lexicon) is another archive that contains a selection of documents and some sections and words within these. These archives (LLI and LGI) can now be searched on-line and enable the user to analyse every documented term in its historic-semantic evolution. IS-LeGI Project (Legal Language Subject Index). has the aim to give a better access to the Institute archives, providing also the context phraseology.

Keywords: Legal lexicography, legal documentation via Internet.

1. Introduction

The Institute of Legal Information Theory and Techniques (Istituto di Teoria e Tecniche dell'Informazione Giuridica, ITTIG) of the Italian National Research Council (Consiglio Nazionale delle Ricerche, CNR) has a long tradition in the study and electronic documentation of legal language.

The origin and development of this language is part of Europe and Italy's legal cultural heritage in that the concepts, the norms and institutions of this discipline are expressed and communicated through it.

Legal sources in all their various typologies are therefore part of the archival and bibliographical capital that constitute the cultural resources that give a people and a nation an identity.

Precisely because we are dealing with historical sources that are often in a poor state of conservation there is always a risk that their contents may be irredeemably lost.

There is, therefore, a pressing need to elaborate digital systems able to convert data held on paper which are in constant danger of physical deterioration into an electronic format.

The legal sector in particular is characterised by the existence of a huge number of sources and documents that need to be classified and easily accessed.

For a long time these have been subject to the limitations imposed by traditional information retrieval systems but changes brought about by the development of new multi-media technologies have had a positive effect in this area.

In fact computing has significantly changed the ways in which material is communicated, stored and disseminated and, at the same time, changes the ways in which data is presented.

The tools and procedures to analyse data are transformed and allow for the creation of exhaustive and representative linguistic corpora of particular legal systems.

The relationship between the new methodologies and legal documentation now allow for a whole series of ways in which cognitive approaches to language can be broadened and take up new and uncharted paths.

Compared to traditional methods of information storage the current possibility of managing a huge quantity of data has led to much more analytical and satisfying research in the field of data documentation.

Over and above this, all documents in an electronic archive can be singled out in their actual physical shape seeing as they are reproduced in image format and this enhances the possibilities of analysing and deepening and understanding of their content.

This has entailed a radical methodological revolution in the study of law as the barriers between different disciplines have become far more flexible.

A trans- and inter-disciplinary area has, therefore, opened up and has permitted an up to date comprehension of sectors that cannot be assigned to one identifiable field.

If this is true at the national level, it is even more so at the European level. It is clearly necessary to compare and to integrate sector languages and systems in order to find a supra-national legal base common to all participating countries.

In order to understand the terms that are not always correctly expressed with literal translation a comparison between the languages of the European States is necessary. This is particularly the case for languages that have acquired pre-eminence in Europe and the world or for specific institutionalised bi- or multilingual contexts.

In fact, the relationship between terms and concepts is certainly not consistent in different languages. Identical terms can even stand for different concepts within a single language and hence the risk that the original meaning of a linguistic legal locution/syntagm may be lost in translation. In order to avoid this, it is important to analyse legal language taking into account the historical connections existing between Europe's legal systems thus allowing a deeper understanding of terminological-conceptual relationships. As far as Italy is concerned, the reception of the French exegetical model first, and the pandectistic German one later has implied a kind of linguistic compliance in Italy to the legal categories developed in those countries that has had profound effects on the characteristics of the Italian legal system or language.

From the outset, the Institute (born in 1968 as the Istituto per la Documentazione Giuridica, IDG) set its primary objective as the creation of a *Vocabolario Giuridico della lingua italiana* (Italian Language Law Dictionary) that documented that language's historical development.

ITTIG researchers considered that this objective would be better accomplished with the help of computer technology rather than via traditional methods.

This led to the creation of electronic lexical archives that were able to provide the user with a considerable quantity of data on legal terms and meanings, as well as search modes that would have been inconceivable in traditional paper archives.

In this context what really matters is the study of techniques and methods of information access that guarantee the retrieval of documents whatever their content, and which have the possibility of diversification with respect to the legal culture of other countries.

2. From Italian legal lexicon to a new on-line dictionary (IS-LeGI)

The *Lingua Legislativa Italiana* (LLI, Italian Legislative Language) is the first archive created by the ITTIG. Today it is accessible on-line and constitutes a valuable and unique consultation tool for understanding the historical development of legal language.

The corpus contains about 190 primary legislation texts in their first official edition, such as codes, constitutions, consolidated law panning across a huge time-span (from 1539- to the present).

These texts were chosen not only because of their significance in the history of Italian law but also because of their impact on legal language that was consolidated precisely via the fundamentally important legislative text. They have been digitalised in a *full text* format and searches are made using headwords or by forms (e.g. their lexical variants) within the *corpus*.

In this sense the LLI[1] is a very important product in the historical-legal-linguistic sector and is a precious consultation tool for legal language through its most significant legal texts.

---

[1] Available at: <www.ittig.cnr.it/BancheDatiGuide/lli/>.

Like its successors the LLI is aimed at a wide category of users (jurists, historians, semiologists, students) interested in this type of material for professional reasons or because they require a better understanding of legal language.

Besides we have the *Lessico Giuridico Italiano* archive LGI (Italian Legal Lexicon), which has been made available on-line.[2] This archive is different from the LLI because it is "selective", that is it contains a selection of documents, and some sections and words within these.

Searching for a particular term in this database, the tool shows the data relative to that term, included the links to the historic works (see fig. 1).

The selected documents in fact have led to the creation of the about 900,000 "source-cards" that make up the archive; by "source-cards" we mean the image format reproductions of the single selected document. The result therefore is direct access to the headword required within its context (see fig. 2).

With this system the user can have directly the image of the historic document that contains the legal term.

Analysing all the images of the archives relative to the single term is so possible to study its historic-semantic evolution.

For example, the Italian legal term *locazione* has more than one legal meaning. It can have the meaning of contract of rent, so that of contract of professional performance, etc.

Reading the document of LGI, we can understand easily which is the meaning of the term in the single historic document, and reconstruct its semantic evolution (see fig. 1 – 2).

In order to complete the documentation obtained in the previous LLI legislative archive it contains circa 2000 legal-historical documents published between the 10th and the 20th centuries and is made up of legislative, legal science and practice texts. The latter includes judicial decisions, notary letters, wills etc. Legislation in this archive does not repeat that found in LLI in that it concerns those aspects of ordinary and day to day law creation tied to the particular and contingent needs that required immediate legislation (e.g. decrees, proclamations, edicts).

The highlighted relationship between these archives is evidence (immediately understood by ITTIG researchers) of the need to consolidate and to rationalise results obtained via a long term view and following European patterns. This in order not to disperse data or duplicate efforts.

From the operative point of view a multiplicity of results in terms of access to documentation is available. It is in fact possible to conduct a search:

— by one or more of the three fundamental legal sources (legislation, legal
   science and practice);

---

[2] The already on-line archive is currently being tested by ITTIG technicians and will in any case be corrected and updated. Available at: <www.ittig.cnr.it/BancheDatiGuide/vocanet>.

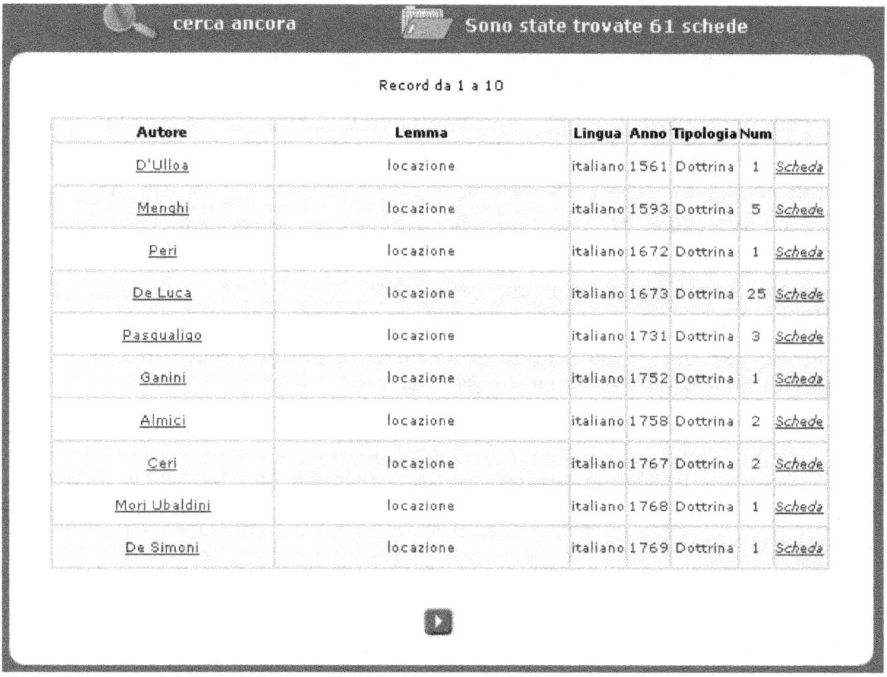

Autore	Lemma	Lingua	Anno	Tipologia	Num	
D'Ulloa	locazione	italiano	1561	Dottrina	1	Scheda
Menghi	locazione	italiano	1593	Dottrina	5	Schede
Peri	locazione	italiano	1672	Dottrina	1	Scheda
De Luca	locazione	italiano	1673	Dottrina	25	Schede
Pasqualigo	locazione	italiano	1731	Dottrina	3	Schede
Ganini	locazione	italiano	1752	Dottrina	1	Scheda
Almici	locazione	italiano	1758	Dottrina	2	Schede
Ceri	locazione	italiano	1767	Dottrina	2	Schede
Mori Ubaldini	locazione	italiano	1768	Dottrina	1	Scheda
De Simoni	locazione	italiano	1769	Dottrina	1	Scheda

Figure 1.

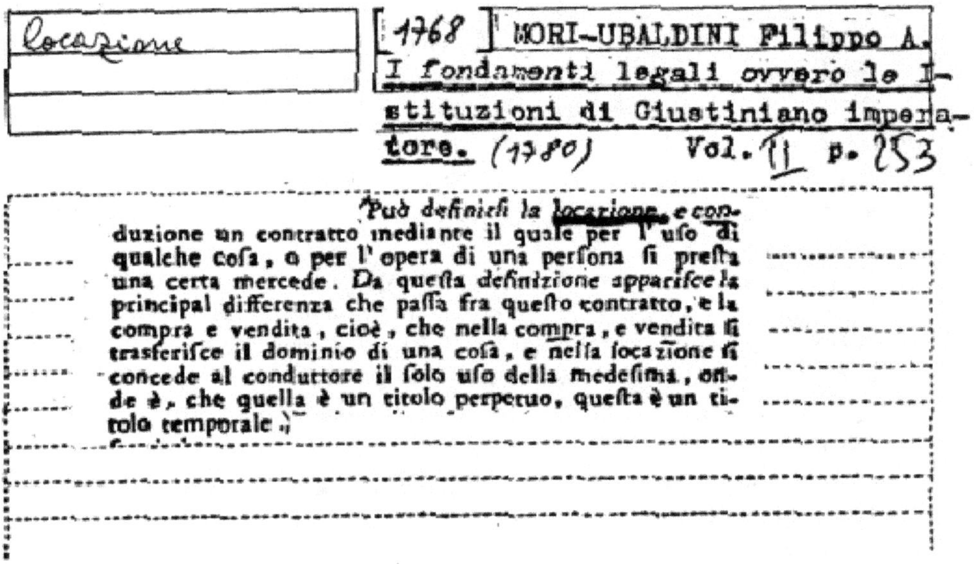

locazione

[1768] MORI-UBALDINI Filippo A.
I fondamenti legali ovvero le Istituzioni di Giustiniano imperatore. (1780) Vol. II p. 253

Può definirſi la locazione, e conduzione un contratto mediante il quale per l'uſo di qualche coſa, o per l'opera di una perſona ſi preſta una certa mercede. Da queſta definizione appariſce la principal differenza che paſſa fra queſto contratto, e la compra e vendita, cioè, che nella compra, e vendita ſi trasferiſce il dominio di una coſa, e nella locazione ſi concede al conduttore il ſolo uſo della medeſima, onde è, che quella è un titolo perpetuo, queſta è un titolo temporale.

Figure 2.

— by term (that includes the use of the whole term or part of it);
— by language. The archive also contains non-Italian head-words that have been found in the Italian documents covered. These are prevalently Latin terms that crystallised in legal language, for example *ab intestato, mortis causa, a latere*, but there are also terms in Greek, English, French, German, etc. This also makes the archive of interest to non-Italian scholars who may want to understand what terms in their own language are to be found in Italian sources, in what period and in what context;
— by date. This also has an important role; through the date, in fact, one can understand when a particular term first appeared or if it has fallen into disuse, or if it has had different meanings at different times and which of these appeared first;
— by author, or by document-type if the author is missing.

For every field, therefore, information required can be selected and the digital images associated with it can be accessed along with relevant bibliographical information.

One of the other important aspects of this archive is the fact that the terms it contains appertain to various legal fields (civil, criminal, commercial, canon etc.) and this makes it of interest to a wide variety of users.

The digitised documents do not just cover Italy's present territorial boundaries but all those areas in which over the years for historical reasons Italian was or still is used (for example Switzerland or Malta).

As an example let us take the English term 'allegiance', that in a generic sense signifies 'faithfulness'. If we perform a search with this word on the LGI, the results obtained show that this term appears twice in the legal science source (Esperson, 1892). It means perpetual subjectivity, a feudal relationship that ties a vassal to his lord. In the historical-legal source, therefore, this term acquires a precise connotation in relation to the historical context in which it is to be found.

LGI is also a source of information with regards to many institutional or honorary functions in Europe and beyond. One has only to note that documented legal locutions/syntagms such as 'consistory court', 'court of audience', 'permanent council' etc. are to found within it.

To take another example, the Latin syntagm *a latere* occurs in nine legal science "source-cards" between the years 1786 and 1949, and is associated with and refers to posts and roles such as that of legate\auxiliary\collaborator *a latere* different contexts.

Amongst German terms *Eigenthumsblatt*, for example, occurs in legal science dealing with transcription (Coviello, 1897) and means 'title deeds'.

These archives (LLI and LGI) can now be searched on-line and enable the user to analyse every documented term in its historic-semantic evolution.

The positive results obtained so far have challenged the ITTIG to carry out another ambitious project: the *Indice ragionato della lingua giuridica* (Legal Language Subject Index).

This will use a different legal-computing methodology because it will be structured as a kind of digital dictionary of legal language that provides documentation for a historical view-point via the evidence contained in the sources.

On the basis of the results obtained by LLI and LGI it is hoped that the Index will be created semi-automatically in order to rationalise efforts and workloads, and to help users in studying the historic-semantic evolution of each term.

This means that some of the information units, such as language, date, frequency etc. will be gleaned automatically from the ready made LLI and LGI archives.

A high level of historical-legal knowledge, as well as expert analysis will however be required to create other units such as: the finding of the single meaning of each term; the links with the "source-cards" that document corresponding meanings, and so on.

In any case, each field will be shown not only in Italian but in English, French and German in order to give non-Italian scholars easier access.

The result would be unprecedented in the historical-legal-linguistic sector and its effects would be felt over a long period.

More specifically, the starting point is LGI, which takes the form of a mixed database (namely, made up of alphanumeric data and images) in which textual data are linked to the descriptive images of the terms: for each of these the author, the year, its variants, the relative legal locutions/syntagms.

For every source-card reproduced, for a given term, there is the passage of a work in which the term is defined and/or put into context.

It is, therefore, necessary to design a program capable of linking the meaning of the term to every source-card in which it is described.

To reach this result, several operative phases have been planned:

- the processing of the LGI information unit in order to build a suitable data processing structure;
- the construction of editorial software for the insertion of the different meanings and for their association to the corresponding images;
- the construction of a software procedure so the Index can be searched by the end user.

3. A software tool for populating IS-LeGI

In order to manage the populating of the Subject Index, starting off from LGI, a descriptive table of every single term is generated in which the absolute frequency of the term in the historic-legal documents are displayed (that is, how many times the term appears in the historical texts in the database) and the frequencies relative to every single area (that is, how many times the term is found separately in legislation, in legal science and practice), together with the time-span.

Every term is linked to a table of the lexical variants and a table of the particularly important legal locutions/syntagms in legal language.

The data processed in this way are electronically retrieved from the LGI database from which the populating of the Subject Index is performed.

As we mentioned earlier, it should, above all, be noted that there is a need to build a software tool and a methodology for creating the Subject Index, which differs from the later query software to be created for the user, because it precedes it from both a logical and operative point of view.

The procedure must allow for the insertion of the meanings relating to every term.

For every term, in fact, the user can display:

— the language;
— the variants;
— the legal locutions/syntagms;
— the absolute frequency with its relative time-span;
— the relative frequencies by sector with their relative time-span.

These data are electronically retrieved from LGI.

The software must be capable of browsing all the images associated with a particular term. The term-image-source-card link can be retrieved from the LGI database, but this requires the analysis of the compiler which has to identify not only the meaning of the term in the legal text but also associate the individual source-cards with their corresponding semantic values.

In brief, for every source-card relating to a term, the software enables one of the following choices to be made:

— to select one of the meanings identified for a given term, and associate it with the corresponding image;
— to edit a new meaning and associate it with an image;
— to modify, both during the analysis and subsequently, one or more meanings previously identified for the term. This will automatically lead to the modification of the associations already made between that meaning and the analysed images.

We would like to stress that, when a meaning is associated to a certain source-card, reference can be made directly to the term or to the term specified in a particular legal locution/syntagm. In fact, sometimes for certain words which have different semantic values, the legal locutions/syntagms orient the user in distinguishing the meanings and contribute to defining or putting the term into context (for example, 'right' and 'law' may have many meanings: it is sufficient to bring to mind the legal locutions/syntagms 'the right to act', 'procedural law', 'acquired right' etc.).

The editorial interface is, therefore, composed of two zones: in the first, the data retrieved from LGI are to be found (the term, with its relative variants and legal locutions/syntagms; the language, the time-span existing between the first and the last meaning, the frequencies); the second is reserved for input activities, understood as: the display of the image and its association with the source-card of one of the available meanings; any insertion of a new meaning or modification of a pre-existing meaning.

There is also a link to the bibliographical data retrieved directly from the LGI database.

4. A software tool for searching in IS-LeGI

As far as the query software is concerned, it enables the user to search by term, by year, by author, and also by using Boolean operators.

The output of the search is represented by the following elements: frequencies; the list of meanings associated with the term and with its legal locutions/syntagms; source-cards relating to every meaning, and bibliographical references.

The applications have been developed in a web environment using the PHP4 language, which is compatible with both the Microsoft Windows server and with Unix, in different dialects.

As a database, mySQL was used.

As we have seen, computer technology has a strategic role in the recouping of enormous quantities of bibliographical resources.

The risk is to lose recuperated material because of the speed with which operating systems and modes change.

ITTIG researchers are particularly sensitive to this issue. The archives referred to here are the result of a "successful migration" in that the Institute has been able to convert their data from one operating system to another over the years. For example, if at first the paper "source-cards" containing information chosen were stored by using magnetic perforation, which allowed the automatic alphabetical ordering of terms, they have now been digitised with the scanner.

Techniques to preserve material are therefore as important as digitisation if we are to avoid the loss of the heritage of our legal culture.

These are very useful tools for learning about and conserving legal language, that is, a specialised and technical language which needs to be analysed in all its aspects. Among these, the historical-semantic aspect is particularly important, because it constitutes the primary dimension from which the law, through its language, expresses itself, transforms and adapts to society.

IS-LeGI software is oriented to web and it is possible to manage it in different platforms, and compatible with Microsoft Windows, Unix, Linux. In the following figure, we can have a brief view and see the different tables that form the working page.

- Card imagine with the word context. We can see the main card identifications (author, legal partition, language, date);
- Headword table with the global frequency and some indications to the historical dictionaries where the word is documented;
- Form table with its phraseology linked;
- Meaning table that is linked with card imagine and the phraseology.

Actually the tool has a data base of 4000 headwords. This is the result of a precise selection developed according the computational linguistics methods.

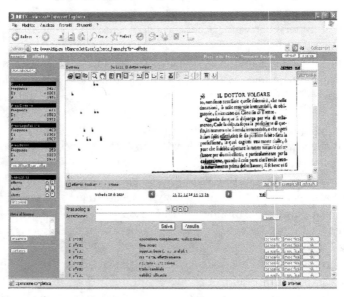

Figure 3.

References

Coviello N. (1897), *Della trascrizione*, Eugenio Marghieri, Napoli, Vol. I., 503 pp.

Esperson P. (1892), *Condizione giuridica dello straniero secondo le legislazioni e le giurisprudenze italiane ed estere*, Milano, Vol. un., pt. 2.

VI SECTION

Strategic Solutions and Sustainability Models for the Diffusion and Sharing of Legal Knowledge

Foundlings on the Cathedral Steps

Thomas R. Bruce

Director, Legal Information Institute, Cornell Law School, USA

Abstract. Legal Information Institutes, which operate extensive search apparatus in their own right, differ from Internet-wide search engines in the way they think about search engine functionality, privacy exposures, and ultimately about user experience. This paper outlines some differences and suggests means of reconciliation.

Keywords: Search, Google, metadata, LII.

1. LIIs in the age of Google

Internet publishers who offer significant amounts of well-ordered information create localized worlds of meaning. That is what information architects do. Most participate in a second world created predominantly by Internet-wide search engines. Google, and to a lesser extent others,[1] create meaning by ordering and presenting information according to a coherent scheme. That benefits the Internet audience simply because it helps them to find things, and to make good guesses about how things might be found.

Publishers want to be in Google's world. The public overwhelmingly use search engines as the first point of entry to the Internet. 61% of the 1.2 million unique visits to the LII last month began with a search engine of some kind. Of those, 80% came from Google, with the remainder divided roughly equally between Yahoo and the English-language version of Wikipedia. Google is, in this way, more than half of public access.

Some information providers choose to secede from that world. Participation is the default, but the architect can more-or-less selectively choose to have Google and other search engines pass her world by. Secession is an affirmative choice made by constructing technical apparatus – robots.txt files and <meta> tags – that selectively limit access to all or part of a web site.

There are parts of Google's world that are not so nice. It rips away privacy protections traditionally enforced by obscurity. In matters of metadata, it is a rigid theocracy that relies on the ignorance of its believers for survival, and allows them little if any self-determination. Yet this is the reason that information consumers overwhelmingly want to live under its dominion. Rigidity is seen as the incorruptible foundation of functionality. But it sometimes results in a system that deals less effectively than it might with particular domains like law.

---

[1] According to Hitwise <**www.hitwise.com/press-center/hitwiseHS2004/ leader-record-growth.php**>, Google accounted for 68% of search traffic in May 2008.

LIIs, like other information providers, may choose whether and when they
want to join Google's world. Some participate fully; others have seceded completely; most join but opt out at times. This paper explores both worlds and
the relative advantages and disadvantages of participation. I am particularly
concerned with what happens as information seekers – the foundlings of the
title – cross boundaries from one world to the other, since so many of them
traverse Google's world to enter our own.

2. Two worlds compared: Philosophy

Google's operating philosophy contrasts sharply with that of LIIs, libraries,
and other large-scale information organizers. (Wolfe, 2005) distinguishes three
important differences in belief, to which I add a fourth:

2.1. SELF-DESCRIPTION

Google believes that all information objects found on the web should describe
themselves, and that they do. For Google, this self-description is limited to the
content of the object itself – metadata doesn't count. By contrast, LIIs and
others don't believe that objects necessarily *do* describe themselves. The most
glaring examples are non-textual objects, whose important qualities elude full-
text indexing. That is why sites like Flickr and YouTube are runaway victories
for user-supplied metadata; social tagging is the most practical means of
making their content discoverable. Multimedia objects are not so common
in law, but there are other, better illustrations of the problem. A simple
and compelling example from American practice is official citation, which
has historically been assigned well after judicial opinions have been collected,
printed, and bound and is thus almost never found within the web-published
version.

Too, under any system that incorporates both precedent and reasoning
by analogy, an index confined to words found in a judicial opinion may miss
its significance entirely.[2] This problem is familiar to law catalogers; it happens when new analogies suggest new meanings for a case. Too, a particular
document may be one chapter in the story of a dispute whose resolution lies
elsewhere. Legal texts frequently omit information about procedural context,
related documents and other bits of information without which it is impossible to understand them. Understanding and utility are often found in a
collection of related documents, and not in any one standing alone. Complete
self-description within a single document can thus be hard to come by.

---

[2] For some interesting views on this relationship, see (Berring, 1986; Delgado and
Stefancic, 1989).

Finally, reliance on self-description assumes that the average reader knows the language of the description. In legal documents, as well as in other specialist domains, this is seldom the case (Tiersma, 1999). Description, and particularly classification, uses a vocabulary that is specialized, technical, and often abstract.

2.2. TRUST AND USER-GENERATED DATA

Google's oft-advertised belief is that publisher-generated metadata is wholly unreliable. This belief is justified by deliberately deceptive metadata practices used by some[3] to raise Google rank for commercial advantage.

That is what makes Google a rigid theocracy. A regime based on trust-related parameters relies crucially on publishers remaining ignorant of the methods used to weight the parameters involved. What publishers understand, publishers will manipulate. Thus, the only way to guarantee accuracy is to keep publishers as ignorant as possible of the workings of the system. The outward-facing version of Google's well-known internal mantra – "don't be evil" – is "thou shalt not lie about your data". In fact, they won't let you. The system is paternalistic (as (Lynch, 2000) termed it) because maintains innocence by enforcing ignorance, pre-empting the occasion of sin. It is theocratic insofar as it relies on, and reinforces, boundless belief in the capacity of clever information science to overcome any disadvantages created by this rejection of publisher-supplied metadata.

LIIs, libraries, and other high-quality data providers don't share this belief. They may be offended by it. They have spent careers in perfecting solid metadata practices that enforce accuracy and integrity, and strengthen the association between metadata and the objects it represents. They believe, in other words, that there is such a thing as a trusted source of high-quality metadata. Most have aspired to this status. Google denies those aspirations.

There is evidence that Google trusts metadata provided by some publishers. It is, of course, impossible to confirm this, because of Goog-le's secrecy with respect to their internal practices. At times[4] they have denied any such preference. Experimental searching on legal citations shows evidence of trust. Searching **540 US 736** (without quotes) produces a list of sites that have *US Postal Service v. Flamingo Industries* (for which 540 US 736 is the official cite) – significantly, sites that are either official or considered similarly reliable sources for Supreme Court cases. By contrast, searching 302 F.3d 905 – the Circuit Court decision it reverses – produces the confused results you would expect if each token in the citation were being treated as an independent term.

---

[3] Numerous articles and blog postings catalog abusive SEO practices. A good example is from about.com, at <google.about.com/od/searchengineoptimization/tp/badseo.htm>.

[4] See generally Weblink SEO, at <www.weblinkseo.com/seo-guides/google-trustrank.jsp>. Despite having registered the mark, Google subsequently denied any use of such an algorithm.

It would appear that, in the case of the Supreme Court decisions, citation metadata from some sites is considered reliable enough to build into the search process in some way.

2.3. RELEVANCE

In Google's world, relevance is a function of popularity. The PageRank system that works so well in determining relevance interprets links as votes; the more heavily linked a site or page is, the better its rank.[5] The simplistic view of this vastly complicated system is that the more people who link to you, the more relevant you must be. This belief rests on the billions of affirmative acts of link-authorship that Google sees as establishing meaning on the Web. There are other ways of establishing relevance. In law, jurisdiction and subsequent history can be much more important than anything else. Systems that help determine the relevance of a case to a given litigant (Wildeboer, Klein, Uijttenbroek, 2007) are possible, but not yet at commercial scale. And some[6] have long suggested alternate methods of determining relevance, such as co-citation.

Indeed, many domains offer better measures of relevance, or at least some worth mixing in. In a way, Google accounts for them – certainly it assumes that some such criteria form part of the authorial decision-making that precedes construction of a link. And it may do so explicitly, as it does when it recognizes statutory citations as phrases rather than a string of tokens. But this is clearly an area where general methods may not work nearly as well as those that recognize domain-specific criteria.

2.4. PRIVACY

Google is an extremely effective information-discovery tool. It demolishes any privacy regime that relies on practical obscurity. This is particularly vexing to LIIs that wish to act responsibly in exposing personal information. I won't rehearse the many policy arguments that have been made around this issue, beyond pointing out that (as many others have remarked[7]) there is an essential tension between principles of openness in the courts and protection of privacy rights that can only be resolved by publicly-debated and agreed-on compromise.

There is no philosophical disagreement about the need to protect individuals. Rather, it is a question of implementation and responsibility. Google offers protection of personal information. It does so in a way that requires the

---

[5] PageRank is explained at <en.wikipedia.org/wiki/PageRank>.

[6] The most recent example is PreCYdent (<www.precydent.com/>), but the literature on co-citation in legal information retrieval stretches back into the 1980s. An interesting related survey is (Martens and Betsy, 2001).

[7] For one view, see (Anderson, 2007).

individual to notify Google that something is awry, and (usually) to notify the actual publisher of the information as well, since any effective remedy typically requires action by whoever operates the site on which the information appears[8] as well as by Google. Google's "policy" consists of a promise to remove any offending object from its indexing process, and a series of prescriptions for avoiding indexing in the first place. It does not – and practically, cannot – require Google to proactively evaluate the documents it indexes before indexing them. It is a simple apparatus by which web publishers may declare exceptions to the default: the belief that publishers want their information to be discoverable. Those publishers are not, typically, the individuals whose privacy is being violated and are not, typically, the real violators – the violation originates with the courts.

Despite their third-party status, public legal information providers have been quick – perhaps too quick – to take responsibility for the problem. This is largely a matter of principle and partly a matter of protecting their supply chain. Courts have always been sensitive to privacy problems, and the very real possibility of identity theft has made them even more so. These sensitivities reflect a certain nervousness about releasing opinions on the Internet at all. To the extent that LIIs believe that courts will refuse to make their opinions available if they see privacy risks, they perceive a potential threat to their operations.

But it is not really the practices of the LIIs that ought to be questioned. The text of decisions originates in courts, and it can most effectively be shaped there. This is really two activities: enforcement of redaction policies,[9] and a vigorous effort to limit collateral damage to privacy that results from heedless administrative practice (such as using personal identifiers as the basis for docket numbers) and careless opinion-drafting (such as exposing information about individuals, even non-parties, that is in no way relevant to the case). Collateral damage of the second type is surprisingly common, and is likely to elude definition in concrete policies.

Publishers who take on the role of privacy-enforcer relieve public bodies of their obligation to formulate and enforce reasonable policies of their own. Moreover, publishers are private actors who often act without public input. The extent to which they act as agents of public bodies may be unclear. In this way, privacy policy becomes the province of well-intentioned vigilantes, and not of public policy publicly arrived at.

---

[8] Google's numerous privacy policies – some are technology-specific – are enunciated at <www.google.com/privacy.html>.

[9] For one thoroughly articulated policy, see the New York State Commission on Public Access to Court Records "Report to the Chief Judge of the State of New York", online at <www.nycourts.gov/ip/publicaccess/>.

3. Shared problems, contrasting remedies

Though they may differ in operational philosophy, Google and the LIIs share some practical problems. LIIs are search-engine operators, just as Google is. Each encounters difficulties inherent in relevance-based search-engine technology itself. It is the remedies for those difficulties that are different from one setting to the other. Because their operations are both smaller and domain-focussed, LIIs can sometimes provide better solutions.

In this section, at last, we meet our foundlings: hapless information-seekers abandoned on the steps of our web sites by general-purpose search engines. This abandonment takes several forms, described in the paragraphs that follow.

3.1. CONTEXT-SMASHING

From the perspective of the information seeker, any search engine is a kind of teleportation device. Click on a search result, and you are transported past information structure and navigational apparatus into a specific document. The seeker arrives without seeing any of the surrounding terrain. In short, she is without context. The user has no immediate way to interpret where what has been discovered fits in the greater scheme of things. Worse, she has no ability to discover other, possibly better, documents that are in some informational sense adjacent to the document she has found. Neither of these well-known problems is likely to be solved by increased precision in the search engine: each happens because the retrieved document is too specific for the user to understand. The solution lies not in drilling-down, but in jumping-up to an overview of the material. That in turn relies on classificatory metadata, possibly automatically generated, as a later section will describe.

3.2. ONTOLOGICAL MISMATCH

Law novices seek legal information – particularly caselaw – based on fact patterns (Dabney, 1999).[10] They select search terms that describe their situation. By contrast, legal information retrieval systems – at least those intended for lawyers – organize and present material that, most of the time, describes itself using formal legal terminology within an expert framework. The user troubled by a neighbor's noisy pet – a "barking dog" – is not likely to use "nuisance" as a search term. This is not merely, as Peter Tiersma has pointed out, (Tiersma, 1999, p. 203) a matter of replacing specialist vocabulary with words that are easier for ordinary people to understand and use. In some cases "law language" is both necessary and irreplaceable, requiring education rather than translation to promote understanding. Other aspects of the problem stretch

---

[10] Considerable evidence confirming Dabney's insight is found in Cornell's search logs.

the limits of what is possible using information architecture and information science.

3.3. PRESENTATION OF RESULTS

Information seeking is more than monotonous, ritual submission of terms to a search engine, and the aim is usually more than the simple amassing of information. There is a target problem in the real world about which information is being sought. Different stages of the problem-solving process require different strategies as understanding of the target problem and its domain increases. Search engines have no way to know what point the information-seeker has reached in this process of discovery, and depend on the user to manipulate their workings differently at each stage. Too often, the capacity to sort and filter both what is searched and what is returned in a result set are too limited to support such strategies effectively. Generally, what is wanted is the ability to restrict or order what is retrieved based on some metadata item, such as the name of the court or judge. Sometimes, too, it is possible that entirely different measurements of relevance would be more helpful at a particular stage of the process. This is the case usually addressed by "law specific" search engines (such as PreCYdent)[11] that use (eg.) co-citation or other document relationships as an important factor in determining relevance.

3.4. ILLUSORY COMPLETENESS

Search engines promise comfort and certainty. They return such a mass of results from so wide a space that we think we must be seeing everything there is to see. But they have blind spots; the problem of reaching into the "deep Web" is well known, which offers a useful literature survey (Zillman, 2008). More, they are not good at distinguishing the object of a search from countless other documents that refer to it. The searcher who wants information about a piece of equipment, and searches for it by model number, will find herself sifting through pages of references to sites that sell the item. And a search on a case by party name commonly produces pages of commentary and media coverage before one reaches the actual text of the decision. Finally, as was pointed out earlier, there are places where relevance is determined entirely by factors that search engines may ignore in their determination of relevance, such as jurisdiction.

---

[11] See the PreCYdent web site at `<www.precydent.com>`.

4. What can be done to bring these two worlds together?

If our goal is to go beyond making law available to making it truly accessible (Kirby, 1999), we need to work out sensible ways for public legal information providers to co-exist with large-scale search engines in some synergistic way. Secession is unrealistic and ultimately damaging. The public uses Internet-wide search engines as its principal means of information discovery. Claiming that shutting spiders out is no big deal because "everyone knows where to find us" really amounts to saying that lawyers know where to find us; first-time users don't. Many prefer, are seduced by, or are habituated to the convenience of using the same apparatus they use when they seek other types of information. We need to give the public entry points along pathways that they are accustomed to follow when they look for other kinds of information.

Failure to do so risks obsolescence, and ultimately irrelevance. The combination of authoritative information offered directly by courts and legislatures with the integrated, Internet-wide search capability is something that will, ultimately, route around third-party free-access providers such as LIIs if we do not find effective means to work with it.

The question, then, is how to create policies and technical apparatus that create synergies with Google and other services like it – ways of taking care of those who have been left on our steps by Internet-wide search engines. Partly this is a matter of doing things that others have done for some time now. We must also improve our own internal information discovery capabilities. We can then build on those accomplishments to create seamless and useful pathways from external to internal search.

4.1. IMPROVE "GOOGLE-FACING" DATA

Improving the way in which we present ourselves to Internet-wide search engines is an important first step. Little that I suggest is novel, though equally little is commonly done by free-access providers.

4.1.1. *End unnecessary use of dynamic pages*
Dynamically-constructed web pages, built "on the fly" from databases, are notoriously hard to index. They are also very much overused in the world of legal information. Even legislation – far less stable than judicial opinions in matters of updating – does not change all that frequently.[12] For example, the performance of most systems run by the US Government Printing Office would be hugely improved by generating static pages from databases only as often as is required by the update cycle. Such an approach produces pages that are easy to index, solves performance problems related to database latency, and

---

[12] For example, even the most chaotic Title of the US Code – tax law – shows only 625 changes since January 3, 2007.

if properly designed makes it easier for other sites to create persistent links that improve navigation and enhance value.

4.1.2. *Recognize the importance of <title>*

Google and others pay little if any attention to site-generated metadata. But they do make extensive use of what they find inside the <title> tag, in two ways. Titles get extra weight in relevance measures, and they reliably appear in search result lists, thus having indicative value for the user trying to decide what to look at first. We could make better use of that; most LIIs and public bodies place only minimal information (often only a cite) in the title. More expansive use (including party names and all other relevant identifiers) would be a great help.

4.1.3. *Improve cross-linkage*

Rich cross-linkage is immeasurably important to navigation, discovery, and relevance ranking. We do less of it than we might, partly because it is difficult for any one site to do at scale using unsupervised software. Public infrastructure that would support cross-linkage among public access legal information providers – particularly citation resolvers – would make this task much easier.

4.2. Improve iInternal Search

We must help the first-time user to find what she is seeking *at the point where an Internet-wide search engine has led her directly to something that is either confusing or inadequate.* This is a matter of offering the context that will provide help in finding what she really wants, and of making our (presumably superior) searching capabilities obvious and attractive. We are competing for the attention of the *second-time* user, who would find her information-seeking task shorter and easier were she to come to us in the first place. For us, the best outcome of a Google search is that the user bookmark our advanced search page.

4.2.1. *Restore adjacencies*

We often emphasize search precision at the expense of effectiveness, which often depends more on the ability to orient oneself on unfamiliar information terrain than it does on immediate arrival at a single focussed result. For the naive user, a table of contents that provides a map of sections adjacent to the one an algorithm has found most relevant may provide a shorter path to what is being sought than direct teleportation into a document whose context is unknown.

4.2.2. *Search and navigate across stovepipes*

We have long recognized the importance of richly-linked collections. Many practical problems remain in reaching the goal of seamless navigation between statutes, regulations, and the judicial decisions that interpret them (not to mention legislation in process, updated materials, legislative history, interpretive guidance documents, and other materials). Barriers to simple availability are going away – perhaps more slowly than we would like, but going away nevertheless. Collection integration is coming to the fore. We need more sophisticated systems for creating linkage with materials as we discover them, and for resolving legacy identifiers such as print citation into meaningful navigation to online materials. Net-wide citation resolvers loom large in this respect, and they in turn rely on painstaking work on namespaces, identifiers, and other scaffolding.

4.2.3. *Expand and improve our use of metadata*

Google has good reason to disregard metadata, but we should make better use of it than we do. Partly this is because we have long seen metadata solely as support for fielded searching (which it certainly is) and ignored its use as a means of relating documents to each other, either across collection-stovepipes or across more abstract boundaries between pools of instances and the explanatory documents that help us understand them.

Practical metadata use is admittedly bound by economics. Human-created metadata, particularly classificatory metadata, is expensive to produce – and still more expensive when nuanced, expert decisions are part of its creation. But computable metadata is relatively cheap and highly functional, and becoming more so as machine-learning and language technologies improve. Automated metadata extraction (Lee and Carroll, 2008) and ontology generation (Yang and Callan, 2008) are techniques that can help tilt the cost-benefit ratio in favor of improved use of metadata. And practical understanding of metadata administration and quality control (Bruce and Hillmann, 2004) are increasing as well, particularly in the world of aggregated digital collections of scientific papers, where much of the work has been done.

4.2.4. *Use novel forms of results presentation*

On most sites, the presentation of search results is inflexible. Ordering and filtering of search results is a particularly good use of metadata. Given a large number of results for the most well-crafted search imaginable, it ought to be possible to order or filter by judge, by jurisdiction, by various types of date, and other domain-specific criteria. Similarly, we ought to be able to aggregate and present results based on structural relationships, co-citation, and other criteria outside conventional ideas of relevance. For example, an interface that structures the results of a search of the US Code in the same manner as the Code itself would provide valuable relevance clues to the user, who can readily distinguish which parts of the structure are relevant to him in ways that machines cannot.

5. Conclusion: improving the transition between worlds

With those things done, we can think about how better to help, rather than abandon, our foundlings. Some simple tricks may be effective. For example, capturing the user's Google search (available in the referer header) and either rerunning it automatically against the site's own search apparatus, or offering the user the option of doing so, may well be useful, and especially so if the search is enhanced by assumptions about intentions that are easier to make in a law specific search engine than in a tool of general application. It is a pretty safe bet that anything with a "v." in the middle is a search for caselaw, at least in the US.

Restoring the context that is stripped away when the user is abandoned inside a relevant-but-too-specific result is more difficult, but it is an important step. This is a matter of first developing or discovering relevant secondary and explanatory resources, and then making them available to the user via some form of navigation. Online newspapers and discussion systems do this successfully now, providing links to related stories and threads. The principal problem for free-access providers is finding the material to point to; useful explanatory resources in law are fairly scarce, though they are growing. Organizing and presenting them is a large-scale problem in standardizing and integrating metadata development in ways that are useful.

No doubt there are other useful means of bringing the two worlds together. Most important is that we stop treating them as something that should be separated; that will have no good result for LIIs in the long run.

References

Anderson, K. (2007), *Balancing Privacy Rights with Accessibility*, 8th International Conference "Law via the Internet", Montreal, 25-26 October 2007, available at: <conf.lexum.umontreal.ca/proceedings_documents/5-Kerry_Anderson.pdf>.

Berring, R.C. (1986), *Full-text Databases and Legal Research: Backing into the Future*, High Technology Law Journal, Vol. 27, No. 1, pp. 27-60.

Bruce, T.R. and Hillmann, D. (2004), *The Continuum of Metadata Quality: Defining, Expressing, Exploiting*, in Hillmann, D. and Westbrooks, E. (Eds.), "Metadata In Practice", Ala Edictions, Chicago, pp. 248-249, available at: <content.nsdl.org/metadata/practice/hillmann/bruce/final.html>.

Dabney, D. (1999), *The mangy dog and other stories my computer told me*, in CALI Conference for Law School Technology Professionals (unpublished talk).

Delgado, R. and Stefancic, J. (1989), *Why do we tell the same stories?*, Stanford Law Review, Vol. 42, p. 206.

Kirby, M. (1999), *Freeing the Law: Beyond the Dark Chaos*, UNSWLJ 8.

Lee, T.Y. and Carroll, J. (2008), *A Genetic Algorithm for Segmentation and Information Retrieval of SEC Regulatory Filings*, in "Proceedings of the 9th International Digital Government Research Conference", Montreal, Canada, May 18-21, 2008, pp. 44-52.

Lynch, C.A. (2000), *Authenticity and Integrity in the Digital Environment: An Exploratory Analysis of the Central Role of Trust*, Authenticity in a Digital Environment, Council on Library and Information Resources, Washington, DC, pp. 32-50.

Martens and Betsy (2001), *Do citation systems represent theories of truth?*, Information Research, Vol. 6, No. 2.

Tiersma, P. (1999), *Legal Language*, University of Chicago Press, Chicago, pp. 203-211.

Wildeboer, G.R., Klein, M.C.A., Uijttenbroek, E.M. (2007), *Explaining the Relevance of Court Decisions to Laymen*, in "Legal Knowledge and Information Systems", IOS Press, Amsterdam.

Wolfe, R. (2005), *The Value of Metadata in the Google Era*, MIT Libraries presentation, available at: <libraries.mit.edu/metadata/presentations/valuemetadatarev.ppt>.

Yang, H. and Callan, J. (2008), *Ontology Generation for Large e-Mail Collections*, in "Proceedings of the 9th International Digital Government Research Conference", Montreal, Canada, May 18-21, 2008, pp. 254-261.

Zillman, M.P. (2008), *Deep Web research*, LLRX.com, available at: <www.llrx.com/features/deepweb2008.htm>.

AustLII's Business Models: Constraints and Opportunities in Funding Free Access to Law

Graham Greenleaf

University of New South Wales and Co-Director, AustLII, Australia

Abstract. The Australasian Legal Information Institute (AustLII) has provided free access to an increasing range and amount of legal information from Australia for thirteen years since 1995. This paper analyses the constraints within which AustLII operates. It then describes the business model – or to be more accurate, the combination of business models – that have enabled it to do so, and some of the challenges involved in it doing so in a sustainable way in the future. The tentative conclusion is that the combination of business models adopted by AustLII, particularly in 2007 and 2008, is capable of sustaining is operations, at least in relation to maintenance of its existing databases, and probably for the creation of new and improved resources to a modest extent.

1. Introduction

1.1. CHANGING BUSINESS MODELS

Grameen Bank gives microcredit.[1] It was founded by Nobel Prize winner Prof Mohammad Yunus of Bangladesh. In 2005 he decided to prove that the bank could extend its model to the lowest strata of society, which it called its 'Struggling (Beggar) Members'. It offered these members credit of less than US$10 at local stores, allowed the (former) beggars to buy small amounts of matches, snacks etc, so as to give their clients a choice of either responding to their begging pleas, or buying something from them. Grameen also offered provision of a mobile phone repayable over 2 years interest-free, allowed its Struggling Members to offer purchase of phone calls as alternative to begging. Within a year over 750 Struggling Members had quit begging. They had become businesspersons. But many others still kept the security of a diversified business model. The moral?: It's never too late to change your business model.

Free-access law providers often start their operations with a grant, perhaps from an academic funding body, an international aid agency, or a philanthropic body. If they are successful, they soon have lots of little databases that are popular with users, and justify the original grant. But after a year or three, or longer if they are lucky, the original grant runs out, and the grant body informs them that it only provides start-up funds, not maintenance. But the little databases keep growing every year, and need more and more resources to sustain them.

---

[1] See: <www.grameen-info.org/>.

1.2. Legal Information Institutes and funding

The hallmark of 'Legal Information Institutes' (LIIs) is that they provide 'free access' to 'public legal information'.[2] There are now 27 such LIIs forming the 'Free Access to Law Movement' (Greenleaf, 2008).[3] From the perspective of their users, the LIIs are free to use, but of course they are not free to build or maintain. However, little has been written on the business models that LIIs have utilised to fund their operations.

The Australasian Legal Information Institute (AustLII) has provided free access to an increasing range and amount of legal information for thirteen years since 1995. In 2007 it faced a funding crisis due to becoming overly dependent on one main source of funding, a competitive academic grant. When it did not obtain that grant for 2007 it had to examine how it could sustain its operations, and diversify its sources of funding. Necessity proved to be the mother of invention once again, and this paper reflects on what can be learned from the last two years.

Since all LIIs operate in different contexts, and with slightly different objectives within the overall goals of their shared *Declaration on Free Access to Law* of the 2002 we can expect that the relevance of AustLII's experience will vary greatly between LIIs. However, sharing experience of business models is of value to all operators of information services based on free or open content.

1.3. Business models based on 'open' content

There are an increasing number of studies which analyse the ways in which successful, sustainable, business models can be developed around various ways of providing content to users without requiring them to pay directly to access or use the content. For example, (Clarke, 2007) attempts to answer the question 'what business models enable content-developers to make their materials available in a content commons by means of open content licences, rather than seeking monopoly rents from the works by means of copyright licensing fees?' He uses the questions (i) 'Who Pays? (Consumers Pay; Producers Pay; Third Parties Pay); (ii) For What?; (iii) Why?; (iv) To Whom?' to categorise a wide array of what he calls open content business models.

Every non-government free access provider to law operates within unique constraints. However, the factors that are probably most common are that (i) funding will usually be very limited; and (ii) funding will rarely be long-term.

---

[2] 'Public legal information means legal information produced by public bodies that have a duty to produce law and make it public. It includes primary sources of law, such as legislation, case law and treaties, as well as various secondary (interpretative) public sources, such as reports on preparatory work and law reform, and resulting from boards of inquiry. It also includes legal documents created as a result of public funding.': *Declaration on Free Access to Law*, 2002 (see the Appendix of this volume).

[3] Since that article, there are six additional members, from Uganda, Argentina, Jersey, France, Thailand and Mexico (see the Appendix of this volume).

As a result (iii) a high level of automation is desirable; and (iv) high levels of editorial intervention are probably unsustainable long-term.

This paper uses AustLII as a case study, starting with an analysis of just what 'open content' means in the context of AustLII's operations, then moving to an analysis of the elements which have made up AustLII's business model, and those which could do so in future.

2. The context of AustLII's business operations

2.1. AustLII's CORE business

AustLII is a free access provider of legal information (AustLII, 2000, 5.4), operated as a joint facility by the Faculties of Law at the University of Technology, Sydney (UTS) and the University of New South Wales (UNSW). It has been supported since its inception through a 1994 funding application by the Council of Australian Law Deans (CALD) as research infrastructure benefiting all law schools. It has been operated on a non-profit basis by its host Universities, who are at present considering restructuring part of its Australian operations as a corporation with charitable objectives, so as to make donations funding easier to manage.

The AustLII website provides over 270 databases of Australian law including: consolidated legislation from all 9 jurisdictions; annual legislation and bills from some; Point-in-Time legislation from three States; decisions from over 120 Courts and Tribunals (half of which are not otherwise available online); all Australian Treaties since 1900; law reform reports from all jurisdictions; and over 40 law journals in full text. The historical depth of its case law is very variable, often extending only 5-10 years, but it extends back to the commencement of almost all federal Courts and Tribunals, including being comprehensive for High Court decisions back to the Court's first decision in 1903. Subject-oriented searchable 'Libraries' are being developed in some subjects. The AustLII-developed open source Sino search engine provides Boolean and proximity operators, fast response times, and displays of search results by relevance, date or database. AustLII's Australian databases obtain over 650,000 accesses per day, and it is the largest online provider of access to Australian law.

The multi-country LIIs (WorldLII, AsianLII and CommonLII) operated by AustLII have a joint function. They are portals which involve the provision of access to about 400 databases developed and maintained by other LIIs. The also include over 250 databases maintained by AustLII), plus the largest Internet catalog of law-related websites (WorldLII Catalog) (Greenleaf, 2008). These databases and Catalog receive around 100,000 accesses per day. They are maintained by a much smaller number of staff, mainly because they are not updated as frequently. This paper does not deal with how those international services are funded.

AustLII's annual budget was approximately A\$1.5M between 2000-06 (as at December 2008, A\$1 is worth approximately US \$0.66). On average, 65-75% of this budget has been expended on AustLII's Australian operations, with the amount varying somewhat depending on the nature of grants obtained from year to year. Subsequent amounts are in Australian dollars.

2.2. CONSTRAINT #1: 'MISSION CONSTRAINTS'

The main constraints within which AustLII works are indicated by its location in two University Law Faculties, and its Mission Statement based on an explicit commitment to 'free public access', according to which it has operated for fourteen years.

Universities place high value on grants for research and research infrastructure, and also a value on reputational benefits that accrue to the Universities from high visibility public service such as providing public access to law. On the other hand, they are very adverse to reputational and legal risks. UNSW has a high commitment to Asian engagement, which assists some of AustLII's international projects. The two Law Faculties have similar values to the Universities, particularly in relation to the obtaining of grants. UNSW Law Faculty places an unusually high value on 'social justice' activities, within which AustLII's provision of public access fits comfortably. Similar values are found at UTS Law Faculty.

2.3. CONSTRAINT #2: 'FREE ACCESS' IS NOT 'OPEN CONTENT'

'Open content' is properly used to refer to content that anyone may reproduce, either because it is in the public domain (in the narrow sense) because of the expiry of copyright, or because the copyright owner has made it available for reproduction by a licence to the public such as a Creative Commons licence. Very little content available for free access via the AustLII website is 'open content' in this sense. First, legislation and case decisions and administrative documents (such as law reform reports) are all subject to Crown copyright in Australia. Although the Berne Convention specifically enables governments to exempt such documents from copyright protection, Australia has not done so, unlike most other countries in the world.[4] The Copyright Law Review Committee (CLRC) recommended that Crown copyright (2005) in legislation and case law be repealed, but that has not yet occurred. AustLII supported such repeal in a submission to the CLRC.

---

[4] For example, of the 27/28 countries in Asia with copyright laws, only a handful (North Korea, Myanmar, Brunei and Singapore) retain government copyright in legislation: (Greenleaf, Chung, Mowbray, 2007); an as-yet-incomplete survey by the author of European countries shows much the same situation.

These factors flowing from Australian copyright law impose a number of very significant limitations on what business models AustLII can adopt. First, most data on AustLII cannot be described as 'open content': neither AustLII nor its users are permitted to republish the data for purposes other than which it is impliedly or expressly provided, with the exception of data from New South Wales or the Northern Territory (where commercial re-use is permitted). Second, AustLII could not knowingly provide at least some of the data it receives to other parties for them to republish for commercial purposes.

Only the State of New South Wales (since the early 1990s) and the Northern Territory (more recently) have made declarations that their legislation and case law may be reproduced for any purpose, subject to some minimal conditions concerning integrity of the information. From some other Australian jurisdictions, when AustLII receives legislation or case law from the government providers of same, it does so on the basis that it is receiving it for the purposes of providing free access to the public via publication on the AustLII website, and consequently receives an implied licence to do so for that purpose. Any use of that information outside the terms of the implied licence would be a breach of copyright by AustLII. From yet other Australian jurisdictions, AustLII receives legislation and case law under formal contracts between the State government and AustLII's host Universities, the terms of which are sometimes even more restrictive. For example, the contracts are explicit that AustLII may only use the data provided for the provision of free access services. The contract concerning legislation from one State even specifies the data formats in which AustLII is permitted to provide legislation to its users.

2.4. Constraint #3: Web spiders and search engines

The environmental factor that Internet-wide search engines used web spiders/robots to make most of the world-wide-web searchable imposes on AustLII privacy constraints concerning case law. Australian courts do not allow web spiders to access their cases, so AustLII cannot do so either (and has not done since 1995, before Australian courts developed their own policies). It would also be fatal to AustLII's reputation, as we find from the sudden rush of complaints every time a search engine web spider makes a mistake and indexes some of our case law content. But this depends on the legal culture of the country concerned.

Internet-wide search engines also pose some other dilemmas for LIIs. Allowing search engines to search other content on AustLII (legislation, law journals etc) increases access rates, and assists in demonstrating value to stakeholders, so it is useful. Search engines benefit through advertisements from the value-adding to source data undertaken by LIIs, without paying any of the cost of that value-adding. The same can be said for any content which content providers allow search engines to make searchable. AustLII, like most other LIIs, has made the strategic decision to let web spiders into all AustLII content except case law.

2.5. ASSESSING OPPORTUNITIES AND RISKS

The expression 'business models' can refer to both profit-making organisations and to non-profit organisations such as AustLII that nevertheless have to cover their costs of operation, usually from a variety of activities which generate revenue, and which we will call 'business activities'. Any activities of an organisation involve some potential risks, even if only the risk of loss of the financial cost of carrying out the activity if it does not generate the expected revenue. Risks to reputation are also important. Business activities also involve the potential to generate revenue. The approach taken in this paper is to broadly categorise actual or possible business activities into those that are more promising and those that are less promising, based mainly on the possible risks involved. In other words it is a moderately conservative 'risk avoiding' analysis.

3. More promising business activities

The business activities described in this part are either ones that Aust-LII has already undertaken (and often would like to undertake more intensively), or has not yet undertaken but it seems would be potentially valuable and involve low risk. The reason that some of these activities have not as yet been undertaken, or not undertaken sufficiently, has been that AustLII has had insufficient staff resources to do so.

3.1. DONATION FUNDING FROM SUBSTANTIAL USERS

From April 2007 AustLII realised that its funding problems would not be solved by finding a single donor to substitute for the major grant on which it had come to rely. Through a public appeal for contributions on its website for the first time, via press publicity, and by direct contact with identifiable[5]

---

[5] AustLII does not require users to identify themselves in order to use its services, in keeping with the principle of 'free and anonymous access' in the Declaration on Free Access to Law, and can therefore only identify users by the IP address through which they access AustLII. Because most users in the commercial sector access the Internet via commercial ISPs, AustLII only sees the IP address of the ISP for these users. In contrast, users accessing AustLII via Universities or government agencies are identifiable by .edu.au or .gov.au IP addresses. This allows separate identification of most Universities, but not of most individual State or Territory government agencies, as they tend to be grouped under one IP address. Some law firms, barristers chambers and businesses have individually identifiable IP addresses and can therefore be referred to as 'identifiable users'.

major users, AustLII communicated its position well enough to expand its contribution base dramatically. AustLII is also progressively contacting all large law firms, barristers chambers and businesses in law-oriented areas (eg banks and accountants), on the assumption that all of them are AustLII users to some extent. This also results in contributions.

In mid-2008 AustLII appointed an External Relations Manager, one of whose main roles is to ensure continuity of contribution income. Details of all contributions are published in (AustLII, 2007) and online.[6]

In 2007 these approaches resulted in 120 legal profession bodies (law firms, barristers chambers, law societies, bar associations etc) contributing up to $50,000 each. Many individual lawyers also contributed, with contributions ranging from $20 to $5,000 (in some cases anonymously). Most of the corporate contributors, have renewed their contributions in 2008, together with new legal profession contributors, contributing over $350,000.

Almost all of the 30 Australian Law Schools contribute over $360,000 between them,[7] with contributions ranging from $30,000 to $500, with a mean contribution of nearly $10,000. All of AustLII's largest identifiable users (particularly large law firms, some ISPs dedicated to the legal profession, some businesses, and other legal publishers) are being progressively informed of their level of usage and requested to contribute. In most cases they decide to do so. On the other hand, many of the contributors to AustLII who can be classified as 'large users' are not identifiable as such through AustLII's logs, and volunteer to contribute without being specifically asked to do so.

Many government agencies are large uses of AustLII (AustLII, 2007, p. 12). Where individual agencies are identifiable they usually make a significant contribution, such as the $25,000 contributions by the Australian Taxation Office attributable primarily to its AustLII usage in 2007 and 2008. However, AustLII has not had success in obtaining 'whole of government' funding based on usage where individual agencies are not identifiable, as discussed later.

To represent the contributors discussed here solely as 'substantial users' is slightly misleading. In many cases they are contributing to AustLII at least in part because they view free public access to law as a worthwhile expenditure of corporate social responsibility funding. Their own usage is not the sole reason for contribution, but also the means by which they provide funding because they perceive AustLII to be of public value. In short, many of these contributions are in part altruistic.

---

[6] Details of all 2007 and 2008 contributors and contributions are at <www.austlii.edu.au/austlii/sponsors/>.

[7] AustLII's host Universities, UTS and UNSW each typically contribute about $100,000 per year in addition, contingent on AustLII success in obtaining a competitive 'research infrastructure' Australian Research Council grant. AustLII has been successful for 2008 and 2009, but was of course not successful in 2007.

3.2. ENGAGEMENT WITH LARGER USERS

Finding what new services, training or recognition larger users value has not been done adequately due to lack of staff resources. This has commenced in 2008 with the appointment of an External Relations Manager and such initiatives as the formation of a Victorian Support and Advisory Committee. It will be expanded as part of AustLII's funding strategy in 2009. As well as its inherent value in improving the quality of AustLII's services to users, improving response to the wishes of organisations who are or may become contributors is one of the most direct ways to increase contributions both horizontally and vertically.

3.3. FUNDING FROM DATA PROVIDERS FOR PUBLISHING

A different aspect of AustLII's business model is that in 2007 and 2008 19 Courts, Tribunals government agencies that provide data to AustLII to publish as part of its over 270 databases have also provided funding. They do so primarily to support AustLII's publication of their content as an effective way of bringing their content to their intended publics (thus also for altruistic reasons). They contribute over $350,000 per year, ranging from $40,000 (for example, from the Department of Foreign Affairs and Trade for publication of Australian Treaties), to between $10,000 - $25,000 from a large federal Court or Tribunal, to a few thousand dollars for a small tribunal. Some of these Courts and Tribunals do not publish their decisions for free access other than through AustLII.

A further development of this approach is where a government agency (or perhaps a professional association) goes beyond simply funding publication of their own content via AustLII, but also provides funding for development of a more general research resource in the area of law in which their agency or association has a particular interest. For example, the Australian Taxation Office is providing $25,000 funding in 2009 for development of the Australian Taxation Law Library on AustLII.[8]

3.4. COMPLEMENTING COMMERCIAL PUBLISHERS

As a free-access provider, AustLII is not in direct competition with commercial legal publishers for market share, and is therefore able to collaborate with both large publishers and boutique publishers to enable them to better use content on AustLII to enhance their own products. Such collaboration leads to contributions, or contract development of facilities to assist collaboration.

Thomson Reuters, one of Australia's largest commercial legal publishers, has automated links to AustLII legislation where it does not publish its own,

---

[8] See: <www.austlii.edu.au/au/special/tax/>.

resulting in its being AustLII's largest commercial sector contributor for the past three years (between \$50-\$100,000 per year).

There is more potential for such collaboration with publishers. Aust-LII holds databases of cases of many Courts and Tribunals the large commercial publishers do not publish, and which are not available anywhere else in electronic form. AustLII's URL formats make such links automatable. Publishers could link to the cases on AustLII that they do not publish themselves, and AustLII can provide services to publishers to automate the linking. This approach does not involve AustLII providing content to other publishers, which it often could not do because of its copyright constraints previously discussed, only linking to content on AustLII. Smaller or niche legal publishers could be assisted to provide links from their content to primary legal materials, since they do not publish these themselves. AustLII currently provides such a facility for Standards Australia, to assist the location of legislation or case law that refers to specified standards, resulting in funding of around A\$30,000 per annum.

Some major legal publishers also use AustLII as a source to find editorial content (eg cases they do not publish), resulting in very substantial levels of access to AustLII's site. AustLII could automate customised complementary services (SDI) to advise other publishers of content they need to know for development of their own facilities.

The development of such complementary relationships with other legal publishers is a potential major funding stream for AustLII.

3.5. ASSISTING USERS TO FIND OTHER PUBLISHERS

A quite different type of cooperation with other legal publishers comes from AustLII's position as the most-used online site for Australian law, with at least eight times the access levels of any Australian commercial legal publisher.[9] AustLII wants its users to find content valuable to them, irrespective of location, so it is not in that sense in competition with commercial publishers. For some years in the early 2000s, AustLII developed with CCH Australia a facility for AustLII users to repeat their AustLII search over all CCH legal content, and obtain lists of search results from CCH, but they could only access the CCH content if they were CCH subscribers. This was useful to existing CCH subscribers who also used AustLII (and possibly preferred its search engine), also had the potential to allow non-subscribers to discover that CCH content was valuable to them and become subscribers. This relationship provided significant funding to AustLII during these years, but did not become a permanent arrangement because it was difficult to quantify the benefits to CCH, and CCH did not have any mechanisms for occasional purchases of its

---

[9] *Hitwise Website Report* for AustLII, November, 2008.

content by non-subscribers. AustLII's position 'upstream' of commercial legal publishers in relation to usage volumes is nevertheless a significant asset.

3.6. ASSISTING OTHER FREE ACCESS SERVICES

AustLII developed the Sino search engine[10] which is used by many other LIIs, and has provided it as open source software since 2007. It regards Sino as a collaborative resource shared between LIIs. AustLII has obtained some modest amounts of funding for assisting development of overseas LIIs (eg BAILII in its formative years, and NZLII more recently), which is more relevant to AustLII's funding of its international activities.

AustLII has not yet obtained funding in relation to assisting development of other Australian free access services, but could do so if appropriate opportunities arose. In particular, if Australian providers intended to use Sino, AustLII would be well-placed to provide support services, a common business model in relation to open source software.

3.7. RESEARCH & INFRASTRUCTURE GRANTS

Success in obtaining competitive grant funds for research or the development of 'research infrastructure' is unpredictable from year to year (as the origins of this paper attest), only lasts from one to three years, and does not provide for maintenance of facilities once built. Nevertheless, it seems likely that a high proportion of AustLII's funding will continue to come from the success of AustLII researchers in obtaining such grants.

AustLII's current competitive grants, obtained since 2007 and relevant to its Australian services, are a grant from the Victorian Legal Services Board of A\$840,000 (2009-11) entitled 'Victoria as the model jurisdiction for free access to law', an Australian Research Council (ARC) 'research infrastructure' grant of \$170,000 (2008-09) to build the 'Australian Legal Scholarship Library', and an ARC 'Linkage' research grant of approximately \$300,000 (2008-11) for research and development on 'Improving case law'. Success in obtaining these grants carries with it commitments to make 'partner contributions' from Universities, Courts and businesses that might not otherwise be available. In particular, UNSW and UTS contribute on average around \$100,000 earch to ARC research infrastructure grant applications, partly because of offsetting financial benefits that success in obtaining competitive grants brings to the whole University. As a result, at least for 2009-10, AustLII will have available to it nearly \$500,000 each year that it would not otherwise have had, to improve and expand its Australian services.

AustLII's main aim in future years is to continue the diversification of the range of funds to which it applies, so as to avoid over-reliance on one type

---

[10] See: <www.austlii.edu.au/techlib/software/sino/>.

of grant. Of course, success is never guaranteed, and depends to a significant extent on successful discharge of previous grant obligations. But an optimistic approach is that grant funding will continue to play a significant role in funding AustLII's Australian facilities. It plays an even larger role in relation to international projects, but that is not the subject here. It is also necessary to consider that success in developing grant-funded new facilities must then be paid for by expansion of donation funding in future to maintain those facilities.

4. Less promising business activities

Some of the business activities discussed in this part are found as part of other open content business models, but for reasons explained they pose a higher level of risks to AustLII's operations than the business activities previously discussed. They have not as yet been undertaken for those reasons, or have been less successful than elsewhere.

4.1. LEGAL PROFESSION OR GOVERNMENT CORE FUNDING

Other LIIs, particularly CanLII have been very successful in obtaining core funding from Law Societies and Bar Associations acting collectively, leading to governance arrangements in which they have a significant role. AustLII has had nearly two years of discussions with the Law Council of Australia and its constituent bodies. This has not resulted in major funding from the organisations of the legal profession, but individual legal profession bodies have between them contributed around $100,000 in each of 2007 and 2008. To put this in perspective, one legal professional indemnity insurer has provided a $50,000 contribution in year because it considers AustLII reduces the liability risks of the legal profession so significantly.

AustLII has had no success as yet in obtaining any 'whole of government' funding from any of Australia's nine governments, as distinct from funding from some individual agencies, Courts and Tribunals whose content AustLII publishes. However, discussions are ongoing which may lead to a 'whole of government' approach to the Standing Committee of Attorneys-General (SCAG) in 2009.

4.2. ADVERTISING MODELS

A report obtained from an experienced consultant (Dixon, 2008) concluded that the net returns to AustLII from the adoption of any type of advertising model would be minimal. Other large legal publishers do not use third-party advertising on their websites, nor do any Courts or Tribunals or government legislation sites, or any University websites, despite their high traffic levels. The costs of advertising brokerage would take a high percentage of any revenues. Loss of reputation to both AustLII and its host Universities, and reduction in contributions would offset any likely revenue gains from advertising.

4.3. OTHER NON-VIABLE FUNDING MODELS

A number of other possibilities need to be mentioned but can be dismissed.

Denial of services to non-contributors. Blocking known significant users who are not contributors would present unacceptable risks to both AustLII's data licences (tied to the provision of 'free access') and its reputation. It would also be discriminatory because not all significant users are known due to the limitations of IP address logging. AustLII has adopted the alternative of making major known users directly aware that their peers do contribute, and this seems to be effective. The Annual Report discloses the extent to which major known users are contributors, but not their identities.

Direct charges for access. These are impossible due to data licences in most jurisdictions. AustLII's national coverage would disappear, its reputation based on free access would be lost, and it would lose most existing contributions, and at least some competitive grant funding.

Charging for republication of content. On-supply of data for republication is not allowed by most of AustLII's data licences. Loss of national coverage would diminish demand significantly.

Operation of closed data services. Paid 'value added' services are often suggested. They create an inherent conflict of interests between what is free and what is 'value added', and the decision as to which services should be value-added is to some extent arbitrary and changes over time. The probable result is that free services will be degraded, and there will be reputational damage to AustLII and its Universities. Use of content in paid value-added services might also conflict with some data licences.

Exclusive arrangements with third parties. Building complementary services on an exclusive basis for one legal publisher would pose dangers to AustLII's reputation and to its University position. We have concluded it is better to provide the same services to any legal publisher on the same funding basis.

5. Conclusions

5.1. AustLII's realistic range of options

The previous sections of this paper have explained how, in 2007, Aust-LII's contributor funding was increased to nearly A$1 million, and this level has been increased in 2008. The number of significant ($5,000 or more) contributors was tripled, providing a broader base for long-term stability of funding. AustLII obtained minimal grant funding for 2007 (the cause of its revised approach to funding), but in 2007 and 2008 it obtained a number of major new competitive grants, sufficient to provide about A$0.5 million for 2009 and 2010. Some of the contributor funding in any given year is 'industry partner' funds applied to research grants and therefore unavailable for maintenance. Contribution funding available for maintenance will have to keep growing funds as services expand.

There seems little prospect of AustLII obtaining a single funding source, or even a small number of major sources, to pay for its Australian facilities. Nor is it realistic for AustLII to consider any form or advertising or paid use (in full or in part) models, because of the constraints within which it operates.

The only realistic option for AustLII is what we could call a 'multi-contributor' model, but is really a mix of different business models. Part of its model will continue to be based on competitive grant funding (from both academic and 'public purpose' sources), with the pressure that this imposes to continue to innovate to provide new services. It appears that 'contributor' funding can, if properly managed, continue to provide the minimum of about A$1 million per year that AustLII needs to maintain its existing databases. However, the expression 'contributor funding' obscures what are in fact quite a variety of business models, few of which have been fully developed by AustLII. None have much to do with being a mendicant.

A multi-contributor funding model is complex and requires considerable resources to service, but it has advantages. It may provide more stability than reliance on one or two major sources, because it is able to cope with loss of any individual stakeholder or group of stakeholders. It also provides more independence from the wishes of any individual stakeholder.

AustLII's financial position is still not certain enough for 2009 onwards, and broader distribution of legal profession, government and business contributors is needed for full stability. However, a full time External Relations Manager was appointed only in July 2008. AustLII will continue to develop the approach to sustainable funding it has taken in 2007-08.

5.2. Possible relevance to other LIIs

The models on which LIIs are funded vary a great deal, and AustLII's 'multi-contributor' model is likely to be of varying relevance to them. BAILII is

G. Greenleaf

similar in having multiple contributors, though fewer. The LII (Cornell) annually solicits funds from the public. Most LIIs have had a considerable deal of academic funding and academic institutional support (particularly HKLII, PacLII, AustLII, LawPhil and BAILII). CanLII is funded primarily by the Canadian legal profession, whereby every Canadian lawyer provides nearly C\$30 per year via their professional associations. Other LIIs have not been able to replicate this. International aid and development agencies have made significant contributions to the development costs of PacLII and SAFLII. A small LII like CyLaw is a personal project. NZLII still lives on 'the smell of an oily rag' (a NZ expression) and help from other LIIs, while - it searches for longer-term funds. Kenya Law Reports is trying to move from a model combining government funding with subscription income to one which does without subscriptions. There is no single path to sustainable free access to law within a country or region, but that doesn't mean it can't be done. It has been done with ever-widening scope for nearly fifteen years. There is not one formula, but as with many other aspects of open content, there are many non-business models by which numerous stakeholders can be engaged.

6. Acknowledgments

Research for this paper was done under the ARC Linkage Project 'Unlocking IP', and also to assist AustLII's operations. Thanks to my Co-Directors, Andrew Mowbray and Philip Chung, and AustLII's External Relations Manager, Annelies Moens, for helpful comments. However, the responsibility for views expressed in this paper remain with me.

References

AustLII, (2007), *Annual Report 2007*, available at: <www.austlii.edu.au/austlii/reports/2007/AustLII_AR_2007.pdf>.

AustLII, (2000), *Mission Statement*, in AustLII Annual Report 2000, pp. 7-8.

Clarke, R. (2007), *Business Models to Support Content Commons*, in: "SCRIPTed", Vol. 4, No. 1, available at: <www.law.ed.ac.uk/ahrc/script-ed/vol4-1/clarke.asp>.

Dixon, R. (2008), *A review of business models for AustLII*, Handshake Media Pty Ltd.

Greenleaf, G. (2008), *Legal Information Institutes and the Free Access to Law Movement*, GlobaLex, February 2008, available at: <www.nyulawglobal.org/globalex/Legal_Information_Institutes.htm>.

Greenleaf, G., Chung, P., Mowbray, A. (2007), *Challenges in improving access to Asian laws: the Asian Legal Information Institute (AsianLII)*, Australian Journal of Asian Law, Vol. 9, p. 152.

The Evolving Ecology of the Legal Information Market

Pierre-Paul Lemyre

LexUM, University of Montreal, Canada

Abstract. For the people involved in the free provision of legal information over the Internet, the permanent alteration of the traditional circulation of legal information is a goal. By insuring the free flow of legal information over the networks, they provide others with the potential to build on top of this shared foundation. Far from weakening the legal publishing industry, this approach promises of creating tremendous opportunities for those capable of developing innovative services and information products.

Notwithstanding the global improvement in the accessibility of legal information, it cannot be denied that this innovative market architecture has yet to replace the previous one. The reason might be that the various players are repositioning themselves in this new environment according to their own individual agenda. History shows that in such a context, the baggage of preconceptions borrowed from the previous period always play an important role in the understanding of a new technology. For legal publishers and public bodies who prospered under the prevailing conditions, the preservation of the statu quo can easily be seen as a necessary condition of its successful implementation. Under their influence, the global efforts to maintain the marketing value of legal information prove to be effective.

As those conflicting visions about the future of the legal data flow collide, it can be difficult to predict which one will ultimately prevail. Nevertheless, it is already possible to discern that not only is the control over access to legal information changing hand, but that the patterns of control are evolving as well.

Keywords: Legal information, effective access, reusability, market, commons.

1. Introduction

In a print-based environment, manipulating information is a costly business. This is particularly true of legal information, which aggregates a complex and often voluminous set of interrelated documents in constant evolution. Those involved in the dissemination of legal information in such a context have to invest in a broad range of operations. Data acquisition first requires regular visits to source institutions by itinerant representatives. The information is input in various ways, and the entire content then needs to be extensively edited, which involves selecting, summarizing and organizing relevant data. In the end, traditional distribution of legal information also involves the self-evident costs associated with paper, printing and subsequent transportation. Understandably, the sum of these costs has led the various legal information providers, whether from the private or public sector, to adopt a commercial approach. Legal information, like all other types of printed information, is marketed as a product. Since it is costly to produce and directed toward professional use, few voices have been heard in favor of subsidizing free, universal access to it. On the contrary, the general perception has been that where a viable market exists, an industry will emerge to meet the demand. Aside from that, the role of the state has been to give minimal access to fundamental texts, others remaining mostly inaccessible.

If the LIIs and other players involved in free provision of legal information over the Internet have demonstrated one thing over the last fifteen years, it is that electronic environments are opening options to this publication model. This is due in part to the introduction of innovative techniques in computerization of legal information that have considerably reduced the level of editorial investment required for basic provision to users (Bruce, 1994). It is also largely recognized that the availability of Internet technologies, coupled with the drastic drop in the price of computer processing and bandwidth, has nearly eliminated the reproduction and distribution costs associated with it (Poulin, 2001). Together, those two factors have contributed to dramatically lowering the entry barriers for potential publishers, effectively allowing a variety of new players to enter the marketplace. Government agencies, academic institutions and dedicated individuals have all realized that they now possess the means to greatly expand the user base of legal information. For the same reasons, they have also been able to expand the scope of access to material previously ignored by the industry. For some of the people involved in these activities, permanent modification of traditional circulation of legal information has become a goal. Instead of being viewed simply as a commodity that can be bought and sold according to the requirements of a market economy, legal information is coming to be seen as a public good. By insuring its free flow over the networks, legal information providers give others the potential to build on it. Far from weakening the legal publishing industry, this approach promises to generate tremendous opportunities for those capable of developing innovative services and knowledge products based on a shared foundation (Susskind, 2000).

Notwithstanding the global improvement in the accessibility of legal information, it cannot be denied that this innovative market architecture has yet to completely replace the previous one. As Ethan Katsh says, the reason might be that the legal field is instead witnessing a process of displacement, during which the various players slowly reposition themselves in the new environment according to their own individual agendas (Katsh, 2008). History has shown that in such contexts, the baggage of preconceptions borrowed from the previous period always plays an important role in the understanding of a new technology (Nazareth, 1994). For private publishers and public bodies who prospered under the previously prevailing conditions, preservation of the status quo can easily be seen as a necessary condition for the success of their businesses. Given their dominant position, they have powerful tools at their disposal to promote their view. Under their influence, global efforts to maintain the marketing value of legal information have proven effective. However, as conflicting visions about the future of the legal data flow collide, it can be difficult to predict which one will ultimately prevail (Martin, 1999).

Nevertheless, it is already possible to discern that not only is control over access to legal information changing hands, but patterns of control are evolving as well.

2. The fate of the information society

From a broader perspective, this polarized attitude towards the adequate shape of the legal information market is simply one specific aspect of the ongoing debate on the fate of the information society (Trosow, 2004). Already discussed in the 1960s, it is only since the turn of the new millennium that development of an economy focused on information resources has started to significantly influence the everyday life of most people. Up to that point, the dominant position had been that if society is to benefit from this transition, content providers require a regulatory framework capable of providing their assets with strong protection.[1] Otherwise, it was argued, the risks and uncertainties generated by the ease of reproducing information in electronic environments would deter investment. In response, legal protection for intellectual property was substantially raised all around the world, taking the form of longer copyright terms, additional database protection and anti-circumvention provisions.

Recently, however, many have started to claim that these measures, coupled with implementation of technical architectures enabling their enforcement, have led to excessive privatization and commodification of information that used to be shared. The end result is the enclosure of many facts and ideas that were not long ago considered common goods (Boyle, 2003). Illustrations of this phenomenon are the patenting of genetic structure and the enforcement of proprietary rights over outcomes of sporting events, and also the attempt to assert copyright over pagination of the United States federal courts reports (Bollier, 2003). For those who contest them, these unintended consequences are unethically enriching a few corporations at the expense of the collectivity, undermining at the same time the positive objectives initially set for the information society. Alternatively, the various success stories of open access over the Internet have led thinkers in all disciplines to reconsider this model not only as a way of distributing information in a more equitable fashion, but also as an innovative method of boosting the production of knowledge (Benkler, 2007). According to this view, justice and wealth are maximized when a wide range of information is accessible for all to consult, use and transform. It is only over the last few years that these ideas have started to

---

[1] Bangemann Group, *Europe and the Global Information Society* - Recommendations of the high-level group on the Information Society to the Corfu European Council, Brussels, European Council, 1994, available at: <`www.cyber-rights.org/documents/bangemann.htm`>.

reach the attention of policy-makers around the world. One recent outcome is the draft Treaty on Access to Knowledge,[2] which originated in a developing nations' call for a development agenda at the World Intellectual Property Organization.

Between those two positions, there is little doubt that a balance must be reached in order to maintain incentives for investment while at the same time protect some invaluable commons. The key, it is said, may be the conjunction of ownership and 'openness' in an ongoing dialectical relationship, each modifying and depending on the other (May, 2005).

Because of their central position, governments should play an active role in pursuing this equilibrium. This is particularly true when information originating from the public sector is involved, since in this scenario great potential for commercial exploitation and added value coexists with citizen rights and expectations to be able to scrutinize the government (Martinez, Marx, 2007). In this regard, the public legal information market perfectly illustrates how states, through their policies, can actively push the pendulum in one direction or another. Past experiences clearly demonstrate that a decision to initiate free dissemination of legal information over the Internet is not the single determining factor. Two additional conditions influence the equation: first, the effectiveness of the access provided, and, second, the possibility of reusing data.

3. Effective access

Because rules can play their regulative role only if they are conveyed to those who are subject to them, legal institutions have generally tried to improve techniques for disseminating legal information. Indeed, official gazettes and journals came to replace the proclamation process for the simple reason that multiplying uniform copies of printed laws was a much more effective technique of spreading the information than having local officials reading potentially inconsistent manuscripts aloud at public gatherings (Susskind, 2000, p. 85). In the early days of printing, however, the various benefits of the new media were not all self evident. For example, it took approximately a century before printers realized that books could be made in a much smaller size than manuscripts, thus facilitating their transportation and accumulation in larger collections (Eisenstein, 1979). For a long period, the mindset of the manuscript era prevented printing from completely transforming access to information. It is only with the passage of time that books finally prevailed.

The recent influence of ICTs on the mode and level of access to legal information leaves little doubt that this process is repeating itself, although

---

[2] "Treaty on Access to Knowledge", Consumer Project on Technology, 2005, available at: <www.cptech.org/a2k/a2k_treaty_may9.pdf>.

at a much more accelerated pace. While most states have initially been eager to improve access to legal information by using new technologies, they have often done so by mechanically reproducing techniques and approaches borrowed from the past. This behavior results in preservation of technical restrictions that can easily be eliminated in electronic environments. Some of them are consequences of an incomplete understanding of the new media, or perhaps of the general passivity characterizing public bodies (Bruce, 2000). Others can be attributed to the willingness to preserve prevailing arrangements with those who have been in charge of printing the law and who have strong incentives to continue selling it online (Martin and Foster, 2000). Together, these reasons account for the fact that free access to legal information is not always enough, and that it is certainly not synonymous with full access.

The most standard type of restriction associated with free provision of legal information on the Internet concerns the exhaustiveness of the data provided. Since they are accustomed to filtering legal information and choosing what is worthy of publication, many institutions are keen to continue doing the same thing in electronic environments. This is true even if the cost of selecting the information is now generally higher than the cost of opening access to the complete set of data. In Quebec, for example, it took a ruling from the provincial Court of Appeal to require the public agency in charge of coordinating and organizing legal information, the Société québécoise d'information juridique (SOQUIJ), to give access to all court decisions instead of a small percentage of them.[3] SOQUIJ, relying on its access monopoly over Quebec's case law to market its own value-added services, was not interested in giving away its major advantage over competition from the private sector (Wilson & Lafleur, 1996).

Elsewhere, similar limitations on the scope of freely accessible material have been based on timing issues. This has generally been achieved by voluntarily delaying updates to freely accessible databases. This problem is particularly acute with respect to legislation: governments are sometimes particularly slow at updating their material (Tjaden, 2005). For instance, the free legislative website of British Columbia is updated only in conjunction with the publication of the printed consolidation.[4] Freely accessible data constantly lags a year and a half behind the actual state of the law so the province's Queen's Printer can sell access to its up-to-date statutes database.[5] Taking the opposite approach, others have implemented restrictions on the historical depth of collections. This is the case in Norway where the Lovdata

---

[3] Wilson Lafleur Inc. c. *La Société québécoise d'information juridique*, 2000 CanLII 8006, available at: <www.canlii.org/fr/qc/qcca/doc/2000/2000canlii8006/2000canlii8006. html>.

[4] "Revised Statutes and Consolidated Regulations of British Columbia", Queen's Printer of British Columbia, 2007, available at: <www.qp.gov.bc.ca/statreg/default.htm>.

[5] "QP LegalEze - British Columbia Legislation", QP LegalEze, available at: <www.qplegaleze.ca/default.htm>.

national legal information system secures a market for its commercial services
by removing Supreme Court and appellate court judgments from its freely
accessible website after six months and four months respectively.[6]

Access restrictions also take the form of technical constraints. More difficult
to identify, they nevertheless create obstacles for third parties interested in
reproducing and adding value to the data. Barriers of this kind are of an
infinite variety and the imagination of web developers is the only limit to their
multiplication. A classic example is the use of PDF files, particularly image
files, where provision in full text format would have been easy. In trying to
control how the information is displayed, some free access providers simply
put a futile burden on those wishing to reuse it (Martin and Foster, 2000).
Another is the hiding of documents behind an interface based on input fields
with no alternative links reflecting the organization of the data. By impeding
users from identifying the complete set of documents included, this technique
makes reproduction of the whole set very difficult. The implementation of
sessions on free access websites constitutes one last illustration. By blocking
downloads when a connection has been open for a certain period of time,
they stop crawlers and other computerized mechanisms from automating the
retrieval of data. By joining several of these restrictions together, free access
providers have the capacity to block massive reprocessing of legal information,
while at the same time allow individuals to consult items one at a time. While
this may be justifiable as a means of blocking abuse of system resources, such
a strategy contributes to preserving the old paradigm.

A final category of restrictions originates in the use of proprietary formats
for dissemination of legal information. Early on, some corporations targeted
public bodies entrusted with the mandate to disseminate law on the Internet
as potential clients for their publishing platforms. Indeed, specialized products
such as the NXT[7] suite (previously known as Folio) have been substantially
customized over the last decade to accommodate legislative material. Notwithstanding how efficient such software may appear to be, it always has the side
effect of making extraction of otherwise freely accessible legal materials subject
to acquisition of a license from a private entity. Moreover, the disappearance
of the corporation, its unilateral decision to stop maintaining the product, or
simply bad technological choices, all have the potential to lock legal information up in obsolete technological architecture. In the case of the Organisation
internationale de la francophonie (OIF), this path has contributed to the
decrepitude of its multi-million dollar project Collecte, gestion et diffusion
du droit (COGEDI). Revolving around dissemination of the proprietary software Edibase in national structures managing legal information, the fate of

---

[6] "Informasjon fra Lovdata", Lovdata, 2008, available at: <www.lovdata.no/info/
lawdata.html>.

[7] "Fast NXT 4", Fast, 2008, available at: <www.fastsearch.com/13a.aspx?m=1058>.

the project was largely influenced by inconsistent decisions by the successive owners of the software (Poulin, 2002).

Whether these restrictions result from conscious deliberations or not is somehow irrelevant. They nonetheless play a part in undermining the effectiveness of online access to public legal information. Being rooted in the premise that the value of the services rendered by the administration lies in the data itself, and not in the improved circulation of information that can result from it, they help keep the old paradigm alive. For this reason, they are all instrumental to preservation of the marketability of legal information and, ultimately, the difficulty of asserting its status as a true common good.

These considerations put aside, some limits on the effectiveness of free access to law initiatives subsist even where there are no technical restrictions. This can be explained by the interrelated nature of legal documents that requires a certain level of integration for them to become truly usable. Early attempts to use the Internet in order to improve access to law showed that

> Fragmentation of [...] information and inconsistencies of different legal documents formats represent historical obstacles to a systematic organization of a normative corpus (Francesconi, 2006, p. 358).

For this reason, it is not always considered enough for each legal institution to publish the results of its law-making activities independently on its own Internet website. In addition, databases need to be either prepared in compliance with standards or consolidated so that they can be searched jointly (McMahon, 1999). Otherwise, the lack of uniformity in publication techniques, access modes and files formats prevent the establishment of any coherence among the multiple sources of law. Web search engines are impotent to fix this problem because numerous public providers of legal information block access to crawlers on privacy grounds (Greenleaf, Mowbray, Chung, 2007). In this context, the will to put an end to the fragmentation of access has been a major impetus to the setup of many legal information systems, including CanLII (Poulin, Salvas, Pelletier, 2000). The same motivation justifies the efforts invested in global ventures such as GLIN and WorldLII (Widdison, 2002).

The challenges generated by fragmentation of access are best illustrated by the situation that prevailed for several years with respect to the opinions of the United States federal courts of appeal. Like similar institutions in this country, each of the thirteen federal circuits hosts a website where full text versions of judgments are made available to the public. However, a large portion of them are not equipped with search engines and a few block external crawlers from indexing the content of their site (Martin, 2007). Fortunately, for several years the LII at Cornell University has managed to bypass the restrictions blocking Google and other search engines in order to provide a single search interface for these multiple databases.[8] Because the United States legal system is so highly diversified, this kind of decentralized approach has been at the center of the LII strategy since its creation (Bruce, 1995). If it were not for this independent initiative, it would have been impossible until very recently to do a complete legal search of American copyrights or federal criminal law without having recourse to one of the private commercial services, even though the state has been making all the relevant information available free of charge on the Internet.

The situation in the United States perfectly illustrates how fragmented access to law is another factor postponing the transition of legal information from product to public good in numerous jurisdictions. Observers noticed years ago that recombination of data from the pool of freely accessible legal information can be daunting. As long as this remains the case, agglomerating the relevant material will be a value-added service for which the market will be ready to pay (Joergensen, 1999). In contrast, if legal information is made available to everyone in consolidated form or, alternatively, if interoperability makes consolidation immaterial, basic control over data ceases to be determining. Whether or not they take steps in this direction, public bodies undoubtedly influence the future of the legal information market.

As understanding of Internet technologies and their overall impact on society constantly improves, issues surrounding the effectiveness of access to public legal information draw people's attention. While the debate is only starting to reach citizens (Markoff, 2007), some public bodies have already started adopting minimal standards. In the United States, the E-Government Act of 2002 has played a role in enjoining federal courts to put all written opinions on their websites in a text searchable format.[9]

It is somehow regrettable that the courts have taken the position that the legislation simply forbids them from posting image files but does not entail any responsibility to provide search capacity.[10] Thus, much of the discussion still lies ahead. In Europe, a more detailed plan of action has been addressed in a recommendation by the Committee of Ministers of the European Council. Although this kind of community document is not binding on member states, it advises European governments to implement comprehensive free legal information services featuring full text searches and point-in-time retrieval of legislation whenever possible, as well as the most widely available technolo-

---

[8] "Search the Opinions of the US Circuit Courts", Cornell law School, 2008, available at: <www.law.cornell.edu/usca/search/>.

[9] E-Government Act of 2002 (US), sec. 205.

[10] "Federal Courts Respond to E-Government Act", The Third Branch 37, No. 4 (2005), available at: <www.uscourts.gov/ttb/apr05ttb/respond/index.html>.

gies.[11] This attitude is representative of a will in the European political class to secure open electronic access to public legal information for the people.

Because of growing consequences in an increasingly connected world, most public bodies have now come to realize that in electronic environments all types of free access are not equivalent. Even though some stakeholders have been slower than others to take action in this regard, the gradual disappearance of many restrictions that were very common only a few years ago and the transition from the initial confusion in the field to an organized framework of free access providers indicate that a significant number of institutions are actively confronting these issues.

4. Reusability of data

As important as it may be, even the provision of total, effective access to citizens does not necessarily lead to unrestricted circulation of public legal information. This can be explained by the simple fact that legal information, even when free, is generally distributed with legally enforceable conditions attached to it. Originating in copyright, contractual agreements or specific statutory requirements, these conditions have the potential to determine quite precisely what can and cannot be done with the material. While we can presume that few government agencies would object to personal, educational and non-profit reuse of legal information (Bond, 2007), some of them still distribute it under generic terms that limit the capacity of others to reproduce or add value to it for those purposes. In the end, such protective control of information might have no real impact on citizen access, but could nevertheless affect use of the content by making the consent of rights-holders a condition on reuse (Janssen and Dumortier, 2003).

Here again, the experience of the last fifteen years shows that strategies based on the print media still strongly influence the current electronic legal information market. In a world where the role of the state was limited strictly to production of information, and the publishing industry was in charge of dissemination, a certain level of control over the data could always be justified by the necessity to secure the integrity and accuracy of content (Bouvet, 1993). The possibility for the state to derive some revenues without substantially influencing the dissemination process also worked in favor of the prevailing scheme. However, these premises have disappeared in parallel with the rapid spread of computer networks allowing public bodies to undertake electronic distribution of official versions of legal documents for a fraction of the previous

---

[11] Committee of Ministers, "Recommendation Rec(2001)3 of the Committee of Ministers to member states on the delivery of court and other legal services to the citizen through the use of new technologies" (European Council, 2001), available at: <https://wcd.coe.int/ViewDoc.jsp?id=188899&Site=CM&BackColorInternet=9999CC&BackColorIntranet=FFBB55&BackColorLogged=FFAC75>.

cost. Since the primary goal of the state is maximization of social wealth, not cost recovery of publicly funded activities, these changes call for a review of prevailing public policies (Stanburry, 1996). While the last few years have been characterized by a shift towards reusability of information originating in the public sector (Bond, 2007), restrictive conditions are still among the major obstacles to free flow of public legal information.

In countries with British legal traditions, these conditions have historically been rooted in the doctrine of Crown copyright. The one major exception is the United States, where the First Amendment to the Constitution has been interpreted as placing state work products in the public domain and the Copyright Act precludes the federal government from claiming ownership of such products (Gellman, 1996). Elsewhere, common law has traditionally recognized a prerogative of the Crown to print certain works, including Acts of Parliament (Tapper, 1985). Extending this protection, the British Copyright Act of 1911 specifically introduced Crown ownership of creations made under its direction or control.[12] From this point on, public legal information has suffered no special treatment and has been protected in the same fashion as other works. Crown copyright implies that legislation and judicial opinions cannot be reproduced without the express permission of the government. Any unauthorized reproduction would result in copyright infringement, opening the door to civil and criminal actions against the counterfeiter.

Although most concerned countries have adopted benevolent regimes under which commercial publishers are free to reuse legal materials on payment of a standard royalty, the mere existence of Crown copyright forbids them from relaxing their grip on subsequent exploitation of information. When applied to online provision of legal information, the requirement to obtain a commercial license from the government not only influences the number and quality of subscription services, but also limits the capacity of the market to provide alternative free services (Saxby, 1998). For some, the control provided by Crown copyright and prerogative is anachronistic and can potentially lead to censorship (Tjaden, 2005, p. 158).

Because it constitutes a direct and evident threat to free dissemination of public information over the Internet, the importance of adapting Crown copyright to electronic environments was identified very early on.[13]

In reaction to this challenge, many different approaches have been promoted and adopted. In some jurisdictions, legislative waivers have been enacted in order to guarantee the free reusability of legal material covered by Crown copyright. This is the case in Canada, where the Reproduction of Federal Law Order allows anyone to reproduce federal law without charge or permission as long as due diligence is exercised in ensuring the accuracy of

---

[12] Copyright Act (UK), 1911, sec. 18.
[13] Canadian Legal Information Council, "Forum on Access to Government Electronic Information on Law: Canada Needs to Resolve the Issues" (Ottawa, 1991).

the materials reproduced and the reproduction is not represented as an official version.[14]

The primary advantage of this approach is that it preserves reasonable conditions in relation to the integrity of databases. Similar results have been achieved in the United Kingdom through an automatic licensing system. By filling in online application forms, users interested in reprocessing specific categories of public information, such as judgments, are provided with computer generated Click-Use Licenses corresponding to their specific needs.[15] While primary information is licensed at no cost, value-added material is charged for in proportion to the type and amount of Crown copyright information being reused.[16] Elsewhere, the possibility of abolishing Crown copyright in primary legal materials has been discussed. In Australia, the Copyright Law Review Committee recently adopted a recommendation to this effect, arguing that the public interest would be best served if copyright did not continue to subsist in legislative, judicial and some executive material.[17]

Even though not all jurisdictions have yet adopted equivalent positions, these developments indicate that the general trend is towards making Crown copyright largely irrelevant in this field (Greenleaf, 2007).

Since the Berne Convention for the Protection of Literary and Artistic Works leaves the protection of official texts of a legislative, administrative and legal nature[18] to the discretion of its signatory states, most countries do not recognize any copyright over them. This has not stopped many states from taking advantage of their central role in the production process to assert effective control over legal information. In the past, this privileged position was often used to barter with publishers, and trade exclusive rights for benefits resulting from the commercialization of the "official version" of legal documents (Martin and Foster, 2000). Although the public domain origin of the data allowed anyone to collect it independently and reproduce it, the practical advantages of close collaboration with the state and the related certification of authenticity meant that competition was generally futile (Leith, 2000). Moreover, publishers involved in providing such services inevitably invested editorial

---

[14] Reproduction of Federal Law Order (Cnd), 1997, available at: <www.canlii.org/eliisa/highlight.do?language=en&searchTitle=Search+all+CanLII+Databases&path=/ca/regu/si97-5/part321381.html>.

[15] "Click-Use Licensing", Office of Public Sector Information, 2008, available at: <www.opsi.gov.uk/click-use/index.htm>.

[16] "Charging for Value Added Material", Office of Public Sector Information, 2007, available at:<www.opsi.gov.uk/click-use/value-added-licence-information/charging-value-added-material.pdf>.

[17] Copyright Law Review Committee, 2005, Crown Copyright, para. 9.48, available at: <www.clrc.gov.au/agd/WWW/clrHome.nsf/AllDocs/4F25A124B6E6F1A4CA256FDB0015D5A7?OpenDocument>.

[18] "Berne Convention for the Protection of Literary and Artistic Works" World Intellectual Property Organization, 1979, sec. 2(4), available at: <www.wipo.int/treaties/en/ip/berne/trtdocs_wo001.html>.

work of their own, resulting in the integration of copyrightable elements into official publications. These additions generated incentives to distribute the final materials under limited licenses. For both of these reasons, the conditions of reuse of legal information could end up being even more restrictive than in countries recognizing Crown copyright.

Due to the positive impact of these arrangements on government coffers, it is not surprising that some public bodies have tried to replicate them online. This happened in the Netherlands, where the government agreed to vest the legal publisher Kluwer with exclusive rights over the development of a national legislation database. Under this agreement, no other publisher was to receive electronic copies of Dutch laws for a period of ten years (Van Eechoud, 2006). Because exclusive licensing of public domain information seems inconsistent with an environment facilitating universal access to it, public pressure eventually forced the Dutch government to back down and renegotiate its contract.

It is precisely to avoid such exclusive contracts and to lower existing barriers to commercial exploitation of public data that the European Union adopted the Directive on the Re-use of Public Sector Information in 2003. Apart from requiring European nations to address reuse requests from the private sector in a fair, transparent and timely fashion, the directive states that

> The re-use of documents shall be open to all potential actors in the market. [...] Contracts or other arrangements between the public sector bodies holding the documents and third parties shall not grant exclusive rights.[19]

This provision formally introduces an equal right to reuse information originating in the public sector in Europe. This development perfectly illustrates how perceptions about the state's role in circulation of information is evolving. The evolution can certainly be felt regarding public legal information where, more than ever before, it is considered a duty to guarantee competitive and maximal exploitation of this public data "deposit" (Poullet, 1999). Going slightly further, the directive also forbids states from imposing conditions unnecessarily restricting reuse possibilities or limiting competition.[20] This obligation undoubtedly limits the capacity of European countries to distribute legal information under unduly restrictive licenses. However, it does not place any obligation on them to make such materials accessible for reuse, since the concept of "generally accessible documents" was removed from the initial directive proposal (Leith and McCullagh, 2004). Moreover, while the directive

---

[19] European Parliament and Council of Europe, Directive 2003/98/EC of the European Parliament and of the Council of 17 November 2003 on the re-use of public sector information, 2003, sec. 11, available at: <eur-lex.europa.eu/LexUriServ/LexUriServ.do?uri= CELEX:32003L0098:EN:HTML>.

[20] Directive 2003/98/EC, sec. 8.

addresses the details of freedom to reuse public data, it does not prevent states from charging for it (Barthe, 2006).

Taken together, the limitations of the European directive highlight the strength of one additional source of restrictive conditions attached to public sector information: state-run publishers. Traditionally, state intervention in the legal publishing industry has been limited to jurisdictions where the market was deemed too small to support competitive offers from the private sector. During the 1970s and 1980s, the large investment required to establish and operate computerized legal databases led some governments to adopt the same reasoning and subsidize national structures dedicated to computerization of legal information. As Internet use grew, many national services initially established on a commercial basis and oriented towards professionals were turned into primary public access points for electronic legal information (Bing, 2003). In particular, this is the case in continental European countries, where the national legal information service approach has been appealing to governments. While these services have been given the mandate to disseminate legal information free of charge to the public, that new responsibility has often been combined with their conventional legal publishing activities. Forbidden from charging individual users for access to basic legal materials, they have adapted: used to capitalizing on the information they control, some of them have chosen to adopt license schemes that either prevent users from massively republishing data or impose fees for such reuse. Implemented in conjunction with some of the technological restrictions discussed above, these maneuvers have kept some revenue flowing in and minimized the financial burden. As a side effect, these policies have also resulted in the creation of de facto monopolies over provision of free access to law (Greenleaf, 2004).

In this regard, France stands out as a perfect example. In its implementation of the European directive, the country surpassed its minimal obligations by adopting principles ensuring freedom to reuse public sector information for any purpose.[21] With respect to legal information, Légifrance, the "public access to law service", fulfils this mandate by providing open access to a large array of legislative, judicial and administrative materials.[22] However, Légifrance makes any quantitatively or qualitatively substantial extraction of data from its website subject to the acquisition of a license. According to its own interpretation, this applies to anyone wishing to reuse more than a tenth

---

[21] "Ordonnance n° 2005-650 du 6 juin 2005 relative à la liberté d'accès aux documents administratifs et à la réutilisation des informations publiques" (JO n° 131 du 7 juin 2005 p. 10021 texte n° 12), available at: <www.legifrance.gouv.fr/affichTexte.do?cidTexte= JORFTEXT000000629684&dateTexte=>.

[22] "Legifrance - Le service public de l'accès au droit" Legifrance, 2008, available at: <www.legifrance.gouv.fr/>.

of the annual flow of a specific collection.[23] In this situation, a free license is available, but apart from including standard integrity and attribution clauses, it also imposes the conditions of not automating data reprocessing and not reproducing the entire content of any single collection.[24] An alternative service providing all of Légifrance's content in XML format has been designed for this specific purpose and those interested in reproducing content are encouraged to subscribe to it. The cost of this service is in proportion of the amount of data required and can reach up to 22,000 euro for entire historical collections and approximately 18,000 euro for annual updates.[25] Although these charges are relatively low for legal publishers, they constitute a major impediment for non-profit organizations wishing to develop efficient and exhaustive complementary free services based on French electronic legal information. Stuck with Légifrance as their unique free access provider, French users of legal information have no choice but to complain about its technical limitations and the state's slowness in dealing with them (Rolin, 2006). In 2005, Légifrance licenses generated revenues of 143,678 euro out of the 928,092 euro budget of the Secrétariat Général du Gouvernement.[26]

Finally, legal publishers have also tried to impose restrictive reuse conditions on the basis of their involvement in the publishing process. Law reports are especially at risk since they are usually privately prepared and edited, even if courts around the world have consistently ruled against private ownership of case law. In its celebrated 1834 decision, Wheaton v. Peters, the United States Supreme Court found that

> No reporter of the decisions of the Supreme Court has, nor can he have, any copyright in the written opinions delivered by the Court...[27].

However, a large portion of reporters' efforts go into the production of headnotes, classification mechanisms and other types of intellectual input, for which they are entitled to claim copyright protection. Some also enhance the body of judgments with typographical and substantive corrections, and by inserting parallel citations. Difficulties started to appear when electronic reproduction of cases proved difficult to achieve without using some of these additions. When the official version recognized by the courts integrates them,

---

[23] "Notice explicative relative à la réutilisation des données disponibles sur Légifrance" Legifrance, 2008, available at: <www.legifrance.gouv.fr/html/licences/licences_notice.htm>.

[24] "Contrat de licence de réutilisation des données diffusées en propre sur le site Légifrance", Legifrance, 2008, art. 1, available at: <www.legifrance.gouv.fr/html/licences/licences_contrat.htm>.

[25] "Tarif des licences Légifrance', Legifrance, 2008, available at: <www.legifrance.gouv.fr/html/licences/licences_tarifs.htm>.

[26] "Question N°: 105950 de M. Le Fur Marc (Union pour un Mouvement Populaire - Côtes-d'Armor)", Questions de l'Assemblée nationale, 2007, available at: <questions.assemblee-nationale.fr/q12/12-105950QE.htm>.

[27] Wheaton v. Peters, 33 U.S. 591 (1834).

it can be debated whether reuse should be subject to obtaining the permission of the copyright holder.

In the United States, West Publishing claimed rights over its West National Reporter system and the Star pagination system in the 1990s and 1980s. The company litigated aggressively on the grounds that it published enhanced version of cases, and it was sometimes successful (Browne, 1999). In 1998 however, West lost its battle in the HyperLaw cases when the Federal Court of Appeal for the second circuit decided that

> star pagination does not create a "copy" of any protected elements of West's compilations[28]

and that

> West's choices with respect to selection and arrangement can reasonably be viewed as obvious, typical, and lacking even minimal creativity.[29]

For both of these reasons, it has been possible for anyone to key in or scan text from the West National Reporter system ever since (Sugarman, 2008). Interestingly enough, it was only a decade later that someone actually started to do so in order to free access to United States federal case law (Gardner, 2008).

In the end, whether they originate in Crown copyright, exclusive contracts, the business model of state-run publishers or private rights, restrictive reuse conditions all imply the need to secure a permission before reproducing and disseminating the law. Based on the presumption that public legal information can be owned and controlled like any other type of intellectual property, they enable public bodies and publishers to maintain their commercial exploitation in raw form even when it is freely distributed over the Internet. As it can be expected, very little has changed in the legal information market where this policy has been pursued. In most countries however, the popularity of this approach is fading with every year passing. But if states are abandoning their copyright in legal materials, adopting legislations banning exclusive licensing of public sector information, and dismissing private rights in it, publicly owned legal publishers stands out as the one remaining obstacle. As Daniel Poulin noted in 2001,

> It is paradoxal that what was yesterday the best solution to guarantee access to [legal] information has today become the main obstacle to this access (Poulin, 2001, para. 50).

Over the last eight years, the challenge of free legal information providers has evolved from securing access to the possibility of reusing the data provided, but the source of the problem is still the same.

This said, the fact remains that availability of legal information is constantly improving all over the world. Restrictions on access and the possibility

---

[28] Matthew Bender & Co. v. West Publishing Co., 158 F.3d 693 (2d Cir. 1998).
[29] Matthew Bender & Co. v. West Publishing Co., 158 F.3d 674 (2d Cir. 1998).

of reusing the material are currently the center of attention because they are implemented in an environment where accessibility is more and more taken for granted. The field is also influenced by the ever increasing involvement of states and publishers in free online provision of legal information. In this sense, they are taking the baton from traditional promoters of free access to law. Although the fight over marketability of legal information will probably continue for many years to come, one major consequence can already be discerned. Access itself is becoming less determining while the mode of access is becoming the main battlefield.

This evolution in the ecology of the legal information market implies that the intrinsic value of providing access to primary legal material will continue to decrease in the near future. For private players in the legal information market, there is a pressing need to focus on quality, added value and improvement of reusability. Only those capable of providing one or more of these elements will survive in the long term. Others will be replaced, including some of the most prominent promoters of free access to law. This is a great challenge for legal information institutes, which have traditionally seen themselves as pure access providers. Since states and publishers are slowing taking over this role, they must take urgent action to secure their place in the legal information market and thereby ensure the sustainability of their initiatives.

References

Barthe, E. (2006), *Le principe de disponibilité des données publiques: mythe ou réalité?*, Precisement.org, 2006, available at: <www.precisement.org/blog/article.php3?id_article=2>.

Benkler, Y. (2007), *The Wealth of Networks: How Social Production Transforms Markets and Freedom*, Yale University Press, New Haven, available at: <www.congo-education.net/wealth-of-networks/>.

Bing, J. (2003), *The Policies of Legal Information services: A Perspective of Three Decades*, in Bygrave, L.A., (Ed.) "Yulex 2003", Institutt for rettsinformatik / Norwegian Research Centre for Computers and Law, Oslo, pp. 40-48.

Bollier, D. (2003), *Silent Theft: The Private Plunder of Our Common Wealth*, Vol.1, Routledge.

Bond, C. (2007), *Reconciling Crown Copyright and Reuse of Government Information: An Analysis of the CLRC Crown Copyright Review*, University of New South Wales Faculty of Law Research, Series 32, available at: <www.austlii.edu.au/cgi-bin/sinodisp/au/journals/UNSWLRS/2007/32.html?query=\%22crown\%20copyright\%22>.

Bouvet, D. (1993), *Crown Copyright: A Quest for a Peaceful Harbour*, Canadian Law Libraries Review, Vol. 18, p. 187.

Boyle, J. (2003), *The Second Enclosure Movement and the Construction of the Public Domain*, Law and Contemporary Problems, Vol. 66, No. 33, pp. 33-74.

Browne, K. (1999), *Does the Law Governing Public Access to Judicial Opinions Mandate Citation Reform? It Depends*, Legal Reference Services Quarterly, Vol. 17, No. 1, pp. 106-114.

Bruce, T.R. (1994), *The Internet and Legal Information: Projects and Prospects*, in "The Electronic Superhighway: The Shape of Technology and Law To Come", available at: <www.lexum.umontreal.ca/conf/ae/en/bruce.html>.

Bruce, T.R. (1995), *Legal Information, Open Models, and Current Practice*, La revue juridique Thémis, Vol. 30, No. 2, pp. 186.

Bruce, T.R. (2000), *Public Legal Information: Focus and Future*, UTS Law Review 2, pp. 16-35.

Eisenstein, E. (1979), *Printing Press as an Agent for Change*, Cambridge University Press, New York.

Francesconi, E. (2006), *The "Norme in Rete" Project: Standards and Tools for Italian Legislation*, International Journal of Legal Information, Vol. 34, No. 2.

Gardner, E. (2008), *An Operating System for Law: Online Cases*, Law.com, available at: <www.law.com/jsp/legaltechnology/pubArticleLTN.jsp?id=1206700930604&rss=ltn>.

Gellman, R. (1996), *The American model of access to and dissemination of public information*, presented at the Access to Public Information: A key To Commercial Growth and Electronic Democracy, Stockholm, available at: <europa.eu.int/ISPO/legal/stockholm/en/gellman.html>.

Greenleaf, G. (2004), *Jon Bing and the History of Computerised Legal Research – Some Missing Links*, in Torvund, O. and Bygrave, L., (Eds.) "Et tilbakeblikk på fremtiden"= "Looking back at the future", Institutt for rettsinformatikk, Oslo, available at: <www2.austlii.edu.au/~graham/publications/2004/Greenleaf_Bing_book.pdf>.

Greenleaf, G. (2007), *Commons-ism in One Country? – National and International Dimensions of the Public Domain*, presented at the Public lecture, AHRC Research Centre for the Study of IP and Technology Law, Edinburgh, p. 7.

Greenleaf, G., Mowbray A., Chung P. (2007), *Networking LIIs: how free access to law fits together*, in Holmes, N. and Venables, J., (Eds.) "Legal Web 2007/2008: Legal Information Topics" Infolaw Limited, London, available at: <www.venables.co.uk/n0703liisnetwork.htm>.

Janssen, K. and Dumortier, J. (2003), *Towards a European Framework for the Re-use of Public Sector Information: a Long and Winding Road*, International Journal of Law and Information Technology, Vol. 11, No. 2, p. 192.

Joergensen, J.P. (1999), *Are Non-Profit Internet Publishers the Future of Legal Information?*, Legal Reference Services Quarterly, Vol. 17, No. 1, p. 40.

Katsh, E.M. (1995), *Law in a Digital World*, Oxford University Press, p. 13.

Leith, P. (2000), *Owning Legal Information*, European Intellectual Property Review, Vol. 22, No. 8, p. 363.

Leith, P. and McCullagh, K. (2004), *Developing European Legal Information Markets Based on Government Information*, International Journal of Law and Information Technology, Vol. 12, No. 3, p. 252.

Markoff, J. (2007), *A Quest to Get More Court Rulings Online, and Free*, The New York Times, August 20, sec. Technology, available at: <www.nytimes.com/2007/08/20/technology/20westlaw.html?_r=1&oref=slogin>.

Martin, P.W. (1999), *The Internet: 'Full and Unfettered Access' to Law–Some Implications*, Northern Kentucky Law Review, Vol. 26, pp. 205-206.

Martin, P. (2007), *Finding and Citing the "Unimportant" Decisions of the U.S. Courts of Appeals*, Cornell University Law School, par. 9, available at: <topics.law.cornell.edu/wex/papers/lir2007-1>.

Martin, P.W. and Foster, J.M.G. (2000), *Legal Information - A Strong Case for Free Content, An Illustration of How Difficult "Free" May Be to Define, Realize, and Sustain*, presented at the Conference on Free Information Ecology, Cornell University, available at: <www4.law.cornell.edu./working-papers/open/martin/free.html>.

Martinez, R. and Marx, B. (2007), *La longue marche de l'information publique, de la liberté d'accès aux documents administratifs à la réutilisation commerciale des informations publiques*, Documentaliste, Vol. 44, p. 219.

May, C. (2005), *Between Commodification and 'Openness': The Information Society and the ownership of Knowledge*, Journal of Information, Law and Technology, No. 2 & 3, available at: <www2.warwick.ac.uk/fac/soc/law/elj/jilt/2005_2-3/may>.

McMahon, T. (1999), *Improving Access to the Law in Canada With Digital Media*, Government Information in Canada/Information gouvernementale au Canada, Vol. 16, available at: <www.canadalegal.com/gosite.asp?s=3364>.

Nazareth, A.M. (1994), *Legal Databases, Legal Epistemology, and the Legal Order*, Law Library Journal, Vol. 86, p. 687.

Poulin, D., Salvas, B., Pelletier, F. (2000), *La diffusion du droit canadien sur Internet*, Revue du notariat, Vol. 102, p. 189.

Poulin, D. (2001), *La démocratisation de l'accès au droit: nouveaux acteurs et nouvelles technologies*, in Monville, C., "Variations sur le droit de la société de l'information", Cahier du CRID, Brussels, Bruylant, para. 9-18.

Poulin, D. (2002), *La diffusion libre du droit des pays francophones*, Mission Report, Agence intergouvernementale de la francophonie, Paris.

Poullet, Y. (1999), *Diffusion des données juridiques et Nouveaux médias: Un enjeu fondamental pour la justice*, in Multimédia Le Cyberavocat, Formation permanente CUP, p. 124.

Rolin, F. (2006), *Sur quelques propositions concrètes et peu onéreuses et désormais urgentes d'amélioration de Legifrance*, Le Blog de Frédéric Rolin, available at: <frederic-rolin.blogspirit.com/archive/2006/11/15/sur-suelques-propositions-concretes-et-peu-onereuses-et-deso.html>.

Saxby, S.J. (1998), *Information Access Policy and Crown Copyright in the Electronic Age: Which Way Forward?*, International Journal of Law and Information Technology, Vol. 6, pp. 19-22.

Stanburry, W.T. (1996), *Aspects de la politique des pouvoirs publics sur le droit d'auteur de la Couronne à l'âge numérique*, La revue juridique Thémis, Vol. 30, No. 2, pp. 262-266.

Sugarman, A. (2008), *Comments Re: Law.Com Article Re HyperLaw v. West Publishing, Matthew Bender, and Carl Malamud: Only HyperLaw Was the Party in the Text Copyright Decision*, HyperLaw, available at: <www.hyperlaw.com/>.

Susskind, R. (2000), *Transforming the Law: Essays on Technology, Justice, and the Legal Marketplace*, Oxford University Press, New York, p. 106.

Tapper, C. (1985), *Copyright in Primary Legal Materials*, Monash Law Review, Vol. 11, p. 79.

Tjaden, T.J. (2005), *Access to Law-Related Information in Canada in the Digital Age*, LL.M. Thesis, University of Toronto, p. 104, available at: <files.slaw.ca/TedTjadenLLMThesis.pdf>.

Trosow, S.E. (2004), *The Ownership and Commodification of Legal Knowledge: Using Social Theory of the Information Age as a Tool for Policy Analysis*, Manitoba Law Journal, Vol. 30, pp. 417-462.

van Eechoud, M. (2006), *The Commercialization of Public Sector Information: Delineating the Issues*, in Guibault, L. and Hugenholtz, P.B. (Eds.), "The Future of the Public Domain" Netherlands: Kluwer Law International, pp. 285-286.

Widdison, R. (2002), *New Perspectives in Legal Information Retrieval* International Journal of Law and Information Technology, Vol. 10, No. 1, pp. 46-47.

Wilson & Lafleur (1996), *L'information juridique au Québec: Des mythes à la réalité*.

Introducing the Legal Taxonomy Syllabus (LTS) on EU Consumer Law

Gianmaria Ajani
Department of Law, University of Turin, Italy

Abstract. The legal orders of the EC Member States are currently on the verge of further convergence of their respective private law – a process which is strongly influenced and directed by European primary and secondary legislation. One tool which might help to increase consistency during this process through the means of highlighting European and national legal terms and concepts is the Legal Taxonomy Syllabus (Consumer Law) which has been developed within the Uniform Terminology programme. This project aims to complement current research activities in the field of European law which is targeting the identification of similarities and differences, common principles and concepts within national and European legal acts. The EU legal terminology is also a priority identified by the European Commission ("rewriting legal texts to render them more coherent and understandable", "developing more user friendly access to consult and use Community law", "gradual modernisation and simplification of existing legislation", overcoming "potential legal uncertainty resulting from inconsistent definitions or terminology, or as a result of Member State transposition which has itself added unnecessary, complicated, detailed or excessive provisions" see Communication from the Commission "Updating and simplifying the Community acquis" COM(2003) 71 final). Indeed, the legal language of the Community encompasses various inconsistencies due to the lack of coherence among different sectoral legislative interventions (see EC Directives on consumer law, like Timeshare, Distant Contract, Unfair terms, and so forth).

LTS could serve as an instrument to describe the content and relevance of consumer law rules both at European and domestic level, taking into account horizontal divergences (i.e. between various legal instruments at European level or between various national legal orders), but also vertical divergences (i.e. differing legal concepts between the European and domestic level). With regard to the European or national legislator, LTS could enhance coherency already at the drafting stage by providing for an insight into the existing consumer law terms and concepts and a better understanding of the impact of any further legislative act within the Member States. With regard to translators, LTS could serve as a specific tool to enhance uniformity of legal language without losing national traditions transposed in different expressions and to select legal terms more consistent with the pre-existent choices of the European legislator.

***

In this short presentation I will be introducing a tool, a software which is the result of an EU sponsored research network, and which aims to reduce the complexity of multilinguism within European private and consumer law.

Here is the background of the project I am going to introduce. While working on a functional comparison in the field of trust law between English law and Continental law, my research group got in contact with colleagues of the University of Torino, who were doing research on Artificial Intelligence (AI) and were developing applied ontologies in the field of law. We decided

to combine the two research groups, linking our expertise in comparative
and European law with their expertise in AI, so to elaborate a multilingual
semantic database, to be used by those facing the difficult task of translating
legal concepts in some of the EU languages. As a result, we developed a data
base and a software, named Legal Terminology Syllabus (LTS).

Its website, <www.eulawtaxonomy.org>, is already available in the Internet.

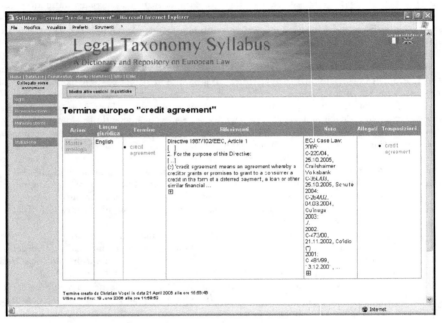

Figure 1.

This output is the result of a research network (Uniform Terminology in
European Private Law) established 6 years ago by seven Universities: Torino
(Italy), which was the leading institution, Barcelona (Spain), Lyon 3 (France),
Münster (Germany), Nijmegen (the Netherlands), Oxford (United Kingdom),
and Warsaw (Poland). The project was sponsored for 8 years by the European
Commission under an IHP network (IHP stands for Improving Human Potential). It provided funded research grants for three years to PhD candidates
and post-doc students, to enable them to spend long research stays within
the network: through this scheme, competent young scholars were asked to
contribute to the building of the data base.

The scholarly background of this project is the following: while investigating comparative aspects and national resistances to the implementation of
EU private law, we found that we were not satisfied with a mere translation
of *words*. The local resistance, and the diversity which derives from it among

the Member States legal orders, is not only a matter of difficult or mistaken translation of legal terms from one to another language. Rather, it is a more complex phenomenon, rooted in a diversified taxonomy at the national level.

We therefore tried to address this issue, not by compiling a dictionary – a multi-language dictionary, but by setting up a pretty more ambitious semantic tool.

"Semantic tool" means that we wanted to take into account the context in which terms are defined and used, and to see how a selection of terms from a bulk of EU Directives terms are defined in the different levels of the European legislation, of the European case-law, of the national implementing acts and of the national case-law. To make this exercise more complete, we also added some doctrinal notes and comments.

Research on legal terminology is something different from research on legal translation. It is also a priority identified by the European Commission. In its communication of 2003 on "Updating and simplifying the Community Acquis",[1] the Commission indicates the need of "rewriting legal texts to render them more coherent and understandable" and of overcoming "potential legal uncertainty resulting from inconsistent definitions or terminology". It is therefore the Commission itself who recognizes that there is a problem in terminology regarding the *Acquis*.

However, regardless how terminology is used, the definition of terminology itself is not coherent. Even in the Commission documents the word "terminology" gets different meanings: sometimes, it is meant as a substitute for searching common principles, some other times it is used as a synonym of legal categories, other times it is used simply as a synonym of "words".

Terminology, in its proper meaning, is actually about something else. It is an analysis on a set of terms linked together by some connecting element and seen into their context. Thus, the reason why we called our tool "Legal taxonomy syllabus", with an emphasis on terminology, is that we wanted to place the definitions of the terms into a context, defined by different national (or EU) legal taxonomies.

We have decided to limit our research to consumer law for two simple reasons. One is that there is a bulk of well identifiable sets of rules: the Directives on consumer law as quoted in the Green Paper on European Union Consumer Protection (COM/2001/0531 final), together with a couple of important Directives which have been added in 2003 and 2005. This made up a distinctive corpus which was narrow enough to permit this exercise, but also general enough to give sense thereto, taking into account that consumer law today is still the core of contract law transformation within the European Union. The *corpus* is therefore composed of the Directives identified in the

---

[1] Communication from the Commission to the Council, the European Parliament, the European Economic and Social Committee and the Committee of the Regions - Updating and simplifying the Community Acquis, COM/2003/0071 final.

2001 Green Paper on Consumer Protection, and of the 2002 Directive on distance marketing of consumer financial services.[2]

We tried to make this tool useful for several groups of users, in particular for those having an interest in getting access to the meaning of consumer law in different languages: lawyers, translators, legislators and scholars. I mention legislators, I'd like to draw your attention to the Common Framework of Reference project, that has been launched by the Commission in 2003, with the aim to set the conditions for a more consistent and better law-making in the regulation of the European market.

Entering now the structure of the "Syllabus" as such, the first thing to say is that it includes 90 terms identified within consumer law Directives. These terms are explored following a two-step approach.

Step 1 gives the horizontal perspective: it maps the occurrence of the selected terms within the EU law and identifies terminological variants. The project takes into account five different national systems: the French, the Spanish, the Italian, the German and the British legal orders. The five boxes related thereto are linked in the sense that the user can move from one legal system to another, from one Directive, one link, to another, surfing through the software.

Step 2 provides the vertical perspective, comparing the terms used in EU law to those used in the national law of Member States. The user can, for instance, go from a term belonging to an European Directive which has been written in Italian, into the Italian national implementing checking out the degree of consistency of the terminological transposition. The same applies to the French, the Spanish, the German and the British legal systems.

In other words, the user can map the occurrence of the words within EU law - horizontal perspective - and between the EU law and the national level – vertical perspective.

Let us take the horizontal perspective first (*Figure 3*). If, for instance, you compare Directive 97/7/CE on distance sales[3] with Directive 2002/65/EC on the distance marketing of consumer financial services, you find that the term "good faith" in the English texts is expressed in the same way, using the same words. The same occurs for the Spanish term "*buena fe*". However, if you come to the French version of the same Directives you realise that what was expressed as "good faith" in English is translated into two different terms ("*loyauté*" and "*bonne foi*"). The same happens as regards the Italian ("*lealtà*" and "*buona fede*") and the German ("*Lauterkeit*" and "*Treu und Glauben*") versions.

---

[2] Green Paper on European Union Consumer Protection COM(2001) 531 final. Directive 2002/65/EC of the European Parliament and of the Council of 23 September 2002 concerning the distance marketing of consumer financial services and amending Council Directive 90/619/EEC and Directives 97/7/EC and 98/27/EC, OJ L 271, 9.10.2002, pp. 16–24.

[3] Directive 97/7/EC of the European Parliament and of the Council of 20 May 1997 on the protection of consumers in respect of distance contracts, OJ L 144, 4.6.1997, pp. 19–27.

"Good faith"

Step 1: The Horizontal Perspective

Several EU directives refer to the general principle of good faith.

Unfair Contract Terms Directive (1993/13/EEC)

Distance Selling Directive (1997/7/EC)

Directive on Distant Marketing of Financial Services (2002/65/EC)

Unfair Commercial Practices Directive (2005/29/EC)

Figure 2.

"Good faith"

Step 1: The Horizontal Perspective

Terminological variants can be identified among various language versions

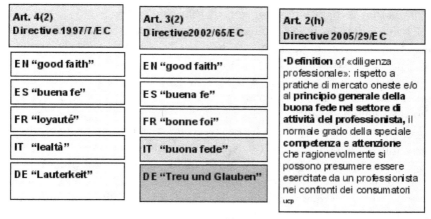

Art. 4(2) Directive 1997/7/EC	Art. 3(2) Directive2002/65/EC	Art. 2(h) Directive 2005/29/EC
EN "good faith"	EN "good faith"	•**Definition** of «diligenza professionale»: rispetto a pratiche di mercato oneste e/o al **principio generale della buona fede nel settore di attività del professionista**, il normale grado della speciale **competenza e attenzione** che ragionevolmente si possono presumere essere esercitate da un professionista nei confronti dei consumatori ucp
ES "buena fe"	ES "buena fe"	
FR "loyauté"	FR "bonne foi"	
IT "lealtà"	IT "buona fede"	
DE "Lauterkeit"	DE "Treu und Glauben"	

Figure 3.

If you now consider the vertical perspective (*Figure 4*), i.e. going from the European to the national level, you will see that the Italian word "*lealtà*" used in Directive 97/7/CE has been converted into "*buona fede e lealtà*" and the term "*buona fede*" from Directive 2002/65/EC was transformed in "*correttezza e buona fede*". I took the Italian example because I am more familiar with it, but you have the same phenomenon as to other implementing measures within the addressed legal orders.

"Good faith"

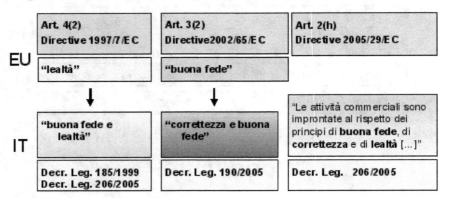

Figure 4.

So, is that recognition important? Is that challenging?

I believe it is both important and challenging, as there is still a kind of understatement, among the jurists working on EU private law, about the creative role played by the languages in the complex process of harmonization.

When we see the call for "a more coherent European law", we have to understand that it is not only European law – the *acquis* – which is at stake. Also the dynamic relationship between the acquis and the national levels has to be transformed in a more coherent correlation. This kind of exercise shows where minor interventions on the legal texts could enhance coherence.

The second aspect of the problem is related to the concept of terminology, or of taxonomy. It is not only a matter of "using different words meaning the same thing". Sometimes, when you swing between different, but similar, words you find yourself facing different taxonomies, that lead to different set of concepts.

Needless to say, an access to the Syllabus through its website will make this presentation clearer.

The homepage offers a short description of how the project was originated, and information on those who have contributed thereto. The software is a new tool, which was tailored by the Department of Informatics at the University of Torino.

Once you have logged you have access to the database, that is organized in 5 languages (English, French, Italian, German, Spanish) and on 3 levels: European and national, or only European or only national. You will find a box where the "term name" has to be typed in. The full list of 90 terms composing the corpus, that has been worked out from the set of Directives on consumer law, can be obtained by typing a little star (*). The whole list represents 55 paper pages, in alphabetical order, in all 5 languages.

Let's now try testing the term "offer", which refers to the English term "offer" used in Directive 85/577/EEC.

The full text of the actual article(s) containing its definition and operation, will appear, together with more information. Furthermore, the user can compare the terminological use of the term "offer" in other linguistic versions by clicking on "Show other linguistic versions". Having done this he will find that "offer" is set in German as "*Angebot*". However, a click on the right column ("Associations"), will show that "*Angebot*" origins to two different terms in the German implementing measures: "*Antrag*" and "*Angebot*".

We have entered now the national level, as we have jumped from the English term "offer" used at European level, to its German, version, and then we have moved into the vertical level. The full text of the articles concerned at the national level also will appear: so, the text of § 145 BGB, which transposed the ruling of the Directive into German law, is available.

The system does not only work on single terms, but also on expressions, as the example of "good faith" showed. By clicking successively on "European", and then "Show other linguistic versions", the user obtains the equivalent of "good faith" in all five languages and sees that there are several French equivalent terms: "*loyauté*"; "*bonne foi*", "*en traitant de façon loyale et équitable*": clicking on "Association" reveals the term used for national implementation, such as, in French: "*bonne exécution des obligations*".

The Syllabus provides also a set specific, quantitative, information on how EU terms have been implemented within the 5 considered in national laws. The "Statistics" function consists of a list terms used at European level and of the corresponding/different terminology adopted at the national level(s). It illustrates how the language of European law differs from the language of national law, even when we are dealing with the same natural language. As an example, European law does say "*Angebot*" for "offer", but German national law says "*Antrag*". The list is rather long and one could speculate whether that was done on purpose, to avoid identification between the EU and the national level, or whether we are facing the results of a mistaken identification of the terms.

As mentioned, the project team tried to make the tool useful for several groups of users. That is why there is an user access for "general users", and another one for "specialists": an ontologist, for instance, who has an interest in designing legal ontologies, can have access to the ontological map which has been prepared to mirror the different terminologies covered by the Syllabus (Ajani et al., 2007).

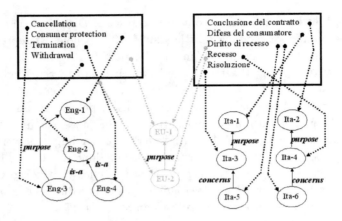

Figure 5.

Appendix
Syllabus - English version - Draft Page

Proposed lemma	Unfair term
Subdivision	-/-
Term	Unfair term
English lemma	Unfair term
Subdivision	-/-
Term	-/-
Sub-Term(s)	-/-
European law (English version)	Council Directive **93/13/EEC** of 5 April 1993 on unfair terms in consumer contracts 1. A contractual **term** which has not been individually negotiated shall be regarded as **unfair** if, contrary to the requirement of good faith, it causes a significant imbalance in the parties' rights and obligations arising under the contract, to the detriment of the consumer. 2. A term shall always be regarded as not individually negotiated where it has been drafted in advance and the consumer has therefore not been able to influence the substance of the term, particularly in the context of a pre-formulated standard contract. The fact that certain aspects of a term or one specific term have been individually negotiated shall not exclude the application of this Article to the rest of a contract if an overall assessment of the contract indicates that it is nevertheless a pre-formulated standard contract. Where any seller or supplier claims that a standard term has been individually negotiated, the burden of proof in this respect shall be incumbent on him. 3. The Annex shall contain an indicative and non-exhaustive list of the terms which may be regarded as unfair." (Article 3)

Term English law	Unfair term
Sub-Term(s) **English law**	-/-
English Law	**The Unfair Terms in Consumer Contracts Regulations 1999** revoke and replace the Unfair Terms in Consumer Contracts Regulations 1994 (S.I. 1994/3159) which came into force on 1st July 1995. Those Regulations implemented Council Directive **93/13/EEC** on unfair terms in consumer contracts (O.J. No. L95, 21.4.93, p. 29). Regulations 3 to 9 of these Regulations re-enact regulations 2 to 7 of the 1994 Regulations with modifications to reflect more closely the wording of the Directive. Regulation 5 of the 1999 Regulations contains the definition of 'unfair terms'. **Unfair Terms** "**5**. - (1) A contractual term which has not been individually negotiated shall be regarded as unfair if, contrary to the requirement of good faith, it causes a significant imbalance in the parties' rights and obligations arising under the contract, to the detriment of the consumer. (2) A term shall always be regarded as not having been individually negotiated where it has been drafted in advance and the consumer has therefore not been able to influence the substance of the term. (3) Notwithstanding that a specific term or certain aspects of it in a contract has been individually negotiated, these Regulations shall apply to the rest of a contract if an overall assessment of it indicates that it is a pre-formulated standard contract. (4) It shall be for any seller or supplier who claims that a term was individually negotiated to show that it was. (5) Schedule 2 to these Regulations contains an indicative and non-exhaustive list of the terms which may be regarded as unfair."

Commentary	**Unfair Terms in Consumer Contracts - what is an unfair term?**
	An unfair term in a contract covered by the UTCCRs is not binding on the consumer.
	Test of fairness
	A term is unfair if:
	contrary to the requirement of good faith it causes a significant imbalance in the parties' rights and obligations under the contract, to the detriment of consumers.
	'Good faith' means that you must deal fairly and openly with consumers. Standard terms may be drafted to protect commercial needs but must also take account of the interests and rights of consumers by going no further than is necessary to protect those legitimate commercial interests.
	The plain language requirement
	According to the UTCCRs, a standard term must be expressed in plain and intelligible language. A term is open to challenge if it could put the consumer at a disadvantage because he or she is not clear about its meaning - even if its meaning could be worked out by a lawyer. If there is doubt as to what a term means, the meaning most favourable to the consumer will apply.
	What terms are not covered?
	Most standard terms are covered by the UTCCRs. The exceptions are those:
	— that reflect provisions which by law have to be included in contracts
	— that have been individually negotiated
	— in contracts between businesses
	— in contracts between private individuals
	— in certain contracts that people do not make as consumers – eg, relating to employment or setting up a business
	— in contracts entered into before 1995.
	Terms setting the price or defining the product or service
	Terms in consumer contracts which set the price or define the product or service being supplied are 'core terms' of the contract and are exempt from the test of fairness as long as they meet the plain language requirement.
	(Source of information: The Department of Trade and Industry/ Consumer & Competition Policy, `<www.dti.gov.uk/ccp/>`)

References

Ajani, G., Lesmo, L., Boella, G., Mazzei, A., Rossi, P. (2007), *Multilingual Conceptual Dictionaries Based on Ontologies*, in Biagioli, C., Francesconi, E., Sartor, G. (Eds.), "Proceedings of the V legislative XML Workshop", European Press Academic Publishing, Florence, pp. 161-172.

After 15 Years, is Free Access to Law Here to Stay?

Ivan Mokanov

LexUM - University of Montreal, Canada

Abstract. The emergence of free access to law has brought about several new realities. Today, law is increasingly available in the public domain thanks to a wide variety of initiatives carried out by many different actors. The process of delivering legal information through many channels other than pricey commercial databases, known also as commoditization of legal information, is of paramount importance for democratic processes and good governance. Moreover, commoditization of legal information has changed the legal information marketplace in an unprecedented way and caused strategic reorientations of all vendors. The success of many projects in the area of free access to law has resulted in the creation of large informational holdings that must be preserved and improved as an invaluable part of the common heritage of humanity.

However, despite its effervescence, the free access to law phenomenon poses several challenges. Because it is happening through various channels and evolving informally, there have been little, if any, studies or analyses. While publishing law is unquestionably of paramount importance on theoretical grounds, there is still little understanding of how it actually operates or the effects of free access to law in the real world.

The following text proposes a broad methodology that can be used to study what free access to law projects do and how they do it so that we can understand the effects they have in society and explore the factors determining their sustainability. This methodology can be translated into a set of tools for issues such as:

Are there any real-world outcomes from free access to law that we could call "successes"?

Are those outcomes creating incentives among LIIs' target audiences or stakeholders acting on their behalf to sustain free law publishing?

What practices have been adopted by LII's that have been successful and by those that have not?

The proposed research methodology will explore the relationship between two central concepts: (1) success, in other words, the ability of a free access to law project to adopt practices that result in positive outcomes and create value for the target audience and (2) sustainability of free access to law projects.

1. Introduction

The following text contains nothing more than lists of questions. The questions are there for anyone to take, adapt, modify and try to provide answers to. Their objective is to help free legal publishers such as us better understand what we do, what works in various sets of circumstances, what value we create and for whom.

In more scientific terms, this text offers a broad methodology for conducting comparative case study research on free access to law. The topic of the research revolves around sustainability. Sustainability is frequently a subject of discussion because it is seen as a potential problem related to free access to law projects. This is paradoxical: How could such commendable initiatives to make law accessible for free to everyone face sustainability issues which bring their continuity into question? This text does not suggest that free access to law is not justified, but a thorough understanding of the value created by free access to law projects and empirical evidence about their positive outcomes seems to be missing.

This paper attempts to provide a preliminary basis for assessing the free access to law phenomenon. The questions and underlying framework could evolve into a more sophisticated methodological tool to be used in various contexts by different stakeholders. Finally, this is also an attempt to encourage free access to law project leaders to engage in research and evaluation of their activities in order to transform the assumptions and beliefs on free access to law into empirical evidence.

The objective is straightforward – maximizing free access to law projects' chances of survival because they serve a worthy cause.

2. The first fifteen years of free access to law

Projects that aim at delivering access to law at no charge have been carried out by various types of organizations – government, the judiciary, academia, law societies, NGOs. Some organizations, namely, Legal Information Institutes (LIIs) are grouped in the Free Access to Law Movement (FALM). FALM has been evolving for 15 years and it now includes over twenty LIIs. LIIs are organizations that collect mainly primary legal information, such as case law and legislation, in order to provide free public access to the information via a website. Both developing and industrialized countries from Africa, Asia, the Pacific, Europe and North America host LIIs. Today, tens of millions of documents are published on various LII websites.

The emergence of free access to law has brought about several developments:

— Today, law is increasingly available in the public domain thanks to a wide variety of initiatives carried out by many different actors;
— The process of delivering legal information through many channels other than pricey commercial databases, known also as commoditization of legal information, is of paramount importance for democratic processes and good governance;
— Commoditization of legal information has changed the legal information marketplace in an unprecedented way and has caused strategic reorientations of all vendors;
— The success of many projects in the area of free access to law has resulted in the creation of large informational holdings that must be preserved and improved as an invaluable part of the common heritage of humanity.

The following assumptions have been formulated regarding the expected benefits of free circulation of legal information: (1) free access to law upholds the rule of law; (2) it contributes to equality in the judicial process; (3) it promotes transparency and accountability of national judicial systems; (4) it strengthens lawyers' competence and the overall quality of legal services; (5) it makes the legal process more efficient; (6) it leads to a wider dissemination of national laws; and (7) it eliminates legal insecurity and thereby encourages entrepreneurship and investment (Poulin, 2004).

These benefits are particularly important rationales in transition-country environments where human rights and rule of law issues are a major concern. The soundness of the free access to law movement's purpose based on the fact that this is obviously "the right thing to do" has generated a lot of support among the legal community and development agencies, and has encouraged many to adopt the movement's mission.

3. Challenges

The free access to law phenomenon poses several challenges. Because it is happening through various channels and evolving informally, there have been little, if any, studies or analyses. Lessons, best practices and successful models have rarely been subject to systematic documentation. The absence of documentation creates obvious limits on sharing and dissemination of know-how, and keeps many programs and initiatives "on their own" with no access to useful guidance and knowledge support.

This is particularly true given the fact that the futures of many initiatives may not be as secure as those of well-established projects. Any free access to law project, especially the ones in the developing world, may face sustainability issues at some point. At the same time, the need to identify ways to keep free access to law projects alive and to preserve their informational assets and the democratic values that they protect seems obvious. Sustainability often refers to access of adequate resources on a recurrent basis.

However, access to adequate knowledge can be even more important.

Furthermore, free access to law projects have rarely been subject to careful assessment or evaluation. Only recently, have some projects been undertaken in an effort to measure and verify the assumptions about the benefits of free access to law.

Among those efforts, we must mention a study conducted by LexUM and supported by the International Development Research Center of Canada, which aims at assessing the outcome of free access to legal information on lawyers' competence and the overall quality of legal services in Western Africa. In a different context, a study is being conducted to assess the impact of free access to legal information on the evolution of law. Some preliminary data

collected in this project show that since the law of the Pacific has become
freely accessible, the courts have started referring more often to cases issued
by those same courts in their opinions. This change in the way judges draft
their reasons is seen as a first step to establishing a body of coherent local
jurisprudence. Finally, the Canadian Legal Information Institute (CanLII)
recently conducted an extensive survey among 2,000 lawyers in Canada in
order to assess its effect on the legal information marketplace. The survey
provided strong evidence about the role played by CanLII in legal research
and legal practice. According to the survey data, 71% of lawyers said that
CanLII reduces their cost of accessing legal information.

While what has been demonstrated by the studies is encouraging, more
global evidence about the benefits of free access to law remains scarce. On theoretical grounds, publishing law is unquestionably of paramount importance.
Unfortunately, there is still little understanding of how it actually operates or
the effects of free access to law in the real world.

4. A need to study free access to law

There is a need to study what free access to law projects do and how they do
it so as to understand the effects they have in society and explore the factors
determining their sustainability. There are many reasons why this would be a
worthy contribution to the continuity of free access to law movement:

— First, we need to verify the assumptions regarding the benefits of free
   access to law;
— Second, we must understand and document factors that have an impact
   on sustainability of free access to law projects;
— Third, we should promote access to knowledge and lessons learned from
   free access to law projects as important tools for the sustainability of
   current programs;
— Fourth, we need to rely on research as a means to support free access to
   law development programs;
— Fifth, we want to help future free access to law projects choose the appropriate context and adopt practices that can maximize their chances
   of survival as well as the benefits they bring;
— Sixth, we must inform donor agencies about factors and conditions that
   can maximize the benefit of aid dispensed to free access to law projects.

5. Success and sustainability

A good starting point for such research would be to clarify and study the link between two central concepts: success of free access to law projects and the sustainability of those projects.

LIIs have always adopted a common purpose, which is to produce benefits in society. Usually these benefits include the public's right to know the laws that bind it, the principle of open government and open legal systems, and the importance of eliminating legal insecurity in economic life. Often, a project that has managed to produce some of those positive outcomes is considered successful. As a first step, we must further explore and develop the concept of success of free access to law projects, which may be seen as their ability to produce the expected benefits.

The concept of sustainability also needs further study and development. It is often defined in more general terms as the ability to deliver services that provide sufficient value to their target audience, so that either that audience or other stakeholders acting on its behalf choose to fund the ongoing operation and evolution of that service. This broad definition also applies to the context of LIIs. Their sustainability may be approached as an ongoing process of locating revenue sources that allows them to operate the service on an ongoing basis and to improve it.

So what do those two concepts have in common? The link between them can be described as follows: By making law freely available, a LII produces outcomes that benefit its target audience, thereby creating incentives among the target audience or other stakeholders to sustain the LII's ongoing operations and development.

6. Questions and hypotheses

The main question that a study on free access to law must try to answer is:

Are LIIs an ephemeral phenomenon and what determines their sustainability?

Several specific questions follow:

— Are there any real-world outcomes from free access to law that we could call "successes"?
— Are those outcomes sufficient to create incentives among LIIs' target audiences or stakeholders acting on their behalf to sustain free law publishing?
— What practices have been adopted by LII's that have been successful and by those that have not?

In this text, we posit the following preliminary hypotheses.

Free access to law produces important outcomes in society. Some of those outcomes include:

— Free access to law promotes outside investment by making rules transparent.
— Free access to law contributes to equality in the judicial process.
— Free access to law promotes transparency and accountability of national judicial systems.
— Free access to law strengthens lawyers' competence and the overall quality of legal services.
— Free access to law makes the legal process more efficient.
— Free access to law eliminates entry barriers for people who choose to assert their rights through the legal system.
— Free access to law leads to wider dissemination of national laws.

By being successful in producing those outcomes, free access to law projects create value for their target audiences and sufficient incentives for those audiences to sustain their operations and development.

Between their creation and the moment they start providing benefits, free access to law projects undergo a lengthy incubation period when they accumulate critical content, increase their quality and gain users' confidence. During that period they are at high risk of disappearance.

7. Defining success

As a first step, we must determine what we call "success" with respect to free access to law activities and how we can measure it. As mentioned above, success is the ability of a free access to law project to adopt practices that allow the project to produce positive outcomes thereby creating value for the target audience. Measuring success involves two dimensions: the external benefits created by the project and its internal practices.

8. Measuring external benefits

The purpose of measuring external benefits is to provide answers to three questions: (1) What were the expectations with respect to the benefits to be delivered by the free access to law project? (2) Were all or some of those expectations met? (3) Did the ensuing benefits result in any value for the target audience?

What were the expectations with respect to the benefits to be delivered by the free access to law project?

In the first place, we must find answers to the following questions:

— When did the project start, who created it and why?

— Were there any identifiable needs that triggered the creation of the free access to law project?

— What were those needs?

— What were the benefits expected from the free access to law project?

— What were the vision, mission and mandate of the free access to law project?

Were all or some of those expectations met in practice?

Once the expected outcomes have been determined, we must focus on measuring to what extent those outcomes have been achieved. Often expected outcomes relate directly to the legal and judicial system. Therefore, qualitative and quantitative performance measurements that have been developed by donor agencies and international organizations acting in the field of legal and judicial reform may be useful.

Moreover, the questions to be answered at this stage revolve around the hypotheses formulated at the outset of this research but also around the expected benefits that were identified in the first step of the research. The questions may include:

— Is the justice system less corrupt?

— Is it more efficient?

— Has the quality of judicial reasons improved?

— Are people asserting their rights more often?

— Are lawyers more competent?

— Has the production of legal scholarly material intensified?

— Was there a positive change in small-business development and entrepreneurship?

— What are the behavioural changes that have resulted from greater accessibility of law?

What value has been created for the target audience?

Finally, we need to verify whether the projects that have been successful in achieving the expected outcomes have created value for their target audiences. While in some cases such value is obvious and does not need to be proven, for example reduction of corruption, in others value creation may depend on the audience. At this stage, answers to the following questions must be sought:

— Who is the audience?

— How is the audience benefitting from the outcomes produced?

— Is the value sufficient in nature and quantity to create incentives among the audience to support the ongoing operations of the free access to law project?

At the outset of this subcomponent, it will be possible to propose a comprehensive definition of what we call success in free access to law activities as well empirical evidence showing which projects have been successful. This leads to the next stage, in which free access to law projects will be studied from an internal perspective in order to determine which practices have contributed to achieving success, and which have not.

9. Measuring internal practices

Once we have determined what success means and which projects have been successful, we must look closely at what free access to law projects do and how they do it.

Measuring the internal practices of a free access to law project may prove an ambitious task. Free access to law programs are complex initiatives with numerous facets. For example, most programs need to find solutions in terms of relations with data sources, data flow procedures, technology and interoperability. Any of those elements can make a difference in the ability of a project to procure the benefits that were expected from it. Thus, every aspect deserves careful attention. The following is a general list of the various facets of free access to law projects and their context. It provides a framework of questions that need to be answered in order to study and understand the project's internal practices and environment:

— Questions regarding the situation in the country with respect to access to legal material and the legal marketplace;
— Questions regarding the content published or targeted by the project in terms of type, format, volume, quality, acquisition, etc.;
— Questions regarding the educational and awareness-raising campaign undertaken by the project, and the success and the impact of the campaign;
— Questions regarding the technological choices made by the project, the standards and applications developed or used by it and related issues and challenges;
— Questions regarding the establishment and implementation of editorial policies that govern the project's publishing activities, coverage of such policies and difficulties related to them;
— Questions regarding the choices made with respect to the website's functional design and search engine and their impact on efficient information retrieval;
— Questions regarding the revenue model chosen by the project or available to the project and related issues;
— Questions regarding the support obtained from the judiciary and government, and the role played by those stakeholders in the project;

— Questions regarding collaboration with other free access to law initiatives.

Quantitative data is essential for a better understanding of the project context and therefore for an adequate interpretation of the findings. Such data may include:

— Demographic data about the countries;
— Economic data about the countries;
— Data about the legal information market, for example number of publishers, number of products, types of products (paper and electronic), size of the market;
— Data about the legal profession, for example number of lawyers and number of law students, number and type of law firms, geographical distribution of lawyers;
— Data regarding the legal practice, for example lawyers' average legal research budget, relative importance of legal research in legal practice, number of self-represented litigants;
— Data illustrating usage of the free access to law website, for example number of visits, number of documents downloaded, origin of the visits, profile of the users in terms of profession and gender, most consulted documents, variance in usage data over the years;
— Data illustrating the awareness of the public about the legislative and judicial activities, for example frequency and intensity of media coverage of those activities; financial data, such as project budget.

10. Does success mean sustainability?

After having determined what success is and having identified which projects have been successful, we need to define the concept of sustainability. This will make it possible to identify which projects are considered sustainable under the proposed definition.

Again, sustainability refers to the ability of a project to deliver services that provide sufficient value to its target audience so that either the audience or stakeholders acting on its behalf choose to fund the ongoing operation and its development. Based on that definition, we can attempt to identify which projects can be considered sustainable by answering the following questions:

— Has the project secured sufficient funding to support its ongoing operations?
— Who provides the funding?
— Can the project operate without donor aid?
— Is the project's future in jeopardy?

— Can project leaders afford to plan several years ahead?
— Can the project raise resources to develop further and beyond its ongoing operations?

The data collected based on the series of questions stated above will allow us to answer the question of whether there is a link between success and sustainability. This in turn will bring is to the essence of this research, which consists in the following analysis: What practices make the difference between a successful (sustainable) and unsuccessful (unsustainable) project?

A tentative approach with respect to this question is outlined in the following section.

11. What do we hope to learn from all this?

With all the answers to our questions, we should be able to perform case-specific analyses of the data. The analyses will provide insight and clarification as to which projects did well and why.

Again, a subset of questions can be used to guide the analysis:

— What are the main factors that contributed to the project's success?
— Was the project's success driven essentially by internal practices?
— What was the impact of external causes?
— Would the success factors be easy to replicate in other contexts?
— Are they context-specific?
— Are successful choices a permanent success factor?
— Do they need adjustment over time?

After the analyses of the individual cases, we should determine what do successful projects have in common. A cross-case comparative analysis will help establish a set of general propositions about what best practices work under various sets of circumstances and with respect to different players. The results of the cross-case analysis will constitute the basis for formulating a set of best practices aimed at strengthening free access to law projects' viability and maximizing their benefits.

12. Conclusion

There is significant value in working together to provide answers to the questions raised in this text. One outcome would be to favour dialogue between free access to law programs around the globe thereby allowing them to share expertise and experiences.

This would leverage the networking effect of inter-connected development programs and contribute to wider dissemination of success stories and lessons learned.

We must also encourage reliance on research as a tool to sustain development projects. Often, since most develop in a dynamic and unstable environment, free access to law programs have evolved through day-to-day operational decisions with little attention to careful analysis of success factors and lessons learned. Studying the issues brought up by this text will allow projects to analyze their own situations and benefit from research results.

A study on free access to law will benefit both current and future programs. On one hand, it will improve existing projects by offering them access to valuable knowledge and experience gained in other contexts similar to theirs. Often, ongoing projects need guidance and advice when it comes to difficult operational and financial choices. Access to best practices and knowledge will also strengthen the projects' positioning with respect to securing funding and building partnerships. On the other hand, future initiatives will be better equipped when entering the field of free access to law and better informed about the challenges to be expected. This will facilitate planning by making project activities more foreseeable. Finally, by making the field better-known and the project benefits clearer, the study will encourage organizations to engage in free a access to law.

References

Poulin, D. (2004), *Open access to law in developing countries*, First Monday, Vol. 9, No. 12, available at: <firstmonday.org/htbin/cgiwrap/bin/ojs/index.php/fm/article/view/1193/1113>.

POSTFACE

Reflecting on Cross-Language Retrieval of Legal Information as an Essential Component of Open Access

Ginevra Peruginelli
Institute of Legal Information Theory and Techniques (ITTIG-CNR), Italy

This postface addresses what I consider to be one of the most relevant aspects of free access to legal information: multilingualism. The free access to law concept has been indeed at the core of the Conference, whose proceedings are published in this volume. Connected to this, a number of speakers have tackled multilingualism in the law domain from various perspectives and in the following pages I will try to resume and further develop this main theme.

The Free Access to Law Movement has progressed rapidly from its beginnings in 1992. Considerable efforts have been made to further extend both its partnership and content coverage, and to ensure legal information quality and authenticity, adoption of open standards, fair relationships between public and commercial services, trying to reaffirm an equitable balance between the interests of rights-holders and the public interest.

Concern has also been raised, in developing legal databases and related services by the various countries, on the requirement of citizens to effectively understand laws in force and judicial decisions and on the need for semantic tools to support users in their searching.

It is a matter of fact that nowadays improving knowledge of the law is imperative for the benefit of a wide category of users: legal professionals, businessmen, scholars and laymen, interacting as they are in an environment of increasing cross-border relations where powerful information and communication technologies are available which can greatly facilitate access to legal material despite its specificity and complexity.

However, language barriers still hinders the exchange of legal information and universal access to law. In a world where linguistic diversity is an undeniable reality, many are the initiatives undertaken by international institutions to foster the preservation of national identities and their languages, while promoting a common approach towards multilingualism by developing strategies and methods for cross-language access to law.

Just a few major international events in this area are provided as examples. The UNESCO General Conferences have systematically recommended and supported equitable and affordable access by all citizens to information communication infrastructures and to knowledge as essential to collective and individual human development in view of the creation of a knowledge-based society. Specific attention is devoted to the requirement that all cultures express themselves and have access to cyberspace in all languages, extensive multilingual capabilities be incorporated as relevant features in information systems, providing availability and access to online dictionaries and terminology tools, automated translation services for all, as well as intelligent linguistic systems such as those performing multilingual information retrieval.

Such synthesised recommendations refer to general domain information, but they perfectly fit to the specific domain of law in the actual environment where internationalisation and increasing globalisation of market economy and social patterns of life have created a situation where the need for legal information from foreign countries and from different legal systems is greater than ever before. This requirement is not new, but is now becoming more and more crucial under the pressure of the rapid and complex cross-border transactions occurring between people of different legal cultures and languages.

At European level a number of relevant measures have been taken in this direction, culminating in a major program, the Political Agenda for Multilingualism. Following its creation in 2007 as a separate portfolio to reflect the political and social dimension of the European Union (EU), the European Commission is committed to preserving and promoting this key feature, supporting multilingualism in view of its contribution to competitiveness, growth, better jobs and intercultural dialogue.

A relevant decision dates back to 2001 concerning the presentation over the Internet of legislative texts free of charge under the EUR-Lex portal common to the European institutions. This is an excellent system providing access to European law including treaties, legislation, case law and legislative proposals as well as to the Official Journal of the European Union. The multilingual material is accessible via a single interface but no search functionalities are offered to retrieve information in a language different from the query language. This facility is partly available in N-Lex, the common portal to Member States' national laws, where a common interface and the implementation of the Eurovoc thesaurus in the form of a dictionary allow, limited to those terms of the thesaurus, search terms to be translated, so as to retrieve related multilingual material following a search in a given language.

The appointment by the European Commission of a special Commissioner for multilingualism, Leonard Orban, supported by groups of scholars and experts in the field of linguistics, culture, education, is a major event in these last few years. Promoting multilingualism in the different policies of the European Union, such as culture, education, communication and employment, is at the moment at the centre of the EU objectives and approached in this spirit, linguistic diversity can become a precious asset, increasingly so in today's globalised world.

After all, what multilingualism has to do with open access to law? They are intimately connected with each other as in the actual multilingual and multicultural environment there is a strong need in the academic world, in the legal profession, in business settings as well as in the area of public administration services to citizens, of common understanding and exchange of legal concepts of the various legal systems, while there is a strong pressure for the preservation of their basic sense and value. Both requirements are quite difficult to meet, complicated by the complexity of legal language and by the variety of modalities used to express law within different legal systems.

Unlike a number of technical and scientific disciplines, where a fair correspondence exists between concepts across languages, serious difficulties arise in interpreting law across countries and languages, due to the system-bound nature of legal terminology. In fact, each legal order is situated within a complex social and political framework originating from the history, uses and habits of a particular community.

In such an environment the challenge of law information systems worldwide lies in providing transparent access to the multilingual information contained in distributed archives and, in particular, allowing users express requests in their preferred language and to obtain meaningful results. Therefore cross-language information retrieval (CLIR) systems can greatly contribute to open access to law, facilitate discovery and interpretation of legal information across different languages and legal orders, thus enabling sharing legal knowledge in a world which is becoming more interconnected every day.

During the Conference of Florence a number of contributions have highlighted the need of this functionality as well as of semantic tools to enhance uniformity of legal language without loosing national traditions.

It is true that multilingualism in the law domain and in particular retrieval of multi-language legal material is unanimously perceived as a complex issue, linked as it is to disciplines like comparative law, linguistics, translation theory and practice. It is a highly debated topic not only among professionals and scholars of these various disciplines, but also among government officials in institutional settings at national and international level. This is demonstrated by the efforts made for the preservation and management of the plurality of languages in a number of countries as a guarantee of cultural diversity. Apart from Europe as a whole, this is the case of Belgium, Switzerland, Canada, etc.

Retrieval systems to legal information across different legal systems represent a practical approach to the confrontation and exchange of legal cultures. Since comparison involves observation and explanation of similarities and differences, comparative research can give a major contribution to the development of these information systems. In fact, the implementation of retrieval functionalities implies taking into account and properly managing the peculiarities of legal concepts across systems, handling the variety of languages used to express these various concepts, addressing the terminological issues of representing the various legal cultures.

Many comparatists are strongly concerned with the implications of the differences existing between the cultural contexts underlying the various legal languages and with the difficulties in transferring legal meanings and legal concepts from one legal system to another, even when the same language is used (Kjaer, 2004).

In addressing the issues related to the development of systems and tools for accessing legal information across legal systems, consideration is to be given to the methods employed in the comparative process of legal systems: integrative as opposed to contrastive (Schlesinger, 1995). The convergence or divergence approaches are key elements for implementing multilingual retrieval tools and services. According to the chosen approach, the methods adopted in these systems will facilitate terms and concepts to be matched across legal orders, adapting concepts of different systems and helping contextualization so to approach the most likely similar concept in the target language and system. In a more restrictive approach, only broad correspondences will be established, focused on broad concepts which are likely to be commonly understood by a variety of users.

It is also a fact that cross-language retrieval of legal information is strongly based on translation, as in order to match search terms and documents to be retrieved either the query or the documents or even both must be translated. On a practical level legal translation implies both a comparative study of the different legal systems and an awareness of the problems created by the absence of equivalents. In fact a particular concept in a legal system may have no counterpart in other systems, or a particular concept may exist in two different systems but may refer to different realities. In other words, law lacks a common knowledge base or "universal operative referents" (Pelage, 2000), which makes it very difficult to find equivalents for culture-bound terms, especially those concerning legal concepts, procedures and institutions. In this context the danger of ambiguity and miscomprehension is considerable. A field where the significance of legal translation is evident in many respects is comparative and international law. Since the right of States to communicate in their own language has been accepted, translation has become more important than ever in these two fields of law, but there is still the danger of the existing communication gap among nations especially translating from the language of a civil law country to the language of a common law country.

One major question concerns the translation strategy to be adopted in order to ensure that users access legal information independently of the language used in a query. Legal translation mainly refers to texts, whereas in cross-language information retrieval what mainly matters is handling single units of information or a combination of them as expressed by users.

Among the different approaches to legal translation the approach of fidelity to the letter of the original document, that is the strict adherence to the original, has long lasted over the centuries. Little by little the method of simple linguistic equivalence has given way to a target-oriented translation adopting a functionalist approach, where non formal correspondence between source and target text is to be sought, but the equivalent legal effects principle (Šarčević, 1997).

The functional equivalence approach is likely to be effective in CLIR systems for its potential to ensure correspondence based on legal effects of source and target concepts. Other methods of translation as borrowing (translation procedure whereby the translator uses a word or expression from the source text in the target text) and creation of neologisms are scarcely significant in cross-language information retrieval, where the objective is to help users to find materials in any language irrespective of the language used in searching.

One major problem connected with translation is the poor quality of actual legal dictionaries, which fail to meet users' expectations for conveying the meaning of the source legal language into the target legal language. Furthermore, apart from the lack of good dictionaries and the difficulty of directly using electronic bilingual dictionaries in information retrieval systems as some kind of pre-processing is required before these tools can be used in automatic systems, limitations are due to the shortage and high cost of development of specialised resources like multilingual legal thesauri and training corpora from where to extract information and context useful for CLIR applications.

Despite these difficulties, so far considerable efforts have been made to develop linguistic tools as well as systems for multilingual retrieval of law (Peruginelli, 2009).

Research studies, tools and systems designed for multilingual retrieval of law material progressed but at the moment a unique model suitable for cross-language retrieval of legal information does not exist and we are far away from an ideal approach to be adopted to overcome the language barriers arising in worldwide searching of law. Even in multilingual retrieval of general domain information, no one-fits-all solution exists ensuring users to effectively access information beyond language barriers.

Systems developed so far greatly concentrate on pairs rather than on multiple languages, the latter being a much more complex endeavour. While lots of experiments and discussions focus on the developments of vocabulary matching over languages as such, a strong need is felt to study some kind of interlingual mechanism allowing the transfer of meanings between languages. This would enable matching to equivalent terms in all languages and realising cross-language retrieval in any of the language combinations.

Furthermore, linguistic tools and multilingual systems developed for the law domain mostly concentrate on a specific theme or field of law: this approach is sound as these systems are likely to provide insights for larger applications and developments.

Various crucial factors hinders the development of effective worldwide cross-language retrieval of law. Shortage of lexical sources like quality bilingual dictionaries, multilingual thesauri, parallel and comparable corpora, ontologies helping to establish correspondences among languages is still a reality for a great amount of languages considered as minor, but spoken by millions of people: this is definitely an obstacle to multilingual information access in general, and in particular to law. The case exists of a large number of languages of countries like India and Africa for which no parallel corpora or machine translation commercial systems are available.

Mostly spoken languages in Europe as English, French, German, Italian and Spanish show a different situation, as well as those languages like Chinese and Japanese and also Arabic and Russian which are the other official languages of the United Nations. The dominance of English is a fact, and this phenomenon is at the origin of the scarce interest, or even the impossibility at practical and economic level, to develop information retrieval systems in less-represented languages.

An additional, relevant issue regards the difficulty to have access to sophisticated technologies for the development and management of information retrieval systems in combination with language processing methodologies. Another factor, of an economic nature, have a major impact on multilingual systems' functionality. So far the major search engines have not ventured in true cross-language information retrieval services also due to the high cost of development of these systems. In fact a reluctance still persists, especially by commercial providers, to develop multilingual information retrieval systems in the form of real consolidated services, beyond what is the most frequently offered functionality, represented by a simple multilingual dialogue interface.

On the grounds of applications developed up to now, there is evidence that a combination of different techniques is needed, consisting, for example, in query expansion and relevance methodologies, to be operated also through users' interaction. To be effective in the area of law, these techniques have to be adapted and properly fitted to the various applications and, if implemented in large scale systems, they raise development costs considerably.

As the real question is how to establish a correspondence among concepts of diverse legal systems expressed in different languages, a comparative analysis of legal concepts and, parallel to this, the study of translation theory and practice to be intended as search of functional equivalents, are fundamental activities in order to reach a satisfactory mediation among different legal identities and ensure intercultural communication.

Leaving untouched that precision in legal language is an essential feature due to the inevitable negative implications of inexactness and inaccuracy in every action where law is involved, it can be stated that in multilingual retrieval systems, where comparison of legal concepts comes into play, less rigid solutions can be acceptable as compared to legal text translation, whose incorrect formulation can have extremely serious implications.

Less rigour does not imply abandoning the principle of clarity and precision which is necessary in comparing legal concepts belonging to different legal orders, rather it means adopting a flexible approach. From legal information retrieval systems it is expected to ensure knowledge communication by providing really relevant documents, even coming to a compromise. This implies, for example, in terms' comparison and therefore in translation, accepting a more general concept as compared to the more specific original one, and also systematically adopting term disambiguation techniques, so as to present more results through users' interaction methods.

On the basis of these considerations, a multilingual model in the law domain requires an orchestration process in which all responsible actors are involved, those operating in the wide environment of the diverse legal orders: legislators, judges, legal professionals, scholars, linguists and also citizens. The challenge is not to choose a given communication language, rather to find a way to make linguistic and cultural diversities coexist in harmony.

In this context multilingual legal information retrieval systems do represent the necessary tools to encourage multilingualism in the law domain and have the chance to make it effective. In view of preparing to develop systems and tools allowing users to retrieve and make use of legal information resources made available through institutional and commercial services, joint activities among actors with quite different skills are recommended: jurists, linguists, jurilinguists, translators should commit themselves to cooperate with researchers in the field of new technologies and promote large-scale comparative studies on several fields of law. In particular, through linguistic-conceptual correspondence definition activities carried out in cooperation among institutional organisations committed to indexing and delivering legal material world-wide, it could be possible to set up experimental applications, pilot projects and systems capable of fostering awareness and understanding of different countries' legal concepts, in a word facilitating worldwide open access to law.

References

Kjaer, A.L. (2004), *A common legal language in Europe?*, in Van Hoecke, Mark (Ed.), "Epistemology and Methodology of Comparative Law", Hart, Oxford.

Pelage, J. (2000), *La traductologie face au droit*, in "Proceedings of the International Colloquium", University of Geneva, February 17-19, Association Suisse des Traducteurs, Terminologues et Interprètes (ASTTI), Ecole de traduction et d'interprétation de Genève (ETI), Berne, pp. 125-131.

Peruginelli, G. (2009), *Multilinguismo e sistemi di accesso all'informazione giuridica*, Giuffrè, Milano, 232 pp.

Šarčević, S. (1997), *New approach to legal translation*, Kluwer law International, The Hague.
Schlesinger, R.B. (1995), *The past and future of comparative law*, American Journal of Comparative Law, Vol. 43, pp. 477-481.

Appendix

Montreal Declaration on "Free Access to Law"

Legal information institutes of the world, meeting in Montreal, declare that:

— Public legal information from all countries and international institutions is part of the common heritage of humanity. Maximising access to this information promotes justice and the rule of law;
— Public legal information is digital common property and should be accessible to all on a non-profit basis and free of charge;
— Organisations such as legal information institutes have the right to publish public legal information and the government bodies that create or control that information should provide access to it so that it can be published by other parties.

Public legal information means legal information produced by public bodies that have a duty to produce law and make it public. It includes primary sources of law, such as legislation, case law and treaties, as well as various secondary (interpretative) public sources, such as reports on preparatory work and law reform, and resulting from boards of inquiry. It also includes legal documents created as a result of public funding.

Publicly funded secondary (interpretative) legal materials should be accessible for free but permission to republish is not always appropriate or possible. In particular free access to legal scholarship may be provided by legal scholarship repositories, legal information institutes or other means.

Legal information institutes:

— Publish via the internet public legal information originating from more than one public body;
— Provide free and anonymous public access to that information;
— Do not impede others from obtaining public legal information from its sources and publishing it; and
— Support the objectives set out in this Declaration.

All legal information institutes are encouraged to participate in regional or global free access to law networks.

Therefore, the legal information institutes agree:

— To promote and support free access to public legal information throughout the world, principally via the Internet;

- To recognise the primary role of local initiatives in free access publishing of their own national legal information;
- To cooperate in order to achieve these goals and, in particular, to assist organisations in developing countries to achieve these goals, recognising the reciprocal advantages that all obtain from access to each other's law;
- To help each other and to support, within their means, other organisations that share these goals with respect to:

  - Promotion, to governments and other organisations, of public policy conducive to the accessibility of public legal information;
  - Technical assistance, advice and training;
  - Development of open technical standards;
  - Academic exchange of research results.

- To meet at least annually, and to invite other organisations who are legal information institutes to subscribe to this declaration and join those meetings, according to procedures to be established by the parties to this Declaration;
- To provide to the end users of public legal information clear information concerning any conditions of re-use of that information, where this is feasible;

This declaration was made by legal information institutes meeting in Montreal in 2002, as amended at meetings in Sydney (2003), Paris (2004) and Montreal (2007).

LIIs - Legal Information Institutes

AsianLII - Asian Legal Information Institute
> `<www.asianlii.org/>`

AustLII - Australasian Legal Information Institute
> `<www.austlii.org/>`

BAILII - British and Irish Legal Information Institute
> `<www.bailii.org/>`

CanLII - Canadian Legal Information Institute
> `<www.canlii.org/>`

Cardiff Index to Legal Abbreviations, UK
> `<www.legalabbrevs.cardiff.ac.uk/>`

CommonLII - Commonwealth Legal Information Institute
> `<www.commonlii.org/>`

CyLaw, Cyprus
> `<www.cylaw.org/>`

Droit.org, France
> `<www.droit.org/>`

Droit francophone
> `<droit.francophonie.org/df-web/>`

GLIN - Global Legal Information Network
> `<www.glin.gov/>`

HKLII - Hong Kong Legal Information Institute
> `<www.hklii.org/>`

IIjusticia, Argentina
> `<www.iijusticia.edu.ar/>`

IIJ-UNAM - Instituto de Investigaciones Jurídicas UNAM, Mexico
> `<www.juridicas.unam.mx/>`

IDT - Institute of Law and Technology, Autonomous University of Barcelona, Spain
> `<idt.uab.es/>`

IRLII - Irish Legal Information Initiative
> `<www.ucc.ie/law/irlii/>`

ITTIG - Institute of Legal Information Theory and Techniques, Italy
> `<www.ittig.cnr.it/>`

Jersey Legal Information Board

> `<www.jerseylaw.je/>`

JuriBurkina, Burkina Faso

> `<www.juriburkina.org/>`

JuriNiger, Niger

> `<juriniger.lexum.umontreal.ca/juriniger/?>`

Juristisches Internetprojekt Saarbrücken, Germany

> `<www.jura.uni-saarland.de/>`

KenyaLaw - Kenya Law Reports

> `<www.kenyalaw.org/>`

LawPhil, Philippine

> `<www.lawphil.net/>`

Legal Information Institute (Cornell Law School), USA

> `<www.law.cornell.edu/>`

LexUM, University of Montreal, Canada

> `<www.lexum.umontreal.ca/index_en.php>`

NZLII - New Zealand Legal Information Institute

> `<www.nzlii.org/>`

Office of the Council of State, Thailand

> `<www.lawreform.go.th/>`

PacLII - Pacific Islands Legal Information Institute

> `<www.paclii.org/>`

SAFLII - Southern African Legal Information Institute

> `<www.saflii.org/>`

ULII - Ugandan Legal Information Institute

> `<www.ulii.org/>`

WorldLII - World Legal Information Institute

> `<www.worldlii.org/>`

Author Index

Agnoloni, T., 327
Ajani, G., 455

Bacci, L., 327
Badeva-Bright, M., 261
Belli, R., 227
Berger, A., 49
Bing, J., 83
Bruce, T.R., 411

Cammelli, A., 359, 399
Casanovas, P., 347
Caso, R., 97
Chan, H.W., 151
Cherubini, M., 337
Chong, C.F., 151
Chow, K.P., 151
Chung, P., 285
Costanzo, P., 111
Cottin, S., 163
Currie, I., 73

De Groote, B., 371

Fameli, E., 359
Faro, S., 139
Fellows, C., 129
Francesconi, E., 327

Galindo, F., 237
Greenleaf, G., 285, 423
Gregorio, C.G., 245

Hietanen, A., 177
Hui, L., 151

Koch, N., 187

Leith, P., 129
Lemyre, P., 437
Lupo, C., 193

Mariani, P., 399
Mercatali, P., 385
Mokanov, I., 465
Montemagni, S., 327
Moret, M., 199
Mowbray, A., 285

Nannucci, R., 271

Paliwala, A., 253

Peruginelli, G., 477
Pietrangelo, M., 41, 111
Poblet, M., 347
Poulin, D., 15
Pun, K., 151

Ragona, M., 271
Rolleri, F., 65
Romano, F., 385

Sarti, D., 123
Schefbeck, G., 207
Scotti, I., 57
Seta, E., 57
Spinosa, P.L., 327

Tiscornia, D., 327
Traunmüller, R., 301
Tsang, W.W., 151

Van Bossuyt, H., 371
Van Engers, T.M., 311
Venturini, F., 219

Wimmer, M.A., 301

Zeno-Zencovich, V., 33